URBAN ANALYSIS:
Readings in Housing
and Urban Development

urban analysis

READINGS IN HOUSING AND URBAN DEVELOPMENT

Alfred N. Page

University of Washington

Warren R. Seyfried

University of Washington

SCOTT, FORESMAN AND COMPANY

PREFACE

The articles in this book deal with various economic aspects of the urban environment. Among the many subjects covered are the demand for housing, the theory of housing location, property values and race, and slums and urban renewal.

Section I, *Housing and the Urban Environment,* is made up of four articles, brought together to provide a perspective on the general subject of urban housing. Joseph J. Spengler's essay, "Population Pressure, Housing and Habitat," emphasizes the necessity of housing our expanding and increasing urbanized population. A paper by John Dyckman, "The Changing Uses of the City," describes the evolution of urban social functions, institutions, and physical facilities, and suggests ways in which the quality of the urban environment might be improved. Lyle C. Fitch's paper, "Goals for Urban Development," discusses problems and needs of the urban environment, including housing. Finally, the article by Britton Harris, "The Uses of Theory in the Simulation of Urban Phenomena," presents an informative critique of the scientific approach to urban development.

Section II, *Economic Analysis of Urban Housing Demand,* presents theoretical and empirical studies of fluctuations in residential housing construction. Because there are strongly opposing viewpoints regarding the causes of these fluctuations, their relative significance, and the proper methods of analyzing them, the articles were chosen to represent several alternative positions.

The article by Leo Grebler and Sherman J. Maisel entitled "Determinants of Residential Construction: A Review of Present Knowledge" gives a comprehensive survey of work in the area. The article by Jack M. Guttentag, "The Short Cycle in Residential Construction, 1946–59" and that by William W. Alberts, "Business Cycles, Residential Construction Cycles, and the Mortgage Market," provide theoretical discussions of the impact of credit on housing fluctuations. Following these, the paper by George Break, "The Sensitivity of Housing Demand to Changes in Mortgage Credit Terms," is an attempt to incorporate such credit variables into a statistical analysis of housing.

Sherman J. Maisel's paper, "A Theory of Fluctuations in Residential Construction Starts," posits an alternative theory of housing fluctuations in which the changing availability of credit is not a deciding factor. The paper by Alfred N. Page, "Residential Construction: Exploration of the Statistical Series," discusses several methods of forecasting changes in construction that do not require attribution of causes. Finally, a major portion of a lengthy housing essay by Richard F. Muth, "The Demand for Non-Farm Housing," shows the use of the time-series data to analyze income and price elasticities in housing demand.

Section III, *Housing and Intra-Urban Location,* consists of eight articles, seven of which attempt to explain the spatial patterns of urban housing. "Equilibrium of the Household," by William Alonso, an economist, and "An Economic Model of the Utilization of Urban Land for Residential Purposes," by Lowdon Wingo, Jr., an urban planner, use economic-equilibrium analysis to determine the best choice among alternative locations for household residence. "An Aggregative Model of Resource Allocation in a Metropolitan Area," by Edwin S. Mills, also an economist, uses a different approach, which considers the interrelations of the three urban activities of production of goods, transportation, and housing. "The Spatial Structure of the Housing Market," by Richard F. Muth, and "The Journey-to-Work as a Determinant of Residential Location" by John F. Kain, provide empirical tests of location models of the kind treated by Alonso and Wingo.

The next two articles are inductive models designed around empirical data. In "An Approach to the Analysis of Metropolitan Residential Extension," Willard B. Hansen, an urban planner, develops a dynamic model to explain residential expansion. Beverly and Otis Dudley Duncan are demographers, and their paper, "The Measurement of Intra-City Locational and Residential Patterns," empirically analyzes a case study relating work place and residence. The final article, "Intra-Urban Location Problems: An Evaluation," is by the late Charles M. Tiebout, an economist who contributed much to the understanding of urban and regional analysis. Tiebout's article evaluates intra-urban location and models and suggests the necessity of government decisions to offset limitations of economic or market models. Following Tiebout's article is a discussion of the author's views by Barbara R. Berman.

Section IV, *Urban Housing and Racial Integration,* is concerned with empirical evaluations of the relationships among race, property values, and rents. Articles were chosen that emphasized the statistical aspects of the problem, in order to offer objective evidence rather than the untested mythology with which the subject is often approached. (The editors feel that considerable work remains to be done in this area, including the gathering of large samples of cross-sectional data.)

The initial article, "Theories of Race and Property Value," by Luigi M. Laurenti, provides a historical survey. The second article, also by Laurenti, "Effects of Non-White Purchases on Market Prices of Residences," was one of the earliest attempts to evaluate empirically the price effects of integration, and was the forerunner for a number of studies done for the Commission on Race and Housing. A summary of the findings of these studies is found in the David McEntire article, "The Housing Market in Racially Mixed Areas." The study by Chester L. Hunt, "Integrated Housing in Kalamazoo," indicates the impact on housing price and popular attitudes when neighborhoods are integrated in a relatively small city. William M. Ladd's paper, "Effect of Integration on Property Values," attempts to analyze the price behavior of integrated areas by evaluating multiple sales of housing. Finally, two related papers, "Note on the Economics of Residential Zoning and Urban Renewal" and "Effects of Race and Other Demographic Factors on the Values of Single-Family Homes," both by Martin J. Bailey, show how regression analysis might be used to study such problems.

Section V, *Slums, Urban Renewal, and Public Policy,* begins with three articles on slums. Arthur D. Sporn's "Empirical Studies in the Economics of Slum Ownership" and George Sternlieb's "Slum Housing: A Functional Analysis," provide analyses of case studies of existing slum conditions. Ira S. Lowry's "Filtering and Housing Standards: A Conceptual Analysis" defines the "filtering" process—the market mechanism for distributing the existing housing stock among households—and evaluates its effectiveness in meeting housing needs. The next four articles pertain to urban renewal. Robert C. Weaver's "Class, Race and Urban Renewal" discusses racial discrimination in the housing market and how urban renewal might help to achieve housing or neighborhood "balance." The long article by Jerome Rothenberg, "Urban Renewal Programs," is a comprehensive discussion of programs, objectives, and methods of urban renewal, including the identification of costs and benefits. James C. T. Mao's article, "Efficiency in Public Urban Renewal Expenditures Through Benefit-Cost Analysis," is an application of cost-benefit analysis to a case study of an urban renewal project. "Urban Renewal: A Strategy for Information and Analysis," by Lowdon Wingo, Jr., discusses the broader aspects of urban renewal, including decision making and the information required in undertaking renewal. The final two articles are concerned with evaluation of urban development programs. Leo Grebler's article is "Criteria for Appraising Governmental Housing Programs." Louis Winnick's article, "Economic Questions in Urban Redevelopment," as well as Irving Morrissett's comments on it, is concerned with costs and benefits of urban renewal programs.

The editors are grateful to the authors and original publishers of these selections for making them available for use in this book.

Alfred N. Page
Warren R. Seyfried

University of Washington

INTRODUCTION

Housing is important to economists with a great variety of interests. The business cycle specialist is interested in studying the peculiarities of construction cycles. The student of industrial organization finds the construction industry to be worth special study. Specialists in demand theory find the demand for housing to be a challenging example of demand for a durable capital good by consumers. The location theorist finds that housing dominates the spatial pattern of the urban economy. Students of financial markets an institutions are interested in the specialized credit institutions that finance the construction and ownership of housing. Students of public policy are concerned with the myriad ways in which the public sector affects housing, including zoning, public investment, mortgage insurance, regulation of financial institutions, and acquisition of land by eminent domain and resale for renewal purposes. The student of welfare economics tries to understand "the anatomy of market failure" in slum housing. Finally, the student of poverty knows that poverty and poor housing are related by complex causal patterns working in both directions.

Most importantly, housing is inextricably related to virtually all the urban and racial problems of our time. Sociologists, political scientists, and city planners, as well as economists, are interested in the relationships between racial segregation in housing and racial segregation in schools, the culture of poverty, inadequate provision of public services, urban crime and violence, and urban blight.

It is obvious that no single volume could survey all these topics and problems. And good studies are lamentably few in many of the most important areas. The purpose of the present volume is to bring together a series of papers that will give the reader the flavor of recent work by economists on the subject of housing. Inevitably, the reader of these papers is struck with the impression that although some excellent work has been done on the economics of housing markets and although our knowledge has been considerably advanced during the last decade or two, appalling gaps remain. We do not know to what extent slums are the result of malfunctioning of markets rather than of residents' low incomes. We do not know to what extent racial segregation and discrimination force up housing prices to Negroes. And we do not know how the pattern of low-density suburban housing affects the optimum transportation systems of a metropolitan area.

Thus, the volume of papers collected by Professors Page and Seyfried should be viewed not only as a report on the current state of knowledge, but also as a challenge for future work.

Edwin S. Mills
Baltimore

CONTENTS

INTRODUCTION

HOUSING AND THE URBAN ENVIRONMENT

Population Pressure, Housing, and Habitat

JOSEPH J. SPENGLER

INTRODUCTION

A house is not a home. This aphorism is usually held to possess validity only in the demimonde. Brief consideration suggests, however, that the validity of this aphorism is not so confined. It fits other worlds as well; in particular, the world of housing upon which the current issue of this journal is focused.

It may still be true in this age of insecurity, anti-privacy, and emerging police states, that "the house of everyone is to him," as Sir Edward Coke declared four centuries ago, "as his castle and fortress, as well for his defense against injury and violence as for his repose." It is also true that a man's house means a great deal more, even to those who agree with Samuel Butler that occasional absence from one's house enhances its attractiveness.

In this article I argue (a) that the subject of housing must be examined in terms of the larger set of *gesellschaftliche* and *gemeinschaftliche* relations within which the house, together with its occupying household, is situated; (b) that this set of relations and hence the role of housing is significantly affected by the growth and concentration of population, control of which is essential to the easing of the so-called housing problem.

The underlying issue is clearly recognized by architects such as Doxiadis who see in the expansion of the impersonal city and the associated elimination of nature a process that is destroying neighborhood and community units and making of man a building-occupying troglodyte subject to "instructions issued from the peak of the pyramid." He suggests that we once again create human communities in our cities, "operating neighborhoods, downtown shopping centers where people can walk freely, can come into natural contact, can enjoy quiet surroundings and create and admire art. These human communities should become the cells which will be interconnected by mechanical means of transportation and communications to form major systems and major cities." [1] While Doxiadis is here referring mainly to communities within large cities he recognizes the interrela-

tion of housing and community and the importance of how man can spend his time, especially in a modern world in need of a moral equivalent to work.

HOME VERSUS HOUSE

How the Greeks, Aristotle in particular, viewed housing may be suggestive since concern for the eudaemonic aspect of life played a very important role in their view of housing—a concern honored more in the breach than in the observance in the United States.[2] Aristotle approaches housing in terms of the overall community and the pursuit of the "highest good." The polis, or city state, as he conceived of it, was a community which, embracing all other communities, aimed at the "highest good." The elemental community of which the state was composed was the household, to whose management Aristotle and those influenced by him devoted attention.[3] Aristotle, defender of simplicity in a simple age, pointed to the smallness of the number of instruments needed within a household to make the "good life" possible.[4] Presumably he agreed with Hesiod that a house was the "first and foremost" requisite of a household [5] and with the statement that "a house must be arranged both with a view to one's possessions and for the health and well-being of its inhabitants." A house must, therefore, "be airy in summer and sunny in winter"; whence it needs to face "north" and be longer

Reprinted from a symposium, *Housing: Perspectives and Problems,* Part I, appearing in *Law and Contemporary Problems,* XXXII, No. 2, Spring 1967, published by the Duke University School of Law, Durham, North Carolina 27706. Copyright © 1967 by Duke University.

1 Doxiadis, *Topics: Of Inhuman and Human Cities,* N.Y. Times, March 11, 1967, at 28, col. 5. *See generally* on *gemeinschaft and gesellschaft,* T. Parsons, STRUCTURE OF SOCIAL ACTION 686–94 (1937).
2 *See, e.g.,* R. E. Wycherly, HOW THE GREEKS BUILT CITIES (2d ed. 1962).
3 POLITICA 1:2. *See generally* OECONOMICA 1:1, a work partly Aristotelian and partly reflective of the influence of Xenophon and others.
4 POLITICA 1:8–9.
5 OECONOMICA 1:2.

than wide.[6] These and other aspects of a house were stressed several centuries later by the architect Vitruvius, a contemporary of Nero, who designed and situated several types of houses to meet specific occupational and climatic requirements.[7]

Aristotle looked upon a house as one of a triad of interrelated elements: house, household, and organic urban community. The house sheltered the members of the household and afforded them access to a good and healthy life. The household itself was relatively self-sufficient, as a rule. The head of a household was united with other household heads in that network of reciprocity which undergirded the state or urban community.

The problems confronting a household in Aristotle's day were fewer and simpler than those confronting a household in the affluent present. Cities usually were small and relatively free of congestion, even of that congestion of which Juvenal was later to complain in Imperial Rome. Getting to work, to recreational and religious centers, or to political responsibilities, presented no serious difficulties. Aristotle wanted to keep the Greek city that way. Not only did he insist that a city not be large, since "a very populous city can rarely, if ever, be well governed," He even suggested that its population not exceed "the largest number which suffices for the purposes of life, and can be taken in a single view."[8] Had he anticipated today's opulent society, he would have found it wanting, along with its conception of housing.

The observations made by Aristotle or imputable to him call attention to the fact that a house is not a solitary, autonomous, self-subsisting unit, even when occupied by a household, but rather a locus in many partially overlapping environments or complexes. It is a locus in the spatial economy of the household; it is a locus in a social environment; it is a locus in a physical environment that varies in salubrity and conduciveness to health. In the parlance of today, we may conceive of a house as a micro-habitat within a larger but highly relevant macro-habitat. The householder may be said to dwell in the former and carry on his extra-dwelling roles and functions in the latter. It is quite evident, therefore, that his well-being and the extent to which he can attain the good life depend in large measure upon the quality of each of these two habitats. This inference is borne out by data assembled on the amounts of time spent by various types of families, upon in-home and extra-house activities, respectively.[9]

Since a house is a micro-habitat within a macro-habitat, it is improper to conceive of housing independently of and in isolation from the macro-habitat within which houses are situated. To do so is on a par with conceiving of Gettysburg in terms of Edward Everett's prolix but forgotten oration. That housing often is so conceived of is a result of the absence of order, or even of ordering values, from the determinants of the growth, organization, and construction of cities. The outcomes resulting are accepted as parts of the scheme of things, with the result that the fundamental significance of the macro-habitat for the quality of housing is underestimated. In consequence, the impact of the growth and concentration of population upon man's macro- and micro-habitats receives little attention.

THE MACRO-HABITAT

The macro-habitat, within which household, house, and micro-habitat are situated, embraces a number of environments. For purposes of illustration we need discuss only a few. Perhaps the most important is the set of spatial economies within which the individuals composing a household seek the good life, directly and/or indirectly through pursuit of material means. Almost equally important are the social, physical, and health environments of the micro-habitat. It is sometimes said, of course, that modern man has become largely free of his external environment.[10] This exaggerated view

6 *Id.* at 1:6.
7 Vitruvius, THE TEN BOOKS ON ARCHITECTURE 24–26, 38–41, 170–92 (M. H. Morgan transl. 1960).
8 POLITICA 7:4.
9 *E.g.,* the excellent account given in J. N. Morgan, I. A. Serageldin & N. Baerwaldt, PRODUCTIVE AMERICANS (1966).
10 For example, R. W. Gerard writes: "Man has, in fact, largely cut himself off from the external environment and created a hothouse internal environment of culture in which he lives in remarkable physical comfort. . . . Our lives are spent overwhelmingly at the symbolic level, and we live in a

suggests a modern Daedalus who pretends to have risen above his physical environment. One must, therefore, agree with Dubos's comment: "As happened to Antaeus of the Greek legend, his [man's] strength will probably wane if he loses contact with the biological ground from which he emerged and which still feeds him, physically and emotionally." [11]

A house is always a locus of household activities and a base from which members of a household operate. The household is situated in a net of activity-loci interrelated from the vantage point of members of a household even if not always connected by exchange as are interrelated markets. Each member of a household moves from his house to a locus of activity and back to his house either directly or via a path connecting diverse activities participated in sequentially. The problem confronting each member of a household is that of minimizing time utilized in moving from house to activity, from activity to activity, and from activity to house. His capacity to minimize time thus expended is quite limited, however, since the loci of these activities, together with the house, are not easily modified. [12]

Economy of time must be mainly sought, therefore, via economy of space, though some economy of time is achievable through reducing the actual time cost if not also the pecuniary cost of traversing space. Economy of space in turn must be sought through optimizing the spatial arrangement of relevant activities in the urban environs of the house and household. [13] When this is done a house begins to be viewed as a home, as the focus of man's search for the good life. This outcome is not likely to be emphasized, however, until both social scientists and those who manage the allocation of resources become space-minded—concerned about terrestrial and urban space rather than about mere lunar and Martian space. For, as Isard observes, excessive emphasis upon time in economic analysis long made for neglect of the role of space in the theoretical and empirical structures of Anglo-Saxon economists. [14]

What constitutes a satisfactory social environment is not easy to define or to realize empirically. It is evident, however, that occupants of micro-habitats or neighborhoods are not likely to agree upon what makes a social environment satisfactory unless they agree on many things.

This condition is overlooked, of course, in much of the discussion of housing that involves the intermingling of households which are quite dissimilar in tastes and conduct-determining norms. Even within a household common standards of value must be present to permit passage from the preference patterns of its individual members to a preference pattern representative of the household as such. [15] At the neighborhood level where the tastes of individuals must be sufficiently similar to permit the construction of "suitable social welfare functions," [16] a minimal though not excessive degree of similarity of tastes is essential to insure agreement on what constitutes a satisfactory social environment. The degree required is less when there is agreement both on the need for day-to-day decisions and on the mechanism or process whereby these decisions are reached. [17] The market mechanism alone is unlikely to bring about this minimal degree under all conditions, though it can be enabled to do so if certain conditions are met. [18] It is true, as a rule, therefore, that a considerable though variable degree of homogeneity in the tastes of those inhabiting a neighborhood or macro-habitat is essential to their settling upon what makes a social environment good. When this degree is not fully attained, whether because

man-made sea of meanings. And the sea is still rising more or less exponentially." Gerard, *Intelligence, Information, and Education*, 148 SCI. 762, 763 (1965).
11 R. Dubos, MAN ADAPTING 279 (1965).
12 An extended inquiry into the relationships between time, space, and activity is being conducted by G. C. Hemmens. A recent progress report is available: The Structure of Urban Activity Linkages, 1966 (mimeo., Center for Urban and Regional Studies, University of North Carolina, Chapel Hill).
13 W. Isard, LOCATION AND SPACE-ECONOMY (1956).
14 *Id.* at 24–27.
15 K. J. Arrow, SOCIAL CHOICE AND INDIVIDUAL VALUES 9 n.1 (Cowles Comm'n for Research in Economics Monograph No. 12, 1951).
16 *Id.* at 81. "[I]t must be demanded that there be some sort of consensus on the ends of society, or no social welfare functions can be performed." *Id.* at 83.
17 Arrow concludes that "we may expect that social welfare judgments can usually be made when there is both a widespread agreement on the decision process and a widespread agreement on the desirability of everyday decisions." *Id.* at 91.
18 The market mechanism does not always take into account all relevant matters, although it can be manipulated to this end. *See* Arrow's discussion, *id.* at 81–86.

of class or other differences, the macro-habitat becomes instable.[19] It can become instable also if the inhabitants and their children become too standardized.

While it appears to be true that whatever unduly reduces the degree of homogeneity of any particular neighborhood or macro-habitat affects it unfavorably, this inference does not support the view that cultural differences *between* macro-habitats should be reduced. There must be room in the all-inclusive community for a sufficiency of diversity which, while a characteristic of individuals, is in part a concomitant of differences between macro-habitats.[20] It may be well, therefore, that the overall community resemble a sea dotted with islands which differ culturally from one another.[21] Unfortunately, the "formal elegance of welfare economics" does not tell us how much homogeneity is essential to a people's happiness.[22]

It may be noted parenthetically that economic as well as social factors have to be taken into account if the current housing shortage confronting nonwhites is to be greatly reduced. For, while housing values in nonwhite areas tend to lie below those for comparable housing in nearby white areas,[23] and while block-busting can enlarge nonwhite housing areas, urban renewal programs tend to raise the price of affected urban land above the level at which it is economically attractive to most nonwhites.[24] Emphasis upon residential desegregation, it is said, is retarding the construction of low-income housing.[25]

The degree of attractiveness of the physical environment of a macro-habitat enveloping a dwelling unit depends upon many circumstances, some of which seem to have been taken into account even in ancient ghetto-ridden Egypt.[26] Among these circumstances are absence of disorder and traffic congestion, the availability of private and public space, and general attractiveness, now usually lacking within as well as outside American urban centers.[27] Closely related is the healthfulness of this environment and its freedom from noise and pollution, both of which are inimical to good health.[28]

An environment's healthfulness usually depends, at least in advanced countries, upon its freedom from pollution, especially chemical pollution of the water and the atmosphere.

19 For example, a retirement city built outside Sacramento for retired military personnel proved a flop. "[I]t turned out that retired colonels did not like to live beside retired sergeants, and neither liked the idea of living on streets named Billy Mitchell Boulevard and Hap Arnold Court." FORTUNE, Feb. 1966, at 158.
20 *See generally* Platt, *Diversity*, 154 SCI. 1132 (1966), for a discussion stressing the importance of cultural and other diversity.
21 In the United States, for example, though unifying common values are present, there are also many local communities which, though they include diverse elements, have evolved each into a somewhat unique constellation of values and institutions. *See, e.g.,* R. E. Engler, Jr., THE CHALLENGE OF DIVERSITY (1964).
22 Mishan, *A Survey of Welfare Economics, 1939–59,* in 1 SURVEYS OF ECONOMIC THEORY 154, 211–13 (American Economic Ass'n & Royal Economic Soc'y 1965).
23 Bailey, *Effects of Race and of Other Demographic Factors on the Values of Single-Family Homes,* 42 LAND ECON. 215 (1966).
24 *See* J. Rothenberg, ECONOMIC EVALUATION OF URBAN RENEWAL (1967); Bailey, *Note on the Economics of Residential Zoning and Urban Renewal,* 35 LAND ECON. 288 (1959); Nourse, *The Economics of Urban Renewal,* 42 LAND ECON. 65 (1966).
25 "The Achilles heel of housing programs has been precisely our insistence that better housing for the black poor be achieved by residential desegregation. This ideal glosses over the importance of the ethnic community as a staging area for groups to build the communal solidarity and power necessary to compel eventual access to the mainstream of urban life. . . .
"If group conflict is at the root of past failures, strategies must be found to improve ghetto housing without arousing the ire of powerful segments of the white community." Piven & Cloward, *Desegregated Housing, Who Pays for the Reformers' Ideal?,* NEW REPUBLIC, Dec. 17, 1966, at 17, 21. That this proposal for the improvement of ghettos is not impractical is suggested by the actions of a number of large building supply companies that are rebuilding parts of slums, to be turned over to nonprofit sponsors, and by plans to establish corporations that can produce housing competitive with public housing. *See* Ridgeway, *Rebuilding the Slums,* NEW REPUBLIC, Jan. 7, 1967, at 22.
26 Perhaps the world's first model village for workmen was that built in Amarna in Egypt in the 14th century, B.C. *See* E. Wells, NEFERTITI 162–63 (1964).
27 *See* L. Halprin, FREEWAYS (1966); Faltermayer, *How to Wage War on Ugliness,* FORTUNE, May 1966, at 130; Larremore, *Public Aesthetics,* 20 HARV. L. REV. 35 (1906). *See generally* R. Starr, THE LIVING END: THE CITY AND ITS CRITICS (1966); Spengler, *The Aesthetics of Population,* 13 POPULATION BULL. 61 (1957).
28 *See generally* on the adverse effects of noise, Beranek, *Noise,* SCIENTIFIC AM., Dec. 1966, at 66; Kryter, *Psychological Reactions to Aircraft Noise,* 151 SCI. 1346 (1966); *Silence at Less than $35 an Ounce,* FORTUNE, Dec. 1966, at 191; *When Noise Annoys,* TIME, Aug. 19, 1966, at 24, and on the destructiveness of the "sonic boom," offset only by an increase in the egg-hatching rate among chickens, THE NEW YORKER, Dec. 18, 1965, at 41.

"[T]he few facts available demonstrate," René Dubos states, "that pathological states can be caused by exposure to concentrations of pollutants of the order of those which exist in the urban atmosphere. On the basis of these results, it can be surmised that pollution can also have deleterious and lasting effects on human beings." [29] "The possibility of delayed and cumulative effects is not limited to any particular class of agent." [30] Dubos, therefore, stresses the "need for *striking* information" because "environmental pollution will not be controlled until physicians and scientists take an active part in its study." [31] Response to this same need on the part of students of urban and housing environments will help place efforts to solve housing problems in a more general context than is common at present; it will help men recognize that since, as Commoner shows, the elements of nature constitute an integrated totality,[32] it must be dealt with as a whole and not in a piecemeal fashion.[33]

POPULATION TRENDS

The rate of population growth has fallen below 1.5 per cent per year, at which rate it increased in 1960–64 when natural increase accounted for eighty-seven per cent of the total growth. Natality has since descended enough to reduce the current rate of natural increase nearly to one per cent per year. In the years just ahead, however, the large increase in the number of females aged 20–29, an echo of the upsurge of natality after the war, should push natality up somewhat. It is likely that the nation's population, nearly 198 million at the beginning of 1967, will number over 250 million by 1985 and 300 million or more by the close of the century. Should this population continue thereafter to grow 1¼ per cent per year it would number a billion or more by the year 2100, by which time population density might exceed 350 per square mile in the conterminous United States. Acres of all sorts per person would then average less than two.

The nonwhite population will increase somewhat faster than the white population, rising from twelve per cent of the total at present to about 13.5 per cent by 1985. At that time the rate of natural increase of the nonwhite popu-

lation may be somewhat in excess of two per cent whereas the white rate will be about 1⅓ per cent. Should that rate differential persist, around one-fourth of the nation's population would be nonwhite by 2085.

While the farm population has continued to decline, from 32 million in 1920 to less than 12 million, increase in population concentration has been extensive rather than intensive. The population formerly defined as rural has continued to increase, though only about half as fast as the nation's population—in 1940–60 about sixteen per cent instead of thirty-five per cent as in the aggregate. The urban population increased more rapidly, of course, about fifty-two per cent; that in places under 100,000 increased about seventy-one per cent while that in places of 100,000 and over grew about thirty-four per cent. Even so, the proportion which the population in places of over 100,000 constituted of the total population changed only slightly.[34] The data just presented do not, however, fully reflect the implosion and megalopolitanization of population in process. But they do reveal how a shifting urban frontier has replaced that westerly moving rural frontier in terms of which some seventy years ago Frederick Jackson Turner interpreted the course of American history up to the 1890s. For a real sense of the change we must turn to metropolitan data.

29 Dubos, *supra* note 11, at 209–10. *See generally* ENVIRONMENTAL POLLUTION PANEL, PRESIDENT'S SCIENCE ADVISORY COMMITTEE, RESTORING THE QUALITY OF OUR ENVIRONMENT 1–9, 91–101 (Report of the Environmental Pollution Panel, 1965).
30 Dubos, *supra* note 11, at 221. *See generally* B. Commoner, SCIENCE AND SURVIVAL (1966); *Ecology*, TIME, Jan. 27, 1967, at 48.
31 Dubos, *supra* note 11, at 225. (Emphasis added.)
32 Commoner, *supra* note 30.
33 *See, e.g.*, COMMITTEE ON POLLUTION, NATIONAL RESEARCH COUNCIL, NATIONAL ACADEMY OF SCIENCES, PUB. NO. 1400, WASTE MANAGEMENT AND CONTROL (1966); SUBCOMM. ON SCIENCE, RESEARCH, AND DEVELOPMENT, HOUSE COMM. ON SCIENCE AND ASTRONAUTICS, 89TH CONG., 2D SESS., ENVIRONMENTAL POLLUTION—A CHALLENGE TO SCIENCE AND TECHNOLOGY (Comm. Print 1966).
34 In 1940, 28.8 per cent of the total population and 51 per cent of the urban population lived in places of 100,000 and over. The corresponding percentages in 1960 were 28.4 and 45. I have used the former census definition of "urban" in order to make the data of 1940 comparable with those of 1950 and 1960.

Continuing population growth may intensify population concentration and urban crowding in two ways. First, it may simply add to the population situated in places of all sizes. Second, should the population-attracting power of cities increase more than in proportion to their numerical size, the rate of growth will be greatest in larger centers and the fraction of the nation's population concentrated therein will increase. This did happen between 1900 and 1930 when the rural fraction of the population fell from 60.3 per cent to 43.8 per cent and when the population in places of 100,000 and over rose from 18.7 to 29.6 per cent of the total population and from 47.1 to 52.7 per cent of the urban population. Then the process slowed down. Between 1930 and 1950 none of these percentages changed markedly. More recently some dispersion has set in. Between 1950 and 1960 the fraction of the nation's population situated in places of both above 500,000 and above 100,000 declined. This increase in dispersion may reflect in part a forty-two per cent increase in 1940–60 in the number of places under 100,000—of which nearly three-fifths were added in 1950–60.[35]

Whether an increasing fraction of the nation's population does become concentrated in the larger centers turns on the strength of the stochastic process apparently underlying what Kendall, describing the work of Zipf and others, calls "a kind of the-higher-the-fewer rule." This rule "says, in effect, that for certain kinds of activity with a measurable size x, the number y of individuals greater than or equal to x is given by

$$y = A/x^p$$

where p is a constant which is often quite close to unity."[36] Here y stands for the rank of a particular city in size of population, x for its size, and p and A are constants, with A denoting the population of the largest center and p approximating unity. Now if A grows faster than a nation's population, it will, after the manner of a Saturn eating his own children, increase at the expense of other communities, especially the smaller ones;[37] but if the number of communities grows rapidly enough, the population will tend to become more dispersed.[38]

It is within the metropolitan population that we find changes taking place of great significance for housing and its macro-habitats. First, the population of metropolitan areas is growing much faster than that lying outside these areas—2.3 per cent per year in the 1950s and 1.9 per cent per year in 1960–65 when the corresponding rates for the nonmetropolitan population were 0.8 and 0.7 per cent per year. The fraction of the nation's population living in metropolitan areas rose from about 60.5 per cent in 1950 to about sixty-three per cent in 1960 and sixty-four per cent in 1965. The metropolitan population in 1960 already approximated nine-tenths of the urban population and it could easily rise to seventy-five per cent of the nation's total population within 40–50 years. Second, while the proportion of the nation's population growth taking place in metropolitan areas is greater than before the Second World War, the proportion taking place in central cities situated within metropolitan areas is declining, especially in those with over a million inhabitants.[39] In sum, while the nation's population is becoming more concentrated, within the larger areas of concentration a redistribution of population is taking place and thus changing or threatening to change many of the macro-habitats within which housing is located. The rate of change underway can be especially significant because it is made up of net in-migration as well as of natural increase. For example, between 1950 and 1960 about thirty-five per cent of the increase in metropolitan population was due to in-migration.[40]

The long continued migration of the Negro to the city in search of better economic opportunity and housing, coupled with the decline

35 U.S. BUREAU OF THE CENSUS, DEP'T OF COMMERCE, STATISTICAL ABSTRACT OF THE UNITED STATES 1965, at 15 (1965); C. Taeuber & I. B. Taeuber, THE CHANGING POPULATION OF THE UNITED STATES 114–15, 118 (1958).
36 Kendall, Natural Law in the Social Sciences, 124 J. THE ROYAL STATISTICAL SOC'Y (ser. A) 1, 4 (1961). See generally Isard, supra note 13, at 55.
37 G. K. Zipf, NATIONAL UNITY AND DISUNITY 55 (1941). In the United States the ratio of New York's population to that of the nation rose between 1880 and 1930 and thereafter fell. Id. at 56. I have computed the ratios for 1950 and 1960.
38 The ratio of places to population rose from 100 in 1900 to 115 in 1930, 118 in 1940, and 126 in 1960.
39 W. S. Thompson & D. T. Lewis, POPULATION PROBLEMS 141–48, 156 (5th ed. 1965).
40 Id. at 151–152.

in foreign immigration, is bringing about a re-distribution of population within metropolitan centers.[41] This redistribution is of very great significance for housing problems since in 1965 about sixty-four per cent of the white population of the United States and about sixty-eight per cent of the nonwhite population lived in metropolitan areas. This redistributive process reflects forces affecting both concentration and congestion as well as the passage of a city's racial composition beyond a so-called tipping point.[42] First, the population outside the central cities has been growing much faster than that in these cities, four per cent per year in 1950–60 and 3.3 per cent per year in 1960–65 compared with annual increases in central cities of one per cent in the 1950s and 0.6 per cent in 1960–65. Second, the nonwhites are displacing the whites in central cities with the result that if this process continues, by 1980 seven or more large cities will be predominantly nonwhite (mainly Negro) and perhaps thirty more about one-third nonwhite. Of the top ten cities in the United States only Houston and Los Angeles will be predominantly white thirty-five years from now.[43]

Illustrative of current redistributive tendencies are those of 1960–65 when the nonwhite population of metropolitan areas increased 2,508 thousand, of whom 2,096 thousand settled in central cities. Meanwhile, the metropolitan white population increased 8,982 thousand, *all* of whom settled outside central cities, together with about 470 thousand who migrated there on balance from central cities. The nonwhite fraction of the total central-city population thus rose from about eighteen per cent in 1960 to nearly twenty-one per cent in 1965; in 1950 it was only about thirteen per cent.[44] Meanwhile the nonwhite fraction of the metropolitan population in the ring of areas outside central cities, about 5.5 per cent in 1950, had declined to five per cent by 1960. An unpublished study of eleven central cities, by my colleague Reynolds Farley, indicates that residential segregation is again increasing.

So alarmed has the present administration apparently become at the current drift and its implications for desegregation of the school system that what amount to legislative and administrative efforts to countervail or reverse the drift are being initiated.[45] This approach

not only is unmindful of potential boomerang effects; it overlooks the advantages to be had from the proposal made below to multiply the number of urban centers to which Negro and white can migrate and through which the problem of concentration can be greatly alleviated, though not solved altogether.

POPULATION EFFECTS

The effects of the population trends described in the preceding section are of two sorts, sequelae to population growth and sequelae to population concentration. Four sequelae to population growth may be noted. The first of these, the accentuation of population concentration or density, has already been touched upon. The second, increase in overall population, is treated largely under the head of population concentration, of which it is a source. Of course, enlargement of areas of population density outside areas of heavy concentration do produce effects of the sort discussed below, though less intense than those found in areas of heavy concentration.

The third effect of population growth is the absorption of inputs which might otherwise have been used to improve the material condition of the existing population and its replacement. Here we may indicate only the order of magnitude of this cost which may then be compared with fixed investment in residential construction that has been running about $22 bil-

41 *See* Newman, *The Negro's Journey to the City* (pts. 1 & 2), 88 MONTHLY LABOR REV. 502, 644 (1965).
42 *See, e.g.,* Grodzins, *Metropolitan Segregation,* SCIENTIFIC AM., Oct. 1957, at 33; Tauber & Tauber, *White Migration and Socio-Economic Differences Between Cities and Suburbs,* 29 AM. SOCIOLOGICAL REV. 718 (1964); Winsborough, *An Ecological Approach to the Theory of Suburbanization,* 68 AM. J. SOCIOLOGY 565 (1963); Winsborough, *City Growth and City Structure,* J. REGIONAL SCI., Winter 1962, at 35.
43 U.S. NEWS & WORLD REPORT, Feb. 21, 1966, at 72–73; U.S. NEWS & WORLD REPORT, March 6, 1967, at 58–62.
44 The fraction that was Negro was slightly smaller than the nonwhite. *See generally* on the suburbanization process, Winsborough, *An Ecological Approach to the Theory of Suburbanization, supra* note 42.
45 *See* U.S. NEWS & WORLD REPORT, Feb. 27, 1967, at 68–69.

lion a year. If we conceive of capital only in terms of hard goods and suppose it costs about four per cent of the national income to support a rate of population growth of one per cent per year, then the cost of America's population growth has been in the neighborhood of $30 billion a year since 1964. If we include under the head of "capital" all expenditure which serves to increase the stream of income in the future and allow as well for the adverse effect of population growth upon the age composition of the population, we may raise this figure to around $45 billion. Another way of arriving at an estimate is to suppose that the cost of adding a cross-sectional thousand people to the nation's population costs between $10 and $20 million. On this supposition, adding about 2.5 million persons a year to the population costs between $25 and $50 billion a year. Whatever be the correct estimate, it represents an annual expenditure far in excess of the current rate of expenditure upon residential construction. Of course, even should fertility fall to the replacement level, it would take a few years for the benefits to materialize fully and then they might be utilized in part in the form of leisure.[46]

The fourth effect is associated with the continual change in city size produced by population growth and discussed earlier. Let us suppose that a country's population is stationary. Its population distribution will then be fairly stable, affected by changes in technology, incomes, and the composition of tastes and amenities, but *not* by the main source of distributive change operative in the past—namely, increase in the nation's population. The urban problem would then become mainly one of keeping particular cities and their macro-habitats intact; it would thus resemble maintaining a stationary economy's capital intact.[47] Financial provision for the maintenance of all components of a city including its housing and macro-habitats could then easily be put on an orderly basis. Planning for changes could be carried out readily since almost any particular change would be but a wave in a sea of stability. Short and long time-horizons would differ less than now. The remaining changes would be small enough so that, were they met sub-optimally, corrective action would be easy and not very costly. Under these conditions demographic metabolism, the replacement of old families

nearing or beyond retirement by younger families, would entail little unfavorable change in the quality of the environment.

Population concentration and density produce a number of somewhat distinct effects, all of which, when intensified beyond a critical point, outweigh the advantages associated with a lesser amount of population agglomeration. These effects are incident on some or all the macro-habitats constituting a community, though in varying degree, and they reduce the contribution that housing can make to welfare. "Welfare," in other words, may be viewed as a joint "product" of (*inter alia*) that which a household's housing and macro-habitat make possible and that which the larger, all-inclusive community makes possible. Agglomeration of population continues to increase the latter contribution after it has begun to diminish that of housing and habitat, until a point is reached where the positive effect is offset at the margin by the negative effect. This is the optimum point; it varies with household, of course, and this variation affects how population distributes itself within urban or metropolitan space.

It is not possible here to catalog and describe all the effects associated with excessive population growth and concentration, but the main ones may be touched upon in order to illustrate the theme of this paper. These effects are contraction of space, pollution, congestion, unproductive use of time, and sub-optimal distributions of population.

Population concentration reduces the ratio of space available per person for household and/or other activities and thus diminishes the contribution of space to the city-dweller's standard of life. In 1960 about twenty-eight per cent of the nation's population occupied only 0.23 per cent of its land area, and about forty-five per cent occupied just under one half of one per cent of this area. Population density ranged from 13,870 persons per square mile in places of a million or more to just over 3,900 per square mile in places of 50-100 thousand and

46 When families earn less than $6,000 per year they tend to put forth extra effort. *See* Morgan, Serageldin, & Baerwaldt, *supra* note 9, at 191. *See generally* on choosing between more work and more leisure, *id.* at 198–202.
47 *See generally* on "maintaining capital intact," A. C. Pigou, ECONOMICS OF WELFARE 43-49 (4th ed. 1932).

about 2,290 per square mile in places of 10 to 25 thousand. Expressed in terms of acres per person, ground space per person ranged from about one twenty-fifth of an acre in places of over a million to one-sixth of an acre in places of 50–100 thousand and nearly three-tenths of an acre in places of 10–25 thousand. Even if we allow four persons per household, the pinch of space is pronounced, for part of this average land quota is required for streets, structures other than housing, and very rarely for parks. Moreover, since the daytime population of cities is much greater than their nighttime population, density within the city in daytime is more pronounced than our data suggest.

Second, population concentration increases the exposure of housing and macro-habitats to pollution of all sorts. Most of it is ultimately of human origin and therefore is in greatest amount where men are concentrated and live, work, and consume, and hence manufacture debris, pollutants, and contaminants of all sorts. Moreover, the impact of this unwelcome product is hard to cushion. For example, since about nine-tenths of United States air pollution "consists of largely invisible but potentially deadly gases," air conditioners cannot defoul the atmosphere; at best they can remove particles.[48] It is doubtful, therefore, if man's natural right to breathe clean air can be made realizable in megalopolitan or other large centers. Indeed, he may find himself hard pressed even to dispose of his refuse and get a sufficient supply of usable water.[49]

We may state the problem generally and in terms of a set of hypothetical flows. Modern life is subjective and objective; it consists largely in symbolic communication and in the flow of men and matter. The volume of each stream tends to increase faster than population, especially in urban settings. Indeed, an urban center, above all, a megalopolis, may be thought of as a network of channels for the conduct of men and matter, together with information, within that center and between it and the world outside its environs. Channel capacities are limited and so are the number of channels actually or potentially available. Let R_e represent the rate of flow of effluent e and C_e the capacity of channels existing for the conveyance and disposal of e into the atmosphere, into waters, and elsewhere, but always in keeping

with the health and good life of all concerned. If $R_e > C_e$, portions of e must be destroyed at points of origin, or stored until R_e falls below C_e. Otherwise e will accumulate within the population center and perhaps in areas immediately nearby. Presumably R_e grows at least as fast as $(p' + g')$ where p' denotes the rate of population growth of an urban center and g' denotes the rate of growth of per capita consumption and/or production of output which gives rise to various forms of effluent within the urban center. Since C_e has upper limits, it is inevitable that as a center's population grows, the probability of pollution of the macro-habitats of housing increases.

Third, congestion of channels for the conveyance of people and perhaps also of those for the conveyance of information tends to increase with population growth and concentration. Consider for example the movement of traffic through the center of a metropolitan area; it can grow nearly as the square of the population. "To keep the degree of traffic congestion constant, road traffic capacity must rise far more than in proportion with the rate of increase of population, and sheer problems of geography and land availability practically preclude such a possibility. Of course, the fact that population tends to cluster and is not spread evenly throughout the city only adds to these congestion problems."[50] This congestion, together with the accompanying noise and disorder, tends to accentuate two interrelated forces which generate the cumulative deterioration of local environment and macro-habitats—namely, urban blight and flight to the suburbs.[51] Dense traffic is not the only form of congestion that inflicts uncompensated costs upon a large fraction of the population. There is also, as Colin Clark points out, a second

48 Ecology, TIME, Jan. 27, 1967, at 48, 49–50; See generally RESTORING THE QUALITY OF OUR ENVIRONMENT, supra note 29, at 1–9, 62–69.
49 New York's garbage dumps will be filled in eight years, N.Y. Times, Feb. 20, 1967, at 27, col. 1. See generally on the water problem, Wolman, The Metabolism of Cities, SCIENTIFIC AM., Sept. 1965, at 179, 181–185.
50 Baumol, Urban Services: Interactions of Public and Private Decisions, in PUBLIC EXPENDITURE DECISIONS IN THE URBAN COMMUNITY 1, 7–8 (H. G. Schaller ed. 1963).
51 Id. at 11–14; G. Neutze, ECONOMIC POLICY AND THE SIZE OF CITIES (1965).

type, "zonal congestion," the dearth of open space for recreational and other purposes.[52] Oddly enough, another British author argues for the "concentration of future population growth in a limited number of major cities as opposed to a balanced and uniform expansion of all existing urban centres."[53] Such concentration will economize on land and thus preserve more land for agriculture and the amenities.[54] He has in mind England where overall population density is very high, greater even than in Japan.

Fourth, two further concomitants of population concentration may be noted, each of which may affect man's macro-habitat adversely. First, a population and its activities may become suboptimally dispersed within a metropolitan region and then perpetuated because the totality of public and private fixed capital outlays undergirding this distribution is so great as to render modifications very expensive. Herein, it is to be noted, we find support for careful anticipational urban planning, together with emphasis upon the preservation of flexibility and the retention of options realizable in the future. Since urban decisions tend to become frozen in steel and concrete as well as in transport systems, they should not be taken and acted upon until and unless the future is relatively clear. Second, a sub-optimal distribution of population and activities makes for high consumption per capita of modern man's most precious possession, time that might otherwise be discretionary and hence contributive to his well-being. Perhaps increasing education will result in countervailing measures. Did not Dante write: "Who knows most, him loss of time most grieves."[55]

POLICY IMPLICATIONS

Certain policy implications may be derived from what has been said. First, it is unlikely that the housing problem can ever be solved satisfactorily so long as population continues to grow and with it the excessive size of cities. For the impact of growth, unless carefully planned for and counterbalanced, will make for continual decay of parts of cities and hence of macro-habitats. Not only central cities but suburbs as well will continue to be subject to this

process of decay which steals in unobtrusively, not as a fast-working pestilence that comes in the night but as a slowly working mutagen which produces a bodily change that in time metastasizes. It will probably be many years, however, before population growth ceases, or, in the absence of nuclear war, becomes negative.

Second, contemporary tax and subsidy systems conduce to the deterioration of many macro-habitats, together with housing, by putting a premium on deterioration or by shunting its costs from those responsible to non-responsible third parties. (a) Buildings and land need to be differentially taxed in order that taxation of real property, usually a deterrent to its maintenance and improvement, will cease to be so.[56] (b) Every business firm or organization must be made to bear all congestion and related costs to which it gives rise, costs currently borne in part by others. (c) Impose the entire cost of urban expansion upon those responsible for this cost, instead of partly upon non-responsible parties as at present.

Third, current financial arrangements for maintaining housing and other forms of urban capital are inadequate to keep this capital intact through repair and/or replacement. Two approaches seem indicated. (1) Requiring the accumulation of adequate, earmarked liquidable assets to permit repair or replacement as it becomes necessary. (2) Require architects to plan construction in much greater measure than now in terms of easily replaceable parts,

52 Clark, *Industrial Location and Economic Potential,* LLOYDS BANK REV., Oct. 1966, at 1, 3–4.
53 Bellan, *The Future Growth of Britain's Cities,* 37 THE TOWN PLANNING REV. 173, 183 (1966).
54 *Id.* at 183–184. *See generally* G. P. Wibberley, AGRICULTURE AND URBAN GROWTH 201–229 (1959).
55 PURGATORY, Canto I.
56 M. M. Gaffney writes of building taxes as distinguished from land taxes that "it would be hard to contrive a tax calculated to throw more risk onto the builder in proportion to the revenues rasied." Gaffney, *Property Taxes and the Frequency of Urban Renewal,* in PROCEEDINGS OF THE FIFTY-SEVENTH ANNUAL CONFERENCE ON TAXATION 272, 284 (National Tax Ass'n 1964). The builder responds by not making improvements since the assessment of his land moves with the assessment of the structure on it. If, however, land is assessed and taxed at its true opportunity cost, it can no longer be economically allocated to sub-optimal uses. *See id.* at 272–85. *See generally* Woodruff & Ecker-Racz, *Property Taxes and Land Use Patterns in Australia and New Zealand,* THE TAX EXECUTIVE, Oct. 1965, at 16.

a point insisted upon by A. Spilhaus in his plan for an experimental city of about 250,000.[57]

Fourth, many problems associated with urban growth and housing flow from inattention to the need to balance *total* costs and benefits at the margin; and this form of inattention tends to grow faster than the size of urban centers. Pollution, congestion, and related costs are among those that need to be offset. A variety of measures is available for this purpose, some of which are better suited than others to particular cases.[58]

Fifth, several implications follow from the irreversible character of decisions or processes determining urban growth after it has taken place. It sometimes happens, as Lösch has pointed out, that production, having been initiated in the wrong place, will be continued there.[59] For such mislocation imperfectly planned investment is responsible. Urban growth and extension entail heavy fixed-capital investment the sacrifice of which, along with that of economy-yielding business connections, makes decision-makers loath to shift location. Given this heavy *ex-post* anchor, should not *ex-ante* decision-making be forced to take into account all expected costs as well as all suppositious advantages? Should not the set of forces currently shaping city growth be brought under more effective control, at least so long as these forces resemble those governing the growth of polyp colonies? Of course, city size could be explicitly limited, and the ownership of all urban land could be vested in cities. Such controls might, however, run counter to economic flexibility and American ideology. The same objectives could probably be achieved through use of a system of taxes and subsidies, calculated to influence population distribution and provide compensation to those on whom discretionary decisionmakers imposed unrequited direct and indirect costs. These tax and subsidy arrangements would be reinforced if a rent-absorbing tax in keeping with, say, the *zonal* opportunity cost of land were imposed on all *land* in and around cities.

Sixth, perhaps the greatest promise lies in the development of an adequate number of additional cities of such size—say, 100–200 thousand —as provides adequate communal opportunity, together with near-optimum conditions for housing and macro-habitats as well as abundant access to amenities and recreational space. Suppose that 600 such cities were established during the next thirty-five years. They could absorb 60–90 million or more inhabitants, or something like 60–80 or more per cent of the prospective population increase, most of which will settle in urban centers. If, say, as much as one-fourth of the population absorbed into these cities were nonwhite, it is possible that more than the anticipated increase in the nonwhite population would be settled there; then the current drift into central cities and ghettoes would be checked and perhaps reversed. Should such cities not be established, the population of most cities now over 100,000 would be greatly increased, for the next thirty-five years will witness the addition of 100 or more million to this nation's population and perhaps that of an equal number to the urban population, which in 1960 already numbered 113 million on the old census definition and 125 million on the new definition.

That this promise is realizable is suggested by two facts: (a) the relevant Key Decisions regarding location and many other matters are made by a very small number of businessmen; (b) big businessmen and corporations are becoming increasingly interested in the development of attractive, rationally-organized cities. We may divide a working population into Primary Job Makers and Job Takers, in which category may be placed Secondary Job Makers. The Primary Job Makers establish and locate the basic enterprises and employments. Around these gather Secondary Job Makers whose enterprises service and meet the needs of the Primary Job Makers and their employees as well as those of all persons who fall in the Job-Taker category. The heads of some but not all governmental agencies and foundations belong in the Primary Job-Maker category as they make Key Decisions affecting location of activities.

(a) That the making of Key Decisions respecting location is highly concentrated is sug-

57 Spilhaus, *The Experimental City*, The News and Observer (Raleigh, N.C.), Jan. 22, 1967, § 3, at 1.
58 *See, e.g.,* Ogden, *Economic Analysis of Air Pollution*, 42 LAND ECON. 137 (1966).
59 A. Lösch, THE ECONOMICS OF LOCATION 258, 330–331 (1954).

gested by the following data. In 1965 twenty-one out of each 100 persons employed in the United States were employed by 750 companies, many of which are describable as Primary Job Makers. About 55.1 per cent of all industrial workers were employed by 500 industrial companies.[60] Brian Berry reports that in the area around Chicago the location decisions of about twenty retailers control those of about 20,000 lesser retailers respecting where they will carry on for the next twenty-five years.[61] It is evident, therefore, that the Key Decisions essential to locating basic employment in new cities may be made by a small number of business firms. The implementation of such locational decisions would entail a redistribution of "brains," now most unevenly distributed because of unequal distribution of economic activities and educational institutions.[62] For "brains" have not merely replaced muscle; they now constitute the most strategic form of mobile and creative capital. "Brains," however, insist on access to cultural and other amenities as well as to good housing and attractive macro-habitats. Of this Key Decision Makers are becoming increasingly aware even if the current urban power structure is not.

A Key Decision Maker or two can launch a new city destined to number 100–200 thousand inhabitants by establishing an economic base capable of multiplying and expanding into around 40–80 thousand jobs.[63] If such base is established, say by introduction of manufacturing plants that employ 10–20 thousand persons, the labor force will expand sympathetically to something like 40–80 thousand gainfully employed. Manufacturing is not, of course, the only possible source of an initiating economic base, particularly in the United States, where the ratio of employment in manufacture to all employment is falling. Other activities, among them collections of services, may provide a base; they need only to supply the exports that enable the community to purchase goods and services not supplied locally.

(b) A Key Decision Maker may be interested in doing more than locating activities at a point in space where, he believes, a city with attractive environs will come into being. He may want to establish a more complete city, one providing not only basic employment but also ordered and abundant space for all ancil-

lary activities and amenities (including even such activities as amateur theatricals and similar activities which seldom yield returns even equal to private monetary costs). In such a city far more than in those described under (a) high priority must be given to housing and its macro-habitats and to averting the diverse costs and dissatisfactions associated with both life in central cities and life in isolated suburbs. Otherwise the collection of houses and macro-habitats constituting this city will not prove convertible into a community that generates a degree of loyalty and collective responsibility. It is probable that planned cities of this sort, together with those referred to under (a), can absorb most of the prospective increase in urban population. Illustrative of the planned type of community is that near Clear Lake, Texas, sponsored by the Humble Oil Company and the National Aeronautics and Space Administration, and intended to evolve over a fifteen-year period into a city of some 140,000 residents living in some 40,000 houses situated in an area of twenty-four miles square that includes a 365 acre town center and a 1,000 acre research park.[64] Somewhat similar cities are planned by General Electric Company, Goodyear Tire and Rubber Company, Westinghouse, and other large corporations. Several are well along—Robert Simon's Reston, Virginia, intended to house about 75,000 people, and James Rouse's Columbia, Maryland, intended to house about 110,000 people. All follow Secretary Udall's advice that "city planning should put people first." [65]

The types of towns referred to have a localized primary base, supplemented in several instances by the activities of inhabitants destined to work in nearby metropolitan centers. The housing problem is solved, though sometimes at

60 *Big Business in American Society, Is It Really Taking Over?*, BUSINESS IN BRIEF (Chase Manhattan Bank), Oct. 1966.
61 NORTH EASTERN ILLINOIS PLANNING COMMISSION, METROPOLITAN PLANNING GUIDE LINES, COMMERCIAL STRUCTURE 94, *cited in* Clark, *supra* note 52, at 3.
62 *See* Lapp, *Where the Brains Are*, FORTUNE, March 1966, at 154.
63 In 1960, 40% of the population was in the labor force. Given lower fertility this fraction might rise slightly.
64 *The Birth of a City*, THE HUMBLE WAY, No. 4, 1963, at 1–3.
65 S. L. Udall, THE QUIET CRISIS 170 (1963).

the expense of considerable cost in potentially discretionary time. This time-cost must be borne also by some of those who live in small planned communities (other than retirement communities) situated near metropolitan centers to which many must journey daily for employment. Again, however, the housing problem is solved.

CONCLUSION

The argument permeating this essay is that the housing question must be examined and carried toward resolution through a systematic approach rather than through the piecemeal approaches of speculators and others who neglect the fundamental importance of macro-habitats and their relations to each other and the larger urban unit. This approach is of increasing significance in an age when discretionary time is increasing and the challenge of the inept may be undergoing intensification, perhaps with Toynbeean implications.[66] It is not inferred that improvement in housing or even in macro-habitats will solve the ills of the day though it may contribute to solutions under appropriate conditions. It is suggested, however, that we are in need of innovation of systematic though diverse arrangements suited to the housing, habitat, and related needs of communities of varying size and situation. It is emphasized finally that our capacity to meet these needs is likely to be inversely related to our rate of population growth.

The Changing Uses of the City

JOHN DYCKMAN

INTRODUCTION: FORCES INFLUENCING THE CHANGING CITY

There is some evidence that men took to the city slowly. The early cities of Eastern culture were built by villagers as sacred centers for religious or ritual retreat. Eventually, the villager moved into the city with the concentration of agricultural surplus, the extended specialization of consumption, the assembly of a labor pool, and the growing economies of scale and social overhead as the urbanites developed technology. Thereafter, the momentum of urbanization took over on its own, freed for action by facilitating noneconomic institutions. Today, when the old economies of the city are dwindling in importance in the wealthiest industrial countries, metropolitan growth rushes on. But the urbanites, some of whom remain in village-like pockets in the hearts of the cities, show signs of resuming the village roots in the new suburbia.

Bertrand Russell once observed, in comment on Lloyd Morgan's optimistic doctrine of emergent evolution, "If indeed the world in which we live has been produced in accordance with a Plan, we shall have to reckon Nero a Saint in comparison with the Author of that Plan." Our emerging metropolitan civilization at times inspires similar sentiments in the hearts of its would-be planners. But if our cities have been produced by neither human nor divine plan, they are nonetheless a faithful mirror of our culture.

In contemporary America, the forces exerting the greatest influence on the changing city are so pervasive they sometimes escape attention. Among them we should surely include:

1. The late-industrial technology, fed by the rapid leaps of modern science rather than the old painfully wrought steps of the industrial arts.

2. The ubiquitous growth of socio-economic *organization,* manifest in the form of
   a. continuation of the long-time trend to "bigness";
   b. extension of process of specialization, with

66 *See* Goode, *The Protection of the Inept,* 32 AM. SOCIOLOGICAL REV. 5 (1967). *See generally* on the internal proletariat, 5 A. Toynbee, A STUDY OF HISTORY 58–194 (1939).

Reprinted with permission of *Daedalus,* Journal of the American Academy of Arts and Sciences, Boston, Mass. Winter 1961, "The Future Metropolis."

its interdependence and hierarchical ordering of parts;

c. development of a self-conscious management rationale and an embryonic theory and science of organization.

3. In the advanced industrial economies, the early signs of the first appearance of a sufficiently large societal surplus to permit the widespread weakening of old economic drives and motivation (this development has thus far been disguised by noneconomic military priorities).

4. A rapid leap in communication facilities and the subsequent growth of world-wide communication (including the upsurge in literacy and shared symbols) which has made the world functionally "smaller" and has raised the potential for changing old boundaries and old definitions of community.

5. The deepening awareness of cultural impoverishment relative to American material prosperity. The task of raising mass culture above the levels of its present vulgarity is inseparable from the awakening of mass interest in public canons of consumption. Respect for the communal arts and public services is a prerequisite for the development of public tastes. So far this awareness is confined to intellectuals, but with the aid of communication resources at their command, they may bring it to broader public attention.

One would wish to add a sixth force, that of a rising concern with organized city planning, but the evidence for it is not yet strong.

These developments are so closely interwoven that it is impossible to separate their contributions to the changing physical form and the changing cultural image of the city. Nonetheless, we shall indulge in some speculation about their individual and combined impact on the urban innovations ahead.

LATE INDUSTRIAL TECHNOLOGY AND THE PHYSICAL CITY

In the early stages of the evolution of the city, industrialization, though only one of many social changes, was the decisive one. Without it the metropolis would have been impossible; without it the metropolis would have been unnecessary. The city, in turn, was an important artifact in the creation of an industrial civiliza-

tion. Now, however, the marriage faces possible dissolution. For one thing, industry is freer than it has ever been to set up outside the city. For another, both the "city" and "industry" are less clearly defined. The former has been submerged in a tide of urbanization which does not respect clear-cut boundaries. The latter has evolved from recognizable processes of shaping and fabricating materials to a range of activities shading almost imperceptibly in some cases from pure science to manipulation of human motives. The change from the technology of steam, coal and iron to electric power has not produced the dirt-free, decentralized city of the Geddes-Mumford[1] dream, but there are few now who would feel it to be impossible. Newer power sources, most notably solar energy, may carry out the job which the gasoline engine has crudely and imperfectly begun.[2]

These developments, of course, will be applied, if they are applied, at first only on the margins. Like progressive education, they will be debated and even superseded long before they have received widespread application. And in the meantime, our cities continue to feel the full impact of the older technology and still reap the whirlwind of its transformation of an agricultural society. Living with this heritage, the contemporary city dweller hopes to escape from the uglier by-products, or waits for "renewal." It is hard for him to see anything in his organizational role that is helping to bring about new living forms which will be free of the mills that usurp the river banks and pollute the lakes, the congestion that burns up a cloud of smog, and the waves of rural workers moving into a chaos of residential decay. But if the city still means excitement, ideas, and license to him, he will not—in the absence of suitable alternatives—want to be far away from it, either. This is the limbo in which the half-empowered city dweller of today finds himself, and the half-

1 The expected transition to a neotechnic complex, earlier formulated by Kropotkin and by Geddes, was applied by Mumford in *Technics and Civilization*, New York, Harcourt Brace, 1934, and *The Culture of Cities*, Harcourt Brace, 1938.
2 It is worth noting that the forecaster who was guided by considerations of engineering efficiency would never have acknowledged the potential since realized by the gas-driven auto. Only by blending in liberal amounts of judgment on income levels, social and individual motivation could he have come to an accurate forecast.

way solutions which he seeks in suburbia are familiar to all.

TECHNOLOGY AND POPULATION DISTRIBUTION

Cheaper, faster transport is potentially decentralizing (and given the same population, density reducing) since it permits workers to achieve the same real costs of travel to work at greater distance from the job. When an improvement of transport technology cuts the costs of assembly and distribution significantly, it may reduce pressure to achieve economies by a particular location, that is, it may leave the activity less space-tied. On the other hand, engineering improvements in site utilization (for example, storage capacity) increase the ability of a site to provide services at a given transport cost, and so may have a potentially centralizing effect.

Thus in a rapidly changing technology conditions are being created which may make both higher densities and lower densities more economic. Since technological innovations are themselves selected by economic factors, however, consumer demand plays a part in making its own bed. The dispersal attained with the relatively costly auto commutation is an indicator of the direction in which that demand leans. Decentralization trends may be boosted further by the exhaustion of the fossil fuels such as coal and petroleum, and their replacement by the direct utilization of solar energy.[3] The amount of space required per unit, the freedom of units from fixed power sources, and the requisite spacing of units indicate a relatively low density of development for residence using this type of energy.

The use of atomic power may serve to postpone this decentralization. The economic size of an atomic power plant is currently very large, and while the plant itself should not, for obvious reasons, be located in the heart of a major population center, it can most efficiently serve a large, concentrated market at some point nearby. Strides in the improvement of space-utilization in buildings are also possible, thus permitting the more intensive use of space "at the center of things." Microfilm, magnetic tapes, transistors, and other devices are achieving this effect in many kinds of data storage essential to business. In a much smaller way, urban renewal has worked to this end in the residential sector by replacing large but inefficient units with smaller and more "functional" ones. Measured in terms of the volume of activity taking place at a given point, rather than by the persons assembled, the capacity of land in our central places has been increased enormously in recent years, though this change has been disguised in central office districts by a more lavish use of space.

At the same time, individuals are less rooted to any one place. With more free time and more income in his hands, the individual's travel costs become relatively smaller. The range of activities within his grasp becomes larger. Under these circumstances, it is not unlikely that the extent and variety of spaces "consumed" by the individual should increase, and that his use of space should become more functionally specialized. This has long been an observable characteristic of the well-to-do, some of whom keep a separate apartment or house for such diverse functions as dwelling, work, theatergoing, duck-shooting, and winter and summer vacationing. On a more significant scale, a limited variant of this kind of special-purpose use of place and structure might be made available to large numbers of persons with technological developments which would make both the individual units and the travel to reach them cheaper.

A nondiscriminating technology, making possible both greater centralization and greater decentralization, might be turned to both uses simultaneously by a wealthy, pragmatic nation. One possible outcome is a kind of permanent oscillation between the dense city center and the sparsely settled outer suburbia; between a tiny but well-equipped cubicle (one-upping the "beats," a super-functional "pad") and a

3 As a recent handbook points out, "Solar energy arrives in the neighborhood of the Earth at the rate of about 1.35 kilowatts per square meter." The capture of this energy for heat and power is the task of a new technology. Direct conversion of this energy into electricity via solar batteries, or into heat through some intermediate fluid or salt, makes possible an "emancipated" unit in which the power plant and the consumer are one. With adjustments in the collectors and the use of some standby conventional sources, this energy is available virtually everywhere.

virtually portable solar-powered house. If the style of life of the multitudes who are electing to live in Southern California at the rate of a thousand a day is symptomatic of a deep American wish, provisions ought also to be made for long periods of living in a boat or trailer.

CENTRALIZATION, DECENTRALIZATION, AND DENSITY

Density of settlement and the spacing of persons, according to persistent beliefs, materially affect the quality of life. In the early industrial era, when the close quarters of the industrial towns were accompanied by bad diet, poor sanitary engineering, little knowledge of the transmission of disease and the low immunity to these hazards of a recently rural labor force, the rapid increase of urban density nearly proved a total disaster. In the later stages of the growth of the city, density has acquired a connotation of urbanity, and has thereby come to be associated with social development and intellectual awareness. Especially when contrasted with a peasant countryside, the city has been championed as the natural habitat of learning and the richest soil for cultural flowering.

It is no longer appropriate to associate high density with plagues, but it may be equally ill-fitting to correlate low density with "the idiocy of the countryside." The distinctions between city and country are in need of revision to fit the realities of present possibilities. Further, the vices and virtues attributed to the city were never wholly assignable to density *per se*. We still know little of the safely realizable densities of human congregation and of their effects on human performance.

Biological populations seem to show some "critical mass" beyond which the individual, as well as the group, exhibits malfunction and breakdown. The National Institute of Mental Health, in its researches, has shown a disposition to attempt to extend the findings on various animal populations to human groups by analogy. While human groups need not suffer as a group from being of a size that presses on a local food supply (at least in United States society), one suspects the existence of some more subtle stresses on the individual under certain conditions. Support for this view is supplied indirectly by recent biological research on the causes of disease and mass "neuroses" in rodents.[4]

At the same time, there is evidence of strong congregating tendencies in human populations, including a tendency to congestion even where space is available, free, and riskless.[5] The possibilities for an efficient storage of information and activity, and so for greater concentrations of persons, are implicit in much of our new communications technology, which tends to be "space" as well as "weight-losing." Given the trends in world urbanization, one does not need a concept of "pathological togetherness"[6] to suggest that we will have much greater massing in future cities than in the present.

Will we then find a way to adjust our rhythm of life to swing gracefully between dense massings and lonely retreat? If this chameleon society should develop, constantly adjusting "tension gates" might need to be developed as part of man's psychosomatic regulation, permitting him to raise or lower the bars to reception of stimuli under dramatically different environmental conditions.

CITIZENS OF A CHANGING CITY

The present effort at urban renewal may, in the long view, appear as the last-ditch attempt to save the old form of the city and the style of life it supported. Paradoxically, the mobilized corporate effort necessary for the large changes has in this instance been devoted to the braking of change. The individuals in the market, voting with their dollars and their feet, have shown little of this nostalgia for the old forms. What is more, the people who show the greatest enthusiasm for the new forms of urban living—the suburban and exurban varieties—are drawn from the ranks of the conformist, security-oriented "organization men." This suggests that there is a covert understand-

4 Edward S. Deevey, "The Hare and the Haruspex," *The Yale Review*, Winter, 1960, pp. 161–179.
5 *Ibid.*
6 Kingsley Davis in a recent paper for a seminar on urbanization in India at the University of California, Berkeley (June, 1960), painted the possibility of cities in India reaching a size of 60 million within the range of present forecasts.

ing that the dominant corporate image is favorable to the new forms, despite a token allegiance to the old city.

The visible changes in the city may suggest a deeper social change than has actually taken place. Middle-class Americans take their style of life with them, with only minor alterations, through various zones of suburbia. The heralded changes in the political affiliations of city workers which were expected to attend their increasing moves to mass suburbia and home ownership have been small. No doubt differences in the superficial aspects of culture, in the traditional symbols of class, nationality, or ethnic group, are reduced in the suburban resettlement of old working-class neighborhoods. But these changes are small compared with those still being experienced by rural in-migrants entering the oldest sectors of the city.

Both these movements, by reducing the backlog of differences, diminish the potential for future change. The long march of the underemployed rural labor force to the city, when seen through the glass of the once proud middle-class neighborhoods in its path, appears precipitate and devastating. It must be remembered, however, that these are the last throes of the change. The new urban recruits are being drawn from the most culturally remote areas, long-bypassed. These laborers in the vineyard will be the last, barring open-door immigration, for whom the move to the city will be a great, cultural, social, and economic leap.

At the same time as the last pockets of rural isolation are being rooted out and incorporated into the disciplined organization of urban society, that organization is changing its rules of enlistment. The transition from an industrial to a "technological" organization has altered the requirements for education, social recruitment, and class distinctions, has changed the meaning of work, has robbed leisure of its release, and cloaked status in more obscure symbols.

The migrant from the subsistence economy of the hills always found it difficult to adjust to the industrial discipline of the factory system. Now that work is further depersonalized, the relation of worker to output less apparent, individual craftsmanship less applicable, and control more remote, the personal impact of the change is staggering. Neither the independence of the mountain man nor the social co-

hesion of the Puerto Rican villager is a usable resource in this new situation.

Even the children of veteran urbanites, the wise young of the cities, find important sources of meaningful activity draining away, as some novelist-critics have underlined.[7] The elaboration of the uses of the automobile, along with hi-fi, boats, etc., is not only a cultivation of the garden of craftsmanship in a desert of routine, but serves even more importantly to give the user a power over the environment which is otherwise denied him even in his work. One need only look to the developing economies of Asia, Africa, and Latin America to see that it is the promise of self-determination contained in technology, not the exercise of a new craft, that beguiles them.

ALIENATION IN THE CITY

The greater separation of the place of residence from the place of work (a hallmark of the modern city) accentuates the separation of man from his productive activity. In space as well as in function, his leisure is freed from the taint of work (the exceptions are the activities of some writers, advertisers, salesmen and communication executives whose work is wrapped around the exploitation of others' leisure). Efforts to re-establish contact through "do-it-yourself" projects are not convincing.

Atomized leisure activities have failed to fuse into any satisfying esthetic of consumption. As Riesman has pointed out, conspicuous consumption (which bequeathed us many of our contemporary antiques and much of the monumental architecture and urban sculpture so revered by city planners) has declined as an avenue to status and has been largely usurped by the corporations.[8] Architectural historians of the future will have to write chapters on clients like Socony, Inland Steel, Crown-Zellerbach and Manufacturers Trust.

The leisure of the old urban villager was meaningful chiefly as a release from work as a

7 Most recently, Paul Goodman, Harvey Swados, and others have updated this Veblenian theme. See Goodman's article, "Youth and Organized Society," *Commentary*, February, 1960.
8 David Riesman, "New Standards for Old," reprinted in *Individualism Reconsidered* (Chicago, The Free Press, 1954), p. 228.

physical break. The leisure of the new suburban villager has increasingly become a status-conferring device. For some contemporaries, the functional uses of leisure, as in business golf, have completely obliterated the old distinctions between leisure and work. For a few, leisure means a search for the ancient meanings of recreation in some forms of self-fulfillment. This last-mentioned constructive leisure, however, is denied all but a few intellectuals in our society. We have invented no goals which would make such an activity truly meaningful for most people.

If the city of today is liberated from the old use of the surplus which created it, the citizens of the United States city find themselves buried under the burden of finding meaningful consumption. J. K. Galbraith, who was an ardent Keynesian in a time when employment and production were faltering in America, has since found the stimulation of employment and output a counsel of aimlessness in an affluent America.[9] To salvage meaning for his economic policy, he proposes using government spending to jack up lagging collective consumption and to redress the balance between "private opulence and public squalor." Private satisfaction from public achievement is little developed in the United States. Perhaps city planning can confer this kind of satisfaction. The task implies vast consumer education as well as proportionate ingenuity and creativity.

THE LEVELING OF URBAN CULTURE

In an environment in which work is meaningless and consumption needs to be constantly refurnished with gimmicks to be acceptable, the rate of the absorption of novelty is terrifying. Television has virtually given up trying for new plots, and has settled down with Westerns, a form of morality tale in which plot is unimportant. The tourism of Americans with money is reaching staggering proportions, expressed in dizzying itineraries in which new places are gobbled up at the rate of one or more a day. We are destined to exhaust our supply of "quaint" places as the speed and availability of transport makes "neighbors" out of the "foreigners."

Perhaps when the visible differences between places have disappeared (in Burchard's words,

when the world is "one great Conrad Hilton chain") more subtle distinctions will be cultivated by the natives of the various cities in order to set the home town apart. But it is also possible that man's identification with a particular place will be weakened. Allegiance to a city or state is even now weaker for many than allegiance to a corporation, a profession, or a voluntary association. National allegiances survive because they have stronger functional implications—political system, economy, money, language, arms, etc. As long as one watches his clues to class and style, he can move from one American city to another with virtually no change in environment, as W. H. Whyte, Jr., has demonstrated.[10]

The second law of urban dynamics, were it written, would postulate that urban variety is running down fast. (Even now old-timers can acquire a semblance of distinction by picturing the "Old Tokyo" or "Old Bombay" before their Westernization.) The leveling has been most marked, not in the matters of subway systems, sewers, and skyscrapers, but in the whiskey-drinking habits of rising young French businessmen and the Coca-Cola breaks of the shop girls; it shows in the "beat" coffee shops of Japan and the omnipresent rock 'n roll of teen-agers everywhere—an ironic comment on the slow progress of jazz up the Mississippi from New Orleans to Chicago in World War I America. Clearly, we have entered on an information-organization drive for the whole world that dwarfs the old task of taking the message to the small towns. Cities play a convenient role in this process, as the metropolis continues to provide a favorable habitat for a large volume of interchanges of information, but they are no longer essential to the task.

THE AUTONOMOUS GROWTH OF ORGANIZATION

Social as well as physical systems usually start out smaller than optimum size, and so can improve their efficiency by growth for a time. Efficiencies of various kinds provide the main

9 J. K. Galbraith, *The Affluent Society*, Boston, Houghton Mifflin, 1958.
10 W. H. Whyte, Jr., *The Organization Man*, New York, Simon and Schuster, 1956.

impetus for organizations to "grow big." After a certain scale is reached, however, the original functions of the organization may change. For at the "optimum scale" either a decline in efficiency sets in, or new tasks, appropriate to even greater size, are found.[11] The bigness in city forms, which is manifest in expressways and skyscrapers, housing projects and superschools, supermarkets and chain stores, is paralleled by bigger metropolitan systems formed by the inclusion of more and more urban units. Within these systems, the individual units have changed many of their functions.

The extension of metropolitan organization to the relatively unorganized environs has been accompanied by restructuring and greater specialization. Settlements caught up in the wake have changed from market or retail centers to dormitories; local transport and utility systems have either been integrated into metropolitan systems or have disappeared in many instances. Most important, the small places have lost much of their sense of self-determination.

New York is the locale of an increasingly large proportion of the nation's economic decisions. Its relative importance as a setting for economic decision is enhanced by two important trends in the growth of economic organization: (1) the consolidations, mergers, and combinations which are grouping many "local" companies in single national organizations,[12] and (2) the extension of the market of regional producers to a national scale, facilitated by the improvement of interregional communication and transport and by the homogenization of regional tastes.

The corporation, which dominates American economic life, is not bound by local restraints. It moves freely across city and state lines. To grow bigger, it must extend its markets. When it extends them geographically, the dependence on any one place becomes relatively weaker.

THE DECLINING SOCIAL IMPORTANCE OF PLACE

To Plato, Aristotle, and Augustine, the "city" was a synonym for the ruling political and social organization of human relations and for the governing of man. In contemporary America, the corporation has largely usurped that image. Scott Buchanan has suggested that the corporation is the archetype of organization itself in our society, and its rules are the guide for the evolving form of our political relations.[13] To the extent that this is so, the concept of place, around which utopian reformers have woven the tapestry of the good life, will lose some of its meaning.

Corporations form larger organizations out of the amalgamation of smaller ones. Within the larger unit there is, after each addition, a careful preservation of the unity of direction. Decisions formerly made in Chicago or Boston must now emanate from New York.[14] Disappearing, together with some of the local-market direction of the society is its counterpart, the local town-meeting democracy. Each now exists in isolated fringes only. Modified versions of local representation may well disappear as the cities themselves lose their old reasons for being. If cities become so specialized in function that citizens are members of the polity only on a part-time basis, while they are making economic decisions, working on a productive process, attending a conference, or vacationing (each in a different city), the old geographical basis for representation will have had the *coup de grâce*. For the wealthiest, most powerful, or most privileged of our society, this is already the case; their influence is exerted through

11 The less flexible species in history often perished from gigantism, particularly as their size reached the point where it generated demands the environment could not meet. As H. G. Wells remarked, "In the record of the rocks it is always the gigantic individuals who appear at the end of each chapter" (*Mind at the End of Its Tether*, New York, Didier Publishers, 1946, p. 25).
12 "Between 1949 and 1954, the number of mergers tripled. In recent years, two-thirds of all mergers have been of small companies into larger ones with assets of over $10 million" (David T. Bazelon, "Facts and Fictions of U.S. Capitalism," *The Reporter*, 17 September 1959, p. 47).
13 Scott Buchanan, *The Corporation and the Republic*, New York, Fund for the Republic, 1959.
14 The firm for which my grandfather worked, which by virtue of its product, building materials, was both locally oriented and politically committed, is a good case. Whereas once it could not afford to be far from the meeting places of Chicago politicians, it has since grown big enough to acquire a different orientation, and recently merged with a firm operating largely in the field of defense contracts requiring it to be close to Washington decision-makers. The head offices of the combine will undoubtedly be in New York, where the nucleus of national decision-making is found.

"corporate," not geographical channels, and it tends to gain primacy thereby.

Margaret Mead's picture of a future studded with highly specialized functional places, and a population traveling, as the occasion and interest demanded, from place to place among them for special purpose conferences,[15] might well be the outcome of the high degree of wealth and transportation which made this movement possible, and of a social and political organization of our society which stripped the local places of any other reason for existence. Men, who came into the city to live only after a period of enjoying it from the relative freedom of afar, might now return to the wilds without giving up the city. What then would be the hold of any particular city?

THE CONSTRUCTIVE CITY

The cosmopolitan skimming of many cities is reserved for the world of affairs and power, for intellectuals and executives. The world of most others is still tied more closely to a single city. The marginal people in our society need the city and its supports, and they cannot afford isolation. For them community has come to mean the city. The aged, the handicapped, and the twenty to thirty percent of our youth who will never get higher education in our time need to be in the mainstream of our society, not isolated from it. Idleness is an affront to their capacities and a barrier to self-esteem. Working mothers who need assistance in child care, minority groups, and deviants of all kinds seek tolerance, understanding and assistance in the city. Our era's rejection of the city is also a symptom of its rejection of the productively underprivileged. The exurban drift of the more able is the fruit of a philosophy of individual survival.

Wherever industrial societies have not rejected the city, or have not used it badly, they have quarantined it. There is a present tendency for societies to turn the old city sections into living museums, as in the old walled center of Krakow.

The real challenge of the constructive city runs deeper than the preservation of medieval town centers girdled by green belts. It lies in the reconstruction of some of the sense of community which previously characterized the town and which inspires a good deal of the nostalgia with which the town is still regarded by some. It is too late to get this community back by any return to the soil or to handicrafts, or by some combination of these earlier technologies, in the manner suggested by Arthur Morgan or Ralph Borsodi or the Hassidic collectives of Israel.

Nor is it very constructive to propose a city in which communities are confined by social walls, with bazaar-like meeting places. The ghetto and the bazaar belong to an earlier society. Urbanization and industrialization have destroyed the old communal and feudal structures of social organization. As they come to maturity, they produce mass societies, pluralistic societies, or totalitarian societies, according to Kornhauser. To the extent that United States society is both pluralistic and organized into collateral systems, the old simple unity of communal life is gone. The community of place is also gone. Even the old pluralistic community of the marketplace has been broken down and replaced by the organization of corporate planning. We reject the corporate state of the totalitarian examples, but we have nothing to put in its place except empty statements about national purpose. National purpose can be immediate rather than remote; it can be addressed to the reconstruction of the world in which most Americans now live—the world of the metropolitan area. The strength of our productive power has prevented neither alienation nor impoverishment of opportunity. The logical heirs-apparent of the task of constructing cities to meet this challenge are the city planners. By tradition and temperament they are dreamers in the grand manner.

But the American city-planning movement has spent so much of its still young history trying to "get its feet on the ground" of local government that it is painfully space-bound. It is tied to the use of land and finds it difficult to rise to legitimate flights of fancy. It is hard pressed to utilize the findings of the army of analysts who have come into the movement to provide it with batteries of forecasts. Meier observes, "Often the study of a single innova-

15 Margaret Mead, "Values for Urban Living," *The Annals*, November, 1957, pp. 10–14.

tion by itself, carrying through all the projections that are associated with it, leads to the conclusion that it should have a trivial impact and that the decisions concerning it should be relatively unimportant. However, it is not uncommon that two or three streams of small-scale innovation converge and a transition with major consequences results." [16]

As an aid to the necessary anticipatory thinking, Meier suggests the use of the fictional constructs employed by H. G. Wells and Edward Bellamy and by many lesser science-fiction writers. If they are to play the wholly warranted utopian role which has been left them by default, the city planners would do well to take up this challenge. Without attempting so ambitious an undertaking here, I would like to list a few of the concerns which might be treated in an imaginative picture of the constructive city of the future.

THE EDUCATIVE CITY

The leitmotiv that might be played throughout the picture is "The City as a Place of Learning." It seems that learning has always been the most powerful lure of the city; the city as a work place was expected to inculcate skills, and the city as a play place was expected to provide vices that were at least slightly instructive. The city as a show place was a place to wander about in, and gape at, and be shown.

The educative uses of the city have always been too numerous to be comprised in the curricula of the schools, but organized education has shown a marked affinity for the urban setting. In its medieval beginnings, the university was a creature of the city. The schools themselves cannot be ignored in the planning of the city. In addition, however, a wide variation in institutional auspices, ranging from the university through adult education and extension to the museums, libraries, and public places of the city, will house the total educational experience of the citizens. The public school itself extends over many of these phases, and our concept of the "common education" can be extended to more of them.

A few years ago a group of architects and educators got together to work out a picture of the school of the future. [17] Their solution was a system in which the school was brought into the city, and the latter was turned into a total campus. This idea received the share of attention given to most novel school proposals, and then receded at the usual rate. It is unlikely that most educators interpreted it as anything more than a scheme for a wider use of field trips, for the proponents left enough conventional props of the school lying around to encourage this notion. But interpreted in more dynamic fashion, the scheme provides a beginning for an exploration of the potential dissolution of the barriers between school and city.

A more radical version of the educators' proposal would undertake the conscious design of the metropolis as an educational experience, rather than on the adaptive use of it. The aim would be to turn the city into an educational construct, with a view to providing a constant presence of meaning and a democratized form of learning.

The city that is devoted to the extension of opportunity would necessarily be an educative city. In the past, the extension of education, particularly to adults, has been aimed at facilitating social assimilation and upward mobility, and at remedying occupational deficiencies. For the genuinely underprivileged, our environment should continually be organized to these ends. But alienation is more widespread, reaching even into the economically more able. Here, education for noneconomic compensation must be extended. For these, it is not the education of the school, but the education of life experience which is most important. No sages can be found who can wisely prescribe the content of such experience, the best we can hope to do is to organize the opportunities for variety.

We live in an era in which formal schooling has largely supplanted apprenticeship, and the demands of skilled jobs have shifted from an emphasis on artistry to an emphasis on scientific literacy and communication skills so standardized that they can best be taught in school.

16 R. L. Meier, "Analysis of the Social Consequences of Scientific Discovey," *The American Journal of Physics*, 1957, 25: 611.
17 "Random Falls," feature article in *The School Executive*, March, 1956.

The early contact with the world of real work cannot be re-established by occasional field trips. For the many who, for reasons of poverty of experience or other handicaps, cannot bridge the great gap between the arid abstractions of school and the conquest of the world of materials and men, schools that are truly "open" to the world and do not shut it out must be devised. If there are not apprenticeships left in industry, law schools, and architects' offices, there is still room for firsthand learning in citizenship, social relations, mass culture, and the management of one's affairs. The great advantage of cities at "human scale," or organized in comprehensible communities, is that an overview of the range of activities of a society is accessible.[18]

The problem, of course, would be more than an exercise in physical design, it would be a challenge to administrative ingenuity and social imagination. It would not do just to provide art and artifacts in ingenious arrangements. Means must be found for dislodging the presently frozen constellations of the urban ecology. For example, access to the educational experience of the *whole* city would have to be provided for all. In today's city, only a small part of the population experiences the whole city; slum dwellers are notoriously rooted to the corners and blocks of the small ethnic slum world, while the cosmopolitan professional middle class ranges the entire city. Free public transit would be an essential minimum step in the educational city. (The partial subsidy of the subway system by New York City makes Manhattan possible; the potential for an extension of this relation is untapped.)

Freedom to experience the city and learn its lessons is more than a matter of transit fares. It is a question of real freedom of choice, of power and acceptability. The West Side Puerto Rican or the Harlem Negro knows that he does not have access to the full meaning of the city of New York. Both the physical space apprehended by the individual and the Lewinian "life space" would have to be expanded. We make much of the city as a center of communication, but the information in the messages is received by a few, while to the many the communication content is chiefly noise.

It will be argued that most inhabitants of the city lack the equipment to receive this information and that their isolation in "ghettos" is self-imposed, a protective device against the confusion, stresses, and possible breakdown from this communication bombardment. There is no evidence, however, that the ordinary urbanite is at the limit of his information-handling capacity. Extension of this capacity is itself a major utopian goal in the constructive city.

Whatever is done, the city will be an instructional milieu. Anyone doubting this should reflect that it is the educative force of the city that many of our families now flee, for it is in the city that plural or strange values are taught their children. Families who would guard the education of their children fear this influence. Only when interclass and interethnic differences in value have been reduced somewhat will communication flow more freely.

THE OPEN CITY

Even the communication specialists will at times find the information interchanges of the city a strain. They will seek escape to relative privacy. Traditionally, it was available in the city, but even the golf course is a major center for information and decision in America. Abercrombie's plan for London sought to accommodate to this condition by providing a precinctal organization of the city along functional and occupational lines. In typical English fashion, these precincts were to offer some of the sociability of the club with a protected, inward-turning privacy, while permitting business to be carried on as usual.

It would be more typically American, however, to provide a truly open city. The open city would not be in the political grip of local cliques. It would be the antithesis of the old-time, one-industry, company town. In fact, in an era of truly cheap transport there is no need for conventional kinds of production to be in the city, and there is no need for people to live full time near their work. The open city belongs to the citizens who participate in its works.

18 The important point in this overview is not a mystical one of any special *Gestalt*, but resides in the power to choose more confidently when the alternatives are comprehensible.

There are many ways in which citizens can participate in experiments in the working of the city if the city is willing to experiment freely. For example, citizens can experience almost any day what it means to overload a highway system; the same lessons can be extended to other workings of the physical city and to its very government. "Tryout" stations can be set up for various kinds of urban apparatus from conveyor sidewalks to expandable houses. The city government can rotate certain civic duties, like dining-room assignments at a boys' camp. It has been seriously suggested recently that citizens be deputized freely for the control of traffic violations. Such an action would be in the tradition of the colonial fire guards and citizen patrols who guarded the city at night. The losses in efficiency from the employment of less than optimum resources would not be crucial in an economy in which these resources were superabundant. It is important, however, that the civic duties in question be more than merely honorific; they must be functional in tangible respects.

Neither is there any need for the city to be the man's world while the suburbs belong to women, as is the case in America today. Only a relatively small part of the time charged to production in the city actually goes for that purpose. Much of the rest goes to a way of life, to the "business game." There is no need, other than the psychic requirements of the players, for maintaining this trend. Given greater choice, women might increasingly reject the exclusive role of consumer-specialist. As a society gets more remote from want, consumption as a class of activity loses importance and prestige. There are also signs that women of the leadership group, upper-middle-class style, are tending to a greater participation in politics. Business and politics, the great games of the city, should be opened to all its citizens.

The home—distant in psychological space and ground space but not in time from the city—would take less of a woman's day. Social planners have been slow to react to the steadily diminishing proportions of the average woman's life that are devoted to child-bearing and infant care.[19] Housewives frequently complain that the advent of a new household technology has actually lengthened their workday, but

some of the additional work is managerial, and some is self-imposed to fill the void left by labor-saving devices. Given a chance to play more meaningful managerial roles, women would be able to divert sizable amounts of household time to the affairs of the city.

The open city is not, by contemporary standards, an efficient city. For a considerable time it would be a difficult and costly place to get things done. Such an open city could come about only as the result of the conscious choice of placing participation above product. Our town-meeting tradition even now does not work in big cities; but it continues to hold a place in our atavistic longings, and might be even more attractive if it could be rescued from the parochialism of suburbia or the dullness of the small town.

The productive technology, which grew in an intimate interdependence with the overhead economies of urbanization, has outstripped these facilitating arrangements and has become independent of them. The urban style of life of a growing proportion of the population has fed the demand for services, private and public. The old forms of the city are no longer needed, but the services the city provides are more than ever in demand. As these demands grow, it is necessary to devise means for "taking in each other's washing." One way to do this is to make rewarding leisure out of community service.

Unfortunately, the ingrained American respect for work and productivity not only prevents us from developing a genuine culture of community leisure but also robs us of respect for activities whose productive consequences are not apparent. This outlook, which is manifest in our treatment of the aged, the infirm, and the intellectually underprivileged, inhibits the full use of national energies and prevents those who cannot master the socially approved developmental tasks from experiencing full adult-

19 Writing of British experience, Titmuss observed that at the beginning of the century, when the life expectation of a woman aged twenty was forty-six years, about one-third of this life expectancy would be destined for these activities. In 1956, however, when the life expectancy of a woman aged twenty was fifty-five years, only about 7 percent of this life would be concerned with child-bearing and maternal care (R. Titmuss, *Essays on the Welfare State*, London, G. Allen & Unwin, 1958, p. 91) .

hood. As we face the prospect of an increasing difficulty in placing new entrants in the labor force,[20] it behooves us to consider some alternatives to the empty extension of education. Instead of brushing the youth out of sight in rural C.C.C. camps, let us consider placing them in the service of the city.

CONCLUSION

The exciting new cities of our time have virtually nothing to do with the old economies of city founding. Brasilia is as much a temple city, remote from the habitat and business of its people, as ancient Edith Shar. Chandigarh is as unessential to the economy of India as Mohenjo Daro. If cities can be built today as monumental symbols of national aspiration in countries poor by our standards, it is not so implausible to consider that we might build cities for our present needs and desired uses. At times cities are turned to vital uses in spite of the intentions of their builders, like the California town which started out to ape Venice and wound up, against its will, as a playground for motorcyclists.

The American construction industry is the world's most efficient, but the imaginative use we have found for it is the building of longer and better autobahns than were built by Hitler. We are unable to renew cities, not for lack of land planning but for lack of economic planning, and, more broadly, social policy. Looking at our metropolitan life, we find a deepened stratification, in social communication even more than in social ecology; a city in which management is in the hands of a meritocracy[21] recruited from the top fifteen percent of the youth (the percent of high school students who now elect the academic major), a city in which a sizable part of the work force is in actual or disguised idleness but in which there are virtually no skills or traditions for making this idleness personally meaningful; a city in which there is a glut of goods and a paucity of public services.

Democracy cannot function where most of the demos is not needed, save as customer or ward. Yet democratic participation may actually get in the way of the functioning of our present cities, as C. Northcote Parkinson has suggested.[22] The answer need not be that of chucking local democracy; it may well be that of recasting our cities. But it is naïve to think that local democracy need be organized around the old notions of place-belonging, just as it is an oversimplification to believe that a physical relocation of the population will solve the functional problems of democracy in our industrial world.

Social invention and innovation in design need to converge on this task. The life style itself would be changed. Traditionally, these patterns are obdurate; but one may easily overestimate the resistance of Americans to a change in life style. Spicer has noted the existence of a marked bias toward imputing such resistance to others on the part of those who are engaged in trying to bring about change or who are especially conscious of cultural differences.[23] People do resist change when it threatens their security; the change in the physical arrangements of city life would have to bulwark security rather than menace it. People tend to resist changes whose implications and workings they do not understand; the "new" forms must have elements of an earlier style (as the suburbs are related to rural small towns) which preserves some continuity. People may resist change if it is too abruptly and forcibly imposed; this is the hardest part of the process, for it requires involvement in change on the part of people who may lack the equipment desired, and so it means a willingness to pay high frictional costs.

20 In recent months (as of June, 1960) there has been some evidence that the seasonal peak in unemployment beginning with the end of the school term has been sharper than usual, and in some areas more than half the unemployed labor force is under 24 years of age. Within the next few years, employment prospects for new graduates are expected to become increasingly gray.
21 Michael Young, in his *The Rise of the Meritocracy 1870–2033* (London, Thames and Hudson, 1958) has sketched the consequences of such a tendency in Britain in a social-fiction exercise much like that proposed here.
22 C. Northcote Parkinson, in an address at a national conference of the American Institute of Architects, San Francisco, 21 April, 1960.
23 E. H. Spicer, Introduction to *Human Problems in Technological Change* (New York, Russell Sage Foundation, 1952), pp. 18–19.

Utopian thinking has a place in this process, not only in painting the consequences of failing to alter the present course, as Young recently, and Orwell, Huxley, and Ignatius Donnelley much earlier, have done, but also in

sketching the possibilities of what might be, as Bellamy tried to do. Clearly, here is meaningful work enough for generations of American urbanists, if they can find in it the reward that will sustain them.

Goals for Urban Development

LYLE C. FITCH

BACKDROP TO THE LAST THIRD OF THE 20TH CENTURY

My suggestions on goals for urban development and the institutional machinery for achieving them are predicated on a few salient facts about the urban scene. In a century we have almost reversed the proportions of rural population to urban—100 years ago the United States was about four-fifths rural and one-fifth urban; now more than 70 percent of the population lives, and by the end of the century more than 80 percent will live, in urban places. Given this reversal, given the rate of population growth— more than sixfold since 1860—and given the profound impact of accelerating technology, we have had a great deal of adjusting to do. It is not surprising that we have had many growing pains.

Despite recently falling birth rates, it appears probable that the national population, now about 200 million, will increase considerably between now and the year 2000. The latest Bureau of the Census projections show the increase, 2000 over 1967, to be in the range of 80 million to 160 million. Recent trends of birth rates make the lower figure appear more probable, but even the lower figure implies an increase of more than 50 percent in urban population (now in the 150 million range) and the high projection, if obtained, would more than double the present urban population—all in 33 years.

Recent projections of the Urban Land Institute [1] indicate that in 2000 the urban population will be concentrated in four great megalopolitan corridors (one in California, one

along Florida's east coast, one around the rim of the Great Lakes, and one along the Atlantic seaboard), in 13 "outlying urban regions," [2] and in six "free-standing" metropolitan areas with a population of a million or more each. [3] The population of these giant centers is projected at 77 percent of the total population of the 48 mainland States, and would occupy 11 percent of the continental land area.

The density of the urban regions and metropolitan areas would average 708 persons per square mile. In some regions, densities would be much higher as in the Atlantic seaboard region (1,050 persons per square mile) and the New York zone (1,860 persons per square mile). In central city areas, densities would remain much higher—thus New York City already averages 25,000 per square mile. Overall densities in urban regions, however, are projected to be lower than those already prevailing in England and Wales (810 per square mile) and the Netherlands (770 per square mile). [4] Average population in the areas outside the centers is projected

From *Urban America: Goals and Problems* by Subcommittee on Urban Affairs (Washington, D.C.: U.S. Government Printing Office, 1967), pp. 19–41.
1 Urban Land Institute, *Urban Land*, February 1967.
2 Carolina-Piedmont, North Carolina-Georgia, north central Alabama, central gulf coast, Texas-Louisiana-gulf coast, north central Texas, south central Texas, Missouri-Mississippi Valley, Salt Lake Valley, Colorado-Piedmont, Puget Sound, Willamette Valley, metropolitan Arizona.
3 St. Louis, Louisville, Memphis, Oklahoma City, Twin Cities, Albuquerque. In addition, Honolulu is projected to have more than 1 million inhabitants.
4 The Urban Land Institute projections assume a year 2000 continental population of 312 million, or an increase over 1967 of approximately 110 million.

to drop from 29 persons per square mile in 1960 to 27 persons per square mile in 2000.

The rate of growth and the pace of technological change in effect condense time. Thus, spokesmen for the Department of Housing and Urban Development are fond of saying that there will be as much construction in the last third of the 20th century as in all of the preceding history of the country. This figure may well be modest, even for the smaller population projection—my rough calculations indicate that the aggregate gross national product in the last third of the century will be from two to three times the aggregate produced in the nation's entire history thus far. Given the volume of output of which the American economy is capable during the next 30 years, and given the rate of accumulation of knowledge and technological know-how, it would appear that we can, by the end of the century, reach levels of material abundance which few now even dream about. This possibility can be quickly dissipated, of course, by catastrophic war, by spending for other unproductive purposes; or it can be dissipated by outdated viewpoints and by obsolete social and governmental institutions.

At the risk of seeming to repeat old bromides, I urge that the best assurance we have of making good use of our promised abundance is to consider what use we should be making of it, and defining goals for our economic, social, and physical development. There is nothing wrong with the goal popularly ascribed to the typical middle-class college graduate—a secure job, a home in the suburbs, an agreeable wife, and several healthy children—but it will hardly suffice to produce the good urban life. It means nothing at all to the increasing number of people who can look forward to nothing better than living out their lives in the slums and ghettos, and it offers little challenge to many of our contemporary younger generation. It is also blithely innocent of the growing problems created by the pace of urban expansion and the tide of migration from the rural areas into core cities. Problems such as the following are already provoking wide protest and demands for more effective solutions:

Air pollution is already a serious menace to health in many cities; even more apparent is the economic cost of stench, airborne dirt, and chemical corrosion. Beginning with cleaning bills, the annual cost to the nation is reckoned in the billions of dollars.

Partly because of the extent of water pollution, large sections of the country are already threatened periodically with water shortages which at the least impair comfort and convenience (New York City had to struggle through much of the summer of 1965 short-rationed on air conditioning) and at most force the shutdown of industries. And a society increasingly oriented toward recreation finds some of its most important recreational resources (lakes, streams, and ocean beaches) preempted for use as sewers.

Uncoordinated, badly planned and inefficient transportation acts to frustrate the economic rationale of cities, which is to reduce transportation and communication costs of satisfying economic wants. It has been a long while since technological innovation has contributed materially to improvement of urban transportation: automobiles, buses, and rail cars are essentially the same vehicles as they were a generation ago, even though mechanical improvements, air conditioning, and radios contribute to comfort.

The migration from southern rural areas to northern urban areas continues. The Nation's 20 largest cities, in the period 1950–65, gained 3.2 million nonwhite population while losing 1.2 million white. In several major cities nonwhites are a majority of the population or soon will be if present trends continue. They come to older core areas for the simple reason that core areas possess the obsolescent housing which is the only housing most of the immigrants can afford and, for Negroes, the only housing to which they will be admitted. Meanwhile, the unskilled and semiskilled jobs they might fill in manufacturing and other goods-handling industries have been moving to the suburbs.

With their spreading stocks of increasingly obsolescent buildings, many of the central cities begin to resemble the slagheaps of our urban civilization. Even in the great national and regional centers such as New York City, urban renewal, exuberant office buildings, and luxury housing have made no more than a dent on the miles of dreary outworn buildings.

The general shortage of housing at rents that low-income people can afford to pay (1) causes serious overcrowding and accelerated deterioration of the housing stock concerned, and (2) poses, in many cities, one of the great obstacles to slum clearance and urban renewal, since there is no way to locate people dispossessed by clearance. Millions of dwelling units are rated as substandards—seriously deficient in one or more respects. Housing construction techniques are still essentially those of a half-century ago, with only minor improvements, and the cost of housing and construction generally mounts disproportionately. Technology is further slowed by archaic building codes supported in turn by fearful labor unions and building supply manufacturers.

The costs of crime and delinquency increase geometrically with population growth, with a consequent decrease in the public's sense of security and enjoyment of life (how enjoy life when one's property, person, and very life are continuously under threat?).

Urban planners, administrators, and physical and social scientists have been pointing out other problems not yet so visible as to arouse wide public concern:

New suburban developments sprawl formlessly over the former countryside, with little consideration of efficient layout in such matters as relating work, residential and recreational centers, providing for open space (not only for recreation but also for hydrological and climatic control), or simply for preserving and creating beauty.

New central city construction repeats the monotonous and inefficient patterns of the old, with buildings located and constructed without consideration of their function or relationships to other buildings, to transportation facilities, or to residential centers. The most fundamental principle of efficient traffic planning—separation of pedestrian and vehicular traffic—has been little observed. Grand Central Station with its separation of motor vehicle, pedestrian, subway, and train traffic, and Rockefeller Center with its grouping of buildings around a central plaza, were the last great innovations in New York City,

but there has been little further use of the principles they employed.

New concepts of organization and management emphasizing systems approaches—extending the scope of planning and management control of an organization or a project to all the interrelated elements—have been too little applied to urban planning and management. One instance is the failure, until recently, to take account of the relationships between intraurban transportation networks and land-use development, or the essential interdependence of transportation modes.

Despite the proliferation of Federal urban programs, the Federal Government thus far has contributed relatively little to urban development *per se*. Thus the amounts laid out for assistance to urban renewals, public housing, community facilities, open space, and pollution control have been largely offset by collections from various programs, mainly insurance premiums derived from housing finance programs. Net Federal expenditures on housing and community development in the first 6 years of the 1960's were in the magnitude of $1.5 billion. Total expenditures on agricultural development and support programs over the same period amounted to some $28 billion; defense expenditures came to $385 billion.

WHAT DO PEOPLE WANT?

Let us accept the propositions that the major development task of the next few decades is raising the standards of urban life, and that without larger goals we shall not mobilize the collective effort necessary to realize our potential. Nonetheless, goals without political substance which can be translated into support at the ballot box are of no avail. So we ask, first, what does the public want enough to vote for and pay for? This question runs into the fact that there are many publics, which want different things. There are different economic classes and groups of different age and family characteristics, racial and ethnic groups, residents of central cities, of high-income suburbs and of low-income suburbs, to mention a few.

Interest in urban goals on the part of the

groups trapped in poverty in the slum stems from deprivations about which these disadvantaged people (particularly the Negroes) are flaring into rebellion. (Whether the vintage 1967 riots have been incited by "agitators" is beside the point that gross deprivation makes fertile ground for rebellion.)

When we look behind the riots, the threats, and the other forms of protest, we find demands which on the face of things are entirely reasonable. People want employment opportunities, better housing, better educational facilities, better social environment beginning with neighborhoods free of violence, dope pushers, and vagrants. They want most of all to be treated as dignified human beings, not as inferiors. All of these things reflect existing middle-class values and middle-class opportunities. For the poverty class, wants are defined by what the majority of Americans already have, despite the offbeat values of the subcultures that tend to form in these groups.

Until recently the contemporary generation of poor have not been politically vigorous or articulate because of their low level of education and sense of alienation. They have tended to look to the welfare bureaucracies rather than to political organization for assistance in meeting pressing needs. Political machines and leaders, which once sought the support of the poor with welfare and other assistance, have been cultivating other constituencies, notably the lower middle class. In both central cities and suburbs, political control has tended to be dominated by the middle class, which demands less from government, rather than by the lower class which demands much, but this situation is changing as Negro and other minorities find strength to protest and numbers to gain political strength.

The working and lower middle classes typically have no great personal aspirations which they expect government, particularly urban government, to fulfill. For improvements in their general condition members of the working class tend to look to increased wages and to union organization. They tend not to seek improvement by upward movement, and lacking this motive for education and self-improvement they tend to resist being taxed for education and other public services. They are typical of the group of which Robert Wood has observed:

"The great bulk of the urban population neither is conscious of its public needs nor anticipates that urban governments will fulfill them." [5] They particularly resist being taxed for welfare and other services to the poverty groups; we may confidently expect that this resistance will be further stiffened by the recent outbreaks of violence.

The higher echelons of the middle class also are oriented to the market but at the same time are prone to make more demands on government for better education (for which they depend heavily on the public sector) and for various urban services such as transportation, health services, recreation, and other utilities.

These groups are likely to be more keenly aware of the need for special services to the "disadvantaged" than are the working and lower middle classes. But frequently they escape the problem. Many of the middle class, along with the more affluent part of the working class, can and do move to the suburbs where they tend to encapsulate themselves in homogeneous communities walled off against incursion by the poor. (Scarsdale and Levittown are examples of wealthy and working class suburbs in the New York City area.) Many have no alternative to suburban residence, for the costs of land and construction are tending to discourage the private sector from building residences on anything less than a luxury scale in central cities.

The upper middle and upper class groups have even wider choices—they can wall themselves off, more or less, from the city's unpleasantness if they choose to live in cities or, like the middle class, they can flee to suburbia or exurbia. In either case, they are likely to absolve themselves of any responsibility for the core city or its problems.

If this were all of the matter, urban development goals for those above the poverty class might well focus on continuing growth and high-level prosperity, which enable the gradual improvement of living standards over time, mainly through increased purchasing power to be spent in the bountiful market. Physical avoidance of the grosser urban problems, along with the fact that urban and suburban political

5 "Contributions of Political Science to Urban Form," in Werner Z. Hirsch, ed., *Urban Life and Form* (Holt, Rinehart & Winston, Inc., 1963), pp. 108–109.

leadership has been dominated by the middle class, helps to explain the weak response of so many urban governments to growing urban problems. Robert Wood has observed that, "The urban political process is not directly concerned with the provisions of goods and services except when these 'problem solving' activities can be translated into useful resources for the resolution of political conflict or its avoidance, or . . . outright failure of law and order seems imminent." [6] Moreover, various circumstances, of which one is perennial financial stringencies, another unimaginative leadership, and a third the lack of well-defined goals around which to mobilize consensus for positive action, have tended to magnify the power of the negative elements in the community.

The worm in the apple is that the kinds of problems listed above are impeding improvement of middle-class living standards and in part offsetting material gains. In many places some things are getting worse—we are sliding back from levels we had once attained. So while we as a society depend on rising incomes and the market for improvement and the things we want, we are forced to turn to collective action to eliminate things we don't want, such as congestion, pollution, crime and delinquency, and urban ugliness. But this is a negative concept of social action; I suggest that we can do better, and possibly avoid some of the problems which happen to us, if we give more thought to what we want our urban communities to be, say, by the end of the century. Here goals come into the picture.

I think there is increasing acceptance of the notion that national and community goals are essential tools of urban physical, social, and economic development.[7] Goals serve somewhat the same purpose in the public sphere that goods in the shop window serve in the market. They educate, arouse interest, and stimulate action, or support for action. Appreciation of this fact is manifested by political leaders and the public in such efforts as, for example, President Eisenhower's Goals Commission, White House conferences on national policy, and citizens' commissions on goals in a number of cities and metropolitan areas, including Dallas, Phoenix, the Twin Cities, and Los Angeles. The business community is taking interest in urban problems and urban goals; thus the Committee for Economic Development has organized a subcom-

mittee on urban goals, in part for the purpose of lending guidance and support to community efforts.

Aspiration goals may spring from many sources: Existing dissatisfactions, the thinking of people in "leverage positions"—business and political leaders, professional specialists, and so on—and from technological and economic developments. Some aspiration goals stem from development of technical knowledge which makes possible their achievement. Probably the greatest triumph for U.S. social planning thus far in the 20th century has been general acceptance, in a generation, of the goal of high-level employment and stabilization. The principal contributing factor was the development of a theory of economic control which would make possible achievement of this goal without unduly impinging on the free market in the process.

I do not think, however, that goals can be formulated by taking public opinion polls. People in the large do not spend time pondering what they would like the society to achieve, any more than they spend time thinking of things they would like to have which haven't yet been invented. Goals, like consumer goods, have to be devised and marketed. Public opinion polls can inform the process of goalmaking but cannot substitute therefor. Goal formulation is the job of experts, primarily, and marketing goals is the job of community leadership.

Despite the forces of inertia which today keep so many urban communities in a swamp of mediocrity, some cities and metropolitan areas have developed a public spirit and forward thrust which demonstrate the latent potentialities of local leadership and local cooperation. Thus Pittsburgh cleans up smoke pollution and rebuilds the Golden Triangle; Philadelphia creates a Penn Center; the San Francisco Bay area undertakes to build a billion dollar rapid transit system; New York City undertakes a broad reorganization of city government to equip it more adequately for the new responsibilities; and New Haven carries forward a wide-ranging program of urban renewal and human resources development. In some cases, the lead-

6 *Ibid.*, p. 107.
7 I distinguish between *aspiration goals, achievement goals,* and *performance goals.* My concern here is with *aspiration goals.*

ership comes from elected officials, in some from the business community, in some from civic organizations. Wide-ranging effective programs, however, usually necessitate the cooperation of all these elements, no matter what the initial source of leadership and ideas. To take one example, the Pittsburgh achievements were made possible by a working partnership between a group of the city's top business leaders, largely Republican, and the Democratic administration of Mayor Lawrence.

GOALS FOR URBAN POLICY

I suggest highest priority should go to two main goals which have already been accepted as objectives of national policy but which have thus far received less than overwhelming support.

The first goal is a decent level of living for all American families.

The other face of this goal is the abolition of dire poverty. I think there is little point in debating with the nitpickers who argue that some people will always be better off than others and that since poverty is only a relative concept we cannot abolish poverty short of absolute leveling. I am referring to poverty which brings hunger and physical discomfort, and social and moral degradation. I mean the poverty implied by the New York City welfare standard, one of the most *generous,* which allows nothing for culture, education, or entertainment (no newspapers, periodicals or books) and for children not even so much as an ice cream cone per week.

Obviously the goal has many dimensions—it requires more emphasis than has thus far been accorded to factors making for individual productivity—good health, aspiration, and motivation; lifelong opportunities for education and training; jobs for everyone who wishes to work. It requires a national policy to provide adequately for those unable to work—the old, the young, the disabled. It necessitates more social innovation and experimentation with ways of providing decently for the economically stranded without spoiling the incentive to work.

The second goal is continuous improvement of the urban (and rural) environment—as to efficiency, convenience, safety, and attractiveness. Here again there are many dimensions, such as—

1. Offering a greater variety of ways of life and opportunities for choosing among them, such as a greater degree of choice as to where one lives and works, as between living in central cities or suburbs, as between living in homogeneous or heterogeneous communities.

2. Freedom from aggression, such as criminal aggression against person and property and such other environmental aggressions as noise, pollution, congestion, and ugliness.

3. Elevation of central cities to be attractive places to live, work, recreate and do business. In the past they have been conceived of largely as centers of commerce and industry, only incidentally as centers of culture and knowledge, and hardly at all as delightful places to live. Nowadays they are in danger of becoming dumping grounds for the socially and economically dispossessed.

4. Planning for metropolitan development outside central cities with specific concern for efficiency and esthetic appeal, orderly relationships between residential, employment, shopping, and other centers, and preservation of open space not only for recreation but also for ecological values.

RESOURCES FOR ACHIEVING URBAN GOALS

In discussing urban goals with businessmen and others, one invariably encounters the reservations, "Yes, but can we afford it?" and "We can't afford everything at once, what should come first?" These questions are pertinent, for even in the affluent society there are not sufficient resources to implement fully, and in a short period, the goals proposed here, including the patching up of defects already discussed. And we can be sure that new goals will suggest themselves, and that new defects will become apparent, as we go along.

If we take a longer view, however, and consider the last third of the 20th century (1967–2000), the potentialities for goal implementation are enormous. The gross national product, despite several technical shortcomings, is still the best measure of available resources. The value of GNP in 1966 was $740 billion. The average annual growth rate in real GNP in the 37-year period, 1929–66, was 3.2 percent, and the aggregate GNP in that period, in 1966 dollars, was approximately $15 trillion. Assuming a growth rate of 3 percent in the 34-year period, 1966–2000, the aggregate GNP would be $42.5 trillion (1966 dollars). A 4-percent growth rate, which many analysts think well within our capacity, would yield an aggregate GNP of $51.5 trillion. The difference, $9 trillion, is equivalent to about 13 years' output at the 1966 rate. The astonishing magnitude of this difference underscores the importance of a high growth rate to all our other objectives.[8]

With a 4-percent growth rate and an overall population increase of 40 percent (the lower Census Bureau projection, which looks reasonable at present) we could accomplish the following by the year 2000.

1. Double average consumption per household. The goal of eliminating poverty would require that we move toward greater equality in consumption by increasing the consumption power of the lowest income groups proportionately more than that of the higher levels. This in turn depends in part on moving toward greater equality of productive capacity by labor force members and more generous income-maintenance programs for those not in the labor force.

2. Provide new dwelling units for all the new households, replace approximately three-fourths of present dwelling units, and provide second dwelling units for 25 percent of households. Meanwhile, raise quality, as measured by real construction costs, by 50 percent over 1966 levels.

3. Double, by 1975, the real expenditure on education per pupil while eliminating elementary and secondary school dropouts and expanding college enrollments by 50 percent.

4. Triple the annual average expenditure, over the 34-year period, on public facilities including transportation, water and sewer lines, recreational and cultural facilities, health centers, hospitals, etc., with provision for such needs as improved pollution control, development and introduction of new transportation devices (separation of vehicular and pedestrian traffic, new transportation technologies), rapidly growing demands for recreation and culture, and generally higher standards of urban design.

5. Increase the rate of private domestic busi-

ness investment, as a proportion of GNP, by approximately 50 percent to allow for developing and introducing new technology, provide new types of consumer goods to meet public and private demand, reduce social costs hitherto imposed on the public (such as air pollution), and replace obsolete equipment.

6. Increase annual Federal Government nondefense purchases by an average of 4 percent per year. [9]

7. Increase State and local government purchases for purposes other than public facilities and education by about 4 percent per year.[10]

The following table shows the aggregate amounts of gross national product that would be absorbed by these various quantitative objectives in the period 1966–2000.

While a 4-percent growth rate would supply the demands as projected in table 1, a 3-percent growth rate would fall $9 trillion short of meeting these projected demands; they would have to be reduced in some degree. But up to a point, lower levels of expenditure on such items as private domestic investment and human

8 I suggest that the aggregate national output will not be greatly affected by the rate of population increase, within the limits of the projections previously mentioned (the range is 80 to 160 million population increase by 2000). The reasons are as follows:

(a) A larger population would require more funds for the support and education of the population differential, part of which alternatively could be expected to go into private and social capital formation. (On this point see Stephen Enke, "Economic Development Through Birth Control," Challenge, May–June 1967. While Enke's analysis is addressed primarily to less developed nations, it has also some relevance for the United States.)

(b) Because the differential between high and low projections would all be borne (except for immigrants) between now and the year 2000, much of it will not be in the labor force by 2000; thus the labor force differential would be relatively much smaller than the population differential.

(c) A relatively high proportion of the differential labor force would come from the low-income, low-culture groups; their productivity in the year 2000 almost certainly would be under average, no matter what we could do in the meantime.

(d) Continued technological progress may keep on depleting the number of jobs for low- and semi-skilled workers, and might make part of the differential portion of the labor force redundant.

9 The crucial element in the Federal account is defense-war purchases which were $60 billion in 1966 compared with $17 billion for nondefense purchases. Here I have optimistically projected defense-war purchases at an average of $65 billion a year (1966 prices) for the rest of the century.

10 This is the approximate increase rate in the 1960's, the period of most rapid recent growth.

Table 1 Projected demands on gross national product, 1966–2000

	Trillions
Consumption	$27.2
Housing	1.6
Education	4.4
Urban public facilities	2.0
Business investment (plant and equipment)	7.7
Federal Government:	
Defense	2.2
Other	1.2
State and local government (excluding education and public facilities)	3.1
Foreign balance, and unallocated	2.1
Total	[1] 51.5

[1] Projections for a population increasing to 280,000,000, with a 4-percent annual growth rate in GNP.

resources development (particularly education and training) themselves dampen the gross national product growth rate.[11] Various other assumptions, such as a larger population increase, would somewhat change the detail of the above projection but would not alter the main point: that the Nation has the power to achieve within the foreseeable future the goals proposed above, if we measure achievement by present standards. Of course, by the end of the century standards will have greatly risen and we will have new and higher goals.

URBAN PUBLIC POLICY AND URBAN GOVERNMENT

I hold that in the last analysis the impetus for improvement in any urban community must come chiefly from the community itself. Federal and State Governments can provide financial and other assistance and a certain amount of stimulation, but only with lively local leadership and citizen participation can a community realize more than a fraction of its potential. Moreover, there are many values and goals which only vigorous urban governments can achieve.

One of the most important objectives is variety and experimentation, along with flexibility in meeting local requirements in ways appropriate to local traditions and conditions. The need for variety and experimentation stems partly from the fact that there is no consensus among urban planners or other urban experts as to what constitutes an ideal city in size, configuration, transportation systems, and other components of urban design. Some experts believe that further deconcentration and lower densities, made possible by the ongoing revolution in communications technology, are the wave of the future; other experts, exemplified by the new housing panel of HUD's 1966 conference on technology at Woods Hole, call for greater densities to facilitate communication and reduce the cost of transportation and other utilities, and promote multiple uses of land devoted to urban purposes.

Many communities have great but unmobilized resources for attacking their own problems, including resources in the private sector which could be put to work on applications of technology and other matters if there were a way of creating the demand therefor. But most urban governments are always fighting holding actions against accumulations of past deficiencies and unforeseen developments. With finan-

11 Leonard Lecht's study for the National Planning Association, "Goals, Priorities, & Dollars (the Free Press, 1966), presents a somewhat more elaborate projection of the cost of meeting the main goals called for by the Eisenhower Goals Commission, in terms of the demands on GNP in 1970 and 1975. The amounts required to meet Lecht's projected demands total about 10 percent more than the projected supply of GNP in 1975, assuming a GNP growth rate of 4 percent. Lecht's projections differ from the ones presented here in that they apply only to selected single years.

cial resources perennially strained, there is little left for innovation except in response to major crises. Recently, most innovation has been stimulated by the Federal Government and by Federal grants for housing and redevelopment, highway construction, antipoverty programs, and health and education.

Urban governments are handicapped also by structure. Most are built around the traditional service functions for which they were responsible in the 19th century—protection, regulation, health, sanitation, sewage disposal, and some aspects of transportation, education, and various utility services.

Beginning in the depression and continuing at an accelerated pace after the Second World War, urban governments began perforce to assume additional responsibilities having to do with the physical and economically disabled, with economic development, urban redevelopment and renewal, poverty, and new kinds of relationships with Federal and State Governments having to do with all of these.

Urban governments have not yet digested these new responsibilities, which tend to be lodged in newly created authorities and special agencies such as housing and redevelopment authorities. Thus the new functions have tended to remain outside the mainstream of planning and decision-making, though intrinsically they are as important to community welfare and as imbedded in community politics as are the old-line service functions. (This fact is being impressed on many urban administrations by the often violent protests of large-city poverty groups against their own deprivation and misery and the inability of the community to supply them with decent housing and amenities or with jobs.)

Many systems of logically related functions cut across traditional departmental lines. For instance, it is now clear that the effective education of children from lower culture home environments may require, in addition to education, the combined resources of welfare, health, police, housing, and other departments which in practice are seldom to be found working together on coordinated programs. Development of efficient urban transportation systems has been impeded by the fact that numerous facilities and controls having to do with the movement of people and goods—private motor

vehicles, bus, rail transit, traffic controls, parking facilities and controls, toll and fare systems, etc.—tend to be lodged in many different, uncoordinated agencies.

And finally, the systems way of thinking has long since informed us that some types of urban services cannot be efficiently provided or provided at all by governments of less than metropolitan scale. Transportation, water supply, air and water pollution control, and efficient land-use planning, are prime examples.

Commenting on the deficiencies of local governments, the Committee for Economic Development's recent policy statement on *Modernizing Local Government* makes the following observations:

> Few local governments are large enough —in population, area, or taxable resources —to apply modern methods in solving current and future problems. Even the largest cities find their major problems insoluble because of limits on their geographic areas, their taxable resources, and their legal powers.
>
> Overlapping layers of local governments abound—municipalities, townships, school districts, special districts—which in certain areas may number 10 or more. They may all have the power to tax the same land, but frequently no one of them has the power to deal with specific urban problems.
>
> Public control of local governments is ineffective or sporadic, public interest in local politics is lagging. Contributing factors are the confusion resulting from the many-layered system, profusion of elective officers without policy significance, and increasing mobility of the population.
>
> Personnel are notoriously weak. Low prestige of municipal service, low pay scales, and lack of knowledge or appreciation of professional qualifications all handicap the administrative process.

State governments by and large (there are exceptions) have a long history of unresponsiveness to needs created by urban growth, central city obsolescence, migrations from rural to urban areas, and the demands for more services. The Advisory Commission on Intergovernmental Relations in a report of March 1967, comments that only a handful of States have moved to meet the problems of their urban areas and that State governments are on the verge of losing control over the mounting problems of central city deterioration and the rapid growth of urban areas.[12] Prof. Roscoe Martin observes that while States are critical "of the growing practice of direct dealing between Washington and the cities, which they regard both as a perversion of the Federal system and a pointed threat to State sovereignty" the States themselves have displayed little interest in taking action.[13]

PLANNING MACHINERY

By now, most large cities and many metropolitan regions have planning agencies, but these tend to concentrate on certain aspects of physical planning such as the location of highways, water and sewer lines, and other public facilities, and on administering zoning controls and subdivision regulations. Most city planning agencies lack resources to develop new concepts and designs for helping their communities find their way in the future. But such basic work is essential to the goal-making process; without it there is no adequate basis for informing public opinion or stimulating political and other community leaders to push for betterment.

Few are staffed to take full advantage of Federal grants now available or to prepare first-rate model cities programs. Little is done to relate planning for commercial and industrial improvement to the needs of slum dwellers. The planning for development of human resources which goes on is generally confined to specialized agencies—education, welfare, and so forth—which deal only with pieces of the problem.

Lacking adequate planning machinery, urban governments predictably will continue staggering from one crisis to the next, continually out of line with the demands of the times. In New York City alone more than a million people live in 40,000 old-law tenements that were outlawed and scheduled for demolition and replacement in 1905. Many more live in other substandard dwellings. The city planning agencies thus far have only nibbled at the problem: there is no grand strategy for providing decent housing for the city's residents in the foreseeable future. And there is even less consideration given to solving the problem arising from the fact that, as in many large cities, the unskilled and low-skilled population congregates in the core while many of the jobs they might fill locate in the suburbs. I do not know how many jobs in the region remain unfilled because of lack of access to people who might fill them, but the figure in Chicago a couple of years ago was put at 35,000.

State planning agencies have been under the same handicaps as urban agencies and (with few exceptions) have had little impact on the course of urban and metropolitan development. The State highway departments, which do substantially affect metropolitan development, have been largely oblivious to planning values not immediately related to moving motor vehicles.

State and urban governments, then, have done little basic planning and introduced little innovation—their bureaucracies and political officials have been resistant to change. Most of the recent spurt of planning activity in these fields has been fostered and financially assisted by the Federal Government; for instance, through the workable program and other planning requirements posed as conditions for Federal aid.

INTERGOVERNMENTAL COOPERATION

The remarkable development since 1930 of Federal, State and local cooperation—in education, highways, urban redevelopment and renewal, health, housing, poverty and other areas—has served to motivate State and local governments to do things they would not otherwise have done, and to raise administrative and technical standards. The response to Federal grant programs, demonstrated most recently by the scores of applications for model city programs, shows that money is still the best incentive and most powerful energizer in the public as well as the private sector of the enterprise system.

I think that testimony by urban officials before the Congress within the past year has made

12 Advisory Commission on Intergovernmental Relations. *Eighth Annual Report*, 1967.
13 Roscoe C. Martin. *The Cities and the Federal System* (Atherton Press, 1965), ch. 6.

clear that in their view the leading difficulty with Federal programs is not simply with red-tape and complexity but with the fact that most are still grossly underfinanced. The urban development goals I have suggested imply much higher levels of Federal grants whereby urban governments take advantage of the Federal Government's superiority as a revenue collector.

If we accept the premises—

1. that the primary responsibility for setting and implementing urban goals must rest on the individual cities and metropolitan areas,
2. that most urban communities can marshal more intellectual and economic resources to solve their problems than they have thus far,
3. that urban (and State) governments need to be modernized and better equipped to handle their responsibilities, but
4. that in the urban political arena the forces of inertia tend to outweigh the forces for innovation,

I think Federal support is justified for State and local innovation in governmental and political arrangements as well as programs. And I believe that encouragement and assistance to urban (and State) governments to improve planning and administrative machinery are better than trying to control every detail of Federal grant programs through minute regulations and supervision.

AGENDA FOR MODERNIZING STATE AND LOCAL GOVERNMENT MACHINERY

If States are to participate more effectively in urban development, most need substantial reorganization and reform of administration, planning, and budgeting systems. Here I draw upon the Committee for Economic Development's recently published policy statement *Modernizing State Government* (1967), which lists the following needed reforms:

Abolition of quasi-independent administrative boards and commissions (frequently they have earmarked funds), insulated from any responsibility for State welfare as a whole.

Concomitantly, centering administrative responsibility in the office of the Governor, and equipping the office with planning, budgeting, and administrative expertise.

Limitation of legislative responsibility to matters of broad policy and budget approval; abolition of legislative budgets and exercise of administrative powers by legislatures or by individual legislators.

Comprehensive merit personnel systems.

Comprehensive budgets covering all funds and expenditure categories; preferably based on program budget concepts (these have been notably unsuccessful thus far for reasons having little to do with their intrinsic merits).

Strict conflict-of-interest laws.

Constitutional provisions affording maximum latitude to local governments which meet reasonable standards of adequacy.

In *Modernizing Local Government* (1966), CED presents an agenda for local government reform which includes:

Reduction in number of local governments by at least 80 percent, and severe curtailment of overlapping layers of local government ("townships and most types of special districts are obvious targets for elimination").

Limitation of popular election to members of legislative bodies and the chief executive in the "strong mayor" type of municipal government.

A single strong executive: elected mayor or city manager.

Modern personnel systems.

Use of county, or combinations of county, jurisdictions to attack metropolitan problems.

Use of Federal (and State) grants-in-aid to encourage local government administrative reforms, particularly reforms having to do with consolidation and organization to meet metropolitan problems.

A FEDERAL ROLE IN STATE AND LOCAL GOVERNMENT MODERNIZATION?

Although I favor, and consider inevitable, much larger Federal grants for urban development and improvement, I am equally concerned about the ability of State and urban governments to make good use thereof. For this reason I have reservations about the formula of the Heller plan distribution of a "national dividend" (a fraction of the annual increase in national output) through the medium of per capita grants to State governments. If Federal tax machinery provides the wherewithal for a "national dividend," would it not be profligate to use Federal funds simply to bolster up existing inadequate and archaic institutions? If we are going to depend, as I think we should and must, on the decision-making and innovational capacities of State and local governments, should we not seek to improve those capacities?

The Congress has attached conditions for administration and performance to many grants, going back at least to the 1930's when State unemployment insurance agencies were required to be under civil service. A few other instances include the design and construction standards required of Federal-aid highways; the requirement that Federal-aid highways in urban areas of more than 50,000 population be based on a continuing comprehensive planning process carried on cooperatively by State and local agencies; the requirement of general State plans for hospital development as a condition for Federal grants for hospital construction; the provision of more general grants for water pollution control under metropolitan-wide plans, as opposed to purely local jurisdiction projects; the requirement for comprehensive community planning and the submission of community "workable plans" as conditions of urban renewal grants; the requirement that Federal-aid community development projects shall be reviewed by metropolitan agencies designated "to the greatest practicable extent" by elected local officials.

While few such stipulations have wrought wonders, many of them have wrought improvements. For example, while many "workable plans" submitted in support of urban renewal applications have been rudimentary and the provisions of many have not been complied with, the requirements have made urban governments more aware of the elements of urban renewal and of the necessity for professional planning than they otherwise would have been.

The instances cited above all relate to specific grant-in-aid programs. Is it possible to establish general standards for planning and administration as a condition of per capita grants or other general grants? Admittedly the task of administering such requirements would be difficult. There is first the job of devising criteria for acceptable standards of administrative organization. Next there is the job of evaluating State and local governments to determine whether they meet established criteria. Inevitably there would be protests from offended State and local interests and congressional protests against adverse rulings.

One possible formula is that set forth in the bill introduced in the House of Representatives by Congressman Henry S. Reuss of Wisconsin in January 1967. Under the Reuss bill, block grants would be made conditional upon the submission by States of acceptable programs of Government modernization; the review and evaluation bodies would be regional coordinating committees and the U.S. Advisory Commission on Intergovernmental Relations, which would certify as eligible programs reflecting "sufficient stated creative initiative so as to qualify that State for Federal block grants." Among the items suggested for consideration in drawing up such programs are:

1. Arrangements for dealing with interstate regional, including metropolitan, problems;
2. Strengthening and modernizing State governments;
3. Strengthening and modernizing local, rural, urban, and metropolitan governments; and
4. Proposed uses of Federal block grants, including provisions for passing on at least 50 percent to local governments.

Any general formula that might be established should be related to administrative standards already imposed by other Federal grants-in-aid. This leads to the point that the Federal Government itself is not a model of organization, least of all with respect to urban programs. The scores of urban-oriented programs and grants administered by the Departments of Housing and Urban Development; Labor; Commerce; Transportation; Interior; Health, Education, and Welfare; the Office of Economic Opportunity; Army Engineers; and General

Services Administration, and others; still suffer from a lack of centralized planning and direction. Down below, State and local governments are handicapped by the number of, and administrative requirements imposed under, the Federal programs ostensibly established to spur, not hog-tie, local initiative. Several coordinating devices established in the last few years have made little impact, and the situation overall is little changed from what it was a decade ago. Obviously more muscular measures, of which several variants have been proposed, are needed.

The prospect of the urban concentrations of the year 2000, as described by the urban land institute, poses still further questions of administrative organization. Two of the great megalopolitan areas projected will be contained within the boundaries of single States (California and Florida), but the metropolitan belts around the Great Lakes and along the east coast will encompass a dozen or more States. Aspects of many of the problems now plaguing metropolitan areas, such as water supply, air and water pollution control, and transportation, will be transferred to the larger areas of the future. The States offer the only organizational building blocks below the Federal level for coping with megalopolitan-scale problems. In some cases, they may be able to organize into regional blocks (as through the device of interstate compacts) for dealing with interstate megalopolitan problems. An interesting possible precedent is offered by the Delaware Valley Authority compact encompassing the States of New York, New Jersey, Delaware, and Pennsylvania with the Federal Government as an equal partner. This may be the megalopolitan counterpart of the emerging federations of municipal governments at the metropolitan level.

I should say at least a word about personnel to man planning and administrative posts in urban governments as well as urban program posts in Federal and State governments. This is, of course, the resource in shortest supply. There are, for instance, no more than a handful of people who can direct the preparations of a first-rate model cities program application. It is no secret that New York City, despite the attractions offered by a reorganization of city agencies along modern program lines, relatively high salaries, and [a] vigorous chief executive,

has had great difficulty in finding competent people for top staff positions in the human resources administration, housing and development administration, and transportation administration, not to mention posts in the top staff agencies.

In the long run, the shortage of personnel trained for modern urban planning and administration will be alleviated only if the universities assume responsibility for attracting and training many more people, and if urban governments become more aware of the nature of their manpower needs and show a willingness to compete for talent. In the short run, Federal assistance for training urban planners and administrators, as in programs backed by Senator Muskie and others, would help to break the logjam.

FOSTERING LARGE-SCALE INNOVATION

There is wide agreement that problems of urban improvement offer the greatest challenge (outside the field of national defense) to innovators of our time. It is offensive to our general notions of progress that many aspects of urban life, for many people, are not improving while some are retrogressing. The lack of progress has a disproportionate impact on people lowest in the income and cultural scale, but no participants in urban life remain unaffected by deterioration somewhere. Everyone endures the irritations of poor transportation and traffic congestion, air and water pollution, noise, lack of recreation facilities, crime and delinquency, and the ugliness of the urbanscape.

The main point is not whether things are better or worse than they formerly were, however, but whether research resources of modern social and physical science and technology have been utilized to the maximum practical extent in the solution of urban problems. The consensus of most physical scientists and engineers, and social scientists, is that they have not been and are not.

Technology, we are assured, can provide means for achieving more efficient, more beautiful, more livable cities. But the engineers, scientists, and designers complain that they have not been given the opportunity to demonstrate what they can do to improve urban environment. This is hardly surprising, because there is little demand for their talent, and there is little demand because much of technology's potential is on the drawing board or in the conceptual or preconceptual stages. (By contrast, the consumer products sold by the private sector are already in existence and are promoted with all the resources of modern advertising.) The politicians and the public can hardly be blamed for failing to demand what does not exist. Somewhat analogous factors impede organizational and political innovation, as illustrated by the slowness to develop machinery for coping with metropolitan-scale problems.

As already implied, technological innovations must depend upon organizational and political innovations, and in many cases innovations in the social sciences as well. So-called systems approaches are an attempt to assemble in packages all the necessary components of solutions to particular problems—thus an urban transportation system involves demographic, economic, physical design, financial, political, organizational, and other policies, all of which depend upon the particular technological approaches selected.

Most of the significant innovations having to do with urban improvement have been stimulated not by State and local governments but by the Federal Government (sometimes, but sometimes not, pushed by urban government interests). But with the exception of the highway program, the amount spent by the Federal Government systematically to stimulate urban improvements has been insignificant compared to expenditures for agricultural improvement and support, or for space programs.

OBJECTIVES AND INCENTIVES

Experience thus far indicates that more resources and energy can be mobilized if there are defined generally accepted objectives, and incentives for pursuing them. Four cases are in point:

1. The urban development and renewal programs have been utilized by many cities with some failures but with some notable successes. In the process there has been a great conceptual development (more significant than the physical development that has occurred thus far), and a great improvement in planning standards and in the number and quality of planners employed.

2. The space effort has demonstrated the potential of technology organized under a public program, with the participation of both public and private sectors.

3. The war on poverty has mobilized a great national effort, again with the participation of both public and private sectors.

4. The competition for the site of the proposed giant (200–300 Bev) nuclear particle accelerator, involving a construction cost of several hundred million dollars and an annual payroll of some $60 million, drew in all the major regions and many individual States and localities in the United States, who spent millions of dollars preparing their cases.

All of these programs have in common (a) clearly defined objectives and (b) large prizes in the form of Federal funds for programs which would galvanize the public sector and furnish incentives for the participation of the private sector. All have in common also the fact that though the objectives were clearly defined the means of achieving them were still to be worked on at the time of their initiation —technological approaches had still to be developed.

A difficulty with most Federal urban improvement programs is that they never concentrate enough resources in any one place to demonstrate what an adequately financed "systems approach" can do in any particular field. The model cities (demonstration cities) program, which seeks to concentrate Federal grants in limited areas of cities, will inevitably be handicapped by fiscal malnutrition as well as Federal redtape; it will end up with some improvements in most areas, no doubt, but with nothing conclusively demonstrated. Much of our experience with Federal grant programs recalls the experience of the 1930's with spending: when toe-in-the-water spending programs did not promptly produce full employment and an economic boom, Government spending to create demand was written off by many as a failure until the very much larger spending of a defense-war demonstrated that the problem of the 1930's had been simply one of inadequate scale.

I suggest that as soon as the military situation is resolved and Federal funds are available, the Federal Government should make a number of substantial grants for urban improvements in a number of selected fields, each designed to produce a major impact. Project designs would employ systems approaches encompassing both technology (applied science, hardware design, etc.) and all the machinery necessary for planning, making decisions, and implementing the projects concerned. Following are some of the areas in which such large demonstration projects might be run:

1. A comprehensive, integrated intraurban transportation system such as exists nowhere at present.
2. A comprehensive, metropolitan areawide health and hospitals program.
3. A 20-year housing development plan, taking into account not only the provision of decent housing to all families in the area but also (a) the efficient location of housing with respect to employment centers, (b) the probable rise in incomes and housing standards over the planning period, and (c) feasible approaches to geographic dispersion of minority groups.
4. A metropolitan area recreation development plan to make recreation facilities available to all inhabitants of the area on approximately equal terms.
5. A design for a new town or a system of new towns in a metropolitan area.

Any project for which a large-scale "innovation grant" is made should meet rigorous specifications. For example, the specifications for a transportation plan (transportation breakthroughs are particularly needed) might include the following:

1. The plan should encompass all forms of intraurban transportation—private motor vehicle, bus, rail transit, traffic controls, parking facilities, parking controls, tolls, fares, and fees (or as many of these as would be appropriate for the particular region). There should be provision for in-

tegration with interurban transportation facilities through such devices as integrating interstate and other highways into physical development plans, and efficient transportation links between air terminals and other points in the area.
2. A project development plan should encompass a period of 20 to 25 years. It should be constructed for maximum flexibility to meet future demographic and economic changes and to take advantage of unforeseen technological developments.
3. The plan-and-program should provide for continuous planning machinery capable of revising plans in accordance with experience gained in developing and operating the system and for keeping transportation and related planning up to date; decision-making machinery capable of taking necessary decisions for implementing various aspects of the transportation plan including highways, streets, parking facilities, bus transportation, traffic controls, etc., and administrative apparatus. The elements of planning, decision-making and administrative machinery should be parts of the same "system," but each element should be constituted to meet the needs and changing institutional framework of the particular urban area.
4. The plan should also lay out the conventional requirements of a conventional intraurban transportation system in terms of capacity for movement of people and goods, and devise a preferred development plan for meeting these requirements, with emphasis on employment of improved technologies.
5. The various systems should be integrated economically as well as organizationally, with each transportation mode bearing appropriate costs consistent with overall criteria laid down for the system. Economic specifications should be devised, first to guard against wasting resources on overelaborate or grandiose plans, but more important, to permit maximum freedom of consumer choice.

A transportation plan of the scope indicated would involve drastic changes in local government organization, arrangements between local governments, State highway departments, and the Federal Transportation Department. But the purpose of the innovation grant would be to stimulate this kind of political and organizational innovation as well as innovations in hardware. In this respect, the program would differ sharply from the usual Federal grant program, which stays within the bounds of existing political frameworks so as to permit everybody to participate without undue strain.

COMPETITION FOR LARGE-SCALE INNOVATION GRANTS

The certainty that there would be intense competition among cities and metropolitan areas to be selected as recipients of large-scale innovation grants suggests that the grants be made through a series of national competitions and awards for best "plans-and-programs" dealing with various urban needs. The awards would be made, in any specified field, for the best plan and program to be submitted by a government or consortium of governments representing a metropolitan area. The plans submitted should meet specifications laid down, such as those suggested for an intraurban metropolitan transportation plan. To qualify for an award, the competing area should give evidence of its willingness and ability to make any necessary organizational changes.

Such a system of awards would, I suggest, have the advantage of attracting wide-scale attention and interest and of drawing a number of metropolitan areas into competition. The activities involved in competing, and coping with specifications of the kind described, would have a high educational value. The "losers" in each competition would benefit in many ways from the experience of competing. It is probable that meritorious plans which did not win awards would be eligible for Federal assistance on a matching or other basis under Federal programs that already exist or which would be enacted in the future. The competitions themselves, if successful, would furnish valuable guidance to the Congress in expanding the Federal grant program.

Many details would have to be worked out, a few of which are considered here: *Selection committees.*—Competition entries should be judged by panels of experts of national reputation in relevant fields, drawn from the universities, industry, and nonprofit institutions. Selection of panels to avoid any favoritism or political influence would be of highest importance in realizing the objectives of the competition. (Experience with the selection of the site for the new accelerator indicates that a certain amount of controversy would be inevitable in any case.) *Financing research and planning.*—Preparation of plans and programs of the scale contemplated would involve, for most communities and most functions, heavy expenditures on research and promotion. Referring again to transportation as an example, preparing an integrated plan and program would entail coordinated work of demographers, economists, city planners, traffic engineers, highway engineers, specialists in urban technology, political scientists, specialists in finance and administration. New hardware (as new types of transportation vehicles) might need to be developed to the point of demonstrating feasibility for purposes of submission as part of the plan. New political arrangements would require time-consuming negotiation, public education, and in some cases legislative action. Private firms should be drawn in. This suggests the possibility of setting up award competitions among private firms for development of various aspects of an overall plan and program, particularly aspects having to do with development of physical technology and systems design. Management consultant firms might be invited to enter competitions for plans for governmental reorganization, financing, and other matters within their competence. The device of competitions has already been successfully employed in several fields, notably architectural design and military and space hardware.

To help finance plan and program preparation, including competitions among private firms, the Federal Government, following established precedents, might make available research and planning funds for plan and program preparation—some funds already available under such legislation as section 701 of the Federal Housing Act, highway-related research funds provided under the Federal Highway Act, and funds for research on health, education, and various other urban-related activities.

Basically, research funds for award competitions should be part of a more general system of encouraging and assisting work on urban problems, just as the proposed awards system should be only one part of an expanded national effort for urban improvement. *Time allowed for plan preparation.*—The time required for plan preparation would depend upon the subject matter of the particular competition. In the case of intraurban transportation plans, a period of 3 years is about the minimum for preparation of a major plan, and the kinds of plans contemplated here are considerably more expansive than any undertaken to date. In addition to the preparation of plans per se, a considerable amount of negotiation and political engineering would be necessary to commit the community fairly definitely in advance to organizational and institutional changes. This suggests that transportation plans might require as long as 3 to 4 years for proper preparation and presentation. Other functions may require less time, and a few are likely to require more. *Amounts of awards.*—One possibility is that the Federal Government meet the capital construction costs of award-winning plans. Where high operating expenses (or deficits) are likely to be a deterrent, the award might also cover operating expenses (or deficits) for a limited period of, say, 5 years.

One hundred percent financing might not go a great distance beyond amounts already available for some kinds of projects, as two-thirds Federal financing for development of urban mass transportation, two-thirds for urban redevelopment, 90 percent for construction of interstate highways, and 50 percent for primary highways, and various other Federal matching grants. In many programs, a major limitation is appropriations rather than the percentage of Federal matching.

The absence of any requirement for local matching under the award program would remove incentives for economy, but extravagance might be held in check by making economy one of the criteria for evaluation and by introducing appropriate pricing systems and other devices to make projects such as transportation, water supply, and so forth, more efficient from the economic standpoint.

The awards would have to be very large to produce innovations of the scale required, however. A transportation plan alone for a major metropolitan area might cost a billion dollars or more. But the amounts should be compared, not to what we have been accustomed to spending on urban improvement, but rather to (1) needs, (2) prospective resources as measured by our rising gross national product, and (3) what we are already spending for innovation in other fields, for example, military hardware, space, the SST, and so on.

It seems obvious that no competition could be devised that would cover urban areas as widely disparate as the New York metropolitan region at one end of the scale and, say, Lubbock, Tex., at the other. The kinds of problems confronting urban areas, and optimal solutions thereto, will vary greatly according to size, age, demographic characteristics, wealth, governmental and political traditions, and other factors. It therefore would be desirable to divide cities into classes for purposes of an awards program, as:

CLASS:	Population
1	100,000 to 500,000
2	500,000 to 1,000,000
3	1,000,000 to 5,000,000
4	over 5,000,000

Areas under 100,000 are not included: first, because of the large number of such areas; second, because their needs for innovation are generally less acute, and third, because it seems unlikely that they could contribute much of interest to larger areas. For such areas, it might be desirable to establish special awards, perhaps administered by State governments with financial help from the Federal Government and with competition on an intrastate rather than an interstate basis.

The Uses of Theory in the Simulation of Urban Phenomena

BRITTON HARRIS

Most of us who are engaged in one form or another of transportation and land use research have focused a very large proportion of our efforts on simulation. This means that we have devoted our efforts to reproducing in some recognizable form certain aspects of human behavior or of the performance of mechanical systems or of a combination of these two. We have done this generally in order to make predictions, and we have been interested in the accuracy of predictions in order to assist our agencies or other policy-makers in making decisions. It is the modest aim of this paper to provide a brief review of some of the ways in which theory can be of assistance in improving the similitude of simulations, and consequently the accuracy of predictions and the wiseness of decisions. There is, I believe, very little which is novel in what I have to say about the relationships which I imagine to exist between theory and practice. Consequently, it might be wise to apologize in advance to the philosophers whose ideas I may abuse and to my readers for serving a warmed-over menu.

Since there is a good deal of popular jargon which tends to imply that practical activities are useful while activities dealing with theory tend to be nonproductive, I intend to devote a part of this discussion to what might be called paradoxically a down-to-earth defense to these impractical activities—and to some extent I shall oppose what I would call crackpot realism with what might be termed realistic idealism. As Bertrand Russell has said, "Nothing is as practical as a good theory."

THEORY AND PRACTICE

In very simple terms, theory is a general statement about the real world. In these simple terms, for example, the Pythagorean theorem is one of many consequences of the theory of Euclidean geometry. As such it makes its own general statement about the properties of right-angle triangles on plane surfaces, and has had tremendous practical influence in surveying and engineering. This theorem provides the basis for all the well-worn formulas of elementary trigonometry, for example. There are two ways in which, however, we need to qualify this simpleminded definition of theory, and it is these qualifications which may tend to give the notion of theory some of its otherworldly character. First, when we say that theory talks about the real world, we have to include in that real world the minds and ideas of men. Thus, theory may deal to some extent with technology and concrete things on the one hand, and on the other hand with mental constructs which are seldom or never encountered in the physical world outside of men's minds until they have been written down. The real world of mental constructs is a very important one, and in the end has many practical applications. The extension of the trigonometry of measurement into trigonometric functions, for example, is the basis for other large parts of engineering. The second qualification is that a theoretic statement about the real world may not be, to the layman at least, a recognizable mapping of the real world, and the nature of the correspondence between the theory and the world and the consequences of the theory may not be readily expressible in everyday language. This sometimes makes it difficult for the layman to conclude at first glance that the theory is in any sense realistic or has any practical consequences.

There is of course an intimate relationship between theory and science or between the verification of theory and the scientific method. Since theories consist of statements about the real world, their degree of correspondence with this reality can be tested. Where the "real" world in question is one of mental constructs, as in logic and mathematics, the testing may be of a special and somewhat different nature, based on internal relations between constructs. It is not in general a requirement of the development of conceptual systems and their theory that any direct correspondence with mate-

Reprinted by permission of the *Journal of the American Institute of Planners*, XXXII, No. 5, September 1966, 258–273.

rial phenomena should be established, but it has frequently proved to be the case that after short or long periods of development, such concepts have found important and unforeseen applications to theories of phenomena. This course of events is analogous to, but not the same as, the laboratory development of methods and devices which for a long while remain mere curiosities, but which ultimately become technologically important.

We live in an age of rapidly expanding scientific endeavor. Science and the scientific method are being newly applied in the first instance to old systems of human thought such as ethics and philosophy, and in these areas, the boundaries of untestable contention are constantly being narrowed. We now not only know that because of the atomic nature of matter only a finite number of angels can dance on the point of a pin; we also feel greater confidence in the rigor and cogency of philosophy. At the same time, new groups of phenomena are becoming the subject of science. Testable rather than speculative hypotheses are developed about these phenomena, and these hypotheses are organized in increasingly unified systems, frequently of a quantitative nature. Some of this movement towards new applications of the scientific method is occurring in the social sciences, and in this field the two tendencies to reduce the area of philosophical and ethical speculation and to systematize our understanding of objective phenomena go hand in hand.

It is hardly necessary to review the practical ways in which the advances of science during the last two centuries have greatly increased man's control over his natural environment through the application of science to technology. It is more useful to point out, first, that not only is science successful in an objective sense, but also that it is widely accepted publicly and politically, as may be judged by the governmental and private resources which are devoted to it, and, second, that the growth and prestige of science have not simplified but have complicated the distinction between practical and theoretical endeavors.

The "customers" of the scientific establishment are basically interested in results and frequently have shorter time horizons than the scientists. This dichotomy expresses itself in the distinction between science and technology as

disciplines, and organizationally in the distinction between mission-oriented research and theoretically oriented research. As Alvin Weinberg has recently emphasized, the objectives of mission-oriented research are externally imposed upon the scientific community by the real or imagined needs of society and by society's control over expenditures, while the objectives of theoretical research are largely generated within the scientific community.

It appears to me that these distinctions, while valid and useful for analyzing and discussing the problems of science and technology, can be unduly overemphasized. Many factors tend to blur the differences. Technology and engineering themselves are becoming more scientific in their basic methods, and consequently engineers are becoming scientists. Mobility between the professions tends to inject mission-orientation and social responsibility into the scientific community, which was in any case never detached from these values. The tremendously accelerated pace of science tends to shorten the scientist's time horizon and bring it more into accord with that of the decision-maker. Finally, the complexities of real life which face decision-makers are driving them away from simplistic commonsense judgments and in the direction of a more comprehensive and quantitative approach to the problems which they face.

It is in fact the magnitude of the problems of societal control in a period of rapid change and development which are providing the impetus for the truly scientific development of the social sciences. Problems such as maintaining peace, feeding billions of people, reducing racial discrimination, and organizing great cities require powerful instruments of control over men and machines. These problems of control can no longer be resolved by an engineering approach which is overwhelmingly oriented towards physical, inanimate, machine systems. Engineers working in transportation planning must pay increasing attention to problems of human behavior, and it is rapidly becoming evident that the relevant behaviors are not only in the fields of transportation demand and transportation system utilization, but also in the field of land use development and locational choice. In a sense, therefore, and almost willy-nilly, the planning-engineering professions find themselves working on a frontier of science. This is the area of social behavior and social control, in which the application of the scientific method has been unduly retarded. In order to explore what implications this situation will have for their work, we must therefore take a closer look at some of the elements of this method.

SCIENTIFIC METHOD

We are used to the idea that man and the other higher primates are endowed with an innate curiosity which leads them to explore their total environment in an apparently insatiable and not entirely purposive way. There is usually no a priori identifiable useful payoff in some of the exploratory activities of monkeys and children, and one is tempted to make an analogy with the data-collection propensities of social science research and transportation studies. It is also perfectly clear, however, that in man at least, curiosity extends beyond the accumulation of data about the environment. First, even the childlike exercise of curiosity involves the exploration of cause and effect. The "experimenter" will employ some of the simpler ploys of the scientific method to discover what worked when and where. And second, there is frequently an effort to *generalize;* there seems to be a tendency to seek out analogies and similar situations in which earlier findings and elementary "theories" can be tested. Thus we have in a primitive form the four main steps in some classic descriptions of scientific method: First, induction: the collection of information and its organization into patterns. Second, generalization: a restatement of the cause and effect relations behind the patterns, or a redefinition of the patterns themselves in a more abstract form which includes the observations as a special case. Third, deduction: the search for new special cases previously unstudied, as suggested by the more general statement, or theory. And finally, testing: a check to see whether the new cases perform as predicted—if not, the theory must be revised. This schema, while useful for analytic purposes, does not correspond in its rigid division of steps with the way in which scientific investigations actually proceed. We will use these categories as a basis for discussion, specifically maintaining,

however, that the classification is artificial and if pressed too far, actually harmful.

The testing of theories about the world of phenomena raises special problems in the social sciences which should be generally understood before we take up other aspects of the scientific method. In this discussion I use the term "testing" in preference to the more usual "verification" because in principle no theory can be established, but only disestablished. A theory does not have verity, but verisimilitude. There are of course many theories which are outstandingly successful and for which there have been an almost unlimited number of successful tests, while the unsuccessful tests are nonexistent or occur only under well-defined special conditions. An especially significant case in which a theory may be regarded as firmly established because no counter-example exists is the correspondence between the counting numbers of everyday experience and the invented set of positive integers as defined in modern algebra by the use of the Peano postulates or otherwise. The theory states that these two systems, one from real life and one from mathematics, have the same form, and no exception to this theoretical statement is known or is likely to be discovered. A second example is the Newtonian statement based on the laws of motion, the law of universal gravitation, and Euclidean geometry. This theory relates the mechanics of the real world to a mathematical system of differential equations (a field of study which Newton, in fact, was forced to invent). Up to the point where by relativistic considerations the Euclidean geometry no longer applies in real space, there are no exceptions to this theoretic statement, and it too may be regarded as firmly established. In this latter case, it is important to note that the correctness of the theory has only been established by eliminating or controlling extraneous factors such as air resistance which affect the theoretically defined unimpeded motion of observed bodies.

THE SOCIAL SCIENCES

The special problems of the social sciences arise, as is well known, out of the difficulties of pursuing this experimental method in which most variables are held constant (the *ceteris paribus* assumption of economics) while a limited subset of possible variables is manipulated. Where a large number of variables is involved, this difficulty can sometimes be overcome if a large number of diverse observations is available to the researcher, but this is unfortunately not the case with regard to the study of the development, and the manipulation, of large urban areas. Here the case material is limited in extent, and experimental manipulation is both extremely slow and vastly expensive with regard to the aggregate phenomena. Experimental *cum* statistical methods are only possible with respect to smaller elements of the total system. In these regards, science as applied to total development of the function of the urban system is in most respects analogous with its use in astronomy which has a few cases of major interest, subject matter which is inaccessible to experimental manipulation, and the capacity for studying in the physics laboratory elements which do not aggregate by simple addition into the whole.

It may however be argued that the disadvantages of the social sciences in establishing an experimental method have been greatly exaggerated. This argument is advanced on the grounds that the most important tests of theories concern their ability to predict new phenomena or phenomena not previously studied in detail and to extrapolate the effects of causes beyond the ranges in which the causes were originally observed. It is curious to note that the literature of engineering and the social sciences abounds with warnings as to the dangers of extrapolation. If we wish to use, as we are almost forced to do, the power of extrapolation of a theory as a test of its credibility, then this cautionary advice is a frank confession that the relationships being extrapolated have no theoretical basis whatever. From the point of view of testing theories, the social scientists should welcome rather than shun opportunities for extrapolation, since this will provide his main basis for justifying a theory or for designing improvements in it.

INDUCTION AND DEDUCTION

Any acceptance of this criterion for testing theory tends to indicate the ultimate futility of a complete reliance on induction for generating theories. Even in the physical sciences, a fairly thorough knowledge of a particular range of joint variation of phenomena does not guarantee any adequate knowledge of cause and effect or even any complete description of relationships outside the range of observation, and this is even more true of the social sciences. Most of us are thoroughly familiar with the situation which arises when we get a good fit of a polynomial to a set of observed data, only to find that it behaves extremely erratically outside the range of observation. Poincaré has pointed out that if we had a complete knowledge of a portion, however small, of a continuous function, we would have a knowledge of the behavior of the function over its entire range. We could attempt to reach this happy state by developing the function as an infinite series and fitting all its coefficients statistically. Unfortunately, this procedure requires an infinity of observations (and a larger infinity than $\aleph$). Even more important, our observations must be free of errors of measurement, and our function must include all relevant variables, each of which must be measured. It is quite clear that even the process of induction from observed phenomena must be guided by theoretical concepts based on previous experience which will suggest the ranges and objects of observation and the character of the functions to be fitted. A simple engineering example might be found in the difference between the parabolic curve and the catenary. These curves arise under different circumstances in the construction of suspension bridges and lie extremely close together over a certain range of the variables. To distinguish between them by induction would be a hopeless task, especially since the formula for a catenary would not intuitively occur to a statistician, yet in extreme cases the distinction is important for engineering design. The differences are well defined a priori on the basis of a theory which may have been suggested by observation, but which does not spring automatically from it. The difficulties of induction are conclusively delineated, in fact, by the difficulties which arise in social science research in selecting functions for curve fitting and interpreting the results. Linear models are most frequently used because of their simplicity, perhaps with the justification that the linear approximation to some unknown function is not unreasonable over the range of the observations. The function being unknown means that theory is out the window. Perhaps a poly-nomial is used as some sort of an approxima-tion to a Taylor expansion of a function. In this case, the catenary is defined as a parabola. Where the choice of function is deduced from a priori considerations and not merely to sat-isfy goodness of fit, we are suddenly in the realm of deduction rather than induction.

Deductive thinking is of very high value in science. Examined closely, the antinomy be-tween induction and deduction is somewhat artificial; on the one hand, as we have just suggested, induction is almost never initiated without some kind of prior theory, however naive, which suggests areas of investigation, relevant variables, and the form which func-tions might take—while on the other hand, if deduction is unsuccessful and does not result in a confirming instance of the theory on which it is based, then the contradictory evidence may be the basis for a new round of induction. But the importance of deduction as a part of the scientific method remains in spite of the partial artificiality of its separation from induction. At the start of the process of deduction, the in-vestigator is forced to make a statement of a general nature about the real world; in other words, he must formulate a theory. The motive for this formulation frequently comes from psychological forces very closely related to in-duction and to the search for generality. To follow the processes of deduction suggested by the theory, the investigator must search out new areas or new modes of application of the theory. It is useful to him in defining sup-posed cause and effect or functional relation-ships and variables to be investigated. In considering, therefore, the nature and power of the deductive process, we are led naturally to the final and perhaps the essential part of our discussion of theory construction, that of generalization, or the actual formulation of the theory. We must consider this in the light of all of the processes and problems which have been discussed up to this point.

GENERALIZATION

Generalization is the bridge by which the sci-entist or theoretician crosses over from induc-tion, or the observation of reality, to deduc-tion, or the testing of theories and their application to new phenomena. For this reason, I rather like the name "transduction," which is sometimes applied to it. No matter how often this bridge is crossed in the course of a scien-tific investigation, the act of transduction al-ways involves some invention on the part of the investigator. The psychology of invention in this field is intricate and fascinating, but a discussion of it is out of place here. The sources of this invention may, however, be better un-derstood through a consideration of its inherent nature.

The construction or invention of a theory involves in essence a precise statement regard-ing formal relationships, usually including re-lationships of cause and effect. There is an in-finity of possible formal statements of relation-ships which may be made in their most abstract form in the language of mathematics or logic. Such statements regarding relationships are purely formal and have no reference to the real world. Within the sciences dealing with con-cepts, they may in fact be developed quite independently of the real world. The problem of theory construction or invention is, then, to make the correct identification between a real phenomenon and a mathematical or logical statement regarding relationships. There are three possible ways in which this may be done, two of which are merely suggestive and one of which tends to satisfy rigorous scientific re-quirements.

First, an analogy may be recognized at the level of phenomena. Thus, for example, a city may be compared with an organism—say a jellyfish. This analogy is scientifically useless unless two conditions are met. First, the com-parative object (the jellyfish) must have a form which has been clearly and logically defined and, second, the object compared (the city) must be unequivocally said to be theoretically identical. In this case, we have identified a cor-respondence of the third type below, but oth-erwise we have merely made a statement which is useful for heuristic purposes.

Second, an analogy may be recognized as be-tween a phenomenon and a mathematical or logical construct, but may indeed be very loosely defined. Thus, for example, the gravity formula recognizes an analogy between the de-cay of trip frequency with distance and the power function X^{-a}. This analogy is extremely crude, seizing as it does on the most obvious and easily manipulated of a host of monotonically decreasing non-negative functions. No statement of the gravity model, to my knowledge, states any causal relationships which would generate this particular function in preference to others. I think that we may designate an analogy between phenomena and a logical function as a *homomorphism,* meaning a similarity of form.

Third, an important qualitative change is introduced if a scientist identifies a particular phenomenon as having a clearly defined logical form. The definition of form may have already been made either in the development of logic and mathematics and unrelated to phenomena, or in connection with the development of theory dealing with some other and perhaps completely unrelated phenomena. The use of formal statements pertaining to other phenomena is indeed often suggested by analogies between the phenomena themselves. On occasion, the study of phenomena themselves and the formulation of ideas about cause and effect necessitates the invention of a new relational calculus. This has been the case in Newtonian mechanics and quantum mechanics. In any event, the essence of a theoretical statement is to identify an *isomorphism* (identity of form) between a set of phenomena and a logical or mathematical relational system. Thus, the Schneider model for trip distribution, in contradistinction to the gravity model, makes a rigorous statement that the decay of trip frequency is isomorphic to the negative exponential function and consequently also to the radioactive decay of fissionable elements; and Schneider identifies the precise cause and effect relationships on which the isomorphism is based.

It should of course be clear that the borderline between homomorphisms and isomorphisms is blurred, partly because it refers to the motivations and psychology of the scientists. A theory which is in fact generated as an analogy must be presented as an isomorphism, and a badly conceived isomorphism may turn out to be only an analogy. The appropriate distinction can be made only upon close examination of the theory and of its results.

In formulating a theory to serve as a bridge between induction and deduction, the analyst has a number of guides as to desirable features of his formulation. Some of the most significant criteria tend to conflict with one another and others to reinforce each other, depending on circumstances. All arise out of the general characteristics of the scientific process as we have outlined it.

The outstanding criterion, of course, is that the theory should be "correct," that is, that the theory if testable should pass its tests successfully. This is the basis for the essentially practical nature of science, that is, that it says "true" things about the real world. We have seen above that such truth is impermanent, always awaiting contradictions. If these arise, it frequently is retained circumscribing the generality of the theory, limiting the circumstances in which it applies, and creating new and more general theories to apply to other combinations of circumstances. This criterion of correctness is in general overriding. However, practical considerations frequently lead to the generally indefensible practice of applying theories which have been inadequately tested or which have known errors.

Thus a theory, if untestable, becomes a non-theory; like Milton, science has "no use for a fugitive and cloistered virtue. . . ." There are of course examples of very important scientific theories, such as Einstein's theory of relativity, which when published appeared very difficult if not impossible to test. These difficulties in relation to a reputable and exciting proposal often serve as a spur to experimental work. In the field of social sciences, however, this particular type of non-theory has two other manifestations. One of these is a normative admonitory description of how things should be done; the other is a literary or pseudo-statistical description of the real world. The fact that these things are merely masquerading as theory can easily be exposed by searching for critical tests which could deny their validity. If such tests do not exist, the so-called theory is in fact a non-theory. Occasionally tests acceptable to the authors of the theory will be so circumscribed with restrictive conditions and assumptions as to expose the fact that the theory is of extremely limited application and has dubious stature.

The testability of a theory is a special case of a more general property of useful theories—productiveness or fruitfulness. Important theories in the development of science not only answer the problems posed in the initial stages of induction, but are pregnant with consequences which are only dimly seen by their inventors and which lay the basis for a wide variety and a great number of deductive experiments. Axiomatic systems in geometry, algebra, and logic exhibit this property, for example. The tremendous accomplishments of modern mathematics follow (although not effortlessly) from a very limited set of carefully considered initial assumptions. Similar examples exist outside of conceptual systems. The quantum theory, which was invented to explain anomalies in black-body radiation, has found innumerable applications to phenomena as diverse as photoelectricity and solar spectrography, and is in fact a key element in all modern physics. The social sciences and the planning-engineering professions are somewhat lacking in such key theories, but some nominations could be made. These might include, for example, marginal substitution and general equilibrium concepts from economics, and applications of general systems theory. In any event, while it is somewhat difficult to define the process by which a theorist comes upon a fruitful theory with many applications while attempting to solve a more limited and more particular problem, it is apparent that solutions of this type are unusually desirable. At the least, theory builders should have this objective in view, especially since this state of mind leads to stripping any problem to its most essential elements, and thus may simplify as well as lead to greater generalities.

Simplicity is in fact an ancient and honored criterion for choosing between otherwise equipotent theories. Occam's Razor, named after a fourteenth century English philosopher, dictates that theories should contain the minimum possible number of hypotheses, and many of the more durable theories elegantly exhibit this characteristic. Because of the large number of conditions, relations, and variables which occur in social science research, this condition is difficult to meet here and frequently conflicts with requirements of realism and testability. It is nevertheless a desirable characteristic, not only for reasons of elegance, economy, and generality, but also for practical reasons which will be discussed in the next paragraphs. Here there

is a special pitfall which social science researchers can dig for themselves by the use of modern computational techniques. It has been suggested that, had computers been available at the time of Copernicus, the ease of computation of epicycles might have removed the practical difficulties which led to the construction of the elegant and economical heliocentric theory and the Newtonian theory of celestial mechanics. By the use of computers in the descriptive system of Ptolemy, navigational tables could have been constructed to any required degree of accuracy, and the practical impetus for the Copernican and subsequent revolutions would have been removed. I feel that we fall into the same trap when, as with the introduction of K-factors into the gravity model, we constantly patch up a nonexistent or inadequate theory with computational amendments.

MODELS

To be testable a theory must be manipulable. The experimental method in the social sciences is, as we have said, forced to rely on paper experiments, and for these our professions commonly talk about the use of models. To quote Harmer Davis, "A model is a smaller copy of the real thing, as the woman said about a model husband." This pointed definition does not permit us, however, to distinguish between a mathematical model and a simulation model on the one hand, nor between a simulation model and a theory on the other hand. We shall devote brief attention to these two distinctions.

As we have tried to emphasize above, there are in principle distinct sources of an understanding of cause and effect in the real world and of formal representations of relationships in the world of mathematics and logic. Science is in many respects an effort to establish isomorphisms between these distinct realms. If we refer to a linear programming model of warehouse location, we are referring to just such an assertion about an isomorphism. We might then be correct in speaking of a *mathematical model of warehouse location*. Frequently, however, people speak of the linear programming model, and more generally of *mathematical models* in the abstract without relation to any particular real world phenomena. I would submit that this application of the word "model" is incorrect, though lamentably ineradicable, because the mathematical linear programming model is not a model or a smaller copy *of* anything.

The distinction between a theory and a simulation model is somewhat more subtle and difficult. A theory in fact could also be said to be a logical or mathematical model of the phenomena to which it refers. It is smaller; it is a copy; and it is *of* the real thing. Yet this identification of a theory with a model somehow goes against the grain. On the basis of very serious consideration, I have redefined models as they are used in the simulation of social and economic events in a way which tends to provoke outraged reactions, but which I believe withstands serious examination and criticism: *a model is an experimental design based on a theory.* Let us examine the implications of this definition somewhat more carefully.

As is well known to workers in our fields, there are many theories which are testable in the sense that a critical experiment can be designed, but which remain untestable in the sense that the data requirements are for practical purposes excessive, that they involve presently unobservable variables, or perhaps most important, that they cannot be cast in a form which will fit into a computer and run economically. These practical considerations do indeed provide a spur to all kinds of experimental ingenuity, and they should by no means dominate the process of theory construction.

In the process of the development of a theory, there are many applications of experimental design in which, however, the theorist must invoke models. First, in exploratory or inductive investigations, he is quite apt to use a severely truncated or patently inadequate experimental design such as a multiple regression model to explore relationships and to provide information as to the direction of his next transductive steps. In a more developed form he will use a model more closely corresponding to theory inductively to establish the parameters of relationships. Second, he will use a model for testing in the deductive sense in order to determine the applicability of his theory under a wider range of conditions.

Third, used scientifically in a context of projections, the model will provide experimental evidence as to the consistency of the theory and possible inductive evidence as to the sensitivity of the real world to changes in conditions. It may be a matter of scientific but not practical indifference to the scientist that the projective use of models also is important to decision-makers.

One may choose to make a distinction between the value of theory building and the value of experimental work with models, imputing a higher value to the first of these activities. However, in the tradition of British and American experimental science, the theorist usually has some responsibility for making feasible the tests of his ideas, and it is only the boldest and most brilliant innovator in pure theory who can expect others to accept a division of labor in which they will devise feasible tests for his "impractical" formulations. It is this experimental difficulty which often leads to emphasis on the false dichotomy between theory and practice, which can only be overcome by a long-run view of the value of theory and by a nice sense of the potential contributions of new theories whose testing and application may appear outrageously difficult.

There are other criteria which may or may not be useful for the construction and selection of theories but which are frequently in the minds both of scientists and lay people. We have mentioned above the fact that for a variety of reasons a theory may not correspond directly with intuitive and popular ideas about the nature of reality. In this case, the theorist or scientist may be accused of being unrealistic and may feel a social obligation to change or alter the tone of his theory in the direction of popularly understood "realism." Such a compulsion grossly distorts the role of the scientist, which is to identify a genuine isomorphism, most frequently not obvious, between the behavior of the real world and a set of mental constructs. Frequently he has to invent the mental constructs in order to disclose the isomorphism. Many of the most pregnant ideas of the physical and biological sciences, such as the quantum theory, the theory of relativity, or the independence of heredity from environment run counter to widely held and deeply rooted popular ideas, yet without the discovery of these theories and their application to everyday life, the world would have given up a great deal of progress. A search for naive realism is counterproductive in science.

Frequently even though a naive demand for realism may be abandoned, the critics of science will continue to take refuge in an unthinking insistence on comprehensibility. In the field of social sciences, this insistence is based on two circumstances. First, every critic is a member of society, a user of cities, and a participant in the political process. He hence feels intuitively that by virtue of this special status he and most other informed people ought to be able to understand directly all of the theories which purport to define the operations of society, of cities, and of politics. In my view, it would be equally ridiculous to say that because we are all made of protein, we should all understand at a glance the theories of molecular biology. A second circumstance resides in the fact that a great deal of social science research is conducted in such a way that the scientists are close to the administrators, the administrators are close to the decision-makers, and the decision-makers are close to the voters, all with no clear separation of function. Because of the personal and normative nature of the communication between these groups, each link in the chain feels that he ought to know all about what the adjacent link is doing. We may contrast this with the somewhat more impersonal relationships which govern research and development in industry. The laboratory scientist may understand solid state physics in detail. The corporation executive will understand the main directions of this research and its potentialities. The sales department understands the capability of the resultant product, and the customer chooses in the market place between the products of competing technologies and competing companies. The man in the street could not care less about the crucial role of, say, quantum mechanics in the production of his transistor radio. Probably when social science theories produce as effective results as quantum mechanics, the administrators, policy makers, and voters will be less inclined to ask questions and more inclined to judge by results.

A possible requirement for theory which requires brief mention is more likely to be generated by the scientist than by the layman. As a result of the complexity of social phenomena which require holding other things constant, and as a result of the drive for generalization which is inherent in theory building, there is a considerable drive to create theories which are "comprehensive." This drive encounters resistance on two fronts. First, a comprehensive theory may in certain cases become so general as to say nothing about everything. Even if this is not the case, the more comprehensive theories may be the most difficult to manipulate for purposes of testing and application. An important part of theory building is therefore a nice sense of discrimination as to when comprehensive theories are necessary and when they may be appropriately avoided by discretion in the subdivision of the problem into manageable parts. In policy-related sciences improper subdivision of the policy-making problems may result in suboptimization, but a subdivision of the problems of the real world and its functioning for purposes of study need not entail this danger.

LAND USE SYSTEMS AND TRANSPORTATION SYSTEMS

In the preceding sections of this discussion, I have developed my ideas with regard to the scientific construction of theory, mainly with respect to the problems of simulating events in the real world of mass behavior in the use of transportation facilities and in the choice of locations, even though this concern has been in the main implicit rather than explicit. There are two other areas related to public decision-making in which theories of a different kind will have to be developed. These deserve brief mention. Transportation and planning literature already recognizes the need for the development of more general theories of decision-making. In crude terms, the questions to be answered by such theories concern what we are planning for, what trade-offs are involved in the public decision process, and what values our plans will satisfy. In more sophisticated terms we turn out to be dealing with difficult problems of public discount rates, collective consumption, spillovers and externalities, the aggregation of utilities, and the reconciliation of conflicting interests. It is to be hoped that the improvement of theories and models in this general area may be expected to reflect backward into the planmaking process so that sketch planning procedures are replaced by optimizing procedures, and so that optimizing is not limited to narrow engineering criteria but is extended to the most general of social objectives. I think it is also predictable that as we explore the problems of decision-making, planning, and optimizing more thoroughly, we will discover that there are ferocious computational problems which arise in the design process as a result of the huge combinatorial variety which exists in the possible combinations of policies and future conditions. Our fraternal theorists in the field of mathematical programming may be able to make contributions of a theoretical nature with practical applications which are related to the needs of decision-making. It is also probable that a clearer formulation of these needs will influence this development of what are essentially design models.

We have now reached the vantage point of a somewhat shaky and perhaps imperfect understanding of some of the processes of science, from which we may view the needs and accomplishments of experimental simulation of transportation systems and land use systems and the behavior of their users. I will not here belabor the point which is now becoming widely accepted in principle—that in many policy-making contexts we are dealing with these systems not independently, but as a part of the larger urban metropolitan system or regional system. I will emphasize the fact that most theories of locational behavior contain ideas about transportation costs and convenience, and consequently that locational models must contain as submodels some replication of the transportation aspects of the system. It will also prove useful in the discussion which follows to consider the salient features of all these problems together from the point of view of theory construction, drawing freely upon examples from any field wherever they may be appropriate.

The range of our interest in these phenomena covers a wide span from very large and complex total systems through subsystems which may be defined in engineering terms, in social and economic terms, or in spatial terms,

down to the smallest elements of the system themselves. These last may be mechanical components, but the greater interest attaches to decision units—a man driving a car, a family looking for a home, or a corporation deciding to build a new establishment. At each of these levels, different problems arise regarding the appropriate form and content of research.

The broadest view of the over-all system is probably not in itself highly productive, but it is a starting point for certain applications of general systems theory which later affect our view of the components and the elements. General systems theory with respect to the total urban, metropolitan, or regional system will ultimately play a direct role in decision models. Meanwhile, it can be particularly useful in defining the appropriate limits of a system and in guiding the structuring of the problem in such a way that its decomposition into subproblems dealing with subsystems will entail a minimum of distortion. Up to now in both transportation and land use analysis these two problems have been approached largely by intuition and induction. I do not feel that the results have been seriously wrong, but a systematic and better informed approach might provide some surprises and prove a useful guide to research design.

With respect to subsystems properly defined and considered as systems in their own right, general systems theory may very well contribute powerful methods for dealing with system stability as a planning objective and with homeostatic or equilibrating tendencies within systems as handles for both planning and analysis. I have my own intuitive feeling that concepts of equilibrium animate a great deal of research and theory in land use and transportation analysis, but that these concepts are inadequately explored and not sufficiently explicit. For example, transportation analysis and the assignment of traffic to networks with capacity restraints imply a whole pattern of equilibrating behavior on the part of individuals which may or may not lead to system equilibrium and may or may not be related to various forms of optimization. These questions have been very lightly explored by brute force iterative methods in modeling experiments, and their full implications remain to be seriously examined. In land use growth model simulations based upon trend data, there is also a set of unexplored assumptions about tendencies to equilibrium. Whether such an equilibrium exists or ought to exist has in fact been slightly examined in theory. Needless to say, one-shot sketch planning or design models and "instant cities" such as Ira S. Lowry's *Model of a Metropolis* are constrained to use either simultaneous determination or optimization, and it seems likely that the former method contains some optimizing assumptions in its behavioral parameters. More generally, I feel that land use behavior as well as land use system performance can hardly be explained without a consideration of land market equilibrium and simultaneous determination—all of which pose major problems for system theory.

COMMUNICATING MECHANISMS

There are a number of interesting problems which arise out of the communication among subsystems and between elements and subsystems and out of the mechanisms by which equilibrating, disequilibrating, and determining forces are transmitted to and from decision units. The organs of the body communicate information leading to action by nerve impulses and those maintaining homeostasis by chemical messengers; what are the messengers in a large city or region? Many of these questions will arise again in the discussion of the behavior of decision units below, but there is some advantage in taking an overview in the context of systems. It is quite apparent that the generic name for these messengers will be information, and it seems quite likely that some gains in theoretical clarity will be achieved if a systematic application of communications theory can be made to the diffusion of information through and about the systems under study. The applicability of this concept is already apparent in the most elementary consideration of the stability of traffic flow systems, and these ideas can probably be extended to land use systems and larger transportation systems. Considered in the communications context, there is some merit in combining the study of decision units with a priori considerations from different disciplines as to what information is likely to be important and available. At one

extreme this type of merger leads to a consideration of the individual's reaction to the visual environment as developed in studies by Lynch and others. At a different extreme, economics suggests that prices are the messengers by which important economic information regarding, say, the housing market is transmitted. Between these extremes lie many combinations of phenomena which are observable, influential in behavior, and to some extent predictable as consequences of other developments.

The importance of prices as a messenger and of the allocation of money to different purposes (that is, of economic behavior) in private decision-making is so great that it deserves special attention. It is a curious fact that in spite of this a priori importance of monetary phenomena, they have really received relatively little emphasis in transportation and land use planning and analysis. For somewhat understandable reasons, transportation planners have been reluctant to explore the importance of pricing policies in alternative transportation systems. Surely, however, this reluctance should not extend, as it frequently does, to the omission of cost factors and the exclusive emphasis on time-distance which is frequently found in network analysis, trip distribution, and even modal split. Fortunately, this default is not universal. In land use analysis, the problem is perhaps even more severe. Housing rents and values are the medium through which consumers communicate with each other their willingness or unwillingness to compete for space, and more commonly land prices are the medium of communication in the competition of residential, industrial, and public uses for land. Yet in the research field, housing value and land prices very seldom appear as variables. So damaging is this omission that expensive and otherwise useful surveys of locational, social, economic, and housing variables by the Penn Jersey Transportation Study and the Tri-State Transportation Committee are partly vitiated by the failure to inquire as to housing value or rent. It must be admitted that the collection of these data and especially of land value information in a research study is fraught with difficulty, but I believe that there is a more serious reason why these values have been neglected in spite of strong theoretical reasons for their inclusion.

If values (prices) are made explanatory variables leading to changes in the behavior of decision units, then future applications of the same theory and its derivative models require that these values be projected under new circumstances. The theorist then faces an ugly dilemma. If he chooses to predict future prices by means of proxy variables, he must build a purely descriptive model for this purpose which contains no ideas about cause and effect; and this being the case, he might just as well have left prices out of the original analysis and included the same proxy variables, admitting from the outset that his theory was in part purely descriptive. If on the other hand he takes the importance of these economic variables seriously, he must face the difficulty of reconstructing a complete market through some form of simulation. This reconstruction is complicated by the existence of submarkets, institutional stickiness, imperfect dissemination of information, and probable lags in equilibrium. If economic considerations were largely peripheral to the theory of land use and transportation systems, there would be less objection to taking the easy way out of this dilemma. I believe, however, that these considerations are so central that economic models must in the future be added to the implementation of transportation and location theory at full scale. This approach will involve much deeper consideration of equilibrium tendencies than was suggested above, and perhaps a much more serious look at some aspects of the behavior of decision units.

BEHAVIOR OF DECISION UNITS

Before turning to a discussion of the theory of the behavior of decision units, I must emphasize a vital distinction between the study of that theory and its application. To a very large extent, the study of the behavior of decision units can be undertaken independently of the simulation of system and subsystem performance which has been the subject of the prior discussion. This is true because at the moment when we examine the actions of decision units, the systems in which they are embedded have already performed their functions, interacted with each other, and thereby generated the environmental conditions and information of which the decision unit has knowledge and on which it acts. In this analysis, the experimental approach consists in searching out instances in which the environment and its informational content differ significantly from other environments, or the decision units differ significantly from other decision units, so that the general application and fruitfulness of the theory may be examined. When, however, the behavior of decision units as understood on the basis of such an analysis is to be explored experimentally under changed assumptions as to policies and technology, an entirely new situation arises. We can no longer assume that various sets of decision-makers are independent of each other. Each reacts with the environment and creates changes which result in messages reaching other decision-makers. This interaction, which is irrelevant to some analyses, becomes critical in system simulation. I thus assume that system simulation and decision analysis interact strongly with each other and that each is necessary for the other. But as a matter of research emphasis, I would give short-term priority to system simulation on the grounds that relevant experiments to test our understanding of the behavior of decision units can probably not be performed without it.

Engineers and planners are vitally concerned with the behavior of households and business establishments in making use of the transportation system and in making locational decisions. Such behavior is the source of transportation demand. Private decisions in respect of automobile ownership, location, and new construction in the aggregate greatly influence the development of cities and regions. Finally, I am sure that if we understood thoroughly the whole constellation of decisions made by individuals and firms, we could understand at the same time the extent to which various urban arrangements satisfy their needs. Such an understanding is a vital key to producing plans and policies which will best serve the public interest.

Some of the differences between practicing planners and engineers can be traced to their different approaches to decision-makers' needs and preferences. The planner typically approaches the problem from the viewpoint of normative standards of behavior and social welfare. This is in part based upon notions of minimum socially acceptable levels of welfare and in part upon an emphasis on the externalities of individual behavior—that is, upon the effects of one's behavior on others. These notions are linked with strong ideas of social control. The engineering approach tends to be more adaptive. Individual behavior is regarded as being largely self-motivated and not widely amenable to control. In dealing with supposed patterns of behavior as necessary inputs to engineering estimates, the engineer approaches the problem with inadequate concepts of motivation and of measurement. Neither planners nor engineers are in general well trained in the intricate issues of choice behavior, and present-day economics, sociology, and psychology offer little which is of general applicability to the problems which they face. The following remarks are therefore observations on a dilemma which will ultimately be resolved only by training people and developing methods which embody a combination of all of these disciplines in a new format.

The basic theory of choices by individual decision units deals in terms of alternatives and trade-offs, yet if we examine transportation and locational theories or models, we find that these trade-offs are remotely reflected, if indeed they may be presumed to have been considered seriously at all. Since the same thing is true of econometric models in related fields, this is not a particularly telling criticism in terms of past performance, but it is clear that it may constitute a barrier which will have to be removed before a great deal of progress can be made.

Much of the difficulty concerns observation and measurement, and perhaps this may best be illustrated with reference to the theory of industrial and commercial location. Industrial location in particular has long been very carefully studied by locational economists and regional scientists, and interregional locational theory is a particularly well developed field. In this location theory three factors are particularly important: internal economies of scale which depend on the size of establishment; external economies of scale or agglomeration economies which depend on the sizes of the geographical assemblages of activities in which the establishment is located; and locational costs which depend mainly on the cost of land and the costs of interaction. In the complicated urban metropolitan scene, these economic variables turn out to be very difficult to define, more difficult to measure, and still more difficult to value. While it may be well known, for example, that the garment industry has large agglomeration economies and is sensitive to its accessibility to a particular labor force and to the cost of industrial space, these variables and their relationships are not well defined. The interaction requirements of offices and the agglomeration economies of retail trade establishments are also imperfectly understood. While these ideas enlighten a good deal of research design, anyone who has tried to set up an industrial or commercial survey knows that it is very difficult to tie them down specifically. Because of this situation and for allied reasons, it is beginning to appear that in spite of the much more sophisticated work over many decades in industrial location, the problems of residential location are more tractable and amenable to sound solution.

In the area of consumer behavior, some difficulty is introduced by the fact that certain decisions are made by individuals, others by households, and still others by individuals in a household context. These difficulties must be faced in research design, but they are relatively minor compared with other more obvious problems. One which has been both recognized and ignored (often simultaneously) is that of aggregation. Some researchers, perhaps moved by data difficulties, are inclined to deal with the means and medians of areal aggregations of data. This method of work is almost enforced by the form of the availability of published census data in certain cases. There is clearly here a latent conception that area averages represent some sort of aggregation of behaviors, but the implicit rules of this aggregation are not explored, and frequently the assumed behaviors are not fully defined. The gravity model of trip distribution clearly takes this approach at a descriptive level, while multiple regression models of modal split may be but a step closer to postulating real cause and effect. The Schneider model of trip distribution postulates more explicit behavioral patterns and works with areal aggregate data. In practice, however, this model reveals unexplained variations in decision behavior because it requires an area-specific determination of the proportions of long and short trips. This specification amounts to a statement that the behavior in the model is incompletely defined.

Those who avoid the implicit assumptions of working with grouped area data by using individual or household observations encounter another level of difficulty which helps to elucidate the problem of aggregation. Behavioral models of individual and household choice invariably produce tests in which only a small part of choice behavior is adequately explained. Typical coefficients of determination are in the range of .15 to .30. While this may mean in some cases that the models and theories employed are inadequate, it is more likely to imply that behavior is influenced by more or less unobservable cultural and psychological factors which (at least at any one time) may be statistically distributed in the population. The delicate problem of research design is to know when to stop trying to identify these factors and when to introduce assumptions about the statistical nature of their distribution in the population. After the first recourse is exhausted or while it is being further developed, it is apparent that the nature of the assumptions about the statistical distributions of behavior around their observed statistical means may strongly affect the characteristics of their aggregation. As a simple example, I have demonstrated elsewhere that if Schneider's L parameter is assumed to have a certain statistical distribution rather than being fixed, his model converts readily to a modified gravity model or to a combined model. Certainly considerable statistical expertise will be required to explore this problem further.

One of the more subtle and neglected aspects of the analysis of decision units is the role of the history of the unit in its behavior. To some extent, the history of certain units is implicit in their state description—for example, a family head aged 20 is probably recently married. But other and more subtle historical aspects may be overlooked. It is quite clear, for instance, that the history of industrial establishments is related to their tendencies to relocate and the ethnic background of many population groups is related to their choice of residence. It has even been reasonably suggested that consumer choice of mode of travel is re-

lated to the individual's history in learning to drive. These historical aspects of the behavior of decision units have two very important relationships with more general systems analysis. The historical aspects of decisions are closely tied to the extent of the lags in movement toward system equilibrium, and only systems in which the history of decision units is unimportant will rapidly achieve equilibrium. At the same time, the introduction of these histories is a means of dealing quite explicitly with trend data, without at the same time building into the theory an assumption that trends will indefinitely continue. It should be apparent that this historical approach does not lend itself to easy application to aggregate data, at least in analysis. And if the histories to be considered become very complex, then Monte-Carlo methods are almost required for any projection simulations.

In the light of this necessarily incomplete review, we may justifiably conclude, I feel, that a theoretically sound and scientific approach to systems simulation of transportation and land use will require a great deal of rethinking of our theory of decision-units' behavior.

IMPLICATIONS FOR PLANNING

Let us now take a brief final view of the workaday implications of the type of program which I have sketched above. The essential elements of this approach are six in number. First, since sound theory has so much to offer for practical progress, the work should be organized on a scientific rather than a mission-oriented or technological basis. We would thus also avoid the dangers implicit in harnessing these activities to suboptimal policies. We would rely on the social and policy motivations of the scientists to maintain a well directed drive toward ultimate application. Second, we would view these problems as related to certain real world systems and would deepen our efforts to achieve successful theories of the operation of those systems. Third, we would give appropriate recognition to the need for the study of the behavior of decision units in the context of larger systems which create their environment. Fourth, we would give explicit recognition to the theoretical problem of communication between the systems, subsystems, and decision units. Fifth, we would recognize that the scope of these investigations will require the unification of parts of different disciplines in institutions and in individuals. Sixth, we would recognize that in a specially defined sense this work is experimental in the best traditions of experimental science and that the experimental method will require special conditions for success.

It would seem to me that the scale of these problems and their importance for long-term policy development tend to argue against scattered research in connection with specific projects. Such projects in any case tend to attempt to impose their mission orientation on individual researchers. The resulting tension between the desire of the researcher to satisfy his scientific conscience and the desire of the management to get the job done sometimes borders on the tragic, or the comic. In any event, the problems are of general and national significance, and if worthy of consideration should not be charged to local or to special-purpose studies. It is also apparent that the variety of ability and knowledge required for an assault on these problems can rarely be assembled even in a large study of an ad hoc nature. Consequently, many such studies are repeating the work and perpetuating the errors of other studies for lack of resources to go further and try new methods. Finally, there are serious difficulties of communication within this scientific community which result from the excessive fragmentation of effort.

Special attention needs to be devoted to the requirements of the experimental method in this field. Consider, for example, that we are designing a laboratory for social, engineering, and planning research. Our experimental material, instead of white mice, is extensive data about metropolitan areas and regions. These data must meet certain rigorous standards and be well organized and accessible. Our main experimental tool is probably the computer, but this will include the software or operating programs which embody many or most of the elementary processes of simulation and analysis which we have discovered. Our experimental design is a model or group of models based on theory and using our experimental material (data) and our experimental tools (computers and software). In any good experimental design, we are apt to discover that some special-purpose tools will have to be made—in this case, that new programs will have to be written and in some cases new data collected. The essential aim of an experiment will be to make critical tests of theories by good experimental design and thus to decide, for example, on a clear definition of the relative merits of the gravity model, the Schneider model, the Tomazinis model, and the Harris model of trip distribution. The essential ingredient for progress in addition to all the niceties which I have so far discussed is quick turn-around so that experiments may be rapidly executed once they are designed. I would estimate that under current conditions, with practically no standing stock of data and widely diversified programs, the turn-around time on experimental work of this type is roughly three to five years. This time should be reduced by a factor of three or more, and the content of the experiments should be far more conclusive than it is today.

I believe that these standards, both of theoretical excellence and mechanical performance, are achievable, and that if achieved they will have tremendous payoffs in improved planning.

REFERENCES

Gerald A. P. Carrothers, "An Historical Review of the Gravity and Potential Concepts of Human Interaction," *Journal of the American Institute of Planners*, Vol. XXII (Spring, 1956).

Britton Harris, "A Note on the Probability of Interaction at a Distance," *Journal of Regional Science*, Vol. V, No. 2 (in press).

Britton Harris (ed.), "Urban Development Models: New Tools for Planning," *Journal of the American Institute of Planners*, Special Issue, Vol. XXXI (May, 1965).

Ira S. Lowry, *A Model of Metropolis*, Memorandum RM–4035–RC (Santa Monica, California: The RAND Corporation, August, 1964).

Kevin Lynch, *The Image of the City* (Cambridge, Massachusetts: M.I.T. Press, 1960).

Henri Poincaré, *Science and Hypothesis* (New York: Dover Press, 1952).

Morton Schneider, "Gravity Models and Trip Distribution Theory," *Papers and Proceedings of the Regional Science Association*, Vol. V, 1959.

Anthony R. Tomazinis, "A New Trip Distribution Model," Paper #347 (Washington, D.C.: Highway Research Board, 1963).

Alvin Weinberg, "But is the Teacher Also a Citizen?" *Science*, Vol. 149:601–6 (August 6, 1965).

II

ECONOMIC ANALYSIS OF URBAN HOUSING DEMAND

Determinants of Residential Construction: A Review of Present Knowledge

LEO GREBLER AND SHERMAN J. MAISEL

INTRODUCTION

List of Potential Determinants

The volume of nonfarm residential construction can conceivably be determined by a large number of factors. Those mentioned in most of the analytical work performed to date may be grouped as follows:

1. Changes in population
    a. Increases in population
    b. Changes in the age-sex composition
    c. Changes in the number, type, and size of households
    d. Internal migration and immigration
2. Changes in income and employment
    a. Total disposable personal income: past, current, expected
    b. Income distribution
    c. Employment and unemployment
3. Consumer asset holdings and their distribution, especially liquid assets and equities in existing houses
4. Changes in the prices of housing
    a. The price elasticity of housing relative to other prices
    b. The shape of the construction supply and cost curves
5. Relationship between occupancy costs and prices of dwellings
    a. Credit availability and the cost of credit
    b. Real estate taxes and operating expenses
    c. Depreciation
    d. Imputed costs of equity funds
6. Consumer tastes and preferences
7. Net replacement demand for dwelling units demolished or otherwise removed from the inventory less net conversions and mergers of existing units
8. Conditions in the existing housing supply
    a. Utilization of the housing inventory
        (1) Vacancies
        (2) Intensity of occupancy
    b. Prices and rents for existing dwelling units

c. Quality, location
9. Reaction to changes in demand
    a. Builders' organization and profit expectations
    b. Investors' organization and profit expectations
    c. Market structure and market information

Analysis of the determinants of residential construction is complicated not only by the large number of potential forces impinging on this sector of the economy but also by interdependence of some of these factors. Thus, changes in income and income expectations influence the number of marriages and births and the ability of married couples, individuals and unrelated groups of individuals to establish households in separate dwelling units, all of which affect changes in the number and size of households. The utilization of the existing inventory is influenced by both demographic changes and changes in income, which also affect the prices and rents for dwelling units in the existing housing inventory. Prices and rents for new housing, as well as the availability and costs of borrowed funds, are not wholly independent of changes in aggregate income. And aggregate income, which is considered one of the determinants of residential construction, is, in turn, partially determined by the volume of such construction.

Analysis is further complicated by the fact that some of the listed factors may be more significant in determining long-run levels of residential construction, while others may have an important bearing on short-run changes—a distinction often not clearly specified or defined in the analytical work done to-date. A further distinction, also often neglected, is between the total housing market in which households demand dwelling units for occupancy and the construction market in which new units are demanded and built.

Moreover, some of the listed items may have a bearing only on the number of additional dwelling units demanded, while others affect total construction expenditures either because the number of units alters or the amount spent on each changes, and still others influence expenditures on both new and existing units. For example, a demand shift to larger or higher-quality units may raise construction expenditures without any increase in the number of new units built; or a decline in the number of new units demanded may be associated with no fall in total expenditures if construction costs, which are determined in nonresidential or nonconstruction markets as well as in the market for new housing, rise.

Finally, many investigators have found it necessary or useful to divide the determinants of residential construction into (a) those which affect the building of new houses for sale to owner-occupants and (b) those which affect the building of new rental housing. This distinction is considered important on the theory that the households demanding new owner-occupied houses behave more like consumers while the entrepreneurs building dwelling units for rent behave more like business firms.

Much of the research work on the subject has been concerned with selecting a few strategic forces among the multitude of factors which can conceivably determine the volume of residential construction, by either qualitative or quantitative methods, and with assigning weights to them through quantitative analysis. This approach has been dictated by the desire for relatively simple, workable models and by lack of adequate data for one factor or the other; and it has often been rationalized by assuming substitutability of some determinants for others. Thus, existing literature often merely mentions some of the potential determinants in our list without analyzing their effects on variations in the volume of residential construction in systematic or quantitative form.

Government housing programs are not specifically listed above as determinants of residential construction. For the most part, those programs are designed to increase the availability and reduce the cost of borrowed funds and are therefore subsumed under a listed item. To the extent that demolitions under the urban renewal program affect replacement demand, it is also subsumed under a listed item. Public housing programs clearly involving cash subsidies are usually not considered in studies of the determinants of residential construction, although they enter into projections of the construction volume required to meet housing "needs." Their volume depends on many factors not susceptible to economic analysis. Moreover, the volume of public housing has been so small that its omission involves no serious error in historical analysis.[1] The present review, then, addresses itself to determinants of what is customarily labelled "private residential construction," although such construction may be financed with loans insured or guaranteed by governmental agencies or with mortgages purchased by the Federal National Mortgage Association but originated by private lenders.

The omission of governmental housing programs from our list reflects the fact that these programs have rarely been systematically and specifically incorporated in analytical work on determinants of residential construction. Nevertheless, it will be necessary for the purpose of this review to probe existing knowledge for what it reveals concerning the influence of government programs on the level, composition, and short-term fluctuations of residential building.

Our list of potential factors determining the volume of residential building includes forces acting on both the supply of new dwellings and the demand. Analytical work to date, however, has been concerned mainly with demand. One can infer that this emphasis is based on the notion that real resources for residential construction, at least in the long run, are potentially available in such volume that their supply will meet effective demand at current prices, and that there are consequently no significant economic problems other than price problems associated with the supply side. The availability of land, building materials, labor, and contractors and other entrepreneurs, as well as an effective market organization that allows all these input factors to be brought together, is taken for granted. This is a realistic assump-

[1] Construction expenditures for public housing, including military housing, equaled only little more than 3 percent of private residential construction expenditures during the postwar period 1946–58, and they reached not more than 5 percent in any single year.

tion for a sufficiently long period of our history, except for interruptions through wars and their aftermaths. Existing literature usually deals with the supply items in our list when it addresses itself to short-run changes.

Main Types of Analysis

Analytical work on the determinants of residential construction can be divided broadly into two types:

1. Models based primarily on a verbal or qualitative analysis of the market. These models follow the classical tradition in economic analysis, being primarily descriptive and putting more or less stress on one or a few variables believed to be significant. These variables are then analyzed on the basis of available statistics, assumed interrelationships, and logical reasoning. The mainly verbal models can be further separated into:
   a. Those which relate residential construction to housing market conditions, without specific consideration of factors external to the housing market.
   b. Those which take account of factors both external and internal to the housing market.
   c. Those which analyze residential construction in terms of secular trends, long swings, or short cycles.
2. Statistical models, primarily econometric, which attempt to account for specific quantitative changes in the volume of construction. They put numbers and values on the effect of specific variables and attempt to measure the extent of lagged relationships. These models can be further classified into:
   a. Those which primarily fit formal equations based upon a limited number of time series.
   b. Those which use a mathematical framework but fit the parameters by reference to various data, judgment as to important relationships, and a verbal analysis of significant changes.

The work described under 1a above has usually been performed by housing analysts who focus on the operation of the housing market as a whole. Most of the work under 1b and c has been done by general economists interested in business cycle analysis or the theory of investment. The models under 2 have been developed usually by economists aiming at econometric models for the entire economy or at general theories of demand.

Summarizing extensive pieces of analysis, sometimes of book length, is always a difficult undertaking. Faithful reproduction of an argument may require about as much space as the original work but would obviously make this report unmanageable. The briefing here employed involves losing or glossing over some of the more subtle points. In general, nonquantitative models are presented in outline form without reproduction of the statistical evidence occasionally used by authors to support them. In the case of econometric models, however, it is necessary to present the salient equations in full. In addition, the main econometric models have been tested in the light of currently available data, which are often revised and improved versions of those used by their authors, and the results of these tests are reported.

VERBAL OR QUALITATIVE MODELS

Residential Construction Related to Housing Market Conditions

One type of analysis concerns itself with the interaction between occupancy and price changes in the market for existing housing units and changes in the volume of construction. It recognizes that exogenous forces, such as population growth or increases in income, may determine both the changes of market conditions in the existing housing inventory and the volume of new construction. But interest here focuses on the way in which external forces work their way through the housing market and eventually cause new building to occur or cease, or expand or contract. This approach attempts also to furnish early housing market indicators considered to be useful for predicting changes in the level of construction.

Basic to this analysis is the common observation that the supply of housing units is relatively fixed in the short run, with annual new construction at most representing 3 percent of the standing stock. When exogenous forces produce an increase in demand for housing services, the first effect under usual market constellations is a greater occupancy rate. When the occupancy rate of the existing inventory reaches a critical zone, rents and house prices are bid up. When the resulting upward valuation of the housing stock leads to prices exceeding construction costs, new building is encouraged. When external forces produce a decline in demand for housing services, of course, the opposite forces are set in motion. In addition to general expositions of this type, there has been some empirical verification of the sequences of the processes described and of critical occupancy zones giving rise to changes in rents and house prices.

This approach deals only indirectly with the determinants of residential building. It highlights the interrelationships between the overall demand for housing and the amount of construction, but it gives little attention to the specific form in which demand is transferred from one market to the other or to the magnitudes of the resulting effects. Nevertheless, a particular aspect of interactions between the general housing market and new construction has a direct bearing on financial determinants of residential construction and is discussed below.

Housing specialists have never tired of spelling out certain undeniable facts on residential financing, that is, a mortgage loan at $4\frac{1}{2}$ percent interest for 30 years results in lower debt charges than a loan at 5 percent interest with a maturity of 25 years, and so forth. Congressional testimony since the beginning of the thirties is replete with tables showing this kind of simple arithmetic. The implication is that more liberal financing terms will enable additional households to obtain new housing or better-quality housing, and this appears to be true when the individual family as demander for a housing unit is considered and other things are held unchanged. Aggregate economic effects of changes in the ease of borrowing, however, are not identical with the arithmetic effects on an individual family's ability to command housing.

Economists, of course, have always been aware of the relationship between changes in the general level of interest rates and changes in the value of capital assets, and of the processes through which easier credit terms are capitalized in the market for such assets. The application of this general principle to the housing market has been most clearly and consistently developed by Ramsay Wood, along these lines: Because the number of new houses available at any one time is very small compared to the existing total supply of housing, prices of new houses are determined to a very large extent by the prices of existing houses. Consequently, the prices of new houses cannot fall far below the prices of comparable old houses. If the costs of new houses to occupants were lowered by reduction of any cost component, financial or otherwise, speculative resale would develop. The market would evaluate the advantages of lower costs of the new houses against the existing stock of housing and the incomes prevailing in the community, and would equilibrate house prices on the principle that comparable houses command comparable prices. In practice, increases in land and construction costs would eventually absorb any initial difference between the cost to occupants of new houses and the market prices of existing houses.

This line of analysis has been further, though somewhat sketchily, pursued by the same author in the development of a model to demonstrate "how changes in credit terms affect the working out of the forces of demand and supply" in the housing market. Among the conclusions relevant to this paper are: (1) easier terms will usually result in higher prices, (2) they will give an immediate advantage to only some bidders for houses, especially those who have few or no savings for downpayments, (3) they will put at a disadvantage bidders prepared to pay all cash or a large proportion of cash, (4) they will result in greater use of credit, and (5) the extent of credit liberalization will be limited by competitive demands for other funds —if these are strong, a sharp rise in the rate of return on mortgages will be required.

A similar line of reasoning, developed by Ernest M. Fisher, takes its starting point from a simple conversion of the standard tables showing the results of changes in credit terms on mortgage debt charges. If it is arithmetically correct to say that a 4½ percent, 30-year loan results in a lower charge than a 5 percent, 25-year loan, it is also arithmetically correct to say that, with a given debt charge, the first kind of loan gives the borrower command over a larger amount of funds with which to buy a house. In a sellers' market, the increased amount of debt that can be carried by a given debt charge under relaxed credit terms will tend to be absorbed in price advances rather than result in improved standards of housing. This reasoning implies that there are severe limits to an expansion of total residential construction through relaxed credit terms in periods of reasonably full resource employment.

In summary, the work discussed in this section is useful mainly in providing a framework for analysis of the processes through which stimulative or contractive forces work themselves out in the housing market as a whole. But the relationship between housing market processes and new construction is typically described only in general, qualitative terms. Moreover, there is a question of completeness even in terms of the limited objective of this type of analysis. There is also doubt over the usefulness of the analysis for periods in which vacancy ratios and rents or house prices move within a narrow range.

The work on effects of changes of the ease of borrowing on the housing market, which has been associated with this approach, addresses itself specifically to financial determinants. Its main value lies in clarifying the impact of altered credit terms on prices for the existing housing stock and associated costs of resources used in residential construction. Here again, most of the analysis is in general, qualitative terms, and only an admittedly partial and merely illustrative model has been developed for tracing the effects of changing credit terms on the housing market and more specifically on the volume of residential building. The elaboration of such a model, cast in a form that lends itself to empirical tests of its validity, is a high-priority item in this area of research.

Some of the models discussed in this section fail to distinguish between short-run and long-term changes or to specify time dimensions. The implicit assumption of a nearly completely inelastic supply curve suggests that the models at best apply to the short run. To make them more useful for analysis, a great deal of additional information is required on the shapes of the supply curve in the markets for both existing housing and new construction. Moreover, the way in which these separate but interrelated markets react to demand movements warrants further investigation. Many of the stated results depend directly upon assumed demand curves, unspecified lags, and only partially tested relationships. The effects of greater availability and easier terms of credit on new construction as against credit on existing property deserve more attention. This kind of differentiation, partly fostered by federal housing programs, prevailed through much of the postwar period. Consequently, the price and supply linkages between the markets for new and existing construction may not have been as strong as some of the analyses suggest. Also, the analytic framework does not allow any quantification of the price effects of stimulative or contractive forces, including changes in the ease of borrowing, and of the effects on the number of dwelling units built.

Residential Construction Related to External and Internal Factors

A few models analyze residential construction as a special case of the general theory of investment and use variables both external and internal to the housing market. Methodologically, they tend toward an intermediate position between purely descriptive analysis and full-fledged quantitative models and attempt to allow for structural and institutional characteristics of the housing and construction markets.

Clarence D. Long, Jr., used such an approach in 1940. His work, however, applies investment theory to new private building as a whole rather than to residential construction, although empirical materials are provided for the latter type as well as nonresidential building. Because of this aggregation of activities influenced by consumer demand and business demand, Long's application of investment theory is not sufficiently specific for inclusion in the present report.

A specific model for residential construction within the framework of investment theory was more recently developed by James S. Duesenberry. This analysis deals not only with determinants of residential building separately from other types of construction but adopts the division between demand determinants for owner-occupied and rental housing. Duesenberry takes his starting point from the total demand for housing. The demand for single-family dwellings by a population with given demographic characteristics depends upon (1) aggregate income, (2) number of families, (3) nonhousing assets, (4) housing assets, (5) prices of houses, (6) level of rents, (7) prices of other goods, and (8) credit terms. Duesenberry attaches particular importance to the amount of nonhousing assets as a determinant of the ability of potential buyers to make downpayments—an item that has been the subject of an independent, small-scale empirical investigation—and to credit policies which influence downpayment requirements. The demand for rental housing depends on the same variables, "except that assets are probably of little importance, and the signs of the effects of rents and house prices are, of course, reversed."

After tracing the effects of changes in house prices and rents on changes in the rate of construction of single-family houses and apartments, and an analysis of supply factors (builders, material, and labor) and costs, Duesenberry concludes that, speculation aside, the rate of residential construction depends on the following factors: (1) rents and house prices relative to other prices, (2) vacancy rates for apartments and the ratio of demand to supply for single houses, (3) the number of speculative builders and the distribution of their assets in the case of single houses, (4) the total amount of assets in the community and the risk preferences of their owners in the case of apartment buildings, (5) the level of building and operating costs.

These factors are transformed into separate equation systems for single-house and apartment building under carefully defined equilibrium conditions. When the latter are dropped, there emerges a "dynamic system whose movements are ultimately governed by the movement of income and population." Erratic shifts in income and population or changes in the parameters of the system, however, may produce movements in the rate of building quite different from those of income. This observa-

tion leads to a descriptive discussion of housing cycles and the suggestion of two types of such cycles: (1) cycles with "normal relations" between housing investment and income movements. In these, housing investment follows income changes, but with different timing explained by lags and with stabilizing effects on total output; and (2) cycles in which structural changes in the housing industry itself, such as wartime backlogs and speculation, generate independent fluctuations which communicate themselves to movements of aggregate income.

In spite of conceptual neatness, the Duesenberry model suffers from several defects. The verbal statements emphasize lagged relationships but the equation systems fail to incorporate them in any specific form. Partly for this reason, it is never clear whether the analysis refers to the short run or long run. Moreover, the model is developed in terms of plausible rather than tested relationships. For example, the level of building costs is included among the independent variables determining the rate of residential construction, although several previous investigators have indicated in their models that costs are inconsequential. Also, no weights are given to the presumed independent variables. On more technical items, the model for total housing demand includes the "number of families" among the independent variables, and it is not clear whether the omission of the rather numerous households other than families is intentional. Likewise, single-family dwellings in that model are equated with owner-occupied dwellings, in spite of the fact that existing single-family houses are an important segment of the rental supply.

As for financial determinants, they are incorporated in Duesenberry's model for total housing demand and ingeniously linked to the amounts of housing assets and nonhousing assets in the hands of potential buyers of houses for owner-occupancy. But they are ignored in Duesenberry's rather extensive discussion of supply factors in new construction. The number of builders and the scale of their operations, for example, may be significantly influenced by the availability and ease of credit. Also, potential influences of credit on the demand for new construction are not specifically examined although they are obvious from the historical description of housing cycles in Duesenberry's work.

Another model of the "intermediate" type considered in this section has been suggested for short-run forecasting by John P. Lewis. In this case, the model is derived from a theory of investment by households in new housing and consumer durables on the ground that these investments have significant economic characteristics in common.

The starting point is a working estimate of the "normal physical requirements for new nonfarm dwelling units." The estimate takes into consideration "expansion requirements" composed of net nonfarm household formation, migration-induced increases in vacancies, net increases in second homes, and "replacement requirements." Among the latter, the rate at which residential units are withdrawn to make way for other urban land uses is a "powerful independent conditioner" of the demand for new housing.

According to Lewis, income has no stable, quantifiable short-run relationship to the demand for new residential construction. Support for this statement is found in a scatter diagram on spendable incomes per household and the amount of residential construction per household. Variations in mortgage credit terms, on the other hand, have a pronounced impact on short-run changes in the volume of residential construction. This point is illustrated by observations for the 1950's. Judgments on supply-price effects are suggested as modifiers of forecasts derived mainly from physical requirements and credit conditions. The remainder of Lewis' work concerns itself with lags and the problems involved in converting data on housing starts into construction expenditures.

Lewis has worked out an admittedly "opportunistic" procedure for forecasting rather than explanatory purposes. There is no question raised nor any pretense made about its applicability to conditions other than those of the 1950's. No effort is made to quantify the effects of the variables considered to be significant and, even if the limited objectives of this contribution are accepted, there is no way of telling how well the forecasting procedure would have "worked" for the period considered. The analysis provides no systematic link between the total demand for housing and the demand

for new construction, nor does it discuss possible interrelations between short-run and long-run changes in the level of residential construction.

The models discussed in this section include at least implicitly, but not in detail, the influence of fluctuations in the availability of construction financing on new residential building. This is also true of much of current commentary in the press and business journals. There is usually some reference to the impact on construction activity of changes in builders' ability to borrow, but the way and the degree in which these changes affect the volume of activity remain unspecified. This contrasts considerably with general business cycle theory in which the analysis of how the availability of producers' credit causes fluctuations in activity is prominent and fairly complete.

Secular Trends, Long Swings, and Short Cycles

Some of the literature on business and building cycles and one analysis of secular trends concern themselves specifically with determinants of residential construction. Other studies of cycles address themselves to purely descriptive analysis of relationships between business and building cycles or of leads and lags, without attempting to identify or quantify determinants of fluctuations in residential construction. These are omitted from the present review.

Secular trends. The work on secular trends, by Grebler-Blank-Winnick, takes its starting point from evidence that both gross and net capital formation in real terms between 1890 and 1950 showed arrested growth or actual decline. Moreover, the per capita value of residential capital in constant prices fluctuated within narrow margins and in 1950 was only slightly larger than in 1890.

As for financial determinants of secular trends in residential construction, the analysis shows clearly (1) an increased tendency to debt-financing, (2) a rising ratio of net increases in residential mortgage debt to housing construction expenditures, and (3) great easing of credit between the twenties and early fifties in the form of lower interest rates, longer loan maturities, and larger loan-to-value ratios for first mortgages. The absence of a strong growth trend in real terms in the face of a trend toward easier external financing emphasizes the importance of nonfinancial determinants.

As for nonfinancial determinants, the analysis by Grebler, Blank, and Winnick deals separately with forces that have operated on the number of dwelling units built and on changes in real input per new unit. In line with other investigations, the growth of nonfarm households emerges as main determinant of long-term trends in the number of nonfarm dwelling units added to the supply. But a large source of additions to the supply since the twenties were conversions of existing structures rather than new construction, with the result of a large gap between net increments to households and the number of new units built. Because of an anticipated decline in conversion potentials, the study projects re-establishment of a closer long-run relationship between new dwelling units and household growth in the period to 1975. While immigration until the twenties has affected the level as well as the timing of new housing construction, internal nonfarm migration apparently did not raise significantly the level of residential building until 1950, though it may do so in the future. Likewise, demolitions and other withdrawals from the housing inventory have been insignificant determinants of secular trends in new construction, but may become more important mainly because of urban renewal, highway, and other publicly aided programs.

According to Grebler and his associates, a strategic force in the arrested growth of residential capital formation was a marked secular decline in real input per new dwelling unit built, in spite of the long-term rise in real consumer income. The factors producing this decline are identified and to some extent quantified, but it suffices to say here that they are nonfinancial. The analysis concludes with a strong presumption that housing has suffered a secular decline in the consumer's scale of preferences and implies that a reversal of past trends in residential capital formation presupposes a reversal of consumer preferences—of which there are some current indications but no conclusive evidence.

This analysis of secular trends has given rise to critical debate too technical for inclusion in this review. For our purpose, it is more important to outline the relevance of this work to an evaluation of our financial system. During the 60-year period covered by the analysis, there were great improvements in our financial system generally and in the organization and practices of residential mortgage lending specifically in terms of mobilizing and channeling savings, adapting institutional policies to changing demands exemplified by the increased desire for home ownership, facilitating the inter-regional flow of funds, greater adoption of the long-term amortized mortgage, and reduction in the cost of mortgage financing. Some of these improvements were initiated or strengthened by federal programs such as the Federal Home Loan Bank System, the FHA, the veterans home loan program, and the Federal National Mortgage Association. Yet, if the Grebler-Blank-Winnick analysis is correct, the perfection of institutional arrangements in mortgage finance seems to have failed to alter an adverse secular trend. This finding may testify to the stubbornness of the underlying forces producing the trend, or, as some hold, to the remaining inadequacy of market devices for the financing of housing in some value-determined sense.

Long swings. Only a few analyses have come to grips with determinants of cyclical behavior in such fashion that they contribute to generalized knowledge of the determinants of residential building. By demonstrating that fluctuations in residential (or total) building exhibit characteristics as to timing and amplitude that cannot be explained by the course of general business conditions, the analyses have led to a search for presumably unique variables to which residential construction is responsive. The classic work of this type is Arthur F. Burns' "Long Cycles in Construction."

Burns starts out by developing a model of the number of housing units built in a collectivistic, nonpecuniary economy (which precludes consideration of any financial determinants). Even in such an economy certain basic forces will produce long cycles. Among these are variability in the rate of population increase, inconstancy of housing standards, the immobility and durability of dwellings, and uncertainties of planning. Even small changes in the rate of population growth and in housing standards are apt to produce large variations in construction volume and shortages or surpluses which take a long time to correct. In a pecuniary economy, the influence of these basic forces is magnified by imperfect market information, psychological factors, market uncertainties, and changes in credit conditions, among other things. Market disequilibrium is normal. Because of the time required for the market to react to external forces, long cycles will result regardless of whether there are long cycles in the demand for the use of dwellings (such as may be associated with long swings in the rate of population growth or of immigration).

The analysis of how external forces such as changes in the rate of population growth work themselves out in the housing market is very similar to the work described earlier, and the previously noted limitations apply here. Except for general recognition that changes in credit conditions in a pecuniary economy will add to the potentials of long cycles, this approach allows no differentiation between non-financial and financial determinants. Its main value lies perhaps in the application of the "acceleration principle," in the sense that small relative changes in the strength of some of the underlying forces will produce very large changes in the volume of construction.

Another contribution in this group of literature is William H. Newman's systematic empirical analysis for the 1875–1933 period or subperiod. Newman concludes that:

1. Long swings in total building activity (of about 15–21 years duration), measured by building permit values, reflect long waves of population changes, which are accentuated by market imperfections producing delayed reactions to changes in underlying demand;
2. There is no consistent relationship between changes in income and long (major) building cycles;
3. Changes in building costs do not explain major building cycles;
4. Major cycles in building activity are not explained by changes in money-market conditions measured by fluctuations in high-grade bond yields;
5. The movement of net incomes from exist-

ing property shows a positive correlation with major swings in building activity.

Although these conclusions and the underlying data relate to total rather than residential building, there is at least a strong presumption that they are applicable to the latter. The finding under (4) has been reaffirmed for long swings in residential construction specifically by Grebler-Blank-Winnick, with ease of borrowing again measured by changes in the yields of high-grade bonds. Clarence D. Long, Jr., likewise finds no positive correlation of movements of mortgage interest rates and long building cycles.

A preview of Moses Abramovitz's current work on long waves in the rate of economic growth suggests that these long waves have been associated with great fluctuations in construction and specifically in residential building, which in turn have corresponded roughly with long swings in the rate of population growth. But it is too early to say whether Abramovitz's contribution will provide a generalized explanation of residential construction volume separate and apart from the relationship between long building cycles and long swings in the rate of economic growth.

Short cycles. William H. Newman's study, referred to earlier, addresses itself to short cycles in total building activity (averaging about 5 years) as well as long swings. He concludes that:

1. There is no consistent relationship between changes in income and short building cycles;
2. Changes in building activity are more likely to cause changes in building costs than vice versa;
3. A significant and systematic relationship between changes in bond yields and short building cycles suggests that expansion in building activity has been associated with greater ease of borrowing, at least in terms of direction of movement (rather than absolute levels).

Here again, there is a strong presumption that these conclusions hold for residential activity as well as aggregate building. More specific analyses of determinants of short-term fluctuations in residential construction have been undertaken for the period since World War II, mainly by Leo Grebler, Jack M. Guttentag, Saul B. Klaman, and Warren L. Smith. While these analyses differ on matters of emphasis and detail, they agree in the conclusion that short-run fluctuations in residential building have resulted mainly from changes in financial conditions labeled as ease of borrowing, availability of mortgage funds, or supply of mortgage credit. They agree also in linking the changes in financing conditions to the course of the moderate general business cycles that occurred during the periods of study. In the form of a synthetic description, the argument is about as follows: Changes in financing conditions have been greatly influenced by the level of general economic activity. When that level was rising and high, the expanded demand for funds by business, which is relatively insensitive to increased cost of borrowing, tended to reduce the availability of funds for housing, which is held to be unusually sensitive to changes in the cost of borrowing.[2] When there was slack in the economy at large and the supply of funds was ample relative to demand, credit for homebuilding and home purchase became more readily available. As a result, residential construction activity in the postwar period has shown a counter cyclical tendency or at least a strong lead in relation to general business fluctuations.

Analyses along this line employ various techniques in examining the possible effects of other than financial determinants on the short-term swings in residential building, such as household formation, income and employment, or prices. They agree in assigning to these determinants an insignificant, if any, influence on building fluctuations in the postwar period. They note at the same time that the dominant effects of credit factors on the cyclical behavior of residential construction may hold only for periods in which long-run demand forces were favorable to a high level of building activity and in which general business fluctuations were relatively short and moderate. Further, they concern themselves typically with time lags between observed changes in the availability and costs of borrowed funds and in residential construction volume. One author concludes that

the strategic financial factors in short-term swings of building activity have indeed been of a countercyclical character, but that actual construction expenditures varied in less than countercyclical fashion because of the time lags in the process of initiating and building residential projects.

The analyses differ in respect to the definition and measurement of credit variables; and one of them, by Guttentag, attempts an articulated distinction between credit availability, defined as variations in the complex of lending terms (downpayment requirements, loan maturities, and interest rates), and the supply of credit or the schedule showing the amounts that lenders are willing to provide at various terms and interest rates. Guttentag stresses also that the countercyclical behavior of residential construction in the postwar period presupposed some inelasticity in the supply of credit. Another point of difference is found in the importance attached by various investigators to the inflexible interest rates on government-underwritten mortgage loans in producing the observed close association between changes in financial conditions and in the volume of residential building and the resulting countercyclical behavior of the latter. Likewise, there are differences in judgment as to whether the inflexible rates are necessary or desirable instruments of general economic stabilization policy.

The basic propositions offered by the analyses of short-term fluctuations in residential construction during the postwar period would bear further, more rigorous examination through quantitative factor analysis or econometric models. Much of the supporting evidence is descriptive and suggests general tendencies without allowing more definitive estimates of variations in the level of housing construction that may be associated with given changes in financial conditions. The often unavoidable use of "proxy" data for measuring the availability and costs of mortgage credit, in the form of bond yields and otherwise, points up the need for developing better direct data, especially

2   Cost of borrowing is defined broadly to include credit terms as well as interest rates. The latter are probably less important in determining the demand for new residential construction than are downpayment requirements and loan maturities.

data on changes in the terms and interest rates on conventional mortgage loans. Further research should also identify more specifically the basic demand conditions for housing under which change in the ease of borrowing becomes the strategic factor in short-term fluctuations of residential construction. It is not clear, for example, whether and to what extent the thesis would hold for periods of low or declining levels of consumer demand for housing associated with major, prolonged recessions, or with a high level of available vacancies. As this volume is being completed, a great deal of uncertainty has arisen over the stimulation of housing construction that may be expected from the easing of credit during the recession of 1960–61, as compared to the experience observed in earlier postwar recessions. This observation highlights the need for further study of the prerequisites in the economy at large, the financial markets, and the housing market that have made the nearly countercyclical behavior of residential building possible.

STATISTICAL-ECONOMETRIC MODELS

In recent years numerous econometric and statistical models of the housing market have been developed. Some of these models have attempted primarily to throw light on the construction market, while others have been prepared as part of the larger task of building a model for the entire economy. What contributions do they offer to a general understanding of the determinants of residential construction?

While the advantages which economists hope to gain from this approach are familiar, a brief discussion of the concepts and procedures will be useful. Econometric-statistical models summarize, simplify, and express basic information in a form that brings out essential interrelationships and allows them to be tested and measured. As the previous section has demonstrated, verbal models are often incomplete and both their content and their accuracy is hard to test. A statistical model or framework, in contrast, lends itself to completeness. One can see where gaps exist. Important areas or essential relationships are less likely to be omitted. The need for formal definitions and assumptions

precludes the vagueness and imprecision of many verbal theories.

A statistical framework also allows quantification. Concepts can be related to specific events. The parameters can be measured and assigned exact weights. Available statistics can be employed more fully and systematically. Perhaps more importantly, new series to fill gaps can be defined and developed. The significance of data can be estimated. Probability values can be assigned. The results of predictions can be tested and, if errors are found, the model can be corrected.

Because parts of a model can be stated in mathematical language, a large number of diverse concepts can be treated in an integrated form. Mathematics is a language developed for the logical expression and manipulation of relationships. Its use helps to ascertain the complementary effects of many factors, a necessity in dynamic analysis. What happens today is heavily influenced by past actions. Delayed influence can be observed much more readily with the tools of mathematics. Much of the search for a workable explanation of the operation of the housing market is a seeking of lagged relationships.

The basic procedures and methodology of statistical and econometric model-builders are simple. On the basis of an examination of past events, a theory is devised and formulated in mathematical terms. It is assumed that the data are related to each other and reflect people's basic behavior patterns. An attempt is made by statistical procedures to uncover the underlying relationships. The object is both to test and to measure the hypothesized structure.

The relationships may be extremely complex. Some depend upon institutional and legal factors, such as the banking and mortgage systems. Some are technological relationships, as the amount of output that results from mixing certain labor, equipment, and materials. Others involve tastes and group or individual reactions, as, for example, the amount families are willing to spend for rent or housing expenditures and the estimates by investors of relative risks.

These behavior patterns are described in terms of functional relationships. In the statistical or econometric treatment of models, the exact form of these relationships is usually specified, and statistical analysis (such as graphical correlation, least squares, or maximum likelihood) is used to give them numerical values. Verbal analysis, in contrast, usually indicates merely directions and expected magnitudes.

The concepts of economic structure, constants, and variables are related directly to the mathematical expressions from which the terms have been adopted. A simple model of a typical structural relationship for the residential construction market, expressed algebraically, might take the form:

$$S = a + b_1i + b_2H + u$$

This states that housing starts (S) depend on the level of the interest rate (i), the number of households (H), and on certain disturbances (u). These disturbances play a most significant part in the theory and in the statistical estimation of the model. It is usually assumed that these disturbances occur with certain specified types of probability distributions.

In addition to the disturbances which cause random movements in the level of starts, two groups of relationships are expressed in this equation. In the first place, the specific number of housing starts in any period will depend upon the values of i and H. Since these are expected to take different values at frequent intervals, they are the variables of the relationship. The second group is expressed by the small letters a, b₁, and b₂. They represent the various institutional and behavioral relationships. These are called constants because in any short period, such as a year or two, they are not expected to vary. Over a longer period, however, these relationships can shift as human habits and institutions change. When analysts want to refer to the possibility of change in these relationships, they speak of them as "parametric constants" or more generally as "parameters" of the system. The econometrician attempting to specify the parameters, therefore, simply endeavors to measure the basic institutional and behavioral relationships. If he does so successfully, it enables him to state the direction and magnitude of changes in the dependent variable that will be caused by changes in an independent variable. Since these parameters express the underlying structure of the system, the concepts of a shift in the structure and alterations in the parameters are largely identical.

The econometric models attempt to explain why a variable (construction) assumes a certain value in a given period. The amount of construction is determined by its interrelationships with the other variables. It depends upon the behavioral structure of the economy and the values of the other variables. If the econometrician has specified the a's and b's—or the parameters—he can then explain how construction varies as the result of new values for the independent variables on the right-hand side of the equation. For example, as the level of the interest rate (i) or households (H) changes, the value of construction starts (S) will change. If the reaction takes time to occur, the change in the first variable leads that of the second, or the second lags behind that of the first. Since the dependent variable may also change as a result of shifts in the parameters (structure), this possibility must also be included in the analysis.

Problems arise if the theory or model explains changes in terms of "derived" rather than real relationships. Suppose that the value of S depends on Z, credit terms in general, instead of i, the interest rate. If for many periods i and Z move together (e.g., the movements in Z reflect solely interest changes because downpayments and loan maturities are not altered), predictions of S from i would be perfectly valid, even though the relationship between S and i is not the true causal but only a derived one. If, however, i and Z stop moving together, the predicted value of S based on i will be wrong. For accurate predictions, the model requires the parameter of Z or of i and the other credit terms to be separately stated. The general aim of the models is to find the true or invariant rather than the derived relationships. The more complete and exact one's knowledge of the real structure, the more likely are explanations and predictions to be valid.

The most common forms of statistical models in this field have been based upon a few aggregative time series and specify a small number of relationships from these rather limited data. While most of the discussion in the present section, since it reviews existing works, is concerned with these limited attempts at model-building, it should be made clear that other, more general econometric approaches are possible. A framework or model need not be complete in every detail. Its form and the information contained within it may allow the analyst to use judgment and to change parameters or estimate variables based upon logical assumptions. Some parts of the model may use exact statistical techniques such as time series analysis; other sectors may utilize parameters derived from cross-section analysis and surveys. When the structure shifts as a result of legal or institutional changes, the analyst may alter his equations in a formal or informal manner. The frequent variations in FNMA policy, for example, have effects that are unlikely to be measurable from annual data, but these could be inserted into a less rigorous model.

One important use of good models is to measure the effect of alternative assumptions or policy recommendations. The analyst can also use the model to test various orders of magnitude to see whether or not they would make significant differences in the predicted results (sensitivity analysis). As an example, only after one puts orders of magnitude on changes in household formation and the relationship of changes in the availability of credit to the cost of establishing a household is it possible to say whether credit changes are likely to have large or small effects on household formation.

References *

Abramovitz, M. Testimony in *Employment, Growth, and Price Levels,* Hearings before the Joint Economic Committee of the Congress, 86th Cong., 1st Sess., April 7–10, 1959.

Burns, Arthur F., "Long Cycles in Residential Construction," in *Economic Essays in Honor of Wes-* *ley C. Mitchell.* New York: Columbia University Press, 1935.

Duesenberry, James S., *Business Cycles and Economic Growth.* New York: McGraw-Hill, 1958, Chapter 7.

Fisher, Ernest M., *Urban Real Estate Markets: Characteristics and Financing.* New York: National Bureau of Economic Research, 1951, Chapter 4.

Grebler, Leo, David M. Blank, and Louis Winnick, *Capital Formation in Residential Real Estate.* Princeton University Press for National Bureau of Economic Research, 1956.

Grebler, Leo, "The Role of Residential Capital Formation in Postwar Business Cycles." *Conference on Savings and Residential Financing,* sponsored by the United States Savings and Loan League, 1959.

Guttentag, Jack M., *Some Studies of the Post-World War II Residential Construction and Mortgage Markets.* Unpublished dissertation, Columbia University, New York, 1958. See also Guttentag's article "Credit Availability, Interest Rates, and Monetary Policy," *The Southern Economic Journal* (January 1960).

Klaman, Saul B., "'Effects of Credit and Monetary Policy on Real Estate Markets: 1952–1954," *Land Economics* (August 1956).

Lewis, John P., *Business Conditions Analysis.* New York: McGraw-Hill, 1959, Chapter 20.

Long, Clarence D., Jr., *Building Cycles and the Theory of Investment.* Princeton: Princeton University Press, 1940.

Newman, William H., "The Building Industry and Business Cycles." *The Journal of Business.* Chicago: University of Chicago Press, Vol. V, No. 4, July 1935.

Smith, Warren L., "The Impact of Monetary Policy on Residential Construction, 1948–1958." *Study of Mortgage Credit* (Subcommittee on Housing of the Senate Banking and Currency Committee, 85th Congress, 2nd Session, Washington, December 22, 1958). This volume includes various other papers, notably by Saul B. Klaman and James J. O'Leary, dealing with the same subject.

Wood, Ramsay, "Housing Needs and the Housing Market," *Housing, Social Security, and Public Works.* Board of Governors of the Federal Reserve System, Postwar Economic Series, No. 6, June 1946.

* The appropriate references were excerpted from an exhaustive and comprehensive list of references appearing at the end of the complete article.

The Short Cycle in Residential Construction, 1946–59

JACK M. GUTTENTAG

Many of the important issues of housing policy that have arisen over the last decade focus on short-run instability in residential construction. Yet compared to the extensive literature on the long cycle in residential construction, the short cycle has been relatively neglected.[1] The purpose of this paper is to examine the determinants of short-run fluctuations in residential construction during the 1946–59 period.[2]

Part I explains how the short cycles are measured and describes some of their characteristics. Part II considers the relationship between fluctuations in residential construction and changes in the supply of mortgage credit. Many observers have noted that residential construction appears to be quite sensitive to credit conditions in the short run but little evidence for this relationship has yet been produced. In Part III the analysis is broadened to show the relationship between fluctuations in residential construction and in aggregate economic activity. Again, it has been widely noted that residential construction has had a generally stabilizing or countercyclical influence on the economy but no very adequate or complete explanation of this tendency has been provided.

SHORT CYCLES IN RESIDENTIAL CONSTRUCTION

Statistical Identification

The procedure used to identify "cycles" in residential construction activity is similar to that used by the National Bureau of Economic Research, except in one respect. Cycles in residential construction are defined here in terms of movements in three related series rather than only one; a movement is not recognized as "real" unless it is found in each of the series. In effect, this rule supplants the amplitude criterion used by the NBER to identify specific cycles.[3] The three series are private nonfarm housing starts, nonfarm mortgage recordings of $20,000 or less, and residential contract awards. In addition, for the period since late 1950 a

series is available on FHA applications and VA appraisal requests.[4] Each of these series, although covering an activity common to the other two (residential construction), is derived from an independent source and corrected independently for seasonal variation. This approach provides considerable assurance that the cycles identified are not the result of the erratic nature of the data or of faulty seasonal adjustment, but are ultimately explainable in terms of basic economic forces.

The most important activity not covered by all three series is the mortgaging of existing houses, which is included only in the mortgage recordings series. This activity generally accounts for more than half of the total volume of mortgage recordings. Nevertheless, there is a presumption that the volume of residential construction activity and the volume of mortgage activity will move in the same direction.[5]

From the *American Economic Review* (June 1961), pp. 275–298. Reprinted by permission of the American Economic Association and the author.

1 An early investigator of the short cycle was W. H. Newman [15]. More recently L. Grebler [6] [8] has intensively examined a relatively short period, and touched upon some of the issues raised in this paper.

2 Space limitations preclude my bringing the findings of this paper to bear on housing policy issues.

3 Burns and Mitchell describe their rule as follows [2, p. 58]: "The lower limit of the range of amplitudes of all fluctuations that we class confidently as specific cycles is our rough guide in deciding whether any doubtful fluctuation . . . is well enough defined to be accepted as a specific cycle." This rule is modified under certain conditions [2, pp. 138–39]. Reflecting the different procedure employed in this study, I have a contraction in 1953 which the NBER has not marked off in the residential awards series, while the dates of my turning points in this series diverge appreciably in a few instances from theirs.

4 With one exception these series measure physical volume. The recordings series measures value and is the only one adjusted for trend. Data on residential awards are published through the courtesy of F. W. Dodge Corp. The author will be happy to provide a complete description of these series, including coverage, turning points, and sources, to interested readers.

5 This is evident where the principal dynamic factor in the market is a change in the supply of mortgage credit. It is likely also to be the case when market changes originate on the demand side be-

Chart 1 Selected series on residential construction and mortgage activity, 1946–1959.

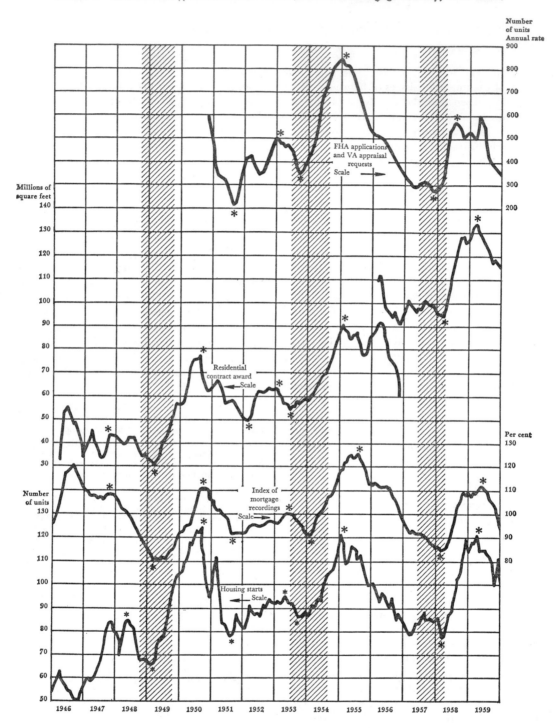

Note: Shaded areas represent reference contractions in general business as established by the National Bureau of Economic Research. Series are three-month averages except for housing starts. All series are seasonally adjusted.

As indicated later, this presumption appears justified for the postwar period, at least after 1948.

The first clearly identifiable turning point in the three series is in late 1947 to early 1948 (Chart 1). Prior to that time, during 1946–47, the brevity and varying duration of movements in the several series make it impossible to relate them to one another with any degree of certainty. These statistical difficulties probably reflect the rather abnormal market conditions of these years. The construction industry was being reconstituted and materials shortages introduced an erratic element into construction activities. The several short movements hardly register in the recordings series, which was dominated during this period by an unusually active market for existing houses.[6]

During the period 1948 through 1959 there are four distinct periods of both expansion and decline in each of the three principal series (Chart 1). The turning points in each of the series can be related to one another with little difficulty since in most cases the timing discrepancies are small. The four complete cycles, measured peak to peak, have an average duration of 31 months in the awards series, 33 months in the starts series, and 35 months in the recordings series. None of the cycles,

whether measured from peak to peak or trough to trough, is shorter than 16 months.

Evidence of a Countercyclical Tendency

A broad countercyclical tendency of residential construction during the 1948–59 period is evident in Chart 1. Construction declined during the late stages of the expansions in general business that ended in late 1948 and mid-1953, and throughout most of the expansion running from late 1954 to late 1957. It rose throughout most of the two brief recessions in 1948–49 and 1953–54, and was a stabilizing influence during the 1957–58 recession.

Employing the familiar reference-cycle technique of the National Bureau of Economic Research, the countercyclical tendency is quite prominent (Chart 2). The average pattern for the three complete business cycles during 1945–

cause (a) the relationship between the incremental demand for housing and the credit demand with which it is associated is very close in the short run, and (b) the mortgage credit demand that arises from sources independent of housing demand is relatively small, and part of it at least apparently is quite stable.
6 This was itself partly a reflection of the fact that new construction was limited.

Chart 2 Average reference cycle patterns.

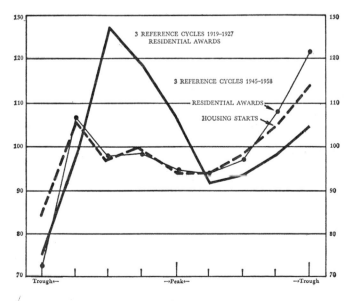

58 is bowl-shaped after the stage of early recovery.[7] This could be described, of course, as a tendency for residential construction to "lead" general business at turning points. The lead and lag terminology leaves open the question of whether the phenomenon described is purely statistical—the residential construction series, for example, might "lead" general business because they record construction at a relatively early stage in the construction process—or whether it is a reflection of how certain economic processes work themselves out over time.[8]

The behavior of the residential sector is here termed countercyclical because the explanation given below of the forces underlying fluctuations in construction appears to support use of this term. Countercyclical forces, however, because they take time to work themselves out, do not invariably produce countercyclical results (to employ Grebler's terminology [8]). That the three major expansions in construction extended into the stage of early recovery in general business reflects both the time-consuming nature of the countercyclical mechanism and the unusual brevity of the postwar recessions.

POSTWAR AND PREWAR CYCLES

The short postwar cycles discussed in this study have a counterpart in the prewar period. Long [13] found 17 cycles in building between 1870 and 1938 averaging 4 years in length. Newman [15] counted 11 minor cycles between 1878 and 1933 having an average length of about 5 years. These cycles were based on building permit data which included commercial and industrial building as well as residential building. Moore [14] found 5½ cycles between 1919 and 1938 in the residential contract awards data.

The reference-cycle patterns for residential contract awards during the three short business cycles of the 1920's have similarities to those of the postwar period (Chart 2). As in the postwar period construction declined during the later stages of expansions in general business and began to rise some time during the recessions. During the 1920's, however, there was a much more pronounced procyclical rise during the recovery phase of the business cycle,

while the rise during recessions was much weaker. Whether the pattern for the 1920's is countercyclical on balance is problematical, but such tendencies clearly were much less pronounced relative to procyclical tendencies than in the postwar period.[9]

Altogether different patterns show up during the two major business cycles covering the period 1927–38, as residential construction declined rather steadily during the entire 1927–33 cycle and fluctuated with unusual sharpness, largely in procyclical fashion, during 1933–38.

The performance of the residential sector in the postwar period has thus been substantially better than in the 1920's and 1930's. We cannot be sure of all the reasons for this because data are not available for a rigorous study of the causes of the prewar cycles. Nevertheless, some obvious points of difference between the prewar and postwar periods—the relatively more stable economy and the existence of the federal underwriting programs during the later period—must evidently have been of some importance. These structural differences will receive further comment below.

Short Cycles and Long Waves

The postwar cycles in residential construction may be placed in perspective by comparing them to the long waves in residential construction, which have been the subject of many investigations.[10] First, and most conspicuously,

7 The rise in construction during early recovery is considerably smaller when the 1945–49 cycle is omitted. Such omission could be justified in light of the abnormal situation in the construction market prior to 1948.
8 One hypothesis (other than the one presented in this paper) which can be used to explain fluctuations in construction and which would attribute causal significance to the "lead" is the familiar acceleration principle. The acceleration hypothesis does not however, for a number of reasons, provide an acceptable explanation for the observed tendency of residential construction to lead general business at turning points. One reason is that it is inconsistent with the evidence presented below that changes in demand were not strategic in the short construction cycles.
9 Also, the dispersion in the reference-cycle patterns of individual cycles was somewhat greater for the cycles of the 1920's than for the postwar cycles.
10 See: [1] [4] [12, Ch. 3] [3, Appendix N] [9, pp. 37–43] [5, Ch. 7] [13] [15] and [18].

the postwar cycles differ from the long cycles in their shorter duration. Measured from peak to peak in the starts series the four postwar cycles cover 20 months, 28 months, 32 months, and 52 months. The long cycles vary in length depending on the unit of measurement used and on the investigator, but their minimum length appears to be about 9 years and they may extend for as long as 25 years.

Second, the postwar cycles have a much smaller amplitude. The average amplitude of three long cycles during 1892–1950, as identified by Grebler, Blank and Winnick [9], was about four times that of the four short postwar cycles. The amplitude of the mildest long cycle was roughly twice that of the most severe short cycle.[11] These relative orders of magnitude fully justify a characterization of the short postwar cycles as "ripples on the long waves."

Third, the short cycles differ from long cycles in their basic causes. Most of the standard explanations of long cycles in residential construction run in terms of fluctuations in the *demand*[12] for housing arising primarily out of changing rates of population growth. The influence of factors affecting the supply of mortgage credit may enter into the explanation but only as a secondary factor, intensifying the force of the movements of both expansion and contraction. In contrast, the short cycles appear to be related mainly to changes originating in the mortgage market. This has been true, at least, during the postwar period. In the prewar period income changes probably played an important role, particularly during major business cycles when such changes were especially large.

THE SHORT CYCLE AND FLUCTUATIONS IN THE SUPPLY OF MORTGAGE CREDIT

The evidence on the central role of mortgage credit is indirect. Inferences are drawn about the principal factor underlying an observed movement in construction from the behavior of three market indicators, which will be discussed in turn. Each of these indicators is shown on Chart 3 along with the recordings series, which can be used to represent the movement of residential construction and mortgage activity.

Construction and Mortgage Yields

Where changes in demand are the chief determinant of changes in construction, we would expect mortgage yields and construction to move in the same direction; where changes in the supply of mortgage credit are the chief determinant, we would expect yields and construction to move in opposite directions.

It is clear from Chart 3 that mortgage yields[13] and residential construction tended to move inversely to each other during the period 1948–59. The timing divergences at most of the turning points (peaks in one case and troughs in the other) are very small. An important exception is the 1950 peak in construction, the one turning point during the period that was caused (initially, at least) by "exogenous" developments—mainly the introduction of credit controls (Regulation X—see p. 81).

The significance of changes in mortgage yields (relative to changes in construction) as an *indicator* of whether supply or demand is the chief influence in the market should be dis-

11   Both the short and the long cycles in this comparison are measured in terms of private housing starts. The method of measuring amplitude is the same in each case except that yearly values are used for measuring the amplitude of long cycles and seasonally adjusted monthly values are used in the case of the short cycles. The method is that of the National Bureau, described in [9, p. 40].
12   In this paper demand will be understood to refer to demand under given mortgage credit conditions, that is under given mortgage interest rates, discounts (when they are paid by the borrower), down payments, maturities, etc. This is sometimes called "basic demand." In a few places the broader concept is used where mortgage credit conditions are also variable, as when speaking of the "sensitivity of demand" to changes in mortgage terms. Where this meaning is intended it will be obvious from the context.
13   The series on mortgage yields shown on Chart 3, which was constructed especially for this study, is based on the prices at which completed FHA home mortgages are traded in the secondary market. For several reasons the series does not measure very precisely the rate of return that can be earned by investors at any given time, or the rate that borrowers must pay for credit; neither does this series represent the average yield over the entire mortgage market, since secondary market transactions, the volume of which is very small relative to the total volume of mortgages written, are atypical. Hence, little significance can be attached to the yield *levels* indicated by the series. However, the series does constitute a fairly sensitive indicator of *changes* in borrower costs and investor returns over the entire market.

Chart 3 Selected mortgage market indicators, 1946–1959.

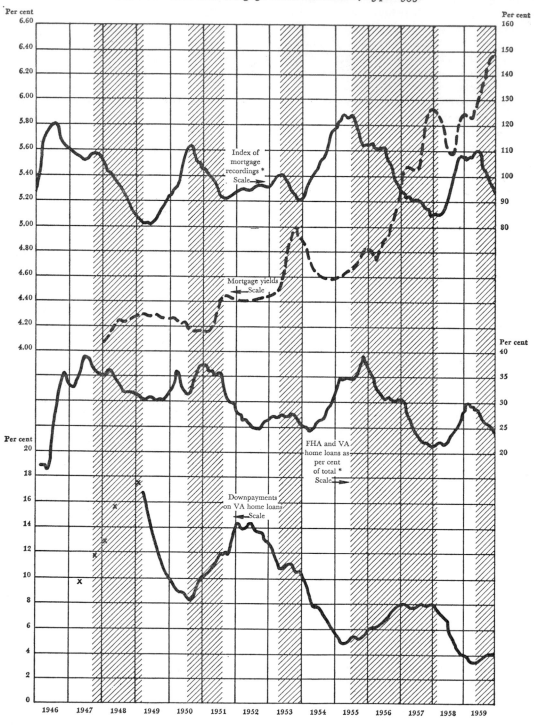

Note: Shaded areas represent contractions in mortgage recordings. Series are three-month averages except for mortgage yields.

* Seasonally adjusted.

tinguished from the *function* performed by yield changes in maintaining market equilibrium. Of course, changes in yields would not serve as an indicator unless such changes also helped to equilibrate the market. It is not necessarily the case, however, that yield changes will bear the brunt of the equilibrating process, especially in influencing the demand for credit. In rationing funds to borrowers, changes in other lending terms, and particularly in the down-payment requirement, probably are as important as, and possibly more important than, changes in rates.

Construction and Mortgage Terms

Changes in mortgage terms themselves constitute an indicator of the principal factors underlying changes in residential construction. Both the supply and demand for mortgage credit are functionally related to mortgage terms. Furthermore, when the supply of credit is a positive function of a given condition of the loan, the demand will be a negative function, and vice versa. The general reason for this is that any change in terms that makes it easier for borrowers with given qualifications to obtain more credit, *ceteris paribus* also increases risk to the lender. For example, the demand for credit is a negative function of the down payment because of the existence of marginal borrowers for whom the down-payment requirement represents an effective constraint on borrowing and spending; the more they can borrow on their existing equity or liquid assets the more they will spend. The supply of credit, on the other hand, is a positive function of the down payment, since the larger the borrower's own investment or equity relative to his borrowed funds, the less the risk that adverse circumstances will wipe out this equity and lead to default.[14]

Hence, within certain institutionally established limits, we can consider the interaction of demand and supply as determining a set of terms just as it determines an interest rate; at the same time, we can draw inferences as to the nature of the principal dynamic factor underlying a movement in construction from the associated changes in terms. Where a change in demand constitutes the chief factor underlying

a change in construction, we would expect an increase in construction to be associated with a restriction of terms. Where a change in the supply of mortgage credit is the chief dynamic factor we would expect an increase in construction to be associated with a liberalization in terms.[15]

Statistics on mortgage terms are sometimes difficult to interpret because they may be influenced by changes in the maximum terms allowed by law or regulation, as well as by changes in the demand or supply of credit. In the case of VA mortgages, however, except for the period 1950–53, the down payment required by law or regulation was either a uniform 2 per cent or nothing at all.[16] Changes in actual down payments reflected almost entirely the influence of market forces and there was ample scope for the play of such forces. A series on actual VA down payments on new houses is shown on Chart 3.

The chart shows that VA down payments tended to move in the direction opposite to recordings during the declines in residential construction of 1948–49 and 1955–57, as well as during the expansions of 1949–50, 1954–55, and 1958–59. (During 1950–53, the series is influenced by the imposition and subsequent relaxation of credit controls.) This evidence supports the thesis that changes in the supply of mortgage credit were the principal dynamic factor underlying the changes in activity. It also suggests, when considered in conjunction with the evidence on mortgage yields, that there may well be considerable variation as between different cycles or phases of cycles, in

14 These points are discussed further in [10].
15 Note that these implications follow only if it can be assumed that changes in demand or supply are not associated with a marked re-evaluation of lenders' attitudes toward the riskiness of mortgages. Ordinarily, for example, a decline in demand would lead to a liberalization of terms (as well as a decline in interest rates). However, if the decline in demand suggests to lenders that borrowers are not as good credit risks as before or that property values may decline, the result may be a restriction of terms rather than a liberalization; this is the paradox where "money gets easy but lenders get tight." It is doubtful that any sharp revision of attitudes occurred during the period covered by this study, since fluctuations in general business were mild and the mortgage repayment experience of lenders was generally very favorable.
16 A 2 per cent down-payment requirement was imposed in July 1955 and removed in April 1958.

the relative importance of yield changes and down-payment changes in rationing credit. Thus, the sharp rise in construction that began early in 1949 was associated in the early stages with only a leveling off of yields and with only a very modest decline (less than one-fifth of a percentage point) over the entire period of expansion. However, down payments declined sharply throughout 1949, and when the 1950 peak in construction was reached the average had fallen to 8 per cent, from about 17 per cent in early 1949.[17] On the other hand, during the 1955–57 period of decline, VA down payments increased only modestly but yields increased by more than 1¼ percentage points.

Construction and the Relative Importance of the Federally Underwritten Sector

Another important clue as to the nature of the forces underlying fluctuations in the level of residential construction is provided by the relationship between such fluctuations and changes in the relative importance of the federally underwritten sector of the market. Where supply-of-credit factors are the chief dynamic influence in the market, we expect changes in residential construction and in the relative importance of federally underwritten mortgages to be in the same direction. There are two broadly different reasons for this.

First, to some extent the federally underwritten and conventional sectors of the market overlap, in the sense that borrowers' demands can be met under either form of financing. Where this is the case, switching occurs between the two sectors in response to market changes. For example, assuming an increase in demand occurs, it is profitable for lenders to switch from federally underwritten to conventional financing. Higher rates can now be obtained on conventional mortgages, whereas the maximum interest rate which can be charged on federally underwritten mortgages is fixed by law or regulation (we are assuming, what was generally the case, that this interest rate ceiling is an effective constraint on the rate charged). In addition, with a stronger demand, lending terms can be tightened so that less risky mortgages are obtained, with the result that the insurance or guarantee feature is less valuable than it had been.

Second, the federally underwritten sector is partially segmented from the conventional sector, in the sense that the credit demands of some borrowers can be satisfied only at the more liberal terms available under the federal programs. The ebb and flow of these "marginal" borrowers into and out of the market is controlled mainly by changes in the market terms on FHA and VA mortgages.[18] Thus when the supply of funds that lenders wish to invest in mortgages increases, terms on FHA and particularly on VA mortgages are eased and the relative importance of these programs in the total rises.[19]

As indicated in Chart 3, the relative importance of the federal programs (as measured by the ratio of federally underwritten home loans to total recordings) varied generally in the same direction as residential construction, although the correspondence between the series is somewhat disrupted by credit controls during the period 1950–53. The same general correspondence appears in the housing starts data beginning in 1951 (when monthly data for federally underwritten starts first became available), and in the nonfarm mortgage acquisitions of life insurance companies. Changes in legislation affecting the federal programs as well as in the regulations of the federal agencies played some role, but with the exception of the 1950–53 period, movements in this indicator appear to reflect the overriding influence of swings in the supply of mortgage credit.

17 In the case of existing houses the decline was somewhat smaller.
18 The VA program is particularly important in this connection because, as already suggested, during most of the period covered by this study no down payment was required of veteran borrowers by law or regulation. This provided ample scope for lenders to adjust the down payment they required on these mortgages in accordance with their changing appetite for mortgages relative to other investments. This has been one important factor underlying the great volatility of VA mortgage lending.
19 The relationship between changes in the supply and demand for credit and changes in the relative importance of the federally underwritten sector holds irrespective of whether or not a change in demand is associated with a change in lenders' attitudes toward the riskiness of mortgages. In the case where demand increases, for example, if lenders are encouraged by this development to believe that mortgages are less risky than they had been, this will have the effect of further encouraging them to shift out of federally underwritten mortgages.

Why the Supply of Mortgage Credit Is Strategic

The reason for the strategic role of mortgage credit in the short cycle is not far to seek. Demographic factors and the relative price of housing, which must be crucially important determinants of housing demand and construction in the long run, ordinarily do not change very much in the short run. The demand for housing, moreover, apparently is not very sensitive to short-run changes in income, so long as such changes are fairly moderate and do not generate sharp swings in consumers' expectations. Decisions to vary housing expenditures are not made lightly since they involve a commitment of substantial magnitude generally extending well into the future. Such decisions are likely to be related to what home buyers consider will be their income over a fairly long period.[20]

At the same time housing demand is extremely sensitive to changes in the supply of mortgage credit. It is estimated that on the average about three-fourths of total expenditures on residential construction during the 1948–59 period was financed with mortgage loans. It is this greater sensitivity of housing demand to changes in the supply of mortgage credit than to changes in the flow of current income, and the considerable short-run volatility in the former, that underlie the counter-cyclical tendency of residential construction. Before analyzing the process in more detail, however, several factors are noted in addition to the supply of credit that exercised a marginal influence on the short construction cycle during the period covered by this study.

Other Influences on Construction in the Short Run

Demand. It is unlikely that the volume of new construction demanded per month under given credit conditions did not change over the 1948–59 period, but in the short run such changes were apparently small relative to changes that resulted from swings in the supply of mortgage credit. I have not been able to find any significant relationships between the short cycles and such factors as house prices, income and employment, marriages, household forma-

tion, etc., which it is reasonable to assume are related to housing demand.[21] These factors, of course, must have been important determinants of the general level of construction around which the short cycles took place.

Changes in Maximum Allowable Lending Terms on FHA and VA Mortgages. Liberalization of maximum lending terms (down payments and maturities) can be effective in expanding the volume of mortgage lending and construction if the supply of mortgage credit exceeds the demand at existing maximum terms. Terms were liberalized on a number of occasions during the 1948–59 period, but since most of these changes came during periods of relative tightness in the mortgage market they had little immediate effect.[22] This was true, for example, of the liberalization of mortgage terms on FHA mortgages in 1948, on both FHA and VA mortgages in 1951 and 1952 (the relaxation of Regulation X), and on FHA mortgages in 1957. On each of these occasions the new more liberal maximum terms did become effective at a later time when an increase in the supply of mortgage credit caused an easing in the market, but the change in supply during such periods was the more important factor in the easing of actual terms to borrowers.[23] On the other hand, liberalizations

20 Calculated estimates of the income elasticity of housing demand that I have seen range quite widely, from .3 to 2.0 and even higher. Margaret Reid [17] suggests that the coefficient relevant to "permanent" income is close to the higher figure, while the much lower coefficients sometimes found reflect the influence of transitory changes in income on the income concept employed.
21 In itself, this cannot be considered conclusive because of inadequacies in the basic data. Indeed, this was why recourse was had to market indicators.
22 This was not altogether fortuitous, since the pressure to "do something for housing" usually was greatest during such periods.
23 This may be illustrated as follows: Assume that the supply of mortgage credit is an increasing function of the down payment (measured as a per cent of value), and that the interest rate is fixed. Initially, when the market is tight, the down payment prevailing in the market is DP_a, or higher than the minimum of DP_m. Under these conditions, a reduction in the minimum to DP'_m has no effect on the market. When S shifts to S_y, however, the new lower minimum becomes effective. If the minimum had not been reduced, the down payment would have fallen only to the old minimum DP_m, where there would have been an excess supply. Even so, the supply of mortgage credit rather than the

during the years 1946 and 1947 (which lie outside the bounds of our cyclical analysis) were an altogether different matter. The supply of mortgage credit in those years was substantially in excess of the demand at existing maximum terms, partly because of the superfluity of liquidity possessed by lending institutions and partly because of certain restrictive aspects of the federal programs at that time. When these restrictions were removed, it was as if a dam had burst, although because of capacity limitations, the impact was more on prices than on output.[24]

Maximum allowable lending terms on federally underwritten mortgages were restricted on only two occasions during 1948–59.[25] In late 1955 there was a minor restriction which had little or no impact because the market had already tightened beyond it. The other restriction occurred in 1950, first in July on FHA and VA mortgages only, and then with even greater severity in October under Regulation X, which applied to conventional mortgages as well. Regulation X and its companion restrictions appear to have been largely responsible for the 1950 downturn in residential construction, and hence represent the one exogenous development during the 1948–59 period that was a strategic factor in a short cycle.[26] Even in this case, during the later stages of the decline the effects of the restriction became inextricably intertwined with the effect of the declining supply of mortgage credit that followed the March 1951 accord between the Federal Reserve System and the Treasury. Hence, Regulation X was only partly responsible for the 1950–51 contraction in residential construction.

The Federal National Mortgage Association (FNMA). The tendency inherent in FNMA's secondary mortgage market operations (consisting of the purchase and sale of FHA and VA mortgages) during the 1948–59 period was to mitigate fluctuations in residential construction activity. The basic reason for this was the Association maintained fixed or "sticky" mortgage purchase prices.[27] Hence, FNMA's mortgage holdings rose most rapidly during periods of declining construction and falling mortgage prices and least rapidly during periods of rising construction and mortgage prices. Since construction tended to move inversely to general

business, this meant that FNMA made the residential construction sector less of a stabilizing influence on the economy as a whole than it would have been otherwise.

FNMA's "natural" tendency to stabilize the mortgage market was, however, disrupted on several occasions by changes in the framework of law and regulations within which it operated. Thus special legislation which became effective during the expansion of 1949–50 when construction and mortgage credit from private sources were rising rapidly, provided an added fillip to FNMA's purchases. Similarly, special legislation enacted during the 1958 recession resulted in $1 billion of purchases at above-market prices as a form of "special assistance," more than offsetting sales that were being made (as a result of the general decline in interest

---

change in the minimum down payment is the more important factor in the situation pictured, since only a relatively small part of the total increase in credit ($Q'_m - Q_m$ of $Q'_m - Q_a$) can be attributed to the change in the minimum.

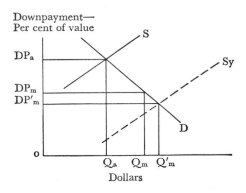

24 This can be illustrated in the diagram above by assuming that initially the supply function is S_y while DP_a is the minimum down payment so that the minimum is the strategic restraint on mortgage lending. When this minimum is reduced to DP_m, the volume of credit increases substantially (by $Q_m - Q_a$). For a further discussion of the tremendous impact of the early postwar changes in the FHA and VA programs see [7].
25 Over the entire period, these restrictions were more than offset by liberalizations. In early 1960, therefore, average down payments on FHA and VA mortgages were lower, and maturities were longer than they had ever been before. Some observers were drawing pessimistic inferences concerning the prospects for a continuation of housing's countercyclical role from this fact (see my concluding remarks below).
26 There has been some reluctance to attribute any great efficacy to Regulation X because of the

rates) under FNMA's regular secondary market operations.

FNMA's influence on the market was of some marginal importance on several occasions. When FNMA's expansionary stimulus was at its peak (in 1949, 1957 and 1959), the Association accounted for about one-tenth of the total net flow into residential mortgages; in most other years, however, its share was considerably smaller.

Rigid Interest Rates on FHA and VA Mortgages. The existence of fixed maximum interest rates on federally underwritten mortgages (set by law or by the federal credit agencies within the authority granted by law), which were usually at or below the market equilibrium rate, probably intensified somewhat the countercyclical tendency of the residential sector. As general interest rates rose during a period of expansion, the inability of lenders to obtain a higher contract rate on federally underwritten mortgages caused the diversion of credit to other sectors to be greater than it would have been otherwise. This tendency was only partly offset by the practice of "discounting" federally underwritten mortgages. And, of course, during a period of contraction the reverse process occurred. The writer's view, however, is that the rate maxima have been emphasized far out of proportion to their real importance. The countercyclical process can be explained quite well, as we shall see, without any reference to them at all.

That the "dial settings" for maximum allowable interest rates or lending terms under the federal underwriting programs were not, in general, strategic in influencing the short construction cycles does not mean that the programs were unimportant. On the contrary, the general availability of FHA insurance or guarantees to lenders when they needed them was an important factor making countercyclical variations in mortgage lending feasible without undue changes in risk exposure.

THE COUNTERCYCLICAL TENDENCY OF RESIDENTIAL CONSTRUCTION

Returning now to our main theme, that changes in the level of residential construction resulted principally from fluctuations in the supply of mortgage credit, what was the cause of these changes in supply? The thesis advanced here is that changes in the supply of mortgage credit were related in large part to changes in the level of general economic activity, so that fluctuations in residential construction resulted from fluctuations in general economic activity.

Thus, the residential sector in the short run assumed a largely passive role in economic fluctuations as opposed to its more autonomous role in the long run. But precisely because the relationship between the residential sector and the general economy was mediated chiefly by the supply of mortgage credit rather than by the flow of current income, this passivity was of an "inverse" sort. The usual picture of a cyclical expansion or contraction is one of a

---

known heavy volume of forward commitments on pre-Regulation X terms that was built up prior to the effective date of the regulation. It has been generally assumed [16] that because of these commitments the impact of the regulation must have been both delayed and diluted. But this view overlooks the following: (a) the fact that there is a stock of outstanding commitments which will permit, say, x months of construction to go forward without being subject to the regulation does not mean (as many observers imply) that there must be a delay of x months before construction is effected. Such a view is unrealistic in assuming that builders will maintain their operations at existing levels until their commitments run out, and then will reduce volume sharply. One of the main problems of builders is finding and holding a cadre of skilled workers, and they usually will go to great lengths to maintain continuity of employment for these workers. A more realistic view of builders' response to controls, therefore, is that they will curtail construction immediately by laying off the most recent additions to the work crew and by reducing overtime; in this way they can husband their commitments and stretch out employment for their basic work force. (b) The July 1950 regulation, a sort of prelude to the more comprehensive restriction imposed in October, must have had considerable impact on the market. This restriction came without any warning and hence without any prior build-up of commitments. Furthermore, by eliminating no-down-payment loans under the VA program, this restriction struck a most sensitive nerve, since these loans had come to account for about three-fifths of all VA primary home loans on new homes at the peak of the 1949–1950 housing boom.
27 Until late 1954 it was FNMA's policy to purchase all mortgages at par. The Housing Act of 1954, effective late that year, stipulated that mortgages acquired under FNMA's principal program be purchased at market prices. Even so, in subsequent years the Association tended to lag well behind the market in adjusting prices.

cumulative process with expansion in one sector leading to expansion in other sectors. In the case we are considering, changes in general business activity set in motion forces leading to movements in the *reverse* direction in construction. Consider the following schematic illustration.

Assume that an expansion in general business occurs, initiated we may suppose by an upsurge in corporate investment. In the early stages of the expansion, the additional demands made upon the capital markets may be small since the corporations have excess liquidity and retained profits are likely to be large. If the expansion follows a period of recession, credit demands will be met with no difficulty and little, if any, increase in interest rates. As expansion develops and spreads, however, the demands upon the capital markets are enlarged, liquidity positions generally are eroded and as capacity ceilings are approached Federal Reserve policy shifts from ease to restraint; interest rates rise and borrowing terms tighten.

Of course, the expansion in general economic activity leads to an increase in disposable income, but the demand for housing is expanded only slightly as a result. At the same time the demand for housing is extremely sensitive to the terms on which mortgage credit is available. After a certain stage of tightness is reached in the capital market, therefore, the reduction in housing demand consequent upon the tightening of credit more than offsets the expansion in demand resulting from the increasing flow of income. While most sectors continue to expand, residential construction turns down.

During a contraction the reverse process occurs. After some point, the easing of credit terms consequent upon a decline in the demand for credit from other sectors (and the easing of monetary policy) has an expansionary effect on housing demand sufficient to offset the effect of the decline in income. Hence, residential construction turns up while other sectors continue to decline. In this way does the residential construction sector act as a sort of countercyclical buffer.

Dynamic Role of the Corporations

It would appear that there are two basic considerations involved in the process. The first,

already discussed, is the unusual sensitivity of the residential sector in the short run to changes in the supply of credit. The second is that the tendency towards economic expansion or contraction is initiated outside of the residential construction sector. This deserves further comment.

In the schematic illustration offered above, the dynamic impetus to economic fluctuations is provided by the corporations. This is a prima facie plausible hypothesis since corporations account for a large proportion of investment spending, generally considered to be the key factor in economic fluctuations. During the 1948–59 period, corporations accounted for about three-fifths of gross private domestic investment (excluding nonfarm residential construction).

The hypothesis implies that corporate investment has quite different characteristics than spending on residential construction (these differences are associated in part with the characteristics of the spenders). The key differences are that corporate investment is (a) more volatile, and (b) less sensitive to changes in the interest rate and less subject to noninterest rate rationing. Thus, when corporate investment demands increase, the associated demands on the capital markets raise interest rates and tighten credit, but the rebound effect of this tightening on the corporations themselves is slight. Potential home buyers, on the other hand, faced with the need to pay higher rates and to make larger down payments, are forced to curtail their expenditures on housing and their mortgage borrowing. Putting the matter crudely, the volume of mortgage credit is a sort of residual, in that home buyers can obtain only that volume of credit which remains after the more volatile and persistent demands of corporations have been satisfied. Although this conclusion must be qualified in several respects, it appears to be basically correct and provides a reasonable explanation for the observed behavior of the residential construction sector during the postwar period.

Some support for this explanation is provided by Chart 4, which shows movements in the net increment to mortgage debt and to corporate securities (including equities) outstanding. The two series shown are virtually mirror images of each other. We can reject out of

Chart 4 Net change in nonfarm mortgage debt and in total corporate securities outstanding, 1949–1959.

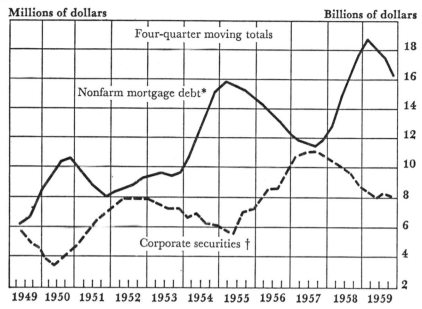

Millions of dollars   Billions of dollars

Four-quarter moving totals

Nonfarm mortgage debt*

Corporate securities †

1949 1950 1951 1952 1953 1954 1955 1956 1957 1958 1959

* Centered at second quarter.
† Centered at third quarter.

hand the possibility that demands for invest- able funds by corporations and by mortgage borrowers are subject to independent influ- ences which happen to be opposite in their effects. The chart suggests instead an organic interconnection between the processes of fi- nancing corporations through security issues and financing home purchasers through the creation of mortgage debt. Moreover, the pos- sible causal relations underlying this intercon- nection are not unlimited. Possibly one type of demand was more volatile than the other; a second possibility is that the demands were equally volatile but that there were sharp dif- ferences in the respective interest rate elastici- ties (or in the degree to which they were sub- ject to noninterest rate rationing). As already indicated, I believe that both were the case.

Role of the Federal Government and the Banking System

How does the federal government fit into this explanation? The characteristics of corpora-

tions noted above, which were said to underlie the dynamic character of corporate spending (as compared to the passive character of resi- dential spending) seem to apply even more to the federal government. The credit demands of the government appear to be more volatile than those of the corporations, for example, while the government's credit demands are in- terest-rate inelastic in the extreme and not to be put off by noninterest rate credit rationing.

As soon as the government is added to our model, it becomes necessary to take into ac- count as well the third dynamic or volatile sec- tor of the economy, namely, the commercial banking system. Broadly, it appears that fluc- tuations in bank credit tend to offset fluctua- tions in government borrowing, leaving cor- porate demands as a sort of residual prime mover in the capital markets. This is not be- cause the monetary authorities are at the beck and call of the Treasury. Rather it reflects the manner in which both government borrowing and Federal Reserve policy are related to the business cycle. During a recession, for example, borrowing by the government increases as receipts from tax payments fall off and expenditures rise. The monetary authorities, following a policy of credit ease designed to cushion the force of the recession and pave the way for recovery, do not allow these heavier borrowing needs by the government to tighten the market. The expansion of bank credit thus offsets the government's increased credit demands. The process may be quite direct, as when the Treasury floats a large cash offering and the Federal Reserve provides the banks with the reserves needed to acquire the new securities without any tightening in their reserve positions. The result is that the recession-induced relaxation of credit demands by corporations has the desired effect of releasing funds for mortgages, as explained above.

During an expansion the reverse process occurs. As government revenues increase, its borrowing requirements tend to fall but because of the policy of restraint followed by the Federal Reserve System this does not have the effect of easing the capital markets. The increasing credit demands of the corporations are thus allowed to tighten the market and draw funds from the mortgage market. Thus, the usual adaptation of monetary policies to the business cycle has the effect of allowing the normal interaction between the corporate and residential construction sectors to proceed without interference from the fluctuating credit demands of the Treasury.

The recession of 1957–58 is a particularly striking example of this because the credit demands of the government rose so sharply as to completely offset the decline in corporate demands. Comparing the year ending June 30, 1958, which roughly demarcates the recession, with the previous year of expansion, external financing by corporations fell from $14 billion to $7 billion, or by $7 billion [28] while net government demands rose by $9 billion.[29] Nevertheless, market conditions eased, as commercial bank credit rose by an unprecedented (for peacetime) $14 billion—$9 billion more than in the previous year.

Some Preconditions

It seems clear that the tendency of the residential construction sector to act in countercyclical fashion involves some basic preconditions. Indeed, the much better performance of the sector in the postwar than in the prewar period can be largely explained in terms of these conditions.

The first condition is that fluctuations in general economic activity be limited, particularly contractions. The increases in the supply of mortgage credit during postwar business recessions had a greater effect in expanding housing demand than the reduced flow of income had in curtailing this demand partly because the reductions in income were small and the confidence of consumers was not significantly affected. However, the amount of ease that can be introduced into the mortgage market is limited by legal and institutional factors; the expansionary effect of easy credit, at the limit, can be largely offset or even swamped by substantial declines in income, such as those experienced in major prewar contractions.

Moreover, when the level of general economic activity declines beyond some point, the supply of mortgage credit may actually begin to tighten rather than easing further, as lenders become apprehensive with respect to the future economic status of borrowers and mortgage loans begin to appear more risky than before. Although lenders under such conditions might have more loanable funds than previously, they would be less inclined to lend. This would be reflected in a greater restrictiveness in lending terms, although interest rates on prime securities probably would continue to decline.[30]

This leads to a second precondition, namely, that lenders are able to make sharp countercyclical variations in their mortgage lending without undergoing large changes in risk exposure. Two possible sources of a change in risk exposure have been noted in this paper. Reference has just been made to a shift in lenders' evaluations of the risks associated with

28 External financing is defined as the net increase in stocks and bonds, mortgage debt, bank loans and federal income tax liabilities plus net reduction in government securities holdings. If income tax liabilities are excluded, external financing declined by less than $5 billion.
29 From debt redemption of about $3 billion to an increase in debt of about $6 billion.
30 This is the paradox referred to above where "money gets easy but lenders get tight."

loans of given characteristics (given type of security, lending terms, etc.). Such changes probably are quite small in a relatively stable economic environment such as we have had in the postwar period. The impact of any re-evaluations of risk that have occurred has been minimized by the federal underwriting programs, although undoubtedly, from this standpoint, these programs have not been very badly needed in the postwar period.

Risk exposure can also change as a result of a shift in the loan mix, for example, toward loans with smaller down payments. Such changes are, indeed, an integral part of countercyclical shifts in mortgage lending. If lenders are to push out more credit during a recession, for example, when basic housing demand is, if anything, weakening, they must stimulate demand by standing ready to make more liberal loans. Here the importance of the federal underwriting programs becomes evident. Credit terms can be liberalized and demand stimulated, without any appreciable increase in risk exposure, by shifting into federally under-written loans. In the absence of such programs credit liberalization may be hampered, either because lenders are unwilling to court the added risk exposure, or are unwilling to do so without a compensating rise in rate (which can be quite large), or are unable to do so because they are already making most loans at the conservative maximum limits established by law for conventional loans. Thus the federal underwriting programs have been an important structural factor facilitating the countercyclical tendency of the residential sector during the postwar period.

Tight Money Before the Accord?

It may appear surprising that a decline in the supply of mortgage credit could have been responsible for the 1948–49 decline in residential construction. Since lending institutions at that time held very substantial amounts of government securities and the Federal Reserve System was supporting the government bond market, how could there have been a contraction of mortgage credit?

The celebrated accord between the Federal Reserve System and the Treasury in March 1951 has tended to overshadow certain important developments in prior years. These developments, which in themselves constituted partial steps back to an effective monetary policy, in a sense prepared the way for the accord, and influenced the mortgage market as early as the second half of 1947. During that period and again in the latter part of 1948, short-term interest rates were allowed by the Federal Reserve System to rise substantially from unusually low wartime levels. The banks appeared to be the only type of financial institution significantly affected by these moves, and their main response to rising short-term yields was to withdraw temporarily from the mortgage market. Between 1947 and 1949 net mortgage acquisitions by commercial banks fell by two-thirds.[31] Since the banks had helped create a climate of extreme ease in the mortgage market in 1946 and early 1947 by aggressively competing for mortgages, their sudden withdrawal from the market had a considerable impact.

The 1948 decline in mortgage credit and residential construction thus resulted from the earliest and mildest of the measures designed to restore the central bank's control over the money supply. This was an unusual instance of developments in the market for short-term instruments of high liquidity directly and seriously influencing the market for long-term instruments of relatively low liquidity. The connecting link, of course, was the portfolio adjustment of the commercial banks, and the fact that the banks had been unusually active in the mortgage market in prior years.

FUTURE PROSPECTS

Will the countercyclical mechanism described above continue to operate in the future? It is not the case, as some have argued, that the process will necessarily come to an end as a result of the gradual weakening of basic housing demand relative to the total housing stock —a result of unfavorable demographic factors over the 1950–60 decade, conjoined with the very substantial additions to the stock during this period. Even if this development presages

[31] Subsequently, the banks re-entered the mortgage market to help spark the 1949–50 expansion.

a decline in the average level of construction, which is by no means certain, credit-induced fluctuations (possibly of reduced absolute magnitude, to be sure) might well occur around this lower level.

Nor does the upward ratcheting of mortgage credit terms on FHA and VA mortgages over the period since the second world war, referred to earlier, limit the scope for easing of credit in the future. Liberalization of credit involves not only a relaxation of terms on FHA and VA mortgages but, possibly of more importance, a greater availability of these mortgages. Each period of credit ease has been accompanied by a rise in the relative importance of FHA and VA mortgages in the total. There has not, however, been an upward trend in this ratio over the 1948–59 period as a whole, and in early 1960 the ratio was lower than during most of the period (see Chart 3).

More germane to future prospects is our assessment of the possibility that fluctuations in general business will be more severe in the future than they were in the 1948–59 period. To be sure the federal underwriting programs will continue to minimize any disruptive swings in risk exposure that could otherwise result from more severe fluctuations in general business. But large procyclical swings in income could still swamp the effects of countercyclical variations in the supply of mortgage credit.

As a further possibility, the intricate mechanism through which business fluctuations generate countercyclical swings in the supply of mortgage credit might develop kinks at one point or another. The time series in Chart 1, for example, suggest the hypothesis that the response of housing to easy credit may be coming progressively later during recessions. This hypothesis warrants careful study, directed at the portfolio responses at crucial junctures of the major types of mortgage lenders (has this response been influenced by the secular erosion of their liquidity positions during the postwar period?); at the timing of governmental policy actions relative to the business cycle; and at the changing structure of housing demand.

REFERENCES

1. A. F. BURNS, "Long Cycles in Residential Construction," *Economic Essays in Honor of Wesley C. Mitchell*. New York 1935.
2. A. F. BURNS AND W. C. MITCHELL, *Measuring Business Cycles*. Nat. Bur. Econ. Research, New York 1947.
3. M. L. COLEAN AND R. NEWCOMB, *Stabilizing Construction: The Record and Potential*. New York 1952.
4. J. B. D. DERKSEN, "Long Cycles in Residential Building," *Econometrica*, 1940, *8*, 97–116.
5. J. DUESENBERRY, *Business Cycles and Economic Growth*. New York 1958.
6. L. GREBLER, *Housing Issues in Economic Stabilization Policy*. Nat. Bur. Econ. Res. Occas. Paper 72, New York 1960.
7. ——, "Stabilizing Residential Construction—A Review of the Postwar Test," *Am. Econ. Rev.*, Sept. 1949, *39*, 898–910.
8. ——, "The Role of Residential Capital Formation in Postwar Business Cycles," *Conference on Savings and Residential Financing*, 1959 Proc., U.S. Savings and Loan League, pp. 57–85.
9. L. GREBLER, D. M. BLANK, AND L. WINNICK, *Capital Formation in Residential Real Estate: Trends and Prospects*. Princeton 1956.
10. J. M. GUTTENTAG, "Credit Availability, Interest Rates and Monetary Policy," *So. Econ. Jour.*, Jan. 1960, *26*, 219–28.
11. ——, *Some Studies of the Post-World War II Residential Construction and Mortgage Markets*. Unpublished Ph.D. dissertation, Columbia University 1958.
12. A. H. HANSEN, *Business Cycles and National Income*. New York 1951.
13. C. D. LONG, *Building Cycles and the Theory of Investment*. Princeton 1940.
14. G. H. MOORE, *Statistical Indicators of Cyclical Revivals and Recessions*. Nat. Bur. Econ. Res., Occas. Paper 31, New York 1950.
15. W. H. NEWMAN, *The Building Industry and Building Cycles*. Chicago 1935.
16. J. J. O'LEARY, "The Effects of Monetary Policies on the Mortgage Market," *Jour. Finance*, May 1958, *13*, 176–87.
17. M. REID, "Capital Formation in Residential Real Estate," *Jour. Pol. Econ.*, Apr. 1958, *46*, 131–53.
18. J. R. RIGGLEMAN, "Building Cycles in the United States 1875–1932," *Jour. Am. Stat. Assoc.*, June 1933, *28*, 174–83.

Business Cycles, Residential Construction Cycles, and the Mortgage Market

WILLIAM W. ALBERTS [1]

INTRODUCTION

Although one might expect house construction to exhibit the same cyclical behavior as the output of other durable goods, it has not done so during the post–World War II period. In general, seasonally adjusted single-family house starts have increased sharply only when gross national product has been depressed and the remainder of the time have either decreased or fluctuated within a narrow range. More precisely, after drifting upward during 1946 and 1947 and then decreasing briefly in 1948, seasonally adjusted house starts turned up sharply after the downturn and just before the trough of the 1948–49 recession, increased over 50 per cent in about four quarters, reached their peak in the summer of 1950, and then decreased over the next five quarters almost as sharply as they had previously risen. Starts were approximately constant for about two years, and then turned up sharply again, this time shortly after the downturn and just before the trough of the 1953–54 recession; they increased about 30 per cent in four quarters, reached their peak in the summer of 1955, and then decreased steadily for almost three years. Starts then reversed their course just at the trough of the 1957–58 recession, increased about 35 per cent in five quarters, turned down in the summer of 1959, and then decreased continuously for the next one and one-half years.[2]

Not surprisingly, a number of economists have become interested in these fluctuations in housing output and have offered explanations of them. All of these explanations are essentially the same: that the postwar housing cycles have been directly tied to the postwar business cycles and that the link has been the fixed interest rates charged on mortgage loans insured by the Federal Housing Administration or guaranteed by the Veterans' Administration. Put another way, these economists have concluded that had interest rates on these insured and guaranteed mortgage loans been free to fluctuate in response to changing market forces, there would have been no, or only very modest, fluctuations in housing output during the postwar period.[3]

It is my contention, however, that fixed interest rates are not the key to the postwar housing cycles; my objectives in this paper are to show why they are not and to present an alternative explanation of the housing cycles.

In Part II, I shall first elaborate the fixed interest-rate theory and then indicate what I think are its shortcomings. In Part III, I shall present an alternative theory of postwar housing cycles and some evidence in support of that theory. My basic thesis will be that business cycles have generated housing cycles not because of fixed rates but primarily because the changes in income associated with periods of business contraction and recovery have had a relatively small direct effect on the demand for housing.

Reprinted from the *Journal of Political Economy* (June 1962), pp. 263–281, by permission of the author and The University of Chicago Press. Copyright © by The University of Chicago Press.

1 I wish to thank, without implicating, Richard Muth, David Meiselman, Arnold Harberger, James Lorie, and Anthony Downs, all of whom have helped a great deal in the development of this paper.

2 The National Bureau of Economic Research places the trough of the 1948–49 recession in October, 1949, the trough of the 1953–54 recession in August, 1954, and the trough of the 1957–58 recession in April, 1958. See Geoffrey H. Moore, *Measuring Recessions* ("Occasional Paper," No. 61 [New York: National Bureau of Economic Research, 1958]), p. 260; and Geoffrey H. Moore, "The 1957–58 Business Contraction: New Model or Old?" *Papers and Proceedings*, (American Economic Association), XLIX (May, 1959), 292. Seasonally adjusted, private, non-farm dwelling unit starts (the Bureau of the Census–Bureau of Labor Statistics series) turned up in the third quarter of 1949, in the second quarter of 1954, and in the second quarter of 1958. I have prepared a seasonally adjusted, single-family house start series which shows about the same upturn dates as the Census-BLS total starts series; this single-family house starts series is exhibited in Chart 1 in Part II of this paper.

3 An exception is Jack Guttentag. See his "The Short Cycle in Residential Construction," *American Economic Review*, LI [June, 1961], 290.

Chart 1 Inspected and non-inspected single-family house starts.

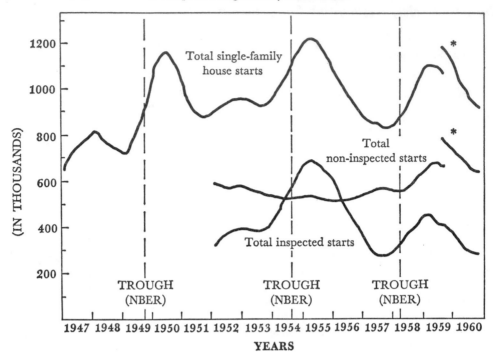

Total single-family
house starts

Total
non-inspected starts

Total inspected starts

TROUGH
(NBER)

TROUGH
(NBER)

TROUGH
(NBER)

(IN THOUSANDS)

1200

1000

800

600

400

200

1947 1948 1949 1950 1951 1952 1953 1954 1955 1956 1957 1958 1959 1960

YEARS

Source: I have derived both the single-family house starts series and the inspected single-family house starts series by converting monthly figures into twelve-month moving monthly averages, summing the monthly averages into quarterly totals, and then stating these totals at annual rates. The non-inspected starts series is the difference between the total starts series and the inspected starts series, that is, it is a residual series. The monthly starts and inspected starts figures are available in United States Housing and Home Finance Agency, *Housing Statistics, Historical Supplement,* June, 1960, and *Housing Statistics,* June, 1961. Although the FHA inspections series goes back to 1935, there are no data on VA inspections prior to November, 1950.

As a consequence of the revelation by the 1956 National Housing Inventory that the Bureau of Labor Statistics had underestimated dwelling units starts by about 20 per cent for the 1950–56 period, the job of estimating monthly starts was transferred to the Bureau of the Census in 1959, and a new estimating method was developed. Monthly starts estimates made with the new method are available beginning with January, 1959. In addition, monthly starts estimates continued to be made with the old BLS method up to April 1, 1960, and as a result there is a sixteen-month overlap in the two series. For 1959, starts under the old method are about 10 per cent less than starts under the new method.

The series marked with an asterisk are derived from estimates made by the new method. Since all FHA and VA data are reported and not estimated, the entire difference between new series starts and old series starts represents non-inspected starts.

THE FIXED-INTEREST RATE THEORY AND ITS SHORTCOMINGS

The Theory

For fixed-rate theorists the main clue to the postwar fluctuations in housing output has been "the fact that almost all the variations in housing starts has been accounted for by fluctuations in that segment of starts financed by government-guaranteed loans [and that] con-

ventionally financed residential construction, despite substantial fluctuations in interest rates, has been remarkably stable." [4] Chart 1 exhibits

4 John P. Lewis, *Business Conditions Analysis* (New York: McGraw-Hill Book Co., 1959), p. 444. A few examples of others who take the same starting point in their analyses of the postwar housing cycles are Warren Smith, "The Impact of Monetary Policy on Residential Construction, 1948–1958," in U.S. Congress, Senate Subcommittee on Housing of the Committee on Banking and Currency, *Study of Mortgage Credit* (85th Congress, 2d Sess., 1958), pp. 248, 253; Albert H. Schaaf, "Federal Mortgage

the data in which this fact has been observed. It shows the quarterly volume (seasonally adjusted at annual rates) of private, single-family house starts broken down into (1) those units whose subsequent construction was inspected by the FHA or the VA for compliance with their own standards of building, and (2) those units whose subsequent construction was not inspected by the FHA or the VA.[5] (The chart also shows the National Bureau of Economic Research estimated trough dates for the 1948–49, the 1953–54, and the 1957–58 business contractions.)

Chart 1 does show that over the course of the 1954–56 fluctuations both the increases and the decreases in single-family house starts were confined entirely to those that had been inspected by the FHA or the VA. Whether this was also the case during the 1949–51 fluctuations we do not know, since data showing combined FHA and VA inspections are not available prior to 1951; it definitely seems not to have been the case during the 1958–60 fluctuations, for Chart 1 shows that non-inspected starts *did* increase and decrease significantly during that period.[6] But when only the 1954–56 figures were available, there seemed an obvious inference to be drawn, and all fixed-rate theorists have drawn it. Colean, writing in 1958, put it this way:

> Because the great unevenness in the volume of house-building since 1950 has been largely centered in that part of it affected by insured and guaranteed mortgage financing, and since similar effects have not been felt in the conventional loan area, it . . . is reasonable to conclude that the violence of the fluctuation is due to qualities peculiar to the insured and guaranteed system.[7]

That is, the fluctuations have been the result of administered contract rates on insured and guaranteed mortgages.[8]

Most fixed-rate theorists have not been very explicit about the precise connection between these fixed rates and the 1954–56 consequences shown in Chart 1, but the following analysis appears to be what they all have in mind.

Because there are interest rate ceilings on VA and FHA mortgages (and even though these ceilings have been adjusted upwards on several occasions since 1953), the rates for these mortgages have tended to lag behind other interest rates in boom periods as the competition for funds became more intense. Indeed, the higher competitive rates became, the less attractive these mortgages became relative to other securities, and the greater the tendency to divert credit to other uses. . . . During periods of business contraction the reverse process occurred. . . . As the general demand for funds fell and was accompanied by declines in interest rates, the fixed rates on these mortgages became more attractive to lenders, and they

Interest Rate Policy and the Supply of FHA-VA Credit," *Review of Economics and Statistics,* XL (November, 1958) , 284–85; and Leo Grebler, "The Role of Residential Capital Formation in Postwar Business Cycles," United States Savings and Loan League, *Conference on Savings and Residential Financing* (1959 Proceedings) , p. 71.
5 There is an interesting and, as we shall see, significant amount of variation in the labeling of this FHA-VA series. *Housing Statistics,* essentially the source publication, and *Construction Review* both label the series "FHA-VA inspections." However, when *Construction Review* has occasionally published staff articles on the housing and mortgage markets, it has relabeled the series as "FHA-VA assisted" starts. The *Survey of Current Business* also uses "FHA-VA assisted" starts. The *Federal Reserve Bulletin* uses the label "government underwritten" starts. Many writers speak simply of "FHA-VA" starts, others of "FHA-insured" and "VA-guaranteed" starts, and still others (e.g., Lewis, *op. cit.*) of starts "financed by government guaranteed loans." The non-inspected starts are invariably spoken of as starts "financed with conventional loans," or "conventional" starts; this should be taken to mean starts "financed either with conventional loans or entirely with cash."
6 Fixed-rate theorists generally exhibit total dwelling unit starts rather than single-family unit starts. However, the fluctuation in total starts from 1953 to 1956 was confined to single-family units; the annual rate at which apartment units were built remained approximately constant over that period. There were significant fluctuations in the volume of apartment unit starts in both 1949–51 and 1957–59, though (see United States Housing and Home Finance Agency, *Housing Statistics, Historical Supplement,* June, 1960) .
7 Miles Colean, "A More Effective Mortgage Insurance Corporation," in *Study of Mortgage Credit, op. cit.*, p. 295.
8 As one of many other examples of the same inference: "The evidence at hand . . . strongly supports the conclusion that the policy of maintaining relatively inflexible interest rates on FHA and VA mortgage loans has been a prime factor in the recent instability of residential mortgage flows" (Saul Klaman, "The Availability of Residential Mortgage Credit," in *Study of Mortgage Credit, op. cit.*, p. 198) .

became more willing to make mortgage loans. On the other hand, a comparatively stable flow of funds went into conventional mortgages, whose interest rates are free to move in response to changes in competing rates.[9]

More succinctly, a combination of three things has generated the fluctuations in housing output: fluctuating bond yields, fixed FHA-VA rates, and a high cross-elasticity of demand for mortgages with respect to bond yields on the part of lenders.

Its Shortcomings

There are three major grounds on which I find this fixed-rate theory vulnerable. (1) It has chosen, in part, the wrong data to explain. (2) Yields on insured and guaranteed mortgages have not been fixed. (3) Even if yields had been fixed, the fixed-rate theory, as I have recapitulated it, still does not actually explain the postwar fluctuations in mortgage lending and borrowing.

1. Fluctuations in outlays for housing have *not* been confined to those financed with insured and guaranteed loans. The problem is not simply the increase and decrease in non-inspected starts during the 1958–59 fluctuations. The problem is that the data in Chart 1 do not represent the volume of insured and guaranteed *loans* and the volume of conventional loans. Instead, these data represent only what their labels indicate: the number of houses inspected during construction by the FHA or the VA and the number of houses not inspected during construction by these agencies. It is true that most insured and guaranteed loans have been made on houses whose construction the FHA or the VA has inspected. However, it is not true that most inspected houses therefore have been financed with insured or guaranteed loans. In fact, during the postwar period, many houses have been inspected during construction and then financed conventionally.[10] Consequently, data on loans tell a somewhat different story than the data on inspections in Chart 1.[11]

Chart 2 shows these data on loans. The chart shows the quarterly volume (seasonally ad-

justed at annual rates) of private, non-farm, single-family house starts, lagged four months to provide a measure of purchases,[12] the seasonally adjusted quarterly volume of insured and guaranteed loans made to finance these purchases, and a residual, which indicates the quarterly volume of purchases financed with conventional loans or with cash alone. The chart shows that the increases in output during

9 United States Federal Reserve Bank of New York, *Monthly Review*, April, 1959, p. 63.
10 Builders have an incentive to have their construction work inspected if they think their buyers will use insured or guaranteed loans. The VA will not guarantee a loan on an uninspected house, while the maximum loan the FHA will insure on any given house is about 5 per cent lower when construction has not been inspected than when it has been inspected. One of the major reasons why more houses have been inspected than financed with FHA-VA loans is that builders who have expected to sell a given percentage of the houses in a proposed development to buyers who would use FHA or VA loans often could not be sure which specific houses would make up the percentage, and therefore have simply arranged for all of the units to be inspected during construction.
11 One fixed-rate theorist, Leo Grebler, has recently noted that the FHA-VA inspection series is not a loan series. See Leo Grebler, *Housing Issues in Economic Stabilization* ("Occasional Paper," No. 72 [New York: National Bureau of Economic Research, 1960]), p. 95. However, instead of FHA-VA loan data, Grebler has examined data showing the dollar volume of mortgages recorded. He has drawn from these data the same conclusion as other fixed-rate theorists have drawn from Chart 1: that during the postwar period the output of conventionally financed houses has been stable while the output of FHA-VA financed output has been unstable. However, recordings data are a very treacherous source from which to draw inferences: (1) they lump together loans made for the purchase of new houses and loans made for the purchase of existing houses, with the latter unquestionably outnumbering the former; (2) they include an unknown number of loans of less than $20,000 made on commercial properties; and (3) they exclude loans of over $20,000 to finance residential properties, the number of which loans has increased significantly in recent years. Aside from all this, I would argue that the annual dollar volume of conventional mortgage recordings was not stable in 1953–56, only more stable than the annual dollar volume of FHA-VA mortgage recordings.
There are no series available showing the dollar volume of the loans that have been made to finance purchases of new houses. However, I am confident that there has been a high correlation between percentage changes in the numerical volume and in the dollar volume of such loans.
12 For some evidence that the average length of the construction period on single-family houses has been about four months in recent years, see United States Department of Commerce, *Construction Review*, June, 1957, pp. 3–8.

Chart 2 The financing of single-family house purchases.

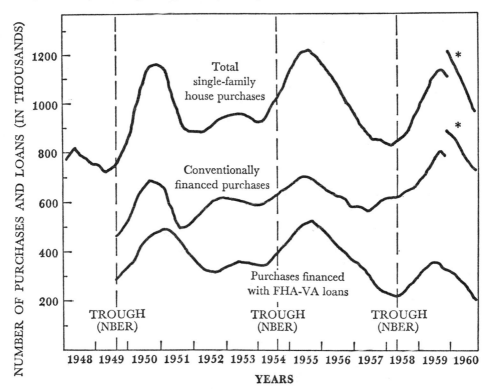

Source: The single-family house purchase series is identical with the starts series in Chart 1, except that I have lagged starts four months (which is about the average construction period of single-family houses) before converting them into twelve-month moving monthly averages. The FHA-VA loan series is the result of converting figures showing the number of loans insured or guaranteed each month (available in *Housing Statistics*) into twelve-month moving monthly averages, summing the monthly averages into quarterly totals, and then stating these totals at annual rates. VA monthly loan data are available only from January, 1949; the loans are those guaranteed under Section 501 of the Servicemen's Readjustment Act of 1944. FHA monthly loan data go back to 1935; almost all of the loans in the FHA series in Chart 2 are those insured under Section 203 of Title II of the amended National Housing Act, and over 95 per cent represent loans on single-family houses, the remainder representing loans on two- to four-family properties.

The series marked with an asterisk are derived from estimates of single-family house starts made with the new Bureau of the Census method referred to in Chart 1.

There is one important flaw in the FHA loan series. When a house has not been built under FHA inspection, but has been financed with an FHA-insured loan, FHA has defined that house as an "existing" rather than a "new" house. The loans underlying the Chart 2 series represent loans on "new" houses only, that is, on houses that are both new *and inspected.* Consequently, this series understates the role of FHA-insured loans in financing new construction. The FHA estimates that the ratio of the volume of loans it insured on new inspected *plus* new non-inspected houses to the volume of loans it insured on new inspected houses was 1.33 for the period 1952–57, 1.22 in 1958, and 1.15 in 1959. Cf. United States Housing and Home Finance Agency, *Eleventh Annual Report*, 1957, p. 58, and *Thirteenth Annual Report*, 1959, p. 62. There is no evidence that this ratio has varied cyclically and that the actual configuration of the FHA-VA loan series has therefore been significantly different from that in Chart 2.

the three cycles were not limited to construction financed with FHA-insured or with VA-guaranteed loans; at least half the increment of purchases in 1949–50, slightly less than half the increment of purchases in 1954–55, and more than half the increment of purchases in 1958–59 were conventionally financed.[13]

2. Concerning interest rates, although *contract rates* on insured and guaranteed notes have been fixed,[14] the prices at which these notes sell have not; and, therefore, by adjusting these prices above or below face value, lenders have been able to earn whatever *yield* they wish. That is, the relation between mortgage contract rates and mortgage yields is analogous to the relation between bond coupon rates and bond yields.[15] Further, published series on yields on insured and guaranteed mortgage loans suggest that these yields have been at least as sensitive to changing market forces as corporate bond yields have. I shall exhibit one of these series in Part III of this paper.

Of those fixed-rate theorists who have found it difficult to ignore the fact that FHA-VA mortgages have sold at discounts for over a dozen years (rarely at premiums because contract rates almost invariably have been set below market yields current at the time), all seem to have tried to depreciate the significance of the fact. Some have simply claimed as Klaman has that "changes in contract rates have been shown to be more effective than discounts in adjusting mortgage yields, and hence in maintaining an even flow of funds" [16] without indicating where or how this has been shown, or, for that matter, why an even flow of funds would be a criterion of "effectiveness." Others have advanced a fairly precise hypothesis to buttress their position. Congress, the argument goes, while allowing discounting and even recognizing its necessity, nonetheless has always been hostile to "high" discounts—most often identified as those over four points—on what they regard as essentially riskless loans. As a result, lenders, anxious to minimize the risk of possible reprisals at some point in the future, have tended to begin to withdraw from the FHA-VA markets when discounts have reached what they thought was the danger level.[17]

13 The increase in the volume of FHA-VA loans relative to the volume of conventional loans in 1951 that Chart 2 shows appears to be connected with the imposition of Regulation X in late 1950. The increase in the volume of conventional loans relative to the volume of FHA-VA loans in 1957 that the chart also shows is undoubtedly connected with the controls on discounts on FHA-VA loans that Congress imposed from August, 1957, to April, 1958. I cannot discuss Regulation X in this paper, but the discount control episode is commented on in n. 17.

14 Since 1948, maximum contract rates on FHA-insured loans have been as follows: 4½ per cent to April, 1950; 4¼ per cent from April, 1950, to April, 1953; 4½ per cent from April, 1953, to December, 1956; 5 per cent from December, 1956, to August, 1957; 5¼ per cent from August, 1957, to September, 1959; 5¾ per cent from September, 1959, to February, 1961; 5½ per cent from February, 1961, to May, 1961; and 5¼ per cent from May, 1961, to the present (July, 1961). Since 1948, maximum contract rates on VA-guaranteed loans have been as follows: 4 per cent to April, 1953; 4½ per cent from April, 1953, to April, 1958; 4¾ per cent from April, 1958, to July, 1959; and 5¼ per cent from July, 1959, to the present.

15 There is one difference between the yield-coupon rate relation on bonds and the yield-contract rate relation on FHA mortgage loans. The proceeds of a bond issue reflect directly any discount (or premium) on the bond. However, the FHA requires that issuers of insured notes receive cash payments equal to the full face value of these notes. Consequently, mortgagors must absorb discounts indirectly. They do so by paying the required discount to the seller of the house, who then passes it to the lender. To obtain this payment, the seller inflates the price of the house by an amount equal to the discount. However, while this payment takes the *form* of a price premium, it is actually an interest premium. A $500 discount on a $10,000, twenty-year, 5½ per cent note raises the cost of the note to 6.1 per cent whether the borrower simply receives $9,500, or receives $10,000 and pays a $500 "premium" for his house.

The question of how discounts are absorbed is more complex in the case of guaranteed notes. To prevent the cost of borrowing to veterans from exceeding maximum allowable contract rates, the VA has tried to prevent borrowers from passing discounts to lenders, not only directly, but also indirectly in the form of price premiums paid to sellers. Its method has been to require that borrowers whose notes it proposes to guarantee pay no more for houses than their "reasonable value" as determined by VA appraisers, where "reasonable value" ostensibly has been intended to be close to market value *exclusive of discounts*. However, someone has had to absorb discounts; otherwise, lenders would not have operated in the VA loan market during most of the postwar period. The only question is whether sellers typically have made the necessary rebates to lenders but have been unable to recover these payments from house-buyers, or whether discounts have come ultimately, as in the case of discounts on insured notes, from house-buyers. Put another way, the question is whether VA appraisers have tended to inflate "reasonable values" by current discounts. Although the evi-

There is no question that some financial institutions have done little lending in the VA market since the middle of 1957 and that discounts on guaranteed loans have been above four points during much of this period.[18] (The FHA has kept its contract rates closer to market yields than the VA has; average discounts in insured loans have rarely reached four points during the postwar period.) However, while these facts may substantiate the hypothesis that the supply schedule of guaranteed mortgage funds has been backward-bending with respect to yields, it is not clear what this hypothesis does to save the fixed-rate theory. First, to say that the supply schedule of guaranteed mortgage funds has been backward-bending need not imply that the supply schedule of *aggregate* insured and guaranteed mortgage funds has been backward-bending.[19] Second, even if the supply schedule of aggregate insured and guaranteed mortgage funds has been backward-bending, this hardly explains how fluctuations in aggregate expenditures have caused fluctuations in residential construction. On the supply side of the mortgage market the problem of the postwar housing cycles is to explain *shifts* of schedules, not movements along schedules.

3. Suppose, though, that yields on FHA-VA mortgage loans *had been* fixed. Given a sufficient high cross-elasticity of demand for mortgage loans with respect to yields on competing investments on the part of lenders, fixed-rate theorists are correct in suggesting that a decrease in yields on these competing investments would have led to an increase in the supply of mortgage funds. But it does not follow from this fact alone that the volume of lending would have increased. Lenders can put more funds into the market only if borrowers are persuaded for some reason to take more funds out of the market at the same time. If periodic upturns and downturns in the output of houses financed with FHA-VA loans are to be accounted for, not only must some explanation be given for the periodic shifts of lenders to and from the mortgage market, but also some explanation must be given for the response of borrowers to these shifts.

I am not saying that fluctuations in the output of houses financed with FHA-VA loans

cannot be explained under a fixed-yield assumption, but only that fixed-rate theorists, in general, have not explained them. In fact, there

---

dence is almost entirely casual or circumstantial, most students of the mortgage market seem persuaded that appraisers have tended to inflate "reasonable values," and, therefore, that the cost of borrowing has been as responsive in the VA market to changes in supply-and-demand conditions as it has in the FHA market.

16 *Op. cit.*, p. 198.

17 This hypothesis is stated in Colean, *op. cit.*, p. 296, and in *Federal Reserve Bulletin*, August, 1958, p. 889. Compare the following comment from a report of Representative Rains's Subcommittee on Housing: "It is one thing to concede the necessity or at least the unavoidability, of moderate discounts in some parts of the country. It is entirely another thing, however, to sanction discounts of 5 or 7 or 10%. A 7% discount, for example, will give a gross yield for a 25 year loan . . . 5.53%. The subcommittee regard this as an outrageous yield on a government-guaranteed obligation at a time when long-term Government loans are yielding less than 3%" (United States Congress, House Subcommittee on Housing of the Committee on Banking and Currency, *Report No. 2, Mortgage Credit and FHA Multi-family Housing* [84th Congress, 2d Sess., 1956], pp. 4–5).

Congressional hostility to discounts culminated in August, 1957, in the imposition of *discount* ceilings (and therefore yield ceilings) on insured and guaranteed mortgages. The FHA discount ceilings were *above* the market at the time and therefore had little or no effect on the quantity supplied and demanded of insured mortgage funds. The VA discount ceilings were below the market at the time, and therefore the supply of VA funds dried up almost immediately. Discount controls were ended in April, 1958.

18 Specifically, life insurance companies and commercial banks allowed their holdings of guaranteed mortgage loans to decrease $800 million and $700 million, respectively, between the end of 1957 and the end of 1960. Mutual savings banks and savings and loan associations increased their holdings in 1958–60, but the increases were quite modest compared with the 1949–50 and the 1954–55 increases. The initial cause of the relative withdrawal of these institutions from the guaranteed loan market was actually not high discounts but discount controls. But soon after the end of discount controls, discounts on guaranteed loans rose to an average of about seven points.

19 All institutional mortgage lenders except life insurance companies appear to have shifted in the aggregate from the VA market to the FHA and conventional markets in 1958–59. Thus, while life insurance company mortgage lending increased sharply in 1949–50 and in 1954–55, it increased only moderately in 1958–59. The reasons for this change in portfolio tastes are not clear. But this behavior of life insurance companies implies nothing, of course, about the shape of the aggregate supply schedule of mortgage funds during the 1958–59 period.

appear to be two possible ways to explain such fluctuations under a fixed-yield assumption. (a) One might argue that prior to each upturn in starts, the supply schedule of FHA-VA funds has intersected the demand schedule for FHA-VA funds above the fixed yield, so that there has been a shortage of funds. As a consequence, each shift to the right of the supply schedule of mortgage funds has caused an increase in borrowing and an increase in the demand schedule for new houses; each shift to the left of the supply schedules of mortgage funds has had the opposite effect.[20] (b) Alternatively, one might argue that the quantity demanded of mortgage funds has depended on such terms of the mortgage loan contract as maturities and ratios of downpayment to price, and that lenders have reduced surpluses and shortages of mortgage funds by varying these terms. As a consequence, each shift to the right of the supply schedule of mortgage funds by its effect on these terms has caused an increase in borrowing and an increase in the demand schedule for new houses; each shift to the left of the supply schedule of mortgage funds has had the opposite effect.[21]

But note that as explanations of the fluctuations in the volume of FHA-VA loans shown in Chart 2, both of these arguments would depend on the same critical assumption: that the demand for insured and guaranteed mortgage funds has remained relatively stable over the course of each business contraction and subsequent recovery. Had this demand decreased each time the supply of mortgage funds increased, borrowing would have tended to remain unchanged, although by the first explanation the shortage of mortgage funds would have decreased, and by the second explanation terms of mortgage loans would have changed. Similarly, of course, it would be difficult to reconcile the increases in the output of conventionally financed houses shown in Chart 2 with decreases in the demand schedule for funds in that sector of the mortgage market in 1949–50, 1954–55, and 1958–59.

Thus, under conditions of fixed yields on mortgage loans, business cycles could not have generated housing cycles unless the demand schedule for mortgage funds had been relatively stable while aggregate expenditures decreased and increased. I shall now suggest that, given

a relatively stable demand schedule for mortgage funds over the course of business contractions and subsequent recoveries, one does not need the assumption that yields on mortgage loans have been fixed to explain how fluctuations in aggregate expenditures have generated fluctuations in the output of houses.[22]

AN ALTERNATIVE THEORY OF THE POSTWAR HOUSING CYCLES

The Theory

In its essentials my theory of the postwar housing cycles reduces to two propositions: (1) Fluctuations in aggregate spending have led to shifts by lenders from the bond market to the mortgage market and from the mortgage market to the bond market (a) because these lenders have had a high cross-elasticity of demand for mortgages with respect to yields on competing investments, and (b) because the schedule showing the quantity of mortgage funds demanded at various interest rates has remained relatively stable over each period of business

20 One fixed-rate theorist, Paul Samuelson, has in fact used this approach. See his "Reflections on Monetary Policy," *Review of Economics and Statistics*, XLII (August, 1960), 266–67; and his "The Current State of the Theory of Interest Rates, with Special Reference to Mortgage Rates," United States Savings and Loan League, *Conference on Savings and Residential Financing* (1960 Proceedings), pp. 18–19.

21 I feel reasonably certain that the great majority of fixed-rate theorists would be inclined to adopt this second explanation. Several have made explicit movements toward it, for example, Lewis, *op. cit.*, p. 445. (Note that the hypothesis that lenders reduce shortages and surpluses of funds by varying maturities and downpayment ratios does not become a "credit rationing" hypothesis until the assumption of fixed interest rates is dropped.)

22 Jack Guttentag, as I indicated earlier, has independently reached the position that fixed rates are not necessary to explain the postwar housing cycles. Guttentag argues, as I do, that the demand for housing, and therefore the demand for mortgage funds, has instead been the critical factor, and presents an analysis of the relation between the postwar business cycles and the postwar housing cycles that is similar in broad outline to the analysis I develop in the next section of this paper (see Guttentag, *op. cit.*, pp. 291, 295). However, Guttentag appears to make the usual assumption that fluctuations in residential construction have been confined to the sector financed with FHA-VA loans; and he does not introduce interest rates, fixed or fluctuating, into his analysis at all.

contraction and recovery. (2) Increases and decreases in the schedule showing the quantity of mortgage funds supplied at various interest rates have caused increases and decreases in the output of new houses (a) because the demand schedule for mortgage funds, whether conventional or FHA-VA, has been not only relatively stable but also elastic, and (b) because the schedule showing the output of new houses at various prices has been elastic. Let me now elaborate these propositions.

When bond yields have decreased (in 1948–49, 1953–54, and 1957–58) as aggregate expenditures outside the housing sector of the economy have decreased, the ratio of mortgage yields to bond yields has increased. Lenders in the aggregate therefore have shifted at the margin from bonds to mortgages, and the supply of mortgage funds has increased.[23] On the demand side of the mortgage market each decrease in aggregate expenditures undoubtedly has led to some decrease in the demand for new houses and therefore in the demand for mortgage funds. However, the built-in stabilizers have moderated significantly the effect of decreases in aggregate expenditures on current disposable income. In addition, there is reason to believe that the effect of decreases in aggregate expenditures on permanent income has been about one-third of their effect on current disposable income, and also reason to believe that the demand for new houses has been a function more of permanent income than of current disposable income.[24] Consequently, I would argue that the decreases in the demand for new houses and for mortgage funds probably have been small absolutely, and almost certainly have been small *relative to* the concomitant increases in the supply of mortgage funds.

Thus, as illustrated in Figure 1, each of the three upturns in residential construction has begun with a shift of the supply schedule of mortgage funds from S_1 to S_2, and with a shift in the demand schedule for new houses and for mortgage funds from d_1 to d_2 and from D_1 to D_2, respectively. As S_2 has moved along D_2, interest rates on mortgage loans have decreased, the marginal cost of investing capital in houses has decreased, and prospective house-buyers have been induced into the market. The demand schedule for new houses has shifted from d_1 to d_2, and the quantity demanded of mort-

gage funds has increased by EF. The output of new houses per time period has increased by mn, and the volume of expenditures on new houses per time period has increased from mp_1 to mp_2. In summary, decreases in aggregate expenditures have produced two major effects on the demand for new houses—a cost of capital effect and an income effect—and the former has dominated the latter. This is the key to the three sharp postwar increases in the output of houses.

Conversely, each time aggregate expenditures have recovered, the demand for new houses has not increased at the same rate, so that bond yields have increased relative to mortgage yields. As a result, lenders in the aggregate have shifted at the margin from the mortgage market to the bond market. This has caused an increase in interest rates on mortgage loans, an increase in the marginal cost of mortgage capi-

23 "In this paper "lenders" refers to life insurance companies, commercial banks, mutual savings banks, and savings and loan associations. However, since savings and loan associations invest almost exclusively in mortgages on single-family houses, changes in the ratio of mortgage yields to bond yields have influenced the volume of mortgage lending of the associations only insofar as it has influenced their inflows. The percentage of mortgage debt on one- to four-family properties held by other lenders (excluding the Federal National Mortgage Association) than these four classes of financial institutions has decreased from 35 per cent in 1945 to about 10 per cent in 1960; in the aggregate these holders have shown no evident tendency to shift toward and away from the mortgage market with increases and decreases in the ratio of mortgage yields to yields on competing investments.

I shall not deal in this paper with the role of the Federal National Mortgage Association in the postwar housing cycles, except to say that there has been a widespread tendency to exaggerate the effect of mortgage purchases by the FNMA on the volume of output of single-family houses. To an important extent the agency's purchases of mortgages have simply supplanted purchases by institutional investors, leaving total purchases largely unchanged.

24 The estimate that permanent income changes only one-third as much as current disposable income in any given year is, of course, Milton Friedman's (Milton Friedman, *A Theory of the Consumption Function* [Princeton, N.J.: Princeton University Press, 1957], esp. chap. iii and ix). By time-series analysis (using annual data from 1915 to 1941, but excluding war years) Richard Muth found that permanent income provides a better explanation of new construction than does current disposable income (Richard F. Muth, "The Demand for Nonfarm Housing" in Arnold C. Harberger [ed.], *The Demand for Durable Goods* [Chicago: University of Chicago Press, 1961], *passim* and p. 76).

Figure 1

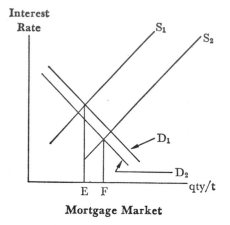

Mortgage Market

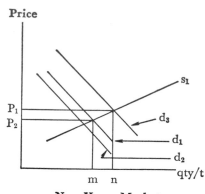

New-House Market

tal, and a consequent decrease in the quantity demanded of mortgage funds and in the demand for new houses. In terms of Figure 1, the supply schedule of mortgage funds has shifted from S_2 back to S_1. The demand schedule for mortgage funds has possibly shifted from D_2 to D_1, and the combined impact of the cost of capital effect and the income effect has been such as to shift the demand schedule for new houses to d_1. Both output and borrowing per time period have decreased to somewhere near their prerecessions levels.[25]

Fundamentally, then, the postwar fluctuations in the output of housing have been contracyclical: periodic decreases in the use of resources elsewhere in the economy have induced compensatory increases in the use of resources in the housing industry; subsequent periodic increases in the use of resources elsewhere in the economy have induced compensatory decreases in the use of resources in the housing industry.[26]

As Charts 1 and 2 show, however, the seasonally adjusted output of houses has begun to increase only just before each of the three troughs in business activity and has begun to decrease each time only after the economy was in its fourth or fifth quarter of recovery. The length of the planning-building-selling sequence involved in residential construction is the major explanation of these lags between turning points in aggregate spending and turning points in the volume of purchases of single-

family houses. Before operative builders (or "tract builders" as they are also called) begin a housing project, they generally secure commitments from lenders to finance the buyers to whom the houses will be sold. The interval between the time when financing is arranged and time when construction actually begins ap-

25 It may well be that some of the house-buyers attracted into the new house market in 1949–50, 1954–55, and 1958–59 had already made plans to buy in some later period, but that what presumably appeared to them as a temporary decrease in the cost of mortgage capital persuaded them to accelerate their purchases. If this is true, fluctuations in the cost of mortgage capital to some extent have redistributed demand through time: some 1949–50 purchases were at the expense of 1951–52 purchases; some 1954–55 purchases were at the expense of 1956–57 purchases; and some 1958–59 purchases were at the expense of 1960–61 purchases. This hypothesis, of course, can explain why the 1960–61 recession generated no upturn in the output of new houses. If the increase in the demand for new houses in 1958 and 1959 shifted the demand schedule for new houses, and therefore the demand schedule for mortgage funds, to the left in 1960 and 1961, an increase in the supply of mortgage funds in 1960 and 1961 would have been followed by a decrease in the cost of mortgage capital, but by no significant increase in the rate of borrowing.
26 Most fixed-rate theorists regarded the postwar housing cycles as a misfortune. Up to the summer of 1961 only four writers (to my knowledge) had pointed to the fact that fluctuations in housing output have run counter to fluctuations in aggregate output: (1) Samuelson, in the two articles cited in n. 20; (2) Grebler, *op. cit.*, pp. 101–8; (3) Guttentag, *op. cit.*, pp. 278–79; and (4) Robert A. Gordon, *Business Fluctuations* (2d ed.; New York: Harper & Bros., 1961), pp. 276, 500.

pears to average three to four months; and construction itself generally takes three to four months, as I noted earlier. As a result, the total lag between the date at which lenders commit funds and the date at which funds are actually disbursed to house-buyers will tend to be from six to eight months.[27] Further, the lag between the date at which lenders commit themselves to buy mortgages and the date at which they add these mortgages to their portfolios can be as much as a year in the case of those lenders (primarily life insurance companies and mutual savings banks) who use mortgage bankers to originate mortgages for them, for there is generally a two- to three-month interval between the date at which mortgage bankers dispense funds and acquire mortgages and the date which they transfer these mortgages to the financial institutions.

Consequently, each of the three sharp increases in the supply of mortgage funds in the postwar period initially has taken the form of an increase in the volume of commitments being made, and only from six to eight months later the form of an increase in dollar lending and borrowing. Each increase in the volume of commitments has first of all induced a fall in the returns demanded by lenders of these funds. Builders have then increased output on the strength of their expectation that the lower cost of mortgage credit would bring about an increase in borrowing and the demand for houses. As their expectations have been fulfilled, dollar lending, borrowing, and buying have increased.

Similarly, each of the three subsequent sharp decreases in the supply of mortgage funds initially has taken the form of a decrease in the volume of commitments made by lenders. Builders have, of course, finished the houses for which they already had arranged financing, but faced with a decrease in the future supply of funds they have cut back on planned production. At the same time, the increase in the cost of mortgage credit brought about by the decrease in the volume of funds being committed has caused a decrease in the demand for houses. (That is, builders have decreased output, and it has been essentially the increase in the cost of mortgage credit that has rationed this smaller supply.) The decrease in dollar lending, borrowing, and buying has followed.

Some Evidence

Charts 3 and 4 provide some evidence in support of the alternative theory I have just stated. Chart 3 shows four yield series for all or part of the period from 1953 through the first half of 1960: (1) average monthly yields on long-term United States government bonds; (2) average monthly yields on corporate bonds of the four highest grades; (3) average monthly yields on FHA-insured mortgage loans on new houses; and (4) average quarterly yields on conventional mortgage loans on new and existing houses combined. Chart 3 confirms that bond yields led mortgage yields down in 1953–54 and 1957–58, and led mortgage yields up in 1954–55 and 1958–59. That is, the ratio of mortgage yields to bond yields first increased with each business contraction, decreased when funds moved into the mortgage market, and then decreased further when funds left the mortgage market.

To show more clearly the relative changes that have taken place in these bond and mortgage yields, I have converted the three monthly yield series in Chart 3 to quarterly yield series and then computed the ratio of average quarterly yields on FHA-insured mortgage loans to average quarterly yields on long-term government bonds and to average quarterly yields on corporate bonds. The results are presented in Panel D of Chart 4. In 1957–58 the ratio of mortgage yields to government-bond yields increased from 1.5 to 1.7 when bond yields decreased, fell back to 1.5 when lenders switched to mortgages, and fell below 1.5 when the economy began to recover from the recession and bond yields turned upward. In 1953–54, however, lenders began to shift to mortgages when the ratio was in the 1.5–1.6 range, while they began to shift from mortgages before the ratio had returned to that level.

The fact that in both 1954–55 and 1958–59 the quarterly volume of mortgage loans in-

27 But from the point of view of the effect of housing upturns (and downturns) on aggregate output and income, the important lag is the three- to four-month lag between the date at which commitments increase and the date at which starts increase. It is increases in *builder* outlays that cause increases in factor incomes. The builders use short-term bank credit to finance these outlays while they are waiting to be reimbursed, so to speak, by house-buyers.

Chart 3 Average yields on mortgage loans and bonds.

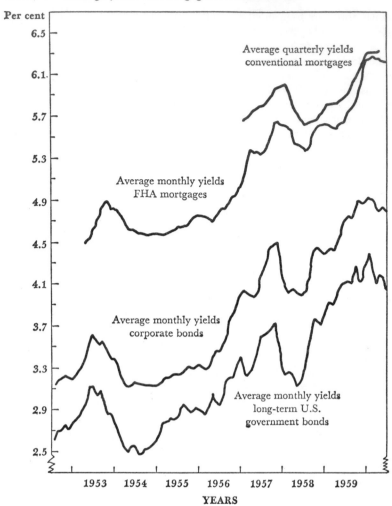

Source: Both bond yield series are available in the *Federal Reserve Bulletin.* The source of the conventional mortgage loan yield series is the FHA. Each quarter FHA field representatives in each of the large metropolitan areas have estimated, largely on the basis of unsystematic sampling, the current average interest rate charged on *all* conventional loans. The estimates of average interest rates for the nation are unweighted averages of the regional averages. All these estimates have been published in the form of press releases.

The FHA is also the source of the series on yields on FHA-insured loans. Each month since April, 1953, field representatives have estimated average *prices* on loans on new houses insured under Section 203 of the amended National Housing Act. From 1953 to 1956 the estimates covered all Section 203 loans on new houses; since 1956 the estimates have covered only Section 203 loans with 25-year maturities and downpayments of 10 per cent or more. National averages are averages of these regional averages, weighted since 1956 by the regional volume of loans and unweighted before 1956. I have converted these estimates of average prices on Section 203 loans into estimates of yields by assuming an average prepayment period of twelve years, the assumption most lenders apparently make in determining effective yield on their own investments. Since 1956 the FHA has published its price estimates in the form of press releases. However, on three occasions when the maximum contract rate on insured loans was increased (December, 1956; August, 1957; and September, 1959), the FHA did not make estimates of average monthly prices for several months after the increase. I have made interpolative estimates of average prices in those months for which the FHA prepared no estimates.

Prior to 1956 the FHA did not publish its price estimates. However, it has since made these estimates available to Jack Guttentag, who converted them to a yield series, using an eight-year prepayment period, for his doctoral dissertation, "Some Studies of the Post-World War II Residential Construction and Mortgage Markets" (unpublished, Columbia University, 1958). Leo Grebler has reproduced Guttentag's series in his National Bureau monograph, *Housing Issues in Economic Stabilization Policy.* I have used the Guttentag data for the 1953–56 period in Chart 3, but I have modified them to conform to my assumption of a twelve-year prepayment period.

Chart 4   Evidence on the cross-elasticity effect.

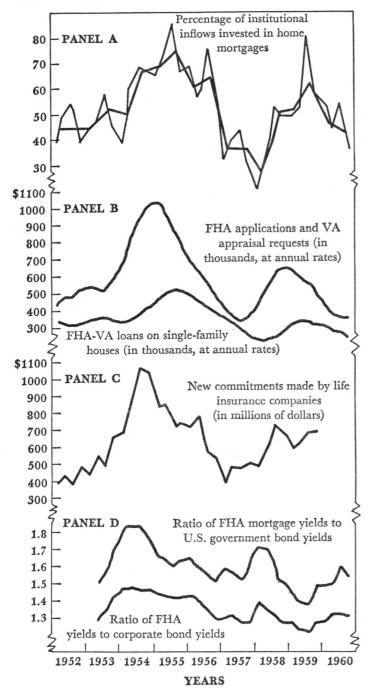

PANEL A

Percentage of institutional inflows invested in home mortgages

PANEL B

FHA applications and VA appraisal requests (in thousands, at annual rates)

FHA-VA loans on single-family houses (in thousands, at annual rates)

PANEL C

New commitments made by life insurance companies (in millions of dollars)

PANEL D

Ratio of FHA mortgage yields to U.S. government bond yields

Ratio of FHA yields to corporate bond yields

YEARS

1952 1953 1954 1955 1956 1957 1958 1959 1960

Source: *Panel A:* Estimates of the quarter-end holdings by life insurance companies, mutual savings banks, commercial banks, and savings and loan associations of mortgage debt on one-to-four family properties are available in United States Housing and Home Finance Agency, *Housing Statistics, Historical Supplement,* June, 1960; and *Housing Statistics,* June 1961. Estimates of quarter-end total assets of life insurance companies and of savings and loan associations, of quarter-end total loans and investments of mutual savings banks, and of quarter-end time and savings deposits of commercial banks can all be found in the *Federal Reserve Bulletin.*

Panel B: I have derived the application and appraisal request series by converting monthly figures into twelve-month moving monthly averages, summing the monthly averages into quarterly totals, and then stating these totals at annual rates. The monthly application and appraisal request data are available in the Housing and Home Finance Agency publications just cited. The FHA-VA loan series is reproduced from Chart 2.

Panel C: The source of the commitment data is the Life Insurance Association of America. The LIAA defines the volume of new commitments in a quarter as the total of monthly commitments made but not used. (*The Federal Reserve Bulletin* now publishes data showing outstanding mortgage loan commitments of all savings and loan associations and of the mutual savings banks located in New York. However, these data have been available on a monthly or quarterly basis only since 1958.)

Panel D: The yields whose ratios I have computed are those that appear in Chart 3.

creased shortly after mortgage yields had decreased is really the only evidence required for the hypothesis that there were shifts to the right of the supply schedule of mortgage funds in 1953–54 and in 1957–58. But the middle two panels of Chart 4 provide some insight into the timing of lender responses to changes in yields. Panel C shows the quarterly dollar volume of new loan commitments made by a group of life insurance companies holding 65 per cent of the total assets of all life insurance companies. Panel B shows the quarterly numerical volume (seasonally adjusted at annual rates) of applications to the FHA for loan insurance and requests made to the VA for appraisals. Generally, as I noted earlier, if builders think houses may be financed with insured or guaranteed loans, they will arrange to have these houses inspected during construction by the FHA or the VA. This involves, first of all, making either loan insurance applications to the FHA or appraisal requests to the VA; many builders will make both applications and appraisal requests on the same houses. Since applications and appraisal requests tend to be made between the dates when buyer financing is arranged and when construction work begins, changes in the volume of these applications and appraisal requests give almost as good an indication of the timing of increases and decreases in the supply of mortgage funds as changes in the volume of commitments made.

Both the Panel C and the Panel B data suggest clearly that lenders had already moved heavily into the mortgage market within about one quarter after the 1953 and the 1957 downturns in aggregate spending, and that lenders had already begun to move away from the mortgage market within one to two quarters after the 1954 and 1958 upturns in aggregate spending.[28] (To give some idea of the interval between the date at which application and appraisal requests are made and that at which loans are actually closed, I have reproduced in Panel B the FHA-VA quarterly loan series of Chart 2; the peaks in the application and appraisal request series led the peaks in the loan series by about two quarters in both 1954–55 and 1958–59, and the trough in the application and appraisal request series led the trough in the loan series by about two quarters in 1957–58.)

Finally, Panel A of Chart 4 provides some confirmation of my hypothesis that it has been a high cross-elasticity of demand for mortgage loans with respect to bond yields on the part of lenders that has caused the shifts in the supply schedule of mortgage funds when the ratio of mortgage yields to bond yields has changed. The heavy line in Panel A shows the percentage of their aggregate inflows in each of the six-month periods during 1952–60 that life insurance companies, savings and loan associations, mutual savings banks, and commercial banks combined have invested in housing mortgages. More precisely, the heavy line shows for each six-month period the ratio of (1) *increases* in mortgage debt outstanding on one-to four-family properties held by these institutions to (2) *increases* in the total assets of life insurance companies and saving and loan associations plus *increases* in the total loans and investments of mutual savings banks plus *increases* in the time and savings deposits of commercial banks.[29] The light line also shows this same ratio, but for three-month rather than six-month periods. (The irregularity in the quarterly ratios stems from the divergence of seasonal patterns in institution inflows and mortgage loan outflows; specifically, inflows tend to be lower in the summer months and higher in the winter months while mortgage

28 The considerably smaller increase in 1958 than in 1954 in the volume of new commitments by life insurance companies to purchase mortgages reflects the shift in portfolio tastes of these institutions discussed in n. 19.

29 With respect to life insurance companies, mutual savings banks, and savings and loan associations, my hypothesis is that changes in the long-term yield structure have caused changes in the portion of *total* inflows invested each time period in mortgages. But with respect to commercial banks, my hypothesis is that changes in the long-term yield structure have caused changes in the portion of increments in time and savings deposits invested each time period in mortgages. Roland Robinson develops the idea that commercial banks relate their mortgage investments to their time and savings deposits rather than to their total deposits at greater length in his *The Management of Bank Funds* (New York: McGraw-Hill Book Co., 1951), pp. 219–20. The National Banking Act limits the mortgage loans of national banks to 60 per cent of time and savings deposits, or 100 per cent of invested equity, whichever is larger.

I speak of increases in time and savings deposits as "inflows" only for expository convenience; time or savings deposit credits, of course, are generally accompanied by demand deposit debits.

acquisitions tend to be higher in the summer months and lower in the winter months.) The percentage of inflows invested in mortgages increased from about 50 per cent in 1952 and 1953 to a high of more than 80 per cent in the summer of 1955, decreased steadily to a low of less than 30 per cent in late 1957 and early 1958, increased sharply to a level of around 65 per cent in the last six months of 1959, and then decreased once again.

There is one further aspect of the data in Panel A that deserves comment. Changes in yield structures have been the primary cause of sharp increases and decreases in the supply schedule of mortgage funds, but they have not been the only cause. Not only has the proportion of inflows invested in mortgage loans increased and decreased with increases and decreases in the ratio of mortgage yields to bond yields, but there has also been a tendency for the inflows themselves to increase (or, more precisely, to continue to increase) at the same time as lenders have shifted to the mortgage market, and to decrease or level off at about the same time as lenders have shifted from the mortgage market. That is, there has been an inflow effect which has tended to buttress the cross-elasticity effect. Apparently each time aggregate spending has decreased and bond yields have decreased relative to mortgage yields *and* to yields paid on claims on financial institutions, individuals and business have tended to shift from goods and bonds to claims on financial institutions; each time aggregate spending has recovered and bond yields have begun to increase relative to yields on claims on financial institutions, individuals and businesses have tended to shift from these claims back to goods and bonds. This inflow effect was especially evident in the case of commercial bank time deposits in 1957–58: there was a very pronounced shift from Treasury bills to time deposits when bill yields fell in late 1957, and a very pronounced shift from time deposits to Treasury bills when bill yields recovered in the last half of 1958.[30]

Table 1 shows two final pieces of evidence in support of my alternative theory of the postwar housing cycles. The first three columns of the table show annual expenditures on private, single-family houses, annual disposable income, and the ratio of the former to the latter. These

data indicate that, during each of the upturn phases of the postwar housing cycles, expenditures on new houses increased at a greater rate than disposable income. By itself, this relationship is consistent with either (1) the hypothesis that decreases in the cost of mortgage capital have shifted the demand schedule for new houses to the right, or (2) the hypothesis that increases in current income have shifted the demand schedule for new houses to the right, assuming a current income elasticity of demand for new houses of more than one. But in conjunction with the fact that mortgage yields have decreased at about the same time that expenditures have increased, allowing for lags in adjustments, the relationship shown in Table 1 is consistent with only the first of the two hypotheses.

The last column in Table 1 shows the percentage changes that have taken place each year in the Boeckh Index of Residential Construction Costs. The Boeckh Index is not ideal for determining changes in the average price of single-family houses. It is essentially a factor price index and consequently includes neither builders' profits nor changes in productivity, both of which probably have fluctuated to some degree in relation to selling prices over the course of each of the three housing cycles. But assuming that percentage changes in the index are a reasonably good approximation of percentage changes in average price, the data in Table 1 support my hypothesis that the supply schedule of new houses has been elastic during each of the upturn phases of the housing cycles. Single-family house starts increased about 45 per cent in 1950 while the index increased 5.5 per cent. Single-family house starts increased about 11 per cent in 1954 and about 15 per cent in 1955 while the index decreased slightly in 1954 and increased 2.9 per cent in 1955. Single-family house starts increased about 12 per cent in both 1958 and 1959 while the index increased 0.9 per cent in 1958 and 3.3 per cent in 1959. However, the fact that the index increased 7.7 per cent in 1951 and 4.5 per cent in 1956 strongly suggests that the supply schedule of new houses shifted to the left in those

30 There is a useful discussion of this shifting between bills and time and savings deposits in United States Federal Reserve Bank of New York, *Monthly Review*, July, 1960, pp. 118–21.

Table 1   Changes in the Relation of Housing Expenditures to Income, and Changes in Construction Costs

Year	Expenditures on Private, Single-Family Houses* (in Billions)	Disposable Income† (in Billions)	Ratio of Expenditures to Disposable Income (Per Cent)	Percentage Changes in Boeckh Index of Residential Construction Costs‡
1948	$ 6.4	$189.3	3.4	—
1949	5.5	189.7	2.9	−2.6
1950	9.8	207.7	4.7	5.5
1951	8.8	227.5	3.9	7.7
1952	8.1	238.7	3.4	2.7
1953	9.5	252.5	3.8	1.8
1954	10.5	256.9	3.9	−0.7
1955	13.8	274.4	5.0	2.9
1956	12.8	292.9	4.4	4.5
1957	11.2	308.8	3.6	1.8
1958	11.0	317.9	3.5	0.9
1959	15.0	337.2	4.5	3.3

* These estimates are the product of single-family house starts lagged four months and annual average construction cost on single-family houses. Average construction cost is defined essentially as the sum of factor payments, excluding those for selling services and including overhead costs and an imputed profit; it excludes land costs. Both the starts series and the construction cost series are available in United States Housing and Home Finance Agency, *Housing Statistics, Historical Supplement*, June, 1960.
† United States Department of Commerce, *Survey of Current Business*, July, 1960.
‡ United States Housing and Home Finance Agency, *op. cit.*

years, thus reinforcing the effect of increases in the cost of mortgage capital on the output of houses.

SUMMARY AND CONCLUSION

I have argued that four conditions have linked the postwar fluctuations in aggregate spending with the fluctuations in the output of single-family houses shown in Chart 2: (*a*) a high cross-elasticity of demand for mortgages with respect to yields on competing investments on the part of lenders; (*b*) a demand schedule for mortgage funds that has been relatively stable over the course of each recession and recovery; (*c*) an elastic supply schedule of new houses; and (*d*) an elastic demand schedule for mortgage funds. I have exhibited evidence in Chart 4 and Table 1 that tends to substantiate the presence of the first three conditions, and if these conditions have been present, the fourth condition has also. Movements in the supply schedule of mortgage funds along the demand schedule of mortgage funds can have caused the increases in borrowing shown in Chart 2 only if the demand schedule has been elastic. A

comparison of Charts 3 and 4 confirms that the percentage decreases in the pure rate of interest (as measured by percentage decreases in government bond yields) at the outset of housing upturns were less than the subsequent percentage increases in the quarterly volume of mortgage borrowing.[31] Following a decrease of about 16 per cent in the pure rate of interest in 1957–58, the quarterly volume of mortgage loans increased about 35 per cent; following a decrease of about 20 per cent in the pure rate in 1953–54, the quarterly volume of mortgage loans increased about 30 per cent; and following a decrease of about 8 per cent in the pure rate in 1948–49 (not shown in Chart 3), the quarterly volume of mortgage loans increased about 50 per cent.[32]

31 Some of the fluctuations in "conventionally financed" houses shown in Chart 2 represent houses financed entirely with equity. However, census data suggest that the percentage of such houses has been less than 5 per cent. See United States Bureau of the Census, *1956 National Housing Inventory*, Vol. II: *Financing Owner-occupied Residential Properties* (1958), p. 3.
32 It is more appropriate to compare decreases in the pure rate of interest than decreases in average yields on mortgage loans with increases in mortgage borrowing. An *n* per cent decrease in the pure rate

But while my explanation of the postwar housing cycles appears to be internally consistent and to fit the data I have exhibited, I must make clear that it is not yet complete. There still remain several unanswered questions concerning the proposition that the demand for mortgage funds has been elastic with respect to the rate of interest. First, I have offered no explanation of the fact shown in Chart 2 that while *absolute* increases in the quarterly volume of FHA-VA loans and in the quarterly volume of conventional loans have been about equal during each of the housing upturns, *percentage* increases in FHA-VA loans have been about twice as large as percentage increases in conventional loans. Second, while I have argued that the marginal cost of investing capital in single-family houses has decreased each time the supply of mortgage funds has increased and interest rates have decreased, I have not determined whether decreases in interest rates have been the *sole* cause of decreases in the marginal cost of mortgage capital. That is, while I have shown that given percentage decreases in interest rates have been *associated* with larger percentage increases in borrowing, I have by no means established that the former completely *explain* the latter.

---

tends to lead to an *n* per cent decrease in yields on given mortgage loans. But a decrease in the pure rate also tends to lead to an increase in the proportion of high risk mortgage loans being made. Consequently, *average* yields on all mortgage loans tend to decrease by less than *n* per cent.

The Sensitivity of Housing Demand to Changes in Mortgage Credit Terms

GEORGE BREAK

Changes in the interest rates, maturities, and loan-to-value ratios prevailing on new home mortgages have an important effect on the demand for housing. This is a proposition that not only commands general acceptance among experts but also forms the basis of the loan insurance and guaranty programs of the Federal Housing Administration (FHA) and Veterans Administration (VA). Yet few economic relationships have defied measurement and verification so successfully. It is the purpose of this appendix to mount—with what will no doubt appear to some as woefully inadequate forces—a preliminary assault upon that citadel, not with the expectation of conquering it once and for all, but with the hope of gathering some useful information concerning its general configurations.

Until quite recently, no comprehensive and reliable time series covering mortgage credit terms have been available. In lieu of such information empirical investigators, if they tackled the problem at all, used series—such as the yields of long-term corporate bonds—which they hoped were closely correlated with mortgage credit terms. Derkson and Tinbergen, for example, found that during the interwar period neither an index based upon the yields of 60 high-grade bonds nor a series showing the average interest rate earned on mortgages held by the 110 largest life insurance companies was closely related to the level of nonfarm residential construction.[1] A similar lack of statistical significance was encountered by Muth when he included Durand's basic yields on 10-year corporate bonds in a least-squares analysis of nonfarm residential construction during the 1915–41 and 1915–53 periods.[2] And Grebler, Blank,

From *The Economic Impact of Federal Loan Insurance* (Washington, D.C.: National Planning Association, 1961), pp. 225–248. Reprinted by permission of the publisher.

1 J. B. D. Derkson, "Long Cycles in Residential Building," *Econometrica*, VIII, April 1940, pp. 97–116, and J. Tinbergen, *Statistical Testing of Business Cycle Theories*, Vol. I, Geneva, League of Nations, 1939, pp. 90–114.
2 Richard F. Muth, *The Demand for Non-Farm Housing*, unpublished doctoral dissertation, University of Chicago, 1958.

and Winnick also noted the low correlation from 1889 to 1952 between residential construction expenditures and either bond yields or average mortgage interest rates in Manhattan.[3] These negative results are suggestive but, applying as they do to variables which may not be closely related to the ones in which we are interested, they cannot be said to demonstrate a lack of relationship between mortgage credit terms and the demand for housing.

During the '50s, the first systematic time series of mortgage interest rates, maturities, and loan-to-value ratios, derived from a sample of urban mortgages taken by the National Bureau of Economic Research,[4] were published. These data were used by John M. Mattila in the most comprehensive and statistically sophisticated analysis of the demand for housing so far undertaken.[5] Unfortunately, Mattila's composite terms-of-credit variable turned out to be highly intercorrelated, over the 1920–41 period studied, with two of his other independent variables, and in the least-squares demand equation its coefficient had the wrong sign and was not statistically significant.[6]

When the present study began, therefore, the quantitative impact of changes in mortgage credit terms on the demand for housing was an intriguing but elusive mystery. It is hoped that the following analysis, which covers both the interwar and postwar periods, will provide sufficient illumination to reveal at least the principal outlines of the complex relationship in which we are interested.

THE BASIC MODEL

Apart from the terms-of-credit variables, our basic model includes those independent variables which other investigators have found to be significantly related to the level of housing construction. The demand for new homes is assumed to be related directly to the level of personal disposable income (expressed in dollars of constant purchasing power), the rate of family formation, and the average maturities and loan-to-value ratios prevailing on home mortgages, but to vary inversely with changes in mortgage interest rates, housing prices (relative to all other prices), and the total stock of housing available for occupancy. Numerous

variations on this theme were explored by lagging the independent variables by different amounts. This was done in order to take into account the varying periods of time that potential home buyers may take to react to changed economic conditions, as well as those time-gaps that typically separate a decision to build a new house from both the initiation and the completion of the resulting construction activity. In addition, the population and housing-price variables were used in some equations only as deflators for other variables, and in other equations as separate estimators in their own right. Finally, for reasons to be given below, it was necessary to employ four different measures of our composite terms-of-credit variable during the postwar period.

The independent variables included in our basic model do not, of course, exhaust the list of factors affecting the level of housing demand. Consumer expectations, as reflected in the attitudes expressed in the Federal Reserve Board's annual Survey of Consumer Finances,[7] may have an important influence, independent of the effects of the variables included in our study, on the buying of new houses. Other things being equal, increasing birth rates and decreasing vacancy rates both should strengthen the demand for housing.[8] These and other factors have been omitted from our analysis either because comprehensive and consistent data were not available for the interwar and post-

3 Leo Grebler, David M. Blank, and Louis Winnick, *Capital Formation in Residential Real Estate: Trends and Prospects*, Princeton, Princeton University Press, 1956, pp. 224–27.
4 J. E. Morton, *Urban Mortgage Lending: Comparative Markets and Experience*, Princeton, Princeton University Press, 1956, Appendix A.
5 John M. Mattila, "An Econometric Analysis of Construction," *Wisconsin Commerce Reports*, IV, Madison, University of Wisconsin, School of Commerce, Bureau of Business Research and Service, 1955.
6 *Ibid.*, pp. 73–76.
7 See, for example, "Preliminary Findings of the 1959 Survey of Consumer Finances," *Federal Reserve Bulletin*, March 1959, p. 253. Two recent discussions of the effects of consumer expectations on consumption expenditures are those of James N. Morgan, "Consumer Investment Expenditures," *American Economic Review*, XLVIII, December 1958, pp. 874–902, and James Tobin, "On the Predictive Value of Consumer Intentions and Attitudes," *Review of Economics and Statistics*, XLI, February 1959, pp. 1–11.
8 See Derkson, *op. cit.*

war periods or because their influence appeared to be less important than that of the variables included. With relatively few observations to analyze, the number of independent variables used had to be severely restricted.

THE DEPENDENT VARIABLES

The basic model just described has been applied to three different measures of the amount of new residential construction:

> The number of private, nonfarm, and permanent housekeeping dwelling units upon which construction was started each year.

> The annual level of expenditures for new, private, and nonfarm dwelling units.

> The average expenditure made each year for new, private, and nonfarm dwelling units.

Since the last two are dollar series which vary both with the level of construction activity and with housing costs, they have been deflated by the Boeckh Residential Construction Cost Index. Each of these series, it may be noted, is subject to important errors. Between 1950 and 1956, for example, it appears that an underestimate of residential construction as large as 20 percent may have been made, and Margaret Reid has shown that the coverage of the housing starts series varied materially during the interwar period.[9] The effects of the latter errors can be eliminated on the basis of Miss Reid's calculations, and an adjusted housing start series (Y'_1) is presented in Table A-1 together with the available statistics for all three dependent variables.

DERIVATION OF THE COMPOSITE TERMS-OF-CREDIT VARIABLE

Given the primary purpose of our analysis, the independent variables of crucial importance are those showing annual changes in the interest rates, maturities, and loan-to-value ratios prevailing on new-home mortgages throughout the entire country. Unfortunately, the data available for this purpose leave a good deal to

be desired, particularly during the postwar period.

As already noted, the National Bureau of Economic Research recently published the first comprehensive mortgage credit-term series for the country as a whole. Derived from a 1947 random sample of 24,000 active and inactive mortgage loans, the data cover the 1920–47 period and show average interest rates, maturities, and loan-to-value ratios for mortgage loans secured by one-family to four-family homes and held by life insurance companies, commercial banks, and savings and loan associations.[10] These time series suffer from a number of shortcomings, the most serious of which arose from a relatively high rate of nonresponse on the part of the smaller lending institutions, the difficulties involved in tracing the complete history of a given mortgage transaction, and the errors to which appraised values (and hence loan-to-value ratios) are known to be subject.[11] In addition, the lending institutions covered by the survey constituted only a part, albeit an important one, of the total nonfarm mortgage market. In 1920, for example, they held 35 percent of the total nonfarm mortgage debt while by 1947 this figure had risen to nearly 58 percent.[12] These are serious deficiencies, the net effect of which is impossible to estimate. Nevertheless, the data are clearly the best available and, accordingly, they have been used for the present study.

For our purposes, the National Bureau series have been combined into a single composite terms-of-credit variable. This was accomplished in two steps. In the first, weighted average interest rates, maturities, and loan-to-value ratios for the three lenders combined were computed (the weights being the relative amounts of new mortgage loans made each year on one-family to four-family homes by life insurance companies, commercial banks, and savings and loan associations).[13] In the second, the three averages thus obtained for each year were combined

9 Margaret G. Reid, "Capital Formation in Residential Real Estate," *Journal of Political Economy,* LXVI, April 1958, pp. 135–37.
10 Morton, *op. cit.,* pp. 173–75.
11 *Ibid.,* pp. 133–38.
12 Computed from the data given by Morton, *op. cit.,* pp. 36 and 169.
13 These weights are given in Grebler, Blank, and Winnick, *op. cit.,* pp. 489–90.

Table A-1 Housing Demand Studies, 1925–1956: Dependent Variables

Year	Y_1 Number of private permanent nonfarm housekeeping dwelling units started (Thousands) (1)	Y'_1 Y_1 adjusted for potential omissions during the interwar period (Thousands) (2)	Y_2 Expenditures for new private nonfarm dwelling units ÷ Boeckh Construction Cost Index (1947–49 = 100) (Billions) (3)	Y_3 Average expenditure (in 1947–49 dollars) per new private nonfarm permanent housekeeping dwelling unit (Thousands) (3) ÷ (1) (4)
1925	937	684	$10.25	$10.94
1926	849	620	10.17	11.97
1927	810	592	9.52	11.75
1928	753	550	8.76	11.63
1929	509	372	6.08	11.94
1930	330	438	3.22	9.77
1931	254	337	2.94	11.57
1932	134	178	1.28	9.52
1933	94	125	0.76	8.21
1934	126	167	0.92	7.30
1935	216		1.76	8.16
1936	305		2.90	9.54
1937	332		3.17	9.53
1938	400		3.38	8.46
1939	458		4.64	10.13
1940	529		5.07	9.56
1941	619		5.57	8.98
1945	208		1.00	4.81
1946	662		4.29	6.47
1947	846		5.85	6.91
1948	913		7.16	7.83
1949	989		7.11	7.19
1950	1,352		10.70	7.91
1951	1,020		8.49	8.32
1952	1,068		8.29	7.75
1953	1,068		8.71	8.16
1954	1,201		10.03	8.35
1955	1,309		12.10	9.24
1956	1,094		10.43	9.53

Sources: Column 1 figures for 1925–28 are from Leo Grebler, David M. Blank, and Louis Winnick, *Capital Formation in Residential Real Estate: Trends and Prospects*, Princeton, Princeton University Press, 1956, p. 332; those for 1929–56 from Department of Commerce, *Business Statistics: a Supplement to the Survey of Current Business*, 1957 Biennial Edition, 1957, p. 38. Column 2 figures for 1925–29 are from column 1 x 65/89; and those for 1930–34 from column 1 x 65/49, (see discussion in text). In column 3, current-dollar values for 1925–52 are from Grebler, Blank, and Winnick, *op. cit.*, p. 335; those for 1953–56, from Department of Commerce, *Construction Review*, February issues, 1955–58, and Boeckh Index; U.S. Department of Commerce, *Construction Review*, various issues and supplements.

Table A-2 The Composite Terms-of-Credit Variable and its Component Parts for One-Family to Four-Family Home Mortgage Loans Made by Life Insurance Companies, Commercial Banks, and Savings and Loan Associations, 1925–47

Year	Weighted average interest rates (1)	Weighted average maturities (years) (2)	Weighted average loan-to-value ratios (3)	Composite terms-of-credit variable (4)
1925	6.6%	8.3	.56	1.42
1926	6.5	8.4	.54	1.41
1927	6.5	8.9	.55	1.34
1928	6.4	8.8	.57	1.28
1929	6.5	9.0	.58	1.26
1930	6.6	8.6	.56	1.36
1931	6.3	8.4	.56	1.34
1932	6.7	8.6	.58	1.33
1933	6.4	7.8	.56	1.46
1934	6.3	9.0	.58	1.21
1935	5.9	11.1	.60	0.89
1936	5.9	11.3	.62	0.85
1937	5.6	12.4	.62	0.74
1938	5.6	14.2	.64	0.61
1939	5.5	14.3	.66	0.58
1940	5.2	15.8	.70	0.47
1941	5.2	15.0	.69	0.50
1946	4.5	14.4	.74	0.42
1947	4.5	15.6	.72	0.40

Sources: In columns 1, 2, and 3, interest rates, maturities, and loan-to-value ratios are from J. E. Morton, *Urban Mortgage Lending: Comparative Markets and Experience*, Princeton, Princeton University Press, 1956, pp. 173–75; and the weights are from Leo Grebler, David M. Blank, and Louis Winnick, *Capital Formation in Residential Real Estate: Trends and Prospects*, Princeton, Princeton University Press, 1956, pp. 489–90.

$$\text{Column 4 equals } \frac{\text{column 1}}{\text{column 2} \times \text{column 3}}$$

into a single value by dividing the interest rate by the product of the average maturity and the average loan-to-value ratio. The result, shown in Table A-2, together with its three component parts, is a mortgage terms-of-credit variable which should vary inversely with the demand for new homes.[14] The use of this composite variable precluded, of course, any assessment of the separate influences on housing demand of its individual parts. This simplification, however, was dictated by two considerations: First is the fact that the three parts were very closely intercorrelated over the period of time covered by the data; and second is the need to limit the number of independent variables included in the studies because of the small number of observations available for analysis.

Comparable information on postwar mortgage credit terms, unfortunately, is not available, and in its place we have set up, relying

14 A similar composite variable was computed by Mattila for his construction model, *op. cit.*, pp. 74–75.

Table A-3 Contract Interest Rates, Average Maturities, and Average Loan-to-Value Ratios on FHA-insured and VA-guaranteed New-Home Mortgages, 1946–56

Year	Contract interest rate		Mean (arithmetic) maturity (years)		Average loan-to-value ratio	
	FHA [a]	VA	FHA	VA	FHA	VA
1946	5.00%	4.00%	21.0	18.8–19.9	.84	.93
1947	5.00	4.00	20.2	19.8–20.6	.81	.90
1948	5.00	4.00	20.1	19.1–20.1	.80	.84
1949	5.00	4.00	22.8	20.9–21.5	.84	.86
1950	5.00–4.75 [b]	4.00	24.1	22.9–23.1	.85	.92
1951	4.75	4.00	23.4	23.9–24.0	.82	.90
1952	4.75	4.00	21.7	23.0–23.1	.80	.87
1953	4.75–5.00 [c]	4.00–4.50 [c]	22.2	23.0–23.1	.83	.89
1954	5.00	4.50	22.9	25.7–25.8	.82	.93
1955	5.00	4.50	25.6	27.4	.85	.95
1956	5.00 [d]	4.50	25.5	27.2	.83	.93

[a] Figures include FHA's insurance premium of 0.5 percent.
[b] Decrease made in April 1950.
[c] Increase made in May 1953.
[d] Rate increased to 5.5 percent on December 4, 1956.
Sources: Figures on FHA are from Housing and Home Finance Agency Annual Reports. Data are for Section 203 single-family homes. The figures for VA are from Veterans Administration, Office of the Director of the Loan Guaranty Service. Maturities computed from a frequency distribution of primary new-home loans. Range represents different assumptions concerning the mean maturity of the 15-year-and-under class.

on a variety of sources listed below, four alternative composite measures. It is hoped that these series provide reasonable boundaries for the true, but unknown, pattern of fluctuation. The remainder of this section is concerned with their derivation. (Readers who are not interested in such details may skip to Table A-4 which presents the final results.)

The measurement of postwar fluctuations in the terms on which new-home mortgage loans were made was carried out as follows:

The first step was to obtain average interest rates, maturities, and loan-to-value ratios for both FHA-insured and VA-guaranteed new-home mortgages. These series, which are presented in Table A-3, are presumably subject to only minor errors, and they are certainly much more reliable than the estimates given below for conventional mortgages.

Next, average interest rates, maturities, and loan-to-value ratios on new-home conventional mortgages were estimated from six principal sources:

a. Open-ended frequency distributions supplied by the U.S. Savings and Loan League. These covered interest rates from 1947–56 and maturities and loan-to-value ratios from 1953–56 on conventional mortgage loans made by savings and loan associations.

b. A series prepared by Saul Klaman for the National Bureau of Economic Research showing average interest rates charged by life insurance companies on conventional one-family to four-family home mortgage loans from 1946–56.

c. Interviews with the financial officers of a number of the larger commercial banks.

d. Qualitative and quantitative information

concerning movements in mortgage credit terms during the postwar period given in building trade journals, *The Wall Street Journal*, and the *Federal Reserve Bulletin*.

e. Median interest rates, maturities, and loan-to-value ratios reported in the 1950 Housing Census for conventional first mortgages made in 1946–48 and 1949–50.[15]

f. Average interest rates, maturities, and loan-to-value ratios for conventional new-home mortgages obtained by the Bureau of Labor Statistics from a sample of 20 cities for use in connection with the Consumer Price Index.[16]

Needless to say, the integration of these bits and pieces of information was a highly subjective process. Separate data for life insurance companies, commercial banks, and savings and loan associations were combined on the basis of the relative shares of the three lenders in annual nonfarm mortgage recordings of $20,000 or less.[17] In many cases, a range of values, rather than a single estimate, was all that it was possible to construct. These minimum and maximum estimates were then arranged into series with high and low degrees of sensitivity to changes in general credit conditions. The

resulting credit-term series for conventional mortgages may be grouped as follows:

1. three insensitive series showing, on the average, relatively stringent credit terms (that is, high interest rates, short maturities, and low loan-to-value ratios);
2. three insensitive series showing relatively liberal credit terms;
3. three sensitive series with stringent terms; and,
4. three sensitive series with liberal terms.

These sets, it is hoped, provide boundaries within which it is reasonable to suppose that the true pattern of postwar conventional mortgage credit terms lies.

The third step was to combine the interest rates on FHA and VA home mortgages with our four interest-rate series for conventional mortgages to form four series covering all three types of financing, and to do the same for

15 U.S. Department of Commerce, Bureau of the Census, *Census of Housing: 1950*, Volume IV, Part I, 1952, pp. 98–100, 145–47, 191–93, and 236–38.
16 See George G. Johnson, "Mortgage Interest Rates in the Consumer Price Index, 1952–57," *Monthly Labor Review*, 80, October 1957, pp. 1240–42.
17 Housing and Home Finance Agency, *Tenth Annual Report*, 1956, p. 278.

Table A-4   Four Measures of the Composite Terms-of-Credit Variable, 1947–57

Year	Z_1 Insensitive and stringent credit terms	Z_2 Insensitive and liberal credit terms	Z_3 Sensitive and stringent credit terms	Z_4 Sensitive and liberal credit terms
1947	0.40	0.40	0.40	0.40
1948	0.48	0.37	0.60	0.47
1949	0.44	0.34	0.48	0.35
1950	0.40	0.32	0.39	0.28
1951	0.42	0.34	0.46	0.34
1952	0.47	0.36	0.53	0.43
1953	0.45	0.34	0.49	0.39
1954	0.39	0.32	0.36	0.30
1955	0.39	0.30	0.35	0.28
1956	0.40	0.31	0.43	0.34
1957	0.44	0.33	0.53	0.39
Arithmetic mean, 1948–57	0.43	0.33	0.46	0.35

Sources: Derived by the procedures described in the text.

maturities and loan-to-value ratios. The weights used for this purpose were the percentages of privately owned, permanent, nonfarm dwelling units started with FHA, VA, and conventional financing. Because shifts from one type of financing to another take place after a housing start has been recorded, these weights are not entirely satisfactory. Alternative computations, therefore, were made for the 1950–54 period using Federal Reserve estimates of the percentages of FHA, VA, and conventional mortgage credit extended on new-home purchases.[18] As it turned out, however, the change in the weighting system did not affect the character of the regression results obtained.

The final step was to combine the comprehensive interest-rate, maturity, and loan-to-value series obtained in the third step into our composite terms-of-credit variable (interest rate divided by the product of the maturity and loan-to-value ratio). The results are shown in Table A-4.

OTHER INDEPENDENT VARIABLES

To measure the effects on housing demand of changes in real disposable income, two basic series were used. The first was the familiar series obtained by deflating Department of Commerce estimates of disposable personal income by the Consumer Price Index. This variable was then used along with a measure of relative housing prices, estimated by computing for each year the ratio between the Boeckh Residential Construction Cost Index and the Consumer Price Index. Alternatively, these two variables were replaced by a single real-income series, obtained by deflating Department of Commerce disposable personal income by the Boeckh Index. These variables were used not only in the unlagged form shown in Table A-5 but also with six-month and 12-month lags behind the dependent-variable values given in Table A-1.

The two remaining independent variables show the annual rate of family formation and annual values of the stock of nonfarm residential wealth (measured in current dollars deflated by the Boeckh Index). Lags of six and 12 months were used here as well. A few studies were also made without the family-formation variable but with the dependent and income variables expressed in per capita terms. The series used, together with their sources, are presented in Table A-5.

Although our postwar measures of mortgage credit terms are undoubtedly the least accurate of the various independent variables, it should

18 Saul Klaman, "Effects of Credit and Monetary Policy on Real Estate Markets: 1952–1954," *Land Economics*, XXXII, August 1956, p. 241.

Table A-5 Other Independent Variables, 1924–41 and 1945–57

Year	X_1 Disposable personal income deflated by the Boeckh Index (1947–1949 = 1.0) (Billions) (1)	X_2 Disposable personal income deflated by the Consumer Price Index (1947–1949 = 1.0) (Billions) (2)	X_3 Boeckh Index divided by Consumer Price Index (1947–1949 = 100) (3)	X_4 Annual increase in total U. S. families (lagged six months) (Thousands) (4)	X_5 Nonfarm residential wealth at June 30 of the preceding year (Billions of 1947–49 dollars) (5)
1924	$141.7	$ 93.8	66.2		
1925	152.0	97.1	63.9	624	$150
1926	155.6	99.6	64.0	572	164
1927	158.5	101.9	64.3	557	174
1928	161.8	105.7	65.4	544	185
1929	166.2	113.4	68.2	507	197

Table A-5 (*Continued*)

1930	$152.8	$104.2	68.2	480	$202
1931	142.1	98.2	69.1	508	198
1932	128.2	83.4	65.1	496	192
1933	120.3	82.6	68.7	442	193
1934	125.9	90.9	72.2	446	203
1935	144.7	99.3	68.6	479	196
1936	158.8	111.6	70.3	501	195
1937	152.4	115.6	75.9	498	196
1938	136.9	109.0	79.6	505	189
1939	144.0	118.5	82.3	542	192
1940	150.7	127.0	84.3	574	195
1941	170.3	143.6	86.8	725	201
1945	$214.6	$195.6	91.2		
1946	206.6	190.8	92.3	675	$192
1947	181.3	177.0	97.6	925	199
1948	179.0	182.5	102.0	1,463	194
1949	184.3	184.9	100.3	1,624	196
1950	191.5	200.6	104.8	1,292	212
1951	194.9	203.7	104.5	1,074	210
1952	198.8	208.6	104.9	845	218
1953	206.4	218.7	105.9	784	224
1954	211.6	221.7	104.8	615	230
1955	218.1	236.0	108.2	927	242
1956	222.0	247.3	111.4	943	248
1957	228.1	250.1	109.7	783	255

Sources: In column 1, disposable personal income in current dollars, 1924–28 figures are unofficial estimates of the Department of Commerce given by J. J. Hughes, Jr., in *Demand Relations in Housing*, unpublished doctoral dissertation submitted at Brown University, 1957. Those for 1929–56 are from U.S. Department of Commerce, *Survey of Current Business*, National Income Supplements and Issues. The Boeckh Residential Construction Cost Index is from U.S. Department of Commerce, *Construction Review*, various issues and supplements. This variable was lagged six months primarily by the use of quarterly data for disposable personal income and monthly data for the Boeckh Index (weighted by the Department of Commerce seasonal index for housing starts). In the earlier years when this information was not available, linear interpolation between the values given in column 1 was used instead. Column 2, Consumer Price Index, is from U.S. Department of Labor, Bureau of Labor Statistics, *Monthly Labor Review*, various issues. And column 3 is derived from sources given above.

In column 4, 1925–47 figures are from C. F. Roos and others, *Statistics and Economics of Housing*, printed for the Joint Committee on Housing, 1948, p. 6. Those for 1948–56 are from U.S. Department of Commerce, Bureau of the Census, *Current Population Reports: Population Characteristics*, Series P-20, No. 76, July 5, 1957, p. 2, Table 3. The annual increase was computed from the number of families in existence at various dates from 1925 to 1947 and from the number of households in existence in March or April of the years 1948–56. Where necessary these figures were shifted backward or forward several months by linear interpolation. A consistent series for nonfarm family formation, which most experts believe to be more closely related to the volume of residential construction than a series based on both rural and urban families, could not be obtained because of a change in the Bureau of the Census definition of nonfarm households in 1950. The data given in column 4 seem to be the best available substitute.

The values in column 5 for 1945–56 were supplied by Raymond W. Goldsmith. Those for 1924–44 are from Raymond W. Goldsmith, Dorothy S. Brady, and Horst Mendershausen, *A Study of Saving in the United States*, Princeton, Princeton University Press, 1956, Volume III, p. 14, their column 4 adjusted to comparability with the 1945–56 values.

be noted that the others are by no means free of error. Perhaps the next weakest series is the Boeckh Residential Construction Cost Index which was used in several places as a deflator as well as in the numerator of the relative-price-of-housing variable. The Boeckh Index is a fixed-weight index number measuring the change in price of a limited number of building materials and types of union labor in 20 large cities. It does not, therefore, reflect the effects on construction costs of changes in the product-mix, of divergent movements in union and nonunion wage rates, or of different rates of change in costs in the 20 cities as compared with the rest of the country. Moreover, the index is not a direct measure of changes in housing prices since it omits builders' profits, closing expenses, and the cost of land improvement, and does not take into account the effects of changes in on-site productivity.

Grebler, Blank, and Winnick have shown that over the 1890–1934 period, for which they were able to construct a housing price index, the Boeckh Index had approximately the same long-term trend but fluctuated considerably less from one year to the next than did housing prices.[19] For our purposes, then, the Boeckh Index probably is unduly insensitive to short-run price fluctuations and, in addition, it may well overstate the long-run price increase because of its inadequate treatment of improvements in quality and productivity.[20] For the present, however, it appears to be the best available measure of changes in housing prices.

With regard to the remaining independent variables, it should be noted that the family-formation series, being based on estimates of the number of families in existence at different points in time, is especially sensitive to small errors in those estimates.[21] In addition, as noted in Table A-5, a series on nonfarm family formation would have been theoretically preferable. Finally, Margaret Reid has raised serious questions concerning the reliability of the available measures of residential wealth.[22] Clearly, much work remains to be done on such series.

One's general impression, therefore, is that attempts to estimate statistically the structural parameters of an aggregate housing-demand function are singularly subject to the disturbing effects of the measurement errors in many of the relevant variables. As a result, it may

well be many years before a definitive study is possible. In the meantime, it is hoped that exploratory analyses of the type attempted here can reduce some of the uncertainty concerning the sensitivity of housing construction to changes in income, mortgage terms of credit, family formation, and other factors.

PERIOD STUDIED AND METHOD OF ANALYSIS

Our basic model and its principal variants were first analyzed for the entire 1925–56 period, with 1942–45 (when the housing market was dominated by wartime conditions) omitted. It was soon apparent that a significant change in the nature of the relationships took place between the interwar and the postwar periods, and separate analyses were accordingly made for 1925–41 and 1946–56. In the postwar studies, 1946 and 1947 typically conformed very poorly with the relationships that appeared to prevail during the other nine years—a result which is not surprising considering the unusual forces to which the housing market was subjected immediately after the end of World War II. The postwar results presented in the next two sections, therefore, were derived for the 1948–56 period only.

Linear regression functions were fitted to the variables both by successive-approximation graphic methods and by classical least-squares analysis. Because of its greater flexibility, graphic analysis was used in every case; the income-construction relationship was treated first, followed in some cases by the relation between family formation and the level of construction, and in others by the relation between mortgage terms of credit and construction. In this and in other ways, every attempt was made to ensure that the terms of credit relationship did not arbitrarily determine the other statistical results, and close attention was paid to the effects of high intercorrelation whenever it

19 Grebler, Blank, and Winnick, *op. cit.*, pp. 344–58.
20 Reid, *op. cit.*, pp. 143–44.
21 That is to say, an error that is small relative to the number of families in existence at a given time may be large in relation to the annual increase in the number of families.
22 Reid, *op. cit.*

existed between pairs of independent variables. The reasonableness of the results obtained by these means was then checked by the computation of a more limited number of least-squares studies.

FINDINGS: EFFECTS OF THE MORTGAGE TERMS-OF-CREDIT VARIABLE

Prior to World War II, residential construction apparently was not sensitive to changes in mortgage credit terms. As column 4 of Table A-6 shows, all of our 1925–41 studies yielded mean elasticities between −0.1 and −0.4. During the first 10 years of this period, mortgage credit terms were relatively stable, but between the first half of the 1930's and 1940–41, our composite terms-of-credit variable fell by 0.85 points (Table A-2). On the basis of the net regression coefficients shown in column 3 of Table A-6, such a decline would be expected to stimulate the construction of 40,000 to 110,000 additional homes, or something between 10 and 30 percent of the actual increase in the number of housing starts that took place between the two periods. Evidently, the liberalization of mortgage credit terms, which began in 1934, had some effect on the level of residential construction but, considering the extent to which the liberalization was carried, its influence was surprisingly small.

During the postwar period, on the other hand, housing construction appears to have been significantly more sensitive to the terms on which mortgages could be obtained. A glance at Part C of Table A-6 will indicate not only that most of the mean elasticities exceeded −0.4 but that a significant number of them were greater than −1.0. The range of values obtained for the net regression coefficients was rather large, the two insensitive terms-of-credit variables, as would be expected, yielding higher values than the two sensitive series. In study G-7, for example, a 0.1-point decline in Z_3 (sensitive and stringent credit terms) was accompanied, on the average, by an increase of 70,000 in housing starts; and the corresponding value for Z_1 (insensitive and stringent terms) was 220,000 housing starts (Table A-6, column 3). Similarly, wide ranges were obtained for the

other postwar studies. If our assumption is correct, however, that our four Z variables represent extreme patterns for the postwar behavior of mortgage credit terms, we can at least say something useful about the minimum influence of that factor. From the results shown in Table A-6, it appears that in recent years a 0.1-decline in the composite terms-of-credit variable stimulated the construction of at least 150,000 new homes and the expenditure of $1 billion or more 1947–49 dollars for that purpose.

It would, of course, be very useful to know something about the relative importance of the three components of the composite terms-of-credit variable. As a step in this direction, our loan-to-value series were taken separately, and the data on interest rates and maturities were then converted into the level monthly payment required to amortize a mortgage loan of $1,000. The two resulting time series, unfortunately, were too highly correlated over the period of time studied to permit a separate estimate of the influence of either. The level-monthly-payment variable, however, did yield results closely similar to those already obtained for the composite terms-of-credit variable. During the postwar period, for example, the elasticity of housing starts with respect to required level monthly payments varied between −0.7 and −2.8, and, with expenditures on residential construction as the dependent variable, the corresponding elasticities ranged from −0.8 to −2.6. Because of the high intercorrelation noted above, these results—which, if anything, show a greater sensitivity of housing demand to mortgage credit terms than does our composite variable alone—should be attributed not only to the influence of changes in mortgage interest rates and maturities, but to the effects of fluctuating loan-to-value ratios as well.

Finally, it must be noted that not all of our studies were successful in yielding reasonable estimates of the influence of mortgage credit terms on housing demand. As already noted, all of the analyses of the entire 1925–56 period, with the single exception of Study G-19, showed either no net regression of the housing variables on the credit series or a positively sloped (occasionally U-shaped) relationship. Nor did Study G-19, with its very small regression coefficients and elasticities, depart greatly from this general pattern. In view of the im-

Table A-6 Sensitivity of Residential Construction to Changes in the Composite Terms-of-Credit Variable: Summary of Findings of Graphic and Least-Squares Multiple Regression Analyses

Type of study and number (G = graphic LS = least-squares) (1)	Dependent variable (2)	Change in the dependent variable accompanying a 0.1-increase in the terms-of-credit variable [a] (3)	Elasticity at the point of means (4)	Other independent variables included in study (5)	$\bar{R}^2$ (6)	R^2 (7)
A. 1925–41 G–1	Y'_1 (housing starts in thousands)	−5 to −13	−0.1 to −0.4	X_1 lagged 6 months; X_4 ; X_5	.81	
LS–1	"	−5 (6)	−0.1	"	.85	
G–2	"	−10	−0.3	X_1 lagged 1 year; X_4 and X_5 lagged 6 months		
G–3	"	−5	−0.1	X_2 lagged 1 year; X_3; X_4	.70	
G–4	Housing starts per capita (thousands per million people)	−0.1	−0.3	X_2 per capita lagged 1 year; X_5		
G–5	Y_2 (real expenditures on residential construction in billions of dollars)	−0.06	−0.3	X_2 and X_3 lagged 1 year; X_4 lagged 6 months		
G–6	Y_2 per capita	−0.3	−0.2	X_2 per capita lagged 1 year; X_3; X_5		
B. 1925–41 and 1946–47 LS–2	Y_1	−15 (7.7)	−0.4	Nonfarm Disposable Income, lagged 1 year ÷ the unlagged Boeckh Index; X_4; X_5	.84	
C. 1948–56 G–7	Y_1 (housing starts in thousands)	−220 Z_1 −160 Z_2 − 70 Z_3 −120 Z_4	−0.9 −0.5 −0.3 −0.4	X_1 lagged 6 months; X_4; X_5	0	.5
LS–3	"	−160 Z_4 (56)	−0.5	"	.66	.8
G–8	"	−155 Z_4	−0.5	X_1 lagged 1 year; X_5 lagged 6 months		

G–9	"	$-290\ Z_1$ $-460\ Z_2$ $-140\ Z_3$ $-180\ Z_4$	-1.1 -1.4 -0.7 -0.5	X_2 and X_3 lagged 1 year	.59	.7
G–10	Y_1	$-170\ Z_1$ $-\ 85\ Z_4$	-0.6 -0.3	X_1; X_4; X_5	.10	.44
G–11	Y_1	$-250\ Z_1$ $-\ 95\ Z_4$	-0.9 -0.3	X_2; X_3; X_5	0	.47
G–12	Housing starts per capita	$-4\ Z_1$ $-5\ Z_2$ $-2\ Z_3$ $-2\ Z_4$	-2.4 -2.3 -1.0 -1.1	X_2 and X_3 lagged 1 year; X_5 lagged 6 months		
G–13	Y_2 (real expenditures on residential construction in billions of dollars)	$-3.0\ Z_1$ $-1.6\ Z_2$ $-1.2\ Z_3$ $2.2\ Z_4$	-1.3 -0.6 -0.5 -0.7	X_1 lagged 1 year	.59	.7
G–14	Y_2	$-1.9\ Z_1$ $-0.6\ Z_4$	-0.9 -0.2	X_1; X_4	.42	.71
G–15	Y_2	$-1.5\ Z_1$ $-0.6\ Z_4$	-0.7 -0.2	X_2; X_3	.57	.73
LS–4	Y_2 (real expenditures on residential construction in billions of dollars)	$-1.5\ Z_4$ (0.7)	-0.6	X_1 lagged 1 year; X_4 and X_5 lagged 6 months	.61	.8
G–16	"	$-3.2\ Z_1$ $-4.0\ Z_2$ $-1.0\ Z_3$ $-1.7\ Z_4$	-1.5 -1.4 -0.5 -0.6	X_2 and X_3 lagged 1 year	.77	.8
G–17	Y_2 per capita (dollars)	$-21\ Z_1$ $-34\ Z_2$ $-\ 7\ Z_3$ $-\ 7\ Z_4$	-1.5 -1.9 -0.4 -0.6	X_2 per capita and X_3 lagged 1 year; X_5 lagged 6 months		
G–18	Y_3 (average housing expenditures, thousands of 1947–49 dollars)	$-.24\ Z_1$ $-.40\ Z_2$ $-.18\ Z_3$ $-.12\ Z_4$	-0.1 -0.2 -0.1 -0.1	X_1 lagged 1 year; X_4 lagged 6 months	.80	.9
LS–5	"	$-.05\ Z_1$ (0.4)	-0.03	X_1 lagged 1 year; X_4 and X_5 lagged 6 months	.82	.9
D. 1925–41 and 1947–56 G–19	Y_1	-9 to -14	-0.1 to -0.2	X_1 lagged 6 months; X_4; X_5		

a Figures in parentheses are the standard errors of the net regression coefficients given immediately above.
Note: For values of the above variables X, Y, and Z, see Tables A-5, A-1, and A-4, respectively.

portant and long-continuing effects which World War II has had on the housing market together with the unsettled state of post-Korean international relations, these failures are not particularly disturbing.

More surprising, however, was the very slight influence which mortgage terms of credit appear to have on the average constant-dollar expenditure for new houses. In a number of cases, no relationship at all was found; in others, the net regression coefficients were very small indeed (see Studies G-18 and LS-5 in Table A-6). As a check on these results, an analysis of the home purchases in 1949 and 1950 of families with 1949 incomes of less than $6,000 was made from data given in the 1950 Census of Housing.[23] Those buying with the aid of a conventional mortgage, for example, spent approximately $6,700 for a single-family home, whereas those receiving an FHA-insured mortgage (and hence more liberal credit terms) spent $8,700 on the average. This $2,000 excess, of course, is only a rough first approximation to the influence on housing expenditures of more liberal loan terms. The FHA families not only had a higher average income than those using conventional financing ($3,900 as compared with $3,200), but also may well have been somewhat smaller in size (FHA families in all income groups contained 3.5 persons on the average in contrast with the 3.7 average size of families obtaining conventional loans). And it is well established that larger incomes and smaller family sizes both tend to increase housing expenditures.[24] When rough allowances were made for the effects of these differences between FHA and conventional home purchasers, however, the amounts spent by FHA families remained higher by some $500, a differential which may, therefore, be largely attributable to the more liberal FHA mortgage terms.[25] The extent to which these terms were more liberal in 1949–50 is indicated by the fact that our composite variable was 0.8 for conventional mortgages (based on a 5-percent median interest rate, a 10-year median maturity, and a 0.61 average loan-to-value ratio), but only 0.3 for FHA mortgages (4.5-percent interest rate, 20-year maturity, and 0.81 loan-to-value ratio).[26] On this basis, it appears that a decrease of 0.1 in the composite measure was associated with a $100 increase in housing expenditures, a re-

sult that falls at the lower end of the range of comparable estimates obtained from the time series studies. Similar values were obtained when the housing expenditures of recipients of conventional and VA-guaranteed mortgages were compared and also when the analysis was made only for families with incomes under $5,000 a year.[27]

23 U. S. Department of Commerce, Bureau of the Census, *op. cit.*, pp. 274–82, Table 16abc.
24 See, for example, H. S. Houthakker, "An International Comparison of Household Expenditure Patterns, Commemorating the Centenary of Engel's Law," *Econometrica*, 25, October 1957, pp. 532–51.
25 The allowances were based on Houthakker's results for all classes of cities in the United States in 1950, *op. cit.*, p. 542—that is, on an average elasticity of housing expenditures with respect to total consumer expenditures of 0.9 and an elasticity of −0.3 with respect to the number of persons in the family. These adjustments are rough because Houthakker's elasticities apply to annual housing expenditures (including property taxes, insurance and interest payments, financing charges, and the cost of repairs and maintenance) rather than to the initial purchase price of a new house, and because our family-size data apply to all income groups rather than to the middle-income and low-income groups only. In addition, we have assumed that the elasticity of housing expenditures with respect to income may be taken to be very close to the elasticity of these expenditures with respect to total consumer spending. Although these approximations appear reasonable in the absence of better data, they may, of course, subject our estimates to an appreciable error.
26 U. S. Department of Commerce, Bureau of the Census, *op. cit.*, pp. 191–93 and 236–38, Tables 5abc and 12abc.
27 The results may be summarized as follows:

Primary Families and Individuals with Annual Incomes of Less than $5,000 and $6,000

	Under $5,000	
	Excess of FHA purchase price over conventional purchase price	*Excess of VA purchase price over conventional purchase price*
Gross amount............$2,200		$1,300
Excess expected on basis of income differential.................. 1,200		700
Excess expected on basis of family-size differential.............. 100		0
Remaining excess (attributable at least in part to more liberal credit terms)............. 900		600
Terms-of-credit differential.................. −0.5		−0.6

Chart continued on pg. 119

None of our studies, therefore, indicated a high degree of sensitivity of average expenditures per house to changes in mortgage credit terms. This finding, it should be noted, is not completely consistent with our estimates of the influence of the composite terms-of-credit variable on the number of new houses constructed and on aggregate expenditures for new homes. If more liberal loan terms do not induce larger average expenditures per house, for example, one would expect that the ratio of credit-induced aggregate housing expenditures to the number of similarly induced new housing starts would be approximately equal to the average expenditure per house during the period of time studied. Most of our regression coefficients for housing expenditures, however, ranged between $1 billion and $4 billion, and when these are divided by the regression coefficients for housing starts which varied from 100,000 to 300,000 (see Table A-6), average expenditures per house of $10,000 or more are obtained. Since the average expenditure per house during the 1948–56 period was only $8,250 (computed from the values of Y_3 given in Table A-1), the implication is that variations in mortgage terms of credit did have an important influence on average home expenditures. The resolution of this inconsistency in our findings must, unfortunately, await the appearance of more (and better) data concerning the factors affecting the volume of residential construction during the postwar period.

FINDINGS: EFFECTS OF OTHER INDEPENDENT VARIABLES

Table A-7 presents the elasticities of housing demand (each measured at the point of means) with respect to the other independent variables included in our model, together with the comparable finds of other empirical studies. Several features of these data are notable:

For all four variables, the elasticities tend to be greater than 1.0 (in absolute terms), indicating that residential construction was relatively sensitive to changes in these factors.

For the most part, our postwar elasticities were less than the corresponding prewar values. As we have already noted, exactly the

reverse relationship prevailed between the prewar and postwar elasticities with respect to the terms-of-credit variable. This shift in the nature of the relationships studied is intriguing, but it cannot be regarded as firmly established until more postwar data are available for analysis.

The majority of the income elasticities fell between 1.0 and 2.0, but the higher values obtained by Mattila and Klein are important exceptions since they were obtained by the application of more advanced statistical techniques than were employed here.

Residential construction typically was especially sensitive to the relative price-of-housing variable, although a few of our postwar studies showed a sufficiently high intercorrelation between prices and the income or terms-of-credit variable to make estimates of the separate influences of these factors difficult, if not impossible. If, as suggested above, housing prices are more volatile in the short run than construction costs (on which our relative price variable was based), the price elasticity of housing demand should be somewhat smaller than our figures would indicate.

The housing-demand elasticities, with respect to both the rate of family formation and the stock of residential wealth were

Primary Families and Individuals with Annual Incomes of Less than $5,000 and $6,000 (Continued)		
	Under $6,000	
	Excess of FHA purchase price over conventional purchase price	Excess of VA purchase price over conventional purchase price
Gross amount............	$2,000	$1,200
Excess expected on basis of income differential..................	1,400	700
Excess expected on basis of family-size differential..............	100	0
Remaining excess (attributable at least in part to more liberal credit terms).............	500	500
Terms-of-credit differential..................	—0.5	—0.6

Table A-7 Sensitivity of Residential Construction to Changes in Disposable Personal Income, Relative Housing Prices, the Rate of Family Formation, and the Stock of Residential Wealth: Comparison of Findings with Results of Other Studies

Study number or authors of other studies	Elasticity [a] of housing demand with respect to:				Period of time covered (5)
	Disposable personal income (1)	Relative price of housing (2)	Rate of family formation (3)	Stock of residential wealth (4)	
A. Housing starts					
G-1	2.0		1.2	−2.5	1925–41
G-7	1.6		0.05	−0.9	1948–56
LS-1	2.0		1.4	−2.4	1925–41
LS-3	5.6				1948–56
G-2	1.3		2.3	−1.3	1925–41
G-8	0.5		0.0	−0.1	1948–56
G-3	1.2	−1.3	3.2	0.0	1925–41
G-9	0.4	−1.9	0.0	0.0	1948–56
G-10	1.1		0.1	−0.2	1948–56
G-11	0.9	−0.7		−0.7	1948–56
G-4	2.0	0.0		−4.4	1925–41
G-12	1.4	−5.1		−1.0	1948–56
Chawner	1.0		4.5		1914–37
LS-2	1.0		1.1	−3.1	1925–41 1946–47
G-19	2.6–2.9		3.2	−0.9	1925–41 1947–56
B. Constant-dollar housing construction					
G-5	1.2	−0.2	5.5	0.0	1925–41
G-13	2.0		0.0	0.0	1948–56
G-14	2.2		0.1	−0.2	1948–56
G-15	1.4	−0.7		0.0	1948–56
G-16	1.3 to 1.8	−2.6 to −5.4	0.0	0.0	1948–56
LS-4	1.7		0.0	−0.5	1948–56
Suits and Goldberger	1.6			−0.02	1929–41 1946–55

Table A-7 *(Continued)*

Study number or authors of other studies	Elasticity [a] of housing demand with respect to:				
	Disposable personal income (1)	Relative price of housing (2)	Rate of family formation (3)	Stock of residential wealth (4)	Period of time covered (5)
B. Constant-dollar housing construction (continued)					
Klein	3.4		1.9		1921–41
Mattila	3.3		0.6	−0.6	1919–41
					1946–50
G–6	2.5	−0.4		−4.5	1925–41
G–17	2.4	−2.9		−0.2 to −0.6	1948–56
Muth	5.4	−5.5		−5.1	1915–16
					1919–41
	1.0	−1.2			1950
C. Average expenditures per house					
G–18	1.3		0.2	0.0	1948–56
LS–5	4.0		1.3	−2.1	1948 56
Reid	2.3	−2.4			1920–29
	2.6	−1.9			1948–56
	2.0	−1.6			1950

[a] Elasticities are measured at the point of means.
Studies cited: Lowell J. Chawner, "The Residential Building Process: An Analysis in Terms of Economic and Other Social Influences," in *Housing, the Continuing Problem*, National Resources Planning Board, 1940.
Daniel B. Suits, "A Statistical Model of Economic Activity as Applied to 1957," *Fourth Annual Conference on the Economic Outlook*, Ann Arbor, Department of Economics of the University of Michigan, 1957, pp. 35–45.
Lawrence R. Klein, *Economic Fluctuations in the United States, 1921–41*, New York, Wiley, 1950.
John M. Mattila, *An Econometric Analysis of Construction in Wisconsin Commerce Reports*, IV, April 1955, published by the Bureau of Business Research and Service of the University of Wisconsin.
Richard F. Muth, "The Demand for Non-Farm Housing," *Econometrica*, 25, April 1957, pp. 365–66 and his unpublished doctoral dissertation filed at the University of Chicago, 1958.
Margaret G. Reid, "Capital Formation in Residential Real Estate," *Journal of Political Economy*, LXVI, April 1958, pp. 131–53.

highly variable, ranging all the way from zero to values as high as four and five. Both of these, of course, are series that are subject to a wide degree of measurement error.

Our own results are reasonably similar to the findings of other empirical investigators. The six studies cited in Table A-7 were selected on the basis of their comparability with our own data but, even so, differences inevitably exist between their models and ours. These divergencies do not appear to be important enough to invalidate the rough sort of comparisons in which we are interested here, and we have consequently not attempted to go into further detail on the point.

SUMMARY

Because of serious deficiencies in the available data, empirical analyses of the parameters entering into the housing-demand relationship are likely to remain in a relatively crude state for some years to come. In the meantime, rough estimates of the effects of various factors can be made, and in this study we have attempted to provide them for mortgage terms of credit. The value of these estimates rests, of course, on their usefulness in predicting fluctuations in residential construction. . . .

A Theory of Fluctuations in Residential Construction Starts

SHERMAN J. MAISEL

Housing production, which has earned the dubious distinction of ranking among the most cyclically volatile industries, is important in the economy because of its large size. Since shifts in housing starts have both an immediate impact on earnings and a delayed reaction on shelter standards, fiscal and monetary policies frequently include programs aimed directly at control of the rate of construction. This article focuses on housing fluctuations and presents a market model designed specifically to aid in their analysis.

Figure 1 illustrates the violent movements which have characterized housing starts. On an annual basis, movements of 30 to 40 per cent from peaks to troughs occurred three times between 1950 and 1962. Starts in the highest quarter exceeded those in the lowest by more than 50 per cent—a difference at annual rates of more than 600,000 dwelling units.[1]

Table 1 relates these starts for 1950–60 to the more basic market forces of demand and inventory changes. Final demand (12,478,000), which approximated 91 per cent of starts, is measured by net household formation plus net removals. For that period, household formations (9,645,000) equaled approximately 70 per cent of private starts; net removals (2,833,000), covering a wide variety of gains and losses to the stock that may offset or augment construction of new dwellings, equaled an additional 21 per cent.[2]

Houses not absorbed by final uses increase the inventory. Table 1 shows a rise in available vacancies and a small drop in the inventory of units under construction. Inventory increases for the decade of only 9 per cent of starts reflect the well-recognized fact that, over any extended period, basic demand normally accounts for a greater percentage of the total.

Figure 1 and Table 2 (Appendix), however, present the opposite picture. For the decade, quarterly changes in inventories accounted for 85 per cent of the variance in starts, while the complementary movements in basic demand were related to less than 15 per cent. In shorter periods such as a quarter or a year, the market forces are reversed. The primary correlation is that between starts and inventory shifts.

The theory of the market developed in this article explains this sharp divergence. The short

From *American Economic Review* (June 1963),— pp. 359–383. Reprinted by permission of the American Economic Association and the author.

[1] The starts data in this article are based on official Census estimates for the period since 1959. For 1950–58 the original data of the Bureau of Labor Statistics have been revised to agree with both the new Census concepts and the 1960 Census. The appendix contains both data and explanations of the revised series of starts, plus those for other series estimated especially for this study.

[2] For the decade of the 1920's, final demand balanced approximately 75 per cent of starts. For the 1930's it was about 110 per cent. The low demand and high vacancy factor for the 1920's was clearly important in aggravating the depression.

Figure 1 Housing starts, final demand, and changes in housing inventories in the United States quarterly totals, 1950–1961.

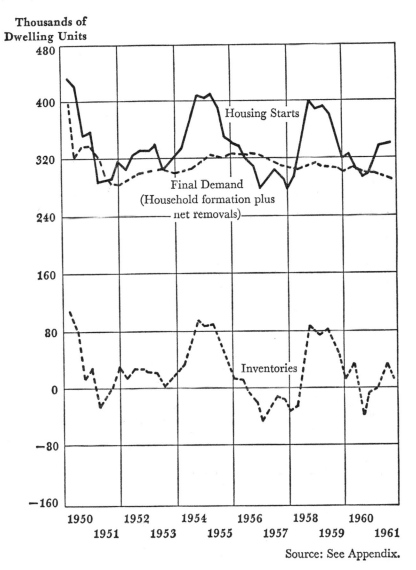

Thousands of
Dwelling Units

Housing Starts

Final Demand
(Household formation plus
net removals)

Inventories

Source: See Appendix.

run instabilities that characterize housing starts have numerous causes deeply imbedded in the construction process. These forces primarily create fluctuations in vacancies and inventories under construction. The movements shown in Figure 1 are of a type similar to the inventory cycles experienced in manufacturing. In contrast, movements in underlying demand form a more stable equilibrium around which inventories fluctuate. While shifts in demand could cause sharp movements in starts, the forces necessary for such reactions—particularly heavy income declines—have not occurred in the postwar market.

Section I describes the logic of this theory and its main variables, contrasting the impact of these variables on inventories and on final demand. Section II presents the statistical testing of the model. Section III analyzes the fitted equation.

Table 1 Disposition of Total Estimated Starts of Private Housing Units in the United States. April 1, 1950 to March 31, 1960

Net Additions to Households:			9,645,000
Net Removals:			
Losses from available stock:			
Mergers from existing units	900,000		
Demolitions	2,050,000		
Other losses	1,947,000		
Vacancies held off market	692,000		
Subtotal:		5,589,000	
Increase in seasonal units:		337,000	
Offsetting gains, (negative removals):			
Public housing completions	425,000		
Trailers, institutional, group quarters, etc.	962,000		
From conversions of other structures, splits, etc.	1,700,000		
Decrease in dilapidated vacancies	6,000		
Subtotal:		−3,093,000	
Total Net Removals			2,833,000
Increase in Available Vacant Units			1,245,000
Change in Inventory under Construction			−37,000
Total Private Housing Starts:			13,686,000

Source: Adapted from *U.S. Census of Housing 1960 Components of Inventory Change,* HD(4), Part 1 A-1, Table C; *U.S. Census of Housing 1950,* Vol. 1, Part I; and 1960 *Advance Reports,* HC(A2)-1. Adaptation necessary because of change in definitions and sampling variability compared to decennial census.

I. A MODEL OF THE HOUSING MARKET

Figure 2 represents the underlying framework of the market for housing and new construction. Around this skeleton, this section constructs a basic model, discusses the necessary interrelationships among the market's components, illustrates the variables, and selects some of the more obvious relationships for analysis and statistical testing.

The figure pictures a typical flow-feedback system. Because of lags, acceleration, partial adjustments, and amplification, such a system tends to have an inherent instability [2] [9] [15].

The major sector (I) represents the existing stock of dwellings which, by definition, equals the number of households plus vacant units. Sector II shows dwelling units completed in the period and their disposition. Completions, by definition, are identically equal to net household formation plus the change in vacancies

and net removals. As net removals drop out of the picture, the other items flow into sector I, modifying the number in each of its segments.

Let us examine the system in equilibrium. Builders (III) start exactly enough units to maintain a constant level (IV) of inventory under construction. The outflow of completed units from this inventory exactly equals basic demand (household formation plus removals and perhaps a normal increase in vacancies). The completions minus removals enlarge the stock of dwellings.

Now assume a shift in an exogenous variable (V), such as income, credit, or relative prices. Such shifts either may affect builders directly or may change the rate of household formation or removals. Changes in the stock become known to builders through data on vacancies, prices, rents, and rapidity of turnover. If the information is favorable, builders raise starts, enlarging the inventory under construction and, eventually, boosting the rate of comple-

Figure 2 Net flows of construction in housing market.

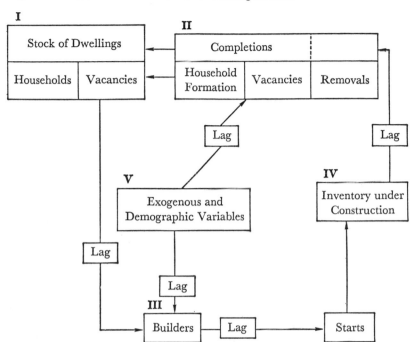

tions. Unless by chance demand rises at the same rate as completions, vacancies will increase. As this fact also filters through to the builder, he will contract his starts.

The model clarifies the types of variables and other influences underlying fluctuations in starts. First come forces outside the housing market which can change the rate of household formation, increase or decrease the number of removals, or cause builders to alter their estimates of future demand and therefore their starts. Internally, as vacancy rates alter, the relationships between rents, prices, and costs of ownership change also. Builders and promoters find their profits affected either directly by price fluctuations or indirectly by the holding costs of vacant units. The lag between starts and completions may also lead to an inventory cycle.

Movements of Final Demand

This section lists the variables determining the level of final demand, and expresses and dis-

cusses their relationhips. In contrast to the numerous forces which may directly influence housing starts, the number of variables about which significant statements can be made is limited. Each general relationship contains the term "disturbance" to account for both omitted and random factors.

Net Household Formation $(\triangle HH)$ depends upon population (Pop), disposable income (Y_d), unemployment (U), credit (Cr), prices (Pr), time (T), and other forces or disturbances (u) :

(1) $\triangle HH = P(Pop, Y_d, U, Cr, Pr, T, u).$

Population (Pop) includes the number, age, and sex distribution of the people in the country. In normal times, this variable dominates net household formation [3] [20] [26]. From 1890 to 1947, over 95 per cent of household formation could be attributed directly to this population factor. In periods such as the 1920's, G. H. Orcutt showed only minor annual movements in the ratio of actual to population-predicted marriage rates [26, p. 84].

The Great Depression and World War II so altered other social and economic variables that their influence tended to dominate those of normal population growth. In 1930–34 the rate of household formation to population dropped sharply as marriages were postponed and existing families doubled up in single dwellings. Between 1947 and 1960, the rate of household formation nearly doubled that expected from demographic forces.

Time (T) represents the social factors that gradually increase the number of households among populations of a given size. Until the war these social pressures were mild but steady, increasing household formation by just under 18,000 a year. In the postwar period a sharp drop in the average age at marriage, accompanied by an apparent unwillingness of families or individuals to share dwellings, boosted household formation by over 400,000 a year. Social changes seem to have diminished recently, with the result that additions to demand from this cause are likely to be far smaller than in the past decade.

Income (Y_d) and unemployment (U) are major indicators of economic well-being and appear significantly related to standardized marriage rates, undoubling, and other household formation [3] [20] [26]. Orcutt found a high correlation between changes in real disposable income per capita and annual marriages for the period 1920–56. Since 1950, a still better explanation can be devised by utilizing a quarterly index of unemployment of young males. Recent recessions have had more serious impacts on groups critical for household formation than on disposable income. Most marriages occur among those under 25, the group that has been among the hardest hit by recessions.

Household formation of non-marrieds also forms a significant segment of current housing demand. It fluctuates as much or more than marriages, and perhaps for the same reasons. Unfortunately, no suitable short-run data exist for movements of non-married households [20, p. 273]. The series in the Appendix is interpolated from changes in the rate of actual to expected marriages.

Credit (Cr) and prices (Pr) of constructing, owning, and leasing houses are frequently listed as important influences on household forma-tion. It is assumed that couples marry and that individuals or couples undouble as a result of lower rents or greater ease in purchasing houses. Section III points out the need to separate credit and price effects on starts and holdings of vacant houses from their influences on household formation. That discussion indicates that both analytically and according to statistical tests the impact of these variables on the rate of marriages appears low [20].

Net Removals from Available Housing—Census Starts Concept

In addition to units required to shelter additional households, the economy must produce houses to replace those removed from the available stock. Final demand for new construction consists of net household formation plus the extremely varied types of forces operating on the housing stock which we define as "net removals."

Under the heading of net removals, Table 1 shows nine types of changes which add or subtract dwellings from the available stock in addition to those cited in Census Series, "Private Housing Starts in the United States" [32]. In the past decade, 283,000 new dwellings were required annually to replace net losses. This is in sharp contrast to the situation during the depression when these nine sources furnished so many additional units that no new construction was needed.

Because net removals can have such an important influence on starts, the possible causes of their fluctuation must be analyzed. Ideally, each of the components lumped under net removals should be treated separately, but unfortunately the required data do not exist. Table 1 is an almost unique attempt to estimate values for some of the subcategories. However, only the over-all decade total can be considered accurate. The subcategories may contain offsetting errors [17] [22].

A general relationship can be expressed as: net removals (Rem) depend upon governmental action (G), income (Y_d), vacancies (V), stock of housing (Hou), time (T), and disturbances (u):

(2) $Rem = R(G, Y_d, V, Hou, T, u)$.

Governmental action (G) has been one of the most important determinants of net removals. Losses in the stock result from the demolition of war housing, clearance for highways and urban renewal, and code enforcements. In the private market, demand from these sources is offset by additions of public housing. Contrary to expectations, administrative data on past and proposed governmental action are at present minimal. This segment remains an important source of uncertainty.

Income (Y_d) is unproven as a determinant of the removal rate for substandard units. We do know, however, that in prosperous times more dwellings are demolished to make way for other uses. Prosperity probably also cuts down on conversions. Some have suggested that higher income should also bring an increased production of seasonal units, but this market remains small, with additions of seasonal dwellings reported by the Census at only 33,700 per year.

These total income-related influences seem to have brought about much larger net losses since 1950 than in previous periods. Furthermore, the rate of removals appears to have risen gradually.

Vacancies (V) of less desirable units might lead to their more rapid removal, but this has not happened as yet. Because the initial cost of housing is so high, it is usually more efficient to repair and remodel existing units, even those in poor condition, than to tear them down and start anew. Only in exceptional cases has the market reduced the value of dwellings in the stock sufficiently to make their removal without a federal subsidy worth while.

Stock of Housing (Hou) would appear to be directly related to certain losses, such as those due to fires, floods, and other disasters. Some theories of fluctuation have been based on the notion that replacements occur as a function of depreciation. However, the probability of a replacement cycle is considered remote because housing's life span remains more an economic than a physical function.

Time (T) is included as a variable because most forces influencing removals work steadily and not erratically. Except through income, there are no obvious reasons for the main components to alter sharply in the short run.

Because there was little information on when removals took place within the decade, we experimented with five possible distributions. Since changes appeared to have occurred regularly, the relationship among these distributions was attributed to time rather than to income or other economic forces. The assumed distributions ranged from a constant amount in each quarter through exponential increases as a function of time.

Our final estimate for this series assumes a constant minimum plus losses equal to .1 per cent of the stock at the end of each previous quarter, to reflect forces which would grow directly with the number of dwellings. Such a distribution is logical only if economic forces either cause no short-run fluctuations or cause conflicts that offset each other's impact. But a disregard for economic forces is basically unsatisfactory, since removals did fall sharply in the depression. Income fluctuations for the past decade have been either too small to influence removals or one of the series in our statistical model, such as interest, carries whatever weight might attach to any cyclically related removals.

Movements of Housing Inventories

Housing inventories consist of units under construction and those held vacant for sale or rent. Figure 1 shows how large and erratic the movements in these inventories have been. In certain quarters the rate of change for each of these series ranged as high as 400,000 units on an annual basis. Fortunately technical factors make extreme movements of both types simultaneously improbable, so that the instability of all inventories has not been much greater than for either of its parts.

Inventories of goods in process are required because of the lag between starts and completions. The number of uncompleted units is determined by the length of the production process and by the feedback system relating starts to completions and final sales.

A normal stock of vacant units is needed for new sales and population mobility. An insufficient supply, as in the postwar period, creates a difficult and nearly intolerable situation for those requiring different accommodations or wishing to migrate. While individual owners desire no vacancies, the aggregate need is met through an equilibrium price or rent which makes it worth while for each to hold his share of vacancies in turn. Many analysts assume that equilibrium vacancies should equal five per cent of the stock. From 1950 to 1962 a linear trend showed an increase of 106,000 units in available vacancies annually. We consider this as a reflection of the rate of increase in the equilibrium level.

Movements of vacancies around this equilibrium have been important. Desired and actual vacancies need not be equal. Because of builders' and sellers' errors of optimism and pessimism, additions to the housing stock diverge from final demand. The resulting shortages or overages influence future starts. The reaction of builders to these vacancies depends on the market's organization. Vacancies may be of various types, spread over many local markets. Cross-elasticities are weak; the gestation period is long. As a result, macro disequilibria may last for long periods before they are adjusted by alterations in the number of starts.

Four major housing submarkets exist: (a) newly constructed single-family houses not yet sold or occupied, (b) previously occupied units being offered for resale, (c) new rental units, and (d) previously occupied units offered for rent.[3]

The level of vacancies in one sector may fall temporarily as that in another rises. Builders of new houses attract a surge of buyers by easier credit or price changes. New rental units entice tenants from older ones with lures of status or amenities. Then adjustments occur through the price mechanism and the type of new construction started. The feedback to starts will vary from short delays for vacancies in new sale houses to several years for existing rental units.

Although information on both total vacancies and its components is increasing rapidly, it is still inadequate [33]. There is difficulty in reconciling the decennial census data with current reports. Since 1955, vacancy rates for all sales-type units have varied between .5 and 1 per cent of all units [33], or from approximately 250,000 to 650,000 dwellings. For-sale vacancies have increased as much as 10 per cent of starts in critical years.

New sales-type vacancies are the smallest and, under normal circumstances, have the most rapid impact on new starts.[4] Because of carry-ing costs, any lengthening of the period of sale rapidly erodes the builder's profits. Furthermore, the volume of unsold new units is controlled by limited builders' capital and by the unwillingness of lending agencies to finance additional starts when the builder has a backlog of unsold units.

Vacancies for sale are also found among existing units. Again owners attempt to keep these at a minimum. Most vacancies result primarily from emergencies, death, foreclosures, or migration. Real estate men advise against vacating a unit prior to its sale because an owner's expenses continue for the empty unit, placing him at a disadvantage.

While vacancies of existing units slow sales and lower prices of competing units, their impact on starts is less immediate than that of new vacancies. The spatial separation of markets may also lead to higher total vacancies. Any particular locality may experience a local economic disaster, with accompanying high vacancies. If basic demand were to drop sharply, as in the early 1930's, the period of adjustment for sales-type units could lengthen.

The probability of sizable movements from equilibrium is greater for rental than for sales-type units. The quarterly Census Surveys indicate that rental vacancies nearly doubled between 1955 and 1961. Moreover, even though rental vacancies rose nearly as fast as new construction, starts continued to expand. In 1961, apartment starts surpassed their previous peak —in 1925—while a new postwar peak for rental vacancies was also established. Total rental vacancies equaled a four- to five-year production level for multi-family units. In recent years,

3 On April 1, 1960 there were 1,975,000 available vacant units with 525,000 for sale and 1,450,000 for rent. (An additional 2,326,000 vacant units were listed as not available.) Never-sold new units may have been anywhere from 5 to 40 per cent of the for-sale type, while new rental units probably were close to 20 per cent.

4 U.S. Bureau of the Census, *Construction Reports: Housing Sales*, Census HHFA: C25–1 (a new series) states that on April 30, 1962 there were only 54,800 completed and unsold new sales units. Similarly, U.S. Bureau of the Census, *Current Housing Reports*, Series H–111 No. 29, shows around 40,000 new vacancies. This would mean that these units were only a two- to three-weeks' level of single family starts, or about a month's inventory of units for sale. Local market information indicates that vacancies of this type have probably fluctuated from a one- to three-months' level of starts.

about a quarter to a third of vacant rental units appear to be located in buildings less than three years old [33]. This would be equivalent to a 30 to 40 per cent vacancy rate for new structures.

In 1960 rental vacancies were nearly three times as large as vacancies for sales-type units. There are several explanations for these higher rental vacancy rates: (1) Since payments would fall on his occupied units also, even the best-informed owner may maximize his returns by allowing vacancies to increase rather than by cutting rents [27]. (2) In a market so complex and diverse as rentals, reliable information is scarce and this tends to breed inaction, hence an increase in vacancies. (3) During the first two years of operation, delays in renting are normal. The total gestation period on new construction covers a three- to four-year period —thus a long period elapses before the market experiences a feedback to new starts [35].

These forces causing vacancies to fluctuate about equilibrium can be expressed in an equation similar to those for final demand. Changes in vacancies about their trend (ΔV) depend upon costs (C), expectations (Ex), credit (Cr), rents (R), prices (Pr), the existing disequilibrium of vacancies (V), and disturbances (u):

$$(3) \qquad \Delta V = V\ (C,\ Ex,\ Cr,\ R,\ Pr,\ V,\ u).$$

Costs (C) exert an important influence on starts. To a large extent, the promoter's costs are externally determined by the amounts he must pay for supplies and labor. If his margin decreases, he must curtail production. Normally, his investment in overhead is minimal, so there is little pressure to maintain output with a prospectively unsatisfactory markup.

Expectations (Ex): Because of the long interval between the start of production and the final sale, expectations play a significant part in forming a builder's decisions. Articles in business magazines and trade papers, talks with other builders and lenders, with customers and tenants—all of these affect his actions. Expectations may move in long or short waves. Clearly, the long delay in building acutely needed rental units in the postwar years can be attributed to the memories of the lean 1930's [35].

Credit (Cr) is a major variable influencing the margin by which starts exceed or fall short of final demand. Tightening of credit affects the terms and prices of construction loans, as well as the discounts that builders of single-family units must pay for financing. Movements in terms have been sufficient to wipe out all potential profits [14]. For promoters of apartments, availability of credit rather than price has been a critical factor, because most often their main concern is to minimize required equities [29, p. 25]. Relative changes in credit availability and terms may also bring about vacancy disequilibrium if they cause households to move from one sector of the market to another, and their vacating of old units has only a lagged impact on starts.

Our model is based on the hypothesis that the cost and availability of credit cause only temporary reactions on starts. This contrasts with the more common view that credit's impact on final demand causes fluctuations.

Rents (R) and prices (Pr) measure the income from building or owning houses. In addition, they reflect the reaction to changed costs, credit, and vacancies. Higher prices and faster sales may increase profits immediately. In other cases, because of weak cross-elasticities, such market movements may influence builders' profits only after considerable lags. Rents indicate possible profits from new apartment units. They also measure the competition between rental units and new sales-type units. Movements either in costs or in rents and prices can clearly advance or retard starts.

Vacancies (V) above the equilibrium are both a cause and effect of the variations in starts. As noted, high vacancies cause the rate of increase in inventories to fall. Speed of reaction depends on the type and location of the empty units.

In addition to changes in vacancies, fluctuations in inventories under construction are extremely important. Annual differences in this series have been as high as 275,000 (see the Appendix) and have accounted for more than a third of the variance in starts.

Changes in Inventories under Construction

Changes in inventories under construction (ΔI) depend upon the difference between starts (St) in a period and completions ($compl$), which are in turn a direct function of previous starts (St_{t-1}):

$$(4) \qquad \Delta I = I \, (St, \, compl \, [St_{t-1}], \, u).$$

When final demand changes, starts must increase by still more in order to raise the inventory level to that required for higher output. This means that current starts are related to previous inventory levels and starts. A simplifying assumption, making completions an exact function of starts six months earlier, allows this inventory cycle to be expressed as a difference equation among starts of separate periods. It is simple to evaluate the form of this equation directly from the statistical estimates, while recognizing that the logical structure might vary somewhat [19].

The homogeneous form of the inventory equation using the parameters of equation (7) (see next section) is:

$$\text{Starts}_3 - .318 \, \text{starts}_2 + .236 \, \text{starts}_0 = 0.$$

This equation has one negative and two complex conjugate roots, all smaller than one. As a result, the inventory levels will oscillate. The period of the underlying cycle is between two and three years. If the system received no new shocks, the cycle would eventually disappear.

Movements in the inventory under construction serve to magnify any shocks arising in the remainder of the system. In mathematical form, the total system is described by a difference equation approaching a moving equilibrium [2] [10]. The form and magnitude of the fluctuations will depend on the coefficients of both the homogeneous equation and the equilibrium which it approaches; or, in other words, on the shifts in basic demand, builders' action, and the feedback-vacancy relations previously discussed.

II THE STATISTICAL TESTING
OF HOUSING MARKET THEORY

The previous section developed a model of the housing market which can be tested statistically. In analyzing results, however, one must constantly hold in mind the inadequacy of the data and their weak conformance to the general criteria necessary for normal statistical techniques. That the parameters found statistically will vary from those of the true world is not only possible but likely. In fact, if the model's only test of reliability depended upon the correlation within the period, it would not be worthwhile to comment on the results. Because of the weakness of the data, I have added four other tests to the traditional one. While these tests are not independent, the fact that all give similar results lends somewhat more credence to the final equation. In addition, the resulting relationships have been checked against bits and pieces of data from cross-sections, from single areas, and from previous periods.

The preceding section discussed market movements in the form of the following four relationships:

(1) $\Delta HH = H \, (Pop, \, Y_d, \, U, \, Cr, \, Pr, \, T, \, u)$
(2) $Rem = R \, (Hou, \, V, \, Y_d, \, G, \, T, \, u)$
(3) $\Delta V = V \, (C, \, Ex, \, Cr, \, R, \, Pr, \, V, \, u)$
(4) $\Delta I = I \, (St, \, compl, \, u)$

We have also made it clear that a necessary identity exists. With changes in vacancies as a residual, the level of starts in any period is identical to the sum of the four dependent variables in the equations previously discussed:

$$(5) \qquad St = \Delta HH + Rem + \Delta V + \Delta I.$$

One approach to statistical testing is to fit statistical parameters to equations (1) through (4), to add the results, and to compare this total with actual starts. It appeared, however, that fitting four separate equations would be demanding too much of the data because of missing variables and inexact estimates. Somewhat conflicting series for households, removals, and changes in vacancies occur. We desired to test the sensitivity of the model to the separate estimates. This was accomplished by utilizing a reduced form of equation (5). The results were then tested in equations (1) through (4). While the separate equations were significant, the statistics would be stretched beyond their true limits if each of the four separate equations were offered as a valid model. Instead, only the single reduced form is discussed.

Equation (6) is the final statistically derived equation. Since no adequate series for expectations and prices which appear in (3) could be found, we assume they are represented in (6) by the rent index. Because household changes and removals are included directly, the variables which influence them do not appear in this equation either.[5]

The estimates in (6) were fitted by least squares to the data for the inter-Census period 1950–60. The lags were found empirically and have no special theoretical value. In fact, from the previous section it is clear that, if four separate series for vacancies existed, each would have a separate lag.

The resulting equation, with its standard error and correlation and Durbin-Watson coefficients, is:

$$(6) \qquad St_0 = -278.0 - 27.92 \frac{1}{3} \sum_{-}^{4} i_{-}.$$
$$(9.47)$$

$$-.1391 \, V_{-1} + .3191 \, St_{-1} - .2958 \, St_{-3}$$
$$(.0393) \qquad (.1652) \qquad (.0810)$$

$$+ 2.212 \left(\frac{R}{C}\right)_{-1} + 3.637 \, Rem_0 + .5677 \, \Delta HH_0$$
$$(.935) \qquad (2.006) \qquad (.3539)$$

Quarterly $R^2 = .878 \bar{S}_u = 16.50$
$$d = 2.09$$
annual $R^2 = .99$

Where:

St = Census type starts of private dwelling units
i = Treasury bill rate new issues
V = Deviation of vacancies at start of quarter from straight trend
R = Rent component of the BLS Consumers Price Index
C = Residential cost component of the GNP implicit price index
Rem = Estimate of new removals
ΔHH = Net household formation in quarter

(For data see Appendix.)

Clearly this model meets the traditional statistical tests, including that of a "d" or Durbin-Watson coefficient, with no indication of severe autocorrelation.

Because the data include estimated series with high possible errors, a second test measured the sensitivity of the model to extreme combinations of different forms of the independent variables. As examples, we used three household series which varied from estimates of no change to the large annual movements reported in the Census Current Population Reports. Similarly for removals, five series covered a range from no change through rates of growth decreasing exponentially and those increasing exponentially. We also tried five different interest rates; a direct estimate of government action through FNMA; and three forms of vacancy estimates.

For each set, shifts occurred in several of the main parameters in addition to those of the altered variables. Correlation coefficients tended to be somewhat, but not much, lower. In almost all cases, however, the general form of the model remained the same; the signs agreed; and the same variables appeared to be significant. The agreement of the equations with the underlying theory did not appear to depend on the particular procedures used to estimate the variables.

A third test was to compare the annual predictions from the quarterly models with actual annual data. As shown, the annual R^2 exceeded .99. This higher R^2 was to be expected since the residuals of the annual data are not independent of the quarterly residuals, but the correlation is satisfactorily high.

A fourth test utilized (6) in predicting the annual values for each of the two years (1960–61) which lay outside the original period used in fitting. Predictions were of two types—one period change and process estimates [6]. In the first type, starts were estimated from the values of the independent variables as they appeared at the end of 1961. This assumes correct knowledge of the variables in the projection period. Projected starts were 1,199,000 for 1960 and 1,336,000 for 1961, compared to actuals of 1,252,000 and 1,304,000. The predictions correctly show two turning points. They also show a sharp drop for 1960 in contrast to almost every available forecast for that period.

[5] For forecasts, of course, their future values must be estimated. In a more general model, their estimates are based on the theory discussed in Section I. Household formation is predicted from population, time, and unemployment. Removals are based on the stock of housing and time.

That year experienced a 17 per cent drop in starts from 1959, which was contrary to the surface trends. As a result, almost all traditional forecasting procedures went far off the mark.

Estimates using actual values of the independent variables give a proper statistical test, but they do not show the model's ability to forecast prior to the availability of such data.

In order to test the model's forecasting ability, the independent variables must be estimated from knowledge available at the time of forecast. The test utilized projections of no change for interest rates, rents, and costs; a basic demographic series for households; and a time trend for removals. The values of lagged starts and vacancies were simulated by operating the model with the naively estimated exogenous variables a quarter at a time. The 1960 and 1961 forecasts from this simulation were 1,184,000 and 1,245,000 respectively. Again the turning points were correctly predicted. Each forecast was about five per cent too low. Given the difficulty of forecasting in this period, these predictions appear good; in fact, better than most.

A final test recomputed the equation to include 10 additional quarters in 1960, 1961, and 1962, which became available after the preliminary work was completed. This recomputation increases the degrees of freedom by more than 25 per cent. It also gives more weight to the official series for starts which begins in 1959. The results of the recomputation are:

$$(7) \quad St_0 = -172.9 - 20.25 \frac{1}{3} \sum_{2}^{4} i_{-i}$$
$$(6.73)$$

$$- .1441 \, V_{-1} + .3177 \, St_{-1} - .2357 \, St_{-3}$$
$$(.0367) \qquad (.1420) \qquad (.0780)$$

$$+ 2.673 \left(\frac{R}{C}\right)_{-1} + 2.456 \, Rem_0 + .5908 \, \Delta HH_0$$
$$(.905) \qquad (1.500) \qquad (.3330)$$

$$R^2 = .85 \qquad \bar{S}_u = 17.01 \qquad d = 2.09$$

Clearly, the significance of the variables did not alter. No basic shift in the structure is indicated. The same variables fit the longer period equally well. The observed differences appear logical in the light of our other market information.[6]

III. THE BEHAVIOR OF HOUSING STARTS IN THE POSTWAR PERIOD

Figure 3 contrasts the actual deviations of housing starts from their means with the deviations estimated by (7). The figure also shows the contribution of the individual variables to the estimates.

The fitted model agrees with both theoretical considerations and other knowledge in assigning a low importance to household formation and net removals as a cause of postwar housing fluctuations. With the exception of a movement in 1950–52 related to the Korean War and reflected in starts, final demand forms a relatively stable equilibrium around which the critical disturbances take place. This theory clashes sharply with those expressed in many recent articles that attribute movements in housing starts primarily to the effect of changes in interest rates, maturities, and loan-to-value ratios on consumers' demand for space[7] [1] [5] [11] [12] [24] [30].

While starts are influenced by credit, as is evident from Figure 3, the channel of causation appears to be through inventories rather than final demand. Both analysis and policy will differ significantly, depending upon whether credit causes a temporary disequilibrium of inventories or a basic change in the number of housing units demanded by consumers.

It is difficult to find any logical channel of causation between credit and household forma-

6 As a final test we used the model to forecast new private housing starts for 1963. The model, on the basis of data at the end of 1962, predicts that housing starts in 1963 will be 1,296,000, or a decrease of 11 per cent from the 1962 level.

7 Break [5, p. 225] correctly summarizes the views of most of those who have been interested in housing fluctuations as a potential area for the use of monetary policy. "Changes in the interest rates, maturities, and loan-to-value ratios prevailing on new home mortgages have an important effect on the demand for housing. This is a proposition that not only commands general acceptance among experts, but also forms the basis of the loan insurance and guaranty programs of the Federal Housing Administration (FHA) and Veterans Administration (VA)."

The approach of this paper, in contrast, builds upon the theories found in much of the business cycle literature [3] [7] [8] [13] [18]. The fact that two different approaches have led to such sharply divergent analyses might make an interesting case study for an historian of the development of economic theories.

Figure 3 Relationships between housing starts and the independent variables (thousands of starts-seasonally adjusted annual rates).

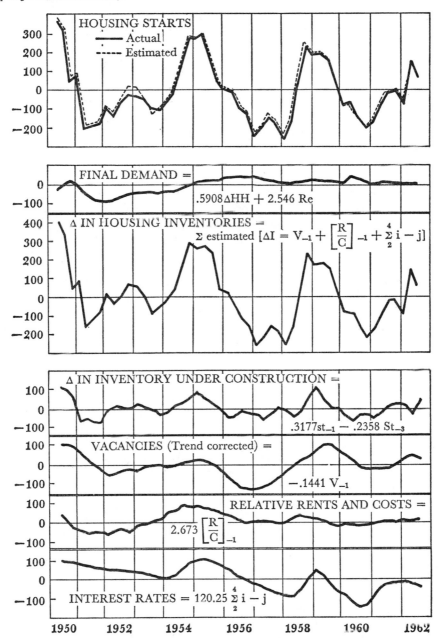

tion.[8] Few newly formed households purchase homes. In 1960 census components of change show that only 7.5 per cent of households formed in 1958–59 owned their own homes. Since these households include a large number

[8] There is, of course, almost certainly a relationship between credit and the average expenditure of households on housing. A failure to distinguish between demand for a certain number of houses and the average value of each leads to some of the errors in analysis.

of reconstituted ones (i.e., households formed by widowed, divorced, separated persons, etc.) whose members probably owned homes under their previous marital status, it is likely that only one or two per cent of new households purchase dwellings during their first two years of existence. Almost certainly, only a small fraction of these, and therefore an insignificant part of the total, would delay marriage or refrain from forming their own households because of credit changes.

For financing to affect the formation of non-owner households, it must first alter rents; then, higher rents must deter people from marrying or undoubling. There is no reason to expect credit to have short-run impact on rents. Furthermore, rents, averaging about 15 per cent of income, are only part of the cost of establishing a household [23]. Given the high psychic costs of delayed marriages or merged households, it appears that reactions to changed prices or rents are likely either to be small or to influence long-run rather than cyclical changes in household formation.

Given the normal situation of a large stock of households growing at a slow rate, an acceleration could make even small percentage increases in total households important for new starts; but such movements do not seem to have occurred in recent years.

Figure 3 shows little relationship between credit and household formation (it actually is negative). This lack of any positive correlation between household change and credit or house prices has generally been found in previous studies as well.

The pictured impact of the other fitted variables reflects both their own weights and the weights of the wider group of variables discussed in Section I. Equation (7) and Figure 3 measure the impact of each variable on both types of inventory movements. The movement of inventories under construction in Figure 3 has a roughly similar path, but less amplitude, than the data in the Appendix. This results from the fact that the fitted variable, Δ in inventory under construction, reflects only the endogenous inventory cycle.

In the three cycles since 1950, actual disequilibrium movements consisted of almost equal changes in inventories of units under construction and available vacancies. The larger actual movements in inventories under construction as estimated in Table 2 result from shocks transmitted through the remaining variables. The amplitudes of the endogenous movements are increased by the other forces particularly in 1954, 1958, and 1960.

The level of vacancies appears to play a role in each cycle. Below-normal vacancies gave impetus to additional building in 1950 and accounted for most of the rise in starts in 1957, 1958, and 1961. On the other hand, the expansion of starts in 1954 and 1955 caused a backlog of empty units which were an important cause of decreased building in 1956–57. A similar reaction occurred in 1959. Throughout the period, vacancies appear to have had far more influence on starts than most observers noted.

The data used to represent the ratio of rents to costs are not as sensitive an index as one would hope for because of the notorious inadequacies in the underlying data. Still the relatively low level of rents resulting from rent control seems to have had a depressing effect on starts through most of 1952, causing demand to be deferred during this period. In 1953 and 1954, rents shot up much faster than costs, thus adding to the expansion.

The high level of starts in 1954 and 1955 led to a rapid rise in costs, which in turn helped to make building or speculating on starts less profitable. Since 1956, except for a small impetus given to the boom of 1958, the influence of these variables has been slight.

The final variable consists of lagged short-term interest rates. According to equation (7), credit, vacancies, and the inventory cycle account for approximately equal parts of the total variance in starts. As explained earlier, our hypothesis states that changes in the cost and availability of credit cause important disturbances in the rate of inventory accumulation. Builders and promoters increase starts because their potential profits grow as discounts fall or the amount of equity required is decreased. In addition, with more favorable terms, they may attract existing households from other parts of the market. As long as their inventories remain low, their profits grow. However final demand does not expand with starts. When the increased inventory is mainly in units under construction, builders feel only slight pressure to change their action. Eventually, however, as the number of empty completed units grows, pressure mounts to cut back starts. Timing depends on both the period of production and the lags between starts and particular types of vacancies.

Because of intricacies in the mortgage market, as, for example, discounting, many seemingly obvious credit variables, such as FHA yields (even corrected for discounts), conventional yields, or the spread between bond yields and FHA rates, are poor measures of the cost of credit. This fact, as well as the probability that changes in availability may be even more significant than costs, explains the earlier finding that short-run interest rates give a considerably better fit in equations (6) and (7) than any of the long-run mortgage credit series.

Because credit is an important government policy variable, significant changes in past relationships may occur which must be considered in analysis and forecasting. Clearly, if the Federal Reserve succeeds in breaking past relationships between the Treasury bill rate and the availability and cost of credit, equation (7) will be affected. Even more important may be the changing policies of the Federal National Mortgage Association. In this study, FNMA intervention in the credit market appeared significant on theoretical grounds, and nearly so on a statistical basis. However, since FNMA action was closely related in time to interest rate movements, it did little to increase our statistical explanation of past movements. Even though this collinearity did result in insignificant coefficients for FNMA policy, it seems logical to assign to direct governmental intervention of this type a good deal of weight, even if only subjectively.

Finally, Figure 3 shows significant longer-run movements. In 1950 there was still a backlog of final demand. Builders were more likely to receive premiums than to pay discounts for their financing; vacancies were below a desirable level; households were still doubled up; rent control was in the process of being dismantled; the high demand allowed only minimum removals. Between 1950 and 1956, most of these after-effects of the war worked themselves out of the system. Since 1957, the number of starts has averaged about 1,366,000 units per year, with a high quarter rate of 1,604,000

and a low of 1,162,000. With this production, available vacancies have accumulated at the rate of about 60,000 per year, slightly below the assumed equilibrium.

There is no obvious reason for the average level of starts to vary much in the near future. Only if sudden economic changes or governmental policy should drastically alter the present levels of basic demand or if vacancies begin to change rapidly, would the number of units constructed over the next five years vary sharply from the previous five.

The probabilities of continued instability also appear to remain unaltered. Basic factors of lags, acceleration, and poor information have not changed, and the system continues to be plagued by unstable forces. The possibility of serious outside shocks remains strong. Only a major increase in knowledge, combined with government policies specifically designed to compensate for, rather than accentuate, normal market instability would appear to offer much hope for improvement.

REFERENCES

1. WILLIAM ALBERTS, "Business Cycles, Residential Construction Cycles and the Mortgage Market," *Jour. Pol. Econ.*, June 1962, *70*, 263–81.
2. R. G. D. ALLEN, *Mathematical Economics*, 2nd ed. London, New York 1960, Chaps. 6, 7, 8.
3. V. L. BASSIE, *Economic Forecasting*. New York 1958, Chap. 9, App. C.
4. E. C. BRATT, "Appraisal of Statistical Information on Construction in the United States," report to the U.S. Budget Bureau, Sept. 1958, (Mimeo.)
5. G. F. BREAK, *The Economic Impact of Federal Loan Insurance*, National Planning Association. Washington 1961.
6. K. J. COHEN AND R. M. CYERT, "Computer Models in Dynamic Economics," *Quart. Jour. of Econ.*, Feb. 1961, *75*, pp. 18–19.
7. J. B. D. DERKSEN, "Long Cycles in Residential Building," *Econometrica*, April 1940, *10*, 97–116.
8. J. S DUESENBERRY, *Business Cycles and Economic Growth*. New York 1958.
9. J. W. FORRESTER, *Industrial Dynamics*. Cambridge 1961.
10. S. GOLDBERG, *Introduction to Difference Equations*. New York 1958, Chaps. 2 and 3.
11. LEO GREBLER, *Housing Issues in Economic Stabilization Policy*, Nat. Bur. Econ. Research Occas. Paper 72. New York 1960.

12. J. M. Guttentag, "The Short Cycle in Residential Construction," *Am. Econ. Rev.*, June 1961, *51*, 275–98.
13. A. H. Hansen, *Business Cycles and National Income.* New York 1951, Chap. 3.
14. John Herzog, *An Analysis of the Dynamics of Large-Scale Housebuilding.* Unpublished doctoral dissertation, Univ. of California, Berkeley, 1962.
15. C. C. Holt and F. Modigliani, "Firm Cost Structures and the Dynamic Responses of Inventories," in Part II of Joint Economic Committee, *Inventory Fluctuation and Economic Stabilization.* Washington 1961.
16. *House and Home*, "Does the U.S. Need More Vacancies," March 1962, pp. 52–53.
17. F. S. Kristof, "Components of Change in the Nation's Housing Inventory in Relation to the 1960 Census," paper presented at the Annual Meeting of the American Statistical Association, Dec. 28, 1959.
18. J. P. Lewis, *Business Conditions Analysis.* New York 1959, Chap. 20.
19. J. P. Lewis, "Building Cycles: A Regional Model and Its National Setting," *Econ. Jour.*, Sept. 1960, *70*, 519–35.
20. S. J. Maisel, "Changes in the Rate and Components of Household Formation," *Jour. Am. Stat. Assoc.*, June 1960, *55*, 268–83.
21. ——— and L. Grebler, "Determinants of Residential Construction," Research Study 4 in Commission on Money and Credit, *Impacts of Monetary Policy.* New York 1962.
22. ———, "Importance of Net Replacements in Housebuilding Demand." *Study of Mortgage Credit*, U.S. Senate Committee on Banking and Currency, Subcommittee on Housing, 85th Congress, 2nd Session. Washington 1958.
23. ——— and L. Winnick, "Family Housing Expenditures—Elusive Laws and Intrusive Variances," in *Proceedings of the Conference on Consumption and Saving*, Vol. 1. Philadelphia 1960, 359–435.
24. R. F. Muth, "The Demand for Non-Farm Housing" in A. C. Harberger, *The Demand for Durable Goods.* Chicago 1960.
25. ———, "Interest Rates, Contract Terms and the Allocation of Mortgage Funds," *Jour. Finance*, March 1962, *17*, 63–80.
26. G. H. Orcutt, M. Greenberger, J. Korbel, and A. Rivlin, *Microanalysis of Socioeconomic Systems: A Simulation Study.* New York 1961.
27. C. Rapkin, L. Winnick, and D. M. Blank, *Housing Market Analysis*, U.S. Housing and Home Finance Agency. Washington, Dec. 1953.
28. M. G. Reid, "Capital Formation in Residential Real Estate," *Jour. Pol. Econ.*, April 1958, *66*, 131–53.
29. P. A. Samuelson, "The Current State of the Theory of Interest Rates, with Special Reference to Mortgage Rates," *Conference on Savings and Residential Financing*, 1960 Proceedings, U.S. Savings and Loan League, 1960.
30. W. L. Smith, "The Impact of Monetary Policy on Residential Construction, 1948–58," Study of Mortgage Credit, *Conference on Savings and Residential Financing*, 1960 Proceedings, U.S. Savings and Loan League, 1960.
31. U.S. Department of Commerce, *Construction Review.*
32. U.S. Bureau of the Census, *Construction Reports—Housing Starts*, C20, especially C20-11 Supplement.
33. ———, *Current Housing Reports—Housing Vacancies*, Series H-111 No. 29.
34. *Wall Street Journal*, July 9, 1962, p. 11.
35. L. Winnick, *Rental Housing.* New York 1958.

APPENDIX

The official series on private housing starts is known to contain serious mistakes. The Department of Commerce, as of December 1962, has promised a revised series shortly. Other data needed to analyze the housing market appear to be missing or available only at infrequent intervals. Similarly, it is difficult to overemphasize the lack of exactitude in housing data [4] [21] [22] [28]. Their quality falls far short of that desirable for economic analysis and necessary for econometric work.

An attempt was made to find the series necessary for econometric testing within local areas. In certain cities or counties, additional series became available, but other gaps widened. However, the additional information on inventories and removals available in some localities did indicate the critical part they play in explaining fluctuations. As a result, revisions were made in the starts series, and estimates were obtained for removals and inventories.

In deriving the required data three steps were followed: (1) It was necessary to obtain a consistent set of estimates for the total changes in all required series for the 10-year period between the 1950 and 1960 decennial censuses. (2) Depending on the availability of other related series, local data, and interim figures, these decennial totals were translated into quarterly time series. (3) The statistical estimates of the market were tested for their sensitivity to a wide variety of conflicting assumptions. The equations were checked against the data, previous periods, local models, and by predictions.

We admit to considerable qualms with respect to individual pieces of data. However, the theory of the market discussed in this paper stands on its own, even if the numbers were to be considered as hypothetical rather than real.

Table 2 shows the data for the nonstandard series which were used in the statistical fitting of the model. These series were derived as follows:

1. Private Housing Starts in the United

Table 2 Quarterly Data on U.S. Housing Starts' Market (*in thousands*)

Years	Qtr.	Private Housing Starts	Net Household Formation	Changes in Inventory Under Construction	Available Vacancies	Net Removals
1950	2nd	432	257	68	730	65
	3rd	422	268	9	772	66
	4th	354	274	−69	851	66
1951	1st	360	263	−59	935	66
	2nd	290	247	−86	1,024	67
	3rd	293	234	−88	1,086	67
	4th	296	222	2	1,166	67
1952	1st	319	220	29	1,171	67
	2nd	307	222	3	1,175	68
	3rd	325	227	− 2	1,189	68
	4th	333	233	34	1,221	68
1953	1st	332	236	14	1,218	68
	2nd	329	236	− 6	1,232	69
	3rd	307	235	−28	1,262	69
	4th	314	233	− 9	1,293	69
1954	1st	325	233	20	1,314	69
	2nd	340	234	19	1,318	70
	3rd	372	238	45	1,335	70
	4th	409	243	69	1,354	70
1955	1st	408	250	35	1,381	70
	2nd	412	252	3	1,434	71
	3rd	391	251	−17	1,520	71
	4th	356	250	−52	1,606	71
1956	1st	342	255	−51	1,695	72
	2nd	339	255	−27	1,762	72
	3rd	321	254	−24	1,801	72
	4th	310	254	−25	1,820	73
1957	1st	282	251	−36	1,828	73
	2nd	292	246	−19	1,822	73
	3rd	304	241	25	1,814	73
	4th	297	236	19	1,779	74

Table 2 (*continued*)

1958	1st	278	235	−14	1,747	74
	2nd	299	232	− 5	1,731	74
	3rd	354	234	74	1,719	74
	4th	401	235	116	1,690	75
1959	1st	389	237	53	1,664	75
	2nd	391	234	− 5	1,688	75
	3rd	382	233	12	1,775	75
	4th	356	231	−19	1,837	76
1960	1st	323	226	−73	1,905	76
	2nd	327	236	−33	1,999	76
	3rd	307	232	−16	2,047	77
	4th	292	227	−40	2,061	77
1961	1st	299	219	−15	2,089	77
	2nd	320	221	+41	2,104	77
	3rd	338	220	+59	2,085	78
	4th	340	219	+26	2,066	78
1962	1st	321	217	−13	2,083	78
	2nd	378	214	+68	2,122	78
	3rd	356	213	−21	2,140	79

Source: Appendix.

States, including Alaska and Hawaii (seasonally adjusted). Source: 1959 to date, New Series Total Private Housing Starts, U.S. Bureau of the Census, *Construction Reports—Housing Starts*, Series C-20. For 1950–58, U.S. Housing and Home Finance Agency, *Housing Statistics* (Historical Supplement, October 1961), p. 3. The data for 1950–56 were inflated by 1.20. For 1957–58 the multiplier decreased evenly per quarter from 1.20 to 1.15.

The control total for this series is shown in Table 1. It was assumed that the BLS starts series showed the correct direction of movement and that the degree of underestimation for 1950–56 did not vary. For 1957–58, the BLS adjusted their estimates upward as a result of the National Housing Inventory. See *Construction Review*, June 1960, pp. 4–10.

2. Change in Households: (the net number of households formed in quarter [seasonally adjusted]). The quarterly fluctuations in the estimated decennial total (Table 1) are derived from National Office of Vital Statistics data on current marriages and divorces related to expected marriages and divorces. These expected net marriages and household formation were estimated from changes in the age-sex composition of households between the Censuses of 1950 and 1960.

3. Changes in the Private Inventory Under Construction (seasonally adjusted).

This series is derived directly from the starts series on the assumption that the time from start to completion is two quarters for single-family units and four quarters for multifamily. The actual amount in this inventory would vary if the construction period changed.

4. Units Vacant Available for Sale and Rent (seasonally adjusted).

Additions to vacancies reported by the 1950 Census were cumulated quarterly. Completions in a quarter were estimated from lagged starts according to series 3. Net change in vacancies is the number of completions minus the number of households formed (2) and units removed (5).

5. Series on Net Removals. Net removals in each quarter were assumed to equal the con-

stant 21,100 plus 0.1 per cent of the available stock at the end of the previous quarter.

6. The following are standard series: Rate on New Issues U.S. Government three months bills: *Federal Reserve Bulletin*.

7. Residential Rent Component of the Consumer Price Index (1947–49 = 100), U.S. Hous-

ing and Home Finance Agency, *Housing Statistics,* October 1961, p. 95.

8. Cost of Residential Construction—GNP Implicit Price Deflator Residential Construction (1954 = 100), Table 6, *Survey of Current Business* (July 1961).

Residential Construction: Exploration of the Statistical Series

ALFRED N. PAGE

INTRODUCTION

Economists have long been concerned with explaining and predicting the observed time series of residential construction. Housing time series are of interest because they seem to exhibit large cyclical swings, and they tend, at least postwar, to be countercyclical to changes in gross national product. However, the existence of significant housing cycles may be seriously challenged in the future as advanced statistical techniques, rarely used in housing analyses, are applied to an ever increasing assemblage of data.

Analyses of housing cycles fall into three different categories. The first category is the use of institutional and descriptive analysis to predict changes in housing activity. Often relying on years of experience and "intuitive feel," such analysis may predict as well or better than more sophisticated methods. This is partly due to the random component in such predictions as well as the random component in the time series. It also is indicative of the current development stage of statistical techniques and the vagaries of data estimation. The principal shortcoming of this category is the usual lack of specification of the underlying model (if any) used for analysis.

The second category is the analysis of variance of housing activity through the use of regression analysis (for a comparison of early housing time series studies, see Grebler and Maisel;[1] for later studies see Muth,[2] Lee,[3] and Maisel[4]). Specific equations representing the

housing market are specified and tested; income and price elasticities are estimated. Such investigations illuminate the intricacies of the market; nevertheless, their quantitative results and predictive ability vary widely. For example, estimates of the income elasticity of demand for housing range from 0.3 to over 2.0. Again, this reflects problems of data measurement as well as the traditional time series problem of serial correlation. It becomes most difficult to obtain good estimates of the postulated relationships. It is also difficult to sort out long-run effects from short-run effects. In addition, the very nature of the statistical data complicates the analysis. That is, as Davis points out, "Differing from the series encountered in the experiments of physical science,

Reprinted from the *Journal of Business* (January 1967), pp. 36–43, by permission of the author and The University of Chicago Press. Copyright © 1967 by The University of Chicago Press.

1 L. Grebler and S. J. Maisel, "Determinants of Residential Construction," *Impacts of Monetary Policy* (Commission on Money and Credit, Research Study 4 [Englewood Cliffs, N.J.: Prentice-Hall, Inc., 1963]).
2 R. F. Muth, "The Demand for Non-Farm Housing," *The Demand for Durable Goods,* ed. Arnold C. Harberger (Chicago: University of Chicago Press, 1960), pp. 29–96.
3 T. H. Lee, "The Stock Demand Elasticities of Non-Farm Housing," *Review of Economics and Statistics,* XLVI (February, 1964), 82–89.
4 S. J. Maisel, "A Theory of Fluctuations in Residential Construction Starts," *American Economic Review,* LIII (June, 1963), 359–83.

every economic time series [including housing] possesses a large random element. But the series themselves are not random, in spite of some popular belief to the contrary, nor are they sufficiently regular to satisfy most mathematical postulates." [5]

The third category is the use of mathematical functions to analyze movements in series over time. The causes of the cycle are ignored, and the generating process of the data may or may not be hypothesized. The purpose of the functional analysis is to describe or gain some useful information about the time series. It is felt by some that more knowledge will be gained about cycles in this way than by attempts to estimate complicated causal relationships through regression analysis. The validity of such a position is still an open question; at present, both statistical techniques are extremely useful. It is with the third category, unexplored by housing economists, that the remainder of the paper is concerned.

DETRENDING

The housing time series $(H_t, t = 1, 2, \ldots, n)$ can be thought of as being composed of four parts, familiarly called trend, seasonal, cyclical, and irregular. For purposes of simplification, yearly data are used in this paper, and thus seasonality is not analyzed.[6] Trend refers to the long-term movement in the series (due to long-term factors such as population growth), and cyclical behavior refers to short-term fluctuations (perhaps due to factors such as flows in mortgage credit). The irregular factor simply refers to random movements in the series.

In order to analyze the time series, it is customary to remove the trend component, a step sometimes called "prewhitening." It should be remembered that the trend and cyclical pattern may be generated by the same statistical process and that it is often difficult to remove a trend perfectly. What appears to be a long-term movement in the existing time series, in retrospect, may appear to be a very short-term movement. Existing observable trends may simply "disappear" when housing series are examined several centuries from now. For example, an existing trend may be part of a cycle with

a period four times the length of the present data.

The trend can be estimated in a number of ways, such as by fitting a polynomial of the form

$$\overline{H}_t = A + \sum_{x=1}^{n} B_x t^x ,$$

or the curve $\overline{H}_t = Ae^{Bt}$ in its logarithmic form, $\ln \overline{H}_t = \ln A + Bt$, to the data. Then, for further statistical analysis, the trend is removed by subtracting the estimated values of H_t from the actual values. Another often successful method of trend removal is the use of the difference formula $\Delta H_t = H_t - kH_{t-1}, \ k \leq 1.0$. For this study, the trend was removed from Department of Commerce data using the estimating equation, $\overline{H}_t = -3297.97 + 4071.75t - 381.26t^2 + 12.36t^3 - .13t^4$ (Fig. 1). The residuals from the trend line are defined as h_t.

The purpose of the trend removal is to obtain, for subsequent analysis, a time series (h_t) which is covariance stationary. Such a series has a constant mean $[E(h_t) = m]$ and a variance which is constant over time $[E(h_t - m)^2 = \sigma^2]$. In addition, the covariances between h_t and h_{t+p}, where p is some arbitrary number, are constant over time and do not depend on where in the time sequence a particular set of observations is obtained. To be specific, an autocovariance function can be defined

$$A_p = [1/(n - p)] \sum_{t=1}^{n-p} (h_t - m)(h_{t+p} - m) .$$

If the series is stationary, the function will depend on only m and p, not on t. If the series contains a strong trend, the autocovariance function will, of course, be a function of t. A useful transformation of the autocovariance function is the autocorrelation function, which for a large number of observations is approxi-

5 H. T. Davis, *The Analysis of Economic Time Series* (Bloomington, Ind.: Principia Press, 1941), pp. vii–viii.
6 H_t represents U.S. construction put in place (residential new housing units plus additions and alterations, 1957–59 constant dollars) as estimated by the U.S. Department of Commerce.

Figure 1   New construction. ($H_t = 3297.97 + 4071.75t - 381.26t^2 + 12.36t^3 - .13t^4$). Construction put in place, United States, 1957–1959 constant dollars. Residential new housing units plus additions and alterations. Source: U.S. Department of Commerce.

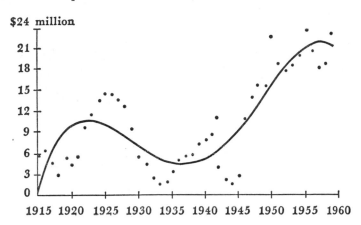

mately equal to the autocovariance function divided by the variance of the series [$R_p = A_p/\sigma^2 = A_p/A_0$].

RANDOMNESS

After the trend has been removed from the time series, it is always possible that the remaining figures represent only random drawings from a distribution. Despite how the residuals look to the eye on a graph, there may be no cyclical behavior present. If the remainder is random, with sampling variation, the values of the autocorrelation function would be expected to equal zero for any p greater than zero. For a large sample, the variance of the function is approximately equal to $1/(n-p)$. Tables of significance for first-order autocorrelations (R_1) are available.[7] For the series h_t, the first-order autocorrelation is approximately .70; the probability of this occurring if the series was random is less than 1 per cent. If the trend was estimated through regression analysis that did not involve distributed lags, the Durbin-Watson d statistic.

$$d = \sum_{t=2}^{n} (h_t - h_{t-1})^2 \bigg/ \sum_{t=1}^{n} h_t^2,$$

can be computed.[8] The estimated d statistic is .57, indicating that serial correlation is present in the residuals.

Finally, a simple test for randomness involves computing the number of complete runs or turning points in the observed data. There are thirteen such runs in the housing sample (h_t). In a random series of n terms, the runs are approximately normally distributed with the expected number of runs equal to $(2n - 1)/3$ and the standard deviation of runs equal to $\lfloor (16n - 29)/90 \rfloor^{1/2}$. Therefore, a standardized normal value can be computed, equal to $[3\,(\text{runs}) - 2n + 2.5]/[(16n - 29)/10]^{1/2}$. In the housing sample, the value of this variable is larger than 5 in absolute value; the probability of obtaining such a number if the series was random would be less than .001. Thus we can reject the hypothesis that h_t is random.

STATISTICAL ANALYSIS

As the housing series (h_t) is not random, the next problem is to hypothesize the generating process or provide some other useful information about the series. As the population-generating function can never be observed and only a single sample is available, it is most

7 R. L. Anderson, "Distribution of the Serial Correlation Coefficient," *Annals of Mathematical Statistics*, XIII (1942), 1–13.
8 J. Durbin and G. S. Watson, "Testing for Serial Correlation in Least Squares Regression II," *Biometrika*, XXXVIII (June, 1951), 159–78.

Figure 2 Autoregressive model ($h_t = .94h_{t-1} - .35h_{t-2} + e_t$).

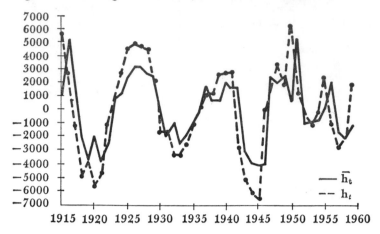

Figure 3 Correlogram.

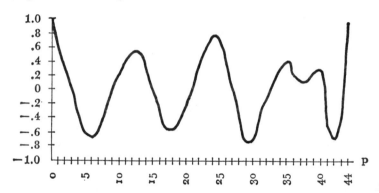

difficult to differentiate among possible generating mechanisms.

One type of possible generator is the autoregressive model suggested by Yule.[9] For example, the series may reflect the following functional relationship:

$$h_t = \sum_{x=1}^{n} B_x h_{t-x} + e_t, \quad E(e_t) = 0.$$

Suppose the hypothesis is $h_t = B_1 h_{t-1} + B_2 h_{t-2} + e_t$. For the housing data, B_1 equals 0.94 and B_2 equals -0.35.[10] The graph of the function against the data appears in Figure 2. Another model may fit the data just as well; how can one discriminate? One device is the correlogram, the plot of the autocorrelation function

against p (Fig. 3). The function will look different for different generating processes; thus, if the above model is correct, the correlogram will start at one and oscillate toward zero as p approaches infinity. This pattern cannot be observed in the graph. The autocorrelation function does not approach zero but instead exhibits the pattern expected of a sinusoidal wave model, often called the "linear cyclical

9 For example, see G. U. Yule, "On a Method of Investigating Periodicities in Disturbed Series, with Special Reference to Wolfer's Sunspot Numbers," *Philosophical Transactions of the Royal Society*, Ser. A. (1927), pp. 267–98.
10 If the second equation is multiplied by h_{t+p} and summed, the result is $R_p - B_1 R_{p-1} - B_2 R_{p-2} = 0$. Setting $p = 1$ and 2, $B_1 = [R_1 (1 - R_2)]/(1 - R_1^2)$ and $B_2 = (R_2 - R_1^2)/(1 - R_1^2)$.

model." Unfortunately, the correlogram is subject to wide sampling variation; in addition, the patterns that would be exhibited by more complicated models are often unknown. An alternative device is the use of a goodness-of-fit criterion, such as a comparison of the coefficients of correlation between h_t and the estimated values of h_t obtained from the models. For the autoregressive model the coefficient is .73, and for the sinusoidal wave model (computed below), the coefficient is .82. However, since these models can only be applied to the existing single sample of the housing time series population, a better fit may simply reflect sampling variation.

The sinusoidal wave model is derived from harmonic analysis, the forerunner of spectral analysis, the most promising statistical technique for analyzing time series. Harmonic analysis, originating in the physical sciences, is the search for hidden periodicities in a time series. For example, given that $h_{t+P} = h_t$ and certain other fairly unrestrictive assumptions, the series $h_t = f(t)$ can be represented by the sinusoidal wave,

$$h_t = \frac{1}{2}A_0 + \sum_{k=1}^{\infty} I_k \sin(2\pi kt/P + a_k).$$

Alternatively, this is written as the Fourier expansion,

$$h_t = \frac{1}{2}A_0 + \sum_{k=1}^{\infty}\Big[A_k \cos(2\pi kt/P)$$
$$+ B_k \sin(2\pi kt/P)\Big].$$

$$I_k = (A_k^2 + B_k^2)^{1/2},$$

$$A_k = (2/P)\int_0^P f(t)\cos(2\pi kt/P)dt,$$

and B_k is defined similarly. Note that if $E(h_t) = 0, \frac{1}{2}A_0 = 0$. The wave has a period of P and harmonic terms with commensurable periods of $P/1$, $P/2$, etc. An alternative formulation sometimes used has harmonic terms with period P_k which need not be commensurable (in which case the function is almost periodic).

The search for hidden periods in the housing data and the construction of a function to simulate the data proceeds as follows. If the period P is divided into n observations, as n approaches infinity,

$$A_k = (2/n)\sum_{t=1}^{n} h_t \cos(2\pi kt/P).$$

and

$$B_k = (2/n)\sum_{t=1}^{n} h_t \sin(2\pi kt/P).$$

In practice, A_k and B_k are averaged over a number of periods, hopefully allowing random deviations to cancel out. That is, if n observations are available, the number mp is formed where m is the largest integer that can be multiplied by the trial period p and still be less than or equal to n. For a trial period p, compute

$$A = (2/mp)\sum_{t=1}^{p} M_{tp} \cos(2\pi t/p),$$

and

$$B = (2/mp)\sum_{t=1}^{p} M_{tp} \sin(2\pi t/p)$$

where

$$M_{tp} = \sum_{w=0}^{M-1} w_{p+t}.$$

If the trial period p is equal to a real period (P/k or P_k), $I^2 = (A^2 + B^2)$ will be high and form a peak.

For trial periods 2 through 20, a graph of I^2 is given in Figure 4. After Schuster, such a graph is called a periodogram.[11] The resulting figure shows a strong peak at $p = 12$, allowing the computation of the function $\overline{h}_t = 4594.59$ $\cos(2\pi t/12) + 249.95 \sin(2\pi t/12)$. Figure 5 plots this function against h_t.

11 Sir Arthur Schuster, "On the Investigation of Hidden Periodicities with Application to a Supposed 26 Day Period of Meteorological Phenomena," *Terrestrial Magnetism*, III (1898), 13–41.

Figure 4 Periodogram.

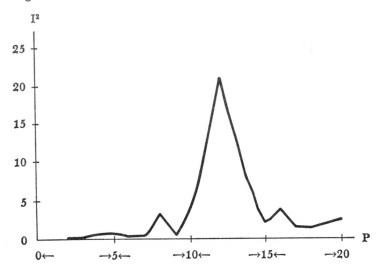

Figure 5 Sinusoidal wave model $[h_t = 4594.59 \cos (2\pi t/12) + 249.95 \sin (2\pi t/12)]$.

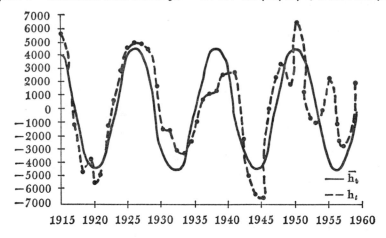

SPECTRAL ANALYSIS

The linear cyclical model, Yule's autoregressive model, and other similar models have not been widely accepted by economists. The reasons are varied and include insufficient data and the possible absence of strict periodicities in the time series. Particularly bothersome is the lack of reliable statistical tests to discriminate among differing models or to evaluate the reliability of a parameter estimation of a particular model. This is the problem of being unable to handle shocks or disturbances to the system which mask the underlying data. This is the problem of handling the situation where the amplitudes in a linear cyclical model become probability distributions and an observed peak may be a random fluctuation.

Currently, research is focused on what might be called a special type of analysis of variance, spectral analysis.[12] The spectrum represents a function which indicates for various frequen-

12 See C. W. Granger and M. Hatanaka, *Spectral Analysis of Economic Time Series* (Princeton, N. J.: Princeton University Press, 1964).

cies (1/period) of a Fourier series the contribution to the variance of a series by a particular frequency band. It provides a means of ascertaining whether a particular frequency accounts for an unusual amount of the total variance, indicating an "important cycle" at that frequency. In turn, the spectrum of one economic variable may be analyzed for its relation to the spectrums of other economic variables, a process called "cross-spectral analysis."

The spectrum can be thought of as a Fourier transformation of the autocovariance function. Suppose

$$h_t = \sum_{k=1}^{n} (A_k \cos P_k t + B_k \sin P_k t),$$

where A_k and B_k are now random variables with constant variances $[E(A_k)^2 = E(B_k)^2 = \sigma_k^2]$ and zero means. Then, the autocovariance function A_p can be defined as equal to

$$\sum_{k=1}^{n} \sigma_k^2 \cos P_k p .$$

When $p = 0$, $A_0 =$ variance of $h_t = \sigma^2$. Thus the variance of the series can be partitioned into a number of variances which are a function of the frequency $(P_k/q\pi)$. In more general terms,

$$A_p = \int_{-\infty}^{\infty} f(P_k) \cos P_k p dP_k ,$$

where

$$f(Pk) = (1/2\pi) \int_{-\infty}^{\infty} A_p \cos P_k p \, dp,$$

and is defined as the spectral density. The graph of $f(P_k)$ against frequencies is called the spectrum.

There are many problems in estimating $f(P_k)$ and several alternative methods. One such method is to compute

$$L_g = (1/2\pi) \left[A_0 + 2 \sum_{r=1}^{m-1} A_p \cos (\pi g p/m) \right. $$
$$\left. + A_m \cos \pi g \right],$$

where m equals the maximum p used in computing the autocovariance function. These crude estimates of the spectrum are further smoothed before they are plotted against the frequencies $\pi p/m$, $p = 0, 1, \ldots, m$.

A spectrum for h_t appears in Figure 6. This graph should be interpreted only as an illustration of the method, not as a valid estimate of the true power spectrum for h_t. The data are simply too short for a reliable estimate. As Granger points out, a desirable minimum of data often may be as much as two hundred observations, an amount that few time series can muster (crude estimates of the spectrum can be estimated with fewer data) .[13] Nevertheless, the exhibited spectrum presents a pattern not too dissimilar to the spectrums of other economic time series. That is, with a larger data sample, the housing spectrum will very probably appear similar to the estimated spectrums of other series. These spectrums tend to be high at low frequencies (which may or may not indicate inefficient trend removal), falling smoothly as the frequency increases. The shape of the spectrums suggests that economic time series may not have important cycles in the usual sense and that simple generating models can simulate these series as well as complicated regression models.[14] Only time and the data will tell for sure.

CONCLUSION

Whether housing economists wish to use casual empiricism, regression analysis, or spectral analysis, the severest constraint at present is the lack of reliable data of any satisfactory length. This enables a large set of analytic techniques to coexist, it being inconclusive which technique is superior. It is quite likely that, as housing data expand, the existing hypotheses used to explain housing cycles will fall away and, indeed, the very existence of

13 *Ibid.*, p. 61. Minimum size of data is dependent upon several factors. For example, if one is testing for the importance of a one-hundred-year cycle, two hundred years data are insufficinet for inference.
14 See I. Adelman, "Long Cycles—Fact or Artifact?" *American Economic Review*, LV (June, 1965), 444–63; and C. W. Granger, "The Typical Spectral Shape of an Economic Variable," *Econometrica*, XXXIV (January, 1966) , 150–61.

Figure 6   Spectrum.

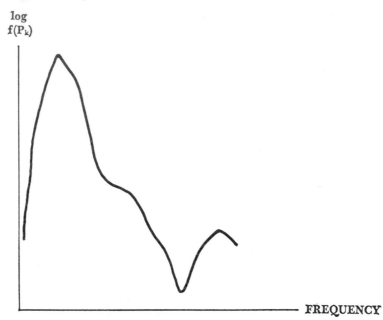

significant cycles will be questioned. One thing is axiomatic: As the housing data grow in quality and quantity, all housing economists will need to use extensively the statistical tools described above in order to understand the nature of the housing market.

The Demand for Non-Farm Housing

RICHARD F. MUTH

INTRODUCTION

In this study an attempt is made to estimate the responsiveness of housing demand to changes in income and in the price of housing. Probably because of the intractability of the data in this field, little work on these questions has been done in the past.

Opinions about the price and income elasticities of demand for housing vary widely. On the one hand, there is the view that housing is a "necessity," in some sense, and that the quantity of housing demanded changes less than proportionally in response to changes in price or income. On the subject of income elasticity, Morton asserts that, "because of the ab-

solute necessity of shelter, housing stands with food very high in the order of urgency. . . . Housing expenditures, accordingly, do not bear a constant but a decreasing ratio to income." [1] This is in direct contradiction to Marshall's

Reprinted from *The Demand for Durable Goods* edited by Arnold C. Harberger by permission of The University of Chicago Press. Copyright © 1960 by The University of Chicago Press.

1   Walter A. Morton, *Housing Taxation* (Madison: University of Wisconsin Press, 1955), pp. 42–43. Sherman J. Maisel in *Housebuilding in Transition* (Berkeley: University of California Press, 1953), p. 274, offers a similar statement to justify his belief that housing demand is highly inelastic with respect to price.

classic comments that "house room satisfies the imperative need for shelter from the weather; but that need plays very little part in the effective demand for house room" and that "where the condition of society is healthy . . . there seems always to be an elastic demand for house room, on account of the real conveniences and the social distinction which it affords." [2]

Morton's assertions and similar opinions expressed by Winnick,[3] among others, are based mainly on evidence of the type presented in Table 1, column (2). This column shows the percentage of current income spent for housing as computed from data from the 1935–36 consumer budget study. This percentage declines steadily as current income increases, as does the percentage of current income spent for all items shown in column (1), suggesting that the income elasticity of demand for housing as well as for all current consumption is less than unity. However, recent research on the consumption function suggests that the relation of consumption to current income as between income classes at a given point in time yields misleading results when attention is focused upon the income elasticity of demand as between different years. This is because the income a consumer receives in a given year may differ from his expectations about his normal income level, and it is the latter which is the more important determinant of consumption.[4] Friedman, in particular, has suggested the hypothesis that consumption is proportional to normal or "permanent" income.[5] If this is correct, the comparison of expenditures for housing with all consumption expenditures would give an estimate of income elasticity more useful for comparisons between different years—the elasticity with respect to permanent income. Column (3) of Table 1 shows that, for these same data, the ratio of expenditure on housing to all current consumption is nearly constant and does not vary systematically with the level of income. This observation suggests an elasticity of about unity with respect to permanent income.[6]

The only published estimate of the price elasticity of housing demand is that of Duesenberry and Kistin.[7] They estimated price elasticity for housing as well as for food and clothing by comparing changes in expenditure in the same city between successive budget studies

with changes in the appropriate Bureau of Labor Statistics city price indexes, holding real income constant. They found significant correlations between expenditures and price for food and clothing; but for housing the correlation coefficient was −.06 and the estimated price elasticity −0.08, neither of which was statistically significant.

This study focuses on housing services as the fundamental object of the "demand for housing." Since these services are provided by the stock of houses in existence at any point in time, we attempt to explain the variations in the stock of housing over time and to estimate how much this stock would ultimately change in response to changes in the price of housing or in income. We view new construction as the means by which the stock of housing is adjusted to changing conditions and attempt to estimate simultaneously from changes in the rate of new construction both the pace at which adjustments take place in the housing market

2 Alfred Marshall, *Principles of Economics* (8th ed; New York: Macmillan Co., 1950), pp. 88 and 107.
3 Louis Winnick, "Housing: Has There Been a Downward Shift in Consumer Preferences?" *Quarterly Journal of Economics*, LXIX (February, 1955), 87–88. Both Morton and Winnick suggest a value of about +0.5 for income elasticity.
4 While the literature bearing on this topic is too extensive to cite here, the reader is referred to Milton Friedman, *A Theory of the Consumption Function* (Princeton, N.J.: Princeton University Press, 1957), and Franco Modigliani and Richard Brumberg, "Utility Analysis and the Consumption Function: An Interpretation of Cross-Section Data," in *Post-Keynesian Economics*, ed. Kenneth K. Kurihara (London: George Allen & Unwin, 1955), pp. 388–436.
5 *Op. cit.*
6 This comparison is meant only to illustrate the point that previous comparisons of housing expenditure with current income by income class at a given time may give a misleading impression as to the elasticity of housing demand with respect to permanent income. If consumption expenditures depend upon the transitory income component, the difference between current and permanent income, as well as upon the permanent income component, and if all current consumption is more sensitive to variations in the transitory component than expenditures for housing, then the comparison made here would result in an underestimate of the permanent income elasticity of demand for housing. And, of course, in this comparison no account has been taken of price or other variables that might affect housing demand.
7 James S. Duesenberry and Helen Kistin, "The Role of Demand in the Economic Structure," in *Studies in the Structure of the American Economy*, ed. Wassily Leontieff (New York: Oxford University Press, 1953), pp. 451–82.

Table 1 * Total Consumption Expenditure and Expenditure on Housing in Relation to Income, 1935–36

| Income Level | Percentage of Income Spent on | | Ratio of Expenditure (Col. [2] ÷ Col. [1]) |
	All Items (1)	Housing (2)	(3)
Under $500	149.3	28.9	0.194
$500–$750	112.7	19.9	.177
$750–$1,000	104.6	18.5	.177
$1,000–$1,250	100.6	18.1	.180
$1,250–$1,500	96.5	16.9	.175
$1,500–$1,750	93.8	16.6	.177
$1,750–$2,000	92.1	16.5	.179
$2,000–$2,500	88.6	15.7	.177
$2,500–$3,000	84.8	14.9	.176
$3,000–$4,000	80.4	14.3	.178
$4,000–$5,000	74.6	13.0	.174
$5,000–$10,000	64.8	11.4	.176
$10,000–$15,000	53.7	10.6	.197
$15,000–$20,000	52.7	8.6	.163
$20,000 and over	35.4	6.5	0.184
Average, all levels	85.6	15.3	0.179

* Source: National Resources Committee, Industrial Committee, *Consumer Expenditures in the United States: Estimates for 1935–36* (Washington, D.C.: Government Printing Office, 1939), Table 6A, p. 78.

and the responsiveness of stock demand to changes in price and income. Our emphasis on stock demand, as derived from the demand for services, distinguishes this effort from a number of studies of new construction which have appeared in recent decades. These studies have been motivated by the interest in short-run fluctuations in aggregate economic activity and have largely neglected the relation of the demand for new construction to stock demand. The emphasis adopted in this study will, I believe, lead to a better understanding of fluctuations in the rate of new construction and their place in the structure of over-all economic change.

A MODEL OF HOUSING DEMAND

This section sets out the model which serves as the framework for the empirical investigation into the demand for non-farm housing discussed in later sections.

Units of Measurement

Before formulating the model of housing demand itself, it is necessary to define precisely certain magnitudes. This is particularly important for the unit of measure of housing stock, since in the real world there is virtually infinite variation among residential structures as to size, type of construction, floor space, and other characteristics to which consumers attach value. Much of the discussion in the literature on housing and several empirical studies have used the dwelling unit as the unit of stock. But these are patently non-homogeneous; a one-room slum apartment and a suburban mansion certainly contain different quantities of "housing" in any reasonable sense, yet both count as one dwelling unit. Because of the infinite variation in dwelling units, it is difficult to find any classification in terms of technological or legal characteristics which results in homogeneous units. One way out of this difficulty is to accept the judgment of the market: to treat as identical those units of "housing" which command identical prices. Thus, to measure the total stock of housing, the market price of each structure might first be observed. (Throughout this study only structures are considered, and land is excluded, unless otherwise noted.) A particular structure would then be selected as standard, that is, as containing one unit of housing, and its price divided into the price of each other structure. The resulting ratios would give for each structure the number of units of housing in standard house equivalents. The total stock of housing would then be the sum of the number of standard house equivalents. But this total is simply the constant dollar value of the stock of housing—the current dollar value deflated by the price of the standard house.[8] Similarly, the price of a unit of housing is defined as the price of the standard house.

In what follows, a unit of quantity of housing service is needed as well. One unit of housing service is defined as that quantity of service yielded by one unit of housing stock per unit of time. The price per unit of housing service, or rent, is the price paid by consumers for the flow of services from one standard house per unit of time. In addition to the net return received by the owner of the structure, this rent includes an allowance for depreciation, maintenance and repair, and taxes.

Demand for Services and Stock Demand

The fundamental demand for housing relates the quantity of housing services, h, to rent, R, income, y, and other relevant variables.[9] This function is shown diagrammatically (for given levels of explanatory variables other than rent) in Figure 1. Now at any instant of time the quantity of housing stock is fixed; thus, by assumption, the quantity of housing services is also fixed. This quantity, say, h_1, together with the position of the demand schedule, determines the level of rent, R_1.

To derive stock demand from the demand for

Figure 1

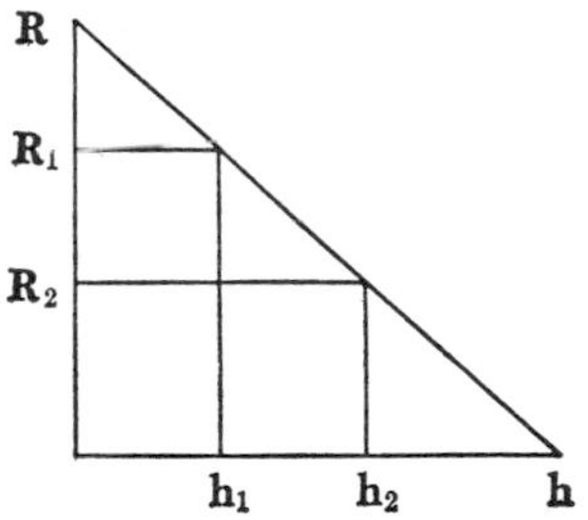

Figure 1

services, we must explore the relation between rent and price per unit of stock. To do so, it is convenient to consider first only positions of long-run equilibrium in the market for stocks. By long-run equilibrium I mean a set of conditions—stock, price, income, and other factors—under which there would be no tendency for the quantity of stock (per capita) to change over time. In such a position, newly constructed housing would only be sufficient to offset depreciation and to provide for additions to population. The stock associated with such a set of conditions is described as the long-run equilibrium, or, for a more convenient term, the *desired* stock of housing, h_d. Now, since the demand for stocks is derived from the demand for services, the desired stock demand will depend upon the long-run equilibrium rent and income. But, if there is to be no net addition to the stock of housing over time, the long-run equilibrium rent, net of depreciation, maintenance and repair expenditures, and taxes per unit of stock must be just sufficient to induce owners of housing to hold this stock. That is, in long-run equilibrium, rent divided by price per unit of stock, p, must be equal to the sum of (1) the rate of depreciation, maintenance, and repair expenditures; (2) the tax rate; and (3) the long-run equilibrium net rate of return on housing. The last of these depends upon

8 This solution to the problem of measurement of stock suffers from the defect common to all index-number solutions. It yields no unique measure if the relative prices of the different units being aggregated change over time.
9 Throughout this study I use lower-case letters to refer to per capita magnitudes of stock and income; capital letters, to refer to the corresponding total or per household magnitudes. Income, rent, and price are all defined in real terms.

the mortgage rate of interest. The ratio of long-run equilibrium rent to price is described as the long-run equilibrium gross rate of return on housing.

Given the gross rate of return on housing, it is easy to derive the desired stock-demand schedule from the demand for services. Take any point on the latter, say, h_1, R_1, and find that price p_1 such that the ratio R_1/p_1 just equals the long-run equilibrium gross rate of return on housing. This price, along with h_1, gives one point on the desired stock-demand schedule, viewed as the relation between price and quantity of stock, given the depreciation rate, the tax rate, the rate of interest, and the variables determining the position of the demand-for-services schedule. The desired stock-demand schedule is illustrated in Figure 2. It is the same curve as the demand-for-services curve in Figure 1, except that the units on the vertical axis are different. That is, if the long-run equilibrium gross rate of return is, say, 10 per cent per year, the point on the vertical axis of Figure 2 which would be labeled "Ten dollars" corresponds to the point on the vertical axis of Figure 1 which would be labeled "One dollar per year."

Because the units of quantity of service and stock are numerically equal, the partial elasticities of the demand for services and desired stock-demand function are equal. An x per cent change in the consumption of housing services as a result of a 1 per cent change in income can come about only through an x per cent change in the stock of housing. Likewise, if in equilibrium rent bears a constant ratio to price, a 1 per cent rise in price must carry with it a 1 per cent rise in the equilibrium rent. Service demand will in response be reduced by y per cent, and the equilibrium stock of housing by the same percentage.[10]

So far only positions of long-run equilibrium, as defined above, have been considered. But at any instant of time the actual stock of housing, h, may not be equal to the desired stock, h_d. Suppose that the price per unit of additional stock is fixed by conditions of supply of newly constructed housing at p_2 and that actual stock is h_1, both in Figure 2. The level of rent as determined by the schedule of demand for services in Figure 1 is R_1 if the actual stock of housing (which is numerically equal to the flow of housing services per unit time) is h_1. The long-run equilibrium rent, that amount just necessary to induce owners of structures to maintain the stock of housing corresponding to the price p_2, is R_2. Hence, if the desired stock of housing exceeds the actual stock, the current level of rent exceeds the long-run equilibrium rent. Thus there is an incentive to add to the stock of housing. As actual stock increases over time, the current rent falls. When actual stock has reached h_2, rent will equal the long-run equilibrium rent, R_2 in Figure 1, and the ratio of rent to price will equal the long-run equilibrium rate of return. There will no longer be any incentive to add to the stock of housing, and the market for stocks will be in long-run equilibrium.

Thus any excess of desired over actual stock means an excess of current over equilibrium rent and therefore an incentive to add to the stock of housing. An excess of desired over actual stock can come about through a fall in price, a rise in income, or a fall in the rate of interest or in taxes.

10 The elasticity of desired stock demand with respect to the rate of interest is but a fraction of the elasticity with respect to price. To see this, suppose that the rate of interest is 5 per cent per year and the depreciation and tax rates 3 and 2 per cent per year, respectively. In these circumstances the gross rate of return on housing in equilibrium is 10 per cent per year. A 1 per cent fall in the rate of interest will lead to a 1 per cent fall in that fraction, here one-half, of rent required to cover interest charges, or to a fall in rent of one-half of 1 per cent. Thus a fall in the rate of interest of z per cent will lead to only one-half the increase in service demand and desired stock that would result from a z per cent fall in price.

Figure 2

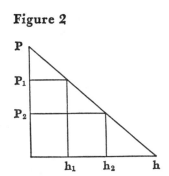

The Demand for New Construction

In dealing with the pace of adjustment of actual housing stocks to the desired or equilibrium level, we assume that a certain fraction, d, of the gap between actual and desired holdings will be filled in a year. If adjustment is rapid, d will be close to 1.0; if it is sluggish, d will be close to 0.

The reasons for slow rather than instantaneous adjustment can relate to either the demand side or the supply side of the market for new housing. On the demand side an increase in income may give, say, 10 per cent of households an incentive to buy new homes or to seek to rent new quarters. But this does not mean that all 10 per cent will try to move to new dwellings in the first year after the income change. It is in the nature of housing decisions that they should be considered carefully, and often moving into new quarters must be meshed with other events—children starting or finishing school, marriage, birth or death of family members, etc. On the supply side it is clear that changes in the scale of the home-building industry may entail changes in price.[11] Likewise, as the demand for mortgage funds to finance new housing increases, the mortgage market may become "tighter." Mortgage rates may rise, or, what seems equally likely under today's institutional arrangements, other conditions of mortgage loans may become more stringent.

We may legitimately ask at this point whether these "supply-side" causes of slow adjustment really fit here in our framework. Have we not already taken account of the effect of price through its effect on desired stock demand? The answer to this question is twofold. First, as a theoretical matter, the changes in demand which follow upon such price changes are governed by a mechanism quite distinct from the long-run price elasticity of demand for housing which we attempt to measure. It is my contention that desired stock demand is determined by the "long-run normal" price of housing, while short-run deviations of price from the long-run normal price govern in part the *rate* at which this desired stock is approached. Short-run price fluctuations about their long-run normal level are by their nature temporary. Houses may be "artificially"

dear for a time after demand has risen, but, when sufficient additions have been made to stock, the normal price will be restored.

Second, as a practical matter, the changes in price which come about from even a sharp rise or fall in demand for new housing are likely to be too small to be captured and isolated by available price indexes. Suppose, for example, that a housing shortage caused by a sudden increase in desired stock demand leads to an increase in rent of 10 per cent and gives an incentive to expansion of home-building. Suppose, further, that conditions of mobility into the home-building industry are such that it can achieve any given output at the normal price within two years[12] but that expansions of output in periods of less than two years entail some price rise in order to hasten the movement of resources into the industry. How far can price rise under these circumstances? The 10 per cent premium in rents cannot last more than two years under our assumptions, so the premium people would be willing to pay for new housing would certainly be no more than 20 per cent of the annual rent. But, since houses usually sell for about ten times the annual rent, the premium for new houses could be no more than 2 per cent.

The argument of the above paragraphs may be illustrated graphically, as in Figure 3, which shows the (total) net demand for new housing, H', as a function of the excess of current over the long-run equilibrium price, p^*, with the mortgage rate of interest held constant at its long-run equilibrium level. The position of the demand curve depends upon the excess of desired over actual stock, E, since E determines the excess of current over long-run equilibrium rent. With an increase in, say, income and hence desired stock, the demand curve shifts from D to D' by an amount measured along the horizontal axis which is generally some fraction of E. In long-run equilibrium D, of course, passes through the origin, since, in such a position, there is no incentive to add to stock. With

---

11 It is also possible that they might entail some deterioration in the quality of newly constructed dwelling units. In our framework, this is reflected in a rise in price of units of given quality.
12 There is impressive evidence that resources are indeed quite mobile. This evidence is discussed in a later section.

Figure 3

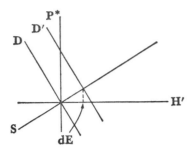

the shift in demand for net additions to stock, the price of new housing tends to be bid up, as indicated by the supply schedule S. Because of the rise in price some consumers who desire new quarters tend to put off acquiring new housing in anticipation of a future fall in price. In fact, for short-run equilibrium to be attained, the increase in price would have to be such that individuals would be indifferent as between acquiring new housing now or in the future. The rise in price in the short run rations additions to the housing stock, so that new construction is less than that quantity indicated by the intersection of D' with the horizontal axis, which is itself but a fraction of the initial excess of desired over actual stock. Thus new construction during the first year after the initial rise in desired stock is dE, where the value of d depends partly on the slopes of the demand-and-supply schedules in Figure 3. Now in the following year the demand curve for new construction shifts downward from D'. This is because the net increase in stock during the first year leads to a decline in the gap between actual and desired stock and, hence, to a fall in current rent.[13]

In an empirical analysis of the housing market, such as is undertaken in later sections of this study, it would be desirable to estimate the short-run supply schedules for new housing and for mortgage funds and the demand function for additions to the stock of housing. There are two reasons, however, why this is not done. First, it is quite unlikely that the measures of price and the interest rate used in this study would reflect changes in these variables accompanying the rate of new construction in the short run. At best, they might be interpreted as

measures of the long-run equilibrium values of these variables. And, second, as was indicated above, such short-run changes are likely to be so small as to be difficult to measure at all. However, Figure 3 suggests that to a linear approximation the net increase in stock per unit time will be proportional to the excess of desired over actual stock, either in total or in per capita terms. Stated in symbols, where h' is the per capita net rate of increase in stock per unit time and d is the constant of proportionality,

$$(1) \qquad\qquad h' = d\,(h_d - h)\,.$$

Here, of course, the numerical value of d depends upon the length of the time period for which net additions to stock are measured. Also it is assumed that replacement demand—depreciation, maintenance, and repair expenditures—is proportional to actual stock. Thus the per capita gross rate of construction of housing per unit of time, h'_g, is given by

$$(2) \qquad h_g = d(h_d - h) + kh = dh_d - (d-k)h\,,$$

where k is the rate of replacement demand. Equation (2) is referred to here as the flow-demand equation; actually, of course, it is a "reduced form" of the demand function for new housing and the supply functions for new housing and for mortgage funds.

While equation (2) specifies the rate at which the stock of housing increases over time,

<hr/>

13 We shall not go into the effects of a short-run rise in the rate of interest in detail. It is sufficient to point out that, if the supply of mortgage funds is not infinitely elastic in the short run with respect to the rate of interest, the latter will rise with any increase in the demand for funds accompanying the increase in the rate of new construction. Also, to the extent that the increase in the rate at which new housing is acquired is accompanied by an increase in borrowing relative to net worth, the risk premium on mortgage loans might rise even if the mortgage rate net of this risk premium remained unchanged. A rise in the interest rate, like a short-run rise in price, will serve to ration additions to the housing stock. In fact, if in Figure 3 and the text above the rate of interest is substituted for price and the schedule S is interpreted as the supply of funds, the argument remains essentially unchanged.

it is of no use for empirical analysis because it contains the desired stock variable, and the latter is not observable. Desired stock per capita can, however, be expressed as a function of its determinants: long-run equilibrium price, p, per capita income, y, and the long-run equilibrium interest rate on mortgages, r.[14] To a linear approximation this function may be expressed by

$$(3) \qquad h_d = b_0 + b_1 p + b_2 y + b_3 r .$$

Substituting (3) into (2) to eliminate the non-observable h_d, we have

$$(4)$$
$$h'_a = db_0 + db_1 p + db_2 y + db_3 r - (d - k)h .$$

Equation (4) is referred to as the "excess form" of the flow-demand equation; it relates the per capita gross rate of new construction per unit of time to the determinants of per capita desired stock and to actual stock per capita. If desired stock increases as income increases, *ceteris paribus*, gross new construction increases as well, since the coefficient of income in (4) is equal to the coefficient of income in (3) multiplied by the adjustment coefficient, d.[15]

However, in interpreting the elasticities of (4), it is important to realize that they depend both upon the point in time of the process of adjustment of actual to desired stock and upon the length of the time period for which additions to stock are measured. To illustrate, consider an initial position of long-run equilibrium and let income increase by 10 per cent. If the income elasticity of stock demand is equal to 1.5, desired stock would increase by 15 per cent. Suppose that in a year's time one-third of the difference between desired and actual stock is added to stock and that the rate of replacement demand is $3\frac{1}{2}$ per cent per year. During the first year after the initial increase in income the net increase in stock would be 5 per cent of the initial stock, while in the second year the net increase in stock would be $3\frac{1}{3}$ per cent of the initial stock. Construction would rise sharply in the year of the change in income, but it would fall from this peak in the second and subsequent years, approaching a new equilibrium level 15 per cent higher than

in the initial equilibrium, and in which construction served only to provide replacement for the now higher equilibrium stock. Thus, in response to a given percentage change in income, we would observe a variety of relative changes in construction, depending on the stage of the adjustment process we looked at. In this study, when estimates are presented of the elasticity of house construction with respect to a given variable, they will refer to the responsiveness of demand during the first year. Hence estimates of, say, the income elasticity of equation (4) refer to what the relative increase in construction would be in the same year as the change in income if prior to the income change the housing market were in full equilibrium.

Another point relating to equation (4) should be noted here. In examining this equation, we note that the coefficients of the desired stock-demand function, the b's in (3), and the adjustment coefficient, d, are not identifiable. That is, to estimate, say, b_2, the coefficient of income in (3), we need an estimate of d. The latter can be obtained from an estimate of the coefficient of h in (4) only if the value of k is known. However, to estimate the *elasticity* of h_d with respect to per capita income, no independent information about the value of k is needed. This elasticity is equal to $b_2 y/h_d$, which, of course, is equal to $(db_2 y) / (dh_d)$. But, comparing (3) and (4), it is easy to see that dh_d is given by (4) with the last term omitted. Hence its value and the income elasticity of desired stock demand can be obtained directly from estimates of (4) without any prior knowledge about k.

In the paragraphs immediately above it is

14 Of course, desired stock also depends upon the property-tax rate, but I omit explicit consideration of this variable here because I have been unable to find satisfactory data to measure it. Also, I assume that the rate of depreciation, k, is constant.
15 We might just as well relate the end-of-year actual stock, h_f, to beginning-of-year stock, h, and the net increase in the year. Thus

$$h_f = h + h' = dh_d + (1 - d) h.$$

We could then substitute (3) and obtain an equation analogous to (4). I prefer to place primary emphasis on (4) because I feel that the data on new construction are of much better quality than the stock data.

seen that the gross rate of new construction can be expressed as a function of the determinants of desired stock and the actual stock of housing. This formulation is especially useful, since it permits estimation of the desired stock-demand elasticities. But for studying the rate of new construction another formulation of the flow-demand equation—the "ratio form"—is useful. Dividing each member of equation (2) by h, we have

$$(2') \qquad (h'_g /h) = -(d - k) + d(h_d/h) .$$

Now the analysis of the preceding section of this chapter suggests that the ratio of desired to actual stock may be approximated by the ratio of current rent to long-run equilibrium price, given the long-run equilibrium mortgage rate

$$(5) \qquad (h_d/h) = c_0 + c_1(R/p) + c_2 r .$$

Substituting (5) into (2'), we obtain

$$(6) \quad (h'_g /h) = [(c_0 - 1)d + k] + dc_1(R/p) + dc_2 r .$$

According to (6), the ratio of gross construction to actual stock varies directly with the ratio of current rent to long-run equilibrium price and inversely with the rate of interest.[16] Estimation of (6) will provide another test of the analysis of this section.

Estimating Stock Demand: A Preview

The principal purpose of this study is to estimate stock-demand elasticities for housing from time-series data. At this point the implications of the analysis of this chapter for so estimating housing demand will be noted. The other comparisons to be made will be discussed when the empirical results are presented.

If, in the real world, individuals tried to add to the stock of housing at such a rate as to make actual stock at the end of any given calendar year equal to desired stock, estimation of desired stock-demand elasticities from time-series data would be similar to estimating

the demand function for the services of any commodity. We would, simply, compare the end-of-year actual stock with price, income, and the interest rate. The set of observations of these variables for any year would give one point on the desired stock-demand function, apart from a random residual. This special set of circumstances will be referred to in this study as the "case of complete adjustment." If it were true that the economy actually operated in this way, new construction could be explained wholly by changes in the determinants of desired stock.

However, we advanced several reasons at the beginning of the last subsection why actual stock might not adjust completely within a year's time to changes in, say, price or income. If the lag in adjustment of actual to desired stock is long enough relative to a year, none of the observed combinations of end-of-year stock, price, income, and the interest-rate needs coincide with a point of the desired stock-demand function. Rather they would lie on a path of dynamic adjustment to the long-run equilibrium stock level. It is precisely for this reason that we considered the dynamics of adjustment at such length in the last subsection. The analysis there indicated that the rate of new construction in any year depends upon two considerations: desired stock expressed as a function of price, income, and the interest rate and the rate at which the actual housing stock moves toward it. Our equation (4) shows how these variables are interrelated. And, as we have shown, from estimates of it we can estimate the partial elasticities of the desired stock-demand function, even though that desired stock corresponding to any particular set of conditions might never be observed. From knowledge about the rate of depreciation parameter, k, the coefficients of the desired stock-demand function, as well as its partial elasticities, can be estimated, as can the rate of adjustment parameter, d. If d were really less than 1.0, and it will be seen that it seems to be substantially less, then new construction can

16 The formulation in equation (6) is similar to that of Charles F. Roos, "Factors Influencing Residential Building," *Dynamic Economics* (Bloomington, Ind.: Principia Press, 1934), chap. vi.

be explained not only by changes in the determinants of desired stock but also by the dynamic lag of adjustment of actual to desired stock. The case where d is less than 1.0 will be called the "case of incomplete adjustment."

THE SUPPLY OF NEW HOUSING

While important in its own right, an understanding of the conditions of supply of home-building is essential for interpreting the response of new construction to changes in the demand for housing. In the last section we saw that reactions on the supply side of the market for new homes provide one reason why the stock of housing might not react immediately to changes in desired stock demand. Likewise, desired stock may itself depend upon conditions of supply, since even in the long run supply might not be perfectly elastic; if it were not, the long-run normal price of housing would increase with an increase in desired stock demand. The evidence presented in this section, however, strongly suggests not only that the supply of new housing is highly elastic in the long run but also that even over short periods of time there is a high degree of mobility of resources into the home-building industry.

In examining the supply of new construction, several factors have to be considered. First, the price of new housing might rise with an increase in the demand for new construction if the prices of materials and labor were to rise along with the rate of new house-building. Even in the absence of this, variations in the price of housing might result from barriers to entry into or exit from the industry or because firms in the industry have differential advantages in producing new housing. Either of these factors would lead to changes in the profits of construction firms, so their importance might be judged by examining profit data. Direct evidence on the behavior of factor prices and rate of entry of firms into the industry is available.

The best time period for examining the relation of factor prices to variations in the level of new construction is that from 1922 through 1929. During this period there was comparative stability in the general level of prices and substantially full employment, as well as large changes in the rate of home-building. Likewise, while residential construction turned down following the middle of the decade, non-residential construction tended to rise well into the latter half. In other periods fluctuations in residential construction were closely related to fluctuations in the general price level and in the gross national product (GNP) as well as to non-residential construction, so that a comparison of annual changes in factor prices and output is less meaningful.

Data on new residential construction and building-material prices are shown in the first two columns of Table 2.[17] Examination of these data shows little or no relationship between new construction and building-material prices. In only three of seven cases did the two series change in the same direction from year to year; in fact, material prices reached a peak in 1923 and declined almost to the end of the decade, while construction continued to rise until 1926. Likewise, the data on the real hourly earnings of unskilled construction workers shown in the third column indicate very little relation to new construction.[18] Except for the years 1925 and 1929, the earnings of unskilled construction workers increased steadily throughout the twenties, despite the fluctuations in residential construction. Sobotka, in examining the influence of unions on the wages of construction workers, has shown that the ratio of average hourly earnings of unskilled

17 Building-material prices are measured here by the Bureau of Labor Statistics index of wholesale prices of building materials, 1935–39 = 100. New construction is measured by the Department of Commerce data, and it includes new dwelling units, additions and alterations, and maintenance and repair expenditures. These are from U.S. Department of Commerce, Business and Defense Services Administration, *Construction and Building Materials, Statistical Supplement, May, 1954* (Washington, D.C.: Government Printing Office, 1954). To convert these value data to quantity terms, they were deflated by the Boeckh index of residential construction costs (brick), which is published in the same source.

18 Both the wages of unskilled and the wages of skilled workers in Table 2 are measured by the *Engineering News-Record* series on average hourly earnings, which are published in the *Survey of Current Business.* It is claimed in the source that these measure wages actually paid rather than union scales.

Table 2   Relation of New Construction to Relative Factor Prices, 1922–29*

| | | Index of | WAGE RATES | |
| | New Construction (Millions of 1935–39 Dollars) | Building-Material Prices (1935–39 = 100) | Unskilled Labor (1935–39 Dollars per Hour) | Ratio: Skilled/Unskilled |
Year				
1922	4,239	90.7	0.369	2.26
1923	4,799	99.6	.425	2.12
1924	5,544	93.4	.454	2.14
1925	6,088	90.5	.429	2.27
1926	6,198	88.3	.434	2.32
1927	5,926	85.4	.447	2.38
1928	5,609	85.6	.454	2.43
1929	4,443	86.9	0.446	2.49

* All current dollar factor prices were deflated by the Consumer Price Index, 1935–39 = 100.

construction workers to those of all manufacturing workers remained virtually constant from 1919 to 1950.[19] This finding indicates a high mobility of labor from construction to other employments and suggests that, for unskilled labor at least, wages are fixed to the home-building industry. While Sobotka's study concluded that unions have influenced the wages of skilled construction workers, the data in the last column of Table 2 suggest that union influence on their wages did not vary with the level of new construction. The ratio of the average hourly earnings of skilled to unskilled workers rose steadily from 1923 to 1929, despite the downturn of home-building following 1926. Here, too, we must conclude that factor prices do not vary systematically with the output of the home-building industry.

Granted that materials and labor are highly mobile into the industry, what about entrepreneurs themselves? There is little evidence to indicate that barriers to entry or exit of firms are a significant source of variation in the price of new housing. Data given by Colean and Newcomb indicate that both the entry and the exit of firms were far more rapid in the construction industry than in any other industrial group during the period 1945–50.[20] According to a recent Bureau of Labor Statistics study, 27 per cent of the dwelling units started

in 1949 were built by owner-builders and 20 per cent by commercial builders who derived income from some source other than construction.[21] Of the operative commercial builders, who started between 45 and 50 per cent of new residential units built that year, 40 per cent had entered the industry in 1949 and 22 per cent had entered in the years 1946–48.[22] It is not surprising that there is such apparent easy entry into the industry. Legal barriers are few, and little specialized knowledge is required, as evidenced by the large numbers of amateurs who built their own homes in the immediate postwar period. Likewise, capital requirements are

19 See Stephen P. Sobotka, "Union Influence on Wages: The Construction Industry," *Journal of Political Economy*, LXI (April, 1953), 127–43.
20 Miles L. Colean and Robinson Newcomb, *Stabilizing Construction* (New York: McGraw-Hill Book Co., 1952), Appendix T, pp. 274–75. These data refer both to residential and to non-residential construction.
21 U.S. Department of Labor, Bureau of Labor Statistics, *Structure of the Residential Building Industry in 1949* (BLS Bull. 1170 [Washington, D.C.: Government Printing Office, 1954]), Table 1, p. 21, and Table 10, p. 26.
22 *Ibid.*, Table 7, p. 25. Operative commercial builders are those who build to their own specifications for future sale, as compared with general contractors, who build to the specifications of a specific buyer.

very low; data gathered by Colcan indicate that equipment per employee averaged only $68 for operative-builders (mostly residential) in 1929.[23] All this suggests that firms, as well as other factors of production, are highly mobile into and out of the home-building industry.

If there were barriers to entry and exit of residential construction firms or if firms enjoyed differential productive advantages, one would expect to find cyclical fluctuations in the profits of construction firms accompanying fluctuations in new construction. This would mean that the price of new housing would fluctuate more over the construction cycle than an index of construction costs. Some evidence on this point is provided by comparing the Department of Commerce GNP deflator for residential construction with the Boeckh index of residential construction costs. The Boeckh index is a fixed-weight index of material and labor costs (it will be discussed further in following sections). The GNP deflator is, essentially, the Boeckh index adjusted for changes in profits and certain other costs of construction firms.[24] The comparison of the two indexes reveals only a slight tendency for the ratio of the adjusted to the unadjusted Boeckh index to vary directly with the level of new home-building in the thirties and with no such tendency in the post–World War II period. Since material and labor costs account for about 90 per cent of the total cost of new housing, it is not surprising that fluctuations in price resulting from changes in profits appear to be minor.

Further evidence on conditions of supply can be obtained by a regression analysis which compares the variables in the supply function for new housing: total new construction in constant dollars, H'_g; the relative price of housing, p'; an index of relative building-material prices, m; the relative wage of unskilled construction workers, u; and the ratio of wages of skilled to unskilled workers, s. All these, except price, are measured by the same data as are presented in Table 2. Price is measured by Blank's index of house prices.[25] Since Blank's index is available only for the period ending in 1934, the regression comparison is limited to the period 1915–34, with war years omitted. Taking H'_g and p' in turn as dependent, the least-squares regression estimates are

$$(7) \quad H'_g = -111p' - 50.1m + 1{,}920u$$
$$(138) \quad (62.0) \quad (3{,}710)$$
$$+ 4{,}800s, \ R^2 = 0.100,$$
$$(10{,}400)$$

$$(8) \quad p' = -0.000425H'_g - 0.0336m$$
$$(0.000530) \quad (0.124)$$
$$+ 21.6u + 54.9s, \ R^2 = 0.804.$$
$$(4.26) \quad (13.7)$$

The first of these shows no relation between the quantity of new construction and the other variables in the supply function, and the regression equation explains only 10 per cent of the variation in new construction. The second indicates that about 80 per cent of the variation in price can be explained by the other variables in the supply function for new housing, but the quantity of new construction contributes nothing to this explanation.[26] Taken together, these results reinforce the conclusions of the earlier parts of this section, namely, that the supply of new housing is highly elastic. While the profit data considered above indicate that, in the short run, prices may show minor fluctuations with changes in the rate of new construction, the evidence is impressive indeed that, in the long run, the price of housing is substantially independent of the scale of the home-building industry.

23 Miles L. Colean, American Housing (New York: Twentieth Century Fund, 1949), Table 20, p. 385. Even for excavating subcontractors, for whom equipment per employee was greatest in the residential construction sector, this figure was only $1,491—very small indeed when compared with capital per worker in manufacturing.

24 See U.S. Department of Commerce, Office of Business Economics, National Income, 1954 Edition (Washington, D.C.: Government Printing Office, 1954), p. 156.

25 David M. Blank, "Relationship between an Index of House Prices and Building Costs," Journal of the American Statistical Association, XLIX (March, 1954), 67–88. This is an index of the market prices of new and existing houses rather than a construction-cost index. Blank's index was not used in the demand analysis presented later because it is not available for years after 1934.

26 That the coefficient of building-material prices in (8) is not significant is not surprising, since there was very little variation in the index of material prices in the period to which the regression refers.

THE DEMAND FOR HOUSING: COMPLETE ADJUSTMENT

We turn now to estimating the stock demand for housing. If the housing stock were to adjust so rapidly to changing prices and incomes that at the end of any given calendar year actual stock would equal the level desired under currently prevailing conditions, estimating stock demand would be no different from estimating the demand for the services of any commodity. Each observed combination of end-of-year stock, price, income, and the interest rate would, apart from sampling fluctuations, give us one point on the desired stock-demand curve. Estimates of stock demand, assuming these conditions, are considered in this section.

In making these estimates, we used the following data:

h_f = end-of-year per capita non-farm housing stock—Grebler, Blank, and Winnick estimates of the non-farm housing stock deflated by the non-farm population of the continental United States [27]

p = Boeckh index of residential construction costs (brick)

y_p = Friedman's per capita expected-income series

r = Durand's basic yield of ten-year corporate bonds [28]

Throughout this study all monetary magnitudes are adjusted for changes in the general level of prices, the base period being 1935–39. Where deflation was necessary, the BLS index of consumer prices was used.

Although a more detailed evaluation of these data will be made in the following section, their essential features should be noted. First, with respect to the stock series, comparisons which Grebler, Blank, and Winnick make with bench-mark-type data for a few selected years suggest that, although their estimates are reasonably close to others for the period prior to World War II and any discrepancies tend not to be cumulative over time, they seriously underestimate the housing stock in the postwar period.[29] For this reason, the time-series analysis of this study is restricted to the period 1915–41 (with war years omitted).

Second, the measures of price and the rate of interest used here are interpreted as measuring the long-run normal values of these variables. Since the analysis of the last section suggests that any short-run fluctuations in price are likely to result from changes in the profits of construction firms, such price changes would not be reflected in an index of material and labor prices. While it might seem surprising that a bond-yield series is used to measure the cost of mortgage funds, there is good reason for this. A measure of mortgage rates would be highly unsatisfactory, since other conditions of mortgage contracts—length of the loan and required down payments—have a significant influence on the cost of mortgage funds.[30] For this reason the bond-yield series, which is a measure of opportunity costs to mortgage lenders, was used.

Finally, with respect to the income variable, it is a matter of common knowledge that people's housing does not change with every short-range change in their income. At the same time it is generally true that individuals' housing is in tune with their normal level of income. This suggests that we need an income variable that is insulated from short-range fluctuations in money receipts and aims at approximating what people appear to believe is their normal income level. Such a variable is provided by Milton Friedman's series of expected or permanent income.[31]

27 Leo Grebler, David M. Blank, and Louis Winnick, *Capital Formation in Residential Real Estate: Trends and Prospects* (Princeton, N.J.: Princeton University Press, 1956) , Table D-1, pp. 360–61.
28 David Durand, *Basic Yield of Corporate Bonds, 1900–1942* (New York: National Bureau of Economic Research, 1942) .
29 *Op. cit.*, Appendix D, pp. 365–76, and especially Table D-3, p. 370. Except for 1950, their estimates diverge from bench-mark estimates by no more than about 10 per cent. For 1950 their estimate is about 22 per cent less than an estimate derived from 1950 housing census data.
30 Data presented by R. J. Saulnier, *Urban Mortgage Lending by Life Insurance Companies* (New York: National Bureau of Economic Research, 1950) , Table B-5, pp. 132–34, suggest that these other conditions changed drastically over the period we are considering. Apart from degrees-of-freedom considerations, measures of mortgage rates, length of contract, and required down payments are highly intercorrelated during this period so that it would be quite difficult statistically to measure the influence of each.
31 *Op. cit.*, chap. v, esp. pp. 142–52.

Turning now to stock-demand estimates assuming complete adjustment, the least-squares regression with h_f as the dependent variables yields

$$(9) \quad h_f = -4.66p + 0.820y_p - 24.7r,$$
$$\quad\quad (1.45) \quad (0.219) \quad (11.4)$$
$$\quad\quad\quad\quad R^2 = 0.448, \, \delta = 0.592,$$
$$E(h_f) - 0.570 + 0.553 \quad -0.131,$$

where δ stands for the Durbin-Watson statistic (see below) and $E(h_f)$ for the partial elasticity of h_f with respect to the several determining variables, as estimated from the slope parameters of (9) and the mean values of the variables for the sample period. Equation (9) indicates that end-of-year stock varied directly with income and inversely with price and the rate of interest, as would be expected a priori. All the coefficients of (9) are numerically greater than twice their standard errors, and the regression equation explains almost half the variance of end-of-year stock. The estimated stock-demand elasticities for income and price are numerically about equal to 0.5. We shall see that these probably seriously underestimate the true elasticities, but even this estimate suggests that housing demand is much more responsive to price changes than the Duesenberry-Kistin estimate, −0.08, would suggest.

In evaluating these results, we note the high positive serial correlation in the residuals, as seen from the Durbin-Watson statistic.[32] An examination of the residuals computed from (9) indicates that they are negative—that is, computed stock exceeds the observed stock—in 1926 and earlier years and positive for the period 1927 through 1935. Now the period 1922 through 1926 was one of greater-than-average home-building, while for most of the period 1927 through 1935 the rate of home-building was below average. This means that, when new construction was proceeding rapidly, the actual housing stock was relatively small for given values of price, income, and the rate of interest and conversely. But this result is just what would be expected if the housing stock did not adjust completely to changed conditions of demand within a year's time. If the housing stock does not respond completely within a year's time to changes in, say, income, then the

coefficients of (9) and the elasticities based upon them might seriously underestimate the ultimate response of the housing stock.

THE DEMAND FOR HOUSING: INCOMPLETE ADJUSTMENT

The results of the preceding section strongly suggest that, if housing demand is to be correctly understood, account must be taken of the dynamics of the adjustment of the housing stock to changing conditions. Our earlier analysis suggests that both the ultimate response of the housing stock to changed demand conditions and the pace of adjustment in the housing market can be determined by comparing new construction, h_g', with the determinants of desired stock and the stock actually in existence, h.[33] When we do so, we see that housing demand appears to be much more responsive than the preceding section suggests and that a period much longer than one year is needed for complete adjustment.

The Basic Estimates of Stock Demand

Taking the least-squares regression with h_g' as dependent yields

$$(10)$$
$$h_g' = -2.49p + 0.438y_p - 8.34r - 0.282h,$$
$$\quad (0.589) \quad (0.0919) \quad (4.47) \quad (0.0695)$$

$$R^2 = 0.621, \, \delta = 1.01,$$

32 For twenty-five observations and three independent variables, the bounds on the 5 per cent point for this statistic are 1.12 and 1.66. Hence we would in this instance reject the hypothesis that the true residuals are serially uncorrelated (see J. Durbin and G. S. Watson, "Testing for Serial Correlation in Least Squares Regression. II," *Biometrika*, XXXVIII [June, 1951], 173, Table 4).
33 Here, the per capita gross rate of non-farm residential construction, h_g, is based upon estimates of the current dollar value of new dwelling units, additions and alterations to existing dwellings, and maintenance and repair expenditures, as published in U.S. Department of Commerce, Business and Defense Services Administration, *op. cit.* To convert to quantity per capita, these estimates were deflated by the Boeckh index and the non-farm population of the continental United States. The variable h is simply the beginning-of-year per capita housing stock and, as such, is h_f lagged one year.

$$E(h'_g) - 5.54 + 5.38 \quad - 0.805 - 5.13$$
$$E(h_d) - 0.904 + 0.879 \quad - 0.131 \ldots$$

New construction varied directly with income and inversely with price, the interest rate, and stock. The coefficients of price, income, and stock in equation (10) are all at least four times as great numerically as their standard errors, while the coefficient of r is almost twice its standard error. The regression equation explains some 62 per cent of the variation in the new construction series. However, the Durbin-Watson statistic indicates that the true residuals are positively serially correlated.[34]

The elasticities of new construction, $E(h'_g)$, are shown in the first line below equation (10). They indicate that home-building is highly responsive indeed to changes in price or income. Either a 1 per cent fall in price or a 1 per cent increase in income leads to an increase in gross construction of about $5\frac{1}{2}$ per cent in the same year as the change in price or income. In the absence of further changes, of course, the annual rate of home-building would decline over time as the housing stock approaches the desired level. The response of new construction depends upon two things: the ultimate change in stock demand resulting from a given change in price or income and the rate of adjustment over time in the housing stock.[35]

The elasticities of desired stock demand, $E(h_d)$, are likewise shown below equation (10). These indicate that a 1 per cent fall in price or increase in income would lead to an eventual increase in stock of almost 1 per cent. These estimates indicate that housing demand is in fact considerably more responsive to price or income changes than is commonly believed. The estimate of income elasticity is almost twice as great as Morton and Winnick inferred from comparisons like that shown in Table 1. Even more striking is the estimate of price elasticity, −0.9 as compared with the Duesenberry-Kistin estimate of −0.08. Likewise, these estimates of price and income elasticity are almost twice as large numerically as those obtained in the preceding section, where it was assumed that the adjustment of the housing stock took place completely within a year's time. This result bears out the suggestion made in the last section that account of the dynamic lag of adjustment of the housing stock must be

34 For twenty-five observations and four independent variables the bounds on this statistic are 1.04 and 1.77, respectively (see Durbin and Watson, *op. cit.*, pp. 173–74). Examination of the computed residuals reveals that equation (10) underestimates new construction during the period 1923 through 1929 and overestimates it from 1930 through 1937. While I have been unable to determine to my complete satisfaction the reasons for this, I believe it is largely due to three factors. First, because of the method by which the estimates of new construction were prepared, it seems likely that any errors of estimation in the 1920's affected the estimates for every year of the decade and that they overestimate new construction in the twenties relative to the thirties. Second, because I have been unable to find a suitable measure of property-tax rates, this variable has been excluded. While it would appear that there was no trend in tax rates during the period considered here, it would seem that they varied contracyclically—falling below the period average in the middle and late twenties and rising above the average in the early and middle thirties (see Colin D. Campbell, "Are Property-Tax Rates Increasing?" *Journal of Political Economy*, LIX [October, 1951], 434–42). (For further discussion of these two points see Appendix B.) And, third, Margaret G. Reid, "Capital Formation in Residential Real Estate," *Journal of Political Economy*, LXVI (April, 1958), 131–53, has argued that the Grebler, Blank, and Winnick stock data overestimate the housing stock in the twenties relative to the thirties. If this is the case, equation (10) would underestimate new construction in the twenties relative to the thirties, producing a time pattern of estimated residuals qualitatively similar to that actually observed.

One might think that taking first differences would tend to eliminate this serial correlation, but here it only makes matters worse. Taking first differences actually increases the serial correlation, $\delta = 0.628$, and results in a substantially worse fit, $R^2 = 0.425$. The presence of serially correlated residuals does not necessarily imply that the regression coefficients are biased, though the traditional least-squares estimators are not efficient. Likewise, the estimated standard errors shown here, which were computed on the assumption that the true residuals are serially uncorrelated, may be poor estimates of the variability of these coefficients in repeated samplings.

35 In estimating equation (10), a measure of the quantity of new construction was used. This is a measure of expenditures for new housing (price times quantity) adjusted for changes in the general level of prices and deflated by the index of relative price. There is, therefore, a possibility of a spurious correlation between measured quantity and price because of errors in the price series. If, however, we compare real expenditures with the independent variables of (10), the possibility of such spurious correlation is eliminated, and quantity elasticities can be obtained. Doing so, the elasticities of quantity obtained are almost identical with those obtained by using the measure of quantity directly, as in (10).

Likewise, if we compute the regression using the logarithms of the same variables as were used in equation (10), the coefficients of the independent variables are simply the elasticities of new construction. These, too, are virtually identical with the

taken for a real understanding of the workings of the housing market.[36]

Further evidence on the dynamics of the adjustment of housing stock is provided by the coefficient of h in equation (10). As equation (4) shows, the coefficient of h is equal to $-(d-k)$, where d is the coefficient of adjustment and k the rate of replacement. Now k is not known exactly, but it is probably about $3\frac{1}{2}$ per cent per year.[37] This, together with the coefficient of h in (10), suggests a value for d of 0.317. This means that individuals seek to add about one-third of the excess of desired over actual stock in any given year. If such were the case, of course, the actual stock of housing would never adjust completely but would come arbitrarily close to desired stock with the passage of time. For this value of d it would take almost exactly *six* years for the adjustment to be 90 per cent completed. Thus the ultimate change in the housing stock that would come about from a change in demand conditions is substantially greater than the change brought about in a single year.

Such are our basic estimates of housing demand. In the following paragraphs we shall consider the more important shortcomings to which they might be subject.

Errors of Measurement

The estimates of equation (10) obtained above might be biased by errors in the statistical measures of the true variables to which our model relates. Such errors are of two kinds, random and systematic measurement errors.

One source of bias in the traditional least-squares estimators of the coefficients of a linear regression equation arises out of measurement errors in the observed values of variables being compared. The case where the measured values of the variables contain normally distributed "random"-error components—error components which are serially uncorrelated and are uncorrelated with the true values of the variables— has received some study. Koopmans has shown that maximum likelihood estimates may be obtained in this case, provided the covariances of the error components are known.[38] These estimates are termed "weighted-regression" estimates. He has also shown that the correctly

weighted regression estimates are bounded by those estimates obtained by computing all the "elementary" regressions—the regression in which it is assumed that only one variable is measured with error and which is simply the conventional least-squares regression with that variable taken as dependent—provided that the error components in the various measured variables are uncorrelated with each other. Thus, even if the covariances of the error components are unknown, it is possible to determine the limits within which the correctly weighted regression estimates would lie.

If four additional regression equations are computed, one for each of the four "independent" variables in equation (10), a set of five stock-demand elasticities for each variable can be obtained. The numerically smallest and largest stock elasticity estimates so obtained

---

elasticity estimates obtained from the linear form of the regression in equation (10).

36 The 95 per cent confidence limits on these elasticities are -0.421 and -1.80 for price and $+0.538$ and $+1.42$ for income. Thus the estimates obtained here are not necessarily inconsistent with numerically larger estimates obtained in some of the comparisons to be made in later sections of this study. The estimated elasticity with respect to the interest rate here is no larger than obtained in the previous section. On a priori grounds, we would expect it to be almost one-half of the price elasticity (see n. 10, above). One reason for this low value is the nature of the interest-rate series used. The bond-yield series might be interpreted as a close approximation to the pure rate of interest. The mortgage rate, in addition, includes provision for administrative costs and risk and, hence, is greater than the pure rate. If administrative costs and the risk premium were fixed rather than varying with the pure rate of interest, the unit increase in new construction and stock demand resulting from a change in the mortgage rate would be correctly estimated using the bond-yield series, but the elasticity of either new construction or stock demand would be underestimated.

37 The rate of depreciation exclusive of maintenance and repair expenditures used by Grebler, Blank, and Winnick in obtaining their cumulated stock estimates is 2 per cent per year. To this should be added an allowance for maintenance and repair expenditures, which averaged about $1\frac{1}{2}$ per cent per year in the period studied here (for a discussion of the appropriate depreciation rate see Grebler, Blank, and Winnick, *op. cit.*, Appendix E, esp. pp. 377–82). While the exact value of the depreciation rate is of great importance in constructing stock estimates by cumulating and depreciating additions to stock, the conclusion reached in the text depends only upon its order of magnitude.

38 Tjalling C. Koopmans, *Linear Regression Analysis of Economic Time Series* (Harlem: DeErven F. Bohn N.V., 1937).

are -0.669 and -1.60 for price and $+0.652$ and $+1.17$ for income. Taking account of the possibility of random errors in the data would have but little effect on the stock-demand elasticity with respect to income but might lead to an estimate of price elasticity which is substantially larger numerically.

Actually, the most serious kind of error in the data with which we are faced is secular bias in the measures of price and stock used. The Boeckh index of residential costs, which was used to measure price, might be seriously biased for comparisons between widely separated years. This is because a fixed-weight index of material and labor costs would fail to reflect changes in the price of housing resulting from technological change or from substitution of inputs resulting from changes in relative factor prices. Such factors are likely to have operated more or less steadily over time, so that a large part of the possible error in the index can be "covered" by introducing a time trend into the regression equation.

In like manner, the most serious kind of error in the stock series used is likely to be a trend-wise bias. The Grebler-Blank-Winnick series used as a measure of housing stock was derived in the following way: an estimate of stock at the beginning of 1890 was prepared using data on mortgaged owner-occupied houses reported in the 1890 census. End-of-year stock for any year is the stock at the beginning plus gross capital formation during the year less capital consumption. Gross capital formation is the current dollar value of new housekeeping dwelling units and additions and alterations to existing dwellings deflated by the Boeckh index of residential construction costs. Capital consumption consists of a depreciation allowance, which is 2 per cent of the beginning-of-year stock plus 1 per cent of gross capital formation, plus an allowance for demolitions.[39] A trend-wise bias in their estimates would arise from such a bias in the construction-cost index used as a deflator for gross capital formation or an incorrect depreciation rate. Such a bias would also arise if, as seems possible, annual estimates of the value of gross capital formation understate the true value. For these reasons, too, it might be argued that a time trend should be included in the regression analysis.

When a linear time trend, T, is included, the regression equation becomes

(11)
$$h'_g = -2.05p + 0.449y_p - 9.72r$$
$$(0.718) \quad (0.0924) \quad (4.66)$$
$$- 0.234h - 0.910T,$$
$$(0.0830) \quad (0.855)$$

$$R^2 = 0.643,$$

$$E(h_d) - 0.870 + 1.05 - 0.179 \quad \cdot \cdot \cdot \cdot \cdot \cdot \cdot$$

The coefficient of T in equation (11) is only slightly greater than its standard error, and it is significant only at about the 30 per cent level. Furthermore, introducing the time trend makes almost no difference in the estimated stock-demand elasticities. It is thus apparent that the possibility of a systematic secular bias in the price and stock variables can be dismissed as unimportant for our purposes. Likewise, including the time trend shows no evidence of any systematic change in consumer preferences or "tastes" for housing, as Winnick has alleged.

Experiments with the Income Variable

In all the comparisons presented so far, Friedman's expected-income series has been used. This series is a weighted average of the current disposable incomes of several recent periods, with the most recent period receiving the greatest weight. It is used in an attempt to measure the normal income level to which the housing stock is adjusted. Here we shall attempt to ascertain whether some other income variable gives us a better explanation of changes in the housing stock.

If, instead of Friedman's series, per capita current income, y_e, is used to measure income,[40]

39 A full description of procedures used is given in Grebler, Blank, and Winnick, *op. cit.*, Appendix D. For a very detailed critical review of their work see Reid, *op. cit.*
40 The series is from Raymond W. Goldsmith, *A Study of Saving in the United States* (Princeton, N.J.: Princeton University Press, 1956), III, 127, Table N-1, and is the series of current income upon which Friedman's series is based. Like Friedman's,

the least-squares regression corresponding to equation (10) is

(12)
$$h_g' = -1.49p + 0.249y_c - 0.106r$$
$$(0.505) \quad (0.0540) \quad (4.43)$$
$$- 0.124h, \quad R^2 = 0.607$$
$$(0.0621)$$

$$E(h_g') - 3.32 + 2.98 - 0.0102 - 2.26$$
$$E(h_d) - 1.02 + 0.913 - 0.00313 \quad \cdots \cdots$$

According to equation (12), an increase of one dollar in current income was accompanied by an increase in new construction in the same year of only about twenty-five cents worth of housing. On the other hand, the coefficient of permanent income in equation (10) indicates an increase of about forty-four cents. This is just the sort of result we would expect if housing expenditures were geared to a consumer's normal income level. Housing demand reacts less to a change in current income precisely because a consumer's expectations of his normal income level change less rapidly than his current income. Note, too, that the coefficients of price and, especially, the rate of interest are much smaller when current income is used instead of Friedman's series.[41]

There is another reason besides the neglect of income expectations for believing that current income is a poor measure for the purposes of this analysis. In his study of automobile demand, Chow found that the rate of personal saving is a significant variable in explaining the purchase of new cars.[42] Now if consumption depends only upon permanent income, as Friedman's hypothesis suggests, then for a given level of permanent income a change in current income represents a change in saving. In particular, let

(13) $c = ay_p$ or $s = y_c - c = y_c - ay_p$,

where c is per capita real consumption, s is the per capita real saving, and a is the average propensity to consume, which, according to Friedman's hypothesis, is independent of the level of permanent income. Then, supposing that new construction depends upon personal saving in addition to the excess of desired over

actual stock, we have, using equations (3) and (13),

(14)
$$h_g' = dh_d - (d-k)h + es = db_0 + db_1p$$
$$+ (db_2 - ea)y_p + db_3r - (d-k)h + ey_c.$$

Equation (14) suggests that the influence of personal saving on new construction can be estimated by including both current and permanent income in the regression analysis. If this is done, we find

(15)
$$h_g' = -2.13p + 0.266y_p - 4.97r - 0.220h$$
$$(0.717) \quad (0.216) \quad (5.88) \quad (0.0988)$$
$$+ 0.110y_c, \quad R^2 = 0.637.$$
$$(0.125)$$

Assuming an average propensity to consume of 0.9,[43] equation (15) can be rewritten as

(16)
$$h_g' = -2.13p + 0.366y_p - 4.97r - 0.220h$$
$$(0.717) \quad (0.124) \quad (5.88) \quad (0.0988)$$
$$+ 0.11os.$$
$$(0.125)$$

The coefficient of y_c in (15) or s in (16) is smaller than its standard error, while the co-

it refers to all persons in the United States rather than to the non-farm population only. However, a current income series for the non-farm population was obtained by deducting estimates of the income of the farm population from total current income. This indicated that fluctuations in per capita current income of the non-farm population were almost identical with those for the whole population. While the mean value of per capita non-farm income was probably somewhat above that for the whole population in most of the period studied here, the effect of this difference on the estimated income elasticity is minor relative to sampling and other errors to which estimated income elasticity is subject.
41 However, the price and income desired stock-demand elasticities inferred from equation (12) are quite similar to those from equation (10), despite the fact that the coefficients of the former are substantially smaller numerically. This is due to the smaller value of the coefficient of h in (12).
42 Gregory C. Chow, *The Demand for Automobiles in the United States: A Study in Consumer Durables* (Amsterdam: North-Holland Publishing Co., 1957).
43 See Friedman's estimate, *op. cit.*, Table 15, p. 147.

efficients of none of the other variables in (16) differ from the corresponding estimates in equation (10) by as much as one standard error. This indicates that the personal savings variable is not very important in determining the rate of new building. But the equations above indicate that if current rather than permanent income is used, as in (12), the income coefficient reflects the influence of saving as well as that of permanent income.

While it is apparent that current income is less satisfactory than Friedman's series for this analysis, might not some other weighted average of past current income be even better? Friedman himself comments:

We have interpreted the exact meaning of permanent income in terms of the horizon of the consumer unit. Now there seems to be no reason why the horizon should be the same for all individual categories of consumption and some reasons why it should differ systematically. For example, it seems highly plausible that housing expenditures are planned in terms of a longer horizon, and so a different concept of permanent income, than expenditures on, say, food.[44]

Specifically, Friedman's expected-income series can be defined by

$$(17) \quad y_p(t) = (1 - e^{-\beta}) \sum_{i=0}^{\infty} e^{-\beta i} \, y_c \, (t - i),$$

where the weight coefficient $\beta = 0.4$ and the symbol t stands for the year.[45] If housing expenditures are planned in terms of a longer horizon than all current consumption, the appropriate concept of permanent income would be a similar series but with a smaller weight coefficient, β. The effect of a smaller weight coefficient would be to give relatively smaller weight to current incomes of the immediate past and relatively more to those of the more distant past.

The hypothesis that the income horizon for housing expenditures is longer than for all current consumption can be tested by computing weighted averages similar to Friedman's but with different weight coefficients. The weighted average appropriate for our purposes is that which maximizes the correlation of new construction with income and the other variables. Table 3 summarizes the results of estimating

Table 3 Housing Demand for Different Expected-Income Measures

β	Estimated $E(h_d, y_p)$	R^2
0.5	+0.869	0.563
0.4	+ .879	.621
0.3	+0.913	0.535

the flow-demand equation for three values of the weight coefficient, β, in the neighborhood of 0.4. In this table the implied estimate of the income elasticity of stock demand and the coefficient of multiple determination for the regression of new construction on income and the other variables in (10) are shown for each of the three income series. The maximum value of R^2 is reached for β equal to 0.4, the weight coefficient for Friedman's series. The second column of Table 3 also shows that the implied income elasticity of desired stock-demand changes very little as the weight coefficient in the expected-income series is varied in the neighborhood of the maximum likelihood estimate, 0.4. Thus the admittedly very plausible hypothesis that consumers plan their housing expenditures in terms of an income horizon which is longer than that for all current consumption is not consistent with our data. It would appear that Friedman's expected-income series is the appropriate one for studying housing demand.

In brief, the results of this section are:

1. The response of housing demand to price or income changes is much greater than is commonly believed. The estimates obtained in this section suggest that the elasticities of desired stock demand with respect to income and price are both about unity.

2. If the adjustment of the housing stock to

44 *Ibid.*, pp. 207–8.
45 Actually, Friedman modifies this formulation to include a time trend. This need not be considered explicitly here, since it results only in the multiplication of the above by a constant. In practice, the infinite summation indicated in (17) can be approximated by a weighted average of current disposable income for a finite number of time periods to any desired degree of accuracy.

changing demand conditions is to be properly understood, account must be taken of the dynamic lag of the adjustment of stock. This lag is substantial. Our estimates indicate that individuals seek to add about one-third the difference between desired and actual stock during a year, which implies that, for the adjustment of the actual housing stock to be 90 per cent completed, six years are required.

3. The rate of new home-building is highly responsive to price and income changes. The elasticities of new construction with respect to price and income are about 5.5, numerically.

4. Including a time trend in the regression analysis indicated that our estimates are not biased by secular bias in the measures of price and stock used. Likewise, it indicated that the demand for housing has not been influenced by a secular change in tastes.

5. Experiments with the income variable suggest that Friedman's expected-income series is indeed the appropriate one for studying housing demand.

HOUSING AND INTRA-URBAN LOCATION

Equilibrium of the Household

WILLIAM ALONSO

INTRODUCTION

An individual who arrives in a city and wishes to buy some land to live upon will be faced with the double decision of how large a lot he should purchase and how close to the center of the city he should settle. In reality he would also consider the apparent character and racial composition of the neighborhood, the quality of the schools in the vicinity, how far away he would be from any relatives he might have in the city, and a thousand other factors. However, the individual in question is an "economic man," defined and simplified in a way such that we can handle the analysis of his decision-making.[1] He merely wishes to maximize his satisfaction by owning and consuming the goods he likes and avoiding those he dislikes. Moreover, an individual is in reality a family which may contain several members. Their decisions may be reached in a family council or be the responsibility of a single member. We are not concerned with how these tastes are formed, but simply with what they are. Given these tastes, this simplified family will spend whatever money it has available in maximizing its satisfaction.

The city in which the individual arrives is a simplified city. It lies on a featureless plain, and transportation is possible in all directions. All employment and all goods and services are available only at the center of the city. Land is bought and sold by free contract, without any institutional restraints and without having its character fixed by any structures existing upon the ground. Municipal services and tax rates are uniform throughout the city. The individual knows the price of land at every location, and, from his point of view, this is a given fact, not affected by his decisions.

In this chapter we shall find how much land and where such an individual would buy in such a city. Finding these things constitutes the equilibrium solution for the individual. It will be found in this chapter by means of classical consumer equilibrium theory, though the unusual nature of the problem will call forth

unexpected turns from the theory. However, though classical theory is satisfactory for the description of individual equilibrium, it does not enable us in this case to aggregate individuals to arrive at a market solution without a radical reformulation. In order to understand this reformulation, the classical solution must be thoroughly grasped. It will be explored in detail in the following pages, first diagrammatically, and later mathematically.

DIAGRAMMATIC SOLUTION OF INDIVIDUAL EQUILIBRIUM

To describe individual equilibrium diagrammatically, we must represent graphically both all of the alternatives open to the individual and his pattern of preferences. By joining these two diagrams, we can observe which of the opportunities open to the individual he will choose.

Opportunities Open to the Individual

The individual has at his disposal a certain income which he may spend as he wishes. Out of this income he must pay for his land costs, his commuting costs and for all other goods and services (including savings). We wish to describe diagrammatically all of the choices open to the consumer, subject to the restriction of

[1] Purposeful simplification for analysis is so much the rule and its advantages and disadvantages have been discussed so thoroughly that further discussion of it here is unnecessary. However, on the particular issue of residential location and urban structure, an interesting polemic was started by Walter Firey (*Land Uses in Central Boston,* chap. 1), who attacked the simplifications of human ecologists. A reply from this group may be found in Amos Hawley, *Human Ecology,* pp. 179–180, 286.

his budget. This restriction may be expressed thus:

Individual's income
= land costs + commuting costs + all other expenditures

First let us examine his expenditures for all goods and services excepting land and commuting costs. The individual may buy greater or smaller quantities of a wide variety of goods. We may denominate the quantity of each good he purchases by $z_1, z_2, \ldots, z_n$, for each of n goods. If the prices of these n goods are $p_1, p_2, \ldots, p_n$, then the expenditure by the individual for any good z_i will be equal to the price of that good times the quantity of the good purchased: $p_i z_i$. His total expenditure for the goods and services in this category will be:

$$p_1 z_1 + p_2 z_2 + \ldots + p_n z_n.$$

However, for the sake of simplicity we shall group all these various goods and services into one composite good, z. The price of this composite good will be a price index, p_z. The expenditure on all goods and services other than land or commuting costs will be $p_z z$. This simplification will not affect the logic of the subsequent analysis. As an alternative, z may be considered to be money, and p_z may be regarded as unity.

Second, let us examine the individual's expenditures on land. From the point of view of the individual, a price structure is given which specifies a price for land at every location. This price structure is represented by curve $P(t)$ in Figure 1. Price of land, P, varies with distance from the center of the city, t.[2] By expressing the price structure in this manner, it is clear that when a location is chosen, a given price of land is implied.

However, in purchasing land the consumer not only chooses a location but must also decide upon the quantity of land he will acquire. We shall represent this quantity by the letter q. The expenditure on land will be equal to the price of land times the quantity purchased: $P(t) q$.

Thirdly, we wish to consider commuting costs. These will increase with increasing distance from the center of the city. We shall

Figure 1 Diagrammatic structure of land prices.

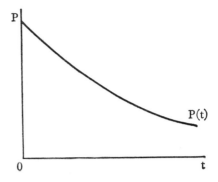

represent these costs by the function $k(t)$ where t corresponds to the same location as in $P(t)$.

We can now write the budget equation that will contain all of the choices open to a person of income y:

$$(2{:}1) \qquad y = p_z z + P(t)q + k(t)$$

where
    y: income;
    p_z: price of the composite good;
    z: quantity of the composite good;
    $P(t)$: price of land at distance t from the center of the city;
    q: quantity of land;
    $k(t)$: commuting costs to distance t;
    t: distance from the center of the city.

Equation $(2{:}1)$ contains within it all the possible alternative ways in which the individual may spend his money. We shall now diagram this function. This can be done in a 3-dimensional set of co-ordinates in terms of the variables z, q, and t. These three variables are the determining ones since income (y) and the price of the composite good (p_z) are given, and the price of land, $P(t)$, and commuting costs, $k(t)$, are functions in terms of t. We shall obtain a 3-dimensional surface that will represent all of the alternatives open to the consumer, and this surface will be called the

2 It will be assumed here that the price of land decreases with increasing distance from the center of the city. Below it will be seen that this is a requirement for the existence of both individual and market equilibrium as well as essentially true for most cities.

locus of opportunities. Every point on the surface is a possible alternative open to the consumer; every point not on the surface is not a possible alternative.[3] To describe the locus of opportunities surface we shall consider sections through it by holding each of the three variables constant in succession and observing the variations of the other two.

First, let us fix t at any distance $t = t_0$. The individual can now choose between varying quantities of land, q, and the composite good, z, while distance is for the moment fixed at t_0. Distance being fixed, so are price of land, at $P(t_0)$, and commuting costs, at $k(t_0)$. Equation (2:1) becomes

$$y = p_z z + P(t_0)q + k(t_0),$$

which may be rewritten as

$$q = \frac{y - k(t_0)}{P(t_0)} - \frac{p_z}{P(t_0)}z.$$

This is a linear equation, with a slope equal to the negative of the ratio of the prices of the two goods. Its intercepts are $q = 0$, $z = [y - k(t_0)]/p_z$, and $z = 0$, $q = [y - k(t_0)]/P(t_0)$. It is shown in Figure 2.

Now let us hold the composite good constant at $z = z_0$, and allow q and t to vary. Equation (2:1) becomes

$$y = p_z z_0 + P(t)q + k(t),$$

which may be rewritten as

$$q = \frac{y - p_z z_0 - k(t)}{P(t)}.$$

This is not a simple linear equation. The price of land, $P(t)$, in the denominator, decreases with increasing distance from the center of the city. Therefore the quantity of land that may be bought, q, increases with distance, since land is becoming cheaper. On the other hand, distance enters into the numerator in the form of commuting costs, $k(t)$. As distance increases, so do commuting costs, and consequently the amount of land that may be purchased decreases. Thus, distance acts in opposing directions upon the quantity of land. The resulting curve is shown in Figure 3. The

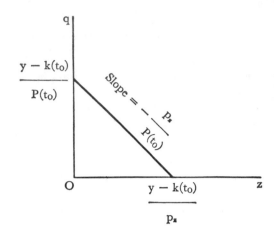

Figure 2   Locus of opportunities between q and z, when t is constant at t_0.

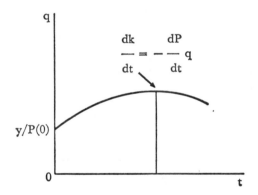

Figure 3   Locus of opportunities between q and t, when z is constant at z_0.

curve of q on t rises up to the point at which marginal increases in commuting costs are equal to the savings realized from the decreasing price of land. Thereafter, the amount of land that may be bought with increasing distance decreases.

3   The locus of opportunities is a generalization of the budget or price line of the usual case. Both describe all of the choices available given a certain income. However, while the budget line considers choices among goods at definite prices, in this case the locus of opportunities considers a good, q, of varying price, $P(t)$, and a good, t, which has no price but determines the price of good q and commuting costs, $k(t)$. Though the budget line is therefore a special case of the locus of opportunities, they both serve the same analytical function.

And lastly, let us hold q constant at q_0 and allow t and z to vary. Equation (2:1) becomes

$$y = p_z z + P(t) q_0 + k(t),$$

which may be rewritten as

$$z = \frac{y - P(t) q_0 - k(t)}{p_z}.$$

The denominator of the fraction is a constant, p_z. The numerator, on the other hand, contains two expressions in terms of t. The first, $P(t) q_0$, will cause z to increase with t since $P(t)$ will be decreasing and the expression is preceded by a negative sign. The second, $k(t)$, also preceded by a minus sign, increases with t and therefore causes z to decrease. The resulting curve is shown in Figure 4. These two opposing effects of distance will cause the amount of the composite good to increase as long as the savings resulting from cheaper land exceed the increases in commuting costs, and the amount of the composite good will decrease when increases in commuting costs exceed the savings resulting from cheaper land.

Now that we have three sections through the locus of opportunities surface, we may draw it in three dimensions. This has been done in Figure 5. A section parallel to the q–z plane would yield a curve corresponding to that of Figure 2. A section parallel to the q–t plane would yield a curve corresponding to Figure 3. And a section parallel to the z–t plane will yield a curve corresponding to that of Figure

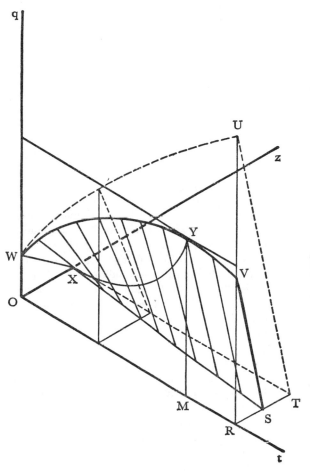

Figure 5   Locus of opportunities surface.

4.[4] The shell-like surface contains all of the combinations of land (q), the composite good (z), and distance (t) open to the consumer, and his equilibrium solution must be a point on this surface.[5] It should be noted that a

Figure 4   Locus of opportunities between z and t, when q is constant at q_0.

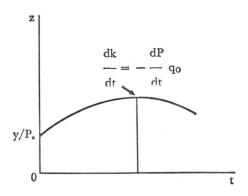

4   At $q = 0$, such a section would show z decreasing monotonically with increases in t. This, of course, is a special case of the typical humped curve, where the high point of the curve occurs at $t = 0$.
5   The surface bounded by dashed lines corresponds to the locus of opportunities that would obtain if there were no commuting costs. It is, of course, higher than the surface for the case with costs of commuting, since these costs are equivalent to reductions in income or reduced purchasing power. As one instance, the quantity of land $q = RV$ bought where there are commuting costs (and no z is purchased) will be $[y - k(R)]/P(R)$, while the quantity of land $q = RV$ that would be bought if there were no commuting costs would be $y/P(R)$. The quantity of land lost to commuting expenses is $k(R)/P(R)$.

higher income would have yielded a locus of opportunities surface of the same shape but above the one in Figure 5, while a lower income would have yielded one below it.

Preferences of the Individual

We now wish to map the individual's preferences. When the mapping of preferences is joined with the mapping of opportunities, individual equilibrium will correspond to that opportunity which yields the individual greatest satisfaction.

Preferences will be mapped through *indifference surfaces*. In this case an indifference surface will be a set of combinations of quantities of land and the composite good and distance, such that the individual will be equally satisfied by any of these combinations. Hence, he may be said to be indifferent among all of the combinations represented by the indifference surface. However, the usual shape of indifference surfaces is that of a bowl propped up against the corner of a box. In this case, the strange nature of the good distance will result in an unusually shaped indifference surface. We shall arrive at the shape of the surface by examining sections through it.

Let us begin by holding the composite good, z, constant, and allowing the quantity of land, q, and distance, t, to vary. Land q is a good of the ordinary type. All other things being equal, the individual will prefer to have more than less of it; that is to say, he will prefer to have ample living space and not to be crowded. Distance, t, on the other hand, is unusual. We assume that, all other things being equal, a rational individual will prefer a more accessible location to a less accessible one. Since t represents the distance from the center of the city, and thus the distance the individual must commute to the principal place of shopping, amusement, and employment, we may say that accessibility decreases as t increases. In other words, the individual would prefer t to be smaller rather than larger, so that t may be thought of as a good with negative utility (that is, satisfaction). Increases in t produce dissatisfaction.

Given these two goods, then, how will they vary while maintaining a constant level of satisfaction? Given any combination of land and distance, a small increase in distance will produce dissatisfaction, and will have to be compensated for by a small increase in the quantity of land for satisfaction to remain the same. The indifference curve, between land and distance, therefore, will be a rising curve, q increasing with t, as in Figure 6. Had we plotted accessibility rather than distance against land, we would have obtained a downward sloping indifference curve of the usual shape. However, since distance can be measured directly, while accessibility implies some subjective pattern of preference (or nuisance value of distance) which may vary from one individual to another, it is better for our purposes to use distance as the variable and to let the shape of the indifference curves take care of the relation between distance and accessibility.

In spite of the direction of the slope of this indifference curve, it remains true, as in the usual case, that lower curves will represent less satisfaction (less land at the same distance, or more distance for the same quantity of land) and higher curves greater satisfaction. It also remains true that curves of this family will not cross.

Now let us hold distance constant at $t = t_0$ and observe the variations between land and the composite good. Given any combination of q and z, a small decrease in one will have to be compensated by a small increase of the other for satisfaction to remain constant. This is the usual type of indifference curve, as in Figure 7. The curve will not only slope down-

Figure 6   Indifference curve between q and t, for a constant z_0.

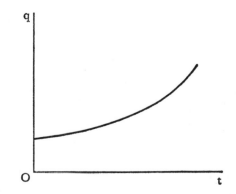

Figure 7 Indifference curve between q and z, for a constant t_0.

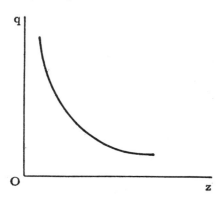

Figure 9 An indifference surface.

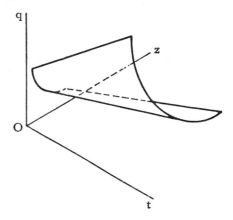

ward to the right, but it will also be convex toward the origin, by reason of the diminishing marginal utility of the goods.

Finally, let us hold the quantity of land constant at $q = q_0$ and allow distance and the composite good to vary. A small increase in distance increases the nuisance of commuting, and requires a small increase in the quantity of the composite good for satisfaction to remain constant. There will result a curve as in Figure 8, sloping upward to the right.

We can now draw an indifference surface in these three dimensions, z, q, and t, by combining these three sections. Figure 9 shows such a surface. Figure 10 shows the same surface; the trace XY on plane A corresponds to Figure 6 above, where q and t vary and z is held constant; trace $QRST$ on plane B corresponds to Figure 7, where q and z vary and t is held con-

Figure 8 Indifference curve between z and t, for a constant q_0.

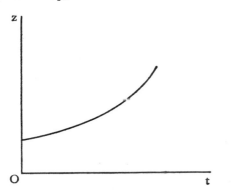

stant; and trace MN on plane C corresponds to Figure 8, where z and t vary, q being held constant.

The indifference surface shown in Figure 9 represents all of the combinations of the three goods, z, q, and t, which yield the same level of satisfaction to the individual. Combinations of these goods yielding different levels of satisfaction would be represented by similarly shaped surfaces, higher ones for more satisfaction and lower ones for less.

Equilibrium of the Individual

We now have a description of the individual's preferences in the indifference surfaces mapping, and a description of all of the opportunities open to the individual in the locus of opportunities surface. If we join the two mappings, we can see which of the available opportunities the individual will prefer. This will be the combination of goods represented by the point at which the locus of opportunities surface touches the highest (that is, most satisfactory) of the indifference surfaces with which it comes in contact. If the point be z_i, q_i, t_i, the individual will purchase quantity z_i of the composite good at price p_z, he will occupy q_i land at distance t_i from the center of the city, for which he pays a price $P(t_i)$, and he will spend $k(t_i)$ on commuting costs.

By examining carefully the shape of the indifference and of the locus of opportunities surfaces, it becomes clear that the point of equilibrium must lie within the portion of the

Figure 10   Sections through an indifference surface.

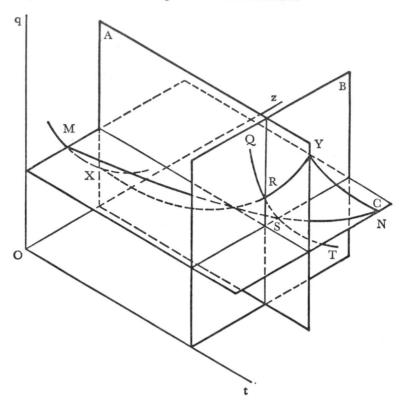

locus of opportunities (Figure 5) bounded by the curves *WX, XY,* and *YW*. At the equilibrium point, the locus of opportunities and the indifference surface must be tangent to each other, since both are smooth surfaces touching at a point. Therefore the two surfaces must be parallel at that point. The indifference surface (see Figure 9) is shaped like a trough, and it moves up and away from the *t*-axis. The locus of opportunities, however, moves up and away from the *t*-axis only over the portion *WXY*. Therefore tangency between the curves and individual equilibrium are possible only in this section.

MATHEMATICAL SOLUTION OF INDIVIDUAL EQUILIBRIUM

The mathematical solution of individual equilibrium parallels the diagrammatic solution but is at once more general and more compact. We may start with the proposition that the individual has a given income, *y*, which he may spend as he pleases between *z* and *q*, after he pays the commuting costs $k(t)$ attendant to his location. This proposition is expressed in the *budget balance* equation

$$(2:1) \qquad y = p_z z + P(t)q + k(t).$$

As before, we assume that we are given the price of the composite good p_z and the functions of the cost of land with distance, $P(t)$, and of commuting costs with distance, $k(t)$. The problem consists of finding the possible set of *z, q,* and *t* which both satisfies the budget balance equation (which corresponds to the locus of opportunities surface) and yields the individual the greatest satisfaction.

The satisfaction of the individual is given in the function

$$(2:2) \qquad u = u(z, q, t),$$

called the utility function. Given a set of values z_0, q_0, t_0, we find u_0 by means of this function. For another set z_i, q_i, t_i, we would find u_i. Then, if u_i is greater than u_0, we may say that the set z_i, q_i, t_i is preferable to the set z_0, q_0, t_0.[6]

The individual will try to maximize his satisfaction within the restraints of his income. In other words, the problem is to discover which combination z_i, q_i, t_i that satisfies the budget balance equation (2:1) yields the highest value for u in equation (2:2). This is done by differential calculus. Differentiating the utility function (2:2) we obtain

(2:3) $du = u_z dz + u_q dq + u_t dt.$[7]

At the point at which satisfaction, u, is maximized, $du = 0$, so that

(2:4) $du = 0 = u_z dz + u_q dq + u_t dt.$

According to the conditions of maximization for multivariable functions, we can hold all variables but two constant, and the sum of the partials times the differentials of the remaining two will still equal zero. Thus, if we hold t constant so that $dt = 0$, equation (2:4) becomes

(2:5) $du = 0 = u_z dz + u_q dq + 0.$

Equation (2:5) may be rewritten as

(2:6) $-dz/dq = u_q/u_z.$

If we hold q constant, so that $dq = 0$, from equation (2:4) we obtain

(2:7) $du = 0 = u_z dz + 0 + u_t dt.$

Equation (2:7) may be rewritten as

(2:8) $-dz/dt = u_t/u_z.$

Now we return to the budget balance equation (2:1). Differentiating we have

(2:9) $dy = y_z dz + y_q dq + y_P dP + y_k dk.$

But y is a given constant, so that $dy = 0$. As we have an explicit statement of the equation (2:1), we can find the partial derivatives.

These are:

$$y_z = p_z; \quad y_q = P(t); \quad y_P = q; \quad y_k = 1.$$

Substituting these into equation (2:9), we obtain

(2:10) $0 = p_z dz + P(t)q + qdP + dk.$

We can solve for dP and dk in terms of dt by the differentials of $P(t)$ and $k(t)$, so that

$$dP = (dP/dt)dt \quad \text{and} \quad dk = (dk/dt)dt.$$

Substituting these into equation (2:10), we have

$$0 = p_z dz + P(t)dq + q(dP/dt)dt + (dk/dt)dt,$$

which may be rewritten as

(2:11) $0 = p_z dz + P(t)dq + dt(q\, dP/dt + dk/dt).$

Equation (2:11) is, of course, merely a rewriting of equation (2:9).

The rule that we may hold all variables but two constant applies to constants as well as maxima. Since y is a constant, from equation (2:11), holding first t and then q constant, we may say that

$$0 = p_z dz + P(t)q + 0,$$
and $\quad 0 = p_z dz + 0 + dt(q\, dP/dt + dk/dt).$

These may be rewritten as

(2:12) $-dz/dt = P(t)/p_z,$

(2:13) $-dz/dt = (q\, dP/dt + dk/dt)/p_z.$

Combining equations (2:6) and (2:8) with equations (2:12) and (2:13), we obtain

(2:14) $u_q/u_z = P(t)/p_z$ and

6 The reader is reminded that the values of u have only ordinal properties, and that they are equivalent to the naming (in some sequence) of the indifference surfaces.

7 For convenience in notation, as is frequently done, we shall denote the partial derivative of a function with respect to a variable by the name (letter) of that function with the variable as a subscript. Thus,

$$u_z = \partial u/\partial z; \quad u_q = \partial u/\partial q; \quad u_t = \partial u/\partial t.$$

$(2:15) \quad u_t/u_z = (q \; dP/dt + dk/dt)/p_z.$

Equations $(2:14)$ and $(2:15)$, together with the budget balance equation $(2:1)$, are three equations which, when solved simultaneously, yield the individual's optimal combinations of the three unknowns, z, q, and t.[8] Finding these unknowns constitutes the solution of the individual's equilibrium.

Interpretation of the Mathematical Solution

The interpretation of the mathematical solution is the same as that of the diagrammatic solution, though it permits greater precision. The budget balance equation $(2:1)$ requires no explanation, since we constructed it by definition. It corresponds to the locus of opportunities of the diagrammatic solution. However, equations $(2:14)$ and $(2:15)$ should be examined closely.

First, let us look at the relation between the utility function and the indifference surface. The indifference surface is the locus of all combinations of goods z, q, and t which yield the same satisfaction to the individual. In terms of the utility function this means that all these combinations of z, q, and t will yield the same value for u. The marginal rates of substitution between goods (the rate at which the individual is willing to exchange small quantities of one good for small quantities of another) are represented in the diagrammatic solution by the slope of the indifference surface. The slope is measured parallel to the plane defined by the axes of the two goods. In the mathematical solution, this slope (that is, the marginal rate of substitution) is represented by the ratio of the marginal utilities of the two goods. The marginal utility of a good is the partial derivative of utility, u, with respect to that good.

Returning now to equations $(2:14)$ and $(2:15)$, we note that the left-hand sides of the equations are marginal rates of substitution. The right-hand sides of the equations make statements about costs. As in the usual case in this type of analysis, these equations state that, at equilibrium, the marginal rate of substitution between two goods is equal to the ratio of their marginal costs. If they were not, the individual would not be at equilibrium since he could increase his satisfaction by acquiring more of the relatively cheaper good.

Equation $(2:14)$ is very simple. It states that, at equilibrium, the marginal rate of substitution (u_q/u_z) between land (q) and all other goods (z) is equal to the ratio of their prices, that is, their marginal costs.

Equation $(2:15)$ is somewhat more complicated. It states that, at equilibrium, the marginal rate of substitution (u_t/u_z) between distance (t) and the composite good (z), is equal to $(q \; dP/dt + dk/dt)/p_z$. In the denominator we recognize p_z, the price and marginal cost of z. The numerator represents the marginal cost of spatial movement. It is the change in the price of land dP/dt (as it changes with distance) times the quantity of land, q, plus the change in commuting costs, dk/dt. Thus, once again the marginal rate of substitution is equal to the ratio of the marginal costs.

We had assumed that a near location was preferred to a distant one, since commuting is generally regarded as a nuisance. This means that u_t is a marginal disutility, and has negative utility; in short, that $u_t < 0$. But we had also assumed that increases in good z had a positive utility $(u_z > 0)$, and implicitly, that $p_z > 0$. It follows, therefore, that the expression $q \; dP/dt + dk/dt$ must be smaller than zero for equation $(2:15)$ to hold.

Let us examine this expression. We can expect that $dk/dt > 0$, since commuting costs increase with the distance traveled. The value of q, the quantity of land, can certainly be no less than zero. We must conclude that dP/dt is negative, for otherwise the expression would be positive. That is to say, the individual cannot arrive at equilibrium except on a negative stretch of the curve $P(t)$. If $P(t)$ were positively inclined—price of land increasing with distance from the center of the city—the individual would move toward the center, where

8 Strictly speaking, we do not have just three equations and three unknowns. We have seven unknowns: z, q, t, $P(t)$, dP/dt, $k(t)$, and dk/dt. The additional four equations are given by the stated functions $P(t)$ and $k(t)$ and their derivatives. This proliferation of unknowns and equations occurs if we regard the four additional unknowns as requiring numerical solution. If we view P, k, dP/dt, and dk/dt as functions in terms of t, then the three original equations are sufficient since we then have only three unknowns. The whole matter of the number of equations between three and seven depends on whether we count unknowns and equations before or after we have effected the substitutions for $P(t)$, $k(t)$, dP/dt, and dk/dt.

he would get cheaper land and do less commuting.

There is a further conclusion. Since, for equilibrium, it is necessary that $(q\ dP/dt + dk/dt) < 0$, the individual will never settle where $-(q\ dP/dt) < dk/dt$. This is the same conclusion we arrived at diagrammatically, when we stated that the individual will only settle where the savings derived from cheaper land exceed increased commuting costs. This is the portion WXY of the locus of opportunities surface in Figure 5.

An Economic Model of the Utilization of Urban Land for Residential Purposes

LOWDON WINGO, JR.

The building of intrametropolitan models bids fair to become an important part of the economic analysis of metropolitan areas.[1] At this moment two large-scale metropolitan studies are engaged in the development of such models: in Philadelphia, the Penn-Jersey Transportation Study is developing a model to help it understand the future implications for the growth of the region of different transportation programs;[2] the Pittsburgh Economic Study will use an intrametropolitan model to distribute projected levels of economic activity among the subareas of the region.[3] It is now clear that urban economic analysis which does not look into the spatial organization of the urban economy stops short of providing the kind of information and understanding which is most needed for rational decision making by public agencies and by private producers and consumers.

The term "intrametropolitan model" is used here to describe a genus of mathematical descriptions specifying at some level the manner in which one or more sectors of the urban economy are spatially distributed within the boundaries of the urban region. Such models may be *comprehensive*, if *all* sectors of the economy are distributed, or *partial*, if a specified set of activities is located under assumptions about the locational characteristics of the activities outside of the set. The two major types of partial models can be identified: those concerned with the locational processes of *producer* activities, such as the siting of industry and the pattern in space of activities servicing the local population, and those analyzing the spatial organization of *consuming* activities, essentially the residential distribution of urban households. The critical distinction between these two types of models is the difference in the nature of the locational choices made by the decision units. In the first case, the pattern results from the profit maximizing calculations of a number of firms. In the latter case, the pattern

From the *Papers of the Regional Science Association*, VII (1961), 191–205. Reprinted by permission of the Regional Science Association.

1 ". . . a major limitation of the whole analysis and description [of the economy of Stockholm] so far, is that all the findings derived or derivable relate to the Stockholm area as a whole. Therefore, a worthwhile extension of the work seems to be to explore whether such findings can be *linked-up* with findings that relate to smaller zones, such as the central business district or a part thereof *within* Stockholm. . . . The ultimate goal of this work will be to establish invariant or predictable *locational* relationships or patterns of urban land use, such that analysis and descriptions of the present type can be pushed one step further: to comprehend, also, the *spatial arrangement* of economic activities *within* the community under study." Roland Artle: *Studies in the Structure of the Stockholm Economy*, Stockholm, 1959, p. 113.
2 "The two models which will be employed for the purpose of this study are: (1) a traffic model . . . and (2) a regional growth model showing how the urban region grows and changes in response to the operation of a variety of factors." Penn-Jersey Transportation Study: *Prospectus*, (mimeo) Philadelphia, 1959, p. 12.
3 ". . . in this phase of the study the intraregional economic model can be regarded as dependent upon and supplementary to the analysis and projections of the aggregate economy, *i.e.*, concerned with allocating to subareas of the region various independently-determined Regional aggregates of activities." Pittsburgh Economic Study: *Prospectus* (mimeo), Pittsburgh, 1959, p. IV-B-1.

results from consumer calculations which are fundamentally individual and subjective.

These models have taken several forms. Generally, they have been deterministic, although suggestions have been put forth for the construction of stochastic models to replicate aggregated consumer behavior in locational decisions.[4] A *linear programming* form has been put forth for the intrametropolitan distribution of producer activities,[5] and has been suggested for the household sector.[6] Akin to these in the way in which the urban region is decomposed into a set of internally-unstructured subareas is a set of non-optimizing allocation procedures typified by the application of gravity or potential constructs to household distributions. These models have been developed chiefly by transportation planners for the projection of urban transportation requirements.[7] Finally, there are the continuous-function, partial-equilibrium models which, in contrast to the "spacelessness" of linear programming and other allocation procedures, incorporates space as a continuous variable in fairly conventional analytical formats.[8]

A final distinction should be made in terms of the dynamic qualities of these models. If one accepts the assumption that each locational decision is independent of all others and that the structural parameters are relatively fixed over long periods of time, a model which simultaneously lays down the final distribution of the population of households in space can be justified. If the household locational decisions are interdependent, or if the structural parameters are subject to exogenous change, then the reliability of the ultimate pattern produced by the model will depend on how faithfully one can replicate the *temporal ordering* of pertinent events. To cope with the problem of parametric variation and interdependence has generally involved a twofold strategy: (1) confining the model to the distribution of an *increment* of population exclusively, accepting the real world distribution as the base given, and (2) of carrying out the distribution through a procedure of fractional iterations of the increment. At the extreme of reducing the iterative fractions one approaches a stochastic procedure in which each population unit is separately located in accordance with alternative probabilities.

This paper will confine itself to the description of a static intrametropolitan model of the urban household sector,[9] in which household decisions are assumed mutually independent and the parameters fixed.[10] It is a continuous-function model: space is structured by transportation costs in continuous fashion, and the consumer decision—a choice based on transportation costs and the space or density preferences of the unit—is continuous rather than discrete, so that it is locational rather than allocational. Our ultimate concern is with the manner in which consumer behavior interacts with the pertinent spatial variables, but because of the central role of transportation technology in the organization of urban space, some special attention will be paid to the manner in which the transportation system enters into the process of consumer location.

A *caveat* is in order at this point. The author is not an econometrician, and the model which will be discussed here is compounded of relatively simple mathematical procedures. Our

4 The first explicit mention of stochastic procedures in conjunction with these models that I am familiar with occurred during a meeting between members of the Penn-Jersey staff and interested scholars in Philadelphia in February, 1960, and was reported by Britton Harris, "Summary of Discussion of February 4 and 5: Patterns of Regional Growth" (mimeo), Philadelphia, February 1960, p. 3. The general application of stochastic procedures in regional economic analysis has been discussed by Guy H. Orcutt: "Microanalytic Models for Regional Analysis" (mimeo), a paper prepared for the Conference on Regional Accounts, Washington University, St. Louis, September 7–8, 1960.
5 Benjamin H. Stevens and Robert E. Coughlin: "A Note in Inter-areal Linear Programming for a Metropolitan Region" in 1:2 *Journal of Regional Science*, pp. 75–83.
6 Such a model was described and extensively discussed at a recent meeting of the Penn-Jersey staff and others, as reported by Britton Harris: "Report on CUE Meeting on Metropolitan Growth Models, July 21st and 22nd."
7 See especially Walter G. Hansen: "How Accessibility Shapes Land Use" in the *Journal of the American Institute of Planners*, May 1959, Vol. XXV, No. 2, pp. 73–76.
8 For an excellent example see William Alonso: *A Model of the Urban Land Market: Locations and Densities of Dwellings and Businesses*, unpub. Ph.D. Dissertation, University of Pennsylvania, 1960.
9 A detailed discussion of this model is in Lowdon Wingo, Jr.: *Transportation and Urban Land*, Resources for the Future, Inc., 1961.
10 Except for the possibility of parametric manipulation to simulate policy.

purpose is to identify some critical components of such models and to explore how technical conditions and the economic characteristics of the inputs influence the nature of the output.[11]

A note on presentation. This model is presented in reverse of conventional order. The general characteristics of the solutions are presented first and reduced by analysis to the pertinent components and inputs. Three appendices are attached to provide an overview of the model, to identify the notation of variables, and to summarize the mathematical relationships discussed in this paper. The order of the mathematical summary is more conventional in that the terminal expressions are synthesized from more particular and logically prior equations.

THE OUTPUT, THE INPUTS, AND SOME BASIC CONDITIONS [12]

The output of this model takes the form of a *density gradient* in which the density M of a given population N at any point in the urban region is expressed as a function of the distance S from the center of the city:

$$(1) \qquad M = M(S)$$

It has been frequently observed that population densities generally decline as one moves outward from the center [13] so that as a general rule $dM/dS < 0$. The relationship of this expression to the total population of the city within m miles of the center is defined by the volume generated in the rotation of the gradient about the center point:

$$(2) \qquad N = 2\pi \int_o^m S \cdot M(S) \, dS$$

and changes in the total population can be introduced into the model by way of this relationship. The burden of this paper, then, is to specify the nature on the general density function $M(S)$.

This model employs four classes of independent variables:[14] those associated with size and composition of the population, those deriving from the transportation system and its technology, those which represent the innate endow-ment of the urban space, and a miscellaneous group of economic and institutional variables. In addition to the general population—density relationship above, the model contains a number of functional relationships: characterizing the spatial conditions of the model are the mathematical statements describing the *functional geometry* of the model; capacity and ingression functions define the load and operating conditions of the transportation system; and consumer characteristics enter the model through marginal value-of-leisure and space demand functions.

As a first step the nature of the density function needs to be refined to be consistent with the decision characteristics of the model,[15] since

11 "All conceptual models provide insight into the mechanism of the processes being studied. . . . However, some models were devised especially for insight, and to allow for manipulation of the parameters in order to increase understanding of the relationships between the inputs and the outputs of the system under study." *Conference on Transportation Research,* Report of a Study Group convened by the National Academy of Sciences at Woods Hole, Massachusetts, August, 1960, p. 66.
12 To provide general overview of the model for the discussion following, Appendix A presents an "information flow" diagram of the total model, while Appendix B identifies the variables. The information flow is generally from left to right in the direction indicated by the arrows. The boxes represent sets of equations or quantitative conditions defining the intermediate variables indicated by the circles, the final output being identified by the larger circle on the right.
13 Colin Clark identified the nature of the gradient with the function, $y = Ae^{-bx}$ and specified the values of the parameters $(A$ and $b)$ for a number of cities. Colin Clark: "Urban Population Densities" in *Journal of the Royal Statistical Society,* v. 114, pt. 4 (1951), Table 1, p. 494.
14 A comment on notation. Most of the variables used in this description are qualified by subscripts. The subscript k preceding the variable symbol relates the variable to population group k; where k is omitted, the variable applies to the total population. Following the variable symbol there may be two subscripts, the first is the origin or location indicator, the second the destination indicator. In either of the positions may be used any one of four indicators: i, representing any point in the urban space, but generally a point of residential location; j represents any point in the urban space except i, but generally a point of location for an employment site; o stands for the center point, and m the margin point, the limit of urban settlement. Again, where there is no following subscript the variable is independent spatially. Thus $_kX_{ij}$ represents the transportation costs to population group k of a set of trips from i to j.
15 Ludlow has pointed out the different ways in which the term "density" can be used: William

density is the relationship of a population n to a quantity of space g, or

$$(3) \qquad M = ng^{-1}$$

refinement can take place through more rigorous specification of both n and g, which relate to two of the four sets of input data.

The set of population inputs relates to the definition

$$(4) \qquad N = \sum_k n_k$$

The appropriate population units are the decision units involved in both the labor market and housing market (the final market from which the residential demand for land is derived). The *household* is the unit best suited to meet these conditions, so that N and n will hereafter express populations of households. The specification of k should replicate the important groups in the real world and at the same time meet the behavioral requirements of the model. For reasons which will become clear later, k indicates a population fraction whose members exhibit similar consumer behavior with respect to marginal-value-of-leisure and space preference functions. To the extent that some marginal-value-of-leisure functions are everywhere greater than others, this specification disaggregates by income; to the extent that large families tend, *caeteris paribus*, to demand more space than small ones, this specification disaggregates by family composition.

The transportation technology is here taken to include all of the relevant characteristics of the transportation system which affect the transportation or locational behavior of the household, ranging from technical features of movement channels and carriers to the pattern in space of transportation opportunities. Integrated with the natural characteristics of the urban space, the transportation technology produces a *functional geometry* which has special areal and linear consequences.

The definition of g in (3) above depends on a density concept related to the market decisions of households seeking to satisfy space and density preferences.[16] Since the amount of land available for residential use is something less than the total "Euclidean space" available, g is confined to that part of the total space which is available for and suitable to residential use. The output of the model accordingly is expressed in terms of *net residential density*.

In most empirical studies distance from the center has been measured "as the crow flies." At a finer grain, however, urban phenomena related to the inter-accessibility of the various parts of the region may be obscured by this too simple spatial framework. A reasonable concern for the context of the locational decision requires more a sense of accessibility than of simple spatial extension. s, then, expresses the shortest distance between two points as *measured along feasible transportation routes*.

Both of these spatial qualifications require revision of the relationship of the total population to the density gradient. Since the net residential density gradient, $q^{-1}(s)$, relates to only a fraction of the total land area which can be expressed as a function of distance, $a(s)$,[17] it follows that

$$(5) \qquad a(s) \leqq 2\pi S$$

and the total population N is really equivalent to a *partial* volume of revolution of the new density gradient.

H. Ludlow: "Urban Densities and Their Costs: An Exploration into the Economics of Population Densities and Urban Patterns" in Coleman Woodbury (ed) : *Urban Redevelopment: Problems and Practices* (University of Chicago Press, Chicago: 1953) , esp. pp. 107–114, and Blumenfeld has actually described the distribution of population densities in Philadelphia by alternative constructs. Hans Blumenfeld: "On the Concentric Circle Theory of Urban Growth," *Land Economics*, v. 25 (1949) , pp. 209–212.
16 Scholars who have investigated urban population density gradients have tended to relate them to a gross geometric expression of area and hence have used a concept of gross population density. Other uses of urban population density concepts have involved a netting out of inappropriate land areas: excessive slopes and swampy land might be excluded to express density in terms of usable land area, or all public uses might be subtracted to relate population to land area in private ownership.
17 John Hamburg identified this proportion for Chicago as part of the Chicago Area Transportation Study, in which it rose from zero at the center to about 40% or $4\pi S$ for $S \geqq 7$ miles, and this seems to check roughly with figures from other cities. John R. Hamburg: "Land Use Projections for Predicting Local Traffic" in Highway Research Board: *Trip Characteristics and Traffic Assignment*, Bulletin 224, Figure 1, p. 74.

Now consider the following analogue of a transportation net. The center point is an intersection in a rectilinear grid, superimposed on which is a system of F radials. If one identifies all points in this analogue s distance from the center and connects them to enclose an area, it can be shown that where $b(s) = (dA/ds)$, S is defined above, and $4 \leq F \leq \infty$:

$$4S \leq b(s) \leq 2\pi S.$$

Then the marginal change in the amount of residential space made available by a unit extension of s, or the *space coefficient*, $A(s)$ is defined as the product of these two modifying elements:

(6) $$A(s) = a(s) \cdot b(s)$$

and

(7) $$N = \int_0^z A(s) \cdot q^{-1}(s) ds$$

The fourth group of inputs consist of several discrete data about the urban economy ranging from the spatial arrangement and temporal organization of producer activities,[18] to the prices of all inputs into the transportation system from auto fuel to parking fees.

With the major inputs so specified, we are now free to investigate the structure of the model itself.

THE LOCATIONAL DECISION

By the simple inversion of net residential density q^{-1} an expression is developed for the net residential space per household which can be expressed appropriately by q.[19] Since the purchase of space pinpoints the locational decision, q can be taken as the principal dependent variable. Here also we can introduce the price of space, or the unit rent, r, which measures the value of space for residential location only.

The identification of r leads to two relationships between r and q. First, the amount of space consumed by a member of group k at point i will be some demand function of the price of space at i:

(8) $$_kq_i = {}_kD(r_i)$$

For the purposes of this model assume that this is a negatively sloped demand curve of a form described by the log linear equation:

(9) $$\log {}_kq_i = {}_kc \log r_i + \log {}_kD$$

where ${}_kc$ and ${}_kD$ are parameters, $c < 0$.

The second relationship of densities and rents is the total outlay by the household for the services of space:

(10) $$_kR_i = r_{ik}q_i$$
$$\text{or } {}_kq_i = {}_kR_i \cdot r_i^{-1}$$

These two functions are expressed graphically in Figure 1, where it is visually demonstrated that if the value of ${}_kR_i$ can be determined, both ${}_kq_i$ and ${}_kr_i$ are determined. Thus, in Figure 1 the determination of R_a yields q_a and $r_{a k} R_i$ is a function of the household budget, but this budget decision may be quite isolated from the household consumption function, a point to be discussed later. For the moment we want to look at ${}_kR_i$ as a rent and to understand how it is generated and how it gets distributed in space. If we can do this, the distribution of location rents and populations follow accordingly.

18 That is, the differentia of the subscript j which would define the degree of centralization or dispersion of employment. Since time is limited here, however, it will be assumed that all employment is concentrated at the center $(j = 0)$, although other assumptions are feasible.

19 The meaning of q in the real world is not quite so simple when one looks beyond the low household densities represented by the single family dwelling in which q stands for lot or parcel size. In the high density, multiple family dwellings site area is enjoyed jointly as a community good by the resident households. In the market it seems likely that consumer decisions in the two cases differ similarly: the purchaser who buys his housing services in the form of a single family, detached dwelling is influenced directly by the *size of site*, while he who purchases his housing services in the form of high density apartment space is influenced by the *density characteristics*, since site size has no meaning for him. Nevertheless, we will assume that there is a continuity in the form of the market decision over the whole range of values for q, so that even though there may be a vast amount of difference between the consumer decision for high densities and that for extensive dwelling sites, there is little basic difference in the choice between q (or q^{-1}) and $q + \Delta q$ [or $(q + \Delta q)^{-1}$] over the whole range of values for q.

Figure 1

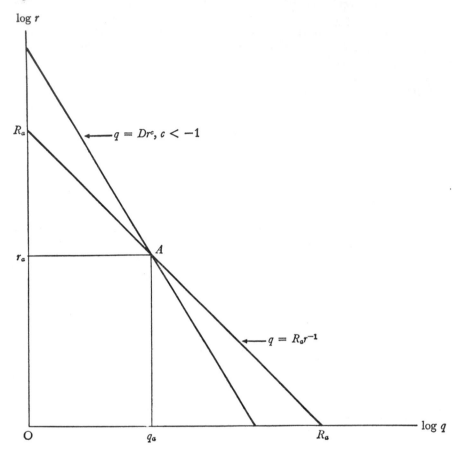

$$\log r$$

R_a $\longleftarrow q = Dr^c, c < -1$

r_a A

$\longleftarrow q = R_a r^{-1}$

O q_a R_a $\log q$

Without any attempt to prove the point here, we begin with the proposition that the crucial locational determinant of household location is its employment linkage with the place of work of the head of the household. This linkage fixes in time and space the immediate destination of approximately forty percent of all trips that engage the household, and the decision by a household to alter its residential location can have significant budgetary consequences through its effect on the trip costs of the journey-to-work.[20]

It is clear that, given the nature of transportation costs, locations in the urban region become differentiated by the extent to which they can yield a saving in transportation costs. This saving will be referred to as *position rent*. On succeeding pages we will demonstrate that $_kR_t$ is, in fact, synonymous with position rent, but

before we do this, it will be useful to specify the nature of the transportation costs generated by the journey-to-work.

On casual analysis these costs appear to have more the nature of a two element vector: one pays the price for movement not only in money but in the amount of time preempted for the trip from other activities. Consumer behavior is apparently influenced to some degree by both elements. Certainly in locational and transportation decisions there are trade-offs among these costs. If this is so, we are confronted with an

20 The head of the household makes approximately five hundred one-way work trips per year. Thus, if one had to choose between two sites identical in every respect except that the trip to work from one costs $.10 more than the other, at an interest rate of 5 percent, the nearer site could demand a price increment of $1,000 over the other by capitalizing an annual saving of $50.00.

analytical difficulty in the fact that the consumer decision will depend on the weights which attach to these costs at any one moment in time. The important question here is whether we can replace the cost vector with a scalar in the form of a cost function which is spatially continuous.

Granting the severe imperfections in the market machinery by which labor services are conveyed, nevertheless there is a persuasive argument on behalf of the convertibility of the time costs of the journey-to-work into dollars and cents. This argument has been obscured by a focus on the hourly wage rate as the form of the purchase of labor services, so that

(11) $W = wu$

where W = the daily wage,

w = the market hourly wage rate,

and u = the time-length of the work day.

This bias can be modified by a shift in perspective: let the daily wage W be viewed as compensation for the total daily time which the worker is compelled to surrender in order to engage in the employment—as a "stoop-to-stoop" payment which includes not only payment for the working day but for the time spent in transit, also:

(12) $W = w'(u + t)$

where w' = the *manifest* hourly wage rate

and t = the time spent in transit to and from the place of employment.

The relationship of these two definitions becomes apparent when set in the framework of the marginal-value-of leisure. Let the following conditions define the pertinent characteristics of the marginal-value-of-leisure function for the purposes of this model: (1) for any given amount of time surrendered by the worker it identifies the value of the marginal hour to him; (2) over the range of interest to us, it has positive slope from the vicinity of the origin and is convex upward. In Figure 2, if $t = 0$, the labor market of classical economic

theory is defined with a *pure hourly wage rate* w'', and a pure daily wage rate of $w''u$. The difference between the market daily wage rate wu and the pure daily wage rate $w''u$ is chargeable to the time separation of work and residence,

Let $_kw$ = "a marginal-value-of-leisure function common to population group k"

so that $_kw(u)$ = pure daily wage rate, and

$_kw(u + t)$ = manifest daily wage rate.

Then let $_kX_i'{}_j$ = the value of the time consumed by the journey-to-work

and $_kX_i'{}_{j'}$ = the money costs of the journey-to-work

so that $_kX_{ij} = {}_kX_i'{}_j + {}_kX_i'{}_{j'}$ (total costs of the work trip).

Then

(13) $_kX_i'{}_j = {}_kw(u + t_{ij}) - {}_kw(u)$

Assuming full employment, indivisibility in the sale of labor services, and short run immobility in the labor market, the daily wage payment for any budget group k will be set by the marginal employee, defined as the employee whose journey-to-work costs are the highest in the group. Since all workers in group k receive the same daily wage, all non-marginal workers will receive a premium over and above the sum of their pure daily wages and journey-to-work costs in proportion to the proximity of their residences to the employment site. This premium enjoyed by the worker over and above the minimum wage which would elicit his employment and resulting from the effects of the positional relationship of home and work site is the source of what was previously identified as *position rent* $_kR_i$.

Thus, the market wage rate obscures the fact that the daily wage is compounded of two components: one, a pure payment for labor services, the other a premium based on the cost to the marginal worker of overcoming the spatial separation of home and workplace. The conversion of the time costs of the journey-to-work is automatic—it is part of the wage bargain. Nor can it be argued that the locational part of the wage payment is an increment to income which will alter the consumption function of the

Figure 2

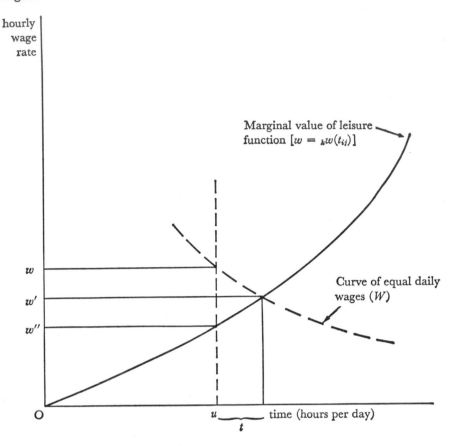

hourly wage rate

Marginal value of leisure function $[w = {}_kw(t_{ij})]$

Curve of equal daily wages (W)

w

w'

w''

O u ——— time (hours per day)

t

household, for the worker is faced with a set of transportation costs which are fixed for him and which determine the location costs for which he is to be compensated. In this basis a scalar rather than a vector expression can be justified for the commuting costs of the worker. ${}_kX_{mo}$, then, not only identifies the transportation costs of the marginal unit, but the *location costs* for all units.

$$(14) \qquad {}_kX_{mo} = {}_kR_i + {}_kX_{ij}$$
or
$$\qquad {}_kR_i = {}_kX_{mo} - {}_kX_{ij}$$

Thus, for every point i in the urban space there is a set of k position rents, and further, following (10) and (11) above, there are a set of densities ${}_kq_i$ and location site rents ${}_kr_i$ similarly for all i and all k.

The conditions for locational equilibrium for population group k can now be defined. If k

bounds on group $k-1$ at $S = K$ and on group $k+1$ at $S = K'$,

$$(15) \qquad {}_kr_i \geqq {}_{k+1}r_i$$

and at the boundaries the rents of bounding groups will be equal:

$$(16) \qquad {}_kr_K = {}_{k-1}r_K$$

These conditions merely state that a population group must outbid all other population groups for the space between K and K'. Given the nature of the demand function which we have postulated, this is always possible at some density of settlement.[21] The final conditions set the control totals for all the groups following:

[21] Assuming, of course, constant costs of construction. In the real world, increasing costs to scale limit actual densities.

(17) $$N = \sum_{k} {}_k n ,$$

where

(18) $${}_k n = \int_{k}^{k'} A(s) \cdot {}_k q^{-1}(s) ds$$

In summary, if the total transportation costs as defined above can be specified for each of k groups in the population and if for each a space demand function can be identified, a distribution of these groups in the urban space is produced which would meet the conditions of locational equilibrium.

TRANSPORTATION TECHNOLOGY AND COMMUTING COSTS

There now remains only the problem of analyzing the relationship of the transportation system to the costs of transportation experienced by the households, by specifying t_{ij} and X''_{ij}. We have already provided for the effect of the system on the supply of space by introducing the space coefficient $A(s)$. The rest of this paper will be devoted to the definition of the impact of the transportation system on the cost calculations of households making locational decisions.

The first step is to describe the pertinent characteristics of an urban transportation system in terms of some spatial organization of routes, and a set of model facilities. Assume then, a single-mode, decentralized system, such as one based on the private auto, operating over a set of F regularly spaced radials superimposed on a rectilinear grid and converging on the employment site at o, where all employment takes place in a single u-hour shift each working day. Two costs are to be analysed: the "money" costs of commuting between any point i in the urban region and the central point of employment at o, or X''_{io}, and the time costs, expressed in units of time, involved in work period commuting between i and o, or t_{io}. These costs are objective consequences of the transportation technology and are pertinent to all groups.

Among the inputs some vary with the length of the work trip, such as fuel costs, and others vary only with the number of trips, such as parking costs or tolls:

(19) $$X''_{io} = \sum_{s} s_{io} p_s x_s + \sum_{h} p_h x_h$$

where s = a distance-associated input
h = a trip-associated input
x = amount of input per unit
p = unit price of input

The time costs emerge from technical relationships which are best described in analogy with a purely physical system. Traffic systems operating under conditions of saturation behave very much as physical systems because the "freedom" of the individual carriers is rigorously constrained, and behavioral and chance variables have a very reduced "play" in such a system. Ours is a saturated system, because all employees report to a common point no later than a given time: units will have to "queue" in such a fashion that the last unit in the queue can meet the deadline. The prevalence of these queues—the complete absence of any unutilized capacity—characterizes a saturated system.

Two kinds of time costs are of interest: those experienced by a carrier moving between i and o in the absence of other vehicles, that is, the *pure time costs* t'_{io}:

(20) $$t'_{io} = V^{-1} s_{io}$$
where V = the "free" velocity [22] of the carrier.

However, the individual must consider the behavior of other units in the transportation system, must, in fact, take account of congestion and waiting time phenomena. These effects, which depend on the capacity characteristics of the system and on the demand imposed upon it, tend to increase the time costs of the trip by what will be known here as *ingression costs*.[23]

Ingression phenomena are related to queue-

[22] That is, the velocity which would be selected under the technical conditions of the system by an operator unrestrained by other vehicles in the system.
[23] Cf. Lowdon Wingo, Jr.: "Measurement of Congestion in Transportation Systems" in Highway Research Board: *Planning and Development in Urban Transportation*, 1959, Bulletin 221, Washington, 1959.

ing phenomena, focusing on system effects of capacity restraints on a system in which time is the currency. However, ingression is concerned mainly with the opportunity time costs which are imposed upon units in the system by the requirement that the last unit meet a deadline. To clarify the nature of these costs requires a brief explanation of the concepts of capacity and demand as they relate to the system.

Capacity in a transportation system must be defined in terms of the velocity at which the carriers move and the "portal width" of the route. In a decentralized system the capacity of a lane of movement tends to have an inverted quadratic relationship to the velocity of the units because of the inertial and feedback characteristics of the system.[24] There is, hence, a velocity at which the lane capacity will be maximized. "Portal width" refers to that point in a route where capacity is the least, so that it governs the ability of the route as a whole to admit units. The capacity of a route is used henceforth to refer to the maximum velocity-specific capacity measured at the point of least capacity along the route. The concept of demand for transportation services pertinent to this system is deadline demand, the number of units which must arrive at o not later than a specified deadline. Assuming a 1:1:1 relationship between households, employees, and demanding units in the transportation system, deadline demand in the system is numerically equal to the population N.

The basic ingression function merely states that in a queue in which the last unit must meet a deadline, the nth unit must experience a waiting time loss at the destination prior to the deadline,[25] which is inversely related to the capacity of the system and directly associated with the number of units following the nth:

$$(21) \qquad y^{(n)} = C^{-1}(N - n)$$

Under conditions of random entry over a large number of trips the ingression costs to any single unit will approach the average ingression costs $\bar{y}$ to all units entering the system, and this fact makes it possible to define the ingression costs between i and o:[26]

$$(22) \qquad \bar{y}_{io} = (C_{io})^{-1}\frac{N}{2}$$

The total time costs of the journey-to-work between i and o can then be defined as the sum of the pure time costs and the ingression costs:

$$(23) \qquad t_{io} = t'_{io} + \bar{y}_{io}$$

CONCLUSION

The total model has now been described and its variables and functions characterized. There is certainly no claim that it is operational in either a research or policy sense. What hopefully it does is to ilustrate how the economic characteristics of a region's population may interact with critical physical and technical dimensions in the environment to develop a distribution of population which is uniquely urban. It suggests the pathways of change by which the conditions of locational equilibrium may be altered through parametric variation and identifies the consequences of change as shifts in the spatial distribution of population throughout the entire urban region. Abstract models such as these may help the construction of their more operational successors by exploring unresolved, or even unanticipated issues and suggesting ways through or around them. If this paper has been helpful in this respect, it has served its purpose.

APPENDIX B. TABLE OF SYMBOLS

a = "a space supply function of"
$A(s)$ = space coefficient
b = "a transportation net function of"
C = capacity of transportation link
c = a parameter
D = "a space demand function of" (also, a parameter)

[24] Calculated lane capacities for automobile traffic from various sources are described in the *Highway Capacity Manual*, (USGPO, Washington, 1950), Figure 1, p. 2, and Table 1, p. 3. These follow the general forms $C = V/ (fV^e + gV + L)$, (where V = free velocity) and differ in their values for the constants f, e, g, and L.
[25] Or elsewhere in this system under certain conditions, in which case ingression is translated into congestion.
[26] It can be shown that this holds for the reverse, or "outflow" movement also.

APPENDIX A. INFORMATION FLOW DIAGRAM

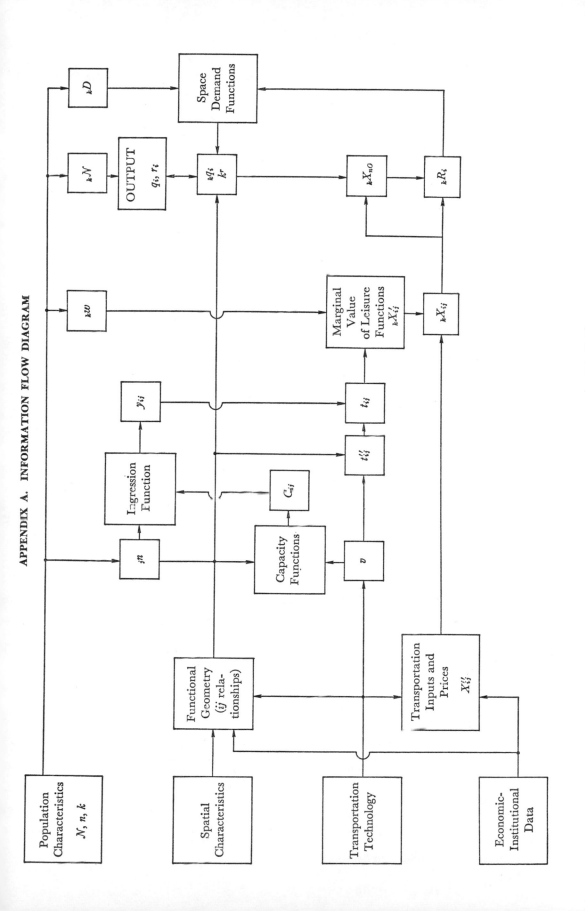

g = a small area

h(subscript) = a "trip associated" input

i(subscript) = (from) a residential location at i (to)

j(subscript) = at (to) an employment site at j

K(subscript) = the boundary between groups "k" and "$k-1$"

K'(subscript) = the boundary between groups "k" and "$k+1$"

k(subscript) = of the kth population group

M = "a density function of"

m(subscript) = the spatial margin (the limit of urban settlement)

N = total population

n = a spatially distinct subpopulation

o(subscript) = at (to) the center point of the city

q = net residential space per household

q^{-1} = net residential population density—(a function of . . .)

R = position rent

r = location rent per unit area

S = geometric distance

s = "functional" distance

t = time spent in the daily journey to and from work

u = length of working day

V = "free" velocity of a carrier

v = effective velocity of route

W = daily wage

w = market hourly wage rate (also, "a marginal value of leisure function of")

w' = manifest hourly wage rate

w'' = pure hourly wage rate

X = total transportation costs per individual

X' = value of the time costs of the work day

X'' = cost of all inputs

y = ingression loss

$\bar{y}$ = ingression loss (average)

APPENDIX C. MATHEMATICAL SUMMARY OF THE MODEL

(1) $C_{ij} = C_{ij}(V)$

(2) $Y_{ij} = C_{ij}^{-1}(n_j/2)$

(3) $t'_{ij} = s_{ij}V^{-1}$

(4) $t_{ij} = t'_{ij} + Y_{ij}$

(5) $X''_w = \sum_s s_{ij}p_s x_s + \sum_n p_n x_n$

(6) $_kX'_{ij} = {}_kw(u + t_{ij}) - {}_kw(u)$

(7) $_kX_{ij} = {}_kX'_{ij} + {}_kX_i{}'_j$

(8) $_kR_i = {}_kX_{mo} - {}_kX_{ij}$

(9) $_kq_i = {}_kR_i r_i^{-1}$

(10) $_kq_i = {}_kD(r_i)$

(11) $_kn = \int_K^{-K} A(S) \cdot {}_kq^{-1}(s) \, ds$

(12) $N = \sum {}_kn$

An Aggregative Model of Resource Allocation in a Metropolitan Area

EDWIN S. MILLS

INTRODUCTION

The purpose of this paper is to put forth a simplified, aggregative model that will help to explain the sizes and structures of urban areas. The viewpoint taken is that the basic characteristics of cities are to be understood as market responses to opportunities for production and income. Properties of production functions are at the heart of the explanation of city size and structure in the model developed here, in much the way that properties of production func-

tions are at the heart of modern neoclassical growth theory.

The general ideas that motivate the selection of the model developed below are commonplace in the voluminous recent literature on urban economics and geography. It has frequently been observed that the large size and rapid recent growth of urban areas are re-

From *American Economic Review*, LVII (May 1967), 197–210. Reprinted by permission of the American Economic Association and the author.

sponses to income and employment opportunities provided there. It is but a small step from this observation to the assumption that the conditions of production differ in crucial respects as between urban and non-urban areas and as between urban areas of different size. Likewise, it is a common observation on the structure of cities that the nature and intensity of land use vary greatly from city to city and from one part of a city to another. Again, it is but a small step to recognize that a major element of factor substitution is involved in this phenomenon and to analyze models whose production functions will explain the observed factor substitution. Indeed, factor substitution is the most dramatic characteristic of urban structure. For example, the relative price of housing varies somewhat from one part of a city to another, but such variation is small compared with the variation in the relative prices of factors used to produce housing—principally land and structures. It is not unusual for land values to vary by a factor of from ten to one hundred within a distance of ten or twenty miles in a large metropolitan area. And the tremendous variation in capital-land ratios—from skyscrapers and high-rise apartments downtown to single story factories and single family homes on two-acre lots in the suburbs—is the market's response to these dramatic variations in relative factor prices.

The model developed below is intended to shed light on these and other factors. To keep the mathematics within manageable proportions, it is necessary to make significant compromises with reality. In the work that follows, two major areas of compromise can be identified. First, the demand side has been slighted almost to the point of exclusion. This has been necessary in order to focus attention on what seem to me to be the crucial factors; namely, input substitution and technology. Second, the degree of aggregation is uncomfortably high. Even with these two areas of compromise, the model is quite cumbersome. Its solution is pragmatic and inelegant.

A WORLD WITHOUT CITIES

It is clear that the existence, size, and structure of cities are closely related to transportation costs. The avoidance of transportation costs is not, however, a sufficient reason for the existence of cities. Indeed, it may help in focusing ideas to state explicitly a set of assumptions—each of which finds a respectable place in important economic models—which imply that there would be no cities.

Consider a general equilibrium model in which an arbitrary number of goods is produced either as inputs or for final consumption. The only nonproduced goods are land and labor, each of which is assumed to be homogeneous. Assume that each production function has constant returns to scale and that all input and output markets are competitive. Utility functions have the usual properties and have as arguments amounts of inputs supplied and products consumed. Under these circumstances, consumers would spread themselves over the land at a uniform density to avoid bidding up the price of land above that of land available elsewhere. Adjacent to each consumer would be all the industries necessary—directly or indirectly—to satisfy the demands of that customer. Constant returns assures us that production could take place at an arbitrarily small scale without loss of efficiency. In this way, all transportation costs could be avoided without any need to agglomerate economic activity.

AN ABSTRACT DESCRIPTION OF A CITY

The two assumptions in the previous section most in conflict with reality are that land is homogeneous and that production functions all have constant returns to scale. Relaxation of either is sufficient to justify the existence of cities. Reasons for relaxing them and for the alternatives to them that are employed below are discussed in the next two paragraphs.

If some land is more productive than other land, it will pay to concentrate production on the better land, thus producing a city. The location of almost all U.S. cities can be understood in terms of land heterogeneity, most having been located near cheap water transportation. There are two ways to represent this heterogeneity in formal models. One is to assume that several variables related to land enter the production functions—natural resources, topography, climate, etc.—and that these variables are available in different amounts at different sites. Another is to assume just one land input, but to assume that different sites have associated with them different efficiency parameters in production functions. For a variety of reasons, the latter representation is chosen in this paper. With this convention, I would say that Baltimore's location results from the fact that some goods—especially transportation services can be produced more efficiently there than further inland. The limited availability of desirable land will show up as decreasing returns as the amount of land used increases, forcing resort to less and less productive land. I will summarize this assumption by saying that efficiency parameters require locational indexes.

Location theorists have identified a variety of factors that lead to "agglomeration economies." The most important and best articulated of these factors is increasing returns to scale. This leads to agglomeration, not only of the activity in question, but also of other activities vertically related to it. Among other sources of agglomeration economies, most can probably be represented approximately as scale economies, at least in an aggregative model. Provided that the notion of scale economies is interpreted broadly, so as to include indivisibilities, it is undoubtedly important in determining city sizes. There are large numbers of specialized business and consumer services for which the per business or per capita demand is so small that a large city is needed to support even a few suppliers.

It is obvious that either locational effects on efficiency parameters or increasing returns will justify the existence of a city. Furthermore, conditions of production impose a finite limit on the efficient size of the city. Suppose we consider the possibility of doubling the population of a city by doubling the height of every building. If this were feasible and if twice as many people now traveled between each pair of points as before, then it would lead to just twice the demand for transportation as before. But if transportation requires land as an input, it must use more land after the doubling of population than before. Thus, some land previously used for buildings must now be used for transportation, thus requiring new buildings at the edge of the city. But the edge of the city has now moved out, and some people must

make longer trips than before, requiring more transportation inputs. Thus, a doubling of the city's population requires more than doubling transportation inputs. For a city of sufficient size, this "diseconomy" in transportation will more than balance any economy of size resulting from increasing returns in production. Another factor that entails the same result is the fact that, as the city's population grows, efficient production of goods requires the use of somewhat more land as well as of somewhat higher structures. At least this is true of any production function that has diminishing returns to factor proportions. Consequently, as a city grows, it moves out as well as up, and this entails diseconomy in transportation resources.

It was suggested above that the exhaustion of favorable land may show up as decreasing returns to scale in production. On the other hand, it was also stated that increasing returns in production is the most important agglomeration economy. It is thus important to formulate a model that is consistent with either increasing or decreasing returns to scale and to let the data tell us which assumption is appropriate.

THE MODEL

A. Production Conditions

The model developed here is an aggregate one. It assumes that only three activities take place in the urban area.

The first activity is the production of goods. The goods production function justifies the existence of the city. The city may be located where the efficiency parameter in the production function for goods is especially favorable. The production function may have increasing or decreasing returns. If there is no effect of location on the efficiency parameter, we must have increasing returns. Otherwise, there would be no city. If there are increasing returns, it is assumed that they are available only if goods production takes place in a contiguous area. If, instead, the city exists because of a site with a favorable efficiency parameter, then goods production will take place at this site. In either case, goods production will take place in a contiguous area and assumptions to be made below will imply that this area plays the role of the central business district (CBD). The production function is assumed to be Cobb-Douglas. Formally,

$$(1) \quad X_1 = A_1 H_1^{\alpha_1} N_1^{\beta_1} K_1^{\gamma_1}$$
$$\alpha_1 + \beta_1 + \gamma_1 = H_1 \gtrless 1$$

where X_1 = total output of goods, and L_1, N_1, K_1 are total inputs of land, labor, and capital in goods production. When written as in (1), the symbols refer to the amounts of inputs and outputs in the city. When reference is made to the value of a variable at a particular distance from the city center, the dependence on distance will be indicated explicitly. Thus, $X_1(u)$ du refers to the amount of goods produced in a ring of width du centered on a circle u miles from the city center. Then

$$X_1 = \int_{\text{city}} X_1(u) du$$

The second activity is intracity transportation. Assumptions will be introduced below that imply that the production of housing and other activities locate in "suburbs" around the CBD in a pattern determined by their bids for land. Transportation links the CBD with these suburbs. A great deal of factor substitution is possible in transportation. At one extreme, subways use little land but much capital. At another extreme, cars use much land but rather little capital. Probably the most realistic representation would be to assume that a choice must be made among a finite number of input-output coefficients relating inputs of land, labor, and capital to output of transportation. An efficient transportation system might then require the choice of a different set of coefficients in different parts of the city. However, the need for an integrated system places limits on this choice. Investigation of an optimal transportation system within the framework of the model developed here is a major goal of this study. The present paper, however, is restricted to studying the implications for city structure of choice of a particular set of coefficients. Thus, the coefficients are assumed to be exogenous in this paper. Actually, only one such coefficient is relevant for further analysis,

as will be shown below. It is the ratio between land and transportation:

$$(2) \quad L_2(u) = bX_2(u)$$

$X_2(u)\,du$ is the number of passenger miles of transportation produced within a ring of width du u miles from the city center, and $L_2(u)\,du$ is the land input in transportation in this ring.

The third activity is designated "housing." The assumption is that all commodities whose production functions have nonconstant returns to scale and whose efficiency parameters are affected by location can be aggregated into the production function for goods (activity one). Competition will force the production of all other commodities to be located adjacent to customers in order to avoid transportation costs. It is assumed that the production of such goods and of housing can be aggregated into a single production function, designated "housing."

$$(3) \quad X_3(u) = A_3 L_3(u)^{\alpha_3} N_3(u)^{\beta_3} K_3(u)^{\gamma_3} \; \alpha_3$$
$$+ \beta_3 + \gamma_3 = 1$$

Once again, the u designates inputs and outputs within a narrow ring u miles from the city center. The assumption that all commodities can be dichotomized into the two groups designated as goods and housing is an approximation. In fact, there are degrees to which conditions of production require central location. Shopping centers display sufficient increasing returns to prohibit neighborhood location, but not enough to require central location except in small towns. To introduce intermediate commodities of this sort would vastly complicate the model, since it would require each activity to be located not only with reference to distance from the center but also with reference to the distance from its neighbors.

B. Market Conditions

All factor markets are assumed competitive, so that each activity pays the same price for a given factor. Furthermore, the wage rate, w, and the rental rate on capital, r, are assumed to be exogenous. These are the appropriate assumptions if the city's size is to be endogenous.

The city's population is determined by the number of workers it can bid for at the going wage rate. Likewise for the city's capital stock. The rental rate per acre of land u miles from the city center, $R(u)$, is endogenous.

Market conditions in the goods industry must be specified carefully. If there are increasing returns to scale, we cannot also have competitive product and factor markets. In this model it is assumed that the goods producer is a monopolist. The demand for X_1 is

$$(4) \qquad X_1 = a_1 p_1^{-\lambda_1} \qquad \lambda_1 > 1$$

where λ_1 is the constant elasticity of demand. X_1 should be thought of as an "export" good. Alternatively, a_1 could be made a function of the city's population, although that possibility has not been incorporated into the subsequent analysis. A careful limiting operation in which λ_1 goes to infinity, but a_1^{1/λ_1} remains finite, would permit perfect competition to be included as a special case of (4).

It follows from the assumptions made in this model that the CBD will be circular. It can therefore be characterized by a single number, k_o, the distance from the city center to the boundary of the CBD. In order to increase land inputs for CBD uses, land must be bid away from suburban uses. Land rent at the boundary of the CBD, $R(k_o)$, therefore determines the use of land in the CBD. CBD land users take this rent as fixed, but its value will be determined by the model. Factor demands by industry 1 are thus determined by the following marginal productivity conditions:

$$\frac{\partial(p_1 X_1)}{\partial L_1} = R(k_o) ,$$

$$\frac{\partial(p_1 X_1)}{\partial N_1} = w .$$

$$\frac{\partial(p_1 X_1)}{\partial K_1} = r$$

Because of (4), these can be written as

$$(5) \qquad \begin{aligned} \bar{a}_1 \frac{p_1 X_1}{L_1} &= R(k_o) . \\ \bar{\beta}_1 \frac{p_1 X_1}{N_1} &= w . \\ \bar{\gamma}_1 \frac{p_1 X_1}{K_1} &= r \end{aligned}$$

where

$$\begin{aligned} \bar{a}_1 &= \epsilon_1 \alpha_1, & \bar{\beta}_1 &= \epsilon_1 \beta_1, \\ \bar{\gamma}_1 &= \epsilon_1 \gamma_1, & \text{and} & \quad \epsilon_1 &= 1 - 1/\lambda_1. \end{aligned}$$

It is assumed that actual rent paid in the CBD just absorbs any monopoly profit. Thus,

$$(6)$$

$$\begin{aligned} R_1 &= \frac{p_1 X_1 - w N_1 - r K_1}{L_1} \\ &= \frac{(1 - \bar{\beta}_1 - \bar{\gamma}_1)}{\bar{a}_1} R(k_o) \end{aligned}$$

the last equation following from (5). We must have $R_1 \geq R(k_o)$, otherwise industry 1 could not bid any land away from the suburbs. This inequality requires

$$(7) \qquad H_1 \leq \frac{\lambda_1}{\lambda_1 - 1}$$

This inequality says that the greater the extent of increasing returns in goods production, the more inelastic must be goods demand in order to be able to pay the factors their marginal revenue products. It shows that the more competitive the goods market (the larger λ_1), the less the extent of increasing returns that is consistent with the model. In the limiting case, perfect competition requires constant or decreasing returns. (7) is assumed to hold in what follows.

Housing is assumed to be produced with competitive output—as well as input—markets, Thus

$$(8) \qquad \begin{aligned} \alpha_3 \frac{p_3(u) X_3(u)}{L_3(u)} &= R(u) \\ \beta_3 \frac{p_3(u) X_3(u)}{N_3(u)} &= w \\ \gamma_3 \frac{p_3(u) X_3(u)}{K_3(u)} &= r \end{aligned}$$

Using (3) and (8), we get the well-known expression for output price when markets are competitive and the production function is Cobb-Douglas.

$$(9) \qquad \begin{aligned} p_3(u) &= [A_3 \alpha_3 \alpha^{\alpha_3} \beta_3^{\beta_3} \gamma_3^{\gamma_3}]^{-1} R(u)^{\alpha_3} w^{\beta_3} r^{\gamma_3} \\ &= A_3 R(u)^{\alpha_3}, \\ A_3 &= [A_3 \alpha_3 \alpha^{\alpha_3} \beta_3^{\beta_3} \gamma_3^{\gamma_3}]^{-1} w^{\beta_3} r^{\gamma_3} \end{aligned}$$

It is assumed that housing consumption per worker is independent of u. Although this is not strictly correct, it is justified by the fact, stated above, that variations in the proportions in which land and capital are used to produce housing are much greater from one part of a city to another than are variations in the amount of housing consumed. We can express this assumption as

$$(10) \qquad X_3(u) = N(u)x_3$$

where $N(u)$ is the number of workers resident at a distance u from the center, and x_3 is the constant per worker housing demand.

It is assumed that a fraction ρ of the workers resident at each u is employed adjacent to their residences in the suburbs. It would be better to allow this proportion to be determined by the model, and presumably the conclusion would be that ρ would increase with u. Efforts to incorporate this possibility into the model have been unsuccessful. The assumption made amounts to the assumption that a fraction ρ of the workers resident at each u are employed in housing and transportation, and a fraction $(1 - \rho)$ commute to the CBD. It is assumed that a transportation system adequate to handle these CBD commuters is also adequate for all other purposes. This is an accurate assumption for radial transportation and no other form appears in the model. With this assumption, the number of passenger miles of transportation needed at each $u \geq k_o$ is proportional to the number of workers who live beyond u and who commute to the CBD. By an appropriate choice of units, the factor of proportionality can be put equal to one:

$$(11) \qquad X_2(u) = (1 - \rho) \int_{u}^{k_1} N(u')du'$$
$$k_o \leq u \leq k_1$$

Here k_1 is the distance from city center to the outer edge of the suburbs. k_1 is endogenous. Likewise, the amount of transportation needed at a $u \leq k_o$ is proportional to the number of workers employed closer to the city center.

$$(12) \qquad X_2(u) = \int_{u}^{k_1} N_1(u')du'$$
$$0 \leq u \leq k_o$$

This ignores the commuting demand of transportation workers. This is legitimate if commuting is by car, since the commuters are then also the transportation workers. Otherwise it is an approximation.

It is assumed that the cost per passenger mile of transportation is proportional to $R(u)$:

$$(13) \qquad p_2(u) = aR(u)$$

This follows literally from (2) if it is assumed that land is the only transportation input. More realistically it is intended to reflect the fact that a major cost of intra-urban travel is the opportunity cost of time spent traveling and that travel is inevitably slower in denser, higher rent areas, even in an optimum transportation system. Although (13) is not necessarily the most realistic assumption that could be made, it greatly simplifies subsequent analysis.

A worker resident at u could decrease his transportation costs by moving in toward the city center. Equilibrium in the location of housing requires that no such move be profitable. This will be so if the change in transportation cost from a short move is just offset by an opposite change in housing cost. This assumption can be expressed by the following equation:

$$(14) \qquad p_2(u) + p'_3(u)x_3 = 0$$

where the prime designates a derivative w.r.t. u. This crucial assumption appears in several models of urban location, but its implications appear not to have been analyzed.

The final assumption concerning market conditions is that urban users must be able to bid land away from some other uses, such as agriculture, at the edge of the urban area. Thus,

$$(15) \qquad R(k_1) = R_A$$

where R_A is the opportunity cost of using land for urban purposes. R_A is exogenous, and (15) provides an "initial" condition for $R(u)$.

Other Conditions

Equilibrium requires that all land be used for some purpose. Within the CBD, land is used to produce goods and transportation, and we must have

(16) $\quad L_1(u) + L_2(u) = 2\pi u \qquad 0 \leq u \leq ko$

In the suburbs, land is used to produce transportation and housing, and we must have

(17) $\quad L_2(u) + L_3(u) = 2\pi u \qquad ko \leq u \leq k_1$

(16) and (17) assume that there is no obstruction to a circular city. Topographical considerations—such as lakes, rivers, and harbors—may make a city of this shape impossible. If the obstruction is shaped like a pie slice, no fundamental alteration is necessary. If an obstruction takes up $(2\pi - \theta)$ radians at each u, then 2π can be replaced by θ in (16) and (17) and wherever 2π appears subsequently. Irregular obstructions cannot be handled within this model.

The relationship that completes the model says simply that all workers must live somewhere. This can be expressed as

(18) $\quad N_1 \equiv \int_c^{ko} N_1(u)du = (1 - \rho) \int_{ko}^{k1} N(u)du$

SOLUTION

Despite the fact that the model presented in Section IV is drastically oversimplified in an economic sense, it is mathematically cumbersome. There does not seem to be any way of checking uniqueness or consistency by counting equations and unknowns, or any simple method of solution. Proceeding pragmatically and taking advantage of special properties of the model, it is, however, possible to solve it. The endogenous variables are input and output quantities and prices in the three activities, the rent of land, and the distribution of residences—all expressed as functions of u. We should also be able to derive k_0 and k_1. Of greatest interest are the expressions giving the rental value of land, the allocation of land among competing uses, and the density of population, each expressed as a function of distance from the center. Exogenous are the parameters of the three production functions, parameters of the demand function for goods, prices of labor and capital, the fraction of the

labor force employed in the suburbs, the demand for housing per worker, and the rental value of land for agricultural purposes.

A. CBD

First, consider k_o and $R(k_o)$ to be fixed. Then from (5) we get the land-labor ratio in CBD goods production. Using (2), (5), (12), and (16), we get

$$L_1(u) + \lambda R(k_o) \int_c^u L_1(u')du' = 2\pi u$$

$$\lambda = \frac{b\beta_1}{wa_1}$$

Differentiating once, we get a first order differential equation in $L_1(u)$. Using the initial condition $L_1(0) = 0$, the solution is

(19) $\quad L_1(u) = \dfrac{2\pi}{\lambda R(k_o)} (1 - e^{-\lambda R(k_o)u})$

This shows that the amount of land available for production increases at a decreasing rate as one moves out from the city center, despite the fact that the total amount of land available grows proportionately to u. The reason is that the land needed for transportation at u is proportionate to the integral of $N_1(u)$ up to u, and this grows much faster than u. Substituting (19) into (16), we have

(20) $\quad L_2(u) = 2\pi \left[u - \dfrac{1}{\lambda R(k_o)} (1 - e^{-\lambda R(k_o)u}) \right]$

If the city is sufficiently large, both k_o and $R(k_o)$ will be large. In that case, for large u, $L_2(u)$ is approximately $2\pi u$. This interesting result shows that, in a sufficiently large city, transportation will require nearly all the land near the edge of the CBD. But it cannot require more land than is available. That is, if CBD factor ratios are those dictated by competitive factor prices, the CBD will always be of a size such that there is enough land at the edge of the CBD to transport all those who work in the CBD.

This result also sheds an interesting light on CBD traffic congestion. Excessive congestion is not inherent in large city size. No matter how large the city there exists an allocation of CBD land that will avoid the need for increases in passenger miles of transportation per acre of CBD land allocated to transportation. Congestion comes about because of the way cities grow. As a city grows (e.g., because of an increase in A_1 or a_1), $R(k_o)$ increases. As can be seen from (20), $L_2(u)$ is an increasing function of $R(k_o)$ for every u in the CBD. This is because an increase in $R(k_o)$ entails an increase in N_1/L_1 (and in K_1/L_1), which requires that a larger amount of CBD land be devoted to transporting the increased number of CBD workers. Congestion results because the adjustment of N_1/L_1 (and K_1/L_1) is relatively quick, whereas the transfer of CBD land from goods production to transportation is relatively slow. The former adjustment takes place mostly in the private sector, whereas the latter normally requires a transfer of land from the private to the public sector.

These and subsequent results can also be used to answer the following question, although the analysis has not been carried out. Suppose that CBD land is now allocated optimally, but that the city is expected to grow. Then three possibilities exist: (1) congestion will take place; (2) land will be transferred from goods production to transportation; (3) input-output coefficients in transportation must change (e.g., a switch from automotive to mass transit). What combination of the three is most economical? As it stands, the model considers only alternative (2), and it assumes that the city starts from scratch in that the cost of using CBD land for transportation is its rental value. For an existing city, the cost of transferring CBD land from goods production to transportation is its improved value, and this is much larger than its unimproved value.

So far we have considered only the input side of goods production. (19) tells us how much land will be available at each u in the CBD if factor proportions are those dictated by competitive factor prices. Taking account of the amount of X_1 that can be sold at the profit maximizing price, we get an expression for the demand for L_1. Making use of (1), (4) and (5), we get

(21)
$$L_1 = \bar{L}_1 R(k_o)^V$$

$$\bar{L}_1 = \left[A_1 a_1^{1/(\alpha_1 - 1)} \left(\frac{\beta_1}{\bar{\alpha}_1 w} \right)^{\beta_1} \left(\frac{\gamma_1}{\bar{\alpha}_1 r} \right)^{\gamma_1} \right]$$
$$\bar{\alpha}_1 \frac{\lambda_1}{\lambda_1 - 1} \Big]^{(\lambda_1 - 1)/(\lambda_1 - H_1(\lambda_1 - 1))}$$

$$V = \frac{(\beta_1 + \gamma_1)(\lambda_1 - 1) - \lambda_1}{\lambda_1 - H_1(\lambda_1 - 1)}$$

It is easy to see that (7) implies $V < 0$, so that the higher are CBD land values, the less CBD land is demanded for goods production. It is also easy to check that an increase in A_1 or a_1 increases X_1 and L_1, as we should expect. We will return to (19) and (21) below where we will see how they can be used to determine k_o and $R(k_o)$.

B. Suburbs

Primary attention will be focused on finding the functions $R(u)$ and $N(u)$. These are the most interesting variables from the theoretical and policy points of view. In addition, once these functions have been found all the input functions can easily be found using (2), (8), (9), (10) and (11).

$R(u)$ will be derived first. Substituting from (9) and (13) into (14), we get a differential equation in $R(u)$. Using the initial condition (15), the solution is

(22) $\quad R(u) = [R_A^{-(1-\alpha_3)} - c(k_1 - u)]^{-1/(1-\alpha_3)} k_o$
$$\leq u \leq k_1$$

$$c = (1 - \alpha_3) a (\alpha_3 A_3 x_3)^{-1}$$

It is sometimes asserted or speculated that land values fall off exponentially as one moves out from the city center. It is interesting to observe that exponential decline is a special case of (22) where $\alpha_3 = 1$. This is the special case where there is no factor substitution possible in housing; land is the only input. In general, (22) indicates a slower-than-exponential decline in land rents. Exponential decline means $R'(u)/R(u)$ is constant, whereas when $\alpha_3 < 1$, $R'(u)/R(u)$ is a decreasing function of u in (22). Another way to put this is to say that the possibility of economizing on land in housing prevents land values from rising as fast as they otherwise would as one moves in toward the city center.

Now turn to population (strictly, labor force) distribution, $N(u)$. Substituting from (2), (9), (10) and (11) in (17), we get

$$b(1 - \rho) \int^{k_1} N(u')du' + BR(u)^{-(1-\alpha_3)} N(u) = 2\pi u$$

Using the solution for $R(u)$ in (22), and differentiating, we get a differential equation in $N(u)$, whose solution is

(23)
$$N(u) = c_1 D^{-1}[BR_A^{-(1-\alpha_3)} - a(1 - \alpha_3)(k_1 - u)]^D$$
$$- 2\pi D, \quad^{-1}k_o \leq u \leq k_1$$
$$B = \alpha_3 x_3 A_3, \qquad D = b(1 - \rho) - a(1 - \alpha_3)$$

c_1 is an arbitrary constant of integration. Using the expression involving $L_3(u)$ in (8) and (9), (10), (15), and the initial condition $L_3(k_1) = 2\pi k_1$, c_1 can be evaluated as

$$c_1 = 2\pi k_1 B^{-(1+D)} DR_A^{(1-\alpha_3)(1+D)}$$
$$+ 2\pi B^{-D} R_A^{D(1-\alpha_3)}$$

It is to be noted in (23) that $N(u)$ is an increasing function of u if $D > 0$, and a decreasing function of u if $D < 0$. It is not possible to specify the sign of D a priori. This is as it should be. As u increases, three things happen: (1) the total amount of land increases proportionately to u; (2) the amount of land needed for transportation decreases; (3) population per residential acre decreases. (1) and (2) tend to increase $N(u)$, whereas (3) tends to decrease $N(u)$. The net effect depends on the strengths of (1) — (3), and these are measured by the coefficients that make up D.

The behavior of population density is generally of greater interest than is $N(u)$. Net density [1] is $N(u)/L_3(u)$, whereas gross density is $N(u)/2\pi u$. Using the first expression in (8) and (9), (10) and (22) net density is given by

(24)
$$\frac{N(u)}{L_3(u)} = [BR_A^{-(1-\alpha_3)} - (1 - \alpha_3)a(k_1 - u)]^{-1}$$

That is, the reciprocal of net density is linear in u. Colin Clark [1] has argued that popula-

tion density falls off exponentially in all cities and at all times. Unfortunately, Clark does not make it clear whether he is using net or gross density and presents his evidence in a way that is difficult to evaluate. (No R^2's or significance tests are given, and there is no statement as to how the excluded CBD was determined.) Nevertheless, it is worth noting that no special case of (24) yields an exponential density function. Nor does any special case of this model yield an exponential gross density function.

The form of (24) makes empirical estimation and testing particularly easy. The reciprocal of net population density can be regressed on distance from city center. Furthermore, although the constant term in this regression (which depends on k_1) will vary from city to city, the coefficient of u should be the same for cities of different size. This provides an extremely simple partial test of the model.

Unfortunately, the effects of parameter changes on population density are not easy to ascertain within this model. Clark [1] asserts that an increase in transportation cost will increase population density near the center and decrease it further out. Within the model presented here, an increase in a represents an autonomous increase in transportation costs. The direct effect of an increase in a is as Clark states. But a change in a will also affect k_o and k_1, and the net effect is difficult to ascertain. Among the questions one would like to answer, the most interesting would concern the effects of taxes and subsidies on the transportation system.

C. Determination of k_o and k_1

All the solutions presented in the last two subsections, and solutions for other variables not presented, contain the two values k_o and k_1 in addition to the autonomous parameters of the model. Equations to determine these values can be specified as follows.

k_o must be such that the land available for goods production in the CBD equals the land

---

[1] Since land used for goods produced in the suburbs is included in $L_3(u)$, the measure of net density used here is not "as net" as the ratio of population to land used for housing.

that can be profitably employed in CBD goods production. The former is an integral of (19).

(25)

$$L_1 = \int_0^{ko} L_1(u)\,du$$

$$= \frac{2\pi}{\lambda R(k_o)} \left[k_o - \frac{1}{\lambda R(k_o)} (1 - e^{-\lambda R(ko)ko}) \right]$$

The latter is given by (21). Equating the two gives

(26)

$$L_1 R(k_o)^V = \frac{2\pi}{\lambda R(k_o)} \left[k_o - \frac{1}{\lambda R(k_o)} (1 - e^{-\lambda R(ko)ko}) \right]$$

Upon inserting the expression for $R(h_o)$ from (22), (26) becomes an equation involving only k_o and k_1 among the endogenous variables.

k_o and k_1 must also be such as to provide enough land for housing in the suburbs to house the workers who work there and those who work in the CBD. (18) ensures this. Upon substituting the solution for N_1 and the solution for $N(u)$, this too becomes an equation involving only k_o and k_1. Thus, (18) and (26) provide two equations for the two unknowns k_o and k_1. Although some progress has been made with approximations, the equations appear too complicated to learn much from them without resorting to numerical methods.

1. Colin Clark, "Urban Population Densities," *J. of the Royal Statis. Soc.*, Series A, 1951, Vol. 114, pp. 490–96.
2. Richard Muth, "The Spatial Pattern of Residential Land Use in Cities" (unpublished manuscript).

The Spatial Structure of the Housing Market

RICHARD F. MUTH

This paper is devoted to an analysis of the forces which determine the pattern of intensity of residential land-use in urban areas. It is especially concerned with the question of why some cities are more "spread-out" than others. While the tendency for the outlying parts of metropolitan areas to grow more rapidly than their inner zones has been widely noted, there has been little combined theoretical and empirical investigation, at least by economists, of the forces which determine the distribution of population within urban areas.[1]

I shall first outline a simple theory of the spatial structure of the housing market. One of the implications of my analysis is a negative-exponential decline of residential population densities with distance from the city center. Such a tendency was first noted by Colin Clark about ten years ago,[2] but there has never been a careful evaluation of the negative-exponential hypothesis. Therefore, in the second section of this paper I consider the goodness-of-fit of the negative-exponential density function to data

From the *Papers of the Regional Science Association*, VII (1961), 207–220. Reprinted by permission of the Regional Science Association.
1 For a summary of the evidence relating to the spread of population within urban areas see Philip M. Hauser, "The Changing Population Pattern of the Modern City," in *Cities and Society*, 2nd ed., eds. Paul K. Hatt and Albert J. Reiss, Jr. (Glencoe, Illinois: The Free Press, 1957), pp. 157–74. The most complete study of urban population distribution I have seen is Donald J. Bogue and Dorothy L. Harris, *Comparative Population and Urban Research via Multiple Regression and Convariance Analysis*. (Oxford, Ohio: Scripps Foundation, 1954).
2 "Urban Population Densities," *Journal of the Royal Statistical Society*, Series A, CXIV (Part IV, 1951), 490–96. The essentials of my analysis were worked out before I became aware of Clark's empirical observations. Hence, I am more confident of the predictive power of this analysis than I would have been had it been constructed for the expressed purpose of yielding a negative-exponential density decline.

The Spatial Structure of the Housing Market   197

for 46 U.S. cities in 1950. The density gradient, or the slope of the regression of log density on distance, yields a natural measure of the spread of urban populations. Finally, in section three I discuss the results of a regression analysis of the differences in density gradients among U.S. cities.

I

The model of residential land-use described in this section is a very simple one, embodying only what I believe are the most important elements of the problem. While this model might obviously be generalized in several directions, I need hardly defend the proposition that simple models can be very useful in themselves. Likewise, it does not seem worth while to complicate matters before determining whether the analysis has any empirical relevance.

I assume that a market exists at some point in space and that land of homogeneous physical characteristics extends in an infinite distance in all directions. This land is used only for residential purposes; all transactions involving the production and sale of commodities other than housing take place at the market.[3] Associated with each point surrounding the market is some transport cost for consumers locating there. It seems quite reasonable to assume as I do that transport costs increase at a decreasing rate with distance from the market. I shall also assume that transport costs are independent of direction from the market, although this is hardly true in a descriptive sense.

For any pattern of residential location to be an equilibrium one, for each consumer at his optimal location the saving in housing costs from a small change in distance must exactly equal the change in transport costs.[4] In symbols,

$$(1) \qquad -qp'(k) = T'(k),$$

where q is the household's consumption of housing, $p(k)$ the price per unit of housing and $T(k)$ transport costs, both a function of distance from the market, k. It is therefore obvious that housing prices must decline with distance. Likewise, it can be shown that price must decline at a decreasing rate with distance.[5]

Equation (1) has two implications of interest to us. First, if the marginal costs of transport fall, at the old equilibrium location, the savings in housing costs from a move a unit distance further from the market would now exceed the increase in transport costs. In such a situation all households would have an incentive to move further from the market. This would result in a bidding up of housing prices in more distant locations relative to central locations, so that in the new equilibrium the rate of decline of price with distance would be smaller. Second, anything such as an increase in income or a fall in construction costs which increases the consumption of housing per household increases the savings in housing costs resulting from an increase in distance, given the price-distance structure. With transport costs unchanged, all households would thus have an incentive to move further from the market, with a resultant decline in the rate of decrease of housing prices with distance.

If one assumes, as I shall, that all households are identical—the same size and with the same tastes and incomes—then all households must be on the same indifference curve in equilibrium, regardless of their location. It follows that the per capita consumption of housing increases with distance, and its change per unit distance depends upon the real-income-constant-price elasticity of demand for housing, and the change in price per unit distance.

I turn now to a consideration of the locational equilibrium of producers.[6] Producers of housing combine land and non-land factors in

3 Throughout this paper, when I speak of housing I mean the bundle of consumer services supplied both by structures and by the land on which they are located.
4 Likewise, for the equilibrium location of a household to be at a finite distance, the savings in housing costs must not increase more rapidly than transportation costs as distance increases.
5 The condition that the net saving on housing and transport cost per unit increase in distance not decrease with distance implies that:

$$p''(k) \geq \frac{-1}{q}\left\{p'(k)\frac{\partial q}{\partial k} + T''(k)\right\}$$

In the neighborhood of the optimal location, real income is constant but $p'(k) < 0$, hence $(\partial q/\partial k) > 0$. Thus, if $T''(k) < 0$, $p''(k) > 0$.
6 Throughout I treat owner-occupants as producers of housing selling housing services to themselves as tenants.

production in such a way as to maximize their income; I assume that all have identical production functions, are competitive, and that the price per unit of the composite bundle of non-land factors is the same everywhere. Under these conditions, the rent per unit of land must fall with distance from the market if the price of housing does.[7] For if rents were everywhere the same but price declined with distance, firms, say, four miles from the market would earn lower incomes than firms only two miles away. It would be in the interest of the former to offer more for land two miles away than the existing users pay, so that the rent of land centrally located would be bid up relative to rents at distant locations.

Given the decline in land rents with distance from the market, the output of housing per unit of land declines with distance as firms substitute land for non-land factors so as to maximize their incomes. The change in output per unit of land with distance depends upon the elasticity of substitution of land for non-land factors and the rate of change in rent per unit distance.

Thus, my model implies that the price per unit of housing, rent per unit of land, and output of housing per unit of land all decline, and the per capita consumption of housing increases with distance from the market. However, data relating to these magnitudes are difficult to obtain and interpret, for reasons I won't enumerate here. Data on population densities, however, are less troublesome in these respects. Gross population density, or population per unit of land, is equal to the output of housing per unit of land divided by the per capita consumption of housing, so my model implies that gross density declines with distance from the market. Making what are probably the simplest possible assumptions about the functional form of the model's fundamental relationships,[8] namely that:

1. The price-distance function declines negative-exponentially with distance,
2. The per capita demand function for housing is linear in the logarithm of price, and
3. The production function for housing is logarithmically linear and exhibits constant returns to scale,

it can be shown that gross population density,

D, declines negative exponentially with distance from the market.[9] In symbols,

$$(2) \qquad D = D_0 \exp. \ (-gk)$$
$$\text{or} \quad \ln D = \ln D_0 - gk,$$

where D_0 is central density or density extrapolated to the city center, and g the density gradient. The latter is equal to the price gradient multiplied by a constant which depends upon the real-income-constant-price elasticity of housing demand and the exponents of the housing production function.

II

The model described in the preceding section, under certain special but not unreasonable assumptions, implies that urban residential densities decline exactly negative-exponentially with distance. Now, one can think of many reasons why this result might not hold. Some of these would produce a scatter about a negative-exponential regression line, while others might work to change the form of the regression line. The only way to appraise the model is to see how well it fits data drawn from the real world.

---

[7] Letting π be the "profits" of a firm producing housing, Q its output, L and R non-land and land, and w and r their respective prices,

$$\pi = pQ - wL - rR$$

Differentiating,

$$d\pi = (Qdp - Rdr) - (pdQ - wdL - rdR).$$

The second parathesis is zero, from the first-order conditions of profit maximization. Hence,

$$d\pi = 0 \quad \text{implies} \quad r'(k) = (Q/R)p'(k) < 0.$$

[8] The negative-exponential price-distance function is to my knowledge the simplest one for which price declines at a decreasing rate with distance. The logarithmically linear approximation is the simplest form of the production function with declining marginal physical productivities. It has been widely used in empirical work. I have found that either a linear or logarithmically-linear housing demand function is a workable approximation using national data; see my "The Demand for Non-Farm Housing," in *The Demand For Durable Goods*, ed. Arnold C. Harberger (Chicago: University of Chicago Press, 1960).

[9] A proof of this assertion is given in the appendix.

Existing estimates of the pattern of urban residential densities are deficient in at least two respects. First, estimates have been made for relatively few U. S. cities, although we are fortunate to have data for several different years in some cases.[10] But more important, the basic data for most estimates are average densities in concentric rings at progressively greater distances from the city center. Such measures hide virtually all the variation about the regression line and are too few in number to test for deviations of the observed pattern of decline from that expected to prevail.

For these reasons I have used data on average (gross) density for census tracts, more specifically for a random sample of 25 census tracts in each city.[11] All told I used data for 46 U. S. cities in 1950. Starting with the list of all tracted cities in the continental U. S., I had to eliminate those for which the central business district tracts could not be identified.[12] I also eliminated three urbanized areas with more than one central city of 50 thousand or more—New York, Minneapolis–St. Paul, and San Francisco–Oakland—because of certain estimation difficulties. The 46 cities studied have urbanized area populations ranging from about 100 thousand to almost 5 million.

Population data for the tracts included in the several samples were obtained from the census tract statistics of the 1950 population census.[13] To obtain densities, the population figures were divided by the areas of the census tracts; in most cases the latter were measured with a polar planimeter using the census tract maps given in the tract statistics reports.[14] The line-of-sight distance from the geometric center of the central business district, the empirical counterpart of my model's market, to the geometric center of the census tract was measured with a ruler; the location of the centers were estimated by eye. Repeated measurements made on the same characteristic suggest to me that measurement errors in the distance variable are small relative to those inherent in the area measurements and, hence, the density variable.

For each city two least-squares regressions were computed with the natural log of density as dependent variable, one linear and one quadratic in distance. The results of these are summarized in Table I. The first three columns

show central density, D_o, the density gradient, g, and the coefficient of determination as estimated from the linear regression. The fourth column shows the F-ratio for testing the significance of the second degree term in the quadratic regression, and the fifth the sign of the second degree term where it is significant.

In all but 6 of the 46 cities the density gradient shown in Table I is significantly greater than zero at the 0.01 level, and in all but three at the 0.10 level. The coefficients of determination, r^2, ranged from about 0.02 in Nashville and Pittsburgh to 0.74 in New Haven, the median being about 0.45. Thus, on the average, distance alone explains a little less than one-half the density differences among census tracts. There is no significant tendency for the goodness-of-fit of the linear regressions to vary with city size or region of the country. Spearman's rho for r^2 and urbanized area population is −0.099. The Kruskal-Wallis H for testing the significance of regional differences, computed

10 See Clark, *op. cit.*
11 In each case I omitted tracts in the central business district and any tract with fewer than 100 residents from the population of tracts sampled on the grounds that in these land is devoted almost entirely to other than residential uses. Likewise, for uniformity the population sampled included only tracts in the central city, since the outlying parts of metropolitan areas are not tracted in all cases.
12 Central business district census tracts are listed in U. S. Bureau of the Census, *1954 Census of Business, Central Business District Statistics, Summary Report* (Washington, D.C.: U.S. Government Printing Office, 1958), pp. APP1–6.
13 U. S. Bureau of the Census, *1950 Census of Population*, Vol. III (Washington, D.C.: U.S. Government Printing Office, 1952), Table 1.
14 *Ibid.* For two cities, Los Angeles and Cleveland, measurements were taken from larger tract maps obtained through the census tract key persons in those cities. In all cases, three measurements of area were made and averaged. If one of the three differed from the average of the other two by as much as one-third it was discarded and another measurement made. For three cities already available area measurements were used. For Boston these were taken from unpublished measurements supplied by the Research Division, United Community Services; for Chicago from Chicago Community Inventory, "Gross Land Area and Gross Population Density of Census Tracts and Community Areas for the City of Chicago, 1950," (Unpublished, November, 1952); for Philadelphia from Philadelphia City Planning Commission, "Population Densities in 1940 and 1950 by Census Tracts—Philadelphia," (Unpublished, August, 1954).

Table I Summary of Density-Distance Regressions, 46 U.S. Cities, 1950.

City	D_0	g	r^2	Linearity F^a	Curvature
Akron, Ohio	38	0.84	0.72	1.0	
Atlanta, Ga.	22	0.48	0.43	0.13	
Baltimore, Md.	69	0.52	0.53	0.19	
Birmingham, Ala.	9.4	0.20	0.35	0.23	
Boston, Mass.	78	0.30	0.35	0.66	
Buffalo, N.Y.	29	0.19 *	0.16	3.6 '	+
Chicago, Ill.	60	0.18	0.47	0.12	
Cincinnati, Ohio	120	0.69	0.67	4.2 '	+
Cleveland, Ohio	22	0.13 ***	0.048	5.2 ''	−
Columbus, Ohio	10	0.19	0.43	0.50	
Dallas, Tex.	26	0.48	0.47	4.5 ''	−
Dayton, Ohio	18	0.32	0.22	0.67	
Denver, Colo.	17	0.33	0.41	0.094	
Detroit, Mich.	19	0.098	0.30	4.7 ''	−
Flint, Mich.	26	0.73	0.42	0.14	
Fort Worth, Tex.	17	0.42	0.73	0.14	
Houston, Tex.	14	0.28	0.58	8.7 '''	−
Indianapolis, Ind.	9.2	0.18	0.30	0.47	
Kansas City, Mo.	13	0.26	0.33	0.059	
Los Angeles, Calif.	14	0.078 *	0.20	2.6	
Louisville, Ky.	29	0.47	0.30	1.2	
Memphis, Tenn.	14	0.22	0.46	0.52	
Miami, Fla.	14	0.24	0.22	7.2 ''	+
Milwaukee, Wis.	61	0.44	0.70	0.044	
Nashville, Tenn.	9.3	0.071 ***	0.022	3.0 '	−
New Haven, Conn.	46	0.99	0.74	0.35	
New Orleans, La.	35	0.41	0.69	1.3	
Oklahoma City, Okla.	16	0.43	0.64	0.21	
Omaha, Nebr.	18	0.38	0.46	3.0 '	+
Philadelphia, Pa.	86	0.40	0.50	0.38	
Pittsburgh, Pa.	17	0.091 ***	0.022	2.0	
Portland, Ore.	11	0.16 *	0.18	0.48	
Providence, R.I.	14	0.41	0.50	1.5	
Richmond, Va.	41	0.82	0.49	0.078	
Rochester, N.Y.	43	0.64	0.54	9.5 '''	−
Sacramento, Calif.	15	0.36	0.38	0.010	
St. Louis, Mo.	47	0.28	0.27	2.7	
San Diego, Calif.	18	0.39	0.62	17 '''	−

Table I (Continued)

San Jose, Calif.	21	0.46	0.24	1.0	
Seattle, Wash.	25	0.31	0.57	0.61	
Spokane, Wash.	5.9	0.34	0.31	0.45	
Syracuse, N.Y.	48	0.92	0.45	0.026	
Toledo, Ohio	6.1	0.20	0.42	0.17	
Utica, N.Y.	51	1.2	0.46	2.1	
Washington, D.C.	20	0.27	0.43	0.49	
Wichita, Kansas	19	0.53	0.36	12 '''	—

[a] With 1 and 22 degrees of freedom.
*** Not significantly greater than zero at the 0.10 level.
* Not significantly greater than zero at the 0.01 level.
' Significant at the 0.10 level.
" Significant at the 0.05 level.
''' Significant at the 0.01 level.

from the ranks of the r^2's, is significant only at about the 0.50 level.

Turning now to the quadratic regressions, in 12 of the 46 cities an F-ratio significant at the 0.10 or smaller level was observed, indicating too much deviation from linearity to attribute to chance variation alone in those particular samples. Now, of course, we would expect some significant results purely by chance in 46 samples. Table III indicates, however, that overall too many deviations from linearity were observed to attribute to sampling variation. However, there is no tendency for departures from linearity to be associated with city size or region. Spearman's rho for F and urbanized area population is +0.15, significant at about the 0.40 level, while the H statistic for testing the significance of regional difference in the F's, was significant only at the 0.98 level.

Also, among the regressions summarized in Table 1 there is no significant tendency for departures from linearity to result in predominantly positive or negative curvature in the relationship between log-density and distance. Nor is there any tendency for the sign of curvature to be associated with city size or region. Of the 12 samples with significant F's, curvature was positive in 8 cases; on the null hypothesis of equally numerous positive and negative departures, the probability of a divergence from expectation as great or greater than observed is about 0.40. Likewise, for all 46 samples curvature was positive in 28 cases, but this is significant only at the 0.20 level. Table V indicates almost identical distributions of curvature for large, medium and small cities. While the distribution of curvature differs among regions, these differences are significant only at about the 0.30 level, as shown by Table VI.

In sum, then, it would seem that the negative exponential function is the best simple ap-

Table II   Mean Rank of r^2 by Region.

Region	No. of Cities	Mean Rank
Northeast	11	21.2
North Central	11	23.2
South	12	20.7
West	12	28.8
Total	46	23.5

$H = 2.70$; Probability $\cong 0.5$.

Table III   Distribution of F-ratios, Observed and Expected on the Hypothesis of Linearity.

F	Probability	Observed	Expected
<1.00	>0.5	25	23.0
1.00–2.94	0.5–0.1	9	18.4
>2.94	<0.1	12	4.6
Total	...	46	46.0

$\chi^2(2) = 16.9$, Probability < 0.001.

Table IV   Mean Rank of F by Region.

Region	No. of Cities	Mean Rank
Northeast	11	23.1
North Central	11	25.3
South	12	23.0
West	12	22.8
Total	46	23.5

$H = 0.256$; Probability $\cong 0.98$.

proximation to the pattern of population density decline with distance from the city center in urban areas.

III

One of the most striking features of the data summarized in Table I is the great variation in the estimated density gradients. While the majority of the gradient estimates range from 0.2 to 0.5, they vary all the way from about 0.07 in Nashville to 1.2 in Utica.[15] This section is devoted to a regression analysis of factors responsible for differences in density gradients among cities.[16]

The analysis of the first section of this paper suggests that the lower the transport costs and the greater the average per household consumption of housing, the smaller the rate of decline of housing prices with distance and, hence, the smaller the density gradient. Transport costs, however, are very difficult to measure, and the best I can do is to use some surrogates for this variable.

Table V   Relation of City Size to Direction of Curvature.

City Size (Rank)	Curvature	
	Positive	Negative
>650 thous. (1–16)	10	6
365–650 thous. (17–31)	9	6
<365 thous. (32–46)	9	6
Total	28	18

$X^2(2) \cong 0$, Probability $\cong 1$.

Table VI   Relation of Region to Direction of Curvature.

Region	Curvature	
	Positive	Negative
Northeast	9	2
North Central	5	6
South	6	6
West	8	4
Total	28	18

$\chi^2(3) = 3.9$; Probability $\cong 0.3$.

From data supplied by the American Transit Association I have computed miles of line of local transit systems per square mile of the urbanized area, X_1, and vehicle miles operated per mile of line, X_2.[17] One might expect that the greater either of these measures the smaller are transport costs, so both should be negatively related to the density gradient.

Two aspects of age were also included, the number of decades since the SMA of which the central city is a part first attained a population of 50 thousand, X_3, and the proportion of the SMA's growth that took place during the period 1920 to 1950, X_4.[18] The older the city on either of these measures, the less adapted I would expect the street system to be for motor vehicles and the greater transportation time and cost. Hence, I would expect X_3 to be positively and X_4 negatively related

15 The median of the g's in Table I is about 0.35.
16 Since the g's are but estimates, part of the reason for differences among them is sampling variability. However, study of the estimated variances of the gradient estimates suggests that sampling variability accounts for only about 10 per cent of the variance of the estimated gradients among the several cities.
17 These measures cover only those local transit companies and public authorities which reported to the Association on their operations for 1950, and are available for only 37 of the 46 cities for which I computed density gradients. The compilations of the Association permit one to calculate passengers carried per vehicle mile operated as well for all but four of these cities. To avoid running too short of degrees of freedom, however, I did not include this variable.
18 The sources for all data used in this part of the analysis are given at the foot of Table VII.

to the density gradient.[19] It might also be argued that the greater X_4 the more nearly adjusted is the actual pattern of densities to the equilibrium one for the auto era. The latter would also imply a negative relation between X_4 and the density gradient. A final surrogate for transport cost is car registrations per capita, X_5. I would expect that where the costs of private automobile transport are low relatively more people would own autos, and I would predict a negative relationship between X_5 and the density gradient.

The most important variable affecting the average per household consumption of housing in a metropolitan area is income. Thus, as X_6, I included the median income of families and unrelated individuals of the urbanized area in the expectation that it would be negatively associated with the density gradient.

Relaxing the assumption made earlier that all transactions other than those involving housing take place at the city center suggests including other variables as well. In general one would expect that the more dispersed are employment centers throughout the area, the less the premium people would pay for locations close to the city center and the smaller the price and density gradients. To the extent that the spatial distribution of retail sales affects the distribution of population, rather than the reverse, one would expect dispersion of shopping centers to have an effect similar to that of employment centers. Thus, as independent variables I include the proportion of SMA manufacturing employment inside the central city, X_7, and the proportion of SMA retail sales within the central business district, X_8.[20] I would expect both to be positively associated with the density gradient if they are significant at all.

In addition to the considerations discussed above, it might be argued that the prices consumers will pay for housing in different parts of the city are influenced by tastes and preferences proper. To the extent that, say, a relatively higher proportion of dwelling units near the city center are dilapidated than elsewhere and consumers have an aversion to living near such residences, the premium they would offer for living close to the center would be smaller than otherwise. Hence, price would decline less rapidly with distance and the density gradient

would be smaller than it would otherwise be. In an attempt to account for the influence of tastes I have included the following variables, which one might expect to be negatively related to the density gradients: X_9, a measure of the condition of central city dwelling units, X_{10}, a measure of industrialization, and X_{11}, a measure of crowding. In addition, X_2 might be interpreted as a taste variable, in which case one would expect a negative association with density gradients.

Finally, as X_{12}, I have included a measure of size in one of the regressions.[21] Casual inspection of Table I suggests a negative relationship between size and g, but size is rather strongly inter-correlated with several of the other independent variables—income, for example. I included X_{12} primarily to see if its relation with g is due to these inter-correlations, as I can think of no very convincing reasons why density gradients should be negatively related to size itself. A significant partial correlation between X_{12} and g, like the presence of serial-correlation in the computed residuals from a time-series regression, would suggest to me that some important variable has been omitted from the analysis.

In all my regressions I used the logarithm of the estimated density gradient as the dependent variable. Logs were used for two reasons. First, scatter diagrams indicated that the simple regressions between g and the independent variables described above are on the whole more nearly linear if the logs of the g's are used. And second, since the estimated variances of the g's tend to vary directly with the estimated gradients, the scatter about the regression line appears to be more nearly homoscedastic when using the logs of the g's.

The results of my regression analysis of differences in the g's are summarized in Table VII. In all cases, the regression results are based upon data for the 36 cities for which

19 The relation of X_4 to density was first suggested to me by an unpublished manuscript of Lowdon Wingo.
20 Data on SMA retail sales were not available for one of the 37 cities for which I have data relating to local transit systems.
21 This is the log of the urbanized area population. Use of logs for this variable resulted in a more nearly linear scatter.

Table VII Simple and Partial Correlation Coefficients, Logs of the Density Gradients with Various Independent Variables, 36 Cities, 1950.

Independent Variable [a]	Simple Correlation Coefficient	Partial Correlation Coefficients, Equation		
		(1)	(2)	(3)
X_1	0.31	0.28	0.26	0.17
X_2	−0.23 *	−0.18	−0.21	−0.21
X_3	−0.066	−0.15	−0.11	0.23
X_4	−0.30 **	−0.38 **	−0.30 *	0.0060
X_5	−0.14	−0.22	−0.38 **	−0.43 **
X_6	−0.24 *	−0.18	−0.31 *	−0.15
X_7	0.28 **	0.44 ***	0.48 ***	0.41 **
X_8	0.41 ***	−0.016	0.025	−0.26
X_9	0.0041	...	−0.43 **	−0.37 **
X_{10}	0.033	...	0.31	0.29
X_{11}	−0.22 *	...	−0.094	−0.089
X_{12}	−0.63	...	...	−0.50
R^2	...	0.47	0.59	0.69

* Significant at the one-tail 0.10 level.
** Significant at the one-tail 0.05 level.
*** Significant at the one-tail 0.01 level.
[a] Definition of Independent Variables Used:

X_1—Miles of line of local transit systems per square mile of the urbanized area, 1950. Data on miles of line and vehicle miles operated (X_2 below) were compiled from data for individual companies or public authorities located in a given urbanized area which reported to the American Transit Association on operations for 1950. These were taken from American Transit Association, *Transit Operating Reports—1950*, Part I (New York: American Transit Association, 1951). Miles of line were divided by the area in square miles of the urbanized area from U.S. Bureau of the Census, *1950 Census of Population*, Vol. I (Washington, D.C.: U.S. Government Printing Office, 1952), Table 17.

X_2—Vehicle miles operated per mile of line, local transit systems, 1950. (See above.)

X_3—Age of the SMA in 1950. Number of decades since the SMA first attained a population of 50 thousand, from Bogue and Harris, *op. cit.*, Appendix Table 1, p. 73.

X_4—Proportion of SMA population growth in the period 1920–1950. Computed from data given by Donald J. Bogue, *Metropolitan Growth and the Conversion of Land to Nonagricultural Uses* (Oxford, Ohio: Scripps Foundation, 1956), Appendix Table II, pp. 28–32.

X_5—Car registrations per capita in principal SMA counties, 1950. Car registrations data are from Automobile Manufacturers Association, *Automobile Facts and Figures*, 31st ed. (Detroit,

1919–41 **55**

Mich.: Automobile Manufacturers Association, 1951), pp. 24–25, while the population data are from U.S. Bureau of the Census, *1950 Census of Population*, Vol. II (Washington, D.C.: U.S. Government Printing Office, (1952), Tables 4 and 5.

X_6—Median income, families and unrelated individuals, urbanized area, 1949. From *ibid.*, Part I, Table 93.

X_7—Proportion of SMA manufacturing employment in the central city, 1947. Computed from data in Evelyn M. Kitagawa and Donald J. Bogue, *Suburbanization of Manufacturing Activity within Standard Metropolitan Areas* (Oxford, Ohio: Scripps Foundation, 1955), Appendix Table A-1, pp. 132–38.

X_8—Proportion of SMA retail sales in the central business district, 1954. From *1954 Census of Business, Central Business District Statistics, Summary Report, op. cit.*, Table 4.

X_9—Proportion of central city dwelling units substandard (in need of major repair and/or lacking running water), 1950. Computed from data in *1950 Census of Population*, Vol. III, *op. cit.*, Table 3.

X_{10}—Proportion of urbanized area manufacturing employment (male) in manufacturing, 1950. Computed from data in *1950 Census of Population*, Vol. II, *op. cit.*, Table 3.

X_{11}—Average density of the central city, 1950. Population per sq. mile of land area, from *1950 Census of Population*, Vol. I, *op. cit.*, Table 17.

X_{12}—Log of urbanized area population, 1950. From *ibid.*

measures of all the independent variables described above are available. The first column on Table VII shows the simple correlation coefficient between the log of g and each of the independent variables. Columns two through four show partial correlation coefficients when different combinations of the independent variables are included in the regression equation. Those coefficients which are significant and of the sign expected on *a priori* grounds are designated with asterisks. The last row of the table gives the coefficient of multiple determination for each of the three multiple regression equations.

The results shown in Table VII indicate some tendency for density gradients to be smaller the lower are transport cost and the greater median incomes, in line with the implications of my analysis. The simple correlation coefficient and all three partials of X_2 are negative, although none of the partials is significant at the 0.10 level. The proportion of SMA growth from 1920 to 1950, X_4 is significantly negatively correlated with g, except when size is added. In equations (2) and (3), car registrations per capita are significantly negatively correlated with g. The simple correlation of income with g and the partial in equation (2) are both significantly negative, though the partial is not when size is added in equation (3).

X_7 and X_8, the variables relating to the spatial distribution of employment and shopping centers, are quite interesting. Except for the size variable, none of the independent variable is more strongly and consistently correlated with g than X_7, the proportion of SMA manufacturing employment inside the central city. The retail sales variable, however, while showing a highly significant and positive simple correlation with g, becomes insignificant when other factors are held constant. These results indicate that the spatial distribution of employment is a very important factor in determining the spatial distribution of population in urban areas. But, in line with central place theory, the spatial distribution of retail sales appears to be a result rather than a cause of urban population distribution.

Of the three taste variables, only dwelling unit condition, X_9, exhibits a significantly negative partial correlation with g. This correlation is consistent with the hypothesis that people prefer outlying residential locations in part because of the dwelling unit characteristics of the central city. But adding X_9 alone increases R^2 only from 0.47 to 0.53, so the condition of dwelling units would appear to have a much weaker influence on the spatial distribution of population than is often ascribed to it.

Finally, the size variable is significantly negatively correlated with g, even when all the other independent variables are included in the regression. This result suggests to me that there are other factors not included in this analysis which have a significant influence on the slope of the density-distance function.

IV

The empirical analysis of this paper shows a strong and highly significant tendency for urban population densities to decline with distance from the central business district. While too many departures from the negative-exponential pattern of decline were noted to be attributable to sampling variability, there was no significant tendency for the log density-distance regressions to exhibit predominantly positive or negative curvature. Hence, the negative-exponential function is probably the best simple approximation to the pattern of urban residential densities in U.S. cities in 1950.

Great variation in the density gradients for 1950 was found and analyzed. The results suggest a significant tendency for density gradients to be smaller for cities more spread out where transport costs are low. If anything it appears that the greater the average income in an area, and hence the average per household consumption of housing, the smaller the density gradient. One of the strongest factors affecting the gradient is the spatial distribution of employment, X_7 being consistently and positively correlated with g. The larger the proportion of central city dwelling units which are substandard the more spread-out is population within the city, a result consistent with the hypothesis that poor-quality housing leads some consumers to seek out residences at greater distances from the center then they otherwise would. Finally, even when all other variables are included in the regression equation, there is a strong tendency for cities to have smaller density gradients the greater their size.

APPENDIX

The purpose of this appendix is to demonstrate the assertion that, if certain simple assumptions are made about the price-distance, demand, and production functions, population densities decline negative-exponentially with distance.

Assuming that housing firms have identical log-linear production functions which exhibit constant returns to scale, the first-order or necessary conditions for firm equilibrium are given by:

$$(3) \quad \begin{aligned} Q^* &= a_0^* + a_1 L^* + a_2 R^*, \ a_1 + a_2 = 1 \\ L^* &= a_1^* + p^* + Q^* - w^* \\ R^* &= a_2^* + p^* + Q^* - r^* \end{aligned}$$

where X^* stands for the natural logarithm of X. Substituting the second and third of these into the first yields.

$$(4) \qquad r^* = \text{const.} - \frac{a_1}{a_2} w^* + \frac{1}{a_2} p^*.$$

Equation (4), which gives the maximum rent firms offer for land as a function of non-land cost and price, when substituted into the third of equations (3), gives:

$$(5) \qquad \left(\frac{Q}{R}\right)^* = \text{const.} - \frac{a_1}{a_2} w^* + \frac{a_1}{a_2} p^*$$

or

$$\frac{d}{dk}\left(\frac{Q}{R}\right)^* = \frac{a_1}{a_2}\frac{dp^*}{dk}.$$

Assuming that price declines negative-exponentially with distance,

$$(6) \qquad p^* = p_0^* - ck, \frac{dp^*}{dk} = -c,$$

so

$$(7) \qquad \frac{d}{dk}\left(\frac{Q}{R}\right)^* = -\frac{a_1}{a_2} c.$$

Likewise, if the per capita demand for housing is

$$(8) \qquad \left(\frac{Q}{P}\right) = \text{const.} \times p^{A_1},$$

where A_1 is the real-income-constant price elasticity,

$$(9) \qquad \frac{d}{dk}\left(\frac{Q}{P}\right)^* = A_1 \frac{dp^*}{dk} = -A_1 c.$$

Since density, D, equals (Q/R) divided by (Q/P),

$$(10) \qquad \frac{dD^*}{dk} = \frac{d}{dk}\left(\frac{Q}{R}\right)^* - \frac{d}{dk}\left(\frac{Q}{P}\right)^*$$

$$= -\left(\frac{a_1}{a_2} - A_1\right) c = -g.$$

Equation (10) says that the log of density declines at a constant rate with distance, and this rate of decline depends upon the price gradient, the real-income-constant, elasticity of demand, and the exponents of the production function. Integrating equation (10), we find:

$$(11) \qquad D = D_0 \exp(-gk), \quad \text{where} \quad D_0 = \frac{Pg^2}{2\pi},$$

the constant D_0 being evaluated by equating the integral of density over the land area used for housing with total population, P.

The Journey-to-Work As a Determinant of Residential Location

JOHN F. KAIN

This study presents some empirical evidence on the manner in which transportation costs influence the household's choice of a residential location. It also describes a residential location model which considers the problem of residential location somewhat differently than have models previously presented before the Regional Science Association or available else-

From the *Papers of the Regional Science Association*, IX (1962), 137–160. Reprinted by permission of the Regional Science Association.

where in the literature.[1] This model makes it easier to understand the empirical tests offered in this paper. The central hypothesis, suggested by this and similar models, and from which I will obtain a number of subhypotheses, is that households substitute journey-to-work expenditures for site expenditures. This substitution depends primarily on household preferences for low-density as opposed to high-density residential services.

THE MODEL

The model deals with the locational choice of a single household. It is assumed that this household's transportation costs increase monotonically with the distance it resides from its workplace. The reasonableness of this assumption may be seen if the household's monthly expenditure for transportation is broken into its component parts. These outlays may be expressed as the sum of the costs of the journey to work, of obtaining residentially oriented services within the immediate residential area, i.e., groceries, elementary school, etc., and of obtaining other services available only outside the residential area. Included are both dollar expenditures for transportation and dollar valuations of time spent in travel. Unless the distinction is explicitly made, transportation costs here will refer to these combined costs.

The household's monthly transportation costs, T, may then be expressed as the sum of its expenditures for those services obtainable within the residential area, t_r, those which vary with the residence's distance from its workplace, $t(w_1)$, $t(w_2)$, $t(w_3)$, $\cdots$, $t(w_n)$, and those which vary with the residence's distance from other points outside the residential area, $t(o_1)$, $t(o_2)$, $\cdots$, $t(o_m)$, where n equals the number of workplace destinations for the household and m equals the number of other destinations outside the residential area. The household's total monthly transportation cost for each residential site may thus be expressed:

$$(1) \quad T = t_r + t(w_1) + t(w_2) + t(w_3) + \cdots \\ + t(w_n) + t(o_1) + \cdots + t(o_m)$$

For our purposes it may be assumed that t_r is invariant with the household's choice of location. The level of t_r may vary with the kind of

residential area the household chooses, i.e., low-density versus high-density, but there is no reason to expect a significant variation between areas of similar characteristics.

If the costs of residentially provided services —retailing, medical services, schools, etc.,— may be considered as invariant, the accuracy of our assumption depends on the relative weights placed on the trips to workplaces and on the trips made to other points outside the residential area. It is my contention that for the majority of urban households the sum of transportation costs to points other than work or within the immediate residential area is small, and that the costs to any one other single point are almost always trivial. The journey-to-work costs, by way of contrast, are large and significant. Thus if these contentions are correct, no serious violence is done in most instances by considering only journey-to-work costs in our residential location model.

It is not at all difficult, however, to find exceptions to the rule I have proposed. For example, there is the large and probably increasing population of households without a member in the labor force. For such households the worktrip term in our equation is equal to zero. For these households the location of other destinations may be of considerable importance. Many retired people desire to live near their children and grandchildren. Single persons and young married couples may make frequent trips to major cultural and recreational centers. The monthly travel costs of these households may vary significantly with the distance from these centers.

Despite these exceptions to the rule, it is my belief that the assumption used in this model is approximately correct for a very large proportion of the population, perhaps for as many

1 See, for example, Edgar M. Hoover and Raymond Vernon, *Anatomy of a Metropolis*, Harvard University Press, Cambridge, Mass., 1959; William Alonso, "A Theory of the Urban Land Market," *Papers and Proceedings of the Regional Science Association*, Philadelphia, Pa., 1960; John D. Herbert and Benjamin H. Stevens, "A Model for the Distribution of Residential Activity in Urban Areas," *Journal of Regional Science*, Vol. 2, No. 2, Fall 1960; Lowdon Wingo, Jr., *Transportation and Urban Land*, Resources for the Future, Inc., Washington, D.C., 1961; Ira South Lowry, "Residential Location in Urban Areas," unpublished Ph.D. dissertation, Department of Economics, University of California, 1960.

Table I Purpose of Trips Originating in the Dwelling Unit in 38 Cities

Trip Purpose	Percent	Trips per 1000 Dwelling Units (Hypothetical)
Work	43.9	1010
Business	6.8	155
Social-Recreation	21.4	490
Shopping	11.9	275
School	4.8	110
All others	11.2	260
Total	100.0	2300

Source: Robert E. Schmidt and M. Earl Campbell, *Highway Traffic Estimation*, The Eno Foundation for Highway Traffic Control, 1956, Table II–4

as 80 or 90 percent of households having a member in the labor force.

The data in Table I illustrate the importance of the journey-to-work in the household's travel budget. Nearly half of all trips from home are made to work. Of the remainder, some portion of social-recreation trips and personal business trips are made to other destinations outside the residential area. The destinations of these trips may be spatially quite separated. Furthermore, many will be to points nearby the workplace, since a large proportion of cultural, recreational, personal business, and other destinations are likely to be nearby employment concentrations.

These trips made to the same destinations may be added to the trips made to the workplace. If a small proportion of the population makes large numbers of these trips, the averages shown in Table I overstate the importance of those trips for the remainder of the population.

The Market for Residential Space

It is also assumed that the household is an atomistic competitor in the market for residential space. That is, it is assumed that there is a market for residential space and that the price a single household must pay per unit for space is given. Residential space is defined as the urban land utilized by the household in its residential activities. For single-family dwelling units this would be closely approximated by lot size. For multiple units it would be some proportion of the total amount of land utilized by the structure. (I am glossing over, at this point, a number of complex relationships among the lot layout, over-all neighborhood densities, and the substitutability between capital and land and residential space.)

I am assuming that the price the household must pay per unit of residential space varies from one location to another. This price is an economic rent which landlords can obtain from households for more accessible sites. The rents on more accessible sites arise because of households' collective efforts to economize on transportation expenditures. For this model, I am assuming that these rents, which I will refer to hereafter as location rents, decrease with distance from the household's workplace. Specifically, I am assuming that the unit price the household must pay per unit of residential space *of a stated quality and amenity* decreases monotonically from its workplace. Of course, the magnitude of the location rents is significant only when there is a significant concentration of employment.

It is possible, as Alonso, Wingo, and others have done, to obtain this second result using only the first assumption.[2] Since I am unable to improve on their solutions in what I consider to be the most important directions, i.e., adequate and explicit treatment of time, depreciation, obsolescence, quality, and other problems of housing-market dynamics, I am instead offering this as a provisional hypothesis. Common sense, the excellent theoretical works cited above, and fragmentary evidence support its acceptance; arrayed against it is the opinion of a number of knowledgeable Institutional Real Estate Economists and other urban researchers. A really adequate empirical verification or rejection of the hypothesis has yet to be accomplished or even attempted.

The Household's Consumption of Residential Space

It is further assumed that residential space is not an inferior good and that the household

2 Alonso, *op. cit.*; Wingo, *op. cit.*

Figure 1　Total iso-location rent curve.

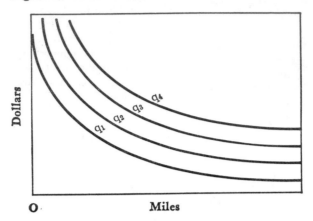

chooses its residential location and its consumption of residential space by maximizing the utility obtainable from a given income. Thus, the quantity of residential space the household will consume depends on the household's income, the price of residential space, and its preference for residential space. These, along with the assumptions about location rents and journey-to-work costs, are the basic components of the model presented in this paper. It will be seen that, if the household's workplace and transportation costs per mile are taken as given,

Figure 2　Marginal location rent and transportation cost functions.

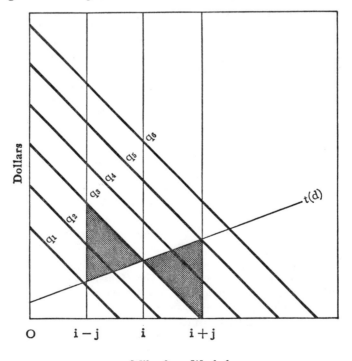

Miles from Workplace

its residential location can be expressed as a function of its space consumption. Similarly, then, the household's residential location may be expressed as a function of its income, space preference, and the price of residential space. These are the nature of the hypotheses to be tested later in this paper. First, however, it is necessary to spell out the implications of our key assumptions more completely. These key assumptions are: (1) the assumption that the household's transportation cost function increases with distance from its workplace, (2) the existence of a market for residential space in which the price per unit a household must pay for residential space of a given quality decreases with distance from its workplace, (3) a fixed workplace, (4) utility maximization on the part of households, and (5) the assumption that residential space is not an inferior good.

The Location Rent Function

The location rent function or schedule of location rents, i.e., the function which describes the decrease in location rents with distance from the household's workplace, describes the savings per unit of residential space the household may achieve by moving farther from its place of employment. What is of interest to the household in making a locational choice, however, is not this amount but its total savings at various distances. If rents per unit of space decrease as the household moves further from its workplace, the absolute amount of the savings possible through longer journeys-to-work depend on the amount of residential space consumed by the household. Since the household's space consumption has not been specified, the decline in total location rents with distance is described by a family of iso-space curves similar to the economist's isoquants. Each curve in Figure 1, for example, illustrates the decline in location rents with distance for a given quantity of residential space. From Figure 1, it can be seen that the absolute dollar savings obtainable by a longer journey-to-work clearly become larger as more residential space is consumed. By way of contrast, the household's transportation costs per mile, $t(d)$, are invariant with the amount of residential space consumed.

It is, however, the combined outlay for transportation costs and location rents that ought to concern the household in selecting a residential site. Since a given dollar spent for transportation or rents has the same disutility, the household's utility maximization combination of the two is included in the set which minimizes the combined outlay for rents and transportation costs for each quantity of residential space.

Marginal Savings in Location Rents and Marginal Increases in Transportation Costs

The characteristics of the solution we seek can perhaps be more easily understood if we use functions which describe the changes in each of these substitutable costs with the household's distance from its workplace. Figure 2 illustrates the incremental savings in location rents obtained by commuting an additional unit of distance for each quantity of space. The area under each curve is equal to the total location rents that would have to be paid by the household if it were to reside at its workplace and if it were to consume the quantity of space specified by a given curve. Since this function describes the manner in which total location rents decrease, the area under each curve to the right of oi equals the total monthly location rents that must be paid to locate at i for each quantity of residential space. For example, the area under q_3 to the right of oi is paid for the quantity of residential space represented by the curve q_3.

Marginal Transportation Costs

The incremental increase in transportation costs can be illustrated in the same manner. The line $t(d)$ in Figure 2 shows the incremental increase in transportation costs with distance. The area under the curve $t(d)$ to the left of oi is equal to the expenditures for the journey-to-work required to reside at oi.

The minimum cost location for each quantity of residential space is given by the intersection of the marginal cost of transportation function and each of the marginal location rent savings functions. For q_3, the minimum cost location is at oi. For larger quantities of residential space, the minimum cost location is farther from the household's workplace; for smaller quantities, nearer.

This solution can be easily verified by using Figure 2. Locations farther from the workplace, say $oi + j$, add the area between oi and $oi + j$ under the $t(d)$ curve to the household's transportation costs. Its savings in location rents amount only to the area under q_3 between oi and $oi + j$. Thus, the household's total location costs for the quantity of residential space q_3 are increased by the shaded area under $t(d)$ between oi and $oi + j$.

Similarly, if the household locates closer to its workplace, say oi-j, it reduces its transportation costs by the area under the $t(d)$ curve between oi-j and oi. At the same time, it increases its rental expenditures by the quantity under the q_3 curve between oi-j and oi. Thus, the household consuming the quantity of residential space q_3 and residing at oi-j rather than oi, makes uneconomic expenditures for location which equal the shaded area between oi-j and oi.

Thus, we have obtained those locations which minimize the household's locational costs for each quantity of residential space. In addition, we have obtained the household's required expenditures for each quantity of residential space. This is all the information we must have to enable us to obtain a unique locational solution for each household.

Total location costs divided by the quantity of residential space is the price the household must pay per unit for residential space. With this price information the household's locational solution is straightforward. Given the price of all other goods and services, the household's preference for residential space, its preference for all other goods and services, and its income, the household's consumption of residential space is uniquely determined. Knowing its consumption of residential space, we have uniquely determined its residential location.

EMPIRICAL TESTING

At the beginning of this paper I stated that the purpose of this model is to provide some testable hypotheses. The variables employed in the model are location rents at each site and transportation costs per mile, from which we obtained a third variable, the price of residential space; incomes; preferences for residential space; and preferences for all other goods and services. I have already stated my willingness to specify the shape of the location rent function. Money costs of transportation are fairly straightforward. The valuation of time is complex. In the empirical tests presented here, it is assumed that similar groups of households place the same valuation on time per mile. Preferences are always difficult to quantify, but we can offer some propositions about the relative space preferences of various classes of households. It is reasonable to assume, for example, that larger households, such as those with children, have higher preferences for space than do smaller households. The income variable is theoretically simple.

Data for the empirical tests presented here were obtained from the origin and destination study conducted in 1953 by the Detroit Area Traffic Study. The data consist of the origins and destinations of worktrips, information on the characteristics of the workers making these trips, information on the characteristics of the households to which the tripmaker belonged, and certain attributes of the trips themselves, for a stratified random sample of approximately 40,000 Detroit households.

The Location Rent Surface for Detroit

For empirical testing of the residential location model, the Detroit metropolitan area is divided into concentric distance rings, numbered from 1 to 6 from the center outward, around the central business district. It is assumed that location rents for a unit of residential space of a given quality and amenity successively decrease from ring to ring outward from the center, with rents very high near the center and very low near the outer circumference. The rate of decrease is assumed to be substantial in the inner rings and very slight in the outer. The surface in the outer rings is assumed to be quite flat, and to decrease only moderately with distance from the central business district.

These assumptions about the shape of the location rent surface are obtained from our premises about the determinants of the surface. It was stated earlier that location rents result from the competition among many workers for residential space near the same workplace or other workplaces nearby. The number of workers employed within each ring may be thought of as representing the number of demanders for residential space within the ring, and the number of acres within the ring as the supply of residential space. Ring 1 includes only 0.2 percent of the available space within the study area, but provides jobs for nearly 11 percent of Detroit's workers. Detroit has 60 percent of its employment located within six miles of the central business district, but only 10 percent of the land within the study area is located there. This indicates a substantial excess-demand situation for space within the close-in rings, and a substantial lessening of demand for space in outer rings. The relatively low level of demand for urban use in the outermost ring is indicated by the large proportion of land which is not in urban use within the ring. A full 68 percent of the available land in Ring 6 is vacant; if land devoted to streets and alleys were subtracted, this figure would be even higher.

Thus it is reasonable to expect that location rents in the central business district and nearby would be very high, while in Ring 6 they would be very low. The high level of demand for residential space in inner rings is indicated by the high employment—and, for that matter, high residential densities. The low level of demand for residential space in outer levels is indicated by low employment densities, low residential densities, and the large quantities of vacant land within these rings.

The Analysis

If workers stratified according to income, sex, race, family size, residential density, or structure type have a common workplace, i.e., the same location rent function, the residential location model would predict different distributions of residence around this workplace for each of these groups. At the same time the model would predict differences in the residential distribution of the same class of workers if the workers are employed at different workplaces, i.e., have different location rent functions.

For the empirical tests presented in this section, the residential distributions of different classes of workers employed within the same ring, having by assumption the same location rent function, are compared with distributions expected *a priori* from the model. In addition, the residential distributions of workers belonging to the same class but employed at different workplaces, i.e., having different location rent functions, are compared for consistency with the expected relationships.

The first finding which supports the appropriateness of the residential location model is a well-known one. The journey-to-work is predominantly from outer residential rings to inner workplace rings. Furthermore, the proportion of a ring's workers residing within the same or adjacent rings increases with the workplace ring's distance from the central business district.

In terms of the model described above, equal transportation costs are incurred with movement in any direction. Reductions in location rents are to be found only away from the central business district. As a result, the minimization of location rents is always obtained in the direction of the periphery regardless of the household's space consumption. Secondly, as the schedule of location rents flattens out towards the rural urban fringe, the space consumption of households becomes less of a constraint and higher proportions of the workplaces' employees live nearby. The model's only justification for a journey-to-work is to reduce the household's total expenditures for location rents. If, as hypothesized for Rings 5 and 6, total location rents do not decrease as the household makes a longer journey-to-work, or decrease only slightly, there is little incentive to make a journey-to-work, at least to economize on rents. Thus, the direction of the journey-to-work is from residences in outer rings where location rents are low to workplaces in inner rings; and larger proportions of worktrips are made to nearby rings as the workplace's distance from the central business district increases.

The distribution of elapsed time spent in reaching work, by workers employed in each ring, also exhibits the expected relationship.

The fewest short trips are made by workers employed in the central business district. Few workers employed in Rings 5 and 6 make long trips. For example, 49 percent of workers employed in the central business district make trips more than one-half hour long. By way of contrast, only 17 percent of those employed in Ring 6, where the location rent surface is hypothesized as being nearly horizontal from the workplace, make trips of longer than a half-hour. The proportion is even lower for Ring 5: 14 percent. If it is assumed that the distribution of travel time valuations, money costs of transportation, incomes, space preferences, etc., are similar for each workplace ring, the model would predict longer journeys-to-work by workers employed in inner rings than for those employed in outer rings. The longer journeys-to-work made by Ring 6 workers is explained by the fact that much of Ring 6 is rural. Workers employed in isolated establishments within the ring may have to make substantial journeys-to-work to obtain an adequate selection of housing.

These results may seem trivial as tests of the appropriateness of the residential location model. It should be noted, therefore, that the empirical results for nonwhites, who because of housing market segregation are unable to compete freely in the market for residential space as we defined it, are exactly the opposite.

The longest trips by Detroit nonwhites are made by those employed in outer rings and the shortest by those employed in inner rings. Similarly the journey-to-work pattern of nonwhites employed in outer rings is from residences in inner rings to workplaces in outer rings. If this economic model lacked relevance, or if residential location resulted entirely from some socioeconomic clustering as many urban sociologists and real estate market analysts have suggested, these regularities would not have to exist. Distributions similar to those observed for nonwhites might be the rule rather than the exception.

Male-Female Differences in Work-Residence Patterns

The work-residence patterns of all workers conceal important differences among the various classes or workers. An understanding of these differences is important for a satisfactory explanation of the relationships between the journey-to-work and the selection of a residential location. Among these is a significant difference in the ring-to-ring movement of male and female workers. Table 2 compares the proportions of males and females residing in each distance ring, by ring of employment.

From Table 2 it is evident that the residen-

Table II Proportion of Males and Females Residing in Each Distance Ring by Ring of Employment.

| Employment Ring | Sex | Distance Ring | | | | | | Total |
		1	2	3	4	5	6	
One	Male	4.8%	9.9%	25.0%	26.8%	23.2%	10.2%	100%
	Female	2.6	15.6	38.0	25.8	12.9	5.0	100
Two	Male	1.0	19.1	31.2	22.9	17.1	8.6	100
	Female	0.8	23.2	39.2	20.9	11.0	4.6	100
Three	Male	0.8	11.3	36.9	24.0	16.9	10.1	100
	Female	0.4	9.7	46.9	25.3	12.5	5.1	100
Four	Male	0.5	6.4	21.0	32.2	24.2	15.7	100
	Female	0.0	4.0	23.0	44.0	19.8	9.2	100
Five	Male	0.4	2.1	10.2	16.6	50.8	20.0	100
	Female	0.0	1.9	8.7	16.6	53.8	18.9	100
Six	Male	0.5	2.0	6.9	10.1	22.4	58.0	100
	Female	0.2	1.6	3.8	6.1	16.6	71.8	100

tial distribution of males around their workplaces is flatter than that of females. Higher proportions of female workers consistently reside in nearby residential rings than do the proportions of male workers.

The tighter locational pattern of female workers is, in terms of the residential location model, consistent with at least three different hypotheses. The first inference that might be drawn is that the direction of causation assumed in the model is wrong for women workers. It might plausibly be argued that the residence is selected for some unspecified reason, and that the wife-and-mother has a greater need to find a convenient job nearby the home. Such an argument would correctly point out that many females, if not most, are secondary wage earners. As such, they tend to seek nearby jobs to augment the family budget, with a more casual attitude in job seeking than that of the primary wage earner. As a result, the place of employment generally has less effect on the choice of a residence. This view suggests that women's selection of a place of employment is more conditioned by the selection of residence.

The second interpretation is that females make shorter journeys-to-work because their workplace is the same as or nearby to that of their husbands. Such households have a stronger incentive to shorten the journey-to-work because the combined journey-to-work costs are higher than for households having only a single wage earner.

Finally, it is likely that a disportionate number of female wage earners belong to households having lower space preference, i.e., to one- or two-person households. For these households both the greater numbers of working wives and the lower space preferences work in favor of shorter journeys-to-work.

I am unable at this time to resolve the question of which hypothesis is most correct; all three, I would expect, contribute to the final explanation. I believe that these three categories include a large proportion of the female working population.

OCCUPATIONAL DIFFERENCES IN RESIDENTIAL DISTRIBUTIONS

The model would postulate that if households had the same location rent function, the same transportation cost function, the same space

Figure 3 Proportion of the central business district's low-, medium-, and high-income workers residing in each residential ring.

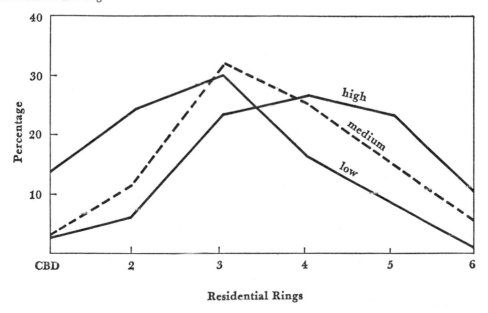

preference, and the same valuation of time, but different incomes, the length of the households' journey-to-work would increase as an increasing function of income. The Detroit origin and destination study did not obtain household income, but the occupations of wage earners can be used as a crude measure of their incomes.

Figure 3 shows the proportion of high-, medium-, and low-income central business district workers residing in each residential ring. Clearly, lower-income workers have the tightest residential pattern; the highest-income workers, the most dispersed.

Analysis of the Data for Occupations Ranked by Median Income

Similar residential distributions were obtained for employment Rings 1, 2, and 3, using eight occupational classifications. For workers employed in Ring 4, however, these relationships show signs of weakening. The hypothesized relationships have all but disappeared for Rings 5 and 6—an expected result. Since the location rent function is very flat from workplaces located in Rings 5 and 6, space consumption provides less of a justification for a journey-to-work. Additionally, the lower-income workers retain their tight adhesion to the workplace observed for inner rings. Of the service workers employed in Ring 6, 77 percent reside within the same ring. The proportion is nearly as large for male service workers—75 percent.

The relationships between occupational earnings and the proportion of each occupation residing in each ring may be subjected to a more rigorous test. The proportion of workers employed in each occupation residing in each ring may be ranked by order of magnitude.

Table III illustrates these rankings for those employed in Ring 2. If the hypothesis is correct, the ranks of the proportions residing in that ring should have the opposite order from those of the median earnings of each occupation. A perfect inverse ranking would show that, in all cases, as the median income increases the proportion of the occupation residing in a residence ring would decrease. This represents the expected pattern for rings near the workplace, where rents decrease significantly with distance from the workplace. A perfect ordering in the opposite direction is expected for Rings 5 and 6. The proportions of the occupations' members residing in Ring 6 should decrease as the average income of the occupation decreases.

It can be seen in Table III that although the order generally accords with the hypothesis, it is not perfect, the imperfection being that lower percentages of sales workers and clerical workers reside in inner rings than their incomes would lead us to expect. By contrast, a higher proportion of operatives and craftsmen resides in inner rings than is consistent with their income rankings. The ordering is also

Table III   Ranked Residential Distributions for Occupational Groups Employed in Ring.

		Residence Ring								
		2		3		4		5		6	
Occupation	Median Income	%	Rank	%	Rank	%	Rank	%	Rank	%	Rank
Managers	$4516	10.6	8	28.8	7	28.8	2	27.4	1	8.5	4
Professionals	4099	12.0	7	27.0	8	29.5	1	22.0	2	8.6	2.5
Craftsmen	3715	19.1	4	29.6	6	24.2	3	16.0	4	10.6	1
Operatives	3002	24.9	3	37.9	1	16.8	7	13.1	6	6.4	6
Salesworkers	2792	15.4	6	33.5	4	24.1	4	18.4	3	8.6	2.5
Clerical	2706	18.0	5	36.3	3	23.2	5	15.3	5	6.5	5
Laborers	2690	34.3	2	30.5	5	18.1	6	6.8	7	6.2	7
Services	2262	35.0	1	36.5	2	15.4	8	6.1	8	2.6	8

very good for residence Rings 5 and 6. If the above two pairs of occupations were exchanged, the order of occupational incomes and the rank of the percentage residing in Ring 5 would be identical. This is a systematic discrepancy for all workplace rings. The operatives group is consistently out of order. Only operatives of the four highest income occupations reside in inner rings at higher-than-average proportions and outer residential rings at below-average proportions. This apparent discrepancy can be largely explained in terms of differences in female participation by occupation mentioned earlier. For this reason we will present results both for all workers and for males only. For the analysis of ranked data which follows, the data for each of the six workplace rings are arranged as in Table III.

The Spearman Coefficient of Rank Correlation provides a powerful and efficient tool for evaluating the degree of association among these ranked relationships. The Spearman Rank Order Correlation Technique is interpreted in a way similar to that applied to the usual correlation technique. For the relationships among these sets of ranked data to be consistent with our *a priori* expectations, the following relationships would have to be exhibited.

The inner employment rings best satisfy the assumptions about the schedule of location rents set forth in the model; therefore, in the innermost three rings, the proportion of an occupation residing in a given ring should be negatively correlated with income. For outer residential rings there should be a high positive correlation between these occupational groups ranked according to median income and ranked according to the proportion of each residing in the residential ring. As the workplace's distance from the urban center increases, the relationship should deteriorate. This would be observed empirically by a decrease in the size of the coefficient of rank correlation for both inner and outer residential rings, and perhaps a non-uniform change of sign in many cases. Where the ring of employment and ring of residence are the same, it is expected that the relationship would always be negative, because low-income workers are small space-consumers and thus make shorter journeys to work. Tables IV and V give the coefficients of rank correlation between occupation and the percentage of that occupation residing in the ring for all six employment rings, for all workers and for males.

The coefficients in Tables IV and V are generally as expected. Reading the tables from left to right, i.e., from inner residential rings to outer residential rings, the coefficients change from high negative correlations to high positive correlations. Reading from top to bottom, i.e., from inner workplace rings to outer, the relationship tends to weaken. Where the residence and workplace rings are the same, the figures are in parentheses; these are the diagonal elements in Tables IV and V. The expected pattern for these rings also material-

Table IV Rank Order Coefficients Between Occupations Ranked by Income and Occupations Ranked by Rate of Residential Selection, for All Employment and Residence Rings: All Workers.

Employment Ring	Residence Ring				
	2	*3*	*4*	*5*	*6*
CBD	−0.86 *	−0.74 *	0.69	0.83 *	0.98 *
2	(−0.81) *	−0.67	0.83 *	0.89 *	0.71 *
3	−0.50	(−0.64)	0.76 *	0.88 *	0.76 *
4	−0.57	−0.71	(−0.48)	0.88 *	0.89 *
5	−0.47	0.04	0.29	(−0.33)	0.19
6	−0.33	0.21	0.42	0.90 *	(−0.61)

Note: Figures are in parentheses where residence and employment rings are the same.
* Differs significantly from zero at the 0.05 level.

Table V Rank Order Coefficients Between Occupations Ranked by Income and Occupations Ranked by Rate of Residential Selection, for all Employment and Residence Rings: Male Workers only.

Employment Ring	Residence Ring					
	1	2	3	4	5	6
CBD	(−0.69)	−0.81 *	−0.74	0.57	0.95 *	0.95 *
2		(−0.50)	−0.55	0.88 *	0.88 *	0.90 *
3		−0.76 *	(−0.95) *	0.95 *	0.86 *	0.83 *
4		−0.88 *	−0.57	(−0.17)	0.48	0.19
5		−0.43	0.29	0.29	(−0.38)	0.38
6		−0.40	0.36	0.36	0.81	(−0.40)

Note: Figures are in parenthesis where residence and employment rings are the same.
* Differs significantly from zero at the 0.05 level.

izes: lower-income workers reside in above average proportions in these rings, i.e., the journey-to-work typically becomes shorter as income falls.

The over-all consistency of the pattern, it is felt, illustrates that the locational selections of households by occupation are generally consistent with the model of residential location.

Family Size by Residence Ring

The relationships between family size and residence are neither as uniform nor as simple to interpret as those between sex and residence and occupation and residence. Family size is employed at this point as an indicator of household space preferences. Larger families undoubtedly spend a greater proportion of their time in the home, using it for a far broader range of social and recreational activities. As a result, it is expected that these households, ceteris paribus, would manifest a greater preference for residential space.

At the same time, residential space beyond minimum requirements is to some extent a luxury. When families reach a very large size, the greater desire to consume space is probably partially offset by a lower per capita income. The minimum levels of food, clothing, and other necessities require a larger proportion of the household budget. Thus, there appears to be some tendency for the space consump-

tion of households to fall off as family size increases beyond a certain point.

The Family-Size Residence Pattern for Inner Employment Rings. Tables VI and VII show the cumulative percentages of those employed in Rings 1 and 2 who reside in Rings 1 through 6. From Table VI it can be seen that the proportion of one-person families residing in inner rings is substantially higher than that of any other family-unit size. The cumulative percentages residing in Rings 2, 3, 4, and 5 fall as family size increases, until a family size of five persons is reached. For families of six or more, the relationship reverses itself. The proportion of six-person families residing in inner rings exceeds the proportions for all family groups except those having more than six persons or unrelated individuals.

The decreasing proportion of central business district workers residing in inner rings, as family size increases, is consistent with a higher space preference on the part of these households. A higher space preference, ceteris paribus, leads to a greater consumption of space and a longer journey to work.

The reversal of the relationships for households having more than five members is consistent with their lower per capita income. Beyond a certain size, the greater space preference is offset for many very large families by an income constraint. Household demand for other needed goods and services causes it to forego the higher space consumption.

Table VI Cumulative Percentages of Ring 1 Workers Residing in Rings 1 Through 6, by Family Size.

Family Size (No. Persons)	Residence Ring					
	1	*2*	*3*	*4*	*5*	*6*
1	26.1%	55.6%	86.0%	97.8%	98.5%	100%
2	2.5	14.8	50.3	76.2	93.4	100
3		9.7	39.8	69.3	90.5	100
4	0.4	10.2	38.8	68.8	90.8	100
5		9.8	35.7	67.3	89.5	100
6		11.2	52.0	77.0	93.4	100
More than 6		15.9	46.8	70.7	92.1	100
All	3.7	16.1	46.8	72.9	91.4	100

Source: Tabulated from Detroit Study Deck.

Table VII shows that these relationship hold for employment Ring 2 as well, with only one unimportant difference: from Rings 3 through 6 the cumulative percentage of families having more than six persons falls below that of six-person families. The percentages still exceed all but those of one- and two-person families, however.

Family Size by Ring of Residence—Outer Employment Rings. In the outer employment rings, we should expect either a reversal of the pattern observed in Rings 1 and 2 or no discernible relationship between family size and residential location. Table VIII shows that one- and two-person families employed in Ring 5 tend to reside in inner rings in the highest proportions of all family-unit sizes. Because of the lower space requirements, living closer to the central business district is less costly for them than for those having higher space preferences. To state that the higher location rents are less of a constraint for these households fails, however, to provide any reason that smaller families should be more willing to pay higher location rents or make a longer journey to work in order to reside nearer the center. The more incomplete specification of the transportation costs of these households provides such an explanation.

It is logical to expect that many of these households make above-average numbers of

Table VII Cumulative Percentages of Ring 2 Workers Residing in Rings 1 Through 6, by Family Size.

Family Size (No. Persons)	Residence Ring					
	1	*2*	*3*	*4*	*5*	*6*
1	9.7%	59.7%	87.1%	94.6%	98.9%	100%
2	0.8	22.6	56.4	79.8	93.0	100
3		16.7	51.1	74.7	93.3	100
4	0.1	15.8	48.9	73.5	91.2	100
5	0.1	17.3	48.3	70.7	89.4	100
6		19.2	53.6	75.0	89.7	100
More than 6	1.4	21.6	58.6	79.2	90.8	100
All	1.0	21.1	54.2	76.6	92.2	100

Source: Tabulated from Detroit Study Deck.

Table VIII   Cumulative Percentages of Ring 5 Workers Residing in Rings 6 Through 1, by Family Size.

Family Size (No. Persons)	*Residence Ring*					
	1	*2*	*3*	*4*	*5*	*6*
1	100%	89.1%	78.3%	52.3%	32.6%	10.0%
2	100	99.8	96.6	83.9	63.6	20.9
3		100.0	98.3	85.6	67.8	19.7
4		100.0	98.0	89.2	72.0	23.1
5		100.0	98.8	92.5	72.5	21.2
6		100.0	99.2	88.8	73.1	27.1
More than 6		100.0	97.6	86.6	70.9	26.6
All	100	99.5	97.2	86.2	67.4	22.5

Source: Tabulated from Detroit Study Deck.

trips to social and recreational centers located in or near the central business district. Their locational choices, therefore, would be heavily weighted by these trips. This should be true for one-person families as well. Unfortunately, one-person households employed in Ring 6 exhibit the tightest locational pattern of all families but those having more than five persons. One-person households employed in Ring 5 exhibit the expected behavior. From Table VIII it can be seen that only 33 percent of those employed in Ring 5 reside either in it or in Ring 6. By contrast, 64 percent of two-person households and 73 percent of six-person families reside in one of these two rings.

Also, it is likely that a large proportion of two-person families have a second wage earner. If the second member of the household is employed in an inner ring this provides an added incentive for the household to live closer to the center. It should be remembered, for all family sizes, that only small proportions of those employed in Rings 5 and 6 live in Rings 1, 2, and 3.

The final relationship exhibited by Tables VIII and IX is an increase in the proportion of a ring's employees residing nearby the workplace as family size increases. This finding is also consistent with the lower per capita incomes of larger families. When changes in total location

Table IX   Cumulative Percentages of Ring 6 Workers Residing in Rings 6 Through 1, by Family Size.

Family Size (No. Persons)	*Residence Ring*					
	1	*2*	*3*	*4*	*5*	*6*
1	100%	93.7%	84.3%	81.1%	79.0%	66.8%
2	100	99.7	96.5	88.0	76.1	56.3
3		100.0	98.7	92.3	81.7	62.7
4		100.0	93.8	93.1	83.5	58.4
5		100.0	97.8	93.4	85.5	62.6
6		100.0	99.6	92.9	90.0	66.4
More than 6		100.0	99.4	95.1	87.3	66.7
All	100	99.6	97.6	91.4	82.2	61.0

Source: Tabulated from Detroit Study Deck.

rents with distance are slight, minimization of transportation costs results in the minimization of total locational costs. Households with lower per capita income may be more sensitive to small differences in transportation costs.

Family Size by Ring of Residence—Rings 3 and 4. Above-average proportions of the very large and very small households employed in Rings 3 and 4 reside in rings near the center. Families with three to six members reside in higher proportions in Rings 5 and 6. The closeness in locational patterns of one- and two-person families employed in Rings 3 and 4 is even more reasonable than is that of the same size families employed in Rings 5 and 6.

Suburban living must be far less attractive to the young married or the childless couple than to those with children; their social and recreational activities are to a much greater degree directed outside the home. For the unattached person, residence in a suburban neighborhood far from the center of activity is even more unsatisfactory.

No adequate explanation in terms of the model can be offered for the locational choices of the very large families. In the case of employment Ring 4, the divergence is great enough that a larger proportion of its workers reside in Ring 3 than in Ring 5. Even so, more workers reside in the two rings away from the central business district than reside in those nearer the central business district.

Space Consumption by Residential Rings

The model of residential location postulates that where location rents are a significant factor, households consuming larger quantities of space will, *ceteris paribus*, make longer journeys to work than those consuming lesser quantities. The distance the household resides from its workplace is expressed by the model as a function of the quantity of residential space consumed. The relationship between space consumption and length of the journey to work, like that between income and the length of the journey, should deteriorate for outer employment rings, where the schedule of rents decreases only slightly or not at all around the workplace.

In this paper, structure type is employed as a measure of space consumption. This is an admittedly inadequate index, especially for single-family dwelling units, where the index fails to differentiate between very significant differences in lot size. Regardless of these deficiencies, structure type undoubtedly represents a dimension of the space consumption relationship. It is probably roughly correlated with the measure of space consumption we would wish to employ. For this reason, we will look at the relationships between residential location and occupancy of single-family, two-family, or multi-family dwellings.

The Residence-Space Consumption Pattern for Inner Employment Rings. Table X shows the percentages of workers occupying each type of dwelling unit in each residence ring, for employment Rings 1, 2, and 3. As might be expected, those choosing higher-density structures —two-family dwelling units and multiple dwellings—reside in well-above-average proportions in the close-in residential rings. For example, 30 percent of central business district workers who live in multiple dwelling units reside in the adjacent ring. In contrast, the adjacent ring is elected by only 5 percent of those choosing single-family structures and 13 percent of those selecting two family structures. This pattern persists through Ring 3, where 50 percent of all central business district workers reside who live in multiple dwelling units. Ring 3 also provides dwellings for 47 percent of those residing in two-family units, as opposed to only 22 percent of those residing in one-family units.

The proportion of those residing in multiple and two-family units in residence Rings 5 and 6, on the other hand, is very low. Less than 2 percent in each case live in Ring 6.

The Residence-Space Consumption Pattern for Outer Employment Rings. The differential pattern of residence by structure type for outer workplace rings is also in basic conformity with the model. These patterns are shown in Table XI. A large proportion of these residents of all three structure types reside in their workplace rings or adjacent rings. Employment Ring 6 encompasses the residences of 64 percent of all single-family households, 40 percent of the two-family households, and 52 percent of house-

Table X Percentage of Inner Employment Ring Workers Residing in Each Ring, by Structure Type.

Structure Type	Residence Ring						
	1	*2*	*3*	*4*	*5*	*6*	*Total*
Percentage of Ring 1 (CBD) Workers							
One-family	—	5.4%	22.1%	29.8%	28.9%	13.8%	100%
Two-family	—	13.1	46.7	32.8	5.8	1.5	100
Multiple	2.4	29.5	50.2	14.7	2.1	1.1	100
All	3.8	12.6	31.1	26.3	18.4	7.8	100
Percentage of Ring 2 Workers							
One-family	—	8.7%	25.5%	28.1%	25.1%	12.5%	100%
Two-family	0.2	26.2	46.8	21.4	4.0	1.4	100
Multiple	1.2	43.6	43.4	9.3	1.7	0.7	100
All	1.0	20.1	34.1	22.4	15.6	7.7	100
Percentage of Ring 3 Workers							
One-family	—	5.3%	27.0%	29.7%	24.1%	13.9%	100%
Two-family	0.1	13.8	60.0	21.4	3.7	1.0	100
Multiple	0.8	25.2	59.9	11.2	2.0	0.8	100
All	0.7	10.9	39.3	24.3	15.9	0.9	100

Source: Tabulated from Detroit Study Deck.

holds choosing multiple units, who work in that ring. Where the rent schedule is relatively flat, as in Ring 6, we would postulate a short journey to work regardless of space consumption. In the case of employment Rings 4 and 5, a similar pattern exists: the residential distribution is tighter than for inner rings, but less tight than for Ring 6. Figure 4 illustrates the contrast in those distributions for Rings 2 and 6. In terms of the model, households employed in Ring 6 tend to live nearby, regardless of space consumption. Those employed in Ring 2, by comparison, tend to live nearby only if they consume limited quantities of residential space. They tend to make a journey to work to outer rings if they consume larger quantities of residential space. Very few of those consuming small quantities of space live in Rings 4, 5, and 6.

Somewhat larger proportions of those employed in Ring 6 and consuming small amounts of space, reside in interior rings.

Income and Substitution Effect

It was pointed out previously that in terms of the way the problem is formulated in this paper, the price of residential space is determined by location rents and transportation costs. As a result, the households employed in inner rings, confronted by higher and steeper schedules of location rents, must pay a higher price for residential space than must be paid by those employed in outer rings. If the assumption of similar incomes, tastes, and transportation costs for those employed in each successive ring is reasonably adequate, it would be expected *a priori* that the relatively lower price of residential space for those in outer rings would lead to higher space consumption.

From Table XII it can be seen that this pattern generally holds. A smaller proportion of central business district workers and those employed in Ring 2 reside in single-family units. A larger proportion select two-family and multi-

Figure 4   Percentage of ring 2 and ring 6 workers residing in each ring, by structure type.

Residence Ring

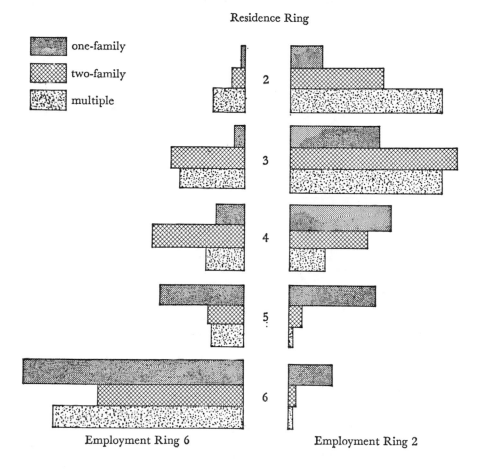

Employment Ring 6   Employment Ring 2

ple units. The proportion employed in Rings 5 and 6 living in one-family structures in turn exceeds those for Rings 3 and 4. Similarly, the proportion residing in multiple and two-family living quarters is smaller.

DERIVED DEMAND FOR RESIDENTIAL SERVICES

There is one final question which I am unable to evaluate with any degree of adequacy, but which should, I feel, be at least alluded to in this paper. A large number of researchers have emphasized the role of good schools and public services, and the supply of new and high-quality dwelling units, in determining residential location.

It is an empirical fact that the mean quality

level of the housing stock, and most likely of government services, increases with distance from the central business district. My intuition, based partially on the findings presented here and those of related research, are that an explanation of residential location in these terms is at best an oversimplification and at worst may be basically incorrect. It is my belief that housing quality is less of a determinant of residential choices than are collective residential choices a determinant of the quality of housing services and of the quality of governmental services. Among other things, this paper solves for a spatial distribution of demand for residential space by different income groups. If, as I would assert, the demand for housing quality and quality of governmental services is a derived demand, the distribution of quality predicted

Table XI   Percentage of Outer Employment Ring Workers Residing in Each Ring, by Structure Type.

Structure Type				Residence Ring			
	1	2	3	4	5	6	Total
Percentage of Ring 4 Workers							
One-family	—	2.6%	13.4%	34.2%	30.7%	19.1%	100%
Two-family	—	8.2	39.4	42.8	7.1	2.5	100
Multiple	—	21.5	43.2	25.5	5.1	4.7	100
All	0.5	6.0	21.4	34.5	23.3	14.4	100
Percentage of Ring 5 Workers							
One-family	—	.7%	6.0%	16.3%	51.8%	25.1%	100%
Two-family	—	5.2	27.0	31.8	30.2	5.9	100
Multiple	—	12.9	34.4	24.2	17.9	10.5	100
All	0.3	2.2	10.5	18.4	46.8	21.8	100
Percentage of Ring 6 Workers							
One-family	—	.8%	3.4%	7.3%	24.0%	64.5%	100%
Two-family	—	3.2	21.2	25.7	10.2	39.8	100
Multiple	—	9.8	18.2	10.3	9.5	52.2	100
All	0.4	2.0	6.2	9.2	21.2	61.0	100

Source: Tabulated from Detroit Study Deck.

by my model and to some extent supported by the evidence presented in this paper would be very similar to that observed empirically. This leads me to the tentative conclusion that observed distribution of housing quality is the result of the long-run operation of an admittedly imperfect market, but one which is possibly less imperfect than supposed.

There is one major exception to my remarks: racial discrimination represents a major market imperfection which distorts the spatial demand for residential space by both whites and nonwhites.

Nevertheless, my suggestion is that the market for residential space has as a whole operated in the direction expected *a priori*. With

Table XII   Percentage Residing in Each Structure Type, by Employment Ring.

Structure Type			Employment Ring			
	1	2	3	4	5	6
One-family	58.4%	56.9%	60.6%	69.0%	79.2%	78.1%
Two-family	18.2	21.7	20.8	18.4	11.8	10.4
Multiple	17.4	17.2	15.4	10.4	6.9	7.5
Other	5.9	4.2	3.2	2.4	2.2	4.0
Total	100.0	100.0	100.0	100.0	100.0	100.0

Source: Tabulated from Detroit Study Deck.

the major exception I have stated, it seems probable to me that many of the *so-called* ills of our central cities are the result of a spatial concentration of employment and insufficient housing expenditures by our low-income population.

There is no need for me to tell anyone that this is an extremely complex problem. My remarks at this point should be taken as highly conjectural. The correct explanation is far more complex than what I have presented here; however, it is my opinion that the findings of this paper suggest the desirability of a rather thorough rethinking of these problems.

CONCLUSIONS

In this paper I have presented a theory or model of residential location and have evaluated this model by examining residential distributions for Detroit whites employed in six concentric rings around Detroit's central business district. These same six distance rings are also used as the residential subareas in the analysis. I have hypothesized that workers employed in each ring participate in a different market for residential space from that of workers employed in every other ring. These markets are differentiated by the fact that the schedule of prices per unit of urban space in each differs with distance and direction from the workplace. It is my contention, therefore, that differences in the length of the journey-to-work and in the locational choices of workers employed in each ring may be comprehended only when the characteristics of the metropolitan schedule of location rents is specified. I postulated, for Detroit, that the surface of location rents tends to decrease with distance from the central business district, and that the rate of decrease was greatest near the center and least near the periphery.

In addition, although housing quality was not explicitly included as a variable in the empirical work, I offered some conjectures about the relationships between the distribution of housing quality and the selection of residential locations by households. These observations were based on the most intuitive of theorizing, but justify, I feel, a rather careful rethinking of a number of our policies of public intervention in the housing market.

The empirical findings are generally in conformity with those expected *a priori* from the model of residential location. This model would predict that where the market for residential space has the characteristics ascribed to the inner rings in Detroit, households will locate at varying distances from their workplaces according to their transportation costs, space consumption, space preferences, and incomes.

It was determined that the commuting pattern was largely from residences in outer rings to workplaces in inner rings, that the average length of the journey-to-work decreased with the workplace's distance from the central business district, and that the proportion of a ring's workers residing in the same or nearby rings increased as the workplace ring's distance from the central business district increased.

Workers employed in higher-income occupations and working in inner rings tended to make longer journeys-to-work and reside in outer rings. When employed in outer rings they made much shorter journeys-to-work and lived within the same ring and adjacent rings at very high rates. Lower-income workers made short journeys-to-work and resided within the workplace ring and in nearby rings regardless of the location of workplace.

Family size as an indicator of space preference had a similar effect on residential location. The smallest and largest families were found to make the shortest journeys-to-work. For the smallest families, I attributed this to low space preferences; the shorter journeys-to-work by the largest families I attributed to a per capita income constraint.

Structure type is used as a measure of the household's space consumption. The longest journeys-to-work were made by those residing in one-family units and the shortest by those residing in multiple units. A marked difference between the locational choices of males and females was also discovered. Female workers, regardless of workplace ring, made shorter journeys-to-work than male workers and resided within the workplace ring and nearby rings in much higher proportions. Finally, it was determined that the proportion of workers residing in low-density structures increased as the workplace ring's distance from the central business district increased.

All the relationships summarized above were very clean-cut for rings near the central business district, where the location rent function with distances from the workplace is believed to be very steep. For peripheral workplace rings, where the function is believed to be very flat, the relationships were much weaker.

In general it is my opinion that the evidence presented in this paper bears out the appro-priateness of the theoretical framework employed. The findings are generally consistent with our *a priori* views on the problem as obtained both from this model and similar models by Alonso, Wingo, and others. The issues evaluated in the paper are still far from settled, however, and will remain so until we are able to take into account more explicitly the dynamics of the housing market both in our models and our empirical work.

An Approach to the Analysis of Metropolitan Residential Extension

WILLARD B. HANSEN

INTRODUCTION

This paper summarizes the results of an analysis of metropolitan residential extension, defined here as "the new occupancy of intrametropolitan open sites by urban housing during specified time periods." Extension is viewed in terms of the residential development levels of metropolitan subregions. A series of models which yield subregional residential development levels are described, and the efficiency of these models is investigated by the regression method using data for the Philadelphia Metropolitan Region, during the periods 1940–50 and 1950–56.

Metropolitan residential extension may be regarded as one aspect of the more general phenomenon of urban residential location. There are several previous instances of the formulation and empirical testing of urban residential location models.[1] These prior models are alike in a number of ways. They are predictive rather than prescriptive, define the entire urban area as their spatial setting, and yield levels of residence for urban subregions (with subregional residence levels being expressed as static distributions at a given point in time, or as distributional change over time). The models are based mainly on empirical observation, exhibit simple algebraic forms, and describe presumed relationships among aggregates, rather than actual behavioral processes. All

embody single equations rather than simultaneous equation systems, and contain parameters whose numerical values must be estimated empirically. Finally, application of the models to projection requires the use of iterative adjustment mechanisms for bringing the output values into conformance with expected subregional residential capacities, and with the residence level anticipated for the urban area as a whole.[2]

Although the models which constitute the subject of this study are generally similar to the ones cited above, they differ from the latter in one important respect. Whereas their precursors treat subregional residence levels as a static or changing distribution of housing or residents, the models of the present study define such levels in terms of open site dwelling construction, i.e., of residential extension. In the writer's view, this distinguishing feature constitutes an important improvement, an im-

From the *Journal of Regional Science*, III (Summer 1961) , 37–55. Reprinted by permission of the author and the Regional Science Research Institute, G.O.P. Box 8776, Philadelphia, Pennsylvania 19101.

1 For example, the work of Blumenfeld [2], Bogue and Harris [3], Clark [6], Hamburg and Creighton [11], Walter G. Hansen [12], Schmitt [16] and Thomas [18].

2 The recent theoretical work of Alonso [1] and of Herbert and Stevens [13] has resulted in relatively complex "behavioral" models of residential location. To the writer's knowledge, these models have so far not been applied empirically.

provement that follows from the relatively greater homogeneity characterizing the determinants of residential extension, and from the strategic role of residential extension in urban locational change.

The homogeneity characterizing the determinants of residential extension in United States metropolitan regions during the 20th Century results from the fact that extension has taken place largely in the form of dwelling construction by private homebuilders and that it has been subject to comparatively few (although steadily increasing) public controls. In contrast, the determinants of population or dwelling distribution are much less homogeneous. Thus, change in the dwelling levels of urban subregions may be the result of any or all of the following:

1. Construction of new dwellings on open sites
2. Construction of new dwellings on cleared sites
3. Conversion of existing structures from nonresidential to residential use, or vice versa
4. Creation of new dwellings through the partitioning of existing ones
5. Elimination of dwellings through the merging of two or more units
6. Demolition of dwellings

Subregional population change, in addition to being subject to the six types of action listed above, may also comprise births and deaths, in- and out-migration, and growth and decline in non-household population (rooming house, college, hospital, military etc.).

The strategic role of residential extension in the locational change occurring in U.S. metropolitan regions is evident in several ways. Extension has accounted for most of the locational change marking metropolitan residence. In its turn, the locational pattern of metropolitan residential extension has determined the distribution of new public and private facilities directly serving the occupants of new housing: e.g. facilities such as stores, schools, parks, water and sewer mains, streets, etc. Finally, new housing has been the single most important consumer of open sites, while a large share of the remaining open-site con-

sumption has been made up of public and private facilities directly serving the occupants of such new housing.[3]

MODELS OF SUBREGIONAL RESIDENTIAL DEVELOPMENT

General Statement

A general model of subregional residential development may be written as:

$$Y_i = \phi(_kX_i),$$

where: Y_i = level of residential development in subregion i

$_kX_i$ = level of residential development factor k in subregion i

ϕ = development function prevailing in the metropolitan region during the development period

$i = 1 \cdots n$ = set of residential development subregions

$k = 1 \cdots m$ = set of residential development factors.

The individual terms of the general model are defined as follows:

Metropolitan Region

A relatively large urban agglomeration containing (1) one or more extensive and densely developed cores, and (2) a sizable fringe area which has lower overall settlement density than the core (s), and the individual parts of which bear a close socio-economic relationship with, or are within commuting distance of, at least one core. This concept is similar to that used by the U.S. Bureau of the Budget [19].

Residential Development Period

A period 2 through 10 years in length, for

3 The relative importance of residential development is illustrated by the growth pattern exhibited by the northeastern portion of Philadelphia County between 1944 and 1954. The area in question comprises 44 square miles, of which fewer than half were in urban use in 1944. Residential uses accounted for 84% of the 4.8 square mile increase in developed land that took place in the area during the 1944–54 period. See Philadelphia City Planning Commission [15], Table 7, Sections K and L.

which residential development rates are predicted.

Development Subregion Set

A set of areas forming part of one given metropolitan region; where each area is bounded and continuous, contains a substantial quantity of open sites available for residential construction during a specified development period, and includes little or no urban housing.

Residential Development

The gross or net change in the absolute or relative number of a given category of residences, that takes place in a development subregion during a development period. The term "residence" refers to an individual unit of shelter, or a set of persons occupying such a unit. Three development rates considered are dwelling construction volumes, dwelling capacity utilization ratios, and incremental population densities.

Residential Development Factor

An independent variable which is used to explain variations in subregional residential development levels. Four development factors are considered: Residential Settlement, Centrality, Residence Access, and Employment Access.

Development Function

An algebraic statement which relates residential development levels to development factor levels. Three development function types are considered: linear, exponential and power.

The dependent variable of the general model expresses metropolitan residential extension in terms of subregional residential development levels, i.e., of change over time in the absolute or relative number of specified types of residences in metropolitan development subregions. The dependent variable was given this broad formulation to enable it to subsume a set of alternative development rates which included both direct and indirect measures of residential extension (see *Development Rates* below).

Two to ten years appeared to be a reasonable range for the time periods during which the development factors under consideration might be expected to influence development rates "unilaterally." Where the period exceeds

10 years, "multilateral" relationships requiring simultaneous equations would be likely. Where the period is less than two years long, special local circumstances might be expected to distort the relationships.

Development Function Types

Three development function types are considered and may be expressed algebraically as follows:

1. Linear Function Type

$$Y = a_0 + a_1(X_1) + \cdots + a_m(X_m)$$

2. Exponential Function Type

$$Y = (a_0)(a_1)^{X_1} \cdots (a_m)^{X_m}$$

3. Power Function Type

$$Y = (a_0)(x_1)^{a_1} \cdots (X_m)^{a_m}$$

where Y is the dependent variable; $X_1 \cdots X_m$ are the levels of independent variables $1 \cdots m$; a is a base parameter; and $a_0 \cdots a_m$, are independent parameters associated with variables $1 \cdots m$.

All three function types are "monotonic" in the sense that the value of the dependent variable will either rise with every increase in a given independent variable, or fall with every such increase, all other variables being held constant. The monotonic property of the forms is in accord with current theory about the nature of the relationships between residential development levels and the individual development factors that were investigated; the relationships in question may be expected to be either consistently positive or consistently negative. At the same time, the small number of parameters ($M + 1$ for any combination of M variables) makes the three function types particularly suitable for regression analysis. Where regression coefficients are interpreted as sample parameters from a "hypothetical universe" the explanatory ability and parametric reliability of the regression equations varies directly with the number of degrees of freedom entailed in their formulation.[4]

Development Rates

Three alternative expressions of development (development rates) are discussed below. Each expression specifies the general term of subregional residential development, which may in turn be regarded as one way of describing the phenomenon of urban residential extension.

1. *Dwelling Construction Volume* (*Q*)

$$Q = H_i$$

2. *Dwelling Capacity Utilization Ratio* (*V*)

$$V = \frac{H_i}{(J_i)(L_i)}$$

3. *Incremental Population Density* (*Z*)

$$Z = \frac{U_i - P_i}{A_i}$$

where: H_i = number of nonfarm dwellings added for sale or rental in development subregion i during a development period, by commercial or owner-builders; on privately acquired open sites, and not as part of a comprehensively designed and executed mass housing project.[5]

L_i = amount of open site area available in subregion i, during a given period, for the addition of new private nonfarm dwellings (H_i); where the term "open site area" denotes land which is vacant or in non-urban use

J_i = mean number of new private nonfarm dwellings (H_i) that can economically be constructed during a given period per unit of open site area (L_i)

P_i = number of persons residing in subregion i at the beginning of a given period

U_i = number of persons residing in subregion i at the end of the period

A_i = total area of subregion i

Development Rates Q and V both constitute direct expressions of the phenomenon of urban residential extension. The former treats dwelling construction volumes in absolute terms, while the latter standardizes these volumes for subregional dwelling capacity.

Development Rate Z constitutes an indirect expression of residential extension. Its formulation was motivated by the need for a measure that could be applied in the Philadelphia Metropolitan Region for an interval earlier than 1950–56 as well as for that period itself (the data required by Rates Q and V were not obtainable for the Region previous to 1950). Rate Z appeared to be suitable for this purpose because population and total area data were available for both the 1940–50 and 1950–55 periods. Moreover, the distribution of Rate Z rather closely resembled the distribution of the "direct" rate, V. This correspondence is reflected by the high degree of association ($\bar{r} = + \cdot 83$) which was registered in the Region for the 1950–55/56 period between Rates V and Z. The correspondence stemmed from the criterion which required the development subregions to contain substantial amounts of open site area, while not permitting them to include sizable quantities of old urban housing. This requirement led to a situation in which subregional population increments were largely brought about by the occupancy of new private dwellings constructed on open sites (as demonstrated by an $\bar{r}$ of $+ \cdot 89$ between 1950–55 population increments and 1950–56 open site dwelling construction volumes). For the same period, the "total area" which is incorporated in Rate Z as a measure of subregional

4 The linear function type is incorporated in the residential location models of Blumenfeld [2], Bogue and Harris [3], Schmitt [16] and Thomas [18]. The exponential form is employed by Hamburg and Creighton [11], while the power form is employed by Walter G. Hansen [12]. In every one of these instances, the forms are employed to specify relationships which are analogous to the development function of the present study, although there are, of course, material differences in the interpretation of the variables involved.
5 It should be noted that the term "dwelling," as used here, includes units in new detached houses as well as units in new row houses, apartment buildings, etc.

dwelling capacity was also markedly associated with the capacity measure, (J_i) (L_i), incorporated in Rate V $(r = + \cdot 67)$. It seems reasonable to assume that the close correspondence observed in the Philadelphia Metropolitan Region during 1950–55/56 between Rates V and Z prevailed there during 1940–50 as well.[6]

Development Factors

Four development factors are considered: Residential Settlement, Centrality, Residence Access and Employment Access.

The *Residential Settlement* variable expresses the degree to which urban housing and local community facilities are present in a given development subregion at the beginning of a particular period. Subregional residential development levels may be presumed to vary directly and substantially with subregional levels of residential settlement.[7] This assumption stems from the types of facilities (e.g., streets, schools, stores, water supply and sewerage systems) which are commonly associated with residential settlement in metropolitan regions. Availability of facilities of the indicated type acts to induce private dwelling construction in one or both of two important ways: by lowering site preparation and building costs, and by providing community services which will tend to make new dwellings more attractive to prospective customers.

The *Centrality* variable expresses the proximity of the development subregion to the dominant intrametropolitan center. Subregional residential development levels may be presumed to vary with centrality because of the opportunities which the dominant center offers prospective dwelling customers by virtue of the fact that it constitutes a transportation hub and a center of government, business and cultural activity.

The *Residence Access* variable expresses degree of subregional proximity to all metropolitan residents at the beginning of given period. Development levels may be presumed to vary with residence access levels because the distribution of residents within the metropolitan region as a whole defines any given home-builder's market population of dwelling customers and the social opportunities that exist for those

customers themselves. Proximity to metropolitan residents thus acts to induce private dwelling construction in two ways: by expediting the disposition of new dwellings, and by yielding transportation advantages which will tend to make the new dwellings more attractive to prospective customers.[8]

The *Employment Access* variable expresses degree of subregional proximity to all metropolitan jobs during a given period. Development levels may be presumed to vary with employment access levels because the intrametropolitan distribution of jobs delimits the employment opportunities of dwelling customers, and length of work-trip is a major factor in the decision to buy or rent a new dwelling.

The four development factors under consideration may be presumed to act in a largely "unilateral" manner on development levels during middle range (2 through 10 year) periods. It should be obvious that the four factors will tend to influence one another, and that still other factors will tend to influence development.

The four development factors are defined as:

1. *Residential Settlement* (B)

$$B = \frac{P_i}{A_i}$$

2. *Centrality* (C)

$$C = D_{ic}$$

6 The correspondence in question may be expected to hold also for other periods and metropolitan regions. Data on the population and total area of small territorial units are obtainable for some of the earliest decennial U.S. Census years. Rate Z therefore suggests itself as a useful "proxy" variable for the comparative analysis of development rates which constitute direct expression of urban residential extension.
7 Note that the concepts of *residential settlement* and *residential development* refer, respectively, to amount of residence at a given point in time, and to change in amount of residence over time.
8 Strictly speaking, the residence access variable expresses two kinds of proximity: *accessibility* with respect to a dispersed market population of dwelling customers, and *access* with respect to the dispersed social opportunities existing for those customers.

3. Residence Access (M)

$$M = \sum_{j=1}^{n} P_j (2.5 + D_{ij})^{\theta}$$

$$\theta \neq 0; \; 2.5 + P_{ij} \leqq 35$$

4. Employment Access (E)

$$E = \sum_{j=1}^{n} T_j (2.5 + D_{ij})^{\theta}$$

$$\theta \neq 0; \; 2.5 + D_{ij} \leqq 35$$

where: $i = 1 \cdots n$ = set of residential development subregions

$j = 1 \cdots n$ = set of opportunity subregions; where the elements of the set together make up the metropolitan region containing development subregions $1 \cdots n$, and include subregions $1 \cdots n$

A_i = total area of subregion i

P_i(or P_j) = number of persons residing in subregion i (or j) at the beginning of a period

c = intrametropolitan center

D_{ij}(or D_{ic}) = number of airline miles between the centroid of subregion i and the centroid of subregion j (intrametropolitan center c); where centroids represent the points which are most accessible to the population residing in a subregion or center during the period

T_j = number of jobs in subregion j during the period

2.5 = terminal airline distance constant prevailing in the metropolitan region

35 = airline distance limit prevailing in the metropolitan region

θ = airline distance exponent

Population levels used in the residential settlement and residence access variables refer specifically to the beginning of the period, whereas the job levels in the employment ac-

cess variable may refer to any time during the period. The condition imposed on population levels obviates the circularity which would otherwise follow from the fact that the course of residential development itself influences population distribution during any given period.

The terminal distance constant of 2.5 miles corresponds to 5 minutes driving time at an average speed of 30 miles per hour. This constant reflects the minimum movement effort required for trips using the available transportation media in U.S. metropolitan regions during the 1940's and 1950's.[9] The mileage limit value of 35 reflects the maximum distance which an individual would be willing to commute. It corresponds to 70 minutes driving time at 30 miles per hour.

The airline distance exponent θ in the residence and employment access factors may take any positive or negative value. Where the exponent is positive the variable may be regarded as a measure of "travel cost." Where the exponent is negative the variable may be regarded as a measure of "potential."[10]

EMPIRICAL TESTS OF THE MODELS

Empirical tests were applied to a series of models incorporating alternative combinations of the function types, development rates and development factors discussed above. The efficacy of these models was investigated by the regression method using data for the Philadelphia

9 In may be noted that the "potential" variables of Walter C. Hansen's [12] residential location models, in which movement effort is expressed as driving time, incorporate a terminal constant of 5–6 minutes.

10 For a discussion of the "potential" concept, see Carrothers [4]. For a comparison of the "potential" and "travel cost" concepts, see Dunn [8].
Indices of aggregate access have been employed as independent variables in location models generally, and in urban residential location models in particular. While access has been expressed as "potential" in nearly all of these cases, there are also some references to the use of "travel cost." Duncan [7] has asserted that the "potential" and "travel cost" concepts are closely related. This view is rejected by Stewart and Warntz [17], who maintain that the "obvious mathematical similarity is merely formal," and who contrast what they call the "sterility" of "travel cost" with the "manifold applications" of "potential."

Metropolitan Region and the periods 1940–50 and 1950–56.

The Philadelphia Metropolitan Region

In addition to meeting practical requirements of data availability, the particular case selected for the statistical tests was satisfactory from a substantive point of view. Between 1939 and 1957 the Philadelphia Region experienced considerable population growth, most of which was accommodated through residential extension. Moreover, with regard to volume, physical and financial characteristics, and type of entrepreneurial organization, homebuilding in the region generally followed the pattern prevailing in U.S. metropolitan regions as a whole during the period under consideration.

The Philadelphia Metropolitan Region was defined as a 4565 square mile area centering on the City of Philadelphia, and having a total population of 4.2 million in 1950. The Region is composed of 11 counties situated in the States of Pennsylvania, New Jersey and Delaware, and comprises the Philadelphia, Trenton, and Wilmington Standard Metropolitan Statistical Areas. (Figure 1) The central district ("downtown") of Philadelphia is the only dominant center. Generally speaking, topography and soil conditions favor urban development.

Between 1939 and 1957, the population of the Philadelphia Metropolitan Region increased by one third, from 3.6 million to 4.8 million. During that same period, approximately 370,000 new dwellings were constructed in the eight-county Philadelphia Standard Metropolitan Statistical Area. Together, they accounted for 88.7% of all additions to the stock of dwelling units. Less than 1% represented farm dwellings, less than 1% were built as public housing, and most were constructed on open land.

During the 1940–50 period, the large majority of new private dwellings were started by small scale commercial builders. In general, this entrepreneurial pattern continued through the 1950–56 period, despite an increase in the number of large scale builders. In addition, however, the latter period was marked by the construction of two private mass housing projects, Levittown and Fairless Hills in the lower part

of Bucks County. They contained about 15,000 and 5,000 dwellings respectively.[11]

Statistical Procedures

Several hundred bivariate and multivariate regression equations were formulated, and their parameters were estimated by least squares. Each equation yielded subregional development levels as a function of subregional levels of one or more of the development factors under consideration: i.e., Residential Settlement, Centrality, Residence Access and Employment Access. The individual equations differed by function type, subregion set, development rate, development factor index, and factor combination. Calculation of the regression coefficients, efficiency measures and access indices ("potential" and "travel cost") necessitated the use of electronic computers.

The development subregion sets selected for study were situated in the Philadelphia Standard Metropolitan Statistical Area. They excluded all portions of the Area which were predominantly in urban use at the beginning of a given development period. Moreover, the sets used for the 1950–56 period excluded the portion of Bucks County containing the mass housing projects of Levittown and Fairless Hills. Most of the equations were based on 44 subregions, with the remainder employing 47 or 71 subregions.

The metropolitan subregions used in the analysis were selected from a set of areal subdivisions, called Planning Analysis Areas, that had been previously delineated by the Philadelphia City Planning Commission and the Philadelphia Urban Traffic and Transportation Board. The Planning Analysis Areas were adopted by the writer because they constituted the only set of suitably sized subregions for which data were available. The subregions varied considerably with respect to shape and size, being relatively small in the densely settled central portion of the Region, and becoming progressively larger toward the fringe. For example, Area No. 2 in Delaware County con-

11 For data on residential construction in the Philadelphia and other metropolitan regions, see U.S. Census [20] and U.S. Bureau of Labor Statistics [21].

Figure 1 Philadelphia Metropolitan Region, 1950.

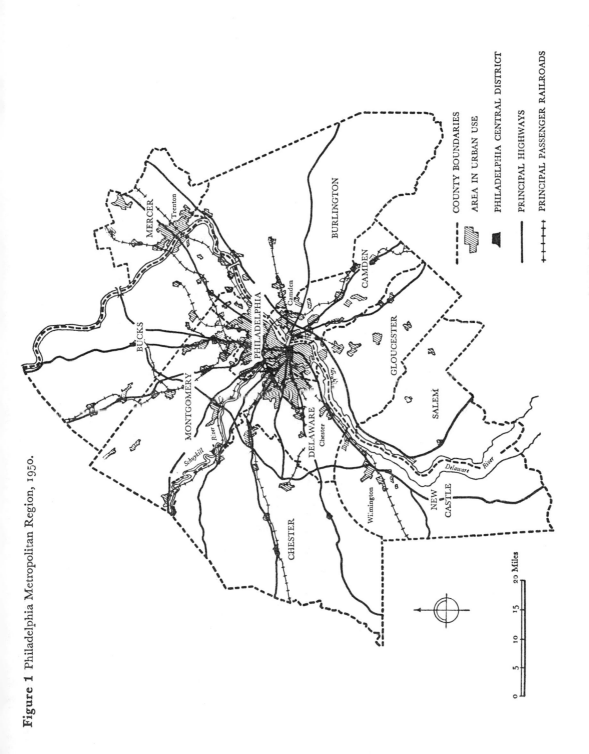

COUNTY BOUNDARIES

AREA IN URBAN USE

PHILADELPHIA CENTRAL DISTRICT

PRINCIPAL HIGHWAYS

PRINCIPAL PASSENGER RAILROADS

tained 10.3 square miles, whereas Area No. 7 in Burlington County contained 377.7 square miles (see Figure 2).

Historical data on the dependent and independent variables were obtained from the U.S. Census and from various local agencies. In some instances, reliability of the local agency estimates was relatively low.

The efficiency of the regression equations was appraised in terms of their explanatory precision and completeness,[12] and parametric reliability and plausibility.[13] The following measures and tests were applied:[14]

1. Explanatory Precision was expressed by corrected residual error ratios (H) for linear equations,[15] and by corrected residual errors $(\bar{S})$ for exponential and power equations.
2. Explanatory completeness was expressed by corrected coefficients of bivariate and multivariate determination ($\bar{r}^2$ and $\bar{R}^2$ respectively).
3. Parametric Reliability was expressed by coefficient error ratios $(_eC)$.[16]
4. Parametric Plausibility was tested by the conformance of the independent regression coefficient signs to generally accepted theory.

Overall Efficiency

The efficiency of the regression equations varied greatly. Levels of explanatory precision ranged from $\bar{H}$ values of 1.82 to 0.62 in the linear cases, and from antilog $\bar{S}$ values of 4.02 to 1.76 in the exponential and power cases. Levels of explanatory completeness ($\bar{r}^2$, $\bar{R}^2$) ranged from .000 to .875. The coefficient error ratios $(_eC)$ of nearly all bivariate regression coefficients were significant at the .01 normal probability level, and their signs conformed to generally accepted theory in every instance. By contrast, a number of the multivariate coefficient error ratios were not significant at even the .05 probability level, and the signs of many multivariate coefficients failed to conform to accepted theory.

By and large, the differentials in efficiency

were consistent between the 1940–50 and 1950–56 periods.

Degree of subregional aggregation affected the efficiency of the regression equations in varying ways. While explanatory precision and completeness tended to vary directly with aggregation, parametric reliability varied inversely with it. Table 1 provides a comparison of results obtained for a "basic" set of 44 development subregions and a "disaggregated" set of 71 subregions (the two sets under consideration comprised an identical 3439 square mile section of the Philadelphia Metropolitan Region, with every one of the 71 subregions of the "disaggregated" set being contained in one of the 44 subregions of the "basic" set).

The explanatory precision of the "basic" equations was moderately superior to the precision of the "disaggregated" equations; the explanatory completeness of the former was still superior, but less so; and their parametric reliability was slightly inferior. Table 1 illustrates this for a pair of equations incorporating Residential Settlement as their independent variable.

Two circumstances help account for the disparate performances of the equations. First, the variability of the dependent variable distribution of the "basic" subregion set was lower than that of the "disaggregated" set.[17] Second, historical data were more reliable in the former case than in the latter, since the "basic" sub-

12 The distinction between explanatory precision and completeness is suggested in Ezekiel [9], p. 159.
13 The first three of these measures must be applied for meaningful comparisons of regression equations which are based on different dependent variable distributions. Investigation of the third and fourth measure is required for all multivariate equations.
14 The measures of explanatory precision and completeness are corrected for the degrees of freedom entailed in the calculation of the regression coefficients.
15 Use of the residual error ratio $(\bar{H})$ is suggested in Bogue and Harris [3], p. 30. The ratio is calculated by dividing the residual standard error by the mean of the dependent variable distribution.
16 The coefficient error ratio is computed by dividing the regression coefficient by its standard error. See Ezekiel [9], p. 322.
17 The coefficient of variability is calculated by dividing the standard deviation of a given distribution by its mean. See Hagood and Price [10], p. 126.

Figure 2. Philadelphia metropolitan region planning analysis areas.

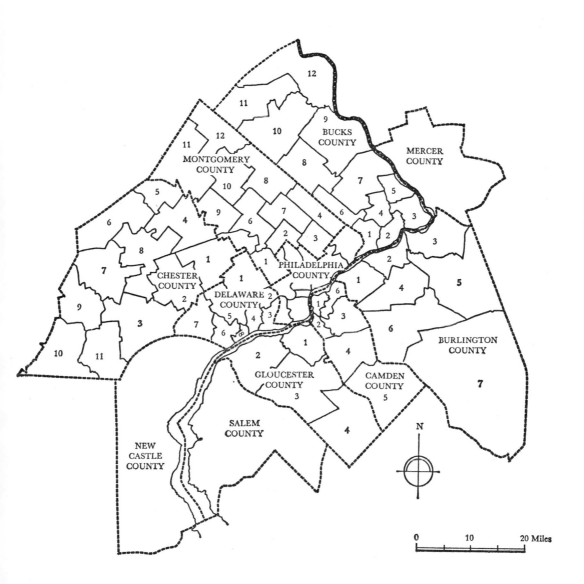

Table 1 Efficiency of Bivariate Regression Equations Yielding Development Rate Z as a Linear Function of Residential Settlement (B): 1950–55

	"Basic Set"	"Disaggregated Set"
	Distributional Characteristics	
Number of Subregions	44	71
Average Size of Subregions	78.1 sq. mi.	48.4 sq. mi.
Mean of Dependent Variable Z	244.8	424.8
Coefficient of Variability of Z	1.67	1.91
	Efficiency	
Explanatory Precision ($\overline{H}$)	1.26	1.54
Explanatory Completeness ($\bar{r}^2$)	.44	.36
Parametric Reliability ($_xC$)	5.89	6.38

regions tended to be larger than the "disaggregated" ones.

The slightly inferior performance of the "basic" equations with respect to parametric reliability follows from the algebraic properties of the coefficient error ratio ($_xC$), which act to translate the substantially higher number of observations underlying the "disaggregated" dependent variable distribution into a sizable increase in the $_xC$ levels of the disaggregated equation.[18]

Function Types, Development Rates and Factors

The efficiency of the power equation forms tended to be moderately to substantially higher than that of the linear and exponential forms, which were similar to each other in overall performance. Exponential equations tended to be better than linear with all the independent variables except the Residential Settlement Factor. Representative results are given in Table 2.[19]

The precision of equations yielding the absolute Rate Q tended to be somewhat higher with all three function types than that of equations yielding the relative rates, V and Z. With respect to completeness, on the other hand, Q tended to be poorer than V and Z. (Because of the algebraic properties of the

measures involved, parametric reliability changed together with explanatory completeness in bivariate cases, while varying directly with completeness and inversely with degree of intercorrelation among the independent variables in multivariate cases.) Table 3 illustrates this for a series of bivariate equations incorporating Residential Settlement as their independent variable.

Two conditions help account for the finding that the explanatory precision of equations yielding the absolute development rate tended to be generally greater than that of equations yielding the relative rates, despite the greater

18 Several regression equations based on a subregion set including the two subregions containing Levittown and Fairless Hills were formulated. The efficiency of this group was compared with the accuracy of a group of equations incorporating identical variables, and differing only by virtue of being based on a subregion set excluding the two subregions in question. In every case, the $\bar{r}^2$ levels of the former series were moderately lower than those of the latter. As might be expected, observed development rates for the two subregions containing mass housing projects were substantially higher than the rates estimated by the equations of the former series.

19 The regression coefficients were calculated by a least squares procedure, which requires logarithmic transformation of the dependent variable in exponential and power cases. See Mills [14], Chapt. 18, and Appendix D of the writer's Ph.D dissertation for a discussion of the comparability of regression results based on, respectively, arithmetic and logarithmically transformed dependent variable distributions.

Table 2 Levels of $\bar{r}^2$ and $\bar{R}^2$ from Regression Equations Yielding Development Rate V as Alternative Functions of Four Development Factors. 1950–56: N = 44

		Linear	Exponential	Power
	Residential Settlement (B)	.7042	.3401	.8003
	Centrality (C)	.3728	.6715	.6415
($\bar{r}^2$)	Residence Access (M.)	.7229	.7929	.8183
	Employment Access (E.)	.6090	.8183	.7845
($\bar{R}^2$)	B, C, M*, E*	.8023	.7909	.8752

Note: The symbol * is used in this paper to denote the aggregate access which registered the highest bivariate coefficient of determination with a particular function type and development rate.

explanatory completeness attained by the latter. First, the variability characterizing the absolute rate, Q, was substantially lower than that of the relative rates, V and Z. Second, the relative rates—unlike the absolute one—standardize subregional residential development levels for amount of subregional dwelling capacity. As a result, the structural correctness of equations yielding the relative rates may be presumed to be concomitantly greater.

As an example of the distribution of a specific development rate, Figure 2 shows subregional dwelling capacity utilization ratios (V) in the Philadelphia Metropolitan Region during 1950–56. While the density of development generally decreases from the center, the preponderance of development on the Pennsylvania side of the Delaware River should be noted. (The lower excluded area on the map comprises territory which was predominantly in urban use in 1950; the upper excluded area comprises the territory in which the mass private housing projects of Levittown and Fairless Hills were built between 1950–1956.)

A comparison of the efficiency of bivariate regression equations incorporating the "most explanatory" indices of the four factors revealed differences in performance that were largely consistent by function type (see Table 2).

The combination of development factors into

Table 3 Levels of Explanatory Precision and Completeness for Bivariate Regression Equations Yielding Alternative Development Rates as a Function of Residential Settlement (B); 1950–55/56; N = 44

	Development Rates		
	Q	V	Z
	1950–56	1950–56	1950–55
Coefficient of Variability	.87	1.38	1.67
Explanatory Precision			
Linear ($\bar{H}$)	.753	.759	1.262
Exponential (antilog $\bar{S}$)	2.47	3.69	4.02
Power (antilog $\bar{S}$)	1.84	2.05	2.53
Explanatory Completeness ($\bar{r}^2$)			
Linear	.2682	.7042	.4414
Exponential	.1363	.3401	.2454
Power	.5344	.8003	.6622

Note: The linear residual errors underlying $\bar{H}$ are additive constants. The antilogs of the exponential and power residual errors are constant ratios.

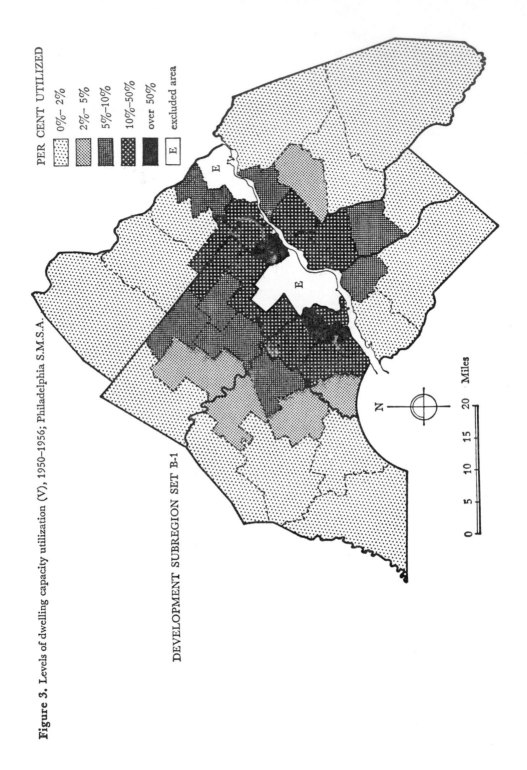

Figure 3. Levels of dwelling capacity utilization (V), 1950–1956; Philadelphia S.M.S.A.

PER CENT UTILIZED

0%– 2%
2%– 5%
5%–10%
10%–50%
over 50%
E   excluded area

N

0   5   10   15   20   Miles

DEVELOPMENT SUBREGION SET B-1

Table 4 Efficiency of Power Regression Equations Yielding Development Rate V as a Function of One or More Development Factors: 1950–56: N = 44

No. of Indep. Variables	$\bar{r}^2$ or $\bar{R}^2$	Parametric Plausibility (Y or N) and Reliability $_x C$ of the Independent Coefficients			
		B	C	M ($\theta = 1.5$)	E ($\theta = 2.0$)
1	.8003	(Y) 13.05			
1	.6415		(Y) 8.82		
1	.8183			(Y) 13.93	
1	.7845				(Y) 12.96
2	.8533	(Y) 3.32		(Y) 3.90	
3	.8637	(Y) 3.99		(Y) 3.69	(Y) 2.03
4	.8752	(Y) 4.50	(Y) 2.16	(Y) 4.41	(N) 2.58

Notes: 1. The letters Y and N denote, respectively, the plausibility or nonplausibility of the algebraic signs of the regression coefficients.
2. Coefficient error ratios ($_x C$) of 1.96, 2.33 and 2.58 are associated with normal probability levels of, respectively, .05, .02, and .01.

multivariate regression equations produced varying effects on efficiency. Generally speaking, while the incorporation of additional independent variables led to moderate gains in the explanatory indices, it also substantially reduced parametric plausibility and reliability. The reduction in structural soundness may be attributed to the high degree of intercorrelation that characterized the development factors being considered. Table 4 illustrates this for bivarite and multivariate regression equations yielding Development Rate V as a power function of four development factors.

Corrected correlation coefficients ($\bar{r}$) between pairs of the independent variables cited in Table 4 registered the following high values in Table 5.

Figures 3 and 4 illustrate the similarity of distribution of Residential Settlement and Employment Access in the Philadelphia Metropolitan Region.

Table 5

	C	M	E
B	−.8310	+.8900	+.9200
C		−.9170	−.8840
M			+.9780

Application of sets of less intercorrelated independent variables might lead to gains in explanatory ability with a much smaller reduction in structural soundness. However, the formulation of such variables is complicated by the fact that most metropolitan phenomena are distributed concentrically around the center, and are therefore strongly associated with one another.

A comparison of the efficiency of two regression equation sets incorporating, respectively, "potential" and "travel cost" indices as independent variables clearly established the superiority of the "potential" construct as a measure of subregional aggregate access. Four distance exponent values (0.5, 1.0, 1.5, 2.0) were alternatively applied with both constructs. Every one of the four "potential" indices attained substantially higher explanatory completeness than any of the "travel cost" indices. Table 6 illustrates this for two series of bivariate regression equations incorporating employment access as their independent variable.

Four alternative values of the distance exponent θ were applied with equations incorporating residence and employment "potential" as their independent variable. While the four alternative values (0.5, 1.0, 1.5 and 2.0) were selected essentially "a priori," their range is in line with values adopted for the "potential" indices of several previous models. Thus, the

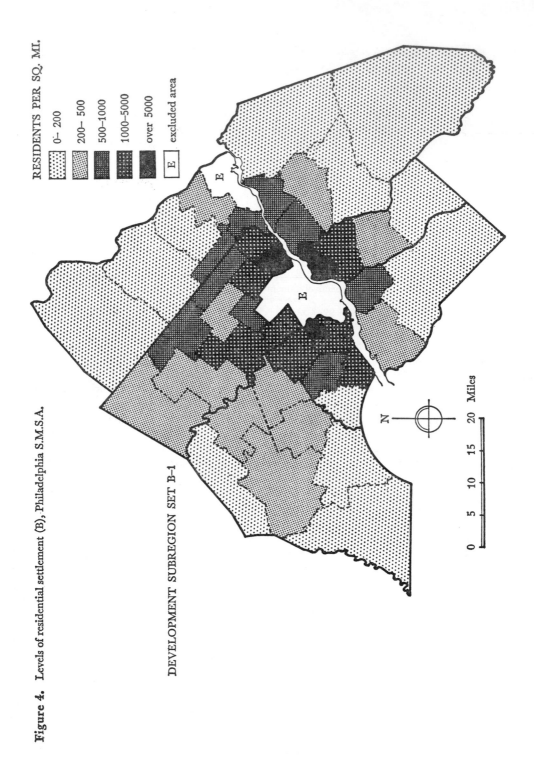

Figure 4. Levels of residential settlement (B), Philadelphia S.M.S.A.

RESIDENTS PER SQ. MI.

0– 200
200– 500
500–1000
1000–5000
over 5000
E   excluded area

DEVELOPMENT SUBREGION SET B-1

N

0   5   10   15   20 Miles

Figure 5. Levels of total employment access (E), 1954–1955; Philadelphia S.M.S.A.

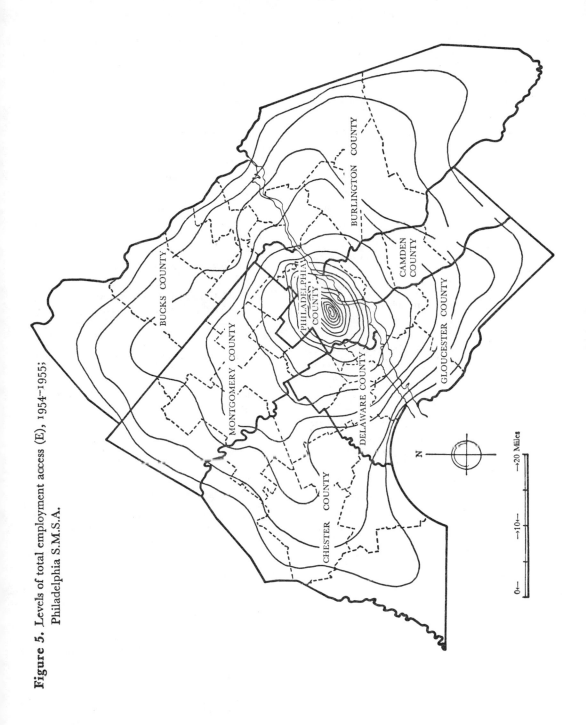

Table 6 Levels of $\bar{r}^2$ for Regression Equations Yielding Development Rate V as a Linear Function of "Potential" and "Total Friction" Indices of Employment Access: 1950–56: N = 44

Value of Distance Exponent (θ)	"Potential" $\bar{r}^2$	"Total Friction"
0.5	.3755	.0000
1.0	.5120	.0205
1.5	.5375	.1166
2.0	.4653	.1750

Note: The employment access indices used in this particular comparison are restricted to 1954 manufacturing jobs.

intra-national location models of Carrothers [5] and Stewart and Warntz [17] contain exponent values of 0.5, 1.0 and 2.0 in the former cases, and 1.0 in the latter. Again, Walter G. Hansen's [12] urban residential location model uses an exponent value of 2.20 with employment "potential," and a value of 2.35 with population "potential."

The relative efficiency of regression equations embodying the four alternative distance exponents was generally consistent for the several opportunity categories, but varied by equation form. With the linear and power function types, "potential" indices incorporating larger exponents (1.5 and 2.0) tended to perform better. With the exponential type, smaller exponents (0.5 or 1.0) tended to give higher levels of accuracy. (See Table 7)

SUMMARY

Metropolitan residential extension was viewed in terms of the residential development levels of metropolitan subregions, and a series of models yielding subregional development levels was described. The individual models incorporated alternative function types, development rates and development factors.

The models were empirically investigated by the regression method with data for the Philadelphia Metropolitan Region during the periods 1940–50 and 1950–56. The efficiency of the resulting regression equations was found to vary significantly by function type, development rate and development factor. Coefficient

Table 7 Levels of $\bar{r}^2$ for Bivariate Regression Equations Yielding Development Rate V as a Function of "Potential" Indices Incorporating Alternative Distance Exponents, 1950–56; N = 44

	Linear	Exponential	Power
Residence "Potential" Index			
$\theta = 0.5$	.4062	.7755	.6557
$\theta = 1.0$	.5828	.7929	.7654
$\theta = 1.5$	.6821	.7319	.8183
$\theta = 2.0$	.7229	.5413	.8122
Employment "Potential" Index			
$\theta = 0.5$	.3768	.7477	.6077
$\theta = 1.0$	.5393	.7616	.7196
$\theta = 1.5$	.6088	.6803	.7814
$\theta = 2.0$	.6090	.5603	.7845

Note: The residence and employment "potential" indices express subregional aggregate access to, respectively, 1950 population and 1954/55 total jobs.

of determination levels ranged from zero to .8752.

REFERENCES

1. Alonso, William. "A Theory of the Urban Land Market," *Papers and Proceedings of the Regional Science Association*, VI (1960).
2. Blumenfeld, Hans. "Are Land Use Patterns Predictable" *Journal of the American Institute of Planners*, XXV (May, 1959), 61–66.
3. Bogue, Donald J., and Harris, Dorothy L. *Comparative Population and Urban Research Via Multiple Regression and Covariance Analysis.* Published Jointly By the Scripps Foundation for Research in Population Problems at Miami University, and the Population Research and Training Center at the University of Chicago. Oxford and Chicago, 1954.
4. Carrothers, Gerald A. P. "An Historical Review of the Gravity and Potential Concepts of Human Interaction," *Journal of the American Institute of Planners*, XXII (Spring, 1956), 94–102.
5. ———. "Population Projection by Means of Income Potential Models," *Papers and Proceedings of the Regional Science Association*, IV (1958). Philadelphia. 121–152.
6. Clark, Colin. "Urban Population Densities," *Journal of the Royal Statistical Society*, Series A, CXIV, Part 4 (1951), 490–96.
7. Duncan, Otis, Dudley. "The Measurement of Population Distribution," *Population Studies*, XI (July, 1957), 27–45.

8. Dunn, Edgar S. "The Market Potential Concept and the Analysis of Location," *Papers and Proceedings of the Regional Science Association,* II (1956) . Cambridge, Mass. 183–194.
9. Ezekiel, Mordecai. *Methods of Correlation Analysis.* Second Edition. New York: John Wiley & Sons, 1941.
10. Hagood, Margaret Jarman, and Price, Daniel O. *Statistics for Sociologists.* Revised edition. New York: Henry Holt Co., 1952.
11. Hamburg, John R., and Creighton, Roger L. "Predicting Chicago's Land Use Pattern," *Journal of the American Institute of Planners,* XXV (May, 1959) , 67–72.
12. Hansen, Walter G. "How Accessibility Shapes Land Use," *Journal of the American Institute of Planners,* XXV (May, 1959) , 73–76.
13. Herbert, John D., and Stevens, Benjamin H. "A Model for the Distribution of Residential Activity in Urban Areas," *Journal of Regional Science* (Fall, 1960) , 21–36.
14. Mills, Frederick C., *Statistical Methods Applied to Economics and Business.* Revised Edition. New York: Henry Hart & Co., 1938.
15. Philadelphia City Planning Commission. *Land Use in Philadelphia 1944–1954.* Philadelphia, 1956.
16. Schmitt, Robert C. "A Method of Projecting the Population of Census Tracts, *Journal of the American Institute of Planners,* XX (Spring, 1954) , 102.
17. Stewart, John Q., and Warntz, William. "Macrogeography and Social Science," *Geographical Review,* XLVIII (April, 1958) 167–184.
18. Thomas, Edwin N. "Areal Association Between Population Growth and Selected Factors in the Chicago Urbanized Area," *Economic Geography,* XXXVI (April, 1960) , 158–170.
19. U.S. Bureau of the Budget. *Standard Metropolitan Statistical Areas.* 1961.
20. U.S. Bureau of the Census. *1956 National Housing Inventory, Vol. I, Components of Change 1950 to 1956,* Part 1, United States and Regions, 1958; Part 9. Philadelphia Standard Metropolitan Area, 1958.
21. U.S. Bureau of Labor Statistics. *Structure of the Residential Building Industry in 1949.* Bulletin No. 1170, November, 1954.

The Measurement of Intra-City Locational and Residential Patterns

BEVERLY DUNCAN AND OTIS DUDLEY DUNCAN

Students of urban structure have lived for some time with the uncomfortable realization that their theories—or rather, their abstract, schematic descriptions—of urban growth and form are not very susceptible to empirical testing. Given a map of land uses and residential characteristics, any investigator can discern evidence of concentric patterning, of multiple nucleation, and of sector differentiation.[1] But evidence favoring one of these does not rule out the plausibility of the others, and no way has been found to assess the relative contribution of the three types of tendency to the total configuration of the city. Such an impasse is perhaps typical of the stage of investigation in which natural-history observation has been followed by the formulation of ideal types. Some methodologists believe that it can be escaped only by resorting to more sophisticated measurement devices and formal multiple-variable analysis. The past decade has, indeed, witnessed a good deal of methodological development along these lines. Given the preoccupation of

much of this work with what are called "social areas," however, the result has been disappointing. Thus far the advocates of "social area analysis" [2] have accomplished little more than further documentation of the already well-known fact that contemporary American cities are differentiated residentially according to social and economic characteristics.[3] There remains the task of explaining such differentiation and of relating its patterns to basic structural determinants and sequences of growth. Our paper tackles one hitherto neglected phase of this task, exploring some relationships between the pattern of location of industry in the city and the pattern of residential differentiation according

From the *Journal of Regional Science,* II (Fall 1960) , 37–54. Reprinted by permission of the author and The Regional Science Research Institute, G.P.O. Box 8776, Philadelphia, Pennsylvania 19101.

1 The best synthetic discussion of these generalizations is still that of Harris and Ullman [11].
2 Shevsky and Bell, [20]; Van Ardsol, Camilleri, and Schmid [23].
3 Hawley and Duncan [13].

ing to the industrial affiliations of the work force. As a case study of one metropolitan community, Chicago, its purpose is to develop appropriate analytical methods and to suggest hypotheses with some preliminary empirical support.

Our point of departure is the observation that the economic efficiency associated with elaborate functional specialization of the urban work force requires a more or less pronounced separation of places of work from places of residence and a marked functional differentiation of areas wherein work is carried on.[4] The intra-community pattern of industrial location presumably evolved as part of the total process of city growth, but also in response to such specific locational determinants as space requirements, linkage to transportation and communication facilities, and site characteristics of available land. The pattern of socio-economic residential differentiation likewise reflects the city's history of growth—on this point the concentric-zone and sector hypotheses are agreed—and in particular the several contingencies as to layout of mass-transit routes, residential amenities, and timing of settlement. In our cross-sectional analysis of about 1950, these locational and residential patterns are taken not as problematic, but as given. Even though we know that they developed together, each changing under the influence of the other, at a given point in time it is possible to characterize them separately and, we believe, to assess at least crudely their interrelation and their independent influences.

Following a description of the data and a presentation of the analytical techniques, the discussion turns to some informal description of the spatial patterns of workplaces and residences. These observations suggest relationships warranting more careful study, making use of a formal analytical model. On the basis of this model it is possible to account for an appreciable part of the areal variation in the proportion of an area's residents affiliated with a given industry in terms of the locational pattern of that industry and the socio-economic level of the area, both factors being independently significant though highly variable in relative importance from industry to industry. Although no satisfactory explanation of this inter-industry variation emerges from our study, its existence argues that the internal residential structure of cities will be found to reflect the industry composition of their economic base and the locational determinants of the basic industries.

DATA

The bulk of this research [5] rests on two bodies of small-area data for the Chicago Metropolitan District c. 1950, one pertaining to the distribution of workplaces by industry and the other to the distribution of the resident labor force by industry. Two features of these data call for special comment. First, statistics are available for the entire CMD (Chicago Metropolitan District), an area approximating the City of Chicago plus the contiguous built-up suburban and fringe areas in 1950. The city, suburbs, and fringe together probably constitute a more or less closed labor market. The city or the suburbs and fringe alone clearly do not. Commutation into the city from white-collar dormitory suburbs has received considerable comment, but equally noteworthy are the flows of manufacturing workers from the city into satellite industrial areas. Only fragmentary information on these flows is available, but data derived from the Six-City Labor Mobility Survey show that eight per cent of the manufacturing workers living in the City of Chicago c. 1950 were employed in establishments located in the suburban area.[6] For industries with major suburban industrial concentrations, the proportion of Chicago residents working in suburban areas was more than double the proportion for all manufacturing workers—16 per cent for primary metals, 25 per cent for electrical machinery, and 29 per cent for transportation equipment except motor vehicles. These outflows are countered, of course, by a relatively heavy in-

4 Duncan, B. [4]; Schnore [19].
5 The initial procurement, processing, and preliminary analysis of the data were accomplished in connection with the Urban Analysis Project of the Chicago Community inventory in 1951–1953. The present analysis was carried out with the aid of a grant to the senior author from the National Science Foundation.
6 The use of these data for measuring the journey to work is described in Duncan, B. [3].

flux of suburban residents to manufacturing and other establishments located in the City. The areal coverage of the available data, therefore, seems particularly appropriate in that it is co-extensive with the physical and economic city. Second, the areal detail with which manufacturing workplaces are reported and the relatively complete coverage of workplaces are somewhat unique although the data suffer certain serious deficiencies as detailed below.

Workplace data of relatively good quality are available for the two-fifths of the labor force in manufacturing, less detailed and comprehensive statistics are available for the three-tenths in the commercial complex, and no workplace information is available for the remaining three-tenths of the labor force. Manufacturing workplaces by major industry for each of the 935 census tracts comprising the City of Chicago were compiled as a part of the Industrial Land Use Survey conducted during 1950–51.[7] Comparable data for the suburban part of the CMD were compiled from published directories of manufacturers and a mail survey of establishments believed to be large.[8] By comparison with counts of the Census of Manufactures and the Illinois Department of Labor or with the Census of Population count of CMD residents employed in manufacturing industries, these small-area data appear relatively complete. The establishment surveys covered 821,400 workplaces in the CMD, and the 1950 Census of Population reported 828,700 manufacturing workers living in the CMD. The total manufacturing workplace and residence counts differ by only one per cent. Discrepancies between workplace and residence counts are substantially greater, however, for individual manufacturing industries. These discrepancies probably reflect both misclassification of establishments and misreporting of industry by residents, as well as omissions and duplications in the workplace counts. Relative to the labor force statistics reported in the population census on a residence basis, the greatest overcount of workplaces is in the transportation equipment (except motor vehicles) industry, amounting to 28 per cent, while workplaces in printing and allied industries were undercounted by some 30 per cent. Workplace statistics for the other durable goods industry exclude employment in miscellaneous manufactures which was erroneously grouped with unknown industry in the Industrial Survey. (See Col. 2 of Table 1.)

Workplace data available for the commercial complex are less detailed in areal distribution and less comprehensive in coverage than are those for manufacturing industries. Commercial workplace statistics were obtained for the 75 Community Areas making up the City of Chicago and 15 to 25 subareas outside the City.[9] The ratio of workplaces to residences in the CMD was 1.03 for retail and .79 for wholesale trade, .52 for finance, insurance, and real estate, and .74 for hotels and lodging places. Workplace statistics of usable quality were not available for any other industry.

Residential distributions for 14 manufacturing industries and 30-odd other industries were obtained from special tabulations of the census-tract summary cards of the 1950 Census of Population. The industrial composition of workers living in each of the 1,178 census tracts making up the CMD was available.

TECHNIQUES OF ANALYSIS

The subsequent analyses rely heavily on a summary measure of the areal distribution of workplaces termed "workplace potential." Workplace potential is analogous to potential of population as defined by Stewart.[10] Instead of dividing persons by their distance away, however, we divide workplaces by their distance away. The workplace potential at a particular site in the CMD is, then, the sum over all workplaces in the CMD of the reciprocals of the distance separating each workplace from the site. We interpret workplace potential as a measure of the accessibility of the site to workplaces in the CMD, on the assumption that accessibility declines as distance increases. Accessibility, conceived as a time-cost factor, need not vary precisely as distance, of course.

7 For a description of the survey see Chicago Industrial Study [2].
8 The compilation of these data is described more fully in Duncan, O. D., and Davis [8].
9 Major sources include: Census of Business publications of the U.S. Census Bureau; Reiss and Breen [17]; Kitagawa and Sholes [15]; Illinois State Employment Service [14], and unpublished tabulation.
10 Stewart [22], reprinted in Spengler and Duncan, O. D. [21].

Table 1 Employment in Manufacturing Industries, on the Basis of Census Resident Labor Force Data, in Relation to Number of Workplaces Covered in Surveys of Manufacturing Establishments, Chicago Metropolitan District: c. 1950.

Manufacturing Industry	Per cent of total resident employed labor force	Reported workplaces as ratio to resident employed labor force
All manufacturing	37.8	0.99
(1) Primary metal industries	5.3	1.07
(2) Electrical equipment, machinery, & supplies	4.6	1.01
(3) Other nondurable goods	2.6	0.98
(4) Food and kindred products	4.4	1.00
(5) Other durable goods [a]	2.9	0.58
(6) Printing, publishing and allied industries	3.4	0.70
(7) Chemicals and allied products	1.5	1.07
(8) Apparel and other fabricated textile products	1.6	1.09
(9) Fabricated metal industries	3.6	1.04
(10) Machinery, except electrical	4.4	0.91
(11) Transportation equipment, except motor vehicle	0.8	1.28
(12) Furniture, and lumber and wood products	1.2	1.07
(13) Textile mill products	0.4	0.87
(14) Motor vehicles and motor vehicle equipment	0.8	1.13
Not specified manufacturing industries	0.3	....

[a] Workplace data exclude employment in "miscellaneous manufacturing industries," which are classified under "other durable goods" in the labor force data.

Several studies in recent years have demonstrated the utility of population potential and a variant thereof, termed "market potential," each conceived primarily as an indicator of accessibility to the national or a sub-national consuming market, in accounting for inter-city or inter-area differences in economic activity.[11] There has, however, been little application of the potential concept in studies of intra-urban structure and function. Exploratory work with workplace potential measures in the investigation of intra-urban residential structure along the lines reported here was initiated under the Urban Analysis Project, 1951–53.

The computation of potential for a series of sites always involves a number of approximations. Because the locational pattern of industrial activity is more clumped and sporadic than the areal distribution of population, the calculation of workplace potential presents some special problems. The procedure developed for computing potential for each manufacturing industry involves first the identification of "major workplace concentrations." Each concentration (minimum of 100 workplaces) on a grid with cells of roughly four square miles was identified, adjacent concentrations sometimes were combined, and workplaces falling outside concentrations were assigned to the nearest concentration. The number of separate concentrations recognized ranged from 11 for textile mill products, an industry with only 7,400 workplaces a fourth of which lie one to two miles from the Loop (CMD central business district) and two-fifths of which lie three to seven miles northwest and west of the Loop, to 54 for the other nondurable goods industry which includes 56,300 workplaces, a sixth located northwest and west some six miles from the Loop, a sixth located southeast some 15 miles from the Loop,

11 Harris [10]; Duncan, B. [5]; Pappenfort [16].

and the remainder scattered over the CMD. (Calculations were carried out with 136 concentrations for the "nonelectrical" machinery industry in the exploratory stage.) The method of calculation was analogous to that described in another publication.[12] Potential was computed for a minimum of 29 sites and a maximum of 102 sites, the number depending on the complexity of the configuration of isolines of potential and the judgment of the investigator. For the commercial complex as a whole, workplace potential was calculated using 30 "concentrations," identified less precisely, for 35 sites scattered over the CMD. Workplace potential for an evenly distributed industry was also computed using 191 "workplaces," one located at each intersection of a grid imposed on the CMD.

Isolines of workplace potential for two industries in the CMD that manifest quite different locational patterns appear in Figure 1. The isolines of potential for the fabricated metal industries (A) summarize a relatively even distribution of workplaces over the CMD with no single dominant concentration, although the density of workplaces is comparatively high in the central manufacturing district to the west of the Loop. The area of highest workplace potential is located slightly to the west of the Loop, and potential falls off more or less evenly in all directions as distance from this area increases. By contrast, areas in which workplace potential is high for the primary metal industries (B) occur along the lakefront at distances ten miles or more southeast of the Loop and also at a lesser distance southwest of the Loop. The locational pattern of the industry is shaped by a few large lakefront establishments which together provide half the primary-metals workplaces in the CMD; a smaller concentration of workplaces is found in the central manufacturing district. It should be noted that, although isolines of potential conventionally are shown with equal intervals, in Figure 1 the interval between isolines of potential increases as the magnitude of the potential increases. Had equal intervals between isolines been maintained in Figure 1, the configuration of contours would apear more "peaked," for more closely spaced isolines would be evident in the areas of relatively high potential.

Estimates of industry-specific workplace potentials for 211 quasi-tracts in the CMD were prepared for purposes of regression analysis. The 211 quasi-tracts are a systematic sample drawn from the 1,053 quasi-tracts making up the CMD. (Quasi-tracts are either single census tracts or groups of tracts combined because each had only a few resident workers.) The preliminary estimate of potential for each quasi-tract was obtained by interpolating between isolines on maps similar to but more detailed than those shown in Figure 1. If the quasi-tract contained 250 or more workplaces in any manufacturing industry, the industry's potential in that quasi-tract was computed more precisely by subtracting from the estimate the potential initially attributed to the workplaces within the quasi-tract itself and adding to it a more careful estimate of potential attributable to these workplaces. (These adjustments were required because somewhat crude approximations were involved in the initial potential calculations.) The preliminary estimate of potential for the commercial complex was multiplied by a factor of 1.3 to take account of the fact that workplace coverage was incomplete. This adjustment assumes that the locational pattern of the total complex is identical with that of known commercial workplaces. The preliminary estimate of potential for an even distribution was multiplied by a factor of 3,513 on the assumption that workplaces for the remaining industries—extraction, construction, transportation and utilities, the entertainment and professional services, public administration—are evenly distributed over the CMD. Total workplace potential for each quasi-tract is the sum of 14 industry-specific manufacturing potentials, the commercial-complex potential, and the "other" workplace potential. Hereafter, the proportion of total potential accounted for by an industry is referred to as the industry's "relative potential" as distinct from its workplace potential *per se.*

Another variable playing an important role in the analysis is termed the "expected" proportion of the resident work force in an industry on the basis of occupational composition. A variation on the "method of expected cases" was selected as a technique for assessing

12 Duncan *et al* [6], appendix.

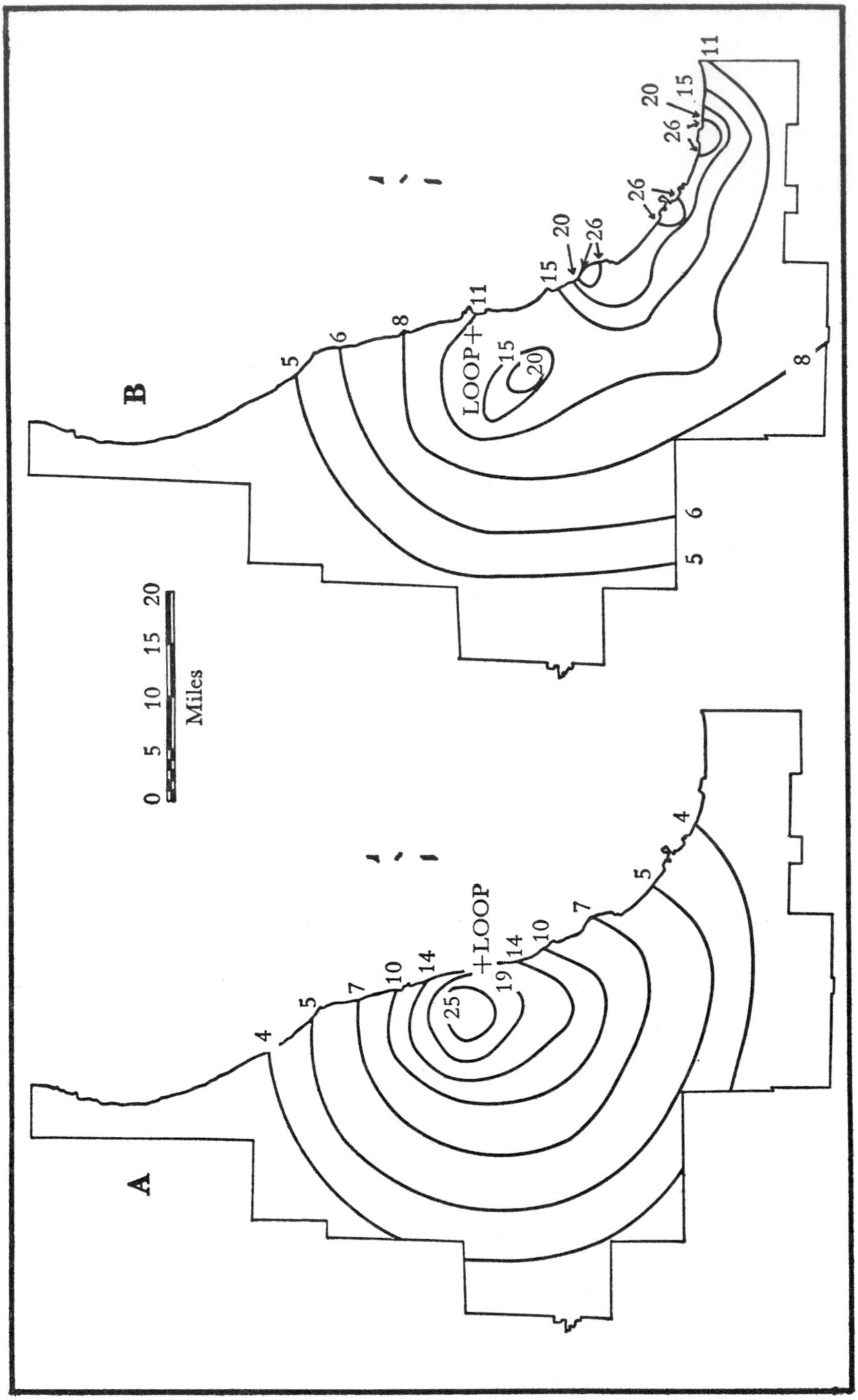

Figure 1 Isolines of workplace potential, in 1000 workplaces per mile, for two manufacturing industries in the Chicago metropolitan district: 1951. (A) Fabricated metal industries; (B) Primary metal industries.

the impact of occupation on the residential patterns of industry groups. The 1950 Census of Population provides data on the occupational composition of each census tract in the CMD and a cross-tabulation of occupation by industry for the Chicago Standard Metropolitan Area, 93 per cent of whose resident labor force was living within the CMD. For a particular tract, "expected" residents in an industry is the sum over all occupation groups of the products of the number of residents in a given occupation times the occupation-specific proportion in that industry in the CMD. The "expected" distribution of workers by industry was obtained for each of the 1,178 census tracts in the CMD on a UNIVAC electronic computer. It was then expressed in proportional terms by dividing by the total work force of the area.

If in fact the sole determinant of areal variation in the proportion of resident workers in an industry were occupation, the observed proportion would correspond with the proportion "expected" on the basis of occupation for each tract, and the coefficient b in the equation describing the regression of observed on "expected" proportions would be unity. It has recently been demonstrated that departure of b from unity can be given a meaningful substantive interpretation in analyses of areal variation.[13] When the slope exceeds 1.0, we know that, on the average, the occupation-specific industry proportion in tracts where occupational composition favors the given industry is higher than in the CMD as a whole, and that the occupation-specific proportion tends to be lower than in the CMD in tracts where the occupation composition is generally unfavorable. Or, to put the matter a little less precisely, this kind of result indicates that "factors associated with occupation" in addition to occupation composition *per se* account for part of the variation in industry proportions.

The special merit of the "expected cases" approach for the present purpose is that it allows the "socio-economic status" of the area (insofar as this may be reflected in its occupational composition) to enter the analysis, not in the form of some generalized and vaguely justified "index," but in a form calculated to capture its particular relevance for the dependent variable at hand. The "expected" propor-

tion in a given industry is both an index of the occupational composition of an area, weighted in a particular manner—as may be seen from its definition—and a norm against which one can measure the influence of occupational composition on variation in the industrial attachments of the work force over a set of such areas.

PRELIMINARY OBSERVATIONS

Before introducing a model to account for the residential pattern of industry groups, some exploratory work which led to the development of the model should be summarized. A series of studies conducted under the Urban Analysis Project pointed to the fact that industry groups differed from one another both in their locational pattern and in the residential pattern of their work force. Moreover, the workplace and residential distributions did not appear to be independent of one another, for the more centralized residential patterns were those of industries whose workplaces were concentrated toward the Loop. Industries which did not conform, i.e., those evidencing a relatively centralized workplace pattern but a relatively decentralized residential pattern or *vice versa*, typically had an occupational composition quite different from the occupational composition of the population residing in areas near their workplaces. The implication of these results was that the residential pattern of an industry group is shaped by the locational pattern of the industry, the occupational composition of its work force, and the residential patterns of the several occupation groups. Any model which sought to account for the residential patterns of industry groups solely on the basis of the location of industrial activity or solely on the basis of the differentiation of the city by socio-economic level would be demonstrably deficient.

There remained, however, the problems of quantifying the locational pattern of the industry and of indexing the socio-economic character of industries and residential areas. Experimentation indicated that the presence of industrial activity within a residential area

13 Borts [1]; Duncan, O. D., Cuzzort, and Duncan, B. [7].

was an inadequate measure of that area's accessibility to workplaces. The contrast between a residential area devoid of industrial activity but ringed by industrial districts and a residential area located at considerable distances from industrial concentrations but including a pocket of industrial activity illustrates the point. Applying the concept of workplace potential, which reflects an area's position with respect to the total configuration of industrial activity, each workplace being weighted by the reciprocal of its distance from the area, seems to capture the relevant aspects of the industry's locational pattern. An index of socio-economic level based on an occupational distribution frequently is constructed by assigning weights to each component occupation and calculating a weighted average. The selection of appropriate weights remains arbitrary, however, in most studies employing such a technique. Our procedure, by contrast, was to weight the occupational distribution, in each tract or residential area by the occupation-specific proportions employed in a particular industry in the CMD as a whole. This means, of course, that the tract has no single index of occupational composition but rather a distinct index for each industry examined. This index, or "expected" proportion of residents in an industry, has special advantages in regression analyses as noted earlier.

Initial studies of the association between industry workplace potential and residential pattern involved a comparison of the residential distribution of workers in a particular industry with that of all workers in the CMD, with the component areas of the CMD ordered in terms of decreasing workplace potential for the industry. The fact that in nearly every case, disproportionate numbers of the industry's work force were living in areas where its workplace potential was high was taken to mean that the locational pattern of an industry shapes the residential pattern of its work force. The three industries evidencing the greatest residential concentration in areas of high workplace potential had a common locational feature: the pattern of each was dominated by a major workplace concentration located some distance away from the districts in which most manufacturing activity occurs. A clustering of small establishments in the Loop area provided two-

fifths of the apparel industry employment. Half the primary metals employment was concentrated in a few large establishments along the lakefront southeast of the Loop, the locations of which can be inferred from Figure 1B. A fifth of the employment in electrical machinery was in a single establishment located some six miles west of the Loop. In an attempt to quantify this locational feature, we measured the concentration of the industry's workplaces relative to all other manufacturing workplaces toward the point of peak potential for the industry. The rank correlation of .7 over the 14 industries between the residential concentration in high potential areas and the workplace concentration toward the peak potential suggests that industries whose locational pattern exerts a relatively strong "pull" on the residential pattern are ones with somewhat distinctive and typically mono-centered workplace distributions.

The finding that workers in industries having similar configurations of workplace potential tend to share common residential areas provides further support for the notion that the residential structure is shaped by the locational pattern of industry. A matrix of correlations between the industry-specific workplace potentials for each combination of two of the 14 manufacturing industries over the 211 quasi-tracts was computed. Coefficients of correlation for the 91 pairs of industries ranged from .9 for "nonelectrical" machinery vs. fabricated metals and for the apparel vs. the printing industry to a nonsignificant −.1 for "other durable goods" vs. primary metals. There was a direct and statistically significant correlation between workplace potentials for nearly three-fourths of the pairs. In the corresponding matrix of correlations between the industry-specific proportions in the resident labor force, the coefficients ranged from .6 for "electrical" vs. "nonelectrical" machinery to −.5 for primary metals vs. the printing industry. The correlation between industry-specific residential proportions was direct and statistically significant for nearly a fourth of the combinations and inverse and statistically significant in four cases. The correlation of .6 between corresponding coefficients in the two matrixes (workplace potential and residential distribution) indicates that the residential distributions of two industries tend to resemble one another when their areas of high workplace potential coincide. The industry pairs which fail to conform to this general tendency are, in themselves, instructive. Three of the four cases in which the residential association is unusually low, given the similarity of workplace-potential configurations, involve printing and publishing, a relatively high status manufacturing industry, in combination with some other industry; five of the seven cases in which the residential association is unusually high involve subdivisions of a broader industry group, e.g., "electrical" vs. "nonelectrical" machinery.

These results also suggest something about the variables that should enter a model purporting to account for the residential patterns of industries. The deviant instances just described reaffirm the importance of the occupation factor. The frequent coincidence of areas of high workplace potential for two or more industries suggests that *relative* workplace potentials may be more efficient predictors of residential structure than workplace potentials *per se*. Such an hypothesis would follow if one conceived of total workplace potential as indicative of the total demand for residence in a particular area, on the assumption that demand varies directly with accessibility to workplaces. The industrial composition of the area's resident work force, then, would mirror the industrial composition of its total workplace potential, assuming the effective demand for residence is constant over all industries.

THE MODEL

The residential pattern of an industry within the metropolitan district, or more specifically areal variation in the proportion of the resident labor force employed in a particular industry, is the phenomenon to be accounted for. Two probable determinants of residential patterns have been identified: inter-area differences in accessibility to the industry's workplaces; and inter-area differences in socio-economic status (occupational composition). Our model assumes that the proportion of the resident work force in a particular industry is a function of the industry's relative potential, i.e., relative accessibility to its workplaces, and the

"expected" proportion of residents in the industry, i.e., socio-economic status. The 14 manufacturing industries are taken to represent 14 "tests" (albeit not wholly independent ones) of the model's goodness of fit.

For each manufacturing industry, the percentage of the total resident work force in the industry varies directly with the industry's relative workplace potential on an area-by-area basis (Col. 1, Table 2). The correlation between the residential proportion and relative potential is significant in the statistical sense in each case, and for half the industries a fourth or more of the inter-area variance in the residential proportion is accounted for by differences among areas in relative potential. Incidentally, the association of the residential proportion with relative potential (Col. 1, Table 2) is stronger than that of the residential proportion with potential *per se* (not shown) for 11 of the 14 manufacturing industries.

It is instructive to look at the regression coefficients as well as the coefficients of correlation. The magnitude of the change in the residential proportion associated with a change in relative potential is substantial for a number of industries. In fact, for half the industries, a change of one percentage point in relative potential is accompanied by a change of more than one percentage point in the residential proportion (Col. 2, Table 2). Inasmuch as the average of relative potential over all areas is very close to the average residential proportion over all areas, the value of the regression coefficient approximates the elasticity of the residential proportion with respect to the relative potential, evaluated at the mean. For the remaining seven industries, a change of one percentage point in relative potential is associated with a change of two- to eight-tenths of a percentage point in the residential proportion.

The percentage of the total resident work force in the industry also varies directly with the area's "expected" percentage in the industry (Col. 3, Table 2). The correlation is statistically significant, however, for only 12 of the 14 industries; and for only four of them does variation in the "expected" proportion account for as much as a quarter of the variation in the observed residential proportion. The "expected" residential proportion or socio-economic level is, on the average, a less efficient predictor of an industry's residential pattern than is relative potential or accessibility to workplaces, as is indicated by a comparison of the correlation coefficients in Columns (3) and (1), Table 2.

The average influence of areal differentials in relative potential on the residential pattern is often less, however, than that of interarea differences in socio-economic level, as measured by the respective regression coefficients, Columns (2) and (4), Table 2. Possibly a more accurate statement would be that the influence of relative potential on the residential distribution may be substantial or negligible, while the influence of socio-economic level is consistently substantial. A change of one percentage point

in the "expected" residential proportion is associated with an average change of more than one percentage point in the observed residential proportion for 13 of the 14 industries; in the other case, it is associated with a change of nine-tenths of a percentage point (Col. 4, Table 2). Moreover, the fact that the values of these regression coefficients exceed unity in nearly all cases means that the residential proportion is higher than "expected" on the basis of occupation in areas where the occupational composition is favorable to residence by members of the industry, and that it is lower than "expected" in areas where the occupational composition is unfavorable. Apparently occupational composition is associated areally with

Table 2 Summary of Regressions of Residential Distributions on Workplace Potentials and "Expected" Residential Distributions, for Manufacturing Industries, Based on Sample of 211 Quasi-Tracts in the Chicago Metropolitan District: c. 1950.

	Correlation and regression coefficients [b]								
	r_{Y1}	b_{Y1}	r_{Y2}	b_{Y2}	r_{12}	$R_{Y·12}$	$R^2_{Y·12}$	$b_{Y1·2}$	$b_{Y2·1}$
Manufacturing Industry [a]	*(1)*	*(2)*	*(3)*	*(4)*	*(5)*	*(6)*	*(7)*	*(8)*	*(9)*
(1) Prim. metal	.86	2.41	.45	2.99	.25	.90	.80	2.23	1.68
(2) Elec. mach.	.65	1.22	.50	2.13	.07‡	.80	.63	1.16	1.95
(3) Oth. nondur.	.78	2.59	.30	2.12	.23	.79	.62	2.49	0.91
(4) Food, etc.	.69	0.74	.41	1.99	.20	.74	.55	0.68	1.38
(5) Oth. durable	.47	0.75	.52	1.49	.12‡	.66	.44	0.65	1.34
(6) Print., pub.	.39	0.55	.36	1.13	−.36	.66	.44	0.85	1.82
(7) Chem., etc.	.64	1.94	.13‡	1.84‡	−.03‡	.65	.43	1.95	2.17
(8) Apparel, etc.	.60	1.01	.42	1.23	.36	.64	.40	0.87	0.70
(9) Fab. metal	.27	0.64	.56	1.83	.18	.59	.35	0.41	1.72
(10) Mach., exc. el.	.29	0.80	.54	2.10	.13‡	.58	.34	0.61	1.99
(11) Trans. equip.	.51	1.31	.10‡	1.44‡	.07‡	.51	.26	1.30	0.85‡
(12) Furn., lumber	.39	1.25	.37	2.07	.37	.46	.21	0.94	1.44
(13) Textiles	.37	0.35	.20	0.89	.13‡	.40	.16	0.32	0.68*
(14) Motor veh.	.20	0.23	.32	1.21	.25	.34	.12	0.15*	1.09

[a] See Table 1 for full titles.
[b] Identification of symbols—
  Y: Per cent of resident employed persons in the specified industry, by quasi-tract.
  X_1: Relative workplace potential of the specified industry, by quasi-tract.
  X_2: "Expected" per cent of resident employed persons in the specified industry, by quasi-tract.
  r_{Y1}, r_{Y2}, and r_{12}: Zero-order correlations.
  b_{Y1} and b_{Y2}: Zero-order regression coefficients.
  $b_{Y1·2}$ and $b_{Y2·1}$: Partial regression coefficients.
  $R_{Y·12}$: Multiple correlation coefficient, Y on X_1 and X_2.
Coefficients not significant at .05 level are marked (‡); significant at .05 level (*); all other coefficients differ significantly from zero at the .01 level.

other factors which are themselves correlates of the residential distribution of industries.

Areas in which relative potential for an industry is high need not have occupational compositions which are conducive to residence by members of the industry. They do not in the case of the printing industry, for which an inverse relationship between relative potential and the "expected" proportion in the industry is observed (Col. 5, Table 2). For six additional industries, the "expected" residential proportion varies over areas more or less independently of relative potential. For only half the industries, therefore, do areal differentials in relative potential reinforce socio-economic level in shaping the residential pattern. Most noteworthy is the typically low correlation between the two predictors: in no case is more than a seventh of the variance in "expected" percentage in an industry accounted for by areal differentials in its workplace potential.

As a consequence of this low correlation between the independent variables, accessibility to workplaces and socio-economic level together more fully account for the residential pattern of an industry than does either alone. For four industries, over half the variance in the percentage of the resident work force employed in the industry is accounted for by the combination of relative potential and "expected" residential proportion (Col. 7, Table 2). The two factors combined account for a quarter to a half of the variance in the residential percentages for seven industries and for less than a quarter of the variance for the remaining three industries.

The effect on the residential distribution of each factor with the other "held constant" is significant for all but three industries (Cols. 8 and 9, Table 2). In two of the exceptional cases, only the partial regression coefficient for the residential proportion on relative potential holding constant socio-economic level is significant; in the other case, only the partial regression coefficient for the residential proportion on socio-economic level holding constant relative potential is significant.

Owing to the generally low correlation between the two predictor variables, the pattern of variation by industry of the partial regression coefficients is much like that of the zero-order regressions. Hence the observation stands

that occupational composition has a more consistently substantial effect on residential distribution, but that relative workplace potential has the stronger effect for a few industries.

Incidentally, since the variables under examination tend to have somewhat skewed distributions when quasi-tracts are arrayed from low to high, it is well to make sure that our results are not a statistical artifact. Hence some of the calculations were carried out using a square root transformation of the dependent variable. The results were only slightly modified, the correlations being a little higher if anything and manifesting only minor shifts in relative magnitude as among the 14 industries.

SOME IMPLICATIONS

We alluded to the fact that industries differ in their residential patterns and then showed that an industry's residential distribution depends in part on its intra-urban locational pattern and the socio-economic differentiation of the city's residential areas. Several aspects of inter-industry variation in residential pattern have been touched on only indirectly, however. The residences of workers in some industries, for example, are distributed over the city in the same pattern as all residences, while the residential distribution for other industries is uneven. We suspect that an uneven residential distribution is evidenced most often by industries whose locational patterns result in substantial areal differentials in accessibility to workplaces and that a coincidence of areas of relatively high accessibility and areas with favorable occupational compositions enhances the unevenness of an industry's residential pattern. In the CMD, nearly half the variance among the 14 manufacturing industries in unevenness of residential distribution (as measured by the ratio of the standard deviation to the mean of the residential proportion) is accounted for by two factors: variability in relative workplace potentials (as measured by the ratio of the standard deviation to the mean of the relative potential) and the coincidence of high potential and favorable socio-economic level areas (as measured by the correlation between relative potential and "expected" residential proportion). This finding provides general support for the notion although the evidence is insufficient as a basis for generalization.

The locational patterns of industries and areal differentials in socio-economic level are taken as given in this study, but they themselves merit attention. Especially important would be an investigation of the way in which the development of the industrial pattern influences the formation of the residential pattern by socio-economic level and vice versa. In the CMD c. 1950, for example, the proportion of professional, managerial, and sales workers among the resident male work force varied inversely with workplace potential for each of the 14 manufacturing industries. (The r's range from −.2 to −.4.) The inverse correlation of the proportion of high status workers with workplace potential, was, in fact, stronger than the direct correlation (r of .2) of socio-economic level and distance from the Loop— the factor that one would emphasize on the basis of extant propositions about areal socio-economic differentiation and city growth.

Inter-industry differences in the efficiency with which the residential pattern is predicted by areal differentials in relative potential and socio-economic level also have been noted. Given the nature of the data, we are certain that errors of measurement obtain in the relative potentials and suspect that the error is not constant over industries. We are reluctant to assume, however, that the observed inter-industry differences are accounted for fully by differential measurement error. The four industries for which the efficiency of prediction is lowest are the smallest of the 14 industries in terms of employment size (see Table 1). Among the ten larger industries, prediction tends to be least efficient for industries whose residential distributions are least variable or most even as compared with the distribution of all residences. Possibly a sizable work force and a variable residential distribution are required if an industry's residential pattern is to be accounted for with gross factors of the type used here.

Industries also differ according to whether inter-area variation in accessibility to workplaces or areal differentials in socio-economic level have the greater influence on their residential distributions. As indexed by the regression coefficients in standard form, the residential pattern is influenced relatively more

by areal variation in workplace potential for eight industries and by areal variation in socio-economic level in three cases. For the remaining three industries, the factors have approximately the same influence. The magnitude of the change in the residential proportion per unit change in the independent variable, however, is typically greater for socio-economic level of the area than for its workplace potential, although the reverse is observed for four industries. We are unable to account for the inter-industry differences in the relative importance of the factors in any systematic fashion, but these differences underscore the observation that areal variation in accessibility to workplaces and socio-economic level jointly and independently shape an industry's residential pattern.

There is reason to doubt that the efficiency of prediction and the relative importance of the two predictors for a particular industry in the CMD would be the same in other cities, although we should expect the residential pattern elsewhere to reflect the locational pattern and the areal differentiation by socio-economic level. The industry "mix"—both the detailed industries included in the major industry groups themselves and the composition of the total work force by major industry—is probably important in shaping an industry's residential distribution. For example, the residential pattern of an industry in a city where that industry was the major source of employment would probably differ from its pattern in a city where it was a negligible source of employment. An industry's residential pattern in a city where employment was concentrated wholly in light manufacturing and nonmanufacturing industries would be unlikely to resemble closely its pattern in a city with a sizable complement of heavy manufacturing.

The issue of how far our findings may be generalized pertains not only to resemblances among cities. A distinct problem is the extent to which findings about the separation of home and workplace for individual workers can be translated into propositions about residential patterns and vice versa. There need be no close correspondence between an industry's rank on the average distance travelled to work by its work force and its rank on a measure of the degree to which residences of its work force are concentrated in areas of high accessibility to its workplaces. In fact, the rank correlation between average distance travelled to work by Chicago residents in each of the 14 manufacturing industries and a measure of the residential concentration in areas of high workplace potential for the same industries is $-.35$. (The correlation rises to $-.6$ if the three industries represented in the sample of Chicago workers by fewer than 30 cases are excluded.) [14] Although there is some tendency for industries ranking high on association between residential and workplace distributions to rank low on the average home-work separation of their work force, generalizations based on comparison of the distributions clearly cannot be transferred to home-work separation on an individual basis and *vice versa* with any great confidence. As another example, the average journey to work is substantially longer for Chicago residents working in the Loop than in less central parts of the CMD. However, the manufacturing industry with the highest proportion of its employment concentrated in the Loop— the apparel industry—ranks sixth among the 14 industries on the index of residential concentration in areas of high workplace potential. It requires no examination of data, however, to identify some cogent reasons why the association of the workplace and residential distributions may differ from the association, or average separation, of home and work for individuals in the work force. If there is little inter-area variation in the proportion of the resident work force in an industry, that industry's index of residential concentration must be low. The average journey to work for persons in the industry, however, can be long or short, depending on the locational pattern of workplaces. Given substantial inter-tract variation in the proportion of residents in a particular industry, the industry's index of residential concentration will be high if areas in which the residential proportion is high are relatively accessible to its workplaces. The average journey to work for its work force, however, can be long or short, depending on whether the areas of high accessibility are proximate to or somewhat removed from workplace concentrations. Industries evidencing considerable variability in their residential proportions will have low indexes of residential concentration should the areas in which the residential proportion is low be areas of rela-

tively high accessibility. The work force of such industries can have a long or short journey to work, however, depending on the locational pattern of the industry. Manifestly, we are confronted here with yet another problem where "ecological correlations" are of truly ecological significance and not mere substitutes for the information needed by analysts of individual behavior.[15]

Despite the restrictions on generalization imposed by having only one city as a case study, the results reported here indicate that any adequate theory of urban residential structure must reckon with both the locational pattern of industrial activity and the socio-economic differentiation of residential areas which comes about through general city growth. To deduce the location of the "zone of workingmen's homes," Burgess, in his schematic presentation of urban residential structure, relied primarily on the latter factor, the sequence of settlement in the course of urban expansion. Characteristics of "workingmen's suburbs," or industrial satellites, have been described,[16] but attempts to reconcile their occurrence with the "zone of workingmen's homes" have been few. Perhaps a more typical response has been the declaration that "ideal type zones" do not exist. We believe there is more promise in a model that assumes both areal differentiation in socio-economic level, stemming at least in part from the process of city growth, and areal differentiation in industrial activity, based on determinants of industrial location.

REFERENCES

1. Borts, G. H., "Comment (on 'Analysis of Interstate Income Differentials,' by Frank A. Hanna)," in Conference on Research in Income and Wealth, *Regional Income*, Studies in Income and Wealth, Vol. 21 (Princeton: Princeton University Press, 1957).
2. Chicago Industrial Study: *Summary Report* (Chicago: Chicago Plan Commission, 1952).
3. Duncan, Beverly, "Factors in Work-Residence Separation: Wage and Salary Workers, Chicago, 1951," *American Sociological Review,* 21 (February, 1956), pp. 48–56.

14 These results are based on data described in Duncan, B. [3].
15 Cf. the statement of this point by Duncan, O. D. and Lieberson [9].
16 Schnore [18].

4. Duncan, Beverly, "Intra-Urban Population Movement," in Hatt and Reiss, [12].

5. Duncan, Beverly, "Population Distribution and Manufacturing Activity: The Nonmetropolitan United States in 1950," *Papers and Proceedings of the Regional Science Association,* 5 (1959), pp. 95–104.

6. Duncan, Otis Dudley, *et al., Metropolis and Region* (Baltimore: Johns Hopkins Press, 1960).

7. Duncan, O. D., R. P. Cuzzort and B. Duncan, *Statistical Geography* (Glencoe, Ill.: The Free Press, 1960), section 3.4.

8. Duncan, O. D., and B. Davis, *Ecological Aspects of the Labor Force in the Chicago Metropolitan Area,* Urban Analysis Project Report No. 20 (Chicago: Chicago Community Inventory, University of Chicago, hectographed, 1953).

9. Duncan, O. D., and S. Lieberson, "Ethnic Segregation and Assimilation," *American Journal of Sociology,* 64 (January, 1959), pp. 364–74.

10. Harris, C. D., "The Market as a Factor in the Localization of Industry in the United States," *Annals of the Association of American Geographers,* 44 (December, 1954), pp. 315–48.

11. Harris, C. D., and E. L. Ullman, "The Nature of Cities," first published in 1945 and reprinted (among other places) in Hatt and Reiss [12].

12. Hatt, P. K. and A. J. Reiss, Jr., *Cities and Society* (Glencoe, Ill.: The Free Press, 1957).

13. Hawley, A. H., and O. D. Duncan, "Social Area Analysis: A Critical Appraisal," *Land Economics,* 33 (November, 1957), pp. 337–45.

14. Illinois State Employment Service; Division of Unemployment Compensation, *Analysis of Employment by Place of Work and Place of Residence: Chicago Area* (Cook and DuPage Counties) (mimeographed, 1949).

15. Kitagawa, E. M., and D. Sholes, *Chicagoland's Retail Market* (Chicago: Chicago Association of Commerce and Industry and Chicago Community Inventory, University of Chicago, 1957).

16. Pappenfort, D. M., "The Ecological Field and the Metropolitan Community: Manufacturing and Management," *American Journal of Sociology,* 64 (January, 1959), pp. 380–85.

17. Reiss, A. J., Jr., and L. Z. Breen, *Geographic Distribution of Retail Trade in the Chicago Metropolitan Area, 1948* (Chicago: Community Inventory, University of Chicago, 1952).

18. Schnore, L. F., "Satellites and Suburbs," *Social Forces,* 36 (December, 1957), pp. 121–27.

19. Schnore, L. F., "The Separation of Home and Work: A Problem for Human Ecology," *Social Forces,* 32 (May, 1954), pp. 336–43.

20. Shevky, E. and W. Bell, *Social Area Analysis,* "Stanford Sociological Series," No. 1 (Stanford, Calif.: Stanford University Press, 1955).

21. Spengler, J. J. and O. D. Duncan, editors, *Demographic Analysis: Selected Readings* (Glencoe, Ill.: The Free Press, 1956).

22. Stewart, J. Q., "Empirical Mathematical Rules Concerning the Distribution and Equilibrium of Population," *Geographical Review,* 37 (July, 1947), 461–85.

23. Van Arsdol, M. D., Jr., S. F. Camilleri, and C. F. Schmid, "The Generality of Urban Social Area Indexes," *American Sociological Review,* 23 (June, 1958), pp. 277–84.

Intra-Urban Location Problems: An Evaluation

CHARLES M. TIEBOUT

The "Frontiers of Economic Knowledge" is the central theme around which papers of this meeting are organized. The topic of this paper, intra-urban location problems, ventures beyond the frontier and off into the wilderness. This is because the topic is too involved, practically limitless, and relatively unexplored.

This paper is concerned with one aspect of intra-urban location problems: the potential of intra-urban location theory to the solution of urban problems. No attempt is made to develop a theory of intra-urban locations. Rather, what is sought is a current appraisal: What are the urban problems? What can we say about them? Finally, where do we go next? It is important to consider such questions as these, for regardless of the state of our theoretical models, planners are planning, developers are developing, and highway engineers are pouring ever more concrete.

After a few words pleading the case for urgent attention to intra-urban location problems, this paper considers: a pure-market,

From *American Economic Review,* LI, No. 2 (May 1961), 271–278, 299–300. Reprinted by permission of the American Economic Association and the author.

intra-urban, "location assignment" problem, the approach to a solution via agricultural location theory which, in turn, highlights the crucial role of governments in intra-urban locations and suggests, possibly, the most important void in the theory of the urban structure.

THE URGENCY OF ATTENTION

Without defining the term "problem," just about everyone agrees that urban areas face problems. Moreover, in the era of "the exploding metropolis" the magnitude of these problems is on the increase. It is of interest to note, for example, that two leading economists, Alvin Hansen and Albert G. Hart, not primarily specialists in urban problems, take the position that urban problems will be the most challenging economic problems in the next twenty-five years.[1]

Other evidence attests to the demand that something be done about urban areas. At the time of this writing, there is speculation that President-elect Kennedy will call for a new cabinet post on urban affairs. Possibly this position is designed simply to co-ordinate the myriad of federal agencies already concerned with urban problems. On another front, the Committee for Economic Development has already issued a policy statement, "Guiding Metropolitan Growth," and further statements by CED are under consideration. Finally, experimentation has gone on in an effort to solve some urban problems as exemplified by the new governmental units created in Miami (Metropolitan Dade County) and in Toronto (Metropolitan Toronto). No doubt a good deal of additional evidence could be cited to illustrate concern about the urban region. What does all this and other evidence point to?

At the risk of being overdramatic, this writer suggests that, just as the depression of the thirties strained public faith in market forces, the failure to solve urban problems in the sixties may again tax public faith in market forces.

Not all of these problems, of course, involve space. Yet, many problems have a spatial context: "gray belts" surround central cores; slums blight whole areas; and congestion affects most urban dwellers. Can intra-urban location theory help us evaluate and solve some of these

problems? For purposes of exposition, it is useful to set forth in a simplified form a conceptual intra-urban, location assignment problem which market forces seek to solve.

THE INTRA-URBAN LOCATION ASSIGNMENT PROBLEM

The nature of a pure, intra-urban, location theory assignment problem may be conceptualized in the spirit of von Thünen and Lösch.[2]

Imagine a bounded nonagricultural region. A large population engaged in a set of productive activities is introduced. Included in these activities are dwelling units.

To keep things simple, eliminate all considerations of geographical terrain; i.e., activities are located on a smooth undifferentiated surface. Further, assume a transport surface exists. This implies that the transport costs of a good are constant for any given distance in any direction. (This says nothing about the level of transport costs; they may be high or low.) In general terms, the task is to find a general equilibrium solution which allocates these activities in urban space. The resulting patterns, leaving the term "patterns" and their measurement undefined, represent the spatial allocation of urban activities via pure market forces.

One approach to the assignment of economic activities in urban space has been to apply agricultural location analysis.[3] Consideration of

1 *Problems of United States Economic Development* (CED, 1958).
2 Johann H. von Thünen, *Der isolierte Staat in Beziehung auf Landwirtschaft und Nationalökonomie* (Hamburg: Fr. Derthes, 1826); August Lösch, *The Economics of Location*, trans. by William Wolgom with the assistance of Wolfgang Stolper (Yale Univ. Press, 1954). The term "assignment" is not used here in the tight technical sense, but as shorthand for the spatial allocation of activities.
3 See William Alonzo, "A Theory of the Urban Land Market," *Regional Sci. Asso. Papers and Proceedings*, 1960, pp. 149–57; Walter Isard, *Location and Space Economy* (Technology Press, M.I.T., and Wiley, 1956), pp. 200–06. An excellent summary and extension of intra-urban analysis is given in Barclay G. Jones, "The Theory of the Urban Economy" (unpublished doctoral thesis, Univ. of North Carolina, 1960). Jones's review of the literature supports my contention that we have not yet developed general equilibrium of the urban economy. What we have are some suggested approaches.

consolidation of agricultural theory not only provides some insight into urban patterns but, in addition, points up certain difficulties which suggest new areas for investigation.

AGRICULTURAL LOCATION ANALYSIS

Agricultural location theory has been relatively well explored.[4] Many of the explorations are variations on a theme by von Thünen. Von Thünen imagines a central city surrounded by farm lands. Some distance away from the city is an impenetrable circular forest bounding the farm lands. His task is that of assigning agricultural crops to various zones.

In essence, transport costs to market for the various products taken in conjunction with demands allocate land to various product belts. In this analysis, the belts are concentric rings around the central city. The technical details of the analysis are not relevant for purposes of this discussion. What is relevant are two of the assumptions common to discussions of agricultural location theory.

One assumption is that of a transport surface, just as Weber and Lösch assume a transport surface for their nonagricultural analysis. True, modifications of simple "cost proportional to distance and weight" analysis have been introduced, but these modifications do not vastly distort the patterns of location. How unrealistic is the assumption of a transport surface?

Let me suggest that for the United States it is not unrealistic. Between the railroads, highways, and waterways, we have a grid that approaches a transport surface. Whole areas are not inaccessible. In consequence, we do see broad belts; cities surrounded by truck garden crops; milk, cream, and butter zones; and other patterns, explicable in terms of transport-demand considerations.

A second assumption, standard in most discussions of market forces, is the absence of externalities; i.e., private costs and benefits are equal to social costs and benefits. In the agricultural sector, this seems to be a reasonable assumption. Robert Frost is our witness. In his "Mending Wall," Frost's neighbor argues that "good fences make good neighbors." His

stand is adamant despite Frost's declaration that:

> He is all pine and I am apple orchard.
> My apple tree will never get across
> And eat the cones under his pines.

Less elegantly, Mr. Frost sees no externalities.

These assumptions plus others combined with market forces enable transport cost-demand variables to assign rents such that agricultural zones are created. A simple piece of casual evidence suggests that the theory and the assignment of agricultural locations is not bad. While we have heard many discussions of agricultural problems, the "problem of bad locations" does not arise.

How does this analysis apply in intra-urban space?

INTRA-URBAN LOCATION PATTERNS VIA AGRICULTURAL LOCATION THEORY

Agricultural location theory does suggest some spatial patterns in terms of the intra-urban location assignment problem specified above.

Given an urban core of some kind, we would expect to find located in that core activities where: (1) face-to-face requirements are high; (2) specialized human labor inputs are needed which may be available outside of the core's large labor pool; and (3) the market is the whole region; i.e., speciality, consumer oriented activities. Outside the core, the single storied manufacturing activities which cannot afford high land rents could be expected. Mingled in with these manufacturing activities are some residential units. And probably the furthest distance from the core would contain the "estate dwellers."

In terms of key variables, these patterns emerge as the result of: (1) technology; e.g., the technology of mass, assembly line production which requires a low single storied manufacturing plant; and (2) communications; e.g., the need for face-to-face contacts versus tele-

---

4 See Edgar S. Dunn, *The Location of Agricultural Production* (Univ. of Florida Press, 1954) and the references cited therein.

phone communication. Transportation facilities and technology are a third key variable. Recall that for our assignment problem a transport surface has been assumed. To the extent that transport costs on the transport surface are low or high, patterns may be expected to expand or contract. Congruent with these patterns, of course, is a rent map of the urban area.

All of this suggests, so far, that the application of agricultural location theory is relevant for intra-urban regions. These patterns are pretty much those described by Hoover and Vernon for the New York metropolitan region.[5] Given the objective of the Hoover and Vernon analysis, which is evidently to take a broad look towards the future, an agricultural type of analysis seems satisfactory.

Yet it does not distract from this type of analysis to suggest that this is not enough. Policy-makers, whoever that group may be, seem to require more specific information; i.e., more detail as to locational patterns. Here an agricultural type of location analysis breaks down.

The difficulty in applying agricultural location theory to the intra-urban region may be simply stated: the assumptions simply do not fit reality. First, urban areas are not transport surfaces and, therefore, simple rings do not emerge. Second, a more critical assumption: the lack of externalities is not valid. Externalities are omnipresent.

The Absence of a Transport Surface

Urban regions, clearly, are not transport surfaces. Even Los Angeles is not an undifferentiated sea of concrete, in spite of the efforts of highway engineers. More often than not, major and minor arteries lead out from the core of cities.

As a result of arteries, urban regions become combinations of rings and arterial spokes; i.e., star shaped. To consider an urban region only in terms of rings can be very misleading. For example, consider the twenty-five to forty mile spoke out of mid-Manhattan running through Connecticut. This segment includes the commuter towns of Greenwich, Stamford, and Dar-

ien. If the segment is moved counterclockwise, a less densely populated region emerges, until the eastern shore of the Hudson River is approached. As even the reader unfamiliar with this area can guess, these denser strips lie along the commuting railroad lines.

This is not the place to ask if there is some optimal number of arteries. Whether a five, six, or n numbered star appears is not relevant. What is relevant is the simple realization that the patterns of urban development we see are not those that emerge from market forces operating on a transport surface. The patterns that result are dependent upon a transport network.

The transport network can well be included as an endogenous variable in any model relying on market forces; e.g., as Lösch has done. No doubt, many intra-urban bus routes are determined by market demands. Yet, the real world is full of imperfections; bridges take time to build; intra-urban railroads may temporarily provide "inadequate" service in the absence of certain tax advantages; some cities may rely on rapid transit for the movement of people while others read the demand for mobility as a call for more freeways. In short, intra-urban location patterns reflect a transport network, and not a transport surface. Thus, agricultural patterns are modified. The transport network may well result from non-market as well as market forces. Hence, patterns are further distorted.

Perhaps the greatest difficulty in applying agricultural location analysis to the urban economy arises when externalities are considered.

Externalities in Intra-urban Space

The usual rules of the game allow only market forces in solving general equilibrium problems. Thus, in imagining any solution to the pure intra-urban location assignment problem stated above, no restrictive governmental actions are allowed. This implies no zoning, control of air pollutions, and other such governmental restrictions and activities. Obviously, it is diffi-

5 Edgar M. Hoover and Raymond Vernon, *Anatomy of a Metropolis* (Harvard Univ. Press, 1959).

cult to imagine what sort of locational patterns might emerge, given the large number of externalities.

The presence of a substantial number of externalities in the urban area arises, in part, in the nature of externalities. Externalities have a spatial extent. While Farmer Jones's chickens and pigs may smell up his barnyard, they do not bother Farmer Brown. Space can isolate or internalize externalities. Yet, as any resident of Chicago can testify, the wafts from the stockyards on ripe days are something less than invigorating. In the case of urban areas, they simply do not have the space to internalize externalities.

Of course, externalities may be positive. Whereas Farmer Jones's attractive front lawn may mean little to Brown, who rarely sees it, in an urban environment the whole neighborhood may enjoy one homeowner's striking landscape.

Geographically, externalities are of varying size. Some are confined only to a neighborhood; e.g., the attractive lawn. Others cover the whole region; e.g., air pollution.

Given the large number of externalities, suppose we seek a stable solution to the intra-urban location assignment problem without government restraints such as zoning. What would be the result? Without rigorous proof, it seems likely that an unending game of musical chairs would result. Maximizing its own advantage, a manufacturing firm may locate in the middle of a residential neighborhood. In turn, the residents may move only to find later another manufacturer in their midst. In short, I am suggesting that a problem exists with even more destabilizing elements than in the simple location assignment problem tackled by Koopmans and Beckmann.[6] Yet, their simple assignment problem had no stable solution.

The achievement of more stable solutions which recognize social costs and benefits may be accomplished when government action is introduced. The control of externalities in the urban region, which can only fall upon governments, removes some of the destabilizing elements. Unlike Frost's view on rural fences, we may analogize that zoning, for example, seeks to make good fences because good fences do make good urban neighbors.

Urban patterns then, to a much greater degree than agricultural patterns, are molded by governmental decisions. The form and mode of transport and the policies to control externalities are all important. In turn, the elements of urban problems are more clearly seen if we reconsider intra-urban location patterns as a joint product of government plus market decisions.

THE INTRA-URBAN LOCATION PROBLEM RECONSIDERED

The twofold source of urban problems is analogous to the sources of error in national income forecasting models. Two sources of error are possible: (1) the endogenous relations are less than perfect; e.g., the consumption function predicts poorly; and (2) exogenous variables are set incorrectly; e.g., government expenditures are higher than assumed.

Suppose we want to solve some urban problem, say traffic congestion. A "good" solution requires: (1) an ability to predict market reactions to an exogenous change; e.g., shopping behavior after the introduction of new one-way streets; and (2) that from the set of possible actions the government chooses the proper action; e.g., new one-way streets versus a new parking lot with shuttle bus service. Errors from either the first or the second imply a degree of nonoptimality.

Stated positively, good solutions require an ability to predict patterns which result from market forces, given governmental actions. Here new theories as well as the extensions of agricultural location theory can help to build better predictive tools. Good solutions simultaneously require appropriate governmental actions. It is the latter requirement that is much neglected and really involves a theory of the spatial aspects of urban finance. Examples will indicate the nature of the problems involved in evaluating the government component.

Consider an urban renewal program. Suppose slums are replaced by low-income hous-

6 Tjalling Koopmans and Martin Beckmann, "Assignment Problems and the Location of Economic Activities," *Econometrica*, Jan., 1957, pp. 53–76.

ing. Assume part of this program is paid for by taxes on the rich. In turn, the rich regroup in a suburban tax colony. As a result of both actions, urban patterns are altered. The slum has been removed, and, hopefully, the neighborhood reclaimed. The rich, now further out in the urban landscape, require commuting facilities. Other ramifications can be imagined.

The question is: Have we a good solution to an urban problem? Clearly, this action has resulted in a redistribution of income. Hence, the goodness or badness of the solution must, at least, consider local governments' function in income redistribution.

Recently, there has been an increased call for area-wide planning as a solution to urban problems. This is a subtle issue.

Area-wide planning is necessarily ineffective in the absence of area-wide government for the functions involved. With area-wide government, such solutions are good only to the extent that, through the political process, the government has somehow ascertained voters'

views on the externalities involved. Without ascertaining preferences, we cannot be sure that governmental actions are solving urban problems consistent with consumer-voter sovereignty.

SUMMARY

In summation, the solution to problems involving the organization of intra-urban space (1) requires a recognition of the role of the government in controlling externalities and influencing the transport network and (2) given governmental restraints, a theory which can predict location patterns. Both are important.

Yet this study, which originated in an attempt to evaluate the possible contribution of intra-urban location theory to the solution of urban problems, leads to the concluding judgment that, in terms of ordering research priorities, further studies on the role of the government win hands down.

DISCUSSION

BARBARA R. BERMAN

Professor Tiebout's paper gives a new and improved prescription for the ingredients of a general equilibrium model of intra-urban location. He would throw out the transport surface in favor of a more realistic cost pattern; he would take account of externalities; and he would elaborate on the effect of governmental decisions on the pattern which emerges.

It would be hard to quarrel with any of these suggestions, so far as they go. To take the last point first, his discussion implies that a single projection of the intra-urban location pattern is useless. What is required is a different projection for each possible set of governmental actions, with the politicians being allowed to choose the one they think most popular in some sense. The proposition that the treatment of government actions as rigidly exogenous to the system is bad practice is true even in the unlikely event that the projection was not explicitly undertaken for the guidance of policymakers.

As to externalities, it can be argued that the effect of the government action is at least partially to internalize them, in the sense that firms which produce external economies are rewarded and those which produce external diseconomies are penalized if they do so. As an example of the latter, zoning laws place artificially infinite rents on sites which would otherwise be eligible; thus forcing a firm to move to a less eligible site and to curtail the external diseconomies it would produce if left to itself. To the extent that externalities are internalized, private optima add up more nearly to social optima. The government fixes the game so that what is good for General Motors *is* good for the country.

When all this is said and done (and easier said than done, of course), we are left with a model—an improved one, to be sure—in which everybody, or all the newcomers in a given period, or, to generalize, a large number optimize simultaneously. I should like to submit that this type of model is inappropriate as a description of the urban location process unless used in a particularly conservative way.

The market for the services of land in an urban area does not operate like Marshall's grain market. In the former, buyers cannot transfer their custom from one seller to another without substantial cost. But it is the possibility of some form of quick and costless recontract which is at the heart of any valid comparative statics approach.

The crops sown on a piece of land can be changed from year to year at relatively small cost, so that one would expect that the method of comparative statics would work quite well in predicting the allocation of agricultural land. But in the urban land market, the order in which buyers attach themselves to particular sellers is crucial. If firm A, with poor or limited foresight, is choosing a location today, it will optimize with respect to the present situation. Firm B, coming along some time after A is established will do the same. Now it may be that the locations of A and B should have been interchanged in the light of the situation after both are established, but the cost of the move will intervene to prevent this from happening.

In the Koopmans and Beckmann article cited by Tiebout, in which the location assignment problem is set up as a problem in linear programming, the authors have this to say about the practical applicability of their model: "Whether a competitive market can find an optimal assignment through a process of alternating adjustments in prices and in choices of location cannot be answered without specifying dynamic characteristics of the market processes in question. [But] there is a possible parallel between the iterative compu-

tation methods for the transportation problem . . . and the market adjustment processes. . . ."

This, I think, is rather egregious. A great gulf of dollars lies between the cost of an arithmetic exercise and the cost of achieving an optimal location pattern in period t, when the particular solution arrived at in period t-1 has turned out to be nonoptimal.

If we look, for example, at the present arrangement of residential areas in a city like New York, it is obvious that if there is any optimizing occurring, it is short-run rather than long-run optimizing. In all truth, how can we expect optimizing with respect to the longer run if the economists themselves have yet to provide projections based on an intellectually respectable model? This might be labeled "the vicious circle of poverty in urban economics."

Thus the urban location problem is, I think, most appropriately tackled by an explicitly dynamic model, or by a series of simultaneous-determination models, each covering a short period. If we are asked the question, "Given that the government will do so and so, and that activities will be carried on at such and such a level, what will the city look like ten or fifteen years from now?" we must, I believe, first answer the question, "What will the city look like one or two years from now?" To answer the latter question may require that we make explicit year-by-year projections of activity levels, and this may be asking too much. So perhaps I had best ask for moderation in quantity rather than a change of quality by restating the point as follows: Great long leaps into the future on the basis of single optimizing models are to be avoided. Just how short the leaps had best be is, I suppose, a matter for practical judgment.

IV

URBAN HOUSING AND RACIAL INTEGRATION

Theories of Race and Property Value

LUIGI M. LAURENTI

Before presenting the factual evidence from the several studies which have been made concerning the effects of racial change on property values, it will be instructive to examine the positions taken on this subject by real estate and finance spokesmen, land economists, and others. Most of their conclusions are unaccompanied by supporting evidence, although such evidence may have been observed by the writers. However, several statements are based on actual field study, and these findings are discussed in later sections of this report.

In examining the statements that have appeared over the past forty years, an evolutionary shift in their scope and tone becomes apparent. Generally, the earlier ones are marked by much more sweeping and unqualified predictions. This is particularly true of statements in real estate textbooks and articles. These are examined first, followed by a survey of the price behavior predictions made by three other groups: real estate brokers, lenders, and builders; professional students of housing; and the Federal Housing Administration.

THE PROFESSIONAL REAL ESTATE LITERATURE

Professional writings have probably played a continuing role in shaping the beliefs that motivate brokers, builders, lenders, and appraisers. They reveal what theories have been and are accepted in the real estate field.

Thirty to forty years ago, the pronouncements of the real estate experts were uniformly gloomy concerning what would happen to prices if a nonwhite should move into a white neighborhood. The following are representative of the 1923–1933 period:

It is a matter of common observation that the purchase of property by certain racial types is very likely to diminish the value of other property in the section.[1]

With the increase of colored people coming to many Northern cities they have over-

run their old districts and swept into adjoining ones or passed to other sections and formed new ones. This naturally has had a decidedly detrimental effect on land values for few white people, however inclined to be sympathetic with the problem of the colored race, care to live near them. Property values have been sadly depreciated by having a single colored family settle down on a street occupied exclusively by white residents.[2]

The mere threat . . . of an undesirable encroachment [differing race or nationality] must many times be recognized by a reduced unit value for the house.[3]

Neighborhoods populated by white persons have been invaded by colored families, and often aristocratic residential districts have suffered tremendous lessening of property values because of the appearance of a Negro resident.[4]

It is in the twilight zone, where members of different races live together, that racial mixtures tend to have a depressing effect upon land values—and therefore, upon rents.[5]

In the next group of statements, dating from 1932 to 1955, there appears a clear tendency to think about the problem more critically.

From *Property Values and Race* (Berkeley: University of California Press, 1960), pp. 8–27. Reprinted by permission of the publisher.

1 Ernest M. Fisher, *Principles of Real Estate Practice* (New York: The Macmillan Company, 1923), p. 116. Cited in Charles Abrams, *Forbidden Neighbors* (New York: Harper and Brothers, 1955), p. 155.
2 Stanley L. McMichael and Robert F. Bingham, *City Growth and Values* (Cleveland: The Stanley McMichael Publishing Organization, 1923), p. 181. Cited in Abrams, *Forbidden Neighbors*, p. 159.
3 George A. Schneider, *California Real Estate Principles and Practices* (New York: Prentice-Hall, Inc., 1927), p. 315. Cited in Abrams, *Forbidden Neighbors*, p. 160.
4 McMichael and Bingham, *City Growth and Values*, p. 370.
5 Homer Hoyt, *The Structure and Growth of Residential Neighborhoods in American Cities* (Washington, D.C.: Federal Housing Administration, 1939), p. 62.

The depressing influence of nonwhite entry is still asserted, but is qualified to various degrees by the recognition of other factors such as socioeconomic levels, physical condition of the neighborhood before entry, and price ranges of homes in the area:

Families in any particular class, who rise in economic status, move to a better district. If they have a degree of inferiority they damage that community, displace the occupying class, and lower values. . . . Most of the variations and differences between people are slight and value declines are, therefore, gradual. But there is one difference in people, namely race, which can result in a very rapid decline.[6]

Certain racial and national groups, because of their lower economic status and their lower standards of living, pay less rent themselves and cause a greater physical deterioration of property than groups higher in the social and economic scale. . . . Land values in areas occupied by such classes are therefore inevitably low. Part of the attitude reflected in lower land values is due entirely to racial prejudice, which may have no reasonable basis. Nevertheless, if the entrance of a colored family into a white neighborhood causes a general exodus of the white people, such dislikes are reflected in property values.[7]

In the appraisal of homes, general data covering the city and surrounding territory must be considered. . . . Even more intensive must be the study of the immediate neighborhoods . . . ; characteristics and background of the residents of the neighborhood; presence or threat of intrusion of discordant racial groups; and other conditions having a bearing on the present and future desirability of the location.[8]

It [the effect of Negroes on property values] has a most important bearing on future developments in our housing program. Appraisers are interested in the problem from many angles. In addition, they desire the problem to be considered objectively from one specific point; i.e., does Negro occupancy have a tendency to blight only the area where it occurs, or does it blight the surrounding white area, with a correspond-

ing decrease in valuation and loss of tenants . . . ? It cannot be denied that his presence in large groups has the effect of blight upon the surrounding property. The first blight which we must mention is the mental blight or the depreciation in psychological worth. Some Negroes may take better care of their property, they may be as law abiding, they may have an equal education, they may in fact be just as fine citizens as their white neighbors, but we all know countless neighborhoods and communities where the presence of one Negro family will cause many white families to move out. There is an immediate falling off in rentals of surrounding property and a corresponding depreciation in value, more Negro families move in and then the returns are greater and the color line blight moves to the next block. . . . In fairness, we must admit it is not always the Negro occupancy alone which causes blight; the contributing factor may be the age and condition of buildings in which these people are housed that causes the trouble.[9]

The third type of depreciation is economic obsolescence. This is a loss of value which comes from conditions outside of the property itself, such as: 1. an oversupply of houses in the area; 2. change in character of use in the neighborhood; 3. legislative enactment, such as zoning changes; 4. proximity to nuisance; 5. racial infiltration; 6. under- or overimprovement. . . . Economic depreciation can be measured by making a careful comparison of value between property in the subject neighborhood and in ideal neighborhoods.[10]

Racial encroachment has less effect on

6 Frederick M. Babcock, *Valuation of Real Estate* (New York: McGraw-Hill Book Co., Inc., 1932), pp. 88 and 91.
7 Homer Hoyt, *One Hundred Years of Land Values in Chicago* (Chicago: University of Chicago Press, 1933), p. 314. Cited in Abrams, *Forbidden Neighbors*, p. 160.
8 David Neiswanger, M.A.I., "Appraising the Small Home," *The Appraisal Journal*, V, no. 2 (April, 1937), 124.
9 Elsie Smith Parker, "Both Sides of the Color Line," *The Appraisal Journal*, XI, no. 3 (July, 1943), 232-234.
10 A. M. McDonald, "Appraising Residential Property," *The Appraisal Journal*, XXI, no. 2 (April, 1953), 264.

high-grade property than upper-medium, medium, or lower-medium grades. Perhaps the reason for this is that only the select representatives of the encroaching race come into high-grade property.[11]

During the 1940's, three new ideas were advanced by several appraisers and other real estate professionals. The first two were (1) that minority occupancy might only "threaten" values, and (2) that while nonwhites might cause market disruptions which would *temporarily* depress prices, eventual neighborhood stability would move prices up again. Some said prices would settle at a level below the old one; others maintained they might return to the previous level, or even higher:

> From this we may generalize that, in the city that houses a large percentage of people of foreign birth, or their children, or that contains a substantial minority percentage of people of races other than white, residential real estate values in the older districts bordering those at present inhabited by the minority peoples will exist in a state of threatened status quo.[12]
>
> Frequently the presence of inharmonious racial, national, or income groups in an adjoining area represents a threat to property values.[13]
>
> That the entry of non-Caucasians into districts where distinctly Caucasian residents live tends to depress real estate values is agreed to by practically all real estate subdividers and students of city life and growth. Infiltration at the outset may be slow, but once the trend is established, values start to drop, until properties can be purchased at discounts of from 50 to 75 per cent. . . . Later, when a district has been entirely taken over, values tend to re-establish themselves to meet the needs and demands of the new occupants.[14]
>
> Should a shift to a buyers' market start in any neighborhood, prices of less attractive houses are the first and most detrimentally affected. This has been markedly true where the shift is from white to Negro population, and the first two or three houses are usually sold to Negroes at a few hundred dollars above the market. In a few months

sales prices drop below prices for comparable houses on white-owned and occupied streets. After the change is past the halfway mark, prices stabilize at an average price of perhaps 10 per cent below prices of comparable houses in white neighborhoods. The loss of price, however, is much greater on a street of mansion-type houses or on a street of sub-standard housing. Rentals are about the same in like quarters, whether rented by whites or Negroes.[15]

In a recent edition of *McMichael's Appraising Manual*, a basic reference, the author modifies the pessimistic predictions about values in transition areas that appeared in earlier versions:

> Whether rightly or wrongly, some families avoid or leave a neighborhood of mixed race or national origin. This reduces the market for homes in the area and consequently may at first affect values adversely. As the neighborhood takes on its new character, and assuming equal maintenance of all property, value trends may reverse.[16]

The third new opinion that developed during the 1940's is that nonwhite entry does not harm—and may even improve—values. In a 1942 ruling on a race restrictive covenant case in the U.S. Court of Appeals for the District of Columbia, Chief Justice Groner evidently

---

11 Thurston H. Ross, "Market Significance of Declining Neighborhoods," *The Appraisal Journal*, XXIII, no. 2 (April, 1955), 203–211. This article analyzes the market problems of declining neighborhoods in general, with only incidental reference to racial factors.
12 Arthur A. May, *The Valuation of Residential Real Estate* (New York: Prentice-Hall, Inc., 1942), p. 75. Cited in Abrams, *Forbidden Neighbors*, p. 165.
13 Arthur M. Weimer and Homer Hoyt, *Principles of Real Estate* (3rd ed.; New York: The Ronald Press, 1954), p. 373.
14 Stanley L. McMichael, *Real Estate Subdivisions* (New York: Prentice-Hall, Inc., 1949), pp. 204–205.
15 George A. Phillips, "Racial Infiltration," *The Review of the Society of Residential Appraisers*, XVI, no. 2 (February, 1950), 8. Quoted with permission of the Society of Residential Appraisers, 7 South Dearborn Street, Chicago 3, Illinois.
16 Stanley L. McMichael, *McMichael's Appraising Manual* (4th ed.; New York: Prentice-Hall, Inc., 1951), p. 169. For his earlier statements, see footnotes 2, 4, and 14.

felt that the technical real estate evidence was favorable to values, for he said:

> The evidence satisfies us that the effect . . . [of a racial change in neighborhood occupancy] is to make the market value of property on Thirteenth Street . . . greater for colored occupancy than for white. There is also evidence to the effect that the local citizens association, upon learning that appellants' vendor contemplated selling to appellants or other Negroes, tried to procure a white purchaser, and that one of the appellee himself had purchased the house . . . from Home Owners Loan Corporation for $2,000 less than the corporation was offered by a colored bishop . . . the covenant would merely depreciate all the property in the block. . . .[17]

Perhaps the best known statement by a professional appraiser supporting the view that nonwhite occupancy may actually be beneficial to values appeared in 1945. In introducing George W. Beehler, Jr.'s article, the editor remarked that "his reasoning and factual support for it establish a new concept for appraising areas under transition of occupancy." In Beehler's own words:

> . . . to show that values have increased, we can cite sections newly occupied by colored during the past two or three years that have increased in value from 60 to 100 per cent on the average. This is due, primarily, to the fact that values in these sections, occupied by white and subject to colored encroachment around the edges, have remained static, while the colored section surrounding has felt the usual increase in values due to the so-called housing shortage and the changing economic value of the dollar as represented by its purchasing power. Then, within a six-month period, when colored occupancy enters a new block it picks up as much as the surrounding sections already occupied by colored people in a much shorter period of time. From that point on the values continue to increase along with other areas.[18]

During the process of racial transition, properties move through three stages of price be-

havior, according to Beehler's analysis. These are (1) an initial period of stagnation followed by (2) continued stagnation or slight price declines, but eventually reaching (3) a period of rising prices:

> White owners ordinarily do not want to be the first to put in colored and the other white people will not buy in the block, so that the only market is that made by the speculator who is buying to hold for a substantially increased price. Then, when the block is first broken, panic sets in among the remaining white owners and sales signs suddenly appear on more than half of the properties. For a short period after that the white owners compete with one another on prices in their desire to vacate. During this period prices either are at the old static figure or in some cases slightly under. When the panic ceases and most of the properties exposed for sale have been sold at this static figure, then gradually prices increase until the block becomes predominantly colored and then the remaining white owners secure a substantially higher price than those who sold earlier.[19]

The new price level holds up firmly and continues to move in accordance with city-wide trends, although Beehler states that the increase in better, newly established nonwhite sections is slightly higher than in similar white areas. Beehler concludes that "Neighborhood values in areas newly occupied by colored people have sharply increased and *will continue to increase.*" He feels this statement will be "startling" to the one out of ten "real estate men [who are] still living fifteen or twenty years in the past when *all* colored occupancy had an adverse effect on real estate values."

Beehler's prediction is challenged by an-

17 *Hundley and Hundley* v. *Gorewitz, Bogikes and Bogikes,* U.S. Court of Appeals for the District of Columbia, December 14, 1942, cited by Robert C. Weaver in *The Negro Ghetto* (New York: Harcourt, Brace and Company, 1948), p. 268, n.
18 George W. Beehler, Jr., "Colored Occupancy Raises Values," *The Review of the Society of Residential Appraisers,* XI, no. 9 (September, 1945), 3–4. Quoted with permission of the Society of Residential Appraisers.
19 *Ibid.* Quoted with permission of the Society of Residential Appraisers.

other appraiser, Oscar I. Stern, well known for his articles in the professional journals. He doubts that colored occupancy will increase values over a period of time in the Philadelphia neighborhoods discussed.[20] Stern agrees that pent-up Negro demand for homes resulted in premium prices, but defines the premium as "exploitation" rather than an addition to value. He concludes that values in transition neighborhoods may be *sustained,* in comparison with similar all-white neighborhoods, but will not stay relatively higher permanently. However, he ends with the firm view that "It is a fact, the axiom that colored infiltration collapses the market is no longer true."

In a later article Stern observed that "Neighborhood mutations have been accelerated. The old notion of Negro infiltration adversely affecting values is now shopworn. We are striking blindly at a situation, ignorant of its causative background. We lack a realistic program to handle it." [21]

In a general analysis of the market significance of declining neighborhoods, the professional appraiser Thurston Ross holds that nonwhites, under certain conditions, may stabilize or possibly enhance values in such neighborhoods.

> In poor and slum sections racial encroachment sometimes raises the economic standards of the neighborhood. There are instances where obsolescence has been arrested and a number of additional years of useful life given a neighborhood by racial encroachment, particularly when older people are displaced by younger groups of the encroaching race. Furthermore, a sufficient identity must be given the neighborhood so that the market is stimulated to encourage additional members of the encroaching race to come into the area, thus keeping the market active, rather than by being depressed by the loss of a favorable identity because of the encroachment of only a few members into the neighborhood.[22]

Reconsideration of long accepted generalizations about race and value is strongly urged by Belden Morgan, formerly deputy chief appraiser of the FHA office in Los Angeles. He writes:

Right now a change is taking place in appraisal thought with respect to the opinion held on the effect of the "infiltration" or "invasion" of minority groups on white neighborhoods. . . . To approach this problem without prejudice is difficult indeed. Over the years we have been brought up with deeply ingrained emotional feelings that we cannot shake off with ease simply by saying we will. Inevitably, some reservation of prejudice will be retained, and we probably will not be free of it for several generations. Most appraisal texts treat the problem from the viewpoint of 20 years ago when it was commonly believed by nearly all that the presence of Negroes or other minorities in a neighborhood was a serious value-destroying influence. . . . There are many locations where such generalizations are no longer true.[23]

These recent statements indicate a readiness on the part of professional real estate people to analyze actual developments as they occur. Evidently, "automatic" reduction of an appraisal because nonwhites are in the neighbor-

20 Oscar I. Stern, "Long Range Effect of Colored Occupancy," *The Review of the Society of Residential Appraisers,* XII, no. 1 (January, 1946), 4–6. Quoted with permission of the Society of Residential Appraisers.
21 Oscar I. Stern, "The End of the Restrictive Covenant," *The Appraisal Journal,* XVI, no. 4 (October, 1948), 439.
22 Ross, *The Appraisal Journal,* XXIII, no. 2, 205.
23 Belden Morgan, "Values in Transition Areas: Some New Concepts," *The Review of the Society of Residential Appraisers,* XVIII, no. 3 (March, 1952), 5–9. Quoted with permission of the Society of Residential Appraisers.

It is significant that Morgan is one of the few real estate representatives writing in the field who encloses words like "infiltration" and "invasion" in quotation marks. Such punctuation suggests that the user does not wish to go along with the implication that nonwhite entry is literally an infiltration or invasion of a white neighborhood.

In this connection, the vocabulary frequently encountered in the literature describing nonwhite population movement around or into a white area is indicative of the tension and hostility felt by many whites. Words like "threat," "encroachment," "encirclement," "penetration," "intrusion," "infiltration," "invasion," "infestation," "inundation," and "infection" appear to be consciously or unconsciously chosen to draw a parallel between the manifestations of war and sickness on the one hand and the entry of nonwhites into white areas on the other.

hood is no longer considered to reflect real value conditions, at least by some appraisers and brokers.

It is possible that the older statements are not so much erroneous as out of date. The years since 1940 have witnessed great changes in social and economic conditions and in the status of nonwhite minorities—changes that have altered the character of racial occupancy in housing. Further changes must inevitably come, and they will in turn qualify present-day statements about race and value.

THE REAL ESTATE BROKER, LENDER, AND BUILDER

As one would expect, the beliefs held by those in the housing industry reflect the professional literature very closely. It is instructive to observe, nevertheless, how the broadly worded theories and generalizations in the literature have more specifically worded counterparts in the field of practice.[24]

The Broker.—Many brokers and salesmen belong to local real estate boards, which in turn make up the National Association of Real Estate Boards. The local boards, numbering over 1,100, control the bulk of real estate selling activity in most communities in the country. Members are known as "realtors" and are bound to operate their businesses in accordance with the NAREB code of ethics, as well as their own local codes. For a quarter of a century, up to its revision in 1950, Article 34 of the National Code stated: "A realtor should never be instrumental in introducing into a neighborhood a character of property or occupancy, *members of any race or nationality,* or any individual whose presence will clearly be detrimental to property values in the neighborhood."[25]

As revised, the article now stipulates: "A realtor should never be instrumental in introducing into a neighborhood a character of property or use which will clearly be detrimental to property values in that neighborhood."[26]

Despite this rewording, most realtors appear to understand the article in the same sense as before, and to continue to act accordingly. In addition, most local real estate boards have their own code of ethics forbidding members to introduce "detrimental" minorities into neighborhoods.[27] Any realtor who violates the code is subject to expulsion or suspension from the local board, a penalty that would have disastrous effects on his real estate business. Property owners in the neighborhood where he handles real estate may take their business elsewhere, and he may lose valuable business contacts. Thus, even those who might be inclined to challenge the old generalizations about nonwhites and property values are given pause by the thought of the direct economic losses and group pressures that could follow.

Very few systematic inquiries into broker and lender attitudes and practices have been made. One recent study, however, is based on interviews with representatives of sixty-four real estate firms and ten mortgage lending institutions in San Francisco,[28] and presents evidence on the general opinions and business methods encountered in the real estate field.

An important aspect of broker behavior emerged in response to the question, "What direct or indirect information do you have regarding what happens when a nonwhite family first moves into a neighborhood?" One broker out of three felt that "there is a sizeable threat to the business of the broker who is thought to have arranged such a sale."[29] Presumably this would occur through local boycott by an-

24 Beliefs and attitudes concerning race and property values held by members of the housing industry are, of course, related to more widely held racial attitudes. The general subject of racial attitudes in housing is treated in two special studies prepared for the Commission on Race and Housing: Claire Selltiz and Stuart W. Cook, "Studies in the Social Psychology of Race and Housing" (unpublished), and Helen E. Amerman, "Studies of Attitudes Toward Housing and Race" (unpublished).
25 National Association of Real Estate Boards, *Code of Ethics,* adopted June, 1924. Italics supplied.
26 *Ibid.,* revised November 17, 1950.
27 The comment made by one broker is typical: "Our Code doesn't mention race, but certain things are understood." Personal interview, San Francisco, October 5, 1955.
28 Constance C. Jensen, John Lindberg, George L. Smith, "The Minority Group Housing Market in San Francisco, with Special Reference to Real Estate Broker and Mortgage Financing Practices" (unpublished Master's research project, School of Social Welfare, University of California, Berkeley, 1955).
29 *Ibid.,* p. 21.

gered property owners in the offending broker's home territory. It follows that many brokers, regardless of their personal beliefs, would not handle a transaction that would bring the first nonwhite into a residential neighborhood.

But the broker's unwillingness to handle such business evidently is not the chief problem: when asked to specify the difficulties nonwhites run into in attempting to buy a home in an all-white area, half the brokers mentioned the owners' unwillingness to sell. About a third gave neighborhood opposition as the reason, with financing problems a close third. Only one broker in five said that the *broker's* unwillingness to sell was a major difficulty.[30]

On the other hand, brokers can set up obstacles to nonwhite purchase even if the sellers do not. To the question, "If the seller says he will sell to anyone, regardless of race, what do you do?" over 85 percent of the brokers replying said they try to avoid handling such sales, while 13 percent said they are willing to carry them through on an unrestricted basis.[31]

The study summarizes three main reasons that impel brokers to restrict nonwhites to a special housing market. To violate an established neighborhood pattern would, they believe, damage their business income and reputation, go against the wishes of most of the white residents, and depreciate property values.[32]

Some of the actual comments made by brokers point up the specific role that the property value question plays in their decisions: [33]

"What happens is that one person sells to a Negro for spite; then a whole block is ruined."

"Property values decline permanently; about 25 per cent in the case of Negroes, less for Orientals."

"When Negroes move into a block, adjoining property goes down in value $1,000 to $2,000."

"If you flood the neighborhood, you cut your own throat. It lowers property values and doesn't help your reputation either."

Additional comments, gathered from interviews conducted during the present study, confirm this pattern among brokers: [34]

Insofar as we can, we try to control the character of occupancy in the neighborhoods in which we sell. The area between 25th and 31st, north of Noriega, is being reserved for high-type whites, and this policy will pay off over time by protecting neighborhood standards and values. By screening applicants we can keep out undesirables, although it isn't always easy to tell who is undesirable. Of course, minority groups aren't wanted out here, and most of them know better than to contact us. The other day the phone rang and it was an answer to our newspaper ad, which hadn't mentioned the location of the property. A dark woman's voice inquired about the location and when told it was in the Avenues she hastily said: "Oh, that's no place for us colored," and hung up. We sometimes have a Chinese or Japanese prospect walk in, but we get rid of them by saying that there is a deposit on the property they're interested in. We haven't yet had to prove we had a deposit, but could easily have one of our office staff make one up if needed.

We San Francisco realtors have adopted the National Code of Ethics which forbids us to be instrumental in introducing a use or character of occupancy which will clearly be detrimental to neighborhood values. It is under this instruction that we feel justified in turning away people who would be undesirable to the community and who would thus harm values.

Values fall about $1,000 or $1,500 in the vicinity of a nonwhite. That is how much the price has to be shaded in order to move it to white buyers. I don't think nonwhites pay more than market to get into a white neighborhood. In fact, in the case of Chinese, they drive a very hard bargain. They will offer perhaps $13,000 for a $15,000 home.

30   *Ibid.*, p. 23.
31   *Ibid.*, p. 30.
32   *Ibid.*, p. 35.
33   *Ibid.*, pp. 44–49.
34   Personal interviews with San Francisco Bay Area brokers during 1951 and 1955.

In a short housing market, there is no difference in income performance of white vs. nonwhite properties. But prospective buyers [of income properties] still demand a discount or refuse to buy, regardless of realistic analysis of income. Perhaps some justification exists for this, in view of possible future unemployment of nonwhites, but much of buyers' behavior seems irrational. Attitudes of whites are changing under pressure of circumstances of the last seven or eight years.

If nonwhites, especially Negroes, hit a white district, where they are not desired, they depress property values in the eyes of other whites. But nonwhites will pay more than whites after the area is entered.

Effect of nonwhite entry or presence is to drop prices about $1,500, on the average. Banks and other lending agencies hasten this process of value loss, since they make financing difficult if subject property is within one block of colored.

Prices drop fully 20 per cent due to colored coming in, because properties just aren't movable to whites. A realtor who sold to a nonwhite in the Sunset area now can't get loans on any property because of anger of financial people, real estate groups, and the community. He is going out of business.

One of the most interesting points made in these broker comments is the recurring theme that while sellers may not get their price from whites (who are reluctant to consider an area undergoing racial transition), they probably can from nonwhites. This is quite different from the unqualified prediction that all prices in an "invaded" area fall.

A public statement by the San Francisco Real Estate Board indicates that the foregoing comments reflect the practices followed by at least those brokers and salesmen who are Board members:

It is a matter of fact and experience that when a Negro or Chinese or Japanese or Filipino moves into a white district, the house values drop. . . . Other whites won't buy into the district. Owners can only sell to other Negroes and so value goes down and down. . . . We don't look at this as a

social problem. That's not our job. For us this is an economic problem. Looking at it this way, the Board has asked that its members "not introduce" into a residential district "any occupancy or race" which will have the effect of lowering values.[35]

The Lender.—The impact of the property value question on lending policies is suggested by the response noted in the Jensen-Lindberg-Smith study in interviews with ten mortgage lending firms. Two-thirds of the lenders felt that "the encroachment of minorities upon a white neighborhood made it more difficult for prospective borrowers in that area to obtain loans." [36]

Lenders, like brokers, especially avoid "first-entry" sales to nonwhites, and for the same reasons:

They were unanimous in giving business considerations as the justification for this practice. Eighty per cent stated that their depositors or policy holders in the neighborhood would threaten to withdraw their accounts, and at least one in three mentioned that the lowered property values would adversely affect their mortgages held on other properties in the neighborhood.[37]

Field interviews for the present study revealed further detail on lender beliefs and policies: [38]

A savings and loan association: We have about 4,000 depositors, most of whom live in the area in which we make loans. Almost all are Caucasian. At least 150 of them have plainly told me that they would not tolerate the use of their funds to install nonwhites in this area, and that they would withdraw their deposits if we adopted such a policy. If the time ever comes when nonwhites in this area make appreciable deposits with

35 "The Negro in San Francisco," *San Francisco Chronicle*, November 6, 1950.
36 Jensen, Lindberg, and Smith, "The Minority Group Housing Market in San Francisco . . . ," p. 40.
37 *Ibid.*, p. 41.
38 From personal interviews with San Francisco Bay Area mortgage lenders during 1951 and 1955.

our association, we may be able to make loans to them here.

A savings and loan association: Nonwhite entry destroys property values only to whites, not to nonwhites. That is, sellers will lose only if they are determined to sell to whites. They can get their price from colored.

Another savings and loan association: We make loans to colored in established areas only. If they were introduced into a new area, values would fall 50 per cent. There are lots of things we would like to do personally, such as treating everybody equally, but we are responsible for millions of dollars and we cannot jeopardize our reputation and business standing by going against community wishes. We will lend on properties up to three blocks away from colored areas, but no closer, because we anticipate such areas will spread, and when they do the values fall to the point where we might be loaning 100 per cent or more of the value.

A large bank: There definitely is a detrimental value impact following establishment of nonwhite residence in a white neighborhood. We refused to finance a 180-unit all-Negro development because of the anticipated value repercussions on surrounding white areas, and have turned down similar smaller projects for the same reason.

A large life insurance company: The effects of racial infiltration are often discussed among the lending agencies and, although we have no factual evidence to present, we are unanimous in the opinion that it harms values. It depresses the neighborhood and thus decreases the amount we will loan on any particular property. A single Negro in a block in the Sunset area would be like a caution flag to us to note the trend of the neighborhood and would probably be sufficient to influence our loans downward in that area.

The Builder.—The apprehension of lenders about property values in areas of racial change is echoed by the builders, who fear marketing difficulties will arise out of mixed racial patterns. A spokesman for one of the largest home building corporations in the San Francisco Bay Area typifies the general position of most builders:

Nonwhite entry has unfortunate effects. In the Richmond area, white owners let their property run down because they lost interest in the standards of the neighborhood after colored came in. It doesn't matter whether colored entrants are "good" or "bad" in type; their color is the thing, and their color stagnates the affected area because white people don't want them as neighbors. . . . We hold many vacant lots throughout the city for future development —perhaps enough for as many as 3,000 new single family units. But our development of those is sensitive to existing and developing racial patterns. If colored have come too close to some of our lots we will sell them and not build, because we couldn't market anything on them.[39]

It is evident, then, that brokers, lenders, and builders—those who create, sell, and resell homes—often believe that nonwhite occupancy is not good for property values. This belief influences their decisions to build, finance, sell, and buy in ways that restrict the opportunities of nonwhites to acquire housing and limit them to certain districts.

PROFESSIONAL STUDENTS OF HOUSING

Experts in sociology and urban land economics have typically taken the position that more knowledge was needed concerning the actual effects of nonwhite entry on an all-white neighborhood. Until sufficient empirical evidence should become available, they have urged the avoidance of fixed opinions in the matter, and have pointed out the theoretical reasons why a number of price behavior patterns are possible.

In his classic study, however, Gunnar Myrdal painted a somewhat pessimistic picture of the economic aspects of "invasion" in the large cities of the North:

When white residents of a neighborhood see that they cannot remove the few Negro intruders and also see more Negro families moving in, they conjure up certain stereo-

39 Personal interview, San Francisco, November, 1951.

types of how bad Negro neighbors are and move out of the neighborhood with almost panic speed. For this reason Negroes are dangerous for property values, as well as for neighborhood business, and all whites are aware of this fact. . . . If white property owners in a neighborhood rush to sell their property all at once, property values naturally are hurt. After the transition to Negro occupancy is made, however, property values rise again at least to the level justified by the aging and lack of improvement of the buildings.[40]

Myrdal's view that prices first dipped, then recovered to their old level or nearly so, was voiced at about the same time that the professional real estate literature was beginning to suggest the same thing.

In 1948, Robert Weaver undertook the most comprehensive survey of facts and theories about the race and value question that had been done up to that time, devoting a chapter of his book, *The Negro Ghetto,* to the topic. After reviewing the scarce and conflicting evidence, Weaver suggested some general theories about the possible economic consequences of nonwhite entry—theories that provide a framework for a variety of empirical findings:

The effect of Negro occupancy upon property values varies from one section of the city to another and from one time to another. Within a given area, the initial result of the arrival of a few colored people may be imperceptible or it may lead to panic among white occupants; the arrival of a few Negroes may be the signal for a great decline in selling prices or it may lead to an appreciable increase. Much depends upon the state of the total housing market and the manner in which colored people enter an area. Or, again, prices may fall with large-scale Negro introduction only to recover again as the transition is completed. Out of all of these possibilities . . . a separate and obviously incomplete theory of the relationship between racial occupancy and property values could be formulated. No such theory would be sound. *There is no one universal effect of Negro occupancy upon property values.*[41]

The manner in which nonwhites affect values in particular areas depends, in Weaver's view, on what is happening to four factors: (1) nonwhite income distribution; (2) general business conditions at the time of nonwhite entry; (3) long-run trend of values in the area before entry; and (4) how nonwhite occupancy actually occurs.[42]

Charles Abrams, author of many works on housing, agrees with Weaver in suggesting that many different price patterns may follow "minority infiltration": [43]

The statement that one race or group inevitably affects prices favorably and another unfavorably disregards the complex of factors which play a part, such as the social and economic status of a particular minority at a particular time; its numbers in relation to the numbers in the majority group; the latter's social and cultural level; the minority's capacity for social improvement and assimilation; the size of the city and the physical condition of its neighborhoods; the particular pattern of minority distribution; the nature of the then current minority stereotype; the type of social and educational leadership and maturity in the community; the social and economic role of the minority in the community; the relationship between the groups in employment, and a host of other factors. . . . . There are no fixed rules as to when minority neighbors raise or lower values; examples may be cited both ways and much study is still needed.[44]

These scholarly approaches to the problem leave the door open to a range of factual answers. They point out that the factor of race is only one of many that affect real estate prices, and that quite often it may by no means be the most important one.

40 Gunnar Myrdal, *An American Dilemma* (New York: Harper and Brothers, 1944), p. 623.
41 Weaver, *The Negro Ghetto,* p. 293. Italics in original.
42 *Ibid.,* pp. 297–298.
43 Abrams, *Forbidden Neighbors,* pp. 285–286. See also, by the same author, "The New 'Gresham's Law' of Neighborhoods—Fact or Fiction," *The Appraisal Journal,* XIX no. 3 (July, 1951).
44 Abrams, *Forbidden Neighbors,* pp. 286, 292.

THE FEDERAL HOUSING ADMINISTRATION

The Federal Housing Administration has altered its earlier adherence to racially homogeneous neighborhoods. Its old view was put forth in the following provision of its *Underwriting Manual* for 1938: "If a neighborhood is to retain stability it is necessary that properties shall continue to be occupied by the same social and racial classes." [45]

Consistent with this theory, the FHA, because of its conviction that declining property values would result from a mixed neighborhood, thus endangering the long-range financing involved, formerly insisted that residential projects desiring FHA-insured financing draw up restrictive covenants against nonwhites. In recent years FHA has adopted the opposite position, refusing to insure projects where a written racially restrictive covenant exists. Concerning property values and race, the *Underwriting Manual* now states: "The tendency of user groups to seek compatible conditions can sustain and enhance, diminish or destroy neighborhood desirability. . . . If a mixture of user groups is found to exist, it must be determined whether the mixture will render the neighborhood less desirable to present and prospective occupants." [46]

THE SELF-FULFILLING PROPHECY

The beliefs, policies, and practices that have been briefly reviewed thus far interweave with each other, and with other real estate market factors, to produce many patterns of price behavior. In the interweaving process, a circular kind of "belief-cause-effect-and-belief" phenomenon often takes place, which operates to magnify and reinforce the barriers affecting nonwhites.

For example, if many white homeowners believe that their new Negro neighbor will cause neighborhood property values to drop, they may "panic," frantically list their homes for sale, and compete with each other for buyers. Such a sudden rise in the supply of homes in a small market area may well mean that not enough buyers can be found, whether white or nonwhite. Homes may not sell for weeks, even months, and when they do it may be at prices that have had to be discounted sharply to at-

tract buyers from a wider radius. The result is that prices have fallen, just as the homeowners expected, and their faith in the formula that "Negroes hurt value" is made stronger than ever.

Again, mortgage lenders in a certain city may all feel the same way about a particular white neighborhood that has recently experienced the entry of one or two nonwhite families: "Its days as a first-class residential area are numbered; values will inevitably drop." Consequently, lending policies for that area will be modified. The percentage of loan to appraisal will be reduced, and appraisals themselves may gradually move downward because of subjective value judgments influencing the appraisers' objective approach. As a result, effective demand for homes in that area will be lower than it would be under ordinary circumstances, because potential buyers cannot get as large loans as before. Prices will fall, relative to other areas where lending policies remain the same, and the lenders' predictive judgment will be vindicated by events.

Probably, neither the homeowners nor the lenders in these examples realize that their own beliefs have influenced them to act in ways that bring about the results they have predicted. It is this very unawareness of their own role in predetermining history that makes the process effective. Considering that the beliefs themselves are open to question, the process demonstrates its capacity for making an unreal definition of a situation produce real results. As Robert Merton's analysis puts it: "The self-fulfilling prophecy is, in the beginning, a *false* definition of the situation evoking a new behavior which makes the originally false conception come *true*." [47] He regards the process as a tragicomic one: tragic in the sense that false or questionable predictions are sanctified by prediction-induced consequences; comic in that "the prophet will cite the actual course of events as proof that he was right from the very beginning."

From these observations on beliefs about race

45 Federal Housing Administration, *Underwriting Manual*, 1938, sec. 937.
46 *Ibid.*, Rev. 1952, sec. 1320.
47 Robert K. Merton, "The Self-fulfilling Prophecy," *The Antioch Review*, VIII, no. 2 (Summer, 1946), 208. Italics in original.

and value, representing many points of view, at least three general conclusions emerge:

1. The fear that property values are seriously damaged by nonwhite neighbors has been very generally felt among both real estate business circles and individual property owners.

2. This widespread fear has for many years contributed heavily to the confining of nonwhites to narrow housing markets. Restrictive selling, building, and lending policies have combined to produce this result.

3. Some questions have recently been raised concerning the precise effects of nonwhite occupancy on property values. These questions have emphasized the contrast between sweeping pessimistic generalizations and the lack of evidence to support them, and have drawn attention to the interplay of socioeconomic factors.

Effects of Nonwhite Purchases on Market Prices of Residences

LUIGI M. LAURENTI

Prior to 1940 the nonwhites in San Francisco were concentrated in two areas—Western Addition and Chinatown.[1] Furthermore, they lived not as home owners in single-family dwellings, but as tenants in multi-family, and usually old, converted properties. Overcrowding and substandard conditions closely approximated those in the long-established racial areas of Chicago and New York, except that nonwhites by no means outnumbered whites in the Western Addition.

Events of the decade following 1940 led to significant changes in the density, racial composition, and personal income of San Francisco residents, ushering in new patterns in nonwhite residential locations and home ownership. Responding to the employment opportunities arising from the defense effort, more than five million persons streamed westward. The Negro population alone increased more than threefold in the eleven Western states, rising from 171,000 to 576,000. San Francisco's total population increased 22.2 percent to 775,357 in 1950, while the nonwhite population rose 137 percent, reaching a total of 81,469.[2] The shift in the Negro group was clearly the most dramatic, amounting to an eleven-fold increase over 1940. The Chinese figure is estimated to have remained fairly stable, whereas the Japanese group, which was dispersed by the wartime relocation orders, had not been sufficiently augmented by individuals returning to San Francisco to regain even its 1940 strength. The new

effect of these changes was to place a heavy strain on housing capacity in those areas of the city where nonwhites had previously been concentrated, causing them to seek shelter in other quarters. The nonwhite demand for housing was further intensified by the considerable rise in personal income levels experienced by most nonwhites.[3] It was inevitable that nonwhite

From *The Appraisal Journal* (July 1952) , pp. 314–329. Reprinted by permission.

1 As used in this paper, the term "nonwhite" refers to persons included in the following racial or national origin groups: Negro, Chinese, Japanese, and Mexican. The last named are not considered as nonwhite by the Bureau of the Census except as to persons who are "definitely Indian or of other nonwhite race." However, in California, at least, the residential pattern of the population of Mexican origin is similar to that of the nonwhite groups; hence, they are considered with the latter for purposes of the present study.

The 1940 Census of Population tabulated a total city population of 634,536, of which 32,136 (or 5 percent) were nonwhite. It was estimated by the San Francisco Public Housing Authority that the nonwhite total included about 18,000 Chinese, 5,000 Negroes, and 5,300 Japanese.

2 Of this total it is estimated by the San Francisco Redevelopment Agency and other reliable observers that about 55,000 (67 percent) were Negro, 20,000 (25 percent) were Chinese, and the balance predominantly Japanese.

3 "Incomes have shot up faster for the average Negro than for the average white person. Actually, incomes of Negro families average only half as much as incomes of white families. Yet the typical Negro family, living on a wage or salary, now has more than three and a half times as much income as it had in 1940. The typical white family, on a wage or salary, has two and a half times as much

families would filter into residential areas which had formerly been occupied solely by whites and that they would do this not as tenants but as home owners.[4]

Statements have often been made concerning the repercussions of changed racial patterns upon property values and market prices. The majority of property owners, appraisers, brokers, lenders, and sideline observers agree that neighborhoods decline and values are harmed by what is termed an "invasion" by nonwhites. Their opinions differ only regarding the *degree* of injury.

Opinions prevailing in the San Francisco area were revealed through interviews with 45 real estate brokers and salesmen, constituting the great bulk of those engaged in any transactions with nonwhites. Of those interviewed, only five believed that introduction of nonwhites into white neighborhoods would *not* result in property devaluation. The rest insisted that losses of 10 to 20 percent—about $1,500 to $2,000 in the price ranges of houses investigated in this study—unequivocally follow nonwhite entry. Out of 15 interviews with top spokesmen for banks, savings and loan associations, and insurance companies, covering the significant sources of institutional credit for home financing, 13 recorded opinions that property values would be adversely affected, with the degree of damage asserted to range from "destroyed" to about a 20 percent discount. One interviewee held that values would suffer only if owners insisted on selling to whites.[5] The prevailing opinion was summed up by another spokesman:

> The effects of racial infiltration are often discussed among the lending fraternity, and, although we have no factual evidence to present in summary form, we are unanimous in the opinion that it harms values. It depresses the neighborhood and thus decreases the amount we will loan on any particular property in that neighborhood. A single Negro in a block in the Sunset district (an all-white, middle-class area) would be like a caution flag to us to note the trend of the neighborhood and would probably be sufficient to influence our loans downward in that area.[6]

As for white private home owners, both in and out of areas undergoing racial change, all but a handful of those interviewed took the position that the value of their property had been, or would be, lowered by reason of that change.[7]

Leading authorities in housing have called attention to the shortage of definitive studies of racial effects upon property values.[8] This is

income as it had in 1940." Special Report, *U.S. News and World Report*, November 16, 1951.

4 Those opposed to nonwhite entry into white neighborhoods have usually been successful in persuading white owners not to rent to nonwhites, but they have not been able to block home purchases by nonwhites completely. A typical comment on this phenomenon is the statement of a Chicago broker: "Of course, if they [Negroes] come in as tenants, we can handle the situation fairly easily, but when they get a deed, that's another matter." Chicago Commission on Race Relations, *The Negro in Chicago* (Chicago: University of Chicago Press, 1922), p. 206.

5 Even this special limitation does not lead to supporting evidence of price decline following nonwhite entry and occupancy. The distribution of price differences for sales to white, as will be noted later, is obviously *not* negatively skewed. Even if it were, this would hardly support the theory advanced above, which would lead one to expect the *bulk* of such sales to be made at prices far below comparable sales in all-white areas. The data show that this has not happened.

6 Interview June 6, 1951. From one of a systematic series of interviews with persons in the field of real estate, conducted during the summer of 1951.

7 The opinions concerning property depreciation probably arise from two sources: (1) observation of older, rundown, multi-family unit areas where nonwhites have entered subsequent to the downturn in the neighborhood's evolution, but have been blamed for it; (2) desire to promulgate the belief that such depreciation takes place, inevitably, for the purpose of profiting by the resulting market psychology.

8 Studies on the racial factors in property value movements include: Elsie Parker, "Both Sides of the Color Line," *The Appraisal Journal*, January 1943, pp. 27–34; July 1943, pp. 231–49. George W. Beehler, Jr., "Colored Occupancy Raises Values," *The Review of the Society of Residential Appraisers*, September 1945, pp. 3–6, 12. Paul F. Cressey, *The Succession of Cultural Groups in the City of Chicago* (unpublished Ph.D. thesis, University of Chicago, 1930). Oscar I. Stern, "The Long Range Effects of Colored Occupancy," *The Review of the Society of Residential Appraisers*, January 1946, pp. 4–6. Homer Hoyt, *One Hundred Years of Land Values in Chicago* (Chicago: University of Chicago Press, 1933). Richard Marks, "The Impact of Negro Population Movement on Property Values in a Selected Area in Detroit," mimeo, summary and conclusions, January 16, 1950, 2 pp., based on an unpublished study made for the Mayor's Interracial Committee of the City of Detroit. Egbert F. Schietinger, *Real Estate Transfers During Negro Invasion: A Case Study* (unpublished M.A. thesis, University of Chicago, 1948), 118 pp. Belden Morgan, "Values in Transition Areas: Some New Concepts," *The Review of The Society of Residential Appraisers*, March 1952, pp. 5–10.

exemplified by the following comment of Robert C. Weaver:

> A review of the arguments designed to prove or disprove an inevitable adverse effect of Negroes' presence upon property values indicates that both sides have often arrived at sweeping conclusions without adequate factual basis to sustain their generalizations.[9]

This same observer emphasizes that no investigation will yield propositions that can be applied for all times and places to the behavior of property values in areas undergoing racial change:

> The effect of Negro occupancy upon property values varies from one section of the city to another and from one time to another. Within a given area, the initial result of the arrival of a few colored people may be imperceptible or it may lead to panic among white occupants; the arrival of a few Negroes may be the signal for a great decline in selling prices or it may lead to an appreciable increase. Much depends upon the state of the total housing market and the manner in which colored people enter an area. Or, again, prices may fall with large-scale Negro introduction only to recover again as the transition is completed. Out of all these possibilities—and the literature is full of examples of each—a separate and obviously incomplete theory of the relationship between racial occupancy and property values could be formulated. No such theory would be sound. *There is no one universal effect of Negro occupancy upon property values.*[10]

Charles Abrams places himself alongside Mr. Weaver in this opinion, holding that:

> As far as I have been able to determine from the limited evidence available, there are at least eight different value reactions (not one or two as claimed) when a minority or class different from the occupiers moves into an area.[11]

Despite the clouded picture as to what actually does happen to property values and market prices when all-white residential neigh-borhoods are newly entered by nonwhites, majority opinion rather confidently asserts that entry as tenants, and particularly as owners, damages or even "destroys" values. It is explained that this comes about in either or both of two ways:

1. Nonwhites physically deteriorate their residences by overcrowding and by failing to engage in adequate maintenance—hence the entire neighborhood is pushed, or led, into decline.
2. White residents who do not wish to have nonwhite neighbors (for any of many reasons) destroy the former equilibrium in the local real estate market by putting up an unusual number of homes for sale, the price-softening effects of such an extension in supply being further aggravated by a weakening on the demand side, since many white prospective customers will turn away from the neighborhood because of the new racial pattern.

Such assertions call for careful investigation of areas experiencing racial change to ascertain, (1) the behavior of prices, (2) the standards of property maintenance, and (3) the presence of any "abnormal" market psychology.

The primary aim of this study was to measure the impact—if any—of changed racial patterns upon market prices of residential real estate.[12] To accomplish this it was necessary to hold constant those price factors other than race.

9 Robert C. Weaver, *The Negro Ghetto* (New York: Harcourt, Brace & Co., 1948) , p. 279. Chapter XV contains an excellent analysis of these attempts.
10 *Ibid.*, p. 293.
11 Charles Abrams, "The New 'Gresham's Law' of Neighborhoods—Fact or Fiction," *The Appraisal Journal*, July 1951, p. 329.
Abrams then proceeds to list these different value reactions, to "put in issue the blunt conclusions rendered ex cathedra about the 'antipathetic racial group' inevitably driving down values or 'threatening' real estate security." *Loc. cit.*
12 Definitive answers to questions involving standards of property maintenance or market psychology will require separate research efforts. In the opinion of the writer, no difference in standards of property maintenance as between nonwhites and whites was discernible during the course of the extensive field work undertaken. One rather informal method of

Chart A   Data Relating to Selected Test Areas Entered by, or in Proximity to, Nonwhites—in San Francisco

Designation of Test Area	General Location in S.F. District	Specific Area Bounded by	Character of Housing									
			% Homes by Age (Yrs.)			Condition[1] Penalty Pts.				Price[2] Class		
			Under 10	10–20	Over 20	Under 20	20–29	30–49	50–100	Low	Middle	High
T-1. Silver Terrace *B*	Bayview	Topeka, Bridgeview, Ledyard, Silver, Quesada, Newhall	80	20		x					x	
T-2. Ingleside Heights	Ocean Avenue	Garfield, Head, Sargent, Byxbee	100			x					x	
T-3. Silver Terrace *A*	Bayview	Topeka, Thornton, Bridgeview	100			x					x	
T-4. Parkside—Sunset	Parkside—Sunset	48th Avenue between Moraga and Pacheco; 42nd Avenue between Taraval and Wawona	50	50		x					x	x
T-5. North of Lakeview	Ocean Avenue	Lakeview, Orizaba, Ashton, Ocean, Harold	40		60	x	x			x	x	
T-6. South of Lakeview	Ocean Avenue	Lakeview, Summit, San Jose, Alemany, Orizaba	40		60	x	x			x	x	
T-7. North of Ridge Lane	Outer Mission	Ridge Lane, Harold, Ocean, Tara, Niagara, San Jose	45		55	x	x			x	x	
T-8. South of Ridge Lane	Outer Mission	Ridge Lane, San Jose, Summit	20		80	x	x	x		x	x	
T-9. Goettingen	Bayview	Goettingen between Ward and Harkness	100			x					x	

METHOD OF MEASURING THE RACIAL IMPACT

The basic approach employed was to make comparisons between market prices of single-family residences which were deemed to differ only in the race of the occupants (or in the proximity to nonwhite occupancy). It was argued that, given two neighborhood areas that displayed clearly comparable characteristics in terms of topography, relation to urban center, land-use pattern, age, type and cost of dwelling units, income class of occupants, and general development over time, there would be no reason for significant differences in price behavior as between the two. If, then, one area experienced nonwhite entry and occupancy, and the

putting this generalization to the test was to attempt to pick out homes occupied by nonwhites *before* obtaining their precise addresses, by noting the condition of all properties in the neighborhood. In only three instances did the writer find the owner of a below-neighborhood-standard home to be a nonwhite.

Racial Characteristics[3]	Entry Date of 1st NW	No. of NW[4] Home-owners July 31, '51	No. of Sales for which Full Information Obtained[5]	
			To NW	To W
No NW, but adjacent to "light" NW area	—	0	—	8
No NW, but adjacent to "medium" NW area	—	0	—	54
"Light" NW	2/18/50	6(N)	6	21
"Very light" NW	3–47	3(C)	0	15
"Light" NW, adjacent to "medium" NW	1948	5(3C)	0	55
"Medium" NW, adjacent to "heavy" NW	1948	9(2C)	5	62
"Medium" NW, adjacent to "very heavy" NW	12/12/47	36(1J) (1C)	20	29
"Very heavy" NW	1945	190 (90%N)	11	8
"Heavy" NW	7/18/49	12(N)	8	2
			50	254

[1] According to a report prepared by the San Francisco Department of City Planning on "Condition of Residential Areas," October, 1949, supplemented by field work. More than one cross indicates a mixture of the indicated conditions.

[2] Price classes arbitrarily defined: low, $3,000–$7,000; middle, $7,000–$13,000; high, above $13,000.

[3] "Very light" NW, 2 or less within a 5-block area; "light" NW, between 3 and 6 within a 5-block area; "medium" NW, between 7 and 50 within a 5-block area; "heavy" NW, over 50 within a 5-block area.

[4] Figures given are minima, except when underlined, in which cases they represent exact counts. (N) Negro; (C) Chinese; (J) Japanese.

[5] It was not possible to utilize every one of these because no comparable control sales could be found for some of them. The total number of "usable" sales was 165, of which 44 sales were to nonwhites and 121 to whites.

other did not, any price differentials could properly be ascribed to the consequences wrought by the only unique factor—race.[13] It is difficult to see how the racial factor in the behavior of real estate prices could be isolated by any other technique, since any method that does not hold the important price-shaping variables constant cannot single out the effects, if any, of racial changes.[14]

In order to determine the sections of San Francisco which experienced nonwhite entry since 1940, data were gathered indicating the

street addresses of all determinable nonwhite residency outside such "established" nonwhite

13 Such consequences might involve "evacuation" by prejudiced whites, property deterioration through changing maintenance patterns, avoidance of the neighborhood by white prospective buyers, or other developments influencing value.

14 True, this method of "comparable sales" did not permit the investigation of the effects of race upon property values in the older urban areas where nonwhites have long resided, population densities are very high, very few single-family homes exist, and land uses are manifold. This is because, for such older areas, no comparable all-white areas

Designation of Control Area	General Location in S.F. District	Specific Area Bounded by	% Homes by Age (Yrs.)			Character of Condition Penalty Pts.			
			Under 10	10–20	Over 20	Under 20	20–29	30–49	50–100
C-1. Silver-Alemany	Outer Mission	Silver, Congdon, Alemany, Cambridge	100			x			
C-2. Geneva	Visitación Valley	Geneva, Parque, Velasco, Santos	100			x			
C-3. Arch¹	Ocean Avenue and Visitación Valley	Arch, between Randolph and Garfield; Head, between Randolph and Garfield; Campbell, 100 and 500 blocks	100			x			
C-4. Ingleside Hts.²	Ocean Avenue	Garfield, Head, Sargent, Byxbee	100			x			
C-5. Standard³	Mixed	Geneva, San Luis, Orizaba, Joost	100			x			
C-6. Sunnyside	Partly Inner Mission, partly Outer Mission	Genessee, Melrose, Baden, Circular, Havelock, Judson	40		60	x	x		
C-7. Glen Park	Outer Mission	Burnside, Surrey, Miguel, Bernal, Bosworth	15		85	x	x	x	
C-8. P	Parkside-Sunset	Selected streets in general area within Noriega, Sunset, Wawona, 48th	50	50		x			

areas as the Western Addition and China-town.[15] The important areas of recent non-white occupancy are preponderantly in the southern sections of the city. Detailed inspections of these areas, coupled with repeated consultations with persons intimately acquainted with the population and construction history of those sections, made it possible to select particular "test areas," that is, neighborhoods which had been all-white in 1940 and had subsequently experienced nonwhite entry under varying circumstances. Chart A lists these test areas together with certain items concerning their location, character of housing, racial characteristics, and the amount of sales information obtainable. Three price classes were arbi-

could be found. Thus, no "control sales" could be set up for comparison with sales in the racially-affected areas. However, this limitation was not too damaging, in that the older areas are not the ones about which concern is expressed as to real estate price movements. It is the "invasion" of all-white neighborhoods that arouses present fears and resentments, and for such cases the method is quite suitable.

15 These data were based upon city birth and death records, health records, racial directories, and information furnished by real estate brokers and others. Its collection involved the arduous efforts of several city departments and agencies, notably the

Housing Price Class			No. of Usable Sales for which Full Information Obtained	Test Area for which Used
Low	Middle	High		
	x		30	Silver Terrace A Silver Terrace B
	x		19	do., also for Ingleside Hgts.
	x		21	Silver Terrace A Silver Terrace B
	x		54	Silver Terrace A Silver Terrace B
	x		8	Goettingen
x	x		38	North of Ridge Lane North of Lakeview South of Lakeview
x	x		23	South of Ridge Lane South of Lakeview
	x	x	21	Parkside-Sunset
			Total 214	

[1] This is a "composite control area" formed by taking sales on streets with characteristics similar to test area, but drawn from three separate neighborhoods.
[2] This was originally chosen as a test area adjacent to a medium nonwhite area, but it was later employed as a control area after determining that it had undergone no price reactions due to race.
[3] Another "composite control area," but built up by noting sales of "standard-built" homes with identical floor plans, constructed on comparable streets in comparable neighborhoods.

trarily defined: low, $3,000–$7,000; middle, $7,000–$13,000; high, above $13,000. All test areas had houses in the middle-price class— some, in fact, had nothing else. But some areas displayed a range of prices as indicated by the chart.

The next step was to find areas similar to the test areas in every respect except that non-white entry was not experienced. Chart B lists and describes these comparable areas, hereafter referred to as "control" areas. The comparability of the control areas with the test areas was checked against the judgment of qualified brokers, appraisers, lenders, and city assessors.[16]

OBTAINING AND ANALYZING PRICE DATA

Price information which would reveal the market behavior of both nonwhite and white-occu-

Redevelopment Agency of San Francisco. Even had the 1950 Census data been classified by race on a tract and block basis at the time the study was started, it would still have been necessary to obtain detailed information on nonwhite occupancy by *street address* and *date of first occupancy*.
16 Similarity in assessed valuations prior to any racial changes assisted in evaluating area comparability.

pied homes in the test areas as compared to market behavior in the control areas was then obtained from several sources. The primary source of actual sales prices was the files of the Multiple Listing Service in San Francisco, covering the period June 1949 to July 1951. These were supplemented by price data obtained directly from real estate brokers operating in the selected areas.[17]

Individual price comparisons were then set up between every house in the test areas for which a selling price was obtained and a *comparable* house in the control areas. An excess of test-house price over comparable house price was labelled as a *plus difference*. If the test house was less, the discrepancy was classed as a *minus difference*. This was the crucial step in the whole method because it required a judgment on the comparability of the two houses involved. As a first step, comparisons were made on the basis of recorded information on the properties concerned. Thus, such obvious factors as age, date of sale, number and size of rooms, garage facilities, and the like were matched. Final comparability of the houses was judged in terms of condition, topography, view, and special features which bear upon market value. This was done by personal inspection of the properties.[18] Wherever possible, the sales of two or more comparable properties in the control areas were averaged in order to provide the best obtainable yardstick.[19]

Chart A shows that complete sales information was collected in the test areas for 50 homes sold to nonwhites and 254 sold to whites. It was possible to find comparable sales in control areas for 44 of the nonwhite and 121 of the white test sales. While these are not large samples, particularly in the case of the individual areas examined, no quantitative or qualitative evidence could be found to indicate they were not typical of all sales to nonwhite and white buyers in single-family neighborhoods entered and occupied by nonwhites. Since most brokers are reluctant to sell to nonwhites in what they regard as their "home territory," whereas they can avoid local censure if the sale is made by a broker from another part of town, there appears to be a mounting tendency towards use of multiple listing as a method of reaching the nonwhite market. If this is indeed the case, the sample sales obtained represents a higher proportion of all sales occurring in the areas studied than would be indicated by the proportion accounted for by all multiple listing sales which amounted to some 20 percent. In the control areas, out of a total of 320 sales for which full information could be obtained, 214 were "useable" in that they involved properties closely comparable to properties in the various test areas.

As described above, pairs of comparable sales were then listed (that is, one test area sale and one control sale) for each test area and its appropriate control area, taking every possible precaution that the matched sales were indeed comparable. Plus and minus differences were tabulated not only in the case of actual list prices, but also for "adjusted" prices resulting from transactions involving secondary financing held by sellers.[20]

17 These sources by no means permitted a complete tabulation of all transactions: sales passing through multiple listing constitute about 15–20 percent of all sales, and the added information from real estate files brings the proportion of observed sales to about 25 percent of all those occurring in the chosen areas. Also the Multiple Listing System was not started until June 1949, so that the development of historical price series was precluded. On the other hand, these sources did permit compiling detailed information about each property, including age, number and size of rooms, special features, types of construction, size and shape of lot, and specific terms of sale. Recorded deeds, to which are affixed federal documentary tax stamps in the amount of $0.55 for each $500 of consideration received, or portion thereof, were not used. Stamps are required only on the difference between sales price and the amount of any assumed loan. Well over half of all transactions involve assumption by the buyer of the existing loan or loans. A sample check revealed that price computed on this basis of the tax stamp figures varied, on the average, by about 5 percent from the known selling prices, with some variations running much higher. Such variations would mean that errors of $500 or more could be present in the comparisons between houses in test areas and control areas and could easily conceal or exaggerate actual price differences. In addition to this objection, recorded deeds do not reveal the terms of sale, which directly and considerably affect not only the recorded price but the net amounts received by the seller and paid out by the buyer.
18 Inspection consisted of careful evaluation of the properties from the outside, in most cases. This was supplemented by interior inspections resulting from 30 interviews with nonwhites and whites in test areas and some spot checks in the control areas.
19 This technique tended to remove unique deviations due to any peculiar buyer-seller behavior.
20 There is some evidence that average cash down is considerably less for nonwhite buyers. This nat-

SUMMARY OF PRICE COMPARISONS

These summaries of price comparisons are set forth in Table I showing the dollar differences between listed sale prices, Table II showing dollar differences between sales prices after appropriate adjustment for secondary loans held by sellers, and Table III showing adjusted dollar differences expressed as percentages of adjusted selling prices. Tables I and II also present the tabulations of dollar differences before and after adjusting for secondary financing held by sellers.

The first point to be made is that, with the exception of sales to nonwhites, the adjustment for secondary financing appears to affect the distribution of dollar differences only slightly. Inspection of Table II shows that for sales to whites the percentages of sales above zero difference was slightly raised by the adjustment, from about 54 to 57 percent. This resulted from the fact that test sales to whites, by comparison with control sales, had relatively fewer cases of secondary financing held by the seller. The writer was not able to discover the explanation for this phenomenon. The adjustment for secondary financing in the case of sales to nonwhites, however, reduced the percentage of positive sale price differences from 77 to 64 percent. This reflected the greater necessity for nonwhites, by and large, to have recourse to secondary financing.[21] This necessity holds, of course, not only as contrasted with sales to whites in the test areas, but also with sales to whites in the control areas.

It is commonly argued by persons engaged in the business of selling real estate, and by property owners themselves, that losses suffered because of changes in the racial character of neighborhoods are intensified because of the *preponderantly* greater use of seller-held secondary financing. This does not seem to be borne out by the analysis insofar as all sales considered together are concerned. It may well be true for individual transactions that whether or not a seller must "take a second" will determine whether he realizes a profit. However, there seems to be no overwhelming evidence that significant amounts of losses could result from this cause for all property owners as a class.

The second, and more basic, point to be de-

veloped from an inspection of the distributions is that they do not appear to support assertions that nonwhite entry and occupancy depress values. If those assertions were true, we should expect to find the distribution of dollar differences concentrated on the "below zero" side. In fact, they are rather evenly tapered out on each side of the zero-difference point. This was also the case for each test area considered individually. For this reason, and because of space limitations, results for each test area are not shown in this paper. It is well worth noting, however, that the *degree* of nonwhite entry appeared to make no difference in the behavior of prices. In the case of sales to nonwhites, however, the largest concentration of differences is slightly on the plus side, as contrasted with sales to whites. The mean difference is plus $256 for nonwhites and $91 for whites. This undoubtedly reflects the differential "fee" that nonwhites who come into a white area are sometimes required to pay by certain sellers who feel that they can extract extra amounts for extending the privilege of residence in such areas. This differential is also tied up with the secondary finance situation because a seller may charge somewhat more in order to make up for the possibility of having to discount the second mortgage that he takes back on the transaction. He thereby hopes to emerge with the same amount of cash in hand as he would have had in the absence of such necessity. It may be noticed that, after adjusting for such secondary financing, the symmetry of the distribution is improved, showing that a portion of the dif-

urally increases the incidence of second and third mortgages. In cases where sellers held this paper, some adjustment of the recorded sales price seems indicated, since it is not equivalent to the sellers receiving their equity (defined as the difference between existing loans and the sales prices as agreed upon) in cash. Investigation revealed that discounting of such paper customarily occurred at rates ranging between 20 and 40 per cent below face value, with a model rate of 30 per cent. Accordingly, this 30 percent rate was applied to all secondary financing held by sellers, and the resulting product deducted from the listed selling price to obtain an "adjusted price," equivalent to an all-cash deal.

21 Racial differences in cash down payments and differences in the extent and size of secondary financing held by sellers will, it is hoped, be examined in detail in a later paper.

Table I   Distribution of Dollar Differences Between Sales Prices of Pairs of Comparable Houses (*One in Test Area, One in Control Area*) Before Adjusting for Secondary Financing Held by Sellers: All Areas

Category of Sales	Total Sales	(.....MINUS Differences:.....) Test House Price Less than Control House Price					(.....PLUS Differences:.....) Test House Price Greater than Control House Price					Percentage		Mean Difference, in Dollars
		$-1999 to $-1500	$-1499 to $-1000	$-999 to $-500	$-499 to $-1	0	$1 to $499	$500 to $999	$1000 to $1499	$1500 to $1999	$2000 to $2499	Below Zero	Above Zero	
To Nonwhites	44	..	..	3	6	1	21	9	2	1	1	20.4	77.4	+$335
To Whites	121	2	9	15	28	1	27	28	8	2	1	44.6	54.5	+ 87
Total	165	2	9	18	34	2	48	37	10	3	2	38.2	60.6	+$153

Sources: Multiple Listing Service and individual brokers' sales records.

Table I   Distribution of Dollar Differences Between Sales Prices of Pairs of Comparable Houses (*One in Test Area, One in Control Area*) After Adjusting for Secondary Financing Held by Sellers: All Areas

Category of Sales	Total Sales	(.....MINUS Differences:.....) Test House Price Less than Control House Price					(.....PLUS Differences:.....) Test House Price Greater than Control House Price					Percentage		Mean Difference, in Dollars
		$-1999 to $-1500	$-1499 to $-1000	$-999 to $-500	$-499 to $-1	0	$1 to $499	$500 to $999	$1000 to $1499	$1500 to $1999	$2000 to $2499	Below Zero	Above Zero	
To Nonwhites	44	..	1	4	10	1	18	4	2	2	2	34.0	63.6	+$256
To Whites	121	4	9	15	23	1	28	30	6	4	1	42.1	57.0	+ 91
Total	165	4	10	10	33	2	46	34	8	6	3	40.0	58.5	+$135

Sources: Multiple Listing Service and individual brokers' sales records.

ferences above zero were not real differences in cash in hand to sellers.

The differences between test house prices and control house prices, before and after adjustment, averaged as follows:

	Before Adjustment	After Adjustment
Sales to nonwhites	+$335	+$256
Sales to whites	+ 87	+ 91
All sales	+ 153	+ 135

These results suggest that, if anything, prices in the neighborhoods undergoing racial change were slightly enhanced, especially for sales to nonwhites. To be sure, the average differences were computed from sample data and may differ to some extent from results that might obtain if it had been possible to collect information on every sale that occurred. However, on the basis of tests commonly employed to evaluate the significance of sampling results, it turns out that for none of the three categories above do the sample results cast doubt on the hypothesis that test-house prices, on the average, exceeded control-house prices. In other words, it is highly unlikely that market prices were driven down in the areas studied; rather, the hypothesis that prices were slightly higher in the test areas may be held with considerable confidence that it corresponds to fact.

Thus, the over-all picture of comparative market prices should be reassuring to those who fear nonwhite entry will harm prices. Approximately half of all sales are within $500 of the prices brought by comparable properties in all-white neighborhoods and are quite evenly divided on each side of zero difference within that range. Random variations of as much as $500 can easily arise as between the sales prices of two identical houses because of unique buyer-seller circumstances and attitudes. Therefore, it may be considered that all the sales within plus and minus $500 of zero difference occurred at substantially "identical prices."

Approximately one-fourth of sales in all categories fell into the difference bracket of *plus* $500–999, and roughly one-tenth into the *minus* $999–500 group. The remaining sales were scattered fairly symmetrically above and below zero. (Sales to nonwhites displayed a few cases of large positive differences.) The reduction in

sales prices resulting from the adjustment for secondary financing shown in Table II confirms the observation from the unadjusted sales prices that no significant differences in price behavior are observable in the test as compared with the control areas.

Such statements as the following, therefore, would not be applicable to the price behavior noted in San Francisco:

> That the entry of non-Caucasians into districts where distinctly Caucasian residents live tends to depress real estate values is agreed to by practically all real estate subdividers and students of city life and growth. Infiltration at the outset may be slow, but once the trend is established, values start to drop, until properties can be purchased at discounts of from *50 to 75 percent* [italics supplied].[22]

CONCLUSIONS OF STUDY

It would appear that the principal contention as to the effects of race upon property values is subject to modification. In San Francisco during the period 1949–1951, areas which experienced nonwhite purchase and occupancy during or shortly before that period did not display the price behavior which the popular theory would predict. Instead, transactions took place at prices closely corresponding to those in comparable all-white areas, although a small fraction of sales differed by plus or minus amounts which may have reflected unusual circumstances: (1) a premium price extracted from a nonwhite buyer anxious to get into that particular locality, (2) a sacrifice price agreed to by a seller desirous of dumping a property in an area believed by him to be on the verge of rapid deterioration.[23]

22 Stanley L. McMichael, *Real Estate Subdivisions* (New York: Prentice-Hall, Inc., 1949) , p. 204.
23 However, the theory given for the premium prices to some nonwhites loses some of its explanatory power when it is observed that a *higher* proportion of the sales to whites—34 percent—showed positive price differences exceeding $500 than in the case of sales to nonwhites—23 percent. The theory concerning sacrifice prices, on the other hand, is indeed strengthened by the evidence, for about 23 percent of the sales to whites showed

Sales to whites involved homes which naturally varied in their distances from nonwhites within the test area. To test the hypothesis that price behavior for test sales to whites might be related to distance from nonwhites, sales to whites in each test area were divided into two groups: sales within two blocks of nonwhite residence and sales more than two blocks away from nonwhite residence. This distance was chosen because it was the one most often mentioned by white homeowners in response to the question, How close would a nonwhite purchase have to be for you to feel concerned?

Inspection of the test sales to whites after being so grouped revealed no regular behavior one way or the other. In all cases, the average difference came out much the same for both groups, with one group or the other displaying a slightly larger figure. It was concluded that the data do not indicate that location within the test area had a differential effect on test sales to whites.

Table III compares the percentage differences in sales between "test" and "control" areas after adjustment for secondary financing. It can be noted from Table III that well over one-half of the total number of sales to both whites and nonwhites showed price differences of less than plus or minus 6 percent. As in the unadjusted price data, a slightly higher proportion of the sales to nonwhites showed plus differences than for sales to whites.

The 11 transactions involving white buyers in the test areas, which occurred at selling prices 12 percent or more below comparable sales in control areas, accounted for 9.1 percent of all sales to whites. Investigation into the circumstances surrounding these sales disclosed that the sellers had reacted strongly to the nonwhite entry into their neighborhood. In several instances, the investigator received the impression that the sellers had been so anxious to move that they would accept almost any price for their properties. Interviews with some white owners in similar circumstances, but who had not yet sold, indicated that they were impelled either by their reluctance to have nonwhites as neighbors or by their sincere belief that property values would be seriously harmed and they would lose heavily if they delayed selling. It was not uncommon to find both reasons motivating a seller. Clearly, such a seller psychology

operating upon the local market, with—very possibly—a white buyer informed as to the racial situation and intent on taking advantage of this in his bidding for the property, would swing the bargaining advantages heavily in favor of the buyer.

On the plus difference side, sales to whites and nonwhites did not differ significantly in their comparability with control sales, except for two sales to nonwhites which showed unusually large plus differences. Evidences pieced together from field interviews and other sources points strongly to the conclusion that these two sales were handled by speculators and involved considerable skillful and advantageous manipulation of the psychological situation. Conclusions based upon examination of percentage price differences are similar to those derived from comparisons of actual dollar differences. Some minor differences in the frequency distributions can probably be traced to the adjustment technique used, although differences were random in nature and did not alter the fundamental structure of the distributions.

SUMMARY

To summarize, the bulk of all sales in the test areas, whether to whites or nonwhites, brought prices slightly above those in control areas, except for two minor qualifications:

1. About 9 percent of the sales to white buyers took place at prices which were between 12 and 22 percent lower than those for comparable properties in control areas, whereas no sales to nonwhites fell in this range.

---

negative price differences greater than $500, whereas only 11 percent of the sales to nonwhites were in this category of differences. Why white buyers should be willing to buy at prices higher than the modal one for the particular type of dwelling involved, when this behavior is usually ascribed to nonwhites who are eager to "buy in" to an area new to them is not readily explainable. Perhaps the answer is that such prices typically occur in a certain proportion of transactions, regardless of the race of buyer, because of buyer ignorance of a "fair market price." Variations also probably reflect to some extent real differences in the test versus control houses, arising from the impossibility of perfectly matching all pairs of houses.

Table III Distribution of Percentage Differences Between Adjusted Sales Prices of Comparable Houses (*one in test area, one in control area*) All Areas

Percentage Differences of Adjusted Selling Prices	Sales to Nonwhites No. of Sales *	Per Cent of No. of Sales	No. of Sales †	Per Cent of No. of Sales
26 and under 28				
24 and under 26	2	4.5		
22 and under 24				
20 and under 22				
18 and under 20				
16 and under 18	1	2.3	2	1.7
14 and under 16	2	4.5	4	3.3
12 and under 14	2	4.5		
10 and under 12			2	1.7
8 and under 10	1	2.3	7	5.8
6 and under 8	1	2.3	8	6.6
4 and under 6	4	9.1	20	16.5
2 and under 4	5	11.4	8	6.6
0 and under 2(a)	10	22.7	17	14.0
0 and under −2(a)	2	4.5	11	9.1
−2 and under −4	4	9.1	12	9.9
−4 and under −6	4	9.1	4	3.3
−6 and under −8	4	9.1	3	2.5
−8 and under −10	1	2.3	5	4.1
−10 and under −12	1	2.3	7	5.8
−12 and under −14			6	5.0
−14 and under −16			2	1.7
−16 and under −18			1	0.8
−18 and under −20			1	0.8
−20 and under −22			1	0.8
Total Sales.............................	44	100.0	121	100.0
Percentages..............................				
under 0 difference.......................		36.4%		43.8%
over 0 difference.......................		63.6%		56.2%

* Range: −10.4 to 24.9; Interquartile Range: −3.5 to 5.0
† Range: −20.7 to 17.6; Interquartile Range: −4.0 to 5.3
(a) Zero differences were evenly apportioned between the classes 0 *and under* −2 and 0 *and under* 2.

2. About 4 percent of the sales of nonwhite buyers took place at prices which were between 22 and 26 percent higher than those for comparable properties in control areas, whereas no sales to whites fell in this range.

These results do not show that any deterioration in market prices occurred following changes in the racial pattern. They should, however, be weighed in the light of environmental conditions previously noted: a large increase in total population; an even larger relative increase in the number of nonwhites; a relative gain in nonwhite personal income; and a severe housing shortage throughout the period of observation. In addition, it may well be that the traditionally polyglot nature of San Francisco's population has produced somewhat unique racial attitudes as contrasted with communities which never experienced a non-white influx. However, San Francisco's cosmopolitan attitude in racial relations may not be unique when contrasted with those apparently now prevailing in some northern cities. According to some experienced observers widespread nonwhite entry into formerly all-white neighborhoods is proceeding apace in such cities as Detroit and Chicago, with no discernible repercussions.

The Housing Market in Racially Mixed Areas

DAVID McENTIRE

Two studies undertaken for the Commission on Race and Housing deal specifically with the impact of racial mingling in residence areas on local housing markets. One is an inquiry into the effects on residential property values of nonwhite entry into formerly all-white neighborhoods.[1] The second study is an analysis of demand for housing in racially mixed areas of one large city.[2]

PROPERTY VALUES AND RACE

According to traditional and widespread opinion, Negroes, and other minorities as well, are dangerous to property values when they seek housing, as they must, outside established minority residence areas. Underlying this belief are two basic propositions: first, that whites will not live in areas entered by nonwhites, and second, that nonwhite demand for housing is not sufficient to replace the vanished white demand and hence, prices must fall.

To many, these propositions seem self-evident, but in recent years both have been challenged. Not only have proponents of racial equality endeavored to demonstrate the error of the "property values myth," but in the real estate appraisal profession, increasing doubts have been expressed about the validity of the traditional doctrines under present-day conditions.

The importance of the problem needs no emphasis. Fear of financial loss gives every property owner in white neighborhoods a direct personal stake in excluding minorities, at least up to a point. Convictions that racial mingling injures property values influence business decisions to build, finance, and sell in ways that restrict the opportunities of nonwhites to acquire housing and limit them to certain districts. In acting on the assumption that values in an area are going to fall, the housing industry and property owners may help to bring about the anticipated result. If major lenders act together to reduce their loans in an area, they may be not merely recognizing but making a shift to lower prices, by eliminating a part of the demand. Similarly, when homeowners in an affected area hasten to sell before the expected price decline occurs, the resulting oversupply of houses may push down their selling prices.[3]

The motive, moreover, of preserving capital, an eminently respectable purpose, often provides moral justification for racial discrimination. People may consider themselves not merely justified but even obligated to exclude minorities for the sake of maintaining values. The real estate board in one large city took this ground in a public statement of policy:

It is a matter of fact and experience that when a Negro or Chinese or Japanese or Fili-

From *Residence and Race* (Berkeley: University of California Press, 1960), pp. 157–171. Reprinted by permission of the publisher.

1 Luigi Laurenti, *Property Values and Race: Studies in Seven Cities.*
2 Chester Rapkin and William G. Grigsby, *The Demand for Housing in Racially Mixed Areas: A Study of the Nature of Neighborhood Change.*
3 This type of collective behavior, akin to panics, bank runs, and hoarding sprees, has been termed by Merton, the "self-fulfilling prophecy." Robert K. Merton, "The Self-Fulfilling Prophecy."

pino moves into a white district, the house values drop. . . . *We don't look at this as a social problem. For us this is an economic problem.* Looking at it this way, the Board has asked that its members not introduce into a residential district any occupancy or race which will have the effect of lowering values.[4]

In similar vein, a savings and loan association executive said in interview: "There are lots of things we would like to do personally, such as treating everybody equally, . . . but we are responsible for millions of dollars. . . . We will lend on properties up to three blocks away from colored areas but not closer. . . ."

Twenty years and more ago, real estate authorities asserted the adverse effect of nonwhite occupancy on values straightforwardly and with few qualifications. Fisher (1923), McMichael and Bingham (1923), Babcock (1932), Hoyt (1933, 1939), and other authors of standard texts and treatises pronounced a common judgment, accepted apparently without dissent.[5] Property appraisal standards of the Federal Housing Administration incorporated the accepted doctrine.

Since World War II, differing theories have been advanced by professional appraisers and others. According to one contemporary theory, the price depression associated with nonwhite entry is only temporary. House prices weaken in areas anticipating a racial change and may continue depressed during the early stages of transition, but after transition, prices rise again.[6] Myrdal espoused this view in the *American Dilemma* (1944).[7] More recently Charles A. Benson, chief appraiser of a leading mortgage-finance institution, reporting on a study of price changes in two Chicago areas—one all-white and one in racial transition—concludes:

. . . prices of residences are depressed from 30 percent to 55 percent when an area is threatened by transition. As soon as transition becomes a fact, prices tend to rise. . . . After transition has been accomplished, prices in the then Negro area compare favorably with prices in the city as a whole and are controlled by supply and demand.[8]

Some appraisers hold that nonwhite occupancy may actually enhance real estate values

in certain conditions. According to the authorities just mentioned, active movement of non-whites into an area is better for values than the continued threat of entry. Thurston Ross writes that "in poor and slum sections racial encroachment sometimes raises the economic standards of the neighborhood." He reports "instances where obsolescence has been arrested and additional years of useful life given a neighborhood by racial encroachment, particularly when older people are displaced by younger groups of the encroaching race."[9]

The newer theories differ from the old in recognizing a variety of conditions under which nonwhite movement into an area can take place, and consequently a range of possible effects on values. Weaver especially emphasizes variation. Reviewing the evidence available in 1948, he wrote:

The effect of Negro occupancy upon property values varies from one section of the city to another and from one time to another. . . . The arrival of a few Negroes may be the signal for a great decline in selling prices or it may lead to an appreciable increase. Much depends upon the state of the total housing market and the manner in which colored people enter an area. . . . *There is no one universal effect of Negro occupancy upon property values.*[10]

Weaver's view is reiterated by Abrams, who finds a complex of factors at work and "no

4 Statement on behalf of the San Francisco Real Estate Board, reported in "The Negro in San Francisco," *San Francisco Chronicle,* November 6, 1950. Italics supplied.
5 The relevant professional writings are reviewed in Laurenti, *Property Values and Race,* chap. ii.
6 George W. Beehler, Jr., "Colored Occupancy Raises Values," *The Review of the Society of Residential Appraisers,* XI, no. 9 (September, 1945) . See also Stanley L. McMichael, *McMichael's Appraising Manual,* p. 169.
7 Gunnar Myrdal, *An American Dilemma,* p. 623.
8 Charles A. Benson, "A Test of Transition Theories," *The Residential Appraiser,* Vol. 24, no. 8 (August, 1958) , 8. Quoted with permission of the Society of Residential Appraisers.
9 Thurston H. Ross, "Market Significance of Declining Neighborhoods."
10 Robert G. Weaver, *The Negro Ghetto,* p. 293. Italics in original.

fixed rules as to when minority neighbors raise or lower values." [11]

Appraisal policies of the Federal Housing Administration reflect the change in appraisal thinking. Where once the FHA flatly asserted the value-destroying tendency of mixed neighborhoods, in successive editions of the *Underwriting Manual* provisions touching race and property values have become steadily more qualified. References to "social and racial classes" have been deleted in favor of the more neutral "user groups," and the *Manual* now states,

> If a mixture of user groups is found to exist it must be determined whether the mixture will render the neighborhood less desirable to present and prospective occupants. If the occupancy of the neighborhood is changing from one user group to another, . . . any degree of risk is reflected in the rating. . . . Additional risk is not necessarily involved in such change. [12]

These judgments of real estate and housing authorities have been based mainly on professional experience and observation rather than on research, for few factual studies have been made of what actually happens to house prices when nonwhites move into new areas. Difficult problems of method confront the study of this question. Merely to observe the course of prices in a neighborhood experiencing racial change tells little, for the movements observed might well be caused by factors other than the racial change. The measurement of racial influence on values is especially complicated by the tendency of minority groups to concentrate in slum and deteriorating sections affected by various adverse influences. To attribute the lower rents and prices in such areas solely to the presence of nonwhites would be obviously misleading.

To isolate the price effects of racial mixture, the price performance of racially mixed areas must be compared with some standard that is free of the racial influence being investigated. Laurenti's research for the Commission on Race and Housing attempts to do this. Twenty neighborhoods, recently become racially mixed, in San Francisco, Oakland, and Philadelphia were chosen for study. Each neighborhood, called a "test area," was matched with a "control" neighborhood which had remained all white. Each pair of neighborhoods was chosen according to criteria to ensure that the two would closely resemble each other in major factors affecting house prices. Criteria for matching included the age, type, and market value of houses, topography, location, land-use pattern, income and broad occupational class of residents, and the character of neighborhood development. A large number of areas were sifted in the search for matching pairs. Comparability of the paired neighborhoods was checked with local real estate brokers, appraisers, lenders, and assessors familiar with the histories of the areas. Informed local judgments were followed in fixing the area boundaries, usually marked by topographic features, arterial streets, or subdivision limits. All areas chosen were away from the central city districts and built up largely with single-unit, owner-occupied houses in the middle-value range. This collection of neighborhoods, therefore, represents the residences of the home-owning middle class in the cities studied. Within this category and subject to the limitations of matching, neighborhoods were selected to give as much diversity as possible in price class and degree of nonwhite occupancy.

The data consist of prices paid for houses in test and control neighborhoods during a period beginning before the entry of nonwhites into the test area and ending in the latter part of 1955. In most of the test areas the first nonwhite buyers arrived during the early postwar years. Sources of price data were the multiple listing services in San Francisco and Oakland, information from real estate brokers, and a real estate directory in Philadelphia, generally considered a reliable source of data for real estate transactions. Approximately ten thousand sales prices were collected, representing about half of all transactions in the San Francisco–Oakland areas and total sales in the Philadelphia areas during the periods studied.

For each neighborhood the collected prices

---

11 Charles Abrams, *Forbidden Neighbors*, pp. 286, 292.
12 Housing and Home Finance Agency, Federal Housing Administration, *Underwriting Manual*, Rev. April, 1958, sec. 1320.

were averaged by quarter years. In some areas with a wide range of prices, ratios of selling price to assessed valuation were computed and averaged by quarters. Using these quarterly averages, the movement of house prices in the neighborhoods entered by nonwhites was compared with price movements in matching all-white neighborhoods. Some of the twenty test areas were sufficiently similar to more than one control area to permit multiple comparisons. In all, thirty-four paired comparisons were made. Analysis yielded the following principal findings:

1. In fourteen of the thirty-four comparisons (41 percent), test prices stayed within 5 percent, plus or minus, of control prices during the observation period. This is considered to mean no significant difference in price behavior.
2. In fifteen comparisons (44 percent), test prices ended relatively higher than control prices, by margins of more than 5 to 26 percent.
3. In the remaining five comparisons (15 percent), test prices ended the observation period relatively lower than control prices, by margins of 5 to 9 percent.
4. From the date of first nonwhite entry to the end of the observation period, twenty

of the thirty-four comparisons showed larger percent increases each quarter for test prices than for control prices.

At the end of the observation period (fall, 1955) the proportion of nonwhite residents in the twenty test areas varied from less than 2 percent to more than 70 percent. The data were examined to determine whether the extent of nonwhite entry affected the comparative performance of test and control area prices, with results given in table 1.

As shown in the table, test areas in all ranges of nonwhite occupancy manifested both superior and inferior price performance as compared with control areas, but in every category, the majority of significant differences favored the test areas.

Distribution of test areas by per cent of population nonwhite corresponds approximately to their distribution by average house value. The three neighborhoods with very limited nonwhite entry are of the exclusive type with houses considerably more expensive than any of the other areas. It is most unlikely that these neighborhoods can become all or mainly nonwhite within the foreseeable future, in contrast to the eight areas at the other end of the scale which were well on their way toward complete racial transition. It is significant,

Table 1 Paired Comparisons of Test and Control Area Prices by Percent of Nonwhites in Test Area Populations

| Test areas by percent of population nonwhite, 1955 | Total | Paired comparisons of price movements | | |
		No significant difference[a]	Test area higher	Control area higher
30 to 75 percent				
8 areas	16	10	5	1
14 to 28 percent				
6 areas	9	3	4	2
6 to 7 percent				
3 areas	5	...	4	1
3 percent or less				
3 areas	4	1	2	1

Source: Luigi Laurenti, *Property Values and Race*, Special Research Report to the Commission on Race and Housing (Berkeley and Los Angeles: University of California Press, 1960), chaps. vi, vii, and viii.
[a] Differences less than 5 percent.

therefore, that in both classes of neighborhoods, nonwhite entry was more often associated with strengthening than with weakening house prices.

The facts of this study contradict the theory that nonwhite entry into a neighborhood must produce a fall in property values. The findings are consistent with newer theories emphasizing a diversity of price outcomes according to circumstances; however, for the areas and time periods studied, the entry of nonwhites into previously all-white neighborhoods was more often associated with price improvement or stability than with price declines.

In assessing the significance of these findings, several factors must be borne in mind. The time period—end of the war through 1955—was one of unprecedented Negro demand for housing generated by large population movements to northern and western cities, by the new economic position of Negroes, and by the increasing availability of mortgage credit. A great backlog of Negro demand had accumulated, and the persistence of exclusion barriers through most of the better housing supply served to concentrate this pent-up demand on the areas open to Negroes.

In the neighborhoods studied, the behavior of white residents seemed to be quite different from the traditional response of whites to nonwhite entry. Although some of the areas showed considerable disturbance, there was almost complete absence of the panic flight of whites which in the past has characterized many zones of racial transition. In many of the neighborhoods, the white residents were anxious to sell but waited until they could get adequate prices from incoming buyers. Under the existing conditions, the nonwhite market offered sufficient demand to move the properties without price weakening—in fact, at prices generally somewhat higher than prevailed in comparable areas not affected by racial change.

These considerations may account for the maintenance of an orderly market and stable or rising prices in those areas heavily entered by nonwhites and evidently destined for complete racial transition. They do not explain the favorable price movements in the neighborhoods with low nonwhite proportions, for these depended upon continuing demand from whites. The conclusion must be that in these

relatively expensive and desirable neighborhoods, a sparse scatter of nonwhites, almost imperceptible to most residents or prospective residents, did not noticeably affect the attractiveness of the areas in the white market.

HOUSING DEMAND IN RACIALLY MIXED AREAS

The second study to be considered goes behind the facts of price movements to analyze the components of demand for housing in areas undergoing racial transition. This study analyzed all house sales recorded during 1955 in four areas of Philadelphia. Two of the areas contained relatively good housing, and in two the housing was mainly poor. Each quality pair further consisted of one area undergoing rapid racial transition and one where the Negro population was growing slowly. In all four areas, Negroes occupied 20 to 30 percent of the dwelling units.

A racial transition zone is commonly pictured as one where whites are leaving and nonwhites coming in. The Philadelphia study found the process to be considerably more complex. Among some two thousand home buyers, 443 or more than one-fifth were whites. Although outnumbered more than three to one by Negroes, the presence of white buyers in substantial numbers is, nevertheless, a significant fact from several points of view. It refutes the notion that whites will not buy in an area once entered by Negroes, and calls for inquiry into the conditions under which whites will continue to buy in such areas. Whether any area can maintain a racially mixed composition depends, of course, on its ability to attract new white residents.

Investigation of the trend of house prices in one area (good housing, rapid transition) revealed a substantial price advance from 1948 through 1955, of approximately the same magnitude as occurred in the city as a whole. The rise appeared most pronounced in the sections of heavy Negro entry and rapid departure of whites. This is further evidence that racial change is not necessarily associated with depressed prices.

Mortgage lenders often take a dubious view of racially mixed areas, but this was not true in Philadelphia. Financing was liberal and played a key role in sustaining demand and prices. Ninety percent of the white buyers and practically all the Negroes depended on mortgage financing to acquire their homes. The loans came almost entirely from established institutional sources. Negroes obtained mortgage terms more liberal than those advanced to whites. A third of the Negro buyers borrowed the entire purchase price and another third received 90 percent or more financing. Only 43 percent of the whites received 90 percent loans or better. Negro borrowers also received more favorable interest rates. Four-fifths of them paid less than $5\frac{1}{2}$ percent, as compared with three-quarters of the whites. The superior terms obtained by Negroes are explained by the higher percentage of VA and FHA loans made to this group. In addition to interest, "points" were generally charged, especially on VA loans, the typical charge being 5 percent. Point charges were usually paid by the seller but, in the judgment of informed observers, passed on to the buyer in the form of higher prices permitted by liberal VA appraisals. The role of easy financing in supporting the price rise is thus doubly apparent. Down payments of 10 percent to zero enabled large numbers of Negroes to buy who could not have met the down payment requirements of conventional loans.

The liberal policies of Philadelphia lending institutions toward these mixed-occupancy areas are a departure from the general practice of mortgage lenders. It should be noted that the loans were both safe and profitable. Nearly all were government insured or guaranteed. The willingness of sellers to pay point charges permitted lenders to combine the safety of guaranteed loans with the higher interest rates associated with conventional mortgage loans. Lenders were also influenced, undoubtedly, by the abundance of mortgage funds available in 1955. Whether they would take the same view of transition-area risks in a period of credit stringency is problematic.

Negro and white buyers paid virtually identical average prices for the homes they acquired except in the one area of poor housing and rapid transition, where Negroes paid substantially more than whites, on the average, and presumably acquired better dwellings. Negroes and whites received about the same value for their housing dollar, paying substantially the same prices for similar houses.

Analysis of the spatial distribution of Negro and white purchases reveals a marked tendency toward racial separation. Among the study areas, the ratio of Negro to white buyers was three to one in the area of good housing and rapid change, but twenty-seven to one in the area characterized by poor housing and fast change. In a third area, where the housing is good but change slow, Negroes were outnumbered by white buyers two to one.

Within the areas some blocks have become wholly Negro occupied, others are mixed, still others have not yet received a Negro resident. In the two areas accounting for the great majority of white purchases, about a third of the blocks were white, but they were the location of the large majority of all purchases by white families.

To measure more strictly the spatial relationship of Negro and white purchases, two calculations were made including the proportion of white purchases made in a mixed block or adjacent to a mixed block,[13] and the per cent of white families who purchased homes on the same street front or directly across the street from Negro residents. The second measure, obviously, is a more critical test of residential proximity, since residents in the same street between intersections are likely to encounter each other frequently in the course of ordinary comings and goings. In the study areas, moreover, the predominant row-type single-family houses are highly homogeneous on any given street, allowing no symbolism of status differences among the residents.

The two measures yielded a striking result. Nearly three-fourths of the white purchases were found in a mixed block or adjacent to a mixed block, that is, within a maximum of three linear blocks from a Negro resident. But only 27 percent of the white buyers acquired homes on the same street front or facing a street front on which Negro families lived, whereas the remainder purchased on all-white

13 The unit of measurement consisted of five contiguous blocks in the shape of a cross in which the house acquired by the white purchaser was in the central block. If any of the five blocks was mixed in occupancy, the whole unit was classified as mixed.

street fronts and facing street fronts. Thus, it seems that the closer the proximity of Negroes, the smaller will be the proportion of white purchasers in any mixed area. This result was, of course, not unexpected. However, the significant finding may not lie in the sharp drop-off in proportion of white purchasers, but in the fact that 119 white families chose to buy homes on mixed streets. The other white families, moreover, by purchasing in an area of transition, exposed themselves to the likelihood of having near Negro neighbors in the not distant future.

White families who choose to buy homes in the same areas with nonwhites, because they go against a behavior norm, may be thought to have some unusual characteristics or motivations which account for their actions. The present study searched for such characteristics but was unable to find any which significantly differentiated the group from the white home-buying population at large. In many ways the white purchasers resembled the resident white population in the areas into which they bought.[14]

As in the general home-buying population, a large proportion of these purchasers were young families. Two-thirds of the family heads were less than forty-five years old. Three-fourths had children less than eighteen and half had children of school age—percentages somewhat higher than among all home purchasers in Philadelphia during 1955 and 1956.[15] About half of the purchasers had attended high school; their educational attainment was similar to that of the resident population of the study areas in 1950. Occupationally, the purchaser family heads showed no unusual concentration in professional or other groups which might be associated with special views on race. Their family incomes, from available scanty evidence, were somewhat lower than those of all recent Philadelphia home purchasers, but averaged about the same as white family incomes in the city as a whole. Two-thirds of the purchaser families were Catholic, a proportion somewhat higher than in the Philadelphia white population but similar to the composition of the study areas.

The Negro purchaser group was quite similar to the white buyers, only somewhat younger, with fewer children, slightly lower family incomes, and a smaller representation in the white-collar and skilled-craftsman occupations.

The white purchasers did not have unique or impelling motives for buying in the mixed areas. Most, in interview, gave commonplace reasons for their choice, mentioning such factors as convenience to work, school, friends and relatives, suitability of the house, or simply, "I'm accustomed to the neighborhood and I like to live here." Familiarity with the neighborhood and attachment to it evidently played an important role in the housing choices of these purchasers, for more than 60 percent of them had lived in the area before buying their homes.

As to racial attitudes, the fact that this group of home purchasers decided to buy in mixed areas implies that they were at least comparatively receptive to the presence of Negroes. However, in interviews, they did not express attitudes of unusual tolerance. If any were motivated by a desire to give a personal example of racial democracy, they were few in number. More than a third of those interviewed expressed varying degrees of dissatisfaction with the presence of Negroes, but strongly negative sentiments were rare. Attitudes of acceptance or rejection were markedly correlated with the degree of hypothetical proximity. Sixty percent of the respondents expressed approval or indifference to the residence of Negroes in the neighborhood; 40 percent to residence on the same block; and 31 percent to residence in an adjacent house. Only 4 percent of the respondents voiced strong disapproval of Negro residence in the neighborhood, but 31 percent were strongly negative toward having Negro neighbors next door.

The racial attitudes expressed by these white home purchasers are fairly consistent with their observed behavior in choosing locations. All of them bought in a general area of mixed occupancy. But as the proximity of Negroes increased, in passing from area to zone to block

14 Data for this phase of the study were obtained by interviews with 194 white families who purchased homes during 1955 in mixed blocks or adjacent to a mixed block, 100 white renter families in mixed blocks, and 196 Negro home purchasers in the study areas.
15 U.S. Bureau of the Census, *1956 National Housing Inventory*, Philadelphia Supplement (unpublished).

to street, the proportion of white purchasers contracted.

CONCLUSIONS

During the time period covered by the present studies, surging Negro demand, supported by growing availability of mortgage credit and concentrated at certain points, was sufficient to maintain and to strengthen house prices in many areas of racial transition. Market stability was helped by the apparently changing attitudes of white property owners which led them generally to refrain from flooding the market with houses on the appearance of Negroes. To an appreciable extent, whites continued to buy into some racially mixed areas, and this too, of course, helped to keep prices up.

In the future, it is certain that Negroes and other minorities will continue to enter many neighborhoods that are now all-white. But some of the conditions which in the recent past generated strong Negro demand for housing in transitional areas are disappearing. Consequently, predictions from recent experience for the future must be heavily qualified. The pent-up housing demand of Negroes which accumulated during the war and early postwar years has by now been satisfied in large part. The increasing market freedom which minorities are gaining, together with the growing social differentiation of the groups, means undoubtedly that their housing demand will be more dispersed and more varied in the future than in the past. Nonwhites are apt to enter more areas than the nonwhite population can fill, and for some areas complete racial transition will be impossible. As noted, this is already true in some higher-priced neighborhoods. Hence there is likely to be an increasing number of neighborhoods where the maintenance of a sufficient market for houses will require white as well as nonwhite buyers in adequate numbers.

The Philadelphia study found white buyers in numbers which may be thought impressive yet were not sufficient to maintain for long the mixed-occupancy pattern. Where four-fifths of the purchasers in a particular area are nonwhite and only one-fifth white, the outcome is plain. The one area where only a third of the purchasers were Negro does have the prospect of a stable interracial balance, if the present ratio is maintained.

The Philadelphia white buyers did not come from any special group in the population nor were they characterized by unusually favorable attitudes toward Negroes. Their motivations for purchase were those of home buyers generally. Similar findings concerning white purchasers in new interracial housing developments are reported. This absence of distinctive traits coupled with the acknowledged general lessening of racial prejudice in the white population during the past twenty years suggests the existence of considerable potential demand by white families for housing in racially mixed areas.

At present, most mixed neighborhoods compare unfavorably with all-white areas in quality of housing, community facilities, or social conditions. But as minority groups gain more freedom in the housing market, an increasing number of good-quality residence areas will be brought into the mixed category. Urban renewal programs may continue to rehabilitate some of the existing deteriorated mixed areas.

The critical racial factors limiting the number of both prejudiced and unprejudiced white buyers who will purchase in mixed areas are the actual or expected number and proportion of nonwhites in the mixed community, and the spatial distribution of nonwhite residences in relation to the homes which white buyers contemplate acquiring. The two factors are related; however, the Philadelphia data show white purchasers to be more accepting of Negroes a short distance away than in the immediate vicinity. An increasing proportion of Negroes in a mixed area is reflected in a shrinkage of white demand, but the behavior of white buyers seems to be related more to the anticipated than to the actual proportion of Negroes.

The level of white demand and consequently the prospects for achieving *both* a stable racial mixture and stable or rising prices in an area depend primarily, therefore, on the expectations of white buyers. In the past, it has been the most common expectation that a neighborhood once entered by nonwhites would become wholly occupied by them, and in most cases events have justified this anticipation. The present outlook, however, is for an increasing number of neighborhoods where this expectation cannot be fulfilled. What this implies for demand and prices in those areas is problematic. If white demand for housing in a given area shrinks in anticipation of racial transition, but Negro buyers do not appear in the expected numbers, the prices of residences may well decline. But present trends may lead to a revision of expectations of white buyers, and to the extent that this occurs, race will tend to lose its importance in the housing market.

Integrated Housing in Kalamazoo

CHESTER L. HUNT

WHAT KIND OF NEGROES MOVE TO NEW RESIDENTIAL AREAS?

Period of Residence

The Negro group in the mixed residential area under study has the type of characteristics that might be expected from a select group of Negro residents in Kalamazoo. Although most of them are not newcomers to the city, fewer are long-time residents than is true of the whites in the same areas. Thus, 15% of the Negroes have moved into Kalamazoo in the last year as compared to 9% of the whites. On the other hand, 20% of the whites have lived in Kalamazoo for twenty years or more and only 4.4% of the Negroes. Approximately half of both the white and Negro population have been living in the city from three to ten years' time.

Education and Occupation

Negroes in the mixed housing areas had more education than either the whites in these areas or the general Negro population in Kalamazoo.[1] In occupational distribution Negroes had a larger proportion of professionals than was true of whites, no business executives at all, and a larger proportion of semi-skilled and unskilled laborers. Negroes in the sample area had a smaller proportion in the semi-skilled and unskilled groups and a higher proportion of professionals than was true of Negroes in the total Kalamazoo area. The relatively high proportion of Negroes in the professional category and the absence of Negro business executives reflects the fact that Negroes have found fewer barriers in some lines of professional endeavor than in business pursuits. The greater proportion of unskilled and semi-skilled workers indicates that thrifty, capable, and educated Negroes still face difficulties in occupational advancement.

The incomes of both Negro and white families were supplemented by working wives. Forty-three percent of the Negro families in the sample and thirty-five percent of the white families had an additional wage earner.

From *Research Report on Integrated Housing in Kalamazoo* (Kalamazoo, Mich.: Upjohn Institute for Community Research, 1959), pp. 3–25. Reprinted by permission of The W. E. Upjohn Institute for Employment Research, Kalamazoo, Michigan.

1 Statements about income and education for all Kalamazoo Negroes are taken from an unpublished study of Negro employment made under the direction of Dr. Jerome Manis for the Western Michigan University Center for Sociological Research in 1956.

Table 1   Education Beyond High School

All Kalamazoo Negroes	18.5%
Whites in mixed area	25.4%
Negroes in mixed area	37.5%

Table 2 Occupation Distribution

	Whites in Mixed Housing Area		Negroes in Mixed Housing Area	
	%	No.	%	No.
Professional	10.5	14	19.6	9
Business Executive	2.3	3	0.0	0
White Collar	15.0	20	4.3	2
Small Business	6.0	8	4.3	2
Skilled Manual	27.8	37	19.6	9
Semi-skilled	21.1	28	30.5	14
Unskilled	17.3	23	21.7	10
Totals	100.0	133	100.0	46

Degree of Pigmentation

Since Negro-white identification is made primarily on the basis of color, it is possible that the degree of pigmentation is a factor in racial attitudes. The Negro respondents were classified by the interviewers as "light," "medium," and "dark." More than half were classed as light. While it is sometimes assumed that light color is an aid to Negroes in securing acceptance by whites, we have little data to justify this belief. Similarly, we have no information by which we could compare the color of the Negroes interviewed with the general Negro population of Kalamazoo. White neighbors sometimes commented favorably on the "light color" of Negro residents; but on a group average, variations in skin color did not seem to be related either to neighborhood acceptance or occupational status.

Conduct and Property Upkeep

In general conversation, whites who are hesitant about mixed neighborhoods sometimes express the fear that Negro residents will fail to maintain their property or will be engaged in noisy, unruly behavior that will disturb community life. Judging from the following table, these fears did not seem to be borne out in the areas surveyed. In fact, Negro and white neighbors were given about the same rating.

Table 3 Reaction of White Residents to Property Maintenance and Behavior of Negro and White Neighbors

CLEANLINESS

Do your next-door white neighbors keep their property neat & clean?

	%	No.
Very Clean	73	51
Fairly Clean	26	18
Not Clean	1	1
Total	100	70

Do your next-door Negro neighbors keep their property neat & clean?

	%	No.
Very Clean	73	46
Fairly Clean	24	15
Not Clean	3	2
Total	100	63

ORDERLINESS

Do you consider your next-door white neighbors to be quiet?

	%	No.
Very Quiet	80	56
Fairly Quiet	19	13
Not Quiet	1	1
Total	100	70

Do you consider your next-door Negro neighbors to be quiet?

	%	No.
Very Quiet	81	51
Fairly Quiet	14	9
Not Quiet	5	3
Total	100	63

APPRAISAL OF LIFE IN A MIXED NEIGHBORHOOD

While the price of real estate is an important topic which is foremost in the minds of many people, it may well be argued that the effect of a mixed neighborhood on people's lives is

Table 4   Reaction to Mixed Neighborhood

(numbers)

Negro	Felt that a mixed neighborhood was		
	desirable	46%	21
	Indifferent	46%	21
	Undesirable	8%	4
White	Felt that a mixed neighborhood was		
	desirable	20%	27
	Indifferent	50%	66
	Undesirable	30%	40

the most important question. The residents of mixed neighborhoods were asked the question, "How do you feel about living in an area where there are both colored and white families?" The answer to this question can be seen in Table 4.

Negroes manifested an almost complete approval of mixed neighborhoods since 92% felt that a mixed neighborhood was either desirable or a matter of indifference, while only 8% had reservations. The whites were less enthusiastic; but 70% felt that a mixed neighborhood was either desirable or a matter of indifference, while 30% felt that a mixed neighborhood was undesirable.

In addition to asking the opinion of people directly, it was also thought that one indication of their attitude might be found by determining what their plans were in regard to remaining in the neighborhood. Respondents (term used for people being interviewed) were asked whether or not they planned to move. Only one of the Negroes said that he was planning to move. When the whites were asked the same question, 80 or 60.1% of the whites said that they planned to remain where they were. Eleven or 8.3% definitely desired to move, and 42 others or 31.6% were undecided as to whether or not they would move. In the interpretation of these figures it might be well to bear in mind that many of the people who were thinking of moving were dissatisfied with the house for reasons not connected with the mixed nature of the neighborhood. On the average, 22% of Kalamazoo people move every year.[2]

"CAUSES" OF MIXED HOUSING ATTITUDES

The "cause" of racial attitudes is difficult to determine. It is possible, however, to ascertain factors that may influence attitudes, and several such factors could be distinguished in the study. None of these factors operate alone and exceptions can be found to any of them.

A favorable attitude towards a mixed racial neighborhood was associated with a long residence in Kalamazoo, a tendency toward sociability in the matter of visiting neighbors and friends, a large number of contacts with the other race, and the age bracket between 20 and 40. A favorable reaction also seemed to be more typical of housewives in the higher-priced dwelling units.

Hostility toward racially mixed housing was associated with a shorter residence in Kalamazoo, a tendency to be withdrawn and not to visit neighbors, few contacts with the other race, the age bracket over 40, and ownership of a lower-priced dwelling unit.

There did not seem to be any relation between occupation or education and the attitude toward mixed housing. One of the allegedly common attitudes toward mixed neighborhoods was seldom expressed in this survey; only two

Table 5   Mixed Housing Attitudes

Favorable Attitude
20–40 years old
More socializing
Higher priced house
More contact with other race
Longer residence in Kalamazoo

Unfavorable Attitude
Over 40 years old
Less socializing
Lower priced house
Less contact with other race
Shorter residence in Kalamazoo

2 Statement based on report of 1950 census that 78% of people in city of Kalamazoo were living in the same house in 1950 in which they lived in 1949.

of the respondents said that they objected to mixed neighborhoods because they were afraid of inter-marriage, and only one mentioned a fear of sexual relationships between adolescents of different races. School relationships evidently are seldom a point of friction, since only one of the white respondents was unhappy about having her children attend a school that enrolled Negroes. This implies white acceptance of mixed classes with a small number of Negroes, since only a few of the people interviewed had children attending the school in the city with the largest Negro enrollment.

NEIGHBORHOOD REACTION TO NEGRO RESIDENTS

Whites Who Moved in Following Negro Entry

Almost one-fourth of the whites interviewed (32) had moved into mixed housing areas *after* Negro entry had occurred and in full awareness of this fact. In this respect, it is interesting to note that 26 of this group said that the presence of Negroes had no effect on their decision about moving into the neighborhood. Six said that the prospect of living in a mixed neighborhood had made them hesitate, but that they had made the move in spite of some misgivings.

Reactions of White Residents in Neighborhood at Time of Negro Entry

The entry of Negroes into the neighborhood apparently was somewhat of a shock to many of the whites in the areas since 39.1% of the whites interviewed described themselves as being unhappy about this event. About one-fourth (26.3%) said it was a matter of indifference to them, and only 3.8% said they had favorable reactions to the entry of Negroes into the neighborhood. The remainder either felt unable to answer the question or were included in the group of whites who had moved in after Negroes were already living in the neighborhood.

The white residents were asked how they felt their neighbors had reacted to Negro entry

Table 6 White Residents' Reaction to Negro Entry

White Residents' Estimate of Neighbor Attitudes Toward Negro Entry		
	No.	*%*
Favorable	4	3.0
Neutral	19	14.3
Hostile	61	45.9
Attempted to oppose	4	3.0
Don't know	45	33.8
Total	133	100.0

White Residents' Own Attitude Toward Negro Entry		
	No.	*%*
Favorable	5	3.8
Neutral	35	26.3
Hostile	48	36.1
Attempted to oppose	4	3.0
Don't know	41	30.8
Total	133	100.0

and gave replies which attributed somewhat more hostility to their neighbors than the respondents admitted themselves.

The Negroes interviewed were asked to indicate how they felt the neighborhood had received their entry, and a majority said they felt that many of their white neighbors were friendly. Negroes were also asked to tell specifically what type of actions their white neighbors had taken when they moved into the block and they mentioned both friendly and hostile acts.

It will be observed that there is a rather striking contrast in the interpretation given by the two races. This difference may be explained in terms of the way that the two groups wished to see the situation and the picture which they wished to present of themselves to the interviewer. Few of the whites described themselves as having been favorable to the entry of Negroes. On the other hand, Negroes said that a majority of their white neighbors were friendly and reported that almost half of them made

Table 7 Negro Impression of White Neighbors' Reaction

Negro Residents' Impression of White Neighbor Attitudes

	%	No.
Friendly	65.3	30
Indifferent	15.2	7
Unfriendly	13.0	6
Don't know	6.5	3

Negro Residents' Impression of White Neighbor Actions

	%	No.
Friendly overtures	45.7	21
No overt action	30.4	14
Hostile acts	15.2	7
Don't know	8.7	4

statements or engaged in acts, such as bringing food or helping with moving, which were interpreted as friendly overtures. It is, of course, possible that Negroes were anxious to be accepted and were inclined to place a more favorable interpretation on the acts and statements of white neighbors than was intended by the neighbors themselves. It is also possible that many whites who were unhappy about the general principle of a mixed neighborhood felt that they should still try to be on friendly terms with the individuals involved.

Only 3% of the whites said that people in their neighborhood had attempted to take action to oppose the entry of Negroes, while approximately 15% of the Negroes reported that they had been the victims of hostile acts. This seems contradictory, but it is possible that the whites who were free to admit unhappiness about the entry of Negroes were somewhat hesitant to admit that their district had been involved in neighborhood conflict, since usually actions of this type are viewed with disfavor in the Kalamazoo community.

Hostile acts included smearing the wall with ink, tearing down foundation walls, making threats, and requesting the Negro family to move out of the neighborhood. There were three cases which had been known to the director of the study and in the community generally as points of conflict in which white neighbors denied knowledge of any overt action to force out their Negro neighbors.

At the time of the interview, the majority of white residents could be classified as being indifferent toward the existence of a mixed neighborhood. Their attitude may perhaps be typified by the lady who said, "It doesn't matter to me as long as each race tends to its own business. My neighbor (Negro) seems to be all right." Some whites said that they were more interested in the person than in his race, and remarked that they would rather have a good Negro family in the block than a "trashy" white family. There were also a few whites whose approval of housing integration led them into attempts to help the Negro family. For instance, one white man visited all the houses on the block and urged them to accept the Negro family as well as inviting the Negro newcomer on the block to visit his house as soon as he arrived. There were others, of course, who took a more hostile position. Some who had been bitter about the change in the neighborhood still retained this attitude. These people felt that there was nothing that they could do about the situation and seemed to regard it as a distasteful but unavoidable pattern.

NEGROES AND WHITES AS NEIGHBORS

How Much Do Neighbors Associate in Kalamazoo?

Before we can discuss intelligently the extent of friendly neighboring relationships between Negroes and whites it is necessary to consider the kind of "neighboring" relationships that are usually found in Kalamazoo. To discover this, we asked people a variety of questions concerning their associations with neighbors. The assumption was that close friendship between neighbors would be reflected in frequent interaction. The results indicated that "neighboring" is less common in Kalamazoo than might be assumed.

More than half of the housewives questioned said they had not visited any of their neighbors in the last month. Nearly 60% said that their husbands spent little or no time with neighborhood friends. When asked whether most of their friends were found in the same area in which they lived or in other parts of the city, only one-fourth of the group said that most of their friends were found in the area in which they lived. People in Kalamazoo are undoubtedly friendly, but it seems that they often have only casual and rather limited relationships with their neighbors and that friendship is not necessarily closely related to "neighboring."[3]

General Pattern of Negro-White Neighboring

Respondents were asked a number of questions concerning their neighboring patterns including such topics as visiting, shopping, exchange of work, exchange of visits, talking, borrowing tools and food, etc. From these questions a scale was computed in which the greatest possible amount of neighboring was indicated by a score of 34 and the least amount of neighboring was indicated by a score of 7.

In evaluating this scale, it will be noticed that the score indicating the greatest amount of "neighboring" (17.6) was made by white residents with white neighbors. Negroes themselves reported a slightly less-active rate of "neighboring" (16.94) and whites with Negro neighbors indicated the least "neighboring" (15.5). These figures indicate that whites and Negroes engage in neighboring activity at a rate only slightly less than is true of whites associating with whites.

It is usually assumed that children play together regardless of social barriers and one would expect acquaintance to cut across racial lines. Only twelve of the Negroes had white

Table 8 General Neighboring Scale

	No.	Neighboring Score
Total Sample	178	16.6
Negroes with white neighbors	45	16.9
Whites with Negro neighbors	63	15.5
Whites with white neighbors	70	17.6

Table 9 Play Between Negro and White Children [1]

	Negro	White
A good deal	8	4
About like other children	4	12
Very little	0	4
None at all	0	4

[1] Based on reports of 12 Negro families and 24 neighboring white families who had children of comparable ages.

neighbors with children of comparable ages. All of these Negro families and most of the white families reported that their children played freely with neighbor children of the other race. A few of the whites stated that their children played either very little or not at all with Negro children. These were white families which had expressed misgivings about the idea of mixed housing and apparently sought to discourage interracial contacts. From these figures one would infer that Negro children in mixed neighborhoods usually found white playmates even though some of the white parents might seek to discourage this pattern of behavior.

Comments on Neighborly Relations

The comments made by the white residents indicate a few of the practices in regard to interracial contacts. Some of the white residents tried to include Negroes in neighborhood social activities, some tried to restrict their social contacts, and some used features such as "light color" to justify a relationship which they may have felt was somewhat unusual.

One white woman mentioned that a Negro child in the neighborhood had been invited to attend her eight-year-old son's birthday party. The Negro child was not shunned by

3 This lack of neighboring is borne out by a study of voting behavior in the Westwood area of Kalamazoo, which found that "nearly half of the residents did not consider any of their neighbors as good or very close friends." Jerome G. Manis and Leo C. Stine, "Suburban Residence and Political Behavior." The Public Opinion Quarterly, XXII, 4, Winter 1958–59, p. 489.

the white children but was simply treated as "one of the gang." The Negro child brought a present to the party that was more expensive than the average, and this was interpreted by the white mother as a gesture of appreciation for the invitation.

Another white resident in a mixed neighborhood said that she knew her daughter played with Negro children at school, but she would not allow her to bring them home. She says her daughter, age 15, argues and doesn't think her mother is right, but the mother feels that when her daughter is older and has children of her own, she will feel differently.

One white mother with a boy of the same age as a boy in a nearby Negro family said that the two boys had an excellent relationship and that the Negro mother frequently took both boys on picnics and other types of play activity. The white mother expressed her liking for the Negro mother and remarked approvingly about the "light color" of the Negro mother.

One Negro mother felt her family had been accepted by the neighbors and related an incident in which white neighbors had rescued her family when their boat overturned on a nearby lake. Another Negro mother said that eventually her family had been accepted but that the first year so much hostility was expressed that she was afraid to transfer her daughter to the neighborhood school.

Visits to Homes

One of the greatest indications of social acceptance is an invitation to a home. Visits to the home of a member of the other race were reported by a majority of Negroes but only by a minority of whites. This difference may be the result of the population proportions since the Negroes in these neighborhoods were far outnumbered and a minority of whites could provide all the home visiting that would normally be expected. However, the fact that about 30 percent of Negroes reported no home visits would seem to indicate some hesitancy on the part of both races in becoming involved in this type of social relationship.

Another indication of the significance of the white visiting rate may be obtained by noticing

Table 10 Have You Visited Homes of Neighbors of a Different Race?

Negro Respondents	No.	%
Yes	32	69.6
No	14	30.4

White Respondents	No.	%
Yes	34	25.6
No	99	74.4

that in most of the two block units used in the survey whites outnumbered Negroes twenty to one. Thus on a normal home visiting rate, regardless of race, many of the whites would not have visited the houses occupied by their Negro neighbors. The 25% rate of such visitation reported certainly compares favorably with a chance average.

People with higher education had a greater tendency to participate in neighborhood interaction both within the race and across racial lines. Visits to the homes of Negro neighbors had been made by 38% of the college educated whites but by only 17% of the whites with a grade school education.

Attitudes of Husbands

If the husband was present during the interview, he was asked to state his attitude toward his neighbor of the other race, otherwise the wife was asked how she would describe his attitude. White husbands were more apt than Negro husbands to be described as having an approving (fine) attitude toward the male neighbor of another race and also more apt to be classified as being reserved (doesn't like them too much). The indication of greater hesitancy on the part of whites than of Negroes is consistent with other findings in the study, but the greater expression of friendliness by whites seems a bit contradictory. This may be due to the fact that attitudes expressed by members of both races reflect the type of response that is considered socially desirable. Presumably the whites who had a friendly at-

Table 11 Attitudes of Husband Toward Neighbors of Other Race

| | Negro Husbands | | White Husbands | |
	No.	%	No.	%
Fine	8	17.4	43	32.3
About like others	17	36.9	18	13.5
Friendly but little contact	13	28.3	19	14.3
Doesn't like them too much	8	17.4	53	39.9
Totals	46	100	133	100

titude were anxious to emphasize this, while Negroes wished a "normal" acceptance and felt this was expressed by the attitude "about like others."

Contacts with the Next-Door Neighbor

To gain still more definite information, respondents were asked about their association with their next-door neighbors. With one exception, all of the Negro families lived next to a white family. About half the white families had one Negro neighbor and the remainder had only white neighbors. Thus we have a comparison of the extent to which Negroes and whites neighbor with the amount of neighboring that goes on when both neighbors are of the white race. The study did not provide a chance to get data on the extent of "neighboring" when both neighbors are Negro.

The following scale measures the interaction of the respondents with their next-door neighbor. The score indicating the greatest possible

Table 12 Next-Door Neighboring Score

	No.	Score
Total Sample	178	50.4
Whites with white neighbors	70	47.9
Negroes with white neighbors	45	49.9
Whites with Negro neighbors	63	53.6

amount of "neighboring" was 76, and the score indicating the least possible amount of "neighboring" was 18. The score is based on such activities as visiting, calling in homes, borrowing or lending tools and household supplies, talking informally, etc.

The results are basically similar to those indicated in the analysis of general neighboring attitudes. In this instance, however, the greatest amount of contact between next-door neighbors was found between white and Negro neighbors, although the difference was very slight.

All of the information that we have on neighborhood relationships supports the same general interpretation. This is, that in many instances, neighboring activity in Kalamazoo is neither frequent nor intimate. Negro and white neighbors, however, seem to have about the same type of contacts as neighbors of the same race. All Negroes in the sample reported some degree of "neighboring" contacts; and this might be explained by the fact that even though their next-door neighbors or some others in the block were not sociable, there were always a few white families who showed some degree of friendship.

The data on neighboring do not support either the fears of those who feel that proximity produces conflict or the hopes of those who claim it leads to close friendship between neighbors of different racial backgrounds. Rather than friendship or hostility, it usually leads to the limited contacts that are typical of an impersonal urban situation. While neighborhood proximity seldom leads to intimate friendship between neighbors, it may be argued that the very fact that people do not rely on neighborhood acquaintances for deep personal friendship makes it easier for them to accept a mixed neighborhood.

HOW MIXED NEIGHBORHOODS DEVELOP

Channels Used by Negroes in Making Purchases

Since it frequently is alleged that Negroes not only face outright opposition to their entry into white neighborhoods but also have difficulty in following the usual channels used in real estate transactions, an effort was made to discover the exact procedures used in the pur-

Chart 1 Prices of homes purchased by Negroes.

%	20.9	62.8	16.3
	Under $8,000	$8,000– $14,999	$15,000 and over
No.	9	27	7

chase of homes by Negroes. The information was not quite as satisfactory in this respect as in other questions, apparently indicating a good deal of vagueness about the financial arrangements of the family, but some data were secured. The emphasis is placed on channels involved in purchases rather than rentals, since only three of the Negro families occupied rental housing.

Sources of Referral

Negro purchasers became aware of a house being available through a variety of means, as indicated by the following table of answers given in response to the question, "How did you learn this house was vacant and available for purchase?"

In two cases the respondent did not remember the name of the real estate agent. Ten specific real estate companies were mentioned in ten separate transactions; eight of these companies were members of the Kalamazoo Board of Realtors. Local realtors estimate that members of the Board of Realtors handle about

Table 13 Means of Locating Property

	%	No.
Real Estate Agent	27.9	12
Advertisements (includes both newspaper ads and signs on property)	23.3	10
Friends	11.6	5
Others and don't know	37.2	16
Totals	100.0	43

80% of the sales of property over $7,000 in value and about 30% of the sales under $7,000. To estimate the total activity of real estate agents, we should also add an unknown number of sales made by real estate agents who are not members of the Board of Realtors.

Since most of the sales made to Negroes in previously white areas are above the $7,000 price level one might expect that real estate agents would be involved in a high proportion of such sales. Although real estate agents are occasionally involved (27.9%) in sales of property to Negroes entering a white neighborhood, it seems apparent that many such sales are arranged without the help of real estate agents. Apparently real estate companies are active in a smaller proportion of the sales to Negroes entering white areas than would usually be expected with houses of the price level involved. This statement should be qualified by the possibility that some of the signs and advertisements mentioned may have been placed by real estate agents.

There was some indication that the white owner of the property was at times hesitant about making the sale, although in only four instances was there an indication of a deliberate effort to conceal what was being done until the neighborhood was confronted with a *fait accompli*. About half of the white respondents said that they felt the neighborhood was critical of the property owner who had sold his house to a Negro. Two instances were mentioned in which neighbors had telephoned local real estate agencies protesting against the sale.

Credit

Financing of the houses was arranged in the manner indicated:

Table 14 Financing Methods

	%	No.
Land contract	27.9	12
Building and Loan Association	37.2	16
Other (cash)	4.7	2
Don't know	30.2	13

The average down payment was $1,864 with payments above this running up to $5,000 and payments below going down to $800, with one instance of no down payment being required. Two of the three building and loan associations in Kalamazoo handled all the loans of this type reported by the Negro respondents. There was no evidence offered by the Negroes interviewed that they had any particular difficulty in financing their purchase, although this does not preclude the possibility that other prospective Negro purchasers may have been deterred by credit difficulty. F.H.A. and V.A. guaranteed loans were not utilized by these Negro purchasers. Agents of financial institutions deny that any discrimination is practiced by these agencies and the reasons for the neglect of this type of financing are not clear.

Effort to Stimulate Property Sales

In several northern cities, neighborhood reaction to the development of a mixed neighborhood has been complicated by a deliberate effort to stimulate real estate turn-over by an approach to white residents from real estate agents warning them that the neighborhood is changing and that they should make an immediate sale. This type of procedure seemed infrequent in Kalamazoo. The white respondents were asked whether anybody had approached them on selling their house since the time of the entry of Negro neighbors. Less than one-third (30.8%) of the whites could remember having been approached by anyone on selling their house. When they were asked what reasons were given for thinking that they might be interested in selling, only 1.5% of the whites mentioned the entry of Negroes. When they were specifically asked whether anyone who approached them on selling the house had men-

tioned neighborhood change or Negroes moving in, 5.2% of the white respondents said that this had been involved. The interviewers did come across charges that real estate agents had encouraged white residents to sell out in one street in the north-central section. While this type of action is rare in Kalamazoo, it has often appeared in other cities. Ethical real estate agents discourage this type of solicitation and feel that most of it is carried on by individuals who have a speculative interest.

It has also been true that sometimes one method of resistance to Negro entry has been to buy out new Negro residents. Approximately one-fourth of the Negroes reported that they had been approached about selling their houses, although only 13.6% felt that this was done in a deliberate effort to get them out of the neighborhood.

"Clustering" of Negro Residences

Some of the white families who were interviewed said that they had no objection to one or two Negro residents coming into the block, but they were afraid that eventually they might be living in a neighborhood that was predominantly Negro. This type of Negro concentration did not seem to have occurred in any of the blocks visited. Rather than speaking of the term "racial dominance" in an area, we are using the term "clustering" to indicate a situation in which two or more Negroes are living within the distance that would normally be covered by a long city block (600 feet).

The survey was divided into four geographical districts, north, south, east, and west; but it became evident that the northern district was somewhat different in its racial occupancy pattern from the other districts. The historic pattern of the city has been that a mixed housing district, in which the large majority of Negroes were concentrated, existed in what might be roughly called the north-central to north-eastern part of the city. Farther north of the mixed district, however, was a fringe of housing that was entirely white in composition. Negroes have been entering this area in the last seven or eight years; and therefore, several houses from this area were included in the survey. The initial assumption was that there were

Table 15 Instances of Clustering or Isolation of
Negro Families in Mixed Neighborhoods

	Total instances
No other Negro families within 600 feet (length of a long city block.)	25
Two families adjacent	2
Two families a block or less apart	3
Three families adjacent	1

a few isolated Negroes who had entered this
area, but the interviewers began to find that
the neighborhood had changed sufficiently so
that this fringe now appeared to be more nearly
half and half rather than one in which there
was a predominance of whites with only an occasional Negro resident. It was not possible for
us to get the exact proportion of whites to
Negroes in this northern fringe, but it seemed
evident that the racial composition would at
least approximate an equal ratio. Data from
families in this northern fringe were compared
with data from families in other areas, but no
significant differences emerged.

In the other three geographical districts there
was no evidence of anything approaching a
large-scale movement of Negroes to any given
area or block. The nearest indication of this
was an occasional clustering of two or three
Negro families fairly close together, although
in most instances the Negro residents were entirely surrounded by white families.

RESIDENTS' ESTIMATE OF REAL ESTATE PRICES

To obtain information on this topic, we
asked the opinion of those interviewed and
used a report of the Kalamazoo Bureau of
Municipal Research compiled from available
records regarding property description and
sales.

In the course of the interview, the respondent was asked the following question, "Is the
price of housing about the same in this area
as elsewhere in the city for the same type of

house?" Replies are indicated in the following
table.

Table 16 White Residents' Estimate of Price
of Real Estate in Mixed Area

	%	No.
Higher here	7.5	10
Same here	70.7	94
Lower here	21.8	29

The white residents who indicated that they
felt the price of housing was different in their
area, either higher or lower, were asked the
following question, "If not the same, how do
you explain the difference?" The answers were:

Table 17 Reason for Price Differentials

	No.	%
Effects of mixed neighborhood	5	12.8
Other reasons	34	87.2

These answers apparently would indicate that
most of the people interviewed did not think
that housing values in their neighborhood were
different from values elsewhere in the city and
that only a small number who felt there was a
variation of housing values blamed the effects
of the mixed neighborhood for this difference.

The respondents were asked if they had tried
to sell their houses within the last ten years'
time. Sixteen had tried to sell unsuccessfully
and nine of these indicated they felt the difficulty in selling the house had been due to the
fact that it was located in a mixed neighborhood. Indirect attitudes toward property values
might also be revealed by a question in which
the respondents were asked, "What do you
most dislike about living in the neighborhood?"
To this question 21.1% of the whites interviewed (28 people) volunteered that they felt
the mixed nature of the neighborhood was a
handicap. It will be noted from these and other
questions that although some whites expressed
reservations about living in a mixed neighborhood the matter of lower property values was
not often mentioned.

DOCUMENTARY PRICE EVIDENCE [4]

Methodology

To gain more information on housing prices, available records on property transactions were checked. For this purpose, the staff of the Bureau of Municipal Research, the Western Michigan University Center for Sociological Research, and a representative of the Kalamazoo Appraisers Society cooperated in the selection of ten distinct types of neighborhoods found in mixed housing areas. These in turn were matched with ten neighborhoods that appeared to have similar characteristics except that they were occupied entirely by white residents. A study was then made of available descriptive records and verified sales reports on properties that had been sold between January, 1953, and June, 1958. Information was obtained on 125 sales, of which 77 were in the "all-white control group" and 48 were in the "mixed" housing areas.

A great many factors affect the price of real estate, and it is difficult to be sure that any two parcels of property are of exactly equal value. However, neighborhoods in which the properties were located were similar in character; and the properties in the mixed area and in the all-white area were also similar in assessed evaluation, number of rooms per house, and age of house. With this type of similarity to go on, it was assumed that if the presence of Negroes in the neighborhood had a marked effect on property values, this should show up on the sales of properties in mixed neighborhoods.

Prices in Mixed and in All-White Neighborhoods

Actually the sales records indicate that mixed neighborhoods have no effect on real estate values. For the total number of houses sold, the price of houses in the mixed area averaged $2,706 higher than the price of housing in the all-white area. When the figures were broken down between sales inside the city and sales outside the city, a more confusing picture emerged. Prices inside the city were $314 lower on the average in the mixed areas than in the comparable all-white areas. Prices outside the city, however, were $5,990 [5] higher on the average in the mixed areas than in the comparable all-white areas. This distribution of prices could hardly be due to racial factors since, in one mixed district, houses in the mixed area had a considerably higher sales value than in the comparable all-white area, while in another district they had a slightly lower sales value than in the comparable all-white area.

The inference that arises from these figures is that the presence or absence of Negroes in a Kalamazoo neighborhood is not reflected in the price of real estate.

The following tables give a more detailed picture of the properties that were sold in these two areas. It will be noted that the information is more complete in the city, since the Bureau of Municipal Research was unable to get information on assessment and age of house in the outlying areas. In looking at Table 14, the reader will notice that line A refers to the average *sales price* of houses in the mixed areas of the city and in comparable all-white areas; Line B refers to the average *assessed valuation* of houses sold in these areas to average sales price; Line C indicates the *ratio* between assessed valuation and sales price; Line D gives the average number of *rooms* per house and Line E gives the average *age* of houses sold in these areas. It is recognized that no one of these figures standing alone would be of great significance, but it is felt that the combination of figures should give a greater understanding of the type of housing involved.

In making use of the assessment figures as one index of comparability, it should be stressed that no claim is made that the assessment figure is a valid indication of the sales price of any specific house. The assessor does, however, make a careful effort to come as close as possible to a figure based on the potential sales price of the property; and it seems logical

---

4 *Source:* Bureau of Municipal Research, A Study of the Influence on Property Values of Negro Family Ownership and Occupancy in Predominantly White Family Neighborhoods, Kalamazoo, September, 1958.

5 Two houses in the mixed suburban area sold for $35,000 each. Eliminating these, houses in the mixed area sold for $3,688 more than in the comparable all-white control area.

Table 18 Housing Data Tabulation

Description	All-White Control Area	Mixed Housing Areas
INSIDE CITY LIMITS		
A. Average price ($)	9,513	9,199
B. Average Assessment Analysis ($)	3,026	2,813
C. Average Ratio—Price to Assessment	3.144	3.270
D. Average House Size (Rooms)	5.786	5.879
E. Average House Age (Years)	37.30	35.80
F. Number of Units	65	23
OUTSIDE CITY LIMITS		
A. Average Price Analysis ($)	8,792	14,782
B. Average House Size (Rooms)	5.098	5.000
C. Number of Units	12	25

to argue that, on a group basis, specific assessments which may be low in terms of market price would be cancelled out by specific assessments which are high in terms of market price.

Rate of Sale

The fear is often expressed that it may be more difficult to sell houses in a mixed area even though prices do not actually drop. In order to

Table 19 Price Level of Mixed Housing Area and Control Group, Kalamazoo and Suburban Area Combined

	Average Price of Parcels Sold	Number of Units
All-White Control Group	$ 9,401	77
Mixed Housing Area	12,107	48

Table 20 Difficulty of Selling Houses June 1, 1953 through June 30, 1958

	Mixed Housing Area	All-White Control Area
Homes offered for sale	68	134
Homes sold	48	77
Homes not sold	20	57
Percent of houses sold	71	57.5

Average price asked of parcels offered but not sold:

All-White Control group	$10,393
Mixed housing area	11,020

test this idea, sales records were checked for reports of houses put on the market but not sold. These figures did *not* substantiate the idea that there are unusual difficulties in selling houses in mixed areas. It should be mentioned that Negroes bought only 7 of the 48 houses listed as sold in mixed areas. The presence of a few Negro purchasers was a slight sales stimulus, but most of the sales were made to white buyers.

Comparability of Houses Located in Mixed Areas and in Similar All-White Areas

Matching individual houses for potential sales price is an almost impossible task; and even matching neighborhoods is difficult, since many factors are involved and it is hard to get an agreement on their relative importance. However, appraisers, assessors, and purchasers of property are constantly making such estimates, and while there may be a difference of opinion on an individual house, it is assumed that on a fair number of houses these differences of opinion will cancel out. Looking at the table of sales data for the city, one will see that there was little difference between the mixed areas and the comparable all-white areas in the age of the houses and the number of rooms. The assessment figures for houses sold in the mixed neighborhoods were slightly lower, but they sold at a slightly higher ratio in proportion to assessed valuation—3.27 times the assessed valuation as against 3.14 times for the houses in the all-white neighborhoods. In the county the only description we had was the number of rooms, and here the houses in the mixed area averaged one-tenth of a room less than the houses in the all-white area.

The overall ratio of assessed valuation to sales price was amazingly close to the intention of the assessor (assessor aims for a ratio of 3.33 to 1). Since this was true of houses both in the mixed and in the all-white areas, the question comes up as to whether the assessor may have considered the supposedly unfavorable effects of a mixed neighborhood in making the assessment. To check this possibility, the Bureau of Municipal Research compared assessments on a before and after basis in similar neighborhoods. This assessment comparison was restricted to houses on which they had reports of sale between 1953 and 1958. It was further restricted to houses which had been built before 1948 and which were located within the city limits prior to the annexation changes since 1948. A systematic reappraisal of all assessment in the city of Kalamazoo was made in 1948 and in 1957 using the same system each year. Thus we have an assessment record on houses which in 1948 were in all-white neighborhoods but which by 1958 had been entered by Negro residents. This is compared to assessment reports of houses which were located in similar neighborhoods which had remained entirely white.

Three neighborhoods were selected that had been all white in 1948 but had been entered by Negroes between 1948 and 1958. These were compared with three similar neighborhoods that had remained all white. While many factors influence assessment changes, it is noteworthy that no evidence was discernible of a tendency of Negro entry to depreciate property assessments.

From this table it would appear that property assessments, like actual sales prices, are influenced by the total housing market without any perceptible effect on racial occupancy. The improvement of individual parcels, fluctuations in the popularity of housing styles, inflationary trends, and general neighborhood changes all influence price. Evidently a racially homogenous neighborhood does not escape the effect of

Table 21 Relative Changes in Assessment in Mixed and in All Comparable All White Areas (1948 and 1958)

Areas	No. of Parcels	% Change in Assessment	
		Increase	Decrease
Area 1 (Mixed)	7	7	
(All white)	18	6	
Area 2 (Mixed)	3	24	
(All white)	14	14	
Area 3 (Mixed)	8	36	
(All white)	9		5

unfavorable changes and the entry of a few minority-group personnel does not retard trends that enhance real estate prices.

SUMMARY OF PRICE DATA

Supposedly people in the area should be sensitive to influences affecting property values, but only 14 of the white respondents (less than 11 per cent of the sample) expressed a belief that property values had been unfavorably influenced by the presence of Negro residents in the neighborhood. This is, of course, substantiated by the evidence of sales price figures, which showed that actual sales prices were higher for homes in mixed neighborhoods than in the all-white control group outside of the city limits and only slightly lower inside the city limits. Compared to assessment figures, houses in the mixed areas sold slightly more favorably than houses in comparable all-white areas. Similarly, in looking at a comparison of houses offered and not sold, the houses in mixed areas had as good a chance of finding a buyer as houses in the all-white areas.

Any one of these situations might be explained away by a number of chance factors, but the total impact leads to the conclusion that the evidence of real estate transactions in Kalamazoo does *not* support fears that mixed neighborhoods necessarily mean lower prices.

While this fact does not show up in the statistics, it would seem obvious that some people with strong objections to mixed neighborhoods would take themselves out of the market for real estate in such an area. The record of price maintenance in Kalamazoo does not prove that all potential purchasers will buy in a mixed neighborhood. It does indicate, however, that a strong market for mixed housing may be found among whites who are willing to accept a mixed neighborhood when other circumstances are favorable.

Effect of Integration on Property Values

WILLIAM M. LADD

The purpose of this paper is to explore the reaction of neighborhood housing prices to racial integration. What happens to property values when one or more Negro families move into a previously all-white neighborhood? The answer arrived at in the analysis to follow is based on a study in Ann Arbor, Michigan.

The data are analyzed in two different ways. First, an analysis is carried out on houses that sold at least two times—once before and once after neighborhood integration. For purposes of comparison, data on similarly-priced houses in all-white areas are also included. However, it may be that integration affects property values some years after the first Negro family moves into the neighborhood. Houses which sold twice at least five years subsequent to Negro entry are studied in an attempt to investigate any longer-run effect of integration on property values.

The second method uses assessed valuations of properties. Comparisons are made over time on the basis of a ratio of market to assessed value for different neighborhoods and for different sections within a neighborhood. The trends established by these ratios over a number of years are examined to see if property values do react to integration and if so in what way. The use of assessed values for this purpose is supported by a regression analysis.

Both methods of analyzing the data point to the conclusion that racial integration does not affect property values.

The approach used here is an alternative to the "control area" technique used by Laurenti [1] and in the Kalamazoo study [2]. In their approach, areas of recent integration are compared to all-white areas which match (as nearly as possible) the integrated areas in all essential characteristics except Negro occupancy. However, because of the many dimensions in which neighborhoods vary, good control areas are difficult to find. Factors such as services available, type of nearby construction, zoning ordinances, and accessibility to schools and business districts are just a few of the elements whose variation can alter the comparability of neighborhoods.

Although differing in method our analysis supports the findings of these earlier studies. Laurenti's basic conclusion is that integration is not associated with any single pattern in housing prices. However, he finds that integration is more often associated with stability of price improvement than it is with price softening [1, pp. 5–49]. Although the Kalamazoo study was primarily addressed to sociological questions, some price evidence is given. The major finding, for this part of the study, is that market values are not affected by integration [2, pp. 20–25].

FIRST METHOD

The starting point in this analysis is a comparison of the values of five houses which sold twice—once before and once after area integration. Data from two integrated neighborhoods covering the period between January

From *American Economic Review* (September 1962), pp. 801–808. Reprinted by permission of the American Economic Association and the author.

Houses	Years Sold	Actual Market Value			Deflated Market Value (1960 $)		
		Before	After	Difference	Before	After	Difference
#1-A	1955, '58	$26,500	$31,500	+$5,000	$30,377	$33,248	+$2,871
#2-B	1954, '59	13,500	14,500	+ 1,000	15,475	14,802	− 673
#3-B	1955, '60	10,000	12,000	+ 2,000	11,460	12,064	+ 604
#4-B	1955, '59	13,000	14,500	+ 1,500	15,466	14,802	− 664
#5-B	1954, '59	12,000	13,400 a	+ 1,400	14,450	13,574	− 876
Average values		15,000	17,180		17,446	17,698	
Average differences				+ 2,180			+ 252
Standard error of average differences (1 sigma)				(690)			(610)

a This is an adjusted figure. It takes account of an improvement made to the property during the time interval between sales.

1950 and December 1960 are used.[1] Integration occurred in 1955 in area A and 1958 in area B. By 1960 only one Negro family had purchased a home in each of these areas. Both neighborhoods consist of houses facing short residential streets. There are 35 such houses in area A and 20 in area B. The houses range in price from $13,000 to $31,500 in area A and $10,000 to $17,500 in area B.[2] Most of the homes have five rooms and were built in the early 1950's. Table 1 shows that the market value for each of the houses was higher after than before integration. The average increase in actual prices is substantial. However, when the inflation that occurred in construction costs is allowed for,[3] only a slight average increase primarily due to the influence of one house is apparent. The observed increase in actual prices is fairly well accounted for by the rise in construction costs. In constant dollars (1960 = 1.00) the average price increase from first to second sale is not statistically significant.

The sales prices of houses in all-white neighborhoods that sold twice between January 1950 and December 1960 are now considered. The houses in the all-white areas satisfy three requirements: First, the initial sales prices of these houses are within the price range of corresponding sales in the two integrated areas. Second, the houses sold twice during the same time-period in which houses in the integrated areas sold. Finally, the assessed value of each house was not changed during the time interval between first and second sale. Table 2 shows price data obtained from all-white areas. The findings are quite similar to those in Table 1. Ten of the twelve houses increased in value from first to second sale. The increase in average price in the all-white area is not as large as in the integrated area, but the standard errors show that the observed differences in real market value between the two cases are not significant at the 5 per cent level.[4]

1   Some of this statistical information as well as that presented later was secured from personal interviews and from the records of real estate brokers. Most of the data, however, was obtained from the City Assessor's Office. A considerable amount of the price information was computed from the face value of the federal tax stamps affixed to property deeds. This is a simple procedure because the tax is paid at a rate of $1.10 per $1,000 of purchase price.
2   The figures show the range in market value for all the transactions recorded for each neighborhood. All of this data is used in the analysis in the second section of the paper.
3   Only prices relevant to the residential housing industry in this part of Michigan are used in the price index. These "Comparative Cost Multipliers" were obtained from the Assessor's Office. For the relevant years they are:

1950 = 1.3595   1954 = 1.2045   1958 = 1.0523
1951 = 1.2783   1955 = 1.1463   1959 = 1.0193
1952 = 1.2568   1956 = 1.0995   1960 = 1.0000
1953 = 1.2295   1957 = 1.0678

4   The standard error of the difference between mean differences is 1.06 sigmas.

Table 2 Prices of Houses in All-White Areas: Houses Which Sold Two Times Between 1950 and 1960

Houses	Years Sold	Actual Market Value			Deflated Market Value (1960 $)		
		First	Second	Difference	First	Second	Difference
#1	1953, '56	$13,500	$16,500	+$3,000	$16,598	$18,142	+$1,544
#2	1952, '56	13,500	14,000	+ 500	16,967	15,393	− 1,574
#3	1953, '59	19,000	20,000	+ 1,000	23,361	20,386	− 2,975
#4	1952, '59	21,000	22,000	+ 1,000	26,393	22,425	− 3,968
#5	1950, '51	14,000	14,000	—	19,033	17,896	− 1,137
#6	1952, '54	16,000	18,500	+ 2,500	20,109	22,283	+ 2,174
#7	1953, '56	7,000	9,000	+ 2,000	8,607	9,896	+ 1,289
#8	1950, '52	14,000	15,500	+ 1,500	19,033	19,480	447
#9	1950, '52	7,000	5,500	− 1,500	9,517	6,912	− 2,605
#10	1956, '59	20,000	20,500	+ 500	21,990	20,896	− 1,094
#11	1957, '59	27,500	30,000	+ 2,500	29,365	30,579	+ 1,214
Average Values		15,681	16,863		19,179	18,572	
Average Differences				+ 1,182			− 607
Standard Error of Average Differences (1 sigma)				(378)			(533)

The final comparison in this part of the study involves houses which sold subsequently to area integration. Area C was integrated in 1945 and as of 1960 about 30 per cent of the occupants were Negro. Some of the houses in this area sold at least twice between 1950 and 1960. An investigation of the price behavior of these houses should reflect any longer-run effect of integration.[5] Area C is much larger and more heterogeneous than the other integrated areas. It consists of about 700 homes, some built prior to the 1860's, others in the early 1950's, with substantial variation in both number of rooms and market value. Sizes range from 4 to 12 rooms and market value from $6,000 to $35,000. Table 3 shows the data on postintegration sales. With one exception, all of the houses increased in actual market value from first to second sale. On the whole the results are very similar to those obtained from the two previous comparisons.

The findings for this part of the study are contrary to the belief sometimes heard that integration depresses property values. The similarity in price behavior of the three cases studied suggests that integration does not affect neighborhood property values.

SECOND METHOD

In this part of the analysis, the behavior of housing prices is expressed in terms of a ratio of market to assessed value.[6]

Two questions concerning the adequacy of assessed values must first be answered. The first question is: Are houses in different neighborhoods assessed at about the same rate? The data in Table 4 suggest that they are. Although differing substantially in average price, the neighborhoods (A, B, C) are quite comparable in terms of the ratio of assessed value to market value. In this respect, two of the areas differ by less than 1 per cent and the total variation is only 1.9 per cent.

The second question is: Are houses in different price ranges assessed at about the same rate?

5 The assessor's records only go back to 1944; otherwise it might have been possible to obtain useful preintegration price data on these houses.
6 Assessments in Ann Arbor are based on "real" cost. Using 1941 price levels, the assessor attempts to compute the replacement cost of properties. Usually, each property is assessed only one time. If improvements to a property are recorded, the assessed-value figure is adjusted accordingly.

Table 3 Prices of Houses in an Integrated Area Selling Between 1950 and 1960: Houses Which Sold at Least Twice After Area Integration (Area integrated in 1945)

Houses	Years Sold	Actual Market Value			Deflated Market Value (1960 $)		
		First	Second	Difference	First	Second	Difference
#1	1954, '56	$12,500	$15,000	+$2,500	$15,056	$16,493	+$1,437
#2	1951, '54	12,500	17,000	+ 4,500	15,979	20,477	+ 4,498
#3	1950, '57	9,500	14,000	+ 4,500	12,915	14,949	+ 2,034
#4	1952, '55	6,500	7,000	+ 500	8,169	8,024	− 145
#5	1950, '59	13,500	14,500	+ 1,000	18,353	14,780	− 3,573
#6	1950, '52	10,000	11,000	+ 1,000	13,595	13,825	+ 230
#7	1951, '58	16,000	18,000	+ 2,000	20,453	18,491	− 1,962
#8	1954, '58	11,000	13,500	+ 2,500	13,250	14,206	+ 956
#9	1952, '53	17,000	17,500	+ 500	21,366	21,516	+ 150
#10	1954, '57	10,000	13,500	+ 3,500	12,045	14,415	+ 2,370
#11	1954, '56	5,500	6,500	+ 1,000	6,625	7,148	+ 523
#12	1953, '55	10,500	11,000	+ 500	12,910	12,609	− 301
#13	1955, '58	12,500	14,000	+ 1,500	14,329	14,732	+ 403
#14	1957, '58	12,500	14,000	+ 1,500	13,348	14,732	+ 1,384
#15	1950, '54	11,000	11,000	—	14,955	13,250	− 1,705
#16	1953, '57	28,000	31,500	+ 3,500	34,426	33,636	− 790
#17	1957, '59	20,500	19,000	− 1,500	21,890	19,367	− 2,523
Average Values		12,882	14,588		15,863	16,038	
Average Differences				+ 1,706			+ 176
Standard Error of Average Differences (1 sigma)				(350)			(400)

A regression analysis was carried out to provide an answer to this question. Treating each area separately, the data points used to determine the regression equation were obtained by averaging all transactions and their associated assessed values for all houses which sold in the same year.[7] The regression line and its scatter are shown in Figure 1. The regression equation is:

$$M.V. = -.079 + 4.31A.V.$$
$$(.26)$$

This relationship is a highly significant one and over 85 per cent of the variation in real market value is associated with quality of house as measured by assessed value.[8] As is apparent in Figure 1, there is no substantial curvature embodied in the relationship: no bias in assess-

ments according to price class is apparent. The use of assessed values as a control for quality of house appears justified.

Let us now see how market values in the three areas vary over time. Figure 2 illustrates the similarity of the three areas with respect to price behavior. A slight decline, common to each area, is observed. In the year following integration (1955 for area A and 1958 for area B), prices improved. The general impression, however, seems to be one of stability; that is, the trend in actual market value parallels, quite

7 There are no sales recorded for some years within the time period covered by this study. The number of average yearly transactions recorded for each area is as follows: Area A: 7; Area B: 6; Area C: 11. The closeness of fit observed in the regression arises from the fact that averages rather than data on individual sales are used in this analysis.
8 $F. = 267$; $F_{.01} = 7.95$; $R^2 = .87$.

Table 4   Housing Data for Three Areas

Description	Area A	Area B	Area C
Average market value (1960 dollars)	$22,160	$13,940	$16,814
Average assessment (dollars)	5,280	3,472	3,851
Average ratio: assessment to price	.238	.249	.230
Number of sales	22	23	135

closely, the trend in construction costs over the relevant time period. This finding is identical to the one found earlier in the paper by a different method. Surely the presence or absence of Negroes is not reflected by the price data.

One may still wonder if any price differential can be observed between market values in all-white sections close to Negro occupants and market values in the integrated sections. Area C is a neighborhood that permits such a comparison. Within area C, some parts are predominantly Negro and other are all-white. A classification was made, selecting those sections having at least a 50 per cent Negro population for comparison with those parts having no Negro population. This information is summarized in Table 5. There is a large difference between these sections with respect to average market value, but in the case of the ratios of assessed value to market value there is only a small difference—1.6 per cent. If anything, prices are higher relative to assessed values in the sections that have the highest percentage of Negro occupants.

REFERENCES

1. LUIGI LAURENTI, *Property Values and Race: Studies in Seven Cities,* Berkeley and Los Angeles, University of California Press, 1960.
2. *Research Report on Integrated Housing in Kalamazoo.* Kalamazoo: W. E. Upjohn Institute for Community Research, July 1959.

Table 5   Housing Data Tabulation on the Basis of Negro Occupancy

	Area C		
	Sections Having No Negro Occupants	Sections Where Negroes are a Majority	All Other Sections (Sections Having about 20 Per Cent Negro Occupants)
Average market value (1960 dollars)	$23,343	$13,794	$14,480
Average assessment ($)	5,506	3,015	3,383
Average ratio: assessment to price	.235	.219	.233
Number of sales	31	44	60

Figure 1   The relationship of assessed value (A.V.) to market value (M.V.).

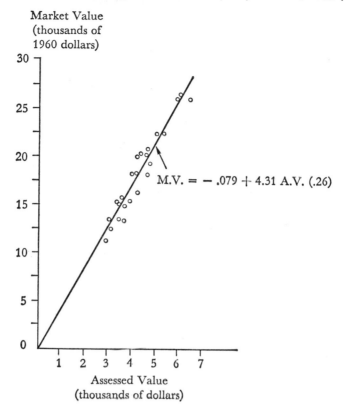

Market Value
(thousands of
1960 dollars)

M.V. = − .079 + 4.31 A.V. (.26)

Assessed Value
(thousands of dollars)

Figure 2   Trend of average price to average assessed value.

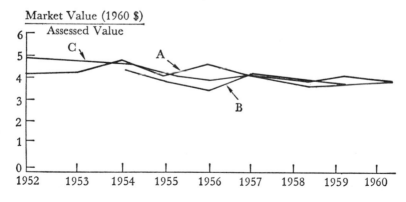

Market Value (1960 $)
――――――――――――
Assessed Value

Note on the Economics of Residential Zoning and Urban Renewal

MARTIN J. BAILEY

The proposition that the completely unrestricted use of land (especially urban land) by its owners according to what each deemed to be in his interest would lead to results injurious to all of them as a group has long been accepted as an essential foundation of public policy on land use. By and large, acceptance of this proposition is based on the obvious fact that some forms of land use in any circumstances, and most forms of land use in some circumstances, have beneficial or harmful effects on neighboring properties. As the owner pursuing his own interest will not take these effects into account, the cumulative effect of many owners' unrestricted decisions will not be conducive to their best interests as a group.

An elementary (and classical) example is that of the smoke nuisance. Each owner in a residential district can heat his home or apartment building more cheaply if he burns cheap coal in a smoky furnace than if he burns high grade coal in a furnace that does not emit smoke. However, the value of their dwellings for their own occupancy or as rental properties, may very well be reduced by more than the saving in heating costs if everyone in the district heats as cheaply as possible. If this is true, they will be benefited by allowing their privacy to be invaded by a regulation, applicable to all of them, restricting the amount of soot and ash their chimneys pour into the air.

The particular kind of nuisance with which this note is concerned is the nuisance of people themselves when they live adjacent to other people whose tastes, habits, and incomes are markedly different from their own. In this case the nuisance may be unilateral rather than mutual. It is generally true that people consider it unpleasant to live near groups of people with lower incomes and with tastes and habits "inferior" to their own, while the reverse is sometimes and perhaps generally not the case.

If the nuisance were mutual there would be no grounds for intervention, as a matter of fact, since the members of each group would gravitate into homogenous residential areas with minimum perimeters bordering the other, mutually repelling, groups' areas. A problem of uneconomic land use, given people's tastes

in these matters, will arise only when the nuisance is wholly or partially unilateral. Consider the opposite extreme, where members of group X prefer living near group Y to living entirely surrounded by other members of group X, while members of group Y prefer to live entirely surrounded by other members of group Y. Suppose that streets A, B, C, and D are occupied entirely by members of group X, while streets E, F, G, etc. are occupied entirely by members of group Y; and suppose that only the occupants of streets D and E consider themselves affected by their proximity to members of the opposite group. Under the assumed conditions, if people do not anticipate any change, the properties along street D will sell (and rent) at prices higher than those along streets A, B, and C, and the properties along street E will sell (and rent) at prices lower than those along streets F, G, etc. Suppose also, for simplicity, that lot sizes and structure types are the same in both groups of streets. (This assumption is not realistic but makes no essential difference to the substance of the argument.)

Now if in the initial situation a property on street A, B, or C sells for the same price as a comparable property on street F or G, then the price of a property on street D will sell at a price higher than a comparable property on street E, and it would pay the owners along street E to convert (or sell for conversion) to group X occupancy. In fact, such conversions would continue to be profitable until properties entirely within the group X district sold at prices below the prices of properties within the group Y district by an amount equal to the sum of the premium and discount on each type of boundary property. In taking this profit, however, the owners along street E would be inflicting a loss on the owners on both sides, since they would cause the owners on street D to lose their (desired) proximity to group Y and the owners on street F to acquire (undesired) proximity to group X.

From *Land Economics* (August 1959), pp. 288–292. Reprinted by permission of the Regents of the University of Wisconsin.

In the initial situation in which properties interior to each group sold at the same prices as in the other, if streets D, E, and F were all under the same owner no conversion would in fact be made because the losses on streets E and F would entirely offset the gain on street D. Conversely, if a final equilibrium under divided ownership were reached, as indicated, with markedly different price levels in the interiors of the two areas, then consolidation of ownership along the boundary would make it profitable for the new owner to convert back to the point at which the price levels of the two interiors were equal. Since such a consolidated owner would make a profit in this operation he could offer higher than market prices for the properties at and between the two locations for the boundary and it would pay the existing owners to sell to a consolidated owner.

However, there would be a bargaining problem as to how the profit was to be divided between the existing owners and the "redeveloper"; and inconsistent expectations could prevent even a mutually profitable bargain from being made. (Such failures are said to be common in real estate experience.) Consequently, there is a case for some form of governmental intervention to maintain or obtain the optimal result: either zoning to keep group X from spreading beyond street D, or a "redevelopment" scheme backed by powers of compulsory acquisition if the overspill has already occurred.

Holding the line at street D is referred to as "optimal" because it implies equal property values (for properties strictly comparable except for type of occupant) within the two areas. If properties within the area occupied by group Y sell above the prices of comparable properties within the area occupied by group X, there is economic waste in the use of the properties; conversion of some of the properties from the less valuable to the more valuable use will secure the increased value at no cost (or at the cost of the conversion). Generally speaking, it is wise policy to employ resources in their most valuable uses since this is equivalent to maximizing the total product obtained from the resources. Following such a policy consistently has an effect for society as a whole comparable to that obtained by landlords in an area who submit to a uniform restriction on the amount of soot and ash their chimneys emit: it tends to raise the general standard of living through maximizing the total net product even though it may be disadvantageous to some individuals in each particular instance.

As has already been indicated, it will not be profitable to convert any properties (move the boundary between the two groups) for a single owner of all the properties if the prices *at a distance* from the boundary are the same on both sides of the boundary. Suppose the price for a standard property within group X (along streets A, B, and C) is P_x, that the price on the X side of the boundary (along street D) is $P_x + p$; that the price within group Y is P_y, and that the price on the Y side of the boundary is $P_y - d$. If the single owner of streets D, E, and F converts street E to occupancy by group X, he will gain on that street the difference between the two boundary prices; i.e., his profit on street E will be $(P_x + p) - (P_y - d)$, since he has converted the street from being on the Y side of the boundary to being on the X side. However, on street D he will lose p on each property, because street D is no longer on the boundary but has become interior to group X; and on street F he will lose d on each property, because street F is no longer interior to group Y but has become the boundary of the group. Hence his total profit on a cross-section of single properties, one on each street, will be $(P_x + p) - (P_y - d) - p - d = P_x - P_y$. If the two interior prices, P_x and P_y, are equal, this total profit will be zero.

More generally, if the types of dwellings and lot sizes characteristic of groups X and Y are not the same, there will be some cost to converting properties from use by one group to use by the other. In this case a single owner of all the boundary and near-boundary properties would not find it profitable to convert unless the price difference between two typical groups of properties, one from each side (each occupying the same total area) is sufficient to cover the cost of conversion. Under divided ownership, on the other hand, occupancy by group X will in this case expand till the boundary price of group X property exceeds the boundary price of group Y property by the cost of conversion: $(P_x + p) - (P_y - d) = c$, where c is the cost of conversion (assumed the same in either direction). That is, it will proceed to the point where $P_x - P_y = c - p - d$. It will pay a single owner to convert part way back, which is to say that "renewal" will be good public policy, if $p + d$ is greater than $2c$; for if so, his profit from renewal, $P_y - P_z - c = p + d - 2c$, will be positive. Otherwise, although a wasteful mistake has been made, the gain from undoing any of it is not sufficient to justify the cost.

The economics of urban renewal, or of zoning by residential type, therefore has the following clear (and unexpected) features: (1) There are two ways, equivalent in principle, to measure whether a proposed urban renewal project (or zoning restriction) is economically justified: it is justified if (a) the price of comparable property is higher in the area of preferred use (group Y use in the example) or if (b) the sum of changes in property values at and around the boundary between uses will be positive if conversion is made toward the preferred use—due allowance being made for costs of conversion in both cases if renewal is contemplated. (2) An "inferior" type of land use, specifically one that causes a nuisance to surrounding properties, should be allowed to expand whenever the price level of properties within the area of that use is higher than the price level of comparable properties within areas of other uses *provided* that the intensity of the nuisance depends only on the distance from the boundary. (This assumption seems appropriate for the type of case under consideration.)

This latter result is especially surprising since we have become quite accustomed to the adoption of renewal projects and of zoning restrictions in the face of substantially higher property values in the inferior use (i.e., slums) than outside it. Clearly the course of policy has not in practice been guided by the considerations mentioned here but has involved other considerations as well.

It is evident from writings and public discussion on this subject that certain types of residential land use, i.e. slums, are felt by most people to be intrinsically undesirable, and that it is thought possible to get rid of them by legislation (zoning) or by demolition and "renewal." Several distinct issues are usually mixed indiscriminately in these discussions and in the present context it will be necessary to separate them. In the first place, people object to the comparative poverty, the low incomes, of most people living in slums. The housing in which they live is largely a reflection of these low incomes although, since there is variation among families as to the amounts they spend on housing and as to the distances they travel to work, it is in part a reflection of differences in tastes in these matters. In the second place, it has been noted that slums and their occupants tend on the average to impose disproportionate tangible costs on the rest of the community because of relatively high morbidity rates (part of which is paid for through public assistance), high crime and delinquency rates, and high costs of fire protection relative to tax revenues.

It is sometimes argued and frequently implied indirectly, that slum clearance would by itself solve these problems although, except in the case of fire risk, there is no relevant evidence indicating that it would. Simple comparisons between morbidity and delinquency rates in public housing and in the slums from which the occupants came make no allowance for the effects of administrative selection among applicants for public housing. A carefully controlled comparison between occupants and nonoccupants of public housing is now in progress in Baltimore, the preliminary results of which indicate that improved housing has no effect on morbidity, i.e. that the observed differences are due entirely to selection.[1] The results on other characteristics are still forthcoming.

Whatever the case for public housing, however, urban renewal is quite another matter, as is restrictive zoning. The effect of these is either to restrict the total available supply of slum housing, holding up prices and rents in the slum areas compared to other areas, or else merely to relocate the slums. Some occupants of slums, at the economically higher margin, may thereby be induced to live in somewhat higher quality housing than would otherwise be the case; and it might be argued that the public will receive benefits from this similar to those, if any, obtained from public (subsidized) housing though to a lesser degree. Even if further study of public housing reveals substantial external benefits, however, this would

1 Daniel M. Wilner, Rosabelle Price Walkley, Marvin N. Glasser, and Matthew Tayback, "The Effect of Housing Quality on Morbidity," Preliminary Findings of the Johns Hopkins Longitudinal Study, *American Journal of Public Health,* December 1958.

not imply that such benefits can be of much importance in the analysis of urban renewal or restrictive zoning. They would arise in connection only with a few marginal families who because they are marginal probably contribute relatively little to the external diseconomies of slums in the first place. Certainly, urban renewal and zoning do nothing to relieve the poverty of people in slums, marginal or otherwise.

Indeed, in the light of the remarks made above concerning the economic criteria for optimal zoning and renewal decisions, it can be said that when these activities hold property values and rents higher in slums than elsewhere they lower the real income of the community and therefore, if anything, increase rather than reduce poverty. It would seem much more sensible, therefore, to adopt programs which alleviate poverty, the fundamental problem, rather than attacking the symptom of poor housing.

The one exception to the above line of reasoning has to do with the costs of fire protection. There is no reasonable doubt that statistics showing higher costs of fire protection per dollar of assessed value of property can be taken at face value. This implies that the protection of slum properties is being subsidized by other property owners. It does not follow, however, that either zoning or urban renewal is the appropriate means of attack on this problem especially since renewal is in practice much more costly than the subsidy to fire protection in slums. The subsidy would disappear if legislation were enacted imposing a surcharge (extra property tax) on inflammable properties corresponding to the extra cost of their protection. This surcharge would in the short run come out of the net incomes of the owners since their ability to raise rents is already being exploited as far as the traffic will bear. If paying the surcharge was more costly than making the buildings fire-resistant the owners would find it profitable to do the latter and would thereby make the economically efficient decision.

A further possible reason for the existing public support for urban renewal projects and zoning, at points where it is uneconomic, is that people do not like to move even if they are able to convert their properties to slum occu-

pancy (or sell their properties to someone who will convert them) at a profit. Indeed, they may not realize in many cases that there is such a profit; and those who do know but prefer to stay may succeed in getting a project adopted because of the ignorance of the others on this point. If those who do not want to move were really numerically dominant in a neighborhood, however, this would be reflected in property values, and the observed disparities would not exist. Insofar as this motive supplies political force for the adoption of renewal and zoning, these forms of interference in land use represent the subordination of policy to a special interest group at the expense of the community as a whole.

Certain instances exist, however, where the economic criteria developed in this article are in fact satisfied even when slums generally have been prevented from expanding to the optimal extent. Although alternative residential users of property may not be unduly harmed by the necessity of moving, certain institutions specific to a relatively high income neighborhood may find that the costs of moving are prohibitive. In this case property values, including the value of the institutional property itself, will in a sense reflect the cost of moving and will accordingly dictate the prevention of the conversion of the neighborhood into slums. If this is true, as might be the case with a hospital or university dependent on a surrounding high-income neighborhood, it would in fact pay the institution to buy up the property surrounding it *even at slum property prices* and to maintain an "island" of the high income, less profitable use. The cost of doing this would, by hypothesis, be less than the cost of moving the institution. Public assistance might be justified on two counts: powers of eminent domain are necessary for the assembly of property in this way because of bargaining problems if the powers are not available; and it may be felt that the institution is deserving of a subsidy.

However, insofar as urban renewal in some cases is in fact a form of federal aid to hospitals and universities, it should be recognized as such and allocated according to principles governing such aid generally. Powers of eminent domain can of course be granted without being accompanied by a subsidy.

The sober appraisal of actual and proposed

urban renewal projects requires better factual information than is readily available on the effects of slums and other "inferior" uses on surrounding property values. Real estate experts are not highly communicative on this subject, mainly no doubt because of the variety and complexity of these and other influences on property values. The present writer is currently engaged in an attempt to sort out these factors as reflected in real estate transaction prices in selected areas of Chicago's South Side in a recent ten-year period. If successful, this study may be broadened to other areas. This should in principle make it possible to estimate the external benefits of urban renewal by either of the two formulas, the one relating to boundary values and the one relating to "interior" values.

Effects of Race and of Other Demographic Factors on the Values of Single-Family Homes

MARTIN J. BAILEY

Whether the arrival of Negro or other non-Caucasian residents in a neighborhood is the cause of a decline in property values has long been a topic of considerable interest in casual conversation and in casual analysis, but it has nevertheless stimulated very little serious research. (Notable, if exceptional, examples of such research are the studies by Laurenti[1] and by Nourse,[2] discussed below.)

A widely held view is that the entry of Negroes into a neighborhood reduces property values, although another widely held view is that those who purchase at reduced prices in such a neighborhood typically resell immediately to Negroes at prices at least as high as those that prevailed before the entry of Negroes. These apparently contradictory views could both be true, even without any element of "panic" or ill-informed action. Negroes and other minority group members might pay prices and rents as high as or higher than others, while prices and rents in areas adjacent to their occupancy could be lower: a similar relationship is possible between slum or low-income areas, irrespective of race, and the adjacent areas. (The economics of this phenomenon, in relation to optimum land and to urban renewal programs, was analyzed in a previous article.)[3] Indeed, because the slum or low-income effect and the effect of race, if either exists, are similar, the question naturally arises whether they are distinct. Inasmuch as non-Caucasians generally have lower incomes and tend, on the average, to live in more crowded circumstances than do whites; an apparent effect of non-Caucasian occupancy on property values in nearby areas might in fact be the same effect as that of occupancy by Caucasians with the same incomes, degree of crowding, etc. Previous work relating to this subject matter is of only limited help in answering questions of this kind.

Although Nourse's study was directed primarily at the measurement of the impact of public housing developments on surrounding area property values in St. Louis, he also obtained some evidence on the effects of race and other demographic variables on contract monthly rents. He found that the effect of non-Caucasian occupancy on rents was insignificantly negative (in the same blocks), and that crowding increased rents in the crowded blocks.[4]

From *Land Economics* (May 1966), pp. 215–220. Reprinted by permission of the Regents of the University of Wisconsin.

1 Luigi Laurenti, *Property Values and Race* (Berkeley, California: University of California Press, 1960).
2 Hugh O. Nourse, "The Effect of Public Housing on Property Values in St. Louis" (unpublished Ph.D. dissertation, Chicago, 1962).
3 Martin J. Bailey, "Note on the Economics of Residential Zoning and Urban Renewal," *Land Economics*, 1959, p. 288.
4 *Loc. cit.* p. 51.

Nourse's method, in the bulk of his study, involved using repeat sales of properties. This has the advantage that it removes unknown and uncertain influences, such as changes in the quality and type of dwelling sold in each area, which could introduce unknown biases into the results and may have done so in the study by Laurenti. Its major disadvantage is that it requires using only those properties that sell more than once in the period of study, a restriction that cuts down the available sample size by a large factor.[5] This limitation makes it difficult or impossible to assemble enough data to analyze demographic influences in detail.

A third, if costly, possibility is to attempt to measure all the major influences on property values and to distinguish their effects by subjecting all sales to multiple regression analysis. It turns out that even here some reduction in sample size results from the unavailability of data but the reduction is not so great as when one is limited to repeat sales. Moreover, this procedure permits cross-sectional analysis of prices in a given year. The disadvantage is that the collection of data on location, size and quality characteristics, and so on, for hundreds of properties is a slow and costly task.

The aim of this procedure was to obtain reliable estimates of demographic effects on property values although it had as a useful by-product estimates of the influences of all other variables considered. Altogether some fifty variables were used, including area demarcators, for a relatively large sample of homes sold in the years 1948–51 in two Chicago southside areas. However, only part of one of these areas had to be selected for more intensive study, in which only some forty-one variables were employed. A parallel study of the same area was also possible for 1954–56.

The dependent variable was the logarithm of the amount of federal real estate transfer tax paid on the transaction when a property was sold. The alternative of using assessed valuation for real estate tax purposes (although this procedure would permit using all properties in the area, rather than merely those sold in a given time period, for the sample for study) was rejected as hopelessly inadequate for the purpose at hand. The results from the sample studied indicate strongly that assessed valuation can be significantly improved upon

as an indicator of value from a general point of view. In particular, although the tax assessment has a higher simple correlation with the tax-stamp "price" than does any other variable, its partial correlation is insignificant in the multiple regression in the case of the 1948–51 data. Moreover, assessed valuation would assuredly fail to reflect the influence of demographic variables under study because such variables do not enter into the typical assessor's formulae for determining taxable valuation.

Although the transfer tax stamp data are of course not absolutely reliable, there is some reason to believe that they can be relied upon for the purpose of such a study as this. In a large part of his sample Nourse was able to check tax-stamp data against actual sales prices recorded in the offices of the real estate firms involved. The only major errors he found involved assumed mortgages, which are rare and which we were able to identify. Other errors were small and appeared random. Of course, the firms he was able to check could be unrepresentative. It is sometimes alleged that the less reputable firms will deliberately overstate sales price in affixing the tax stamps in the hope of selling another property later at an inflated price by quoting this "price" as evidence. If such is sometimes the practice, the question arises, does it bias any of the regression coefficients reported below? Conceivably it would and it might, for example, account for the positive coefficient found for the N-Density variable in Tables I and II below: the less reputable firms are more likely to be dealing in areas of high density of occupancy. Apart from this relatively minor aspect of our findings, however, we see no way that such a practice would affect our results except to lower significance levels.

The sample was further limited to single-family residences for the sake of simplicity. The values of apartment buildings and commercial property are almost certainly affected by the demographic variables in ways different from the effects of the latter on the values of single-family residences. These types of buildings would very likely present special difficulties of specification and measurement as well.

5 In the present work less than five percent of the sales in a ten-year period were repeat sales.

For these reasons and because single-family residences have attracted the most interest in this context, we restricted our attention to them.

The demographic variables employed at one stage or another include three types of variables, relating to race composition, density of occupation, and income. Income is available only by census tract and, surprisingly, proved entirely unsatisfactory as did all other tract data. Density of occupation reflects slum or near-slum conditions or, more generally, is correlated negatively with income. These data are available for 1950 by census blocks in the form of the number of dwelling units having 1.51 or more persons per room. A special tabulation by the Bureau of the Census at our request yielded average persons per room on a half-block basis, as described below. The racial composition of the population is published on a Census tract basis only; the special tabulation provided it on a half-block basis.

At an early stage it was decided that the standard census blocks would likely prove an inappropriate geographic concept for measur-

ing the effects under study. A Census block, the contiguous group of buildings bounded by four streets (where the street pattern is regular), is a convenience for enumeration but is not the neighborhood concept of the block. The latter consists of the buildings on both sides of a street between two intersections. Because nearly all the single-family houses in the area under study face on the north-south streets, we considered a block in effect to be a one-block-long area between two north-south alleys (instead of that between two north-south streets). To test the hypothesis that demographic variables for a given block affect values in neighboring areas differently from the way they affect them in the block itself, we constructed measures of these variables for the ring of blocks around the block in which each property sale occurred as well as for the block itself. The meanings of the different block concepts for a set of blocks in the area studied are illustrated in Figures 1 and 2. The special "neighborhood" blocks we constructed are designated as N-Blocks, in Figure 2; the Census block counterparts for which

Figure 1   Area definitions of C-density and C-ring.

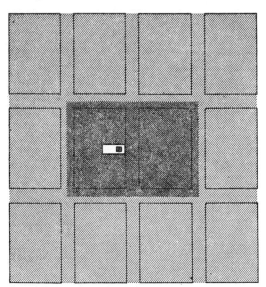

Legend:

⬛ Location of a property sold.

▨ Census blocks for C-density for that sale.

▨ Census blocks for C-ring for that sale.

Figure 2   Area definitions of N-density and N-ring.

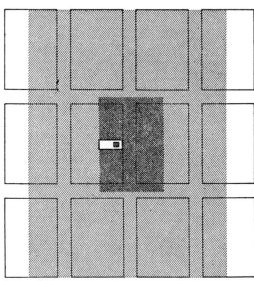

Legend:

⬛ Location of a property sold.

▨ N-block area for N-density for that sale.

▨ Area for N-ring for that sale.

we aggregated the published data are referred to as C-Blocks, illustrated in Figure 1. For the block of sale, we averaged the two Census blocks on opposite sides of the street on which the sale took place, for the C-Density concept. The ring of blocks just referred to has an N-Ring and a C-Ring variant, both shown in the respective figures. Inasmuch as the Census block data on crowding (relating to density) are readily available, it seemed appropriate to use them to see whether they serve as well as the data obtained, at a non-trivial cost, by special tabulation.

The independent variables considered, besides the demographic ones, include taxes, dimensions of the house and lot, building material, access to shopping and public transportation, and others.[6] The successful ones appear in Tables I and II. For 1948-51, in Table I, some eight of the non-demographic (control) variables and four of the demographic variables were significant, with correct signs, at not less than the 10 percent level and of these six were

significant at the one percent level. With due allowance for variables considered and then dropped, the number of variables we would expect to reach these levels of significance by chance alone would be five at the 10 percent level and zero or one (i.e., one-half) at the one percent level. The adequacy of significant variables confirms the conclusion we reach if we evaluate the significance of the multiple R^2 by deducting from the degrees of freedom remaining in the final regression the number of variables considered and then dropped because of non-significance or wrong sign. By this test the overall regression is significant at the .005 level. (The number of variables "significant" but with the wrong sign was roughly the num-

6 Sources include the Recorder's office, the Assessor's office (Cook County), the Chicago publication, *Realty and Building*, the Chicago Title and Trust Company, the Chicago Bureau of Maps and Plats, Sanborn Maps, the Southeast Chicago Commission, and the National Opinion Research Center.

Table I Regression Coefficients and Standard Errors for the Demographic Variables: 1948-51 Data

Variable	Coefficient	Standard Error	Standard deviation of the variable (demographic variables)	Significance **
(1) C—Density	−.00221	.00128	11.6	.10
(2) C—Ring	.00782	.00333	6.06	.05
(3) N—Density	.165	.138	.144	—
(4) N—Ring	−.777	.207	.118	.005
(5) N—Race	*	*	.098	—
(6) N—Race Ring	−.612	.153	.136	.005
(7) Log Floors	.676	.180	—	.005
(8) Log Front feet	.527	.111	—	.005
(9) University Access	.0363	.0166	—	.05
(10) Years of Sale				
(1950)	−.119	.042	—	.01
(1951)	−.092	.049	—	.10
(11) Common Wall	−.0710	.0340	—	.05
(12) Alley	.114	.042	—	.005
(13) Conversion	−.122	.073	—	.05

* Deleted because the coefficient was smaller in absolute value than its standard error.
** This regression had 82 degrees of freedom. All tests are one-tailed except C—Density, C—Ring, N—Density, N—Race, and years of sale.

Effects of Race and of Other Demographic Factors on Single-Family Homes 323

Table II Regression Coefficients and Standard Errors for the Demographic Variables: 1954–57 Data

Variable	Coefficient	Standard Error	Significance *
(1) N—Density	.0321	0.230	—
(2) N—Ring	−.0802	.0351	.05
(3) N—Race	.0534	.0703	—
(4) N—Race Ring	−.246	.105	.05
(5) Log Taxes	.351	.081	.005
(6) Log Floor Area	.157	.119	.10
(7) Log Floors	.226	.184	—
(8) IC and El Access	−.0366	.0165	**
(9) Log Age	−.230	.219	—
(10) Years of Sale			
(1956)	.0686	.0411	.10
(1957)	.0578	.0470	—
(11) Common Wall	−.0338	.0240	.10
(12) Partial Common Wall	.0537	.0358	**
(13) Corner	.0633	.0448	.10
(14) Conversion	−.0442	.0476	—
(15) Dilapidation	−.00071	.00050	.10
(16) Wall Spacing	−.00563	.00374	**
	.01428	.00777	.05
(17) Basement	.115	.057	.05

* This regression had 62 degrees of freedom. All tests are one-tailed except N—Density, N—Race, Taxes, and Years of Sale.
** Wrong sign.

ber one would expect due to chance variation.)

These results are reasonably strong in view of the small geographic area in the sample. Collinearities between some variables were high (e.g., floor area and lot size), and the range of variation within the sample too small to permit reliable estimation with our modest sample sizes. Also, of course, the arbitrary specification of some control variables may have been at fault and some significant ones may have been overlooked. The results shown in Tables I and II reflect these considerations and show several differences in the two lists of significant variables. More reliable estimates of the influences of the demographic and control variables would be possible only with a much larger sample and a larger and more varied geographic area—as may be attempted with the 1960 data.

The principal results for the demographic variables in the more reliable 1948–51 run, shown in Table I, are that (1) the N-Block density and race variables are insignificant, (2)

the C-Block density variable is weakly significant and the C-Block ring is significant with a positive sign, and (3) race and density have the negative neighboring-block effect discussed at the beginning of this article. Thus the effort involved in setting up the special block concept appears to have been justified and the null hypothesis is accepted on the first of the race variables. There is no indication that Negroes, as such, pay more for housing than do other people of similar density of occupation. High-density occupancy and, independently of this effect, non-Caucasians have significant negative effects on property values in the blocks near to but not those including their own residences. This result implies the existence of a racial factor in neighborhood value effects. In blocks of high non-Caucasian occupancy values are higher, if at all, only through their higher density of occupancy.

The density effects are pronounced. Although housing values in this sample are about the same, other things equal, in blocks of high-density occupancy as in blocks of low-density occupancy, they are lower in neighboring blocks. This phenomenon was anticipated in this author's earlier article previously cited. The C-Density effect is very small and is a mixture of N-Block and N-Ring effects. The C-Ring result indicates that neighborhood effects outside the N-Ring are negligible. The C-Ring effect is numerically very small and may represent what amounts to a non-linear adjustment to the N-Ring effect. (These remarks on the relative sizes of the C-Block and Ring effects are true even after due allowance for the large variances of the C-Variable relative to those of the N-Variable.) These overall results strongly support the use of the N-Blocks in preference to the C-Blocks and the use of average density rather than frequency of high-density dwelling units.

Table II presents results from the parallel set of runs for the years 1954–57, using data on the demographic variables gathered and tabulated by the National Opinion Research Center in a special survey in late 1955. The Center took a fractional sample of households, the fraction varying over the area covered and being highest in the part of the area nearest the University. For this study we had these data tabulated over the area in which the fraction sampled exceeded 10 percent which, as it happened, included virtually all sales in the entire sample area in the indicated years. The demographic data were aggregated using the N-Block concepts only.

Generally speaking the regression coefficients from these data agree with those using the Census data. The density effect in the N-Block of the property sold is insignificant; the density effect for the ring of blocks surrounding that of the property sold is significantly negative. The race effects are also about the same as in the other run; an insignificant effect in the block of sale but a significantly negative effect of non-Caucasian occupancy in the surrounding blocks. In the runs involving the Census data, sale price was sufficiently well explained by the control variables that the tax effect became insignificant. The runs with NORC data were less successful in this respect: here the tax effect remained strongly positive, though it has a much lower partial correlation than simple correlation with the dependent variable. The

improvement in explanatory power of the regressions through the use of many variables turns out to be highly significant, and very necessary for the purpose at hand.

The results with the demographic variables in no way contradict the widespread belief that "blockbusting," the conversion of neighborhoods to low-income and to non-Caucasian occupancy, may have been a profitable activity. The N-Ring and Race ring effects directly support this belief in the sense that such conversion is profitable in Caucasian, higher-income areas whose values have been depressed by a nearby slum as long as slum values remain above those in the bordering area. When immigration to the slum area creates a high enough population density to raise values there above those in areas well away from the slum, conversion is even more profitable and tends to relieve the over-crowded condition. In the area under study, however, the process had evidently worked itself out enough by around 1949–50 to have reduced relative values in crowded and non-Caucasian areas to approximate parity to those in the bordering, less crowded areas a couple of blocks or more away.

On the major question, discussed at the beginning of this paper, whether slum-dwellers and non-Caucasians pay more than others for equivalent housing, these data not only fail to support this idea but on the contrary point to the opposite situation. If values within the slum were to be as high or higher than those outside, there would have to be a jump in values just as one crossed the boundary into the slum to offset the decline in values as one approaches it; that is, there would have to be a strong positive own-block effect to offset the ring effect. That is, areas well inside the slum have a value differential compared to areas well outside it given by the *sum* of the own-block effect and the ring effect; where the own-block effect is zero or insignificant, the sum is the same as the ring effect. Thus the area under study appeared to be in the equilibrium position described in this author's previous paper, where divided ownership prevents values from settling down at the relationship that maximizes the total net product of housing. Values in slum and Negro areas in this instance, relating of course only to single-family dwellings, seem to have fallen below the values of comparable housing within the middle-income areas nearby.

V

SLUMS, URBAN RENEWAL, AND PUBLIC POLICY

Empirical Studies in the Economics of Slum Ownership

ARTHUR D. SPORN

While the subject of slum profiteering has received almost limitless journalistic coverage, seriously documented studies of the economics of owning and renting substandard housing are rare.[1] Detailed and quantitative economic studies of slum housing have much more frequently approached the problem from the tenant's point of view. The reasons for this predominance in approach are perhaps understandable. Slum tenants are as a group much more accessible than their landlords, who have often proven difficult to locate even for law enforcement officials armed with compulsory process, and, even if he could be located, the problem of inducing the usual slum property owner to make his records available to the investigator would remain.

In Wisconsin a highly unusual opportunity for studying the economics of slum ownership exists owing to the fact that the state's income tax returns are available for inspection for research purposes.[2] The comparative rarity of such an opportunity is emphasized by the fact that federal income tax returns are in general open to inspection only by employees of the Internal Revenue Service, state tax officials, and Congressional committees,[3] while the use of state returns to investigate many of the cities where such a study might prove most valuable is foreclosed by the fact that the pertinent taxing jurisdiction either imposes no local income tax[4] or preserves for its returns a degree of secrecy as great as or greater than that maintained by the federal government.[5]

The availability of the Wisconsin income tax returns prompted the writer in 1958 to 1960 to investigate the ownership history and the owners' financial operating record for two separate samples of substandard housing in the City of Milwaukee. The initial purpose of the study was to obtain data on the frequency with which the properties had changed hands and the rates at which they were being depreciated for income tax purposes, and also as to the relation between the market price of such properties and the price at which they might be acquired by a public agency in eminent domain.

These data were sought to test two separate hypotheses:[6]

(1) that the availability under state and federal income tax laws to successive purchasers of residential property of repeated depreciation deductions, based upon each owner's separate acquisition cost, stimulates an unhealthy turnover in such property by encouraging each owner to operate it irresponsibly while writing it off in the shortest possible time and then to pass it on to a purchaser who repeats the process; and

(2) that the prospect or actuality of condemnation proceedings to acquire substandard housing exerts an inflating effect on its market price, with the result that the process of public acquisition confers an indirect subsidy upon such property's owners.

The immediate results of these investigations, and their possible bearing on the hypotheses mentioned, are reported and discussed below. In addition to this information an item believed to be of even more general interest and significance emerged: it proved possible in a number of cases to determine the rate of return which the property was yielding to the owners on their capital investments.

From *Land Economics*, XXXVI, No. 4 (November 1960), 333–340. Reprinted by permission of the Regents of the University of Wisconsin.

1 For one of the few studies with which the writer is familiar, see Leo Grebler, *Experience in Urban Real Estate Investment* (New York, New York: Columbia University Press, 1955), pp. 183–6 ("Profits from Slums").
2 See Wis. Stat. § 71.11 (44) (c) (1959).
3 See Internal Revenue Code of 1954 §§ 6103–6106.
4 E.g., Illinois, Michigan, New Jersey and Ohio.
5 E.g., 47 District of Columbia Code § 1564c (1951 ed.); 81 Annotated Code of Maryland § 300 (1957 ed.); 59 McKinney's Consol. Laws of New York Ann. §§ 202, 384, 386-j (Perm. ed.); 72 Purdon's Pennsylvania Statutes Annotated § 3402–506 (c) (Perm. ed.).
6 See A. D. Sporn, "Some Contributions of the Income Tax Law to the Growth and Prevalence of Slums," *Columbia Law Review*, December 1959, p. 1026.

The Properties Studied. The principal sample investigated was a group of properties on Milwaukee's near north side in the area bounded by West Walnut, West Cherry, North 11th and North 6th Streets. These properties are currently (1960) being acquired by the Milwaukee Redevelopment Authority in connection with its Hillside Neighborhood Redevelopment Project UR Wis. 1–2. Of the 155 parcels into which the Authority has divided the area for acquisition purposes, 128 contained buildings devoted either wholly to residential or partly to residential and partly to commercial use, and these last 128 comprised the subject proper of the study.[7] The buildings included brick, brick and frame and frame structures ranging in height from one to three stories and in age from 30 to 75 years, with an average age of 57.4 years. They contained an average of 2.4 dwelling units per structure. While the condition of the buildings varied widely the area in general was considerably run down and was determined by the Milwaukee Common Council to be blighted and in need of redevelopment in November 1958.

In addition to the Hillside Project, the study covered a dozen purely residential properties located throughout the city which had been found guilty of repeated violations of the Milwaukee Housing Code[8] (convictions ranged from 18 to 73 in number) and which were suggested by the Housing Division of the Milwaukee Health Department as representative of the worst offenders in the city. The buildings involved ranged in age from 30 to 75 years with an average age of 64 years, and an average of 19.6 dwelling units per structure. While the same information (except for that pertaining to public acquisition) was sought for these properties as for those at Hillside, the data obtainable for the former proved much more fragmentary. Principally, this was because among the Health Department properties the corporate form of ownership was much more prevalent, and the Wisconsin income tax returns somewhat irrationally permit a corporate taxpayer to lump all of its rental properties in a single account in reporting its operating results but require individuals and partnerships in reporting to detail separately their results for each separate property held.

Ownership Turnover. The record owner-ship of each property studied was traced for the thirty years from 1929 through 1958. A period thus limited was chosen chiefly because ownership history was of interest primarily in the attempt to establish whether there was any correlation between frequency of transfer and income tax depreciation practice; and depreciation figures proved to be available only for the nine-year span from 1949 to 1957. From the ownership record the number of bona fide conveyances undergone by each parcel was determined.[9] The results of this study and classification appear in Table I. The average number of Hillside bona fide conveyances was 2.3; the median, 2.5.

Depreciation Rates. While the Wisconsin Department of Taxation has retained the income tax returns filed with it since the inception of the tax in 1911, the returns' depreciation schedules are systematically preserved only for the nine most recent years. Hence, it was

7 While the Hillside data for buildings partly residential and partly commercial were recorded and analyzed separately from that for those entirely residential, no significant difference in the characteristics for these two groups appeared and consequently the data for the two are lumped in the results reported and discussed herein.
8 Milwaukee Code of Ordinances, Chapter 75.
9 The classification of transfers as bona fide conveyances was basically the same as that employed by Leo Grebler in his comprehensive study of the history from 1900 to 1950 of some 958 parcels on New York City's Lower East Side. In brief, all transfers were considered as bona fide sales and hence as bona fide conveyances unless indications to the contrary appeared in the record. Tax foreclosures and both mortgage foreclosures and voluntary surrenders where possession was taken by an institutional mortgagee were counted only when the property was subsequently conveyed out to a private purchaser within the period investigated and then the two stages were counted (unlike the method of the Grebler study) only as a single bona fide conveyance. While such a sequence of events could hardly be equated to a voluntary transfer it seemed appropriate to take it into account in view of the possibility it afforded of a new cost basis for depreciation purposes. Excluded as bona fide conveyances were death transfers, inter vivos conveyances within a family, agent-principal conveyances (chiefly intermediate transfers involving a real estate broker), conveyances to nominal corporations, and miscellaneous transfers such as quitclaim and correction deeds. See Leo Grebler, *Housing Market Behavior in a Declining Area* (New York, New York: Columbia University Press, 1952), Chapter VI and Appendix G, for a fuller description of this classification scheme and of the methods employed and the uncertainties inherent in assigning transfers within it.

Table I Bona Fide Conveyances Undergone by Hillside and Health Department Parcels: 1929–1958

Number of Bona Fide Conveyances 1929–1958	Hillside Project		Health Department Parcels
	Number Parcels	% of Total	
0	10	8.1	1
1	37	30.1	1
2	28	22.7	5
3	25	20.3	3
4	10	8.2	
5	8	6.5	
6	5	4.1	2
	123	100.0	12

Table II Rates at Which Hillside and Health Department Properties Were Depreciated Under the Wisconsin Income Tax: 1949–1957

Depreciation Rate	Hillside Project		Number of Health Department Properties to which Applicable
	No. of Properties to which Applicable	Per-cent of Total	
2–2.9%	21	16%	6
3–3.9%	50	39	2
4–4.9%	18	14	9
5–5.9%	30	23	2
6–9.9%	5	4	5
10%	4	3	1
	128 [1]	100	25 [1]

[1] These totals exceed the number of properties covered since a single building was usually depreciated at different rates by successive owners, and sometimes by a single owner, during the period investigated.

possible to obtain depreciation figures only for the period 1949–57. These data were obtained for 95 of the Hillside and 11 of the Health Department properties; the distribution of rates among these is shown in Table II.

The rate referred to is in each case that applicable to the principal structure; fixtures and improvements were usually separately depreciated at a considerably faster rate. Depreciation on all properties studied was taken on a straight line basis; the Wisconsin Department of Taxation has not sanctioned any of the accelerated methods permissible under the federal tax.[10]

The average depreciation rate, weighted to take into account number of tax years (but not size of capital investment) to which applicable, was 3.8% for the Hillside properties and 4.7% for those in the Health Department group. The median depreciation rate for the former was 3.9%.

Correlation Between Depreciation and Turnover Rates. Since depreciation was obtainable for only 9 of the 30 years for which ownership turnover was investigated, no definitive analysis of possible correlation between them was possible. Even if one adopted the tenuous assumption that the properties being depreciated at a rapid rate from 1949 through 1957 were those

that experienced the same treatment throughout the 30-year period, no significant correlation emerged: the high turnover properties, those that had experienced 6, 5, and 4 bona fide conveyances, showed average depreciation rates of only 3%, 4%, and 4% respectively, compared with an average for the entire sample of 3.8%; while the high depreciation properties, those subjected to rates of 10%, 6-10%, and 5-6%, showed a bona fide conveyance average of 2.8, 2.8 and 2.3, respectively, compared with 2.3 for the sample as a whole.

Return on Capital Investment. In the case of 48 owners of 45 properties in the Hillside group and four owners of two of the Health Department properties, it proved possible to construct from the returns the taxpayers' capital investment, since the returns showed not only the original purchase price but also all improvements subsequently made and the various rates at which the different capital items were being depreciated. When such a return also indicated the owner's net profit for the

10 See CCH *Wisconsin Tax Reporter* (Chicago, Illinois: Commerce Clearing House, Inc., 1959) Vol. 2, para. 200–664.

year, it was also possible, of course, to determine his rate of return on capital invested. All periods during which any property was (partially) owner occupied were excluded from these calculations on the ground that the net profit in such a case almost undoubtedly represented, to an indeterminable extent, a return on such taxpayer's labor as well as on his capital investment. The results of these determinations appear in Table III.

The average rate of return on the Hillside properties, weighted to take into account the number of years (but not the size of capital investment) to which applicable, was 19.8%.

Redevelopment Authority Acquisition Prices and Owner's Invested Capital. The information that the Milwaukee Redevelopment Authority proposed to acquire the Hillside properties for its project was first released to the public in March 1957. The Authority began to acquire the properties, through purchases negotiated with their owners (occasionally with the intermediate step of obtaining a purchase option), in November 1959; and the process of acquisition, through negotiation and condemnation, was still going on in June 1960. The number of conveyances that took place in the sample between the time the Authority's proposed action became public and the close of the

Table III Return on Owners' Invested Capital in Hillside and Health Department Properties, 1949–1957

Rate of Return	Number of Taxpayers to whom Rate Applicable	
	Hillside Properties	*Health Department Properties*
Under 2%	2	1
2–3.9%	2	1
5–6.9%	2	—
7–9.9%	5	—
10–14.9%	13	1
15–24.9%	13	—
25% and over	11	1
	48	4

period surveyed was insufficient to permit any evaluation of the direct impact of the pending redevelopment upon the market for the properties affected. But, apart from this paucity of conveyances, any attempt to analyze the market effect of imminent public acquisition by a comparison of the sale prices before and after news of the redevelopment was released and by a comparison between such prices and the eventual public acquisition price would have encountered a further difficulty. That is, that while it would have been possible to trace these prices for a given property, the sequence would hardly have any significance unless any intermediate improvements which the owners might have made between successive sales were taken into account. For the most part, information concerning such improvements was not available.

In the case, however, of the properties already mentioned for which it was possible to construct the owners' total capital investment, this difficulty could in part be overcome. Where such owners' invested capital as of December 31, 1957, was determinable, if one adopts the plausible assumption that there were no substantial capital improvements made in the approximately two years between that time and the Authority's purchase (more precisely, that any such improvements did not substantially exceed further depreciation), the relation between acquisition price and invested capital should be of considerable significance. This relation appears in Table IV. The average ratio for the group was 2.89.

EVALUATION AND DISCUSSION

The frequency with which the Hillside properties changed hands (an average of 2.3 [11] and a median of 2.5 bona fide conveyances per parcel during the period surveyed), although high enough to be compatible with a practice of rapid writeoff and turnover, cannot be considered excessive or even exceptionally high

11 This figure, indicating that the average Hillside parcel changed hands every 13 years, compares with a change on the average of every 10 years among old-law tenements and on the average of every eleven years among all properties surveyed, in Grebler's study of New York City's Lower East Side. See Grebler, *op. cit. supra* note 9, pp. 75–77.

Table IV   Ratio of Authority's Acquisition Price to Vendor's Invested Capital as of December 31, 1957

Ratio[1]	Number of Properties to which Applicable	Percent of Total
Less than 1	3	7.7%
1.00–1.49	4	10.3
1.50–1.99	5	12.8
2.00–2.49	11	28.2
2.50–2.99	5	12.8
3.00–3.99	4	10.3
4.00–4.99	2	5.1
5.00–5.99	3	7.7
6.00 and over	2	5.1
	39	100.0%

[1] The acquisition prices on which these ratios are based were the Authority's actual gross purchase price, or the price at which it had obtained a binding purchase option, in every case but one, where the ratio is based upon a proposed acquisition figure for which the Authority had obtained the initial approval of the federal Urban Renewal Administration.

for the type of property concerned. Moreover, the rates at which these properties were being depreciated for tax purposes, an average of 3.8% and a median of 3.9%, are hardly such as to warrant questioning as excessive, even in the occasional case where depreciation ranged as high as 10%, in light of the general age and condition of the buildings concerned. As mentioned, no complete measure of correlation between depreciation and turnover was possible.

In view of the nature of the property surveyed, it is doubtful whether one can draw any conclusions from this data as to whether a pattern of rapid income tax writeoff, encouraging frequent changes in ownership, is prevalent in our cities today. The Hillside neighborhood is too sprawling and sparsely built up to be representative of the more intensively developed, densely occupied tenement neighborhoods found in many metropolitan centers larger than Milwaukee.[12] About all one can say is that, if a significant pattern had emerged in the instant sample, one might reasonably have inferred its presence in more pronounced form in areas of the latter type. In this connec-

tion it may be significant that the properties suggested by the Health Department, with their more substantial structures believed to be more representative of those to be found elsewhere, showed appreciably higher turnover frequency (an average of 3.50 against 2.26) and depreciation rates (an average of 4.7% against 3.8%) than did Hillside, although one must add the caution that the Health Department sample proved too small to permit drawing any definitive conclusions from it. The Health Department results, as well as the higher rate of turnover reported in the New York City study mentioned in Footnotes 9 and 11, suggest that it would be worthwhile to investigate the correlation in a more typical large city tenement neighborhood—presumably employing federal income tax returns if these could be made available.

The results as to the owners' return on capital are believed to speak for themselves. With almost a quarter of the group surveyed showing an annual return greater than 25%, it is hard to avoid the conclusion that, for many property owners in the Hillside area, substandard housing represented a very profitable investment indeed. And the figures reported are undoubtedly on the conservative side since all deductions claimed by the taxpayer were accepted at face value in determining his net profit; the size of the repair deductions taken on a number of returns suggested that some of the items claimed were more properly classifiable as capital improvements.

In the case of the few properties showing a poor yield, heavy repairs appeared to be the principal factor responsible, along with a 10% depreciation rate in one case and the apparent current payment of several years' back taxes in another. The four Hillside properties yielding a net return of less than 4% all reported substantial gross rentals but showed an average ratio of net to gross income of only 7.1%.

The discrepancy between the prices paid for

12 Indeed, there is some question as to how indicative the results of slum landlords operating anywhere in Milwaukee would be of the pattern of more intensive exploitation found in many larger cities, in view of the Milwaukee Health Department's unusual record of long term effective enforcement of the City's Housing Code. See Miles L. Colean, *Renewing Our Cities* (New York, New York: Twentieth Century Fund, 1953), pp. 45–47.

the properties by the Redevelopment Authority and the invested capital of the persons bought out also seems to require little comment. Undoubtedly, a portion of this excess is accounted for by the current expensing and the ultra-rapid writeoff of capital improvements just referred to, and in good measure by the steady rise in price levels that has occurred in recent years. But even if generous allowance for these factors is made it is hard to conclude that a process in which almost 30% of the persons affected are bought out at a price more than three times their investment is not exerting a subsidizing influence. The figures suggest that in at least some of the blighted urban areas now being reclaimed we may have reached a point where market prices are being set with a view to acquisition in condemnation proceedings and not vice versa.

In view of the unusualness of income tax returns as material for investigation and of the widespread speculation and interest as to the value of the federal returns in particular as a source of economic data, a word as to sources and methods in the instant study may be of interest. The writer's experience suggests that, for the detailed investigation of economic phenomena of any duration or complexity, the use of such returns confronts one with difficulties that may seriously limit their value.

The most obvious of these difficulties, and that most frequently encountered, was an inability to find any account at all of the property or transaction under investigation. This obstacle was confronted at a number of stages. First, was an inability to locate any file at all for the party in interest indicated by other sources, such as the registry of deeds or the Redevelopment Authority's or Health Department's records. With the state returns here employed, this absence appeared in some cases attributable to out-of-state ownership, although such an owner is liable for the Wisconsin tax on income from local real estate. When located, the file frequently had returns missing for some of the years under investigation. In a few cases this seemed due to the taxpayers' having received less gross income than the statutory minimum ($600) requiring the filing of a return but more frequently gaps were created by unexcused failure to file, followed by a default or doomage assessment. Even when a return

was found, the property or transaction under scrutiny was sometimes either missing or unidentifiable as the result either of simple omission or of the arbitrary difference already mentioned in the detail required for individual and for corporate returns.

Where a return did contain the details sought, further problems arose on account of inconsistencies between returns for successive years [13] as well as from arithmetical errors and other discrepancies within a single return. Almost invariably these errors produced a result in the taxpayer's favor. The temptation initially arose to correct at least the more straightforward errors encountered but this was soon found to lead into a morass of reconstructing entire returns and a more practical policy had to be adopted of uniformly employing the taxpayer's figures except in the few cases where complete nonsense would have resulted.

The difficulties just mentioned were undoubtedly intensified beyond the ordinary by the fact that the Hillside property owners included many persons of a low level of literacy and even a limited command of English. A few were persons with taxable incomes so low that they can hardly be criticized for failure to use greater precision or consistency in making out their returns; the extra trouble would not have been worth either their own while or that of the tax authorities. It should be mentioned, however, that the incidence of error, and especially of inconsistency from year to year, did not appear appreciably lower on those returns prepared with professional (or at least outside) assistance. Even in the case of persons making a genuine effort to compute accurately their tax liability, the attitude taken towards the prescribed details of the income tax return by the majority of taxpayers (and by their auditing officials) may be too practical a one to make the returns as valuable a source of data as their theoretical contents would indicate.

It should also be pointed out that, while these source difficulties necessarily limit the precision of the results reported, they are not

13 For example, an increase from one year to the next in the cost basis on which depreciation was being taken could readily be explained by additional capital improvements but returns for still later years in some cases showed a reduction to the original basis or to some other lower figure.

believed to affect to any great extent such significance as these results may have, or that of the conclusions drawn from them above. This is so for two reasons. First, the general policy which was followed of accepting all figures reported by the taxpayer, particularly his deductions, at face value offers virtual assurance that the critical item of annual net profits and the rates of return based upon them, err on the conservative side. Secondly, in the case of all returns posing a problem of ambiguity, inconsistency, or omission, the practice was followed of resolving any doubt in favor of the alternative producing the most conservative result. For example, in the case of those depreciation schedules that did not clearly indicate the

owner's separate investment in land, in constructing his invested capital an allowance was made for this item which was considerably more generous than that indicated by the returns for comparable and more completely reported properties. It is not at all certain that such an allowance was necessary or warranted, in view of the indications appearing on the Hillside returns that at least eight and possibly twenty or more of the owners were depreciating land along with their investment in improvements. Indeed, the returns suggested some question as to how widely the basic overall limitation of depreciation deductions to the total cost of the taxpayer's investment was being observed.

Slum Housing: A Functional Analysis

GEORGE STERNLIEB

INTRODUCTION

A sharp division is opening in the ranks of American social activists between the institutionalists and what may be termed the "marketers." The axiomatic role of present housing policy as a social input similarly is under challenge. Congress reflects this uncertainty on optimum action for the future.

The institutionalists are those individuals who, harking back to the lesson of the 1930s, believe in the disposition of social welfare funds through channels clearly defined and structured by the government. There is a strong acceptance by them of certain given tools and values: external guidance of the poor reflected in strong advocacy of public housing, efforts to strengthen the ministrations of the welfare worker, and so on.

The marketers, at least in the socially activist area, are much newer and harder to describe. Essentially they are united in believing that the poor should have greater options—for example, that social welfare funds should be utilized directly to enhance the buying power of the underprivileged, without an intervening structuring of the disposition of these funds.

The use of guaranteed incomes in some form is a frequently advocated instrument. Inadequacies of housing are seen as reconcilable by giving the poor more money—and permitting them at their option to buy better shelter.

Obviously, the dichotomy indicated above does not do justice to the broad range of in-between belief, of tools such as rent subsidies which are usable by either group, and of the diversity of consumers to be serviced by the low-end housing market. Accepting these strictures, however, I am still impressed by the speed with which the concept of bringing the poor into the market mechanisms, as against direct governmental servicing of their needs, has progressed.

In substantial part this change in attitude mirrors the change in the perspective given the problems of the poor. A very short time ago, for example, the expression "urban problems" would have been used in place of "problems

Reprinted from a symposium, *Housing: Perspectives and Problems*, Part I, appearing in *Law and Contemporary Problems*, XXXII, No. 2, Spring 1967, published by the Duke University School of Law, Durham, North Carolina 27706. Copyright © 1967 by Duke University.

of the poor." In part this would have been an euphemism—in part, however, it mirrored the confusion in thinking and motivation prevalent at the time.

There has been a confusion between efforts at rehabilitating the city on the one hand, and helping people who happen to be presently concentrated within cities, on the other.

THE NEGRO IN THE CITY

"If There Were No Negroes"

"If there were no Negroes, the city would be . . . ." Any of a number of "good" things are proposed by all too many people of the United States as a function of this introductory clause. The sins of the city: its decay, its lack of relevance to the current folkways of middle class America, and not infrequently all of its problems generally, are seen as a function of the change in the racial mixture which has taken place in this last generation. I would suggest that this is romantic hogwash. The city is an antiquated form of social organization; its social and economic relevance to the growth frontiers of American society are and have been increasingly tenuous over a lengthy period of years.

The inadequacies of municipal government, revealed strikingly by the series of riots which seems to be a commonplace of every summer, are neither new nor unique. It is not that municipal government is less adequate; to the contrary, a good case can be made for its being much more adequate than was true historically. It is rather that the realities of the city simply cannot provide the standard of living and amenities which the new focal points of American civilization—the new cities, the suburbs—hold out as a measuring stick of adequacy.

Black Power Romanticism

The efforts of Black Power advocates, in this context, can similarly be seen as completely anachronistic in aspiration; the city which they attempt to secure is a bankrupt entity.[1] It is bankrupt not merely in answers, but in its capacity to deliver the improved standard of living which is the universal of American middle class aspiration levels. The "traumas" of the city have been with us probably since its inception.

The city is falling into discard, not because its population distribution has been altered, but rather because the world around the city, the competition faced by the city as an organization, has changed. It is competition, rather than decline in the absolute level of service, that has altered its role. Any efforts at changing this situation must take this basic premise into account. Unfortunately, this has not been the case. Past governmental policy in the city was substantially one, at least initially, or rebuilding some conceived-of Golden Age in the past.

The city must be made a way station toward middle class America for the new immigrants, just as it was for older groups. It is as a means to an end that the city and its housing is to be utilized, rather than as an end in itself.

USING THE SLUMS

The very slums of the city provide a potential takeoff place in this regard, if we can move toward owner residence. This can provide a key element in the development of capital accumulation for the core dweller.

If a gross oversimplification may be permitted, the problem of the slums is one both of plumbing and morale. It has largely been viewed in the past as consisting solely of the plumbing. This is not to denigrate the latter; the provision of appropriate housing amenities is certainly an essential step toward improving the outlook and aspiration level of slum dwellers. However, the morale problem cannot be cured merely by providing these physical amenities.

The present market situation is one of virtual stagnation in the hard core slum areas. The combination of risk, decreasing profitability, and loss of potential for capital gains has substantially restricted the kinds of professional owners who are willing to invest in slum properties. It takes a pretty hard-shelled

1 A clear case in point is the effort to secure Negro ownership of the traditional central core small stores in the face of the discount house and supermarket.

individual to become a professional nonresident owner of slum property, given present societal attitude. And this is not an individual who is easily influenced to invest his money unless an appropriate return can be secured. Given the relative weakness of the slum apartment market, the professional landlord has been faced with the choice of basically two alternatives: to stand pat and not increase his investment, or to attempt to improve his parcel in order to secure higher rentals.

The pattern that we have seen in our studies indicates that the choice has usually been the former. The observer cannot fail to be struck by the "heads we win, tails you lose" nature of this phenomenon. When the apartment market is very strong the landlord need not improve; when the apartment market is very weak the landlord fears for his investment and does not improve.[2]

WHAT IS, OR SHOULD BE, PUBLIC POLICY TOWARD SLUMS AND SLUM DWELLERS?

The goal of government policy towards the slums must have as its primary aim the improvement of the morale of the inhabitants thereof: tax policy, code enforcement policy, financing aid, municipal service policy, all of these must be viewed within the context of the overall objective.

The community must face the realities of the slum situation fairly, without self-deception or romanticism, and at the same time move for change. Let us review the slum conditions as they exist.

1. In Northern industrial cities, the overwhelming majority of hard core slum area residents are Negroes. The decreasing number of whites are typically an elderly remnant of earlier immigrations.

2. There is little evidence of a substantial return of the white middle class to the slum areas of the city.

3. The bulk of slum tenements are owned by absentee white owners. These owners are not merely absentee from the slums per se, they are also absentee at least as residents, from the city in which they own property.

4. The single most basic variable which accounts for variations in the maintenance of slum properties is the factor of ownership.

Good parcel maintenance typically is a function of resident ownership.

5. Subject to major programs of land clearance for the purposes of urban renewal or highway construction or both, a population vacuum is developing in the slums. The tidal wave of southern Negro migration has slowed down and is substantially bypassing some of the northern cities which were its traditional goal. With a virtual stability in Puerto Rican migrant population size, there is no new depressed group on the horizon to fill the older slums.

6. While this population decrease makes the problem of relocation much simpler, it also tends to limit the landlords' capacity and will to improve parcels.

7. Given a substantial dependence upon land taxes in the face of increased demands upon the municipality for services, taxes have become a major inhibitor of entrepreneurial activity in the central city. Particularly in terms of the uncertainty which surrounds their administration, current municipal tax policies are leading to further degeneration of the slums.

8. The relationship of client and patron, which plays a dominant role in the dealings between government, both municipal and federal, and the poor population of the slums, is deleterious to the morale of the individuals concerned.

BOOSTING THE PROPORTION OF RESIDENT LANDLORDS IN SLUM TENEMENTS

There is no question of the significance of local landlord residence, particularly of single parcel landlords, in ensuring proper maintenance of slum tenements. Given the priority accorded by multiple-parcel owners to tenant problems and the lack of feeling on this score by resident landlords,[3] the latter's good record

---

2 *See generally* G. Sternlieb, THE TENEMENT LANDLORD (1966); J. Meyer, H. Schwartz *et al.*, ECONOMIC DESCRIPTION OF THE REAL ESTATE MARKET ON THE LOWER EAST SIDE OF NEW YORK (1967).
3 When asked to rank his problems, the resident landlord cites tenants as minor. The absentee owner, however, puts tenants problems in first place.

in maintenance is most significant. It is the resident landlord, and only the resident landlord, who is in a position to properly screen and supervise his tenantry. No oneshot wave of maintenance and a paint-up, sweep-up campaign, can provide the day-to-day maintenance which is required in slum areas. This can only be accomplished by a resident landlord. The record of these landlords as we have noted in our studies is such as to inspire confidence in their future behavior on this score.

By making it feasible for more residents to become owners, we further encourage the development of local leadership which is so sorely lacking in most slums. The role of resident owners as guides and creators of life patterns for the youth of the slums to follow is clearly evident. Most important of all, we can encourage the growth of capital accumulation which is an essential of social mobility within our society.

Financing

How could this type of development be stimulated? There are several prime requirements. The first of these, obviously, is financing help. The term of mortgages is much more significant from a cash flow point-of-view than are interest rates. For example, a mortgage at six per cent which is written for a fifteen year period involves less cash flow than an equivalent size mortgage for a ten year period at 3½ per cent. Given the dearth of available financing which is currently the case in the slums, there is obviously no alternative but to provide something in the way of long-term FHA-guaranteed mortgages for slum tenement purchases by residents. The analogy with the early Homestead Act springs readily to mind.[4] In that case government lands were provided to those who would live on them, at relatively reasonable rates and with liberal financing. The same thing must be done in the slums.

Advisory Services

Financing, however, is merely one of the several steps which is required. The relatively innocent new resident buyers of slum tenements are frequently victimized by a variety of home improvement services. Thus, a moneylender, interviewed by the writer, pointed to the fact that commonly, when he has to repossess a parcel, the typical cause is that the owner has burdened the parcel with two, three, or more home improvement loans. Just as the Agriculture Department provides a variety of advisory services for the farmer, so the city or the federal government, or both, must provide equivalent advisory services for the new home owner in the slum areas. These advisors must be competent not merely in home improvements, but also in financing and appraising parcels. It would seem entirely possible that among the ranks of senior savings and loan people, as well, possibly, as within the ranks of the present FHA personnel, such individuals could be found. Technical competence, however, must be linked with a basic sympathy with the aspiration level of the new owner and with none of the *deus ex machina* attitude that so often exists in government relations with the poor.

Tax Policy

The question of tax policy is a most significant one on this score, as it is with respect to the general problem of slums. It may well behoove the city to continue its policy of full assessment based upon market values. Obviously, where broad-based taxation is available on a basis other than land, it may reduce some of the strain. Reassessment policy, however, must be more clearly defined than is presently the case. The landlord should have no reason to fear city reassessment as a result of a new coat of paint.

It is essential that the city not merely adopt a more reasonable attitude toward taxation, but also sell the facts of this attitude to those who may be influenced by misconceptions as to its reality. In addition, in the long run it may very well pay the city to provide the equivalent of homestead rebates for resident landlords. This is a format (which will be recognized by those who are familiar, for example, with tax policy in a city such as Miami Beach) in which the homesteader—*i.e.,* the resident landlord—receives either a reduction

4 Ch. 75, 12 Stat. 392 (1862).

or a rebate in his real estate taxes. This might well be coupled with a stipulation that the rebate be employed in the improvement of the parcel in question. The area of uncertainty and suspicion which surrounds current taxing procedures must be clarified. Its existence clearly inhibits improvements.

Municipal Services

There seems to be ample evidence that the level of municipal services required by the slum areas is higher than that required by non-slum equivalent areas. At the same time, there is reason to believe that the actual delivery level of these services is reversed, with poorer areas being slighted.

Every effort must be made by the city to provide an optimum level of services within the slums. Such functions as police protection, street lighting, parking restrictions, garbage collection, and a host of others could be named here. Not least among these is the question of educational facilities. While this is a subject whose depth is beyond the scope of this article, it can not be omitted. Without substantial efforts on all of these fronts, the efforts at utilizing the slums as ladders toward upward mobility will fail.

Code Enforcement

Parallel with all of the above suggestions is the requirement that code enforcement be made much more rigorous. But, prior to this, there is required a much more adequate definition of just what the code should be. Adequate insect and rodent control, plumbing that works, paint, and general cleanliness may be much more significant to the inhabitants of a tenement, both physically and spiritually, than the existence of central heat or plaster walls. Whether the studs used in a repair are sixteen inches on center or are twenty inches on center may be completely irrelevant to a tenant. A building which is completely satisfactory on the basis of existing codes may be completely unsatisfactory in terms of its effect upon its occupants.

Code enforcement, therefore, must require a much more subjective approach than has here-tofore been the case. This is particularly the case with those buildings in the hands of land-lords who cannot afford repairs. In those cases, it may be necessary to work out a long-term plan of rehabilitating the parcel in question—with major emphasis being given to the paint and cleanliness functions, those most easily encompassed by "sweat equity." Good maintenance and resident landlordism are much more significant than mechanical adherence to a mechanical code.

THE FUTURE OF THE HARD CORE SLUM

I would seriously question the potential of hard core slum areas for rehabilitation. Given the relatively loose housing market, which presently exists in many center cities, the bulldozer approach to such hard core areas would seem to be the only answer. This should not wait upon redevelopers. The existence of such hard core blight drags down the neighborhoods peripheral to it.[5]

The loss of tax revenue to the municipality through this process of demolition must be accepted as surgery essential to preserve the surrounding areas from the spread of deep-seated blight. Obviously, the scale of this blight will require considerable discretion on the part of municipal authorities on the phasing and speed of demolition. Given the present functioning of the market, as has earlier been indicated, we cannot depend upon private enterprise to remove no longer useable buildings.

There is some question in my mind as to whether a change in tax policy to encourage demolition might not be in order. The city's need for more open space, and the potential of already assembled and cleared substantial size tracts in encouraging further development, must be depended upon to generate future use for the areas in question. Their maintenance by the city, given the facts of alternative housing availability, cannot be justified upon tax income reasons alone.

5 Current gross vacancy rates, for example, in the twenty-five core census tracts of Newark are on the order of 10% in the midst of a tight housing market. This incongruity is a function of the lack of desirability of core vacancies. In the seventy-five tracts outside the core, the vacancy rate is under 4%. G. Sternlieb *et al.*, VACANCY RATE ANALYSIS (in preparation).

CONCLUSION: NO FALSE ROMANTICISM

The self-help capacity of the poor is limited. Some resident landlords are elderly, others are uneducated, and some lack an appropriate aspiration level. The fact remains, however, that as a group, they are presently the best landlords in the slums, and provide probably the major hope for better maintenance in the future. It will require a talented and understanding guidance operation to help generate landlord enthusiasm, while restraining overexpenditure. The problems here should not be underestimated. It is essential if this operation is to be truly successful, particularly from a morale standpoint, and also from the standpoint of securing long-run improvement, that the advisory service be a guide and an inspiration, not a directorate.

The present and future strains on the municipality's budget, coupled with limited increases in revenue, will make it most difficult to pay for the services that are required. The alternative, however, of increasing degeneration is all too clear-cut. From a fiscal point of view, the program outlined above is a most burdensome one; this point should not be evaded. There is no other answer, however, from the city's standpoint.

Tax policy must be directed toward aiding the good landlord and penalizing those owners who do not properly maintain their properties. A tax policy based on sales value can easily have the reverse effect. The potential of homestead exemption, of rigorous code enforcement, and of self-help stimulating devices must be rigorously exploited.

There is a well-founded fear on the part of the tenantry that rehabilitation leads to rent increases. This must be accepted as a fact of the market. Although tax policy can somewhat relieve this factor, particularly when coupled with more adequate financing, this fact should be faced. The potential of rent subsidies for the under-incomed, with which they can afford better rents, is clear-cut here. The reward in terms of the aspiration level and general morale of the slum dweller will, I think, outweigh the cost. This is particularly true when the cost/benefits are contrasted with those of institutionalized public housing.

The key to improving the slums from a "people" point of view is the creation of a resident responsible middle class within those areas—not a middle class which while physically in the area does not belong to it, as is the case with the efforts to create new middle class housing within slum areas cleared by urban renewal. This has no organic unity with the tenements per se and can only provide frustration, rather than leadership and emulation. These goals can best be accomplished and living conditions within the slum areas most enhanced, by increasing the number of owner residents of slum tenements. This will require a highly coordinated effort in terms of tax policy, financing help, code enforcement, and advisory services. The rewards of a successful program are very great. The cost of present policies are equally evident.

Filtering and Housing Standards: A Conceptual Analysis

IRA S. LOWRY

For some years, discussions of public policy in the field of urban housing have been haunted by an argument which may be briefly summarized as follows: A general improvement in housing standards can be achieved within the framework of the private housing market by a process described as "filtering." Direct government programs which provide subsidized new housing for lower- or middle-income families interfere with an orderly market process that would otherwise provide second-hand—but socially adequate—housing for these same families at prices within their means.

The proponents of the filtering method of

From *Land Economics*, XXXVI, No. 4 (November 1960), 362–370. Reprinted by permission of the Regents of the University of Wisconsin.

raising housing standards seem to agree that the provision of "decent, safe, and sanitary housing" for all members of the community is a legitimate concern of public policy; they also seem to accept current definitions of minimum standards. The issue is rather the efficacy of alternative means for achieving an accepted goal. We are not faced with a knotty problem in welfare economics but with a clear-cut problem of the behavior of the market mechanism in a particular and somewhat peculiar setting.

My intention, therefore, is to scrutinize the model of housing market behavior presented by the partisans of filtering. Since they have never put anything in writing (so far as I can discover), I run the danger of dissecting a straw man. If this is in fact the case I may at least hope to provoke an enlightening rejoinder.

Because the analysis of filtering is largely an oral tradition the meaning of the concept itself is fuzzy. I am familiar with only four publications which deal with the subject at any length.[1] None provides a satisfactory conceptual framework for dealing with the policy issue around which the argument revolves. Professor Ratcliff's definition of the filtering concept is a neat case of implicit theorizing; he describes filtering down as "the changing of occupancy as the housing that is occupied by one income group becomes available to the next lower income group as a result of decline in market price, i.e., in sales price or rent value."[2] Though his discussion of the hypothesis *ex definitio* contains many trenchant observations, it does not really grapple with the argument of the partisans of filtering as I have presented it above. Fisher, Winnick, and Grebler are precise in their use of the term but define it so as to deprive it of most of its analytical usefulness in the present context: "Filtering . . . . is a change over time in the position of a given dwelling unit within the distribution of housing rents and prices in the community as a whole."[3] Rodwin is never clear whether filtering is something that people do, or something that houses do.

For the purposes of the analysis to follow, I propose to define "filtering" simply as *a change in the real value (price in constant dollars) of an existing dwelling unit.* This definition has the advantage of clarity and sim-

plicity. It has an empirical correlate which is at least theoretically quantifiable although it does not avoid the index number problem. (Any analysis relevant to the policy question posed above *must* face this difficulty.) Finally, the definition contains a minimum of implicit theory—that is to say, it makes no attempt to stipulate the causes or consequences of filtering. By this definition the dwelling unit can filter up in value as well as down; occupancy may change as a consequence, or it may not; other units may be similarly affected, or not. These matters are not pre-judged.

To analyze filtering as a market process, its causes and consequences, four basic constructs should be kept in mind: (1) An array of all dwelling units according to their real values (prices in constant dollars). (2) An array of all dwelling units according to their quality (by some quantifiable measure other than price). (3) An array of all households according to their real incomes (incomes in constant dollars). (4) An array of supply prices of *new* dwelling units of each quality class (in constant dollars).

It may be noted that implicit in these constructs is also the magnitude of the total housing inventory and the total number of households. Concerning these constructs, we make the following assumptions: (1) There is a rank, but not necessarily cardinal, correlation of quality and value of each dwelling unit. (2) There is a rank, but not necessarily cardinal,

---

1 Richard U. Ratcliff, *Urban Land Economics* (New York: McGraw-Hill, 1949), pp. 321–34, and E. M. Fisher and Louis Winnick, "A Reformulation of the Filtering Concept," *Journal of Social Issues,* 1951, pp. 47–58 are analytical in approach; the Fisher and Winnick article draws heavily on Leo Grebler's *Housing Market Behavior in a Declining Area* (New York: Columbia University Press, 1952), which is an empirical study of "filtering." Lloyd Rodwin also reports on filtering in, "The Paradox of Boston's Middle Income Housing Progress," *Appraisal Journal,* January 1951, pp. 42–55.
2 *Op. cit.,* pp. 321–22.
3 Fisher and Winnick, *op. cit.,* p. 52. The advantage claimed for this definition is the ease with which filtering can be measured when the problem of price deflation is evaded. About the only clear use for such a measure is in the analysis of differential rates of value depreciation for housing in different neighborhoods of the urban area under consideration. Even so, its interpretation under conditions of changing population and new construction becomes rather ambiguous.

correlation of tenant income and value of dwelling unit. We thus suppress variations in taste and household size within income groups. (3) As a first approximation, all dwelling units will be assumed to decline in quality with the passage of time, without respect to other variables in the system. (4) As an analytic starting point, we will assume the market to be in equilibrium; that is, given the costs of new construction, consumer tastes and incomes and the number of households, all households have balanced their quality requirements with their incomes within the standing stock and there is at the moment no new construction.

The number of households, their real incomes and tastes, and the supply price of new construction are all variables which bear on housing standards. By means of conventional supply and demand analysis it can be demonstrated that changes in these variables will affect the price level and distribution of the standing stock of dwelling units, that such changes will cause filtering, whether up or down, of the entire inventory or some of its component parts. Furthermore, it can be shown that, frictions aside, filtering up must cease when the price of an existing unit of given quality exceeds the supply price of a new unit of that quality. Filtering down will cease when expected revenue no longer covers prime costs, in which case the dwelling unit has only scrap value. Within these limits, demand price rules the market.

However, the above variables are exogenous to the market process with which we are concerned. If the partisans of private housing base their argument on rising real incomes, and on falling supply prices of new dwellings, etc., as a premise for rising housing standards, their disagreement with the "doubters" is essentially trivial. For the filtering argument to have force and content, it must be based on endogenous changes in variables—the relationship between quality and value in abstraction from exogenous influences and, in particular, from those which are in no realistic sense subject to policy control insofar as they influence the housing market.

The partisans of filtering as a means of implementing housing policy have frequently drawn the analogy of the automobile market where upper-income households purchase new automobiles every year or two; their old autos enter the used car market, selling at a substantially lower price although they still have a good many years of useful life.

It is not altogether clear whether the argument is that the housing market *is* like the automobile market or that it *could become* like the automobile market. In either case we might trace the endogenous market process which this analogy suggests: Since quality declines with age, the demand of those households with the highest quality-preferences cannot be satisfied by even the best of the standing stock for very long. Therefore resort to new construction is necessary for such households to maintain their quality standards. Furthermore, the supply price of new construction in this quality class is at least proximate to the prices of existing structures.

When such households decide in favor of new construction the dwellings vacated by them form a price-depressing surplus which causes a filtering-down of all units in the inventory and a subsequent shift in occupancy as prices decline so that the income distribution shifts upward relative to the quality scale. At the bottom of the quality scale will be the residual of surplus housing, now unoccupied. It is thus conceived that the price decline of the entire inventory has its source in the quality decline of new units in the early portions of their lives.

Simultaneously—and independently of the filtering process—there is a gradual general deterioration of quality over time so that each unit moves lower on the quality scale. The effectiveness of filtering as a means of raising housing standards thus hinges on the speed of value decline relative to quality-decline. If the value of the standing stock depreciates so rapidly that even low-income households can afford [4] units which are still above the quality standards of social adequacy, the private market is a satisfactory instrument of public policy.

4 Strictly speaking, what the low-income household can "afford" is a metaphysical question. As a matter of practical politics, however, we can make reasonably accurate estimates of what such a household would be willing to pay; and if necessary, public policy may be implemented by limiting the household's choice to socially adequate housing—given its availability—through the police power.

The above constitutes the filtering argument as it has been presented to the present writer. As we suggested earlier, it is not always clear whether the model is meant to represent actuality or possibility. Moreover, contestants on both sides frequently shift to the ambiguous grounds of changes in the exogenous variables of household population or real incomes, etc. My concern, however, is only with the process of quality decline and its relationship to value.

It will be recalled that for the purposes of the above model we assumed that quality decline is a pure function of time—that is to say, that it is "caused" by forces irrelevant to our analysis which operate regularly over time. Let us consider this further. What is actually involved in quality decline?

In the automobile market we can immediately name design or style obsolescence as a (perhaps *the*) major factor in quality decline. Identifiable newness per se is a very desirable attribute in an automobile and it is evident mostly in body styling. Much less significant would be technological obsolescence in the sense of innovation which contributes to the measurable efficiency of operation, so that a car embodying the innovation would be preferable to an equally new car which did not. Finally, there is a physical deterioration—the actual wearing out of the machine due to use and the elements. All three of these elements of quality decline also appear to operate in the housing market as influences on price although the relative magnitudes of their influences are more problematical.

Style obsolescence as a production policy appears to have been borrowed by the automobile industry from the women's clothing industry and has recently spread to the appliance industry. In house building there are clearly defined fads in architectural style which differ from those of the automobile industry (but not from women's fashions) in that they frequently evoke past styles. Moreover, identifiable newness per se does not seem to be so desirable a quality; people tend to be apologetic about the raw look of very new houses. Concomitantly, identifiable age, particularly antiquity, is not per se derogatory. While it seems unlikely that style obsolescence is very influential in the decision of home owners to change residence, it is almost certainly a consideration to renters who are considering a move to other rental quarters or the purchase of a home.

The question of technological obsolescence has considerably more importance. There have been significant changes in the lifetime of most of our housing inventory, in heating and lighting systems, plumbing, the arrangement of rooms and the efficient utilization of space, general coordination with and provision for modern appliances and modes of family life. Some of this obsolescence is intrinsic in the structure or layout of the building; a substantial portion can be overcome at reasonably low cost within the framework of the existing structure—e.g., installation of floor furnaces, or 220-volt wiring for electrical appliances.

Physical deterioration has always an ambiguous meaning and strikingly so in the case of housing. The roof may sag, dry rot may undermine the foundations, the building may settle. These are difficulties not easily remedied and involve a real decline in structural quality. Deterioration of this type is either implicit in the structure from the beginning as an incident of fraud or miscalculation or it is the inevitable or unpredictable consequence of the passage of time.

But the greater part of the category of physical deterioration seems to consist of those minor incidents of wear and tear and of the elements which, summed together, form a fairly regular and substantial component of annual housing costs: flaking paint, broken windows, cracked or warped siding, leaky roofs, clogged plumbing or drains, worn-out screens, scuffed floors or linoleum, etc. The point is that with adequate maintenance a house need not depreciate in these respects. Of course, the *reductio ad absurdum* of the notion of maintenance would be the demolition of the existing structure and the erection of a similar one on the site. But there seems to be a significant portion of the physical inputs of a dwelling unit which evidence little or no deterioration over time, of which the most obvious is masonry. The surprising age of many well-kept houses is evidence for the proposition that a periodic outlay which is small in relation to the total value of the unit will usually preserve it in close to its original condition.

It might also be noted that much of what has been termed technological obsolescence can be overcome in the course of normal maintenance. For example, when a furnace or water-heater wears out, it is generally cheaper to replace it with an up-to-date one. The same is true of bathroom and kitchen fixtures.

We may reasonably suppose that all three elements of quality decline affect the demand price for a dwelling unit. However, from the point of view of public policy, quality decline includes only the latter two. A house does not fall below the standards of social adequacy by reason of style obsolescence. It may do so because of technological obsolescence but the current standards of social adequacy are so minimal that the impact of this type of quality decline is greatly reduced. Physical deterioration is probably the most important factor of the three in the emergence of substandard housing.[5] This distinction lends plausibility to the filtering argument in that it suggests a slower decline of "social quality" than of "market quality." The magnitude of this difference cannot be defined within the limits of an analytic model.

Let us consider once more the filtering model developed above. In abstraction from changes in income, population, etc., a decline in the market value of recently-built houses must hinge on quality decline—and it is reasonable to suppose that this quality decline takes the form of style or technological obsolescence rather than significant physical deterioration. As top-bracket occupants periodically insist on *new* housing their former dwellings enter the used-house market. Because the supply (standing stock) in the second quality bracket is now increased relative to the demand (number of households) the prices of all dwelling units in this quality bracket will fall, whether there is any further quality decline or not. This price decline would continue until some of the occupants of the third quality stratum took advantage of the low market to improve their housing standards. Thus value depreciation would be propagated throughout the entire inventory.

Suppose we view this value decline from the point of view of a landlord. Abstracting from the other elements of quality decline, we will assume that with "normal" maintenance the quality of the dwelling unit could be preserved indefinitely.[6] But if the demand price (say, annual rent) falls below the landlord's total annual operating costs (without reference to the

historical cost of the structure) his logical response is disinvestment, so that the current outlays may be applied elsewhere to yield a better return.

The landlord's expenses may be divided into (1) *user costs,* which would not be incurred if the unit were vacant—e.g., heat and janitorial service—but excluding depreciation due to tenant-induced wear and tear; (2) *fixed costs,* which would be incurred whether or not the unit were vacant—e.g., taxes, insurance, administration—but also excluding any form of depreciation; and (3) *normal maintenance costs,* which would offset that part of depreciation due to physical deterioration and technological obsolescence (insofar as the latter can be controlled by maintenance).[7] Graphically, using vertically additive curves, this is represented in Figure 1.

5 Other factors of considerable import for standards of social adequacy are (1) overcrowding, whether or not implemented by structural conversion and (2) "neighborhood deterioration." The former can be, in a sense, a consequence of value decline, as suggested later in this essay. If the latter is unrelated to the quality of the structure itself, such deterioration is either implicit in the socio-economic characteristics of the tenants or the result of the invasion of incompatible land uses. These are all matters of theoretical interest but independent of the point which I wish to develop as to the internal behavior of the market.
6 This asumption may appear contradictory to the earlier one that the depreciation of *new* houses is outside the scope of the maintenance problem, being due rather to style and technological obsolescence. There is an element of paradox here; but it should be possible for the major factors in "market quality" depreciation to alter over the life of a durable good, particularly a prestige good. And if maintenance could entirely prevent the quality decline of *new* houses there would be no grounds for the initial value decline on which the filtering model is premised. I might take this opportunity to express some reservations as to the role of structural characteristics in motivating upper-income movements; it seems likely to me that a goodly portion of such moves are predicated on changes in social status and the goal is not "better housing" but a "better neighborhood" in the sense of one commensurate with the new status. This can often be achieved only by new construction in peripheral areas. But we are not here concerned with the effects on the housing market of rising status (e.g., rising income). The effect of this qualification and others made in the course of this essay is to raise the question, whether the filtering hypothesis, true or untrue, is of major significance in the context of rapid changes in population and income.
7 The reader will note that we have defined these cost categories somewhat differently from the usual. If he prefers to attach other names to them it is of no consequence for the analysis.

Figure 1

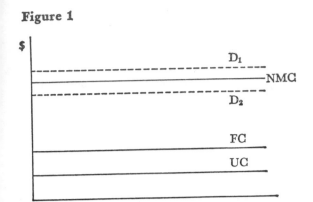

Figure 2

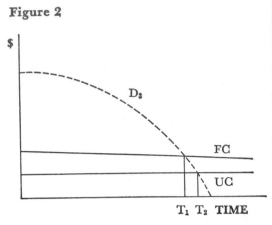

If the demand price falls from D_1 to D_2, the landlord is faced with a perpetual loss. On the other hand, if he discontinues or decreases maintenance outlays, this will accelerate quality decline in the eyes of the market. We can build this consequence into the demand price by giving it a negative time-slope. This is represented by D_3 in Figure 2.

As a dubious concession to reality, we will also allow the tax and insurance components of fixed costs to decline as quality falls. Under these circumstances, the landlord will continue to rent so long as revenue covers what we have defined as *user costs*. Until Time T_1, his revenue will yield a surplus over current outlays, and at T_2 revenues will cease to contribute to *fixed costs* and he will board up the structure. If demolition will save *fixed costs*, he will follow this course between T_1 and T_2.

Thus, under-maintenance is an eminently reasonable response of a landlord to a declining market. This argument is reinforced by the presumption that there will be a delay between the time at which normal maintenance ceases and that at which the consequent quality decline becomes obvious to the market. Furthermore, if all landlords follow the same course, the *relative* quality of dwelling units would remain more or less the same as the *absolute* quality declines. The consumers would not have the alternative of a better house at the same price; only a choice between housing and other goods. This would mean a lesser slope to the revenue curve D_3 than would be the case if our landlord's reaction were unique.

On the other hand, our model assumes that the landlord expects the lower demand price to obtain indefinitely. If he expects it to rise again, so that the house will once more be a paying proposition, his calculation will be whether the costs of normal maintenance in the interim would be sufficiently less than the cost of renovation that the difference would cover the opportunity costs of the interim investment plus the uncertainty as to the eventual returns from the maintenance program. Some types of maintenance could be postponed for a considerable period without incurring extra cost.

The effect of a general policy of under-maintenance would be an accelerated decline in the quality of the housing inventory. But after a time the tenants of housing of the second quality stratum would find their dwellings deteriorating below their optimum quality levels and the competition for such better dwellings as remained would force prices up once more to the point at which maintenance costs were covered and the former quality level was maintained by adequate current outlays on the part of the landlords.

And so filtering would be halted in the successive value strata as the flow of units from above was shut off. Because of the phenomenon of under-maintenance, quality decline throughout the inventory would have been hastened in terms of physical deterioration, while the style and technical obsolescence of the units would be less, relative to price, than if the value-depreciation had not occurred.

This model has particular relevance to proposals for accelerated value-depreciation as a means of raising housing standards. If value-decline is the premise for under-maintenance and under-maintenance is an important element in quality decline (particularly "social quality"), the program seems to be in some measure self-defeating.

Would an owner-occupant respond differently from a landlord to value-depreciation? So far as his own dwelling is concerned, this change in market valuation takes the form of a decline in imputed rent—a rather ghostly category. To be sure, there are now available on the market other units of superior quality whose price is equal to the historical cost of his own; but to make the change, he must take a "loss" on the sale or rental of his present home. If he stays where he is, he can maintain his customary quality level by means of his customary outlays, and it is hard to see why he should not do so.

For completeness, we may also consider the tenant. If our estimation of landlord reaction is correct, the tenant can maintain a given quality standard either by (1) offering a rent above the market in exchange for a mainte-nance guarantee—in which case no filtering would occur for that unit; (2) paying the mar-ket rent but moving frequently as houses pass out of his optimum quality stratum; and (3) entering the free market. If he remains where he is, at a reduced rent, he will encounter a continuous decline in quality which may in turn be the premise for further rent reduc-tions. But presuming that as quality declines the price elasticity of the consumer's quality demand decreases, the eventual shortage of better quality units will force the price back up and the tenant would find himself eventually in his former (equilibrium) position with regard to rent and quality.

Having so far developed the view of under-maintenance as a means of disinvestment, it seems worthwhile to call attention to certain other circumstances in which it may occur. These are not directly relevant to the "filtering argument" but are presented for what light they may cast on the general problem of blighted areas and slums.

Let us consider the owner of rental property on the fringe of the business district. We will suppose that the value of his land is rising (rel-ative to the value of land elsewhere in the city) due to its increasing suitability for busi-ness uses. To continue the use of this property at its present intensity is to incur a rising op-portunity cost. His alternatives are (1) to in-crease his rents concurrently with his rising op-portunity cost, a possibility which is contingent on whatever influence the encroaching commer-cial area may have on the market evaluation of the property for residential uses; or (2) to dis-invest by under-maintenance until the revenue stream falls below prime costs, then to demol-ish the structure.

The mechanics of the latter course may be shown by the use of a graph similar to those employed earlier (Figure 3). We add a separate *opportunity cost* curve. Assuming that the de-mand price, D_1, will not rise because of the en-croaching business district, the dwelling unit ceases to yield a profit at T_1, and maintenance will be reduced or discontinued. As quality de-clines, demand price follows the path D_2, with demolition at approximately T_2 (since there is an alternative use for the land).

A third possibility which may occur to the landlord is an increase in the intensity of resi-dential use through conversion into smaller units. We may assume that this would have been done even without the rising opportunity cost if the space demand in that quality bracket had been such that this would have been a profitable course. But if, as a consequence of under-maintenance and the subsequent quality-decline, the dwelling unit falls into a lower price-class, the consumers in this market, having

Figure 3

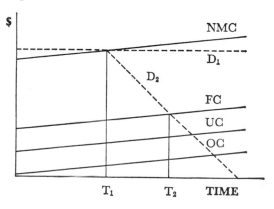

lower incomes, may also have a different pattern of space demand.

We have heretofore completely suppressed space requirements as a feature of housing markets, considering only quality. For the broad purposes of our argument this was a legitimate suppression. Nevertheless, it is clear that consumers economize on space as well as "quality per room." It is also reasonable to suppose that there is an "income effect" on space as well as quality. Consequently, in this new market the landlord may find that total revenue is greater from two four-room apartments (or worse) than from one eight-room house. Thus the rise in land values may be the premise not only for under-maintenance but for increasing density. In this way it has a dual impact on housing standards.

Finally, we may consider the case of the aging homeowner. Presuming that he is concerned only with maximizing household utility during his own lifetime, without reference to posterity, he is faced with the problematic advantage of owning a fixed asset whose value is unlikely to be consumed by the time of his death. His most "rational" course would be to sell the house and use the liquid capital realized as a means to a higher standard of living as a tenant in a dwelling of equal or superior quality. We must recognize, however, that the household differs from the firm in that the market evaluation of assets, to the firm, is the relevant one. To the householder, market value is likely to be appreciably below his subjective evaluation of his dwelling, particularly when many of his other assets—tangible and intangible—are especially adapted to the particular structure and location.[8]

This is the difficulty that economic analysis always faces in dealing with household decisions in the frame of reference of subjective utility. There is no "market" for many of the components of personal satisfaction so it is difficult to estimate the subjectively "economical" choice. The consequence is generally a turbid regression into assumptions about psychic cost.

We will confine ourselves, therefore, to pointing out the second in the rank of measurably "rational" decisions: disinvestment through under-maintenance. It seems a likely choice where the owner-occupant has reason to believe that the quality of his dwelling will not decline intolerably before his death.

It is apparent that our model of the housing market behaves in a way that was not envisaged by the advocates of filtering as a means of implementing housing policy. The price decline necessary to bring a dwelling unit within reach of an income group lower than that of the original tenants also results in a policy of under-maintenance. Rapid deterioration of the housing stock would be the cost to the community of rapid depreciation in the price of existing housing.

The divergence between this analysis and that which we have attributed to the partisans of filtering can be traced to a divergent treatment of the notion of quality decline. The partisans of filtering have stressed the roles of style and technical obsolescence. It is their position that lower-income groups can jolly well put up with the inconvenience of outmoded style and awkward design—although there may be a public commitment to insure that these groups have "decent, safe, and sanitary dwellings."[9]

It hardly seems likely that many persons would dissent from this standard of social welfare—certainly not the present writer. But those who suggest that the standard can be attained by a policy designed to accelerate value depreciation or by the operation of the free market (in the absence of changes in construction costs or in real income) have overlooked the essential nature of physical deterioration and its relationship to maintenance: They have regarded the dwelling unit as an object which, once erected, is no longer subject to human influence. Quality decline related to style and technical obsolescence does not imply any change in the dwelling unit—only a change in human standards of evaluation. To be sure, this viewpoint does admit physical deterioration

8 The Federal Housing Administration has recognized this fact in its appraisal techniques. In capitalizing imputed rent of owner-occupied houses it included at one time an "amenity rent" component (*Underwriting Manual,* Washington, D.C.: United States Government Printing Office, 1938), Par. 1420; this was later abandoned in favor of a direct increase in the gross rent multiplier to allow for "owner-occupancy appeal" (*ibid.,* 1947, Par. 1215).
9 This is the language of the George-Healey Act of 1936 (49 Statutes 115) which has reappeared in virtually all of the housing legislation of the federal government since that date.

—but it is attributed to the relentless passage of time, not to human agency.

I have attempted to demonstrate that owners and tenants will respond to changes in the market evaluation of a dwelling unit with behavior which accelerates or delays the physical deterio- ration of the dwelling. If the two events are linked in this fashion, it is evident that a policy which implements price decline within the standing stock of housing cannot also nourish the hope of using this stock to raise housing standards.

Class, Race, and Urban Renewal

ROBERT C. WEAVER

INTRODUCTION

Urban renewal has opened Pandora's Box in several fields. It has occasioned a fresh look at slums; it has given rise to renewed discussion of racial balance in neighborhoods; it has inspired new thought and approaches relative to the racial and class composition of schools in the central city; and of course it has intensified research in the fields of housing, city planning, and municipal government.

Since one of the principal objectives of urban renewal is to attract more middle-class families back into the central city and slow down the exodus of middle-class families from the inlying areas, much of the current discussion about color and class is oriented around these goals. There is, however, a tendency to treat current problems as though they were unique and devoid of historical precedents. Actually, this is not only untrue but dangerously misleading. As Oscar Handlin has most recently pointed out, the flight of older, middle-class families from proximity to the latest newcomers is as old as immigration. What is unique is not the human behavior but the physical limits of the city and the multiplicity of local governments.[1]

Since in many American cities a principal wave of low-income migrants is composed of readily identifiable members of color minorities, there is a tendency to identify the problem as one of race alone.[2] This is inaccurate and unfortunate. Cities which have few non-white migrants are experiencing the same problems [3]—a fact suggesting that this is a class as well as a color phenomenon. Should further proof of this be required, the experiences of Chicago, Cleveland, Detroit, Cincinnati, and a score of other cities with Appalachian Mountain whites will provide convincing documentation.[4]

Identification of the decline of central cities with the encroachment of non-whites (and in a few places Puerto Ricans) upon established middle-class neighborhoods reflects our consciousness of color. It does more. Such superficial analysis weakens our capacity to deal effectively with the problems of our cities. The color and class aspects of these problems are frequently intertwined but neither should be ignored. Any workable program must recognize both and learn to deal with each.

On the other hand, it would be sheer sophistry to deny that, under existing demographic and ecological changes, long-standing racial attitudes, and the current economic forces which operate in the housing market, the arrival of increasing numbers of non-white families may, and often does, lead to the departure of previ-

From *Land Economics*, XXXVI, No. 3 (August 1960), 235–251. Reprinted by permission of the Regents of the University of Wisconsin.

1 Oscar Handlin, *The Newcomers* (Cambridge, Massachusetts: Harvard University Press, 1959), pp. 14–16, 30–5.
2 See especially Morton Grodzins, *The Metropolitan Area as a Racial Problem* (Pittsburgh, Pennsylvania: University of Pittsburgh Press, 1958); and "Metropolitan Segregation," *Scientific American*, (October 1957), pp. 33–41.
3 Robert C. Weaver, "Non-White Population Movements and Urban Ghettos," *Phylon*, Third Quarter (Fall), 1959, pp. 235–8.
4 For an interesting account of the Chicago experience, see Albert N. Votaw, "The Hillbillies Invade Chicago," *Harpers*, February 1958, pp. 64–7.

ous middle-class whites.[5] This long recognized phenomenon has recently been expressed in terms of a "tipping point" theory, which says that there is in any neighborhood a point at which whites will move out when the proportion of non-whites reaches a certain size.[6]

Many factors are involved in the desertion of a neighborhood. First there is the economic climate. In a period of general prosperity transition is accelerated; the same occurs in a loose housing market. The location of the neighborhood involved is important, too. Factors tending to stabilize middle-class occupancy include proximity to, and identification with, institutional facilities, such as in the area around a university or college or around long-established religious facilities.

Access of minority and low-income families to a formerly white middle-class neighborhood is not always a consequence of whites' desertion of an area in the face of the encroachment of new user groups. Often it results from vacancies caused by the movement of earlier residents and failure of other middle-class whites to replace the former occupants. The cause of the desertion of such neighborhoods is usually the attractiveness of other areas: they may be suburban subdivisions or, as in the case of the East Side of Manhattan, a new prestige location in the central city. Once the vacancy rate becomes high, as it did in New York City's West Side, owners and property managers are happy to substitute new user groups rather than suffer greater losses.

THE IMPACT OF NEWCOMERS ON THE HOUSING MARKET

From early days, middle-class Americans have wanted distance between themselves and the newcomer; that desire has been accentuated by two recent developments—the rise of prestige-laden, single-class, homogeneous suburban areas and the identification of color with a large number of low-income migrants. The recent concern of Americans with the quality of education has, of course, occasioned increasing emphasis upon good schools.

As long as there was ample space within the city limits and no effective modes of rapid transportation, most of the outward movement

of middle-class families occurred within the city proper. The streetcar, automobile, and bus changed the situation, opening for housing development large areas of virgin land removed from the central city. The fact that estates of the wealthy were already located on such lands augmented their appeal to medium-income groups intent on upward social mobility. Real estate operators, developers, and land speculators, readily joined the commuting railroad lines in selling the exclusiveness of these developments.[7] This was the stage when the great impetus to Negro migration occurred during World War I. Low-income colored Americans from the South poured into many Northern cities, replacing, as the new source of unskilled and semiskilled labor, the earlier European immigrants who were no longer available during and after the hostilities. Not only were the newcomers mostly poor and ill-prepared for urban life, but they were also dark skinned. As the readily-identified descendents of slaves, they had the least amount of social prestige of any ethnic group. Race and color joined class in rendering them forbidden neighbors.

Middle-class whites, led by the real estate fraternity, frequently resorted to racial housing covenants and zoning to contain non-whites in a restricted area. Low-income whites, only slightly less undesirable in the eyes of the middle-class, sometimes used intimidation, violence, and threats to assert their Americanism. On the part of the former, this was a manifestation of class as well as racial prejudice; on the part of the latter it was primarily racial. Yet lower-class whites and Negroes frequently

5 For an excellent account of this process, even when the in-coming Negroes were middle-class, see Albert J. Mayer, "Russell Woods: Change Without Conflict," in Nathan Glazer and Davis McEntire, ed., *Studies in Housing and Minority Groups* (Berkeley, California: University of California Press, 1960), pp. 198–220. There are, however, in this article and Nathan Glazer's Introduction to the volume, unsupported assertions about the absence of racial prejudice on the part of the former Jewish residents.
6 Morton Grodzins, *op. cit.,* pp. 6–7. While the author of this concept is probably over-pessimistic due to his involvement with Chicago's experience, his is a useful idea.
7 For an excellent description of this process, see Charles Abrams, *Forbidden Neighbors* (New York: Harper and Bros., 1955), Chapter XII.

shared the same residential areas and faced the same disabilities of poor neighborhoods. Class was often more important than color in neighborhoods which failed to offer prestige or adequate protection and public services to any residents, regardless of race.[8] The early governmental policy of segregation in public housing subsequently served to accentuate color consciousness in low-cost housing at the same time that it reflected the strategic role of authority in establishing racial patterns.

World War II brought in a new stream of Negro, Mexican-American, and Puerto Rican migrants to the urban North and West. It also brought greater residential segregation. This too represented, first, resistance to the expansion of land space available to non-whites and, most recently, abandonment of segments of the central cities to them. Several factors played an important part in this. The federal government through the Federal Housing Administration had facilitated phenomenal expansion of suburban construction, and low downpayments and a longer period for mortgages had made a large part of this available to middle- and lower middle-income families. At the same time FHA accepted the concept of homogeneous neighborhoods and until 1947 the instrument of the racial restrictive housing covenants.[9] Higher incomes during the War enabled a vast number of families to accumulate down payments and sustained prosperity facilitated their meeting monthly carrying charges. At the same time government housing policy made home ownership more attractive than rental[10] and practically all new construction was in lily-white suburbs.

Not only was it possible for the upper-middle class to desert the central city but many of lesser means—if they were white—could follow suit. Even the low-income white family could hope for homogeneity—either in the suburbs with a little more money or perhaps in the grey areas of the core city if the expansion of non-whites was contained. Racially homogeneous neighborhoods had achieved a new prestige and this was increasingly apparent in slums and blighted areas where residents sought to emulate dominant racial attitudes.

Rapid movement of whites to the suburbs was but a part of the population trend. For example, over 7,000,000 persons entered the suburbs between 1940 and 1950. While a large volume of long-term residents left the cities, an even larger number of individuals moved from non-urban areas directly to the suburbs. Meanwhile a much smaller number of whites moved into than moved out of central cities while many non-whites entered the in-lying areas. "The process of losing one net migrant to the suburbs actually was the end result of a larger process whereby for each two non-white persons moving into the central city about three white persons moved out."[11]

These movements have brought interesting changes in the housing market. Throughout the North and West, non-whites have acquired a much larger number of housing units and frequently a more diversified and a better quality of housing. In the process they have expanded into many areas which were formerly all white. The Chicago experience of 1940–50 suggests the human components of this development. Those who initiated the movement were long-term rather than newer residents, resulting in no significant changes in socio-economic characteristics;[12] and the first arrivals had had to "pay a premium rental, which they are able to finance only by using residential space very intensively, e.g., by doubling up families in the household or by including relatives or lodgers in the household."[13]

While it is true that only in a quite general sense has succession in Chicago followed a pattern of radial expansion of the Negro com-

8 Findings of recent research challenge the oft-repeated assertion that the source as well as the center of anti-Negro prejudice and discrimination in this country is in the lower socio-economic classes. See Robert K. Merton, "Discrimination and the National Creed," in R. M. MacIver, ed., *Discrimination and National Welfare* (New York: Harper and Bros., 1949), p. 111; and National Committee on Segregation in the Nation's Capital, *Segregation in Washington* (Chicago, Illinois: The Committee, 1948), p. 38.
9 R. C. Weaver, *The Negro Ghetto* (New York: Harcourt, Brace & Co., 1948), pp. 71–3, 152–3.
10 Louis Winnick, *Rental Housing: Opportunities for Private Investment* (New York: McGraw-Hill Book Company, 1958), Chapter 3.
11 Donald J. Bogue, *Components of Population Change, 1940–50* (Miami, Ohio: Miami University, 1957), p. 34.
12 Otis Dudley and Beverly Duncan, *The Negro Population of Chicago* (Chicago, Illinois: The University of Chicago Press, 1957), pp. 125, 191, 206, 223, 225.
13 *Ibid.*, p. 236.

munity outward from the center of the city, it is significant that:

". . . within both the Negro and the white community, high-status groups tend to share residential areas and to be residentially segregated from low-status groups. Apparently, the selective forces which produce differentiation of residential areas in the urban community operate in somewhat the same way upon the Negro and the white population. This is also in line with the finding that patterns of interarea differentiation with respect to physical characteristics of the area and social and economic characteristics of the residents tend to be maintained under the impact of succession from white to Negro occupancy." [14]

These developments in Chicago, which are fairly typical of larger northern industrial centers, reflect the interaction of many events. Such expansion of housing accommodations for Negroes as took place was facilitated largely by the decline in the white population. It reflected a growing demand for shelter on the part of an expanding non-white population in which a significant number were able to pay higher rents and prices for housing and it enabled some whites to sell profitably and buy new suburban houses. Even where sales were not profitable the availability of Negro purchasers and renters greatly accelerated the liquidation of property in the central city and the acquisition of new homes elsewhere on the part of previous residents in the core areas. To a degree, this greater effective demand for housing on the part of non-whites sustained property values in many parts of the central city and accelerated the purchase of new homes by whites who were replaced by non-whites, many of whom paid higher prices than could otherwise have been secured.

Had there been less racial segregation in the suburbs, a larger number of non-whites would have joined whites in moving from the central cities to the suburbs and going directly to them rather than to the central cities. Even in the face of a most effective color bar, about one-third of a million Negroes did join whites in the 1940–50 trek to the suburbs. Most of those involved were in the South but there was a

pronounced desire of Northern middle-class Negroes to escape from central cities,[15] and there are indications that some of the colored migrants to the North avoided the central city and moved directly to older Negro settlements elsewhere. This seems to have occurred in the industrial cities of New Jersey and the larger cities in New York's Westchester County.

One upshot of residential segregation has been to contain most Negro middle-class families in the core cities.[16] Another, and much more serious consequence for the cities has been the concentration of demand for housing on the part of the growing middle-class Negroes on certain city areas. This too has often sustained property values but it has tended to accelerate the exodus of middle-class whites. Were middle-class Negroes able to compete freely in the total market, their volume in most neighborhoods would have been so slight as to have occasioned little concern. There would have been much less premium payment incident to initial non-white occupancy and white owners would have had less economic incentive to forsake attractive neighborhoods and homes. Even the real estate operators would have had slight impetus to engineer flight of middle-class whites since the principal source of effective demand—the middle-class Negro purchaser— would be more discriminating and less available for any one neighborhood.[17]

For the process described above to have taken place, there would have had to have been a

14 *Ibid.*, p. 298.
15 Handlin, *op. cit.*, pp. 125–31.
16 Actually, this is due to factors other than residential segregation, but it is primarily a consequence of the color line: see Weaver, "The Effect of Anti-Discrimination Legislation upon the FHA- and VA-Insured Housing Market in New York State," *Land Economics*, November 1955, pp. 305–7.
17 There can be no better illustration of the confusion between emotion and economics than the implications of this analysis. Without a color line, housing in certain areas of the central city would probably have fallen in value. This would have been accounted for in economic terms—architectural obsolescence, loss of neighborhood prestige, age of structure, competition of more desirable facilities and neighborhood location, and resulting weakness in demand for the affected housing. Under conditions of color concepts the experience in these areas is cited (and rightfully) as evidence that non-white occupancy does not necessarily adversely influence property values. See, Luigi Laurenti, *Property Values and Race* (Berkeley, California: University of California Press, 1960).

much larger volume of low-priced housing available to non-whites in metropolitan areas. Without such a supply the sheer pressure of numbers occasioned the growth of non-white areas of concentration. In some instances this involved expansion of one or several major Negro ghettos, engulfing surrounding housing regardless of its price or suitability. In other instances it involved the development of new pockets of non-white residential concentration. Invariably, it occasioned over-crowding, undesirably high densities, and blight.

However, in a situation where the supply of low-cost housing available to non-whites is limited, the entrance of middle-income, non-white families into a neighborhood and its subsequent desertion by whites has benefited the mass of colored home-seekers. For, had there been less turnover, there would have been less filtration. This, in turn, would have delayed the improvement in the quality of housing occupied by non-whites. In the present situation of enforced residential segregation in many segments of the housing market, rapid racial transition of desirable housing in parts of the central city has made a larger amount of physically good housing available to non-whites. It has also resulted in more intensive and often socially undesirable occupancy patterns in the areas recently accessible to non-whites and it has made it difficult to sustain the middle-class characteristics of the affected areas, even when higher-income non-whites have attempted to do so. Relatively high vacancy rates, as in Philadelphia and Cleveland, have accelerated racial transition in certain neighborhoods with the result of substantial upgrading in the quality of the occupied housing stock and instability in some middle-class housing areas.

Modern cities can absorb a large supply of low-income migrants without subjecting the newcomers to economic exploitation and greatly augmenting slums and blight only by building more low-rent housing on open sites, solving the problem of rehabilitation without excessive costs and providing a free housing market. The central city has a stake in open occupancy throughout the metropolitan area because it is necessary in order that the market may operate most efficiently. Under conditions of open occupancy a much smaller number of areas of middle-class housing need be threatened by in-

undation by non-whites and it is possible to make the most effective use of the existing supply of housing—particularly the low-rent sector.[18]

EFFORTS TO ATTRACT MIDDLE-CLASS FAMILIES TO THE CENTRAL CITY

It is against this background that urban renewal programs' efforts to attract and maintain middle-class families in the central city must operate. Regardless of any social, political, or moral considerations, the economics of the situation require concern for retention of white middle-class families in central cities because their numbers far exceed those among non-whites.[19] In any given locality the problem has three manifestations: creation of new areas in which middle-class families will establish stable communities, rehabilitation or partial renewal of areas which will attract and hold middle-class families, and the arresting or preventing the desertion of middle-class families from existing areas of residence.

In the larger cities of the South, new segregated middle-class Negro communities have been developed. This has been possible for several reasons. In some instances it results

18 This is the economic rationale for open-occupancy (fair housing) legislation. As in all non-discriminatory legislation, enactment of a law is but a first step. To be effective, such laws need implementation—and that not only involves enforcement but also positive action on the part of minority groups. Thus the Philadelphia Commission on Human Relations is encouraging Negroes to seek homes in all-white neighborhoods, saying: "To break the stubborn pattern of segregated housing many Negro citizens must have the courage to live in 'new' neighborhoods." *The New York Times*, March 6, 1960, p. 49.
19 "What the city needs is a core of upper-middle-class people to support its theatres and museums, its shops and its restaurants—even a Bohemia of sorts can be of help. For it is the people who like living in the city who make it an attraction to the visitors who don't. It is the city dwellers who support its style; without them there is nothing to come downtown *to*." William H. Whyte, Jr., "Are Cities Un-American?" *Fortune*, September 1957, pp. 124–25. Despite significant recent improvement in the economic status of non-whites and a significant increase in the number of middle-class Negroes in urban areas, the number of the latter is not now able, nor does it have a potential in the near future to provide a large or affluent enough population to perform the functions outlined above by Whyte.

from annexation of new areas by the central city after informal agreements have been made concerning the color identification of land. Atlanta is a prime example,[20] New Orleans has had somewhat similar experience.[21] In cities like Charlotte, Greensboro, and Winston-Salem, North Carolina, and Austin, Texas, availability of vacant land contiguous to, or in the path of, existing centers of Negro concentration has afforded sites for new, segregated FHA-insured housing. In Houston, Texas, where availability of good housing has made the owning of attractive homes an important source of status among Negroes, there has been an appreciable amount of new construction and a significant source of excellent middle-class housing in a good neighborhood available to Negroes during the last decade.

Clearly, by creation of new segregated areas in most of these cities and restriction of Negro encroachments upon middle-class white neighborhoods to a few locations in others, the impact of the non-white market has had but limited effect upon the desertion of the central city by middle-class whites. In Houston, where there seems to have been a rather loose housing market,[22] Negro expansion into one good neighborhood served to sustain values and thereby accelerated movement of the older residents to the suburbs. However, some of those who sold to Negroes may have replaced other central city whites moving to the suburbs and thereby supported property values elsewhere in the central city.

In Northern cities the establishment of all-Negro suburbs is usually impossible. This is due to the spatial distribution of non-whites [23] and rejection of segregated patterns by non-whites in the North.[24] The latter fact is, of course, supported by legislation: a score of northern states and cities have non-discrimination housing laws, and racial discrimination in urban renewal areas is banned in several states and many cities. In all of these and other cities, the capacity and willingness of Negroes to pay for better housing in middle-class neighborhoods has increased significantly during the last decade at the same time that the low-income non-white population has grown appreciably. Indeed, the growth of non-white urban populations has been much greater in border and northern cities than in their southern

counterparts. Thus the pressure of Negroes for more housing has had greater impact in the North than in the South. Also, it has had less outlet via expansion into new, vacant areas. The consequence is that Negroes have expanded to a much greater degree into areas formerly occupied by whites in northern than in southern cities.

Efforts to attract and retain middle-class families in the central urban centers of the North and border states must recognize the pressure

20 Robert A. Thompson, Hylan Lewis and Davis McEntire, "Atlanta and Birmingham: A Comparative Study in Negro Housing," Glazer and McEntire ed., *Studies in Housing and Minority Groups* (Berkeley, California: University of California Press, 1960), pp. 22–40; and "Civil Rights Official Lauds Atlanta's Gentleman's Agreement," *House and Home,* May 1959, p. 91. For a discussion of the implications of the use of new, segregated middle-class Negro housing in the South, see R. C. Weaver, "Southern Comfort: A Possible Misapplication of Federal Funds," *Journal of Intergroup Relations,* Fall 1960.
21 Forrest E. LaViolette, "The Negro in New Orleans," Glazer and McEntire, *op. cit.,* pp. 124–30; also "Minority Housing," *House and Home,* April 1955, pp. 146–7.
22 Jack E. Dodson, "Minority Group Housing in Two Texas Cities," Glazer and McEntire, *op. cit.,* pp. 101–9.
23 See R. C. Weaver, *The Negro Ghetto,* pp. 91, 138, 154–6.
24 "In certain ways, the North presents more problems for upper-income Negroes than the South, for here the problem is not only to get good housing—and if Atlanta can supply a Negro market for extensive Negro subdivisions, unquestionably this can also be done in northern cities—but to get good *unsegregated* housing." Glazer, "Introduction," Glazer and McEntire, *op. cit.,* p. 6. Of course, where there is the base of a Negro settlement which originally housed domestics, as on the North Shore of Chicago's suburbs or in cities and towns of Westchester County and Long Island or clusters of industrial workers in suburban towns and cities, growing Negro populations—mostly in ghettos—are developing in northern suburbs. Also, a small number of upper middle-income Negroes have bought homes outside areas of non-white concentration. Current developments suggest that, were the suburbs open to Negroes, they would attract a large segment of the still relatively small number of middle-income non-whites. As the same time, concentration of industry in fringe areas has already attracted a significant number of non-white workers. Many are now commuting from the core areas, but there are indications of a desire for, and a trend to, suburban living on their part. Competent studies suggest that there will be an outward movement of Negroes and Puerto Ricans in the New York City Metropolitan area in response to job opportunities. (Edgar M. Hoover and Raymond Vernon, *Anatomy of a Metropolis* (Cambridge, Massachusetts: Harvard University Press, 1959), pp. 212–13.

for housing occasioned by a growing Negro population. Some of these cities also face the arrival of large numbers of Appalachian Mountain whites, Puerto Ricans, and Mexicans. Since the Negro presents problems of class as well as color, concentration upon his impact is fruitful. Glazer, while minimizing the problem of the dark-skinned Puerto Ricans and Mexican-Americans, has set forth the peculiar disabilities of the Negro in American society:

"... it may seem far-fetched to consider the implications of a social situation in which Mexicans, Puerto Ricans, and Negroes show roughly the same social constitution as the rest of us. However, in the case of the Negroes such large middle-class groups are already developing. They will change greatly the whole character of anti-Negro prejudice in America. But—and this is the point of this last observation—the Negroes will still be a long way from taking up the status in American society of assimilated European ethnic groups. The Mexicans and Puerto Ricans, because of their physical characteristics, will find it easier to achieve this status."[25]

Survival of healthy, central cities requires recognition and solution of this problem. First, there needs to be an acceleration of the size of the middle-class among non-whites. Second, this will be achieved in large measure in proportion to the degree that the middle-class Negro is accepted as his immigrant prototype was accepted.[26] Third, unless the achievement of American norms of success on the part of Negroes is rewarded, as it has been among others who started at the bottom of the economic and social scale, there will be a loss of motivation (already apparent among Negroes) with consequences which are inimical to the economic, political, and cultural health of the central city. Fourth, such results would be tragic for the nation—and western democracy—in the world of the cold war and the emergence of Asian and African nationalism.

Northern cities, if they are to maintain a sound economic base, must strive to adjust to continuing in-migration of low-income Negroes, Puerto Ricans, Appalachian whites, and Mexicans. A first step in this direction is to understand the nature of cities and the historical precedents. A second step is to face up to the unique problems of the present migrant groups. These can be summarized in a single statement: All of certain ethnic groups, because of their physical identification, are assumed to be a threat to a middle-class neighborhood, regardless of the individual's or the family's income, education, or behavior. Centuries of slavery, generations of color discrimination, repeated instances of economic disadvantage via perpetuation of a color line, and a liberal amount of guilt have perpetuated color concepts. These are most apparent and effective in situations involving areas of living and schools.

Most liberals and many social scientists advocate heterogeneous neighborhoods. The majority of them would favor a community of homes in which low-, medium-, and upper-income groups lived; as a minimum, they would mix low- and medium-income people. Some have equally strong feelings about racial heterogeneity, affirming that in the modern world it behooves us in the United States to learn and demonstrate how a multi-racial society can live together under democracy. Recently an outstanding land economist has dissented, questioning the innate superiority of multi-income neighborhoods.[27] In this paper no

25 Nathan Glazer, op. cit., pp. 11–12. For a more realistic discussion of the Puerto Rican, see Handlin, op. cit., pp. 59–60.
26 Oscar Handlin, op. cit., pp. 78–80, 100, 103, 117–19.
27 "It is not clear why economically heterogeneous neighborhoods are innately superior to the homogeneous. We do not really know whether economically diverse groups truly mix or merely live side by side. And casual observation indicates that many exclusively high-income or middle-income neighborhoods seem to have withstood neighborhood decline extremely well while many economically-mixed neighborhoods have proven quite vulnerable. The social gains of mixture and the social losses from homogeneity have yet to be demonstrated." (Louis Winnick, Facts and Fictions in Urban Renewal, p. 12. Mimeographed: a speech delivered before the Forum of the Philadelphia Housing Association, January 28, 1960). Most planners, however, believe that there are such social gains. A recent forum composed of citizens and professionals who met to consider what neighborhoods should be like "pleaded for variety—variety of housing types . . . available at a variety of prices and rentals so that a varied neighborhood population could result, all races, young and old, rich and poor, and people falling between these extremes." Ironically enough,

attempt will be made to pass moral, social, or political judgments on this issue; rather, the problem will be treated from the point of view of the survival of central cities. Our orientation will be primarily economic, recognizing that enforced racial residential segregation is under attack and in the process of change in the nation.

From this point of view, it must be recognized that the middle class in America is keenly conscious of the threat of lower-class encroachments. As was pointed out above this has long been a national characteristic, perhaps an inevitable consequence of a socially mobile people who are status-conscious. During the last quarter of a century, it has become more acute. This leads to the conclusion that many middle-class families will not long voluntarily remain in an area which they believe threatened by lower-class engulfment; few will migrate to such areas. The second fact that has to be recognized is that the white middle class fears neighborhood deterioration on the entry of non-whites—an attitude that has partial roots in the history of decline in city services, lax enforcement of housing codes, and overcrowding in areas inhabited by non-whites. Actually, the degree of this fear is often a function of the speed and intensity of non-white penetration, although it is today an almost immediate reaction upon the first evidence of non-white entry.[28] Most white middle-class families will not long remain in a neighborhood where they are a racial minority. Should they fear this eventuality, they usually act so as to assure its fruition. On the other hand, there are many evidences of whites' accepting a few Negro neighbors, particularly if they are of comparable economic and social status.[29]

THE IMPACT OF URBAN RENEWAL

Urban renewal activity concerned with attracting and holding middle-class households in the central city must be geared to creating neighborhoods which offer good schools, a reasonable degree of cleanliness, protection from violence, and physical attractiveness. They need not be single-class neighborhoods,[30] but there is a limit —a class tipping point—to which they can at the present be heterogeneous from a class point

of view. Similarly, they can absorb some minority group families of middle-class attributes as well as some of lower-incomes.[31] The class and racial mix will vary from new urban redevelopment sites, partial redevelopment and rehabilitation efforts, and conservation areas. The greatest flexibility is in the newly reconstructed redevelopment areas—if for no other reason because new areas and new houses have a snob appeal in themselves.

---

zoning as currently practiced was considered a chief deterrent to such mixture. (Howard W. Hallman, "Citizens and Professionals Reconsider the Neighborhood," *Journal of the American Institute of Planners,* August 1959, p. 123). For a somewhat similar point of view, see Arthur L. Grey, Jr., "Los Angeles: Urban Prototype," *Land Economics,* August 1959, pp. 237–8.)
28 This is a most complex phenomenon. Its manifestation varies from city to city, from time to time, and from area to area within a given city. For example, in the color-conscious Washington, D.C. of the present writer's youth, whites did not hesitate to enter Brookland (a suburb of the central city) despite the presence of a few middle-class Negro families. (R. C. Weaver, *The Negro Ghetto,* pp. 290–91.) As Negro incomes rose in the District of Columbia, an increasing number of middle-class colored families moved into Brookland but, until World War II, it remained a racially mixed area. By 1952, non-whites had penetrated adjoining Woodridge and Michigan Park, areas of white middle-class occupancy. The official organ of the Rhode Island Avenue Citizens' Association exhorted whites to remain in Woodridge. (Weaver, "Relative Status of the Housing of Negroes in the United States," *Journal of Negro Education,* Summer 1953, pp. 351–52). But the combined force of the pent-up non-white demand for good housing and the lure of the suburbs in surrounding Maryland and Virginia for whites was too much. Today Brookland is largely Negro, Woodridge and Michigan Park house many non-white families, and Brookland's Negroes are no longer almost exclusively middle-class. The new prestige area for Washington's middle-class Negro families is in the far Northwest, where a relatively few reside among white neighbors.
29 See Gus Turberville, "The Negro Population of Duluth, Minnesota, 1950," *Sociology and Social Research,* March–April, 1952, pp. 231–38; Arnold M. Rose, Frank J. Atelsek and Laurence R. MacDonald, "Neighborhood Reactions to Isolated Negro Residents; An Alternative to Invasion and Succession," *American Sociological Review,* October 1953; Davis McEntire, "A Study of Racial Attitudes in Neighborhoods Infiltrated by Non-Whites," *Bay Area Real Estate Report* (San Francisco), Second Quarter 1955, pp. 126–29.
30 Those who insist on this will probably move to the suburbs anyway.
31 For an analysis of the experience of builders of interracial private developments during the last decade, see Eunice and George Grier, *Privately Developed Interracial Housing* (Berkeley, California; University of California Press, 1960).

Proximity to an established blighted non-white slum complicates or deters white occupancy in redevelopment projects. Either large-scale demolition, or extra value for the housing dollar, or both are required to offset this circumstance. Chicago illustrates well this situation. The New York Life Insurance Company financed and constructed Lake Meadows, a large redevelopment, medium-cost rental project in the heart of what had been some of the worst of the city's Negro slums. Although it announced open occupancy from the start and, despite the scope of the redevelopment and its inherent desirable location in relation to downtown and in proximity to city-wide health and educational institutions, the attractive new facilities failed to appeal to a large number of white tenants.[32] Intensive efforts and tangible evidences of a new neighborhood achieved 20 percent white occupancy and, currently, 25 percent of the tenants are white.

Prairie Shores was subsequently constructed on the site of a former Negro slum and on the edge of the Negro ghetto. But it was adjacent to Lake Meadows and the upgrading of the neighborhood was well under way. Indeed, the promotion of Prairie Shores describes it as "an entirely new community immediately adjacent to the Michael Reese Hospital campus." In the words of its developer—who incidentally evidenced his commitment to the project by selling his house in the suburbs and moving into Prairie Shores—"people just recognized a hell of a good buy when they saw it." The nature of this buy is indicated by the fact that apartments rented for an average of $33 a room as against $45 to $65 for comparable new accommodations elsewhere in the city. And the first 342 units in the initial structure of this five-building development rented quickly. Seventy-seven percent of the occupants were white but most households were childless and none had children of high school age.[33] As of May 1960, two buildings in Prairie Shores had been completed. Both were fully rented and leases were being signed on a third which will be ready for occupancy in late summer. The racial mix remained about 80 percent white and, while few families with school-age children were in occupancy, there were many with pre-school children.

With rare exceptions a small island of me-dium-cost redevelopment housing in a sea of non-white slums will not attract whites. This was the experience of the attractive—but not relatively competitively-priced—Longwood Redevelopment in Cleveland. An exception was the reasonably priced (single-family, sales house) and slow moving redevelopment project in Richmond, California.[34] On the other hand, redevelopment in an area which is fairly large and marked for total treatment can attract middle-class whites when a minority of non-whites are housed in it. This has been demonstrated in architecturally attractive Capitol Park Apartments of the Southwest Redevelopment in Washington, D.C. and in the Gratiot Redevelopment in Detroit. Both of these are fairly high-rent and that fact alone has greatly limited non-white participation.

Partial redevelopment and rehabilitation present more difficult problems. In the first place, frequently the old neighborhood which is the symbol of the threat of lower-class and minority families is not destroyed. Even if a new type of area is planned the physical evidences of the old remain. Where, as in the area around the University of Chicago, there is a sizeable amount of good housing and an enduring institutional base, the possibilities of success are enhanced. The urban renewal plan for the West Side of New York,[35] which also involved spot clearance and a great amount of rehabilitation, is also favorably located. On the north is a large middle-income redevelopment project partially occupied and nearing completion, on the east an attractive predominantly upper middle-class residential strip on Central Park West, on the south a middle-class strip on 86th Street, and on the west a traffic artery.

32 Lake Meadows is located on a 100-acre site and rented initially from $30 per room per month—about a quarter less than comparable accommodations elsewhere in the city. The first building of slightly less than 600 units attracted only about three percent white tenants. Subsequent special efforts appreciably increased white participation. (Eunice and George Grier, op. cit., pp. 106–7).
33 "Open Occupancy Builder Lands 77% White Tenants," House and Home, March 1959, p. 76.
34 "Pilot Project Survives FHA Red Tape, Starts Blighted Area on Road Back," House and Home, February 1959, p. 59.
35 Urban Renewal (New York: New York City Planning Commission, undated) and West Side Urban Renewal Area (New York: Urban Renewal Board, 1959).

In the Chicago and New York projects there has been great controversy as to how much public housing will be provided. In both instances the amount has been limited so that low-income families will be a definite minority of those in the areas. New York's West Side will also have a sizeable amount of lower medium-rent facilities or reasonably priced cooperatives, but most of the shelter will be priced so as to attract middle-income households. There is no question that both the New York and the Chicago neighborhoods will be predominantly middle class. Both will have some nonwhite, low-income families and some nonwhite, middle-income households. But they will be predominantly middle- and upper-income white communities.

Since conservation areas are subjected to the least amount of physical change, they share characteristics with most of the standard areas of existing housing. While the structures in such areas of the old city may be imposing in size and appearance, frequently they are architecturally obsolete. This may occasion new property uses—rooming houses, conversions to apartments of varying degrees of adequacy, or other forms of multi-family occupancy. Seldom are they suited for small families and their utilization by low-income households usually involves undesirable economic and social consequences.

In some instances the location of conversion areas (in terms of proximity to present concentrations of non-white families) inspires acute fear of minority inundation on the part of present residents. Thus, the possibility of panic selling is real and immediate upon the entrance of non-whites. There is another complicating factor. Present residents of these areas have not elected to live with non-white neighbors. The latter have come in after the neighborhood has been established as a racially homogeneous one. Thus there may be a feeling on the part of old residents that they had lost the opportunity to exercise freedom of choice in selecting non-white neighbors. In this regard they differ from those who move into a new or existing bi-racial community.[36] The physical attributes of conservation areas and the process of change involved in establishing racial mixture complicate the process in such neighborhoods.

Thus conservation areas present perplexing problems to those who would attract and hold middle-class whites in the central city. At the outset it must be recognized that many parts of the core city are destined to be occupied by non-whites. Under present conditions they will provide the almost sole supply of housing for Negroes and other non-whites who seek better shelter and are achieving or have achieved sufficiently high earnings to pay for it. In addition, if the past is any indication of the future, many areas of this type will, should they lie in the path of the geographic expansion of existing racial ghettos, be occupied by house-hungry lower-income non-whites.

The degree to which low-income minority families enter these areas depends upon several things. If there is an alternative supply of good housing which better fits the family needs and pocketbooks of non-whites, the process will be delayed. If housing and occupancy standards are enforced—a thing that is unlikely unless there is an alternative supply [37]—this too will slow up racial displacement. And of course the

36 Henry G. Stetler, *Racial Integration in Private Residential Neighborhoods in Connecticut* (Hartford, Connecticut: Connecticut Commission on Civil Rights, 1957) pp. 72–5. Of course, as has been observed, when one buys or rents in any neighborhood, one has no vested right in its composition. This was emphatically delineated by the 1948 decision of the Supreme Court which outlawed judicial enforcement of race restrictive housing covenants and in the rise of non-discrimination housing legislation. As a practical matter, however, many people do react to what they consider their freedom of choice in this regard and nothing in the law prevents families from moving away from neighbors they do not like.

37 "For many years a high-class residential enclave around the University of Chicago, Hyde Park-Kenwood began developing pockets of slums, then found itself turning from a white to a Negro neighborhood. Concerted community action, with citizen participation on a scale perhaps unmatched in the nation, has done much to slow the drift toward blight. Moreover, the neighborhoods set out to do so on a deliberate interracial basis . . . . Leaders of the effort found out how to make the city government help them enforce decent living standards. But continuing Negro pressure for more housing raised doubts as to whether this unique and pioneering effort could succeed in the face of overwhelming odds . . . . By the end of 1955 physical conversion of apartments into cell-like slum structures . . . . had been stopped cold . . . . But conversion by use—moving three or four families into one apartment—had not been stopped." (Martin Millspaugh and Gurney Breckenfeld, *The Human Side of Urban Renewal* (Baltimore, Maryland: Fight-Blight Inc., 1958), pp. 91 and 105–6).

extent to which the central city becomes more attractive to whites will lessen the availability of such housing to non-whites. At the same time, however, the volume of migration of non-whites to urban centers will be a major factor in determining the demand for housing on their part. Finally, in proportion as we continue to concentrate upon clearing slums inhabited by non-whites the process of racial displacement will take place elsewhere in the city.

In recent years there has been a series of attempts on the part of middle-class neighborhoods to stay the departure of whites with the arrival of colored residents. To date, most if not all of these have been delaying tactics at best.[38] Perhaps if such efforts were a part of an over-all program involving new open-occupancy construction, action for spreading the non-white demand over a larger area of the central city, prevention of the engineering of panic selling by real estate operators, better enforcement of housing and occupancy codes and effective action to open the suburbs to non-whites, such programs might succeed in maintaining the bi-racial character of some well-located and attractive neighborhoods.[39]

THE ROLE OF GOOD SCHOOLS

Up to this point little has been said of family composition and its implications for middle-class residence in the central city. Most of the urban renewal projects mentioned are designed for small families and the most successful of them house few young people of school age. A recent analysis of the demand for renewal and redeveloped housing in downtown Philadelphia eliminates families with children as a source of occupants, suggesting that such families would gravitate to "the massive sections of slums and deterioration that lie beyond the central core."[40] There they would look for single-family houses or garden-type apartments.

Obviously, the needs and requirements of upper- and middle income families without children are quite different from those who have youngsters. For the latter, schools are important. Among those of large incomes (and to some degree among the less prosperous) the possibility of using private schools may cause little concern for public educational facilities. In many

northern cities parochial schools serve a similar purpose.[41]

Most knowledgeable observers consider schools a basic factor in attracting or holding middle-class families in the central city.[42] Indeed in the Russel Woods area of Detroit, concern for education of children seemed to be the most important element motivating liberal families to leave their desirable homes.[43] This too is often as much of a class as a racial phenomenon. In Cleveland, for example, middle-class Negroes entered the comfortable homes in the outlying Glenville section of the central city after World War II. More recently, as large numbers of low-income non-whites have entered the area, some of the earlier Negro residents have moved a second time, entering the more exclusive and prestige-laden Shaker Heights section. Many of those involved explain their action on the basis of the superior schools in the latter location. On the other

38 Loc. cit. See also Mayer, op. cit.
39 The same analysis applies to the use of quotas as a means of effecting and perpetuating interracial neighborhoods. Aside from the troublesome questions of their violation of fair housing laws, they do not offer permanent barriers against the economic pressure of a concentration of non-white demand on one or a few locations. (For a description of the case for quotas, see Oscar Cohen, "The Benign Quotas in Housing," Phylon, First Quarter (Spring) 1960, pp. 20–29). My analysis suggests that benign housing quotas are as temporary a means of stabilizing bi-racial areas as race restrictive housing covenants were to do the opposite. For a discussion of the latter point, see Weaver, The Negro Ghetto, Ch. XIII.
40 Chester Rapkin and William G. Grigsby, Residential Renewal in the Urban Core (Philadelphia, Pennsylvania: University of Pennsylvania Press, 1960), p. 118.
41 "A significantly high percentage of purchasers in nonhomogeneous 'mixed' areas have been found to be families who, if they had school-age children, were sending them to relatively homogeneous (Roman Catholic) schools." (The Demand for Housing in the Eastwick Redevelopment Area, Interim Report, June 1956, Table XXIV, p. 42 (Philadelphia) cited by John W. Dyckman, "Comment on Glazer's School Proposals," Journal of the American Institute of Planners, November, 1959, footnote 2, p. 197.)
42 "Studies . . . provide confirmation for the general hypothesis that in certain large northern cities, choice of school is at least as sensitive as choice of residence to the pull of 'homogeneity,' and for some may play an important part in residential choice." (Dyckman, "Comment on Glazer's School Proposals," op. cit., p. 197) .
43 Albert J. Mayer, "Russel Woods: Change Without Conflict," op. cit., pp. 215–16, 219.

hand, in Russel Woods and elsewhere, the existence of synagogues and other institutions related to Jewish life and religion was a strong factor in holding the white residents. Provision of similar facilities in the suburbs facilitated subsequent departure of many of these families.[44]

One student of the racial aspects of housing has proposed abandonment of the rule requiring children to attend a neighborhood public school and provision of special facilities for the middle-class oriented families. Thus, heterogeneity in residential patterns would be purchased at the cost of homogeneity in public schools.[45] It has been pointed out that special schools of the type suggested might well fail to preserve or facilitate heterogeneity in residential patterns, reinforcing "islands of upper-income white occupancy in an ethnic sea of educational proletarianization." [46] In light of the growing political power of non-whites in northern urban areas such a consequence would sow the seeds of its own destruction—and that of urban renewal in the process.

Public schools are a symbol and an instrument of democracy. While their programs can and should be tailored to meet the needs of students, the whole trend in the nation, as dramatized by the Supreme Court decision of May 1954, is away from racial segregation. This of course is not to say that every child receives the same training but it does call for no arbitrary assignment to schools on basis of color or class. It is compatible with an open system which, within a given school, assigns pupils to educational programs which meet their needs, provided that the system is fluid and based upon some universally applied criteria for assignment. The latter must be a reflection of ability and not social status. The track system now in operation in Washington, D.C. is one which seems to meet these requirements.

But there is still another requirement. It is a system which avoids the implications or consequences of separate identification by tracks. This has been accomplished in one school on the West Coast where there are several curricula for students of differing aptitudes. However, all students of a given grade have a common homeroom or common homerooms, regardless of differences in educational programs. Such arrangement is not only productive of identifi-

cation with a common institution for all but it is also compatible with the concept of a democratic public school.[47]

Just as most middle-class families, if they have an alternative, will not long remain in a neighborhood where they are a minority so they will not long send their children to a school where they are a minority. Middle-class whites with children will remain in the central city in large numbers only if they have access to a middle-class oriented, educationally satisfactory public school or can afford private or parochial schools. The degree of possible class and racial mix in a neighborhood is lessened, therefore, when school-age children are involved. It can be conceived however that as the number of stable bi-racial neighborhoods increases, tolerance for this type of living will grow. In light of the importance of prestige considerations in the selection of housing, it may well be that this process will be accelerated through the creation of attractive, newly constructed, racially mixed neighborhoods in the central city. The efficacy of the latter will be minimized as long as the suburbs remain essentially racially homogeneous.

Public schools in the central city cannot compete with their suburban prototypes on terms of the latter. The city public schools can never match the snob appeal of many suburban ones. Seldom can they assure the same degree of class or racial homogeneity nor can they equal the spaciousness of the surrounding campus. But they can be good schools. Indeed if they are specialized high schools concentrating on specific fields, they can be better schools. This is demonstrated by certain technical schools, fashion schools, and performing arts high schools in New York City. Emphasis must be upon high scholastic standards, adequate discipline in the school, and exploitation of the opportunities for cultural enrichment which urban life offers. While these potentialities will not be given a chance to flower if middle-class

44 *Ibid.,* pp. 212, 216, 219.
45 Nathan Glazer, "The School as an Instrument in Planning," *Journal of the American Institute of Planners,* November 1959, pp. 191–6.
46 J. W. Dyckman, "Comment on Glazer's School Proposals," *op. cit.,* p. 196.
47 See James B. Conant, *The American High School Today,* New York: McGraw-Hill Book Company, 1959, p. 74.

white parents feel that low-income and minority group children are to be a large element in the student body, they are possible of achievement in a city school which is not homogeneous. Proof of this is the effort prestige private schools have made for years to attract and enroll children of poorer parents and from non-white households. The administrations and parents of many of these schools lament the fact that such enrollment is not larger.

At the same time the central city public school has a unique character to sell—a degree of class and racial heterogeneity which will teach young people to live with other children of varying backgrounds.[48] Many middle-class families are acutely aware of the importance of this in a democracy; in the world today it has even more pressing international implications. Unfortunately, realization of its desirability is far from accepting situations in which there is heterogeneity.[49] This is due largely to fear that some class and racial mixture will lead to an inevitable lowering of academic and discipline standards and an ultimate minority status for white children in the school. It is also manifestation of apprehension lest there may be loss of social status in living in a predominantly non-white neighborhood or having one's children in a school with large Negro enrollment. If, however, the public school is geared primarily to the educational goals of middle-class families, it can and will attract and hold many middle-class white children even though some lower-income and middle-class minority pupils are included.

Another attraction which the school in the central city can have is to afford a richer and more meaningful education. This suggests delineation and exploitation of the educational advantages of the central city. The many cultural institutions located in the central city—its theatres, museums, concerts, and the like—are great assets. The school program should utilize fully and dramatically these facilities of the central city.

With all of this, there will be fear and apprehension on the part of middle-class parents. Over the long run, this can be met only as the living standards, opportunities, and assimilation of those least advantaged in the city are increased. Here too the public schools have a basic but not an exclusive role. In those areas where the schools serve large numbers of migrant, low-income, and minority families, programs need to be developed to accelerate their adjustment to urban life. Included among these are activities for remedial work, the discovery and nurture of talent, curriculum enrichment, reaching parents and involving them in community problems related to schools, and the preparation of teachers who understand the cultural problems involved.

All of these programs and activities will hold only some of the middle-class families now in the central cities. They will be more effective in attracting back to the city others who are exhausted or disillusioned with suburban life. But unless we begin now to deal with them, the trend of certain groups away from the city will continue—and probably at an accelerated rate. Certainly, in assessing the potential demand for medium-priced housing in the central city, an important variable is the success we have in creating and maintaining public schools which have an appeal to the families involved.

THE CLASS AND RACE MIX OF THE CITY TOMORROW

This analysis suggests that in northern and border cities there can be a degree of class and racial mixture compatible with attracting and holding middle-class whites. In the expensive and upper medium-rental apartments and sales houses this presents few problems of planning. The income structure assures only token participation by non-whites and of course eliminates the low-income group. If the desirable mix (from the point of view of maintaining large numbers of medium-income families) involves limited participation of low-income households, this too can be achieved by rede-

48 *Ibid.*, pp. 75–6.
49 The inclination of liberal, middle-class white families to offer lip-service to the desirability of racial heterogeneity in schools results in some peculiar situations. Frequently, in an effort to establish the form of bi-racial student bodies, a few non-whites are either admitted or actively sought. This is most prevalent in private schools and the minority group students are "special" in more ways than the obvious. While potential guilt of liberal whites may be assuaged, the non-white symbol of integration may suffer from a forced and artificial gesture.

veloping or renewing areas large enough to establish their own identity and limiting the amount of low-cost housing. This however implies the responsibility for providing in attractive locations an adequate supply of low-cost units and cessation of such widespread dislocation of families as has typified urban renewal to date.

It is at the level of medium-cost housing that real problems arise. The non-white and particularly the Negro housing market includes a growing number of families ready, willing, and able to purchase or rent such shelter. If the market is open to them in only a few locations at any one time the "tipping point" may soon be reached in any one or two developments. As was indicated above, opening the suburbs to non-whites is one of the necessary prices for attracting and holding middle-income whites in the central city.[50]

Cessation of widespread dislocation of low-income families was suggested in the earlier discussion of high and upper-medium-cost housing. It was proposed there from the point of view of political expediency and equity. It is pertinent to the discussion of medium-cost housing for another reason. As long as large numbers of low-income families are uprooted by slum clearance they are a potential source for the displacement of middle-income families elsewhere in the community. This is especially true when they are colored and limited to a racially restricted market.

A final approach, applicable chiefly to conservation areas, is to perfect techniques for stabilizing racially transitional neighborhoods. To be effective they must be an element in a comprehensive program for expanding the supply of housing available to non-whites at all price levels. Also, it must be realized that there are some neighborhoods which, because of location in relation to the growth of areas of non-white concentration, will not respond to this treatment. This only illustrates that cities are not static institutions. Their physical facilities change and their people move. The problems of class and color can never be solved in any one neighborhood. Today they cannot be solved in the central city. They are problems of metropolitan areas.

If this analysis is valid, it has significance for the kind of cities we may expect in the next generation. While the size and squalor of slums may be decreased we shall not clear all of them. Poverty, rejection, and a certain amount of individual choice [51] will dictate their perpetuation. Through better schools—in terms of plant, quality of teaching and effective programs to reach low-income families—the economic and social status of many slum residents can be raised. If we perfect and apply techniques to give the newcomers a feeling of belonging and provide meaningful assistance to the normal as opposed to the problem family, there can be greater occupational, educational and residential mobility among this group. For these approaches to work, our urban populations will have to be less color-conscious; and anti-discrimination housing legislation affecting the suburbs as well as central cities will be required. We need also to develop more tolerance to variations from established middle-class values and behavior.[52]

American urban centers will not soon, if ever, become a total of class and racial heterogeneous neighborhoods. Realistic and courageous planning, constant progress toward open occupancy, continued economic advancement on the part of the disadvantaged, progress in dealing with transitional neighborhoods, an expanding supply of housing suited to the family needs and pocketbooks of low-income and lower medium-income households, good schools, and the development of techniques to upgrade at a reasonable cost much of the existing housing supply will enable our cities to develop and maintain neighborhoods with varying degrees of class and color heterogeneity. But most of these will be predominantly of one income level; some will be almost exclusively non-white; a few will have a small number of medium-income non-whites; and others will be integrated in varying degrees.

What of the central cities? They will survive.

50 This is a complex matter. It would operate as suggested above by (1) syphoning off some of the middle income demand for housing among non-whites from the central city; (2) removing the attraction of racial homogeneity from the suburbs; (3) reducing the snob appeal of racial exclusiveness since no area could assure it; (4) reducing the threat of "tipping" in any one racially open neighborhood.
51 John R. Seeley, "The Slum: Its Nature, Use, and Uses," *Journal of the American Institute of Planners*, February 1959, pp. 7–14.
52 R. C. Weaver, "Human Values of Urban Life," *Proceedings of the Academy of Political Science*, June, 1960.

Indeed, their demise, largely on the same grounds cited as threatening them today, has been foretold many times in the past.[53] Of course, they will be different. For years to come they will have trouble attracting and holding middle-income white families with children. As long as there are private and parochial schools, some such households will remain. To the degree that redevelopment, renewal, and conserved neighborhoods, as well as areas which are left alone, become or continue to be identified as middle class, there will be middle-income whites with children in the central cities. Good public schools and other satisfactory public facilities will augment the number. Almost equally important will be the success we have in utilizing housing codes and other tools to raise the general level of housing, in developing realistic school programs to raise motivation and achievement in all schools, and in applying effective techniques for accelerating the occupational, residential, and social mobility of the growing number of newcomers who are entering and will continue to enter our cities.

53 Louis Winnick, *Facts and Fictions in Urban Renewal*, p. 18.

Urban Renewal Programs [1]

JEROME ROTHENBERG

The federal urban renewal program was born in 1949. By the end of 1961, 587 local projects had major contracts under the Urban Renewal Administration. For 574 of them the total gross project cost was $2.9 billion, of which $1.3 billion was federal money, and $0.7 billion local government money. The private development resources which were, or will eventually be, associated with these projects are probably three or four times these amounts. And the many resources involved are used in ways that make diverse and far-reaching changes in the lives of millions of people. It is important to be able to evaluate the program and its components, making use of the experience of about fourteen years.

This paper attempts to set forth a conceptual framework for making benefit-cost analyses of portions of this program. It will be concerned with what was originally the pre-eminent component of the program—urban redevelopment—but which has recently been somewhat de emphasized, although it has accounted for the lion's share of resources since the program's inception. My attention here is largely devoted to trying to specify the nature of the benefits from a single redevelopment project, and how they may be measured. The problem of specifying the real resource costs involved is not examined in any depth, although the final section presents a numerical illustration of the application of the procedure, and crude money cost figures are given. These are intended for illustration only, and do not pretend to be derived from a serious analysis.

To begin with, I shall briefly sketch the operation of a typical redevelopment project under the federal Urban Renewal Program. A "local public authority" (LPA)—sometimes organized specifically to formulate projects under the program, sometimes already in existence with other operations—declares a certain area blighted and legally condemns it. Then, by the right of eminent domain, the LPA buys up all sites within the area, paying the owners "fair value." Land assembly is followed by demolition of structures in the site (clearance) and preparation of the land for redevelopment. This includes the local government's adjust-

From *Measuring Benefits of Government Investments*, Robert Dorfman (ed.) (Washington, D.C.: The Brookings Institution, 1965), pp. 292–341. Reprinted by permission of the publisher.
1 An extensive treatment of this whole subject is contained in my study, "Economic Evaluation of Urban Renewal," in preparation for the Brookings Institution. [This study has since appeared in *Studies of Government Finance*, The Brookings Institution, Washington, D.C., 1967—Ed.]

ment of streets, sewers, schools, and other utilities. In addition, any families displaced as a
result of clearance are relocated elsewhere by
the LPA, under an explicit relocation program.
Public processing of the area under the auspices
of the LPA is now complete. The next step is
the sale or lease of the area to a private redeveloper; but sometimes part of the area is
given to a government agency for construction
of public housing or other public purpose. Under the private redeveloper, the area is typically
subjected to significant change in land-use—
often high-rise or large-scale housing projects
for people in the upper-middle-income bracket,
and, more recently, modern commercial centers.

The role of the federal government in this
process is to approve the advance planning for
the overall project, to lend working capital
funds for detailed planning, surveys, and acquisition, and to finance up to two thirds of
the LPA's "net project cost," which is defined
as the LPA's total expenditure on the project
less the receipts realized by selling prepared
land to redevelopers. Under the 1949 Act the
federal government was authorized to spend $1
billion in loans and $500 million in grants over
a five-year period. Amendments in 1955, 1957,
1959, and 1961 steadily increased the amounts
of the grants; as of the 1961 amendments,
grants could be as large as $4 billion.

In the version of benefit-cost analysis used in
this paper, the policy alternatives are specified,
and one of them—the status quo policy—is
treated as the point of departure alternative.
The consequences of the other alternatives are
considered to be the positive and negative
changes in well-being of everyone affected.
Where possible, these changes are calculated in
money terms. Where this is not possible,
changes are specified in terms of types of events
which are presumed to affect well-being. Complete specification of consequences may therefore involve a multidimensional vector of effects, only one dimension of which is monetary.

Many benefit-cost studies distinguish between
total income (production) and distribution of
income effects, typically including the first and
excluding the second in the effects to be considered. The presumption is that undesirable
distributional effects stemming from some policy can be offset through auxiliary income transfer policies unrelated to the specific policy area

at issue. This presumption may be warranted
for policy areas at the federal level, since the
federal government has powerful means available, such as the income tax and other transfer
programs, to achieve many redistributional
aims. Most local governments do not have such
means; distributional consequences of major
local programs must typically stand uncorrected.
In the case of urban renewal, which involves
local projects, we shall therefore specify both
total income *and* distributional effects of alternative policies.

The alternative policies that must be compared in this area are three:

1. The status quo policy of allowing land-
   use to be determined by private market
   decisions, subject to the various present
   governmental regulations and enforcement, including tax and credit policy.
2. Redevelopment projects, designed to supersede market decisions in the way described above.
3. A composite of ameliorative public actions other than redevelopment, to "improve" on private performance in those
   respects where private performance is suboptimal. (This third alternative is not
   unique, and we do not attempt to specify
   any one such composite for evaluation in
   this paper. But the nature of some possible components for such a composite are
   strongly suggested by the analysis of the
   kinds of benefits to be derived from redevelopment. And once a composite has
   been specified, the methods presented in
   this paper can be straight-forwardly applied to evaluate its benefits.)

Every benefit-cost analysis requires aggregat-
ing effects for groups of individuals to facilitate computation, and every such method of
aggregation is an arbitrary compromise away
from the "true" value of the social welfare
change. We propose to aggregate together, as
a single group, all individuals who are similarly affected by each type of consequence of a
given policy. Moreover, for each of these
groups a subgrouping may be performed in
terms of a few stereotype characteristics most
perceived in local political decision-making:
for example, rich vs. poor, central city dwellers

vs. suburbanites, minority groups vs. majority groups. A rationale for this procedure is that the lumping-together of benefits and costs in the analysis will parallel the kind of lumping-together that actually informs local political choice.

The selection of this type of benefit-cost analysis automatically decides an important question about evaluative criterion. The criterion is not maximization of property values within a certain area but maximization of welfare among a relevant population. Choice of the relevant population is not easy. In formal terms, since the federal level is involved in at least part of the financing, the well-being of the entire United States population should be consulted. But the truly distinctive benefits and costs of urban renewal are almost entirely contained within the population of the pertinent metropolitan area. It is unwise to narrow the relevant population further—to the central city, or even project neighborhood—because specific alterable features of projects can have significant effects on individuals residing outside such narrower boundaries. (Projects designed to attract middle- and upper-income groups back to the city from the suburbs are of this type.)

Our decision about a relevant population may seem to introduce an anomaly. Renewal projects are typically creatures of central city planning and execution (with federal cooperation). Noncentral city residents of the metropolitan area have no close representation in the projects. This introduces a methodological slippage into our procedure. It is tacit in benefit-cost analysis that policy-makers will be attracted to benefits and repelled by costs. But where these policy-makers have no legal responsibility for—or feel no political pressure from—a numerous portion of the affected population, costs and benefits to the latter will fail to carry the appropriate incentive force. Indeed, they may bear perverse force—policy-makers attempting to impose costs on and deny benefits to the outlying populations. However, many projects do in fact offer benefits to suburbanites, in the form of an enlarged set of city housing alternatives. Costs are typically imposed on them, not by specific structural characteristics of renewal projects, but via the general redistribution of federal taxation to support its financing share. Nonetheless, the

divergence between policy responsibility and policy consequence very likely leads to suboptimal choice. By including the wider population in our criterion we point up the need to change jurisdictional boundaries—whether formally or informally—or otherwise directly modify planners' incentives in projects of this sort.

THE NATURE OF REDEVELOPMENT BENEFITS

The consequences of redevelopment are varied, extensive, and complicated. It is not obvious *a priori* which environmental indications one would have to observe to measure any relevant individual's well-being. As a short cut, we look for the directions of significant influence by examining the purposes of the redevelopment program. Such an examination, in addition to suggesting the distinctive types of benefits to be found from redevelopment, can suggest alternatives to redevelopment by clarifying the status quo deficiencies that redevelopment is designed to correct—and, therefore, what other measures can also be so designed.

Redevelopment has had a variety of explicit and implicit aims. The more significant ones seem to be:

1. The elimination of blight and slums.
2. The mitigation of poverty.
3. Provision of decent, safe, and sanitary housing in a suitable environment for all.
4. Revival of downtown areas of the central city.
5. Attraction of middle-income families from suburbs back to the central city.
6. Attraction of additional "clean" industry into the central city.
7. Enhancement of the budget balance of the central city government.

Of these purposes the elimination of blight and slums has been officially considered by far the most important, but there are indications that local policy-makers have substantial incentives for some of the others, especially in more recent projects. We shall argue that only the first of the aims, and to a more limited extent the fourth and fifth, provide benefits of the sort that an economic benefit-cost evaluation can consider. The others largely involve public subsidies to achieve "public goals," the treatment of which our approach does not handle. This does not mean that such goal achievement does not count as a benefit in an overall evaluation of urban redevelopment. It means only that valuations must be given by decision-makers themselves, since they cannot be calculated within the traditional economic benefit-cost focus.

Elimination of Blight and Slums

Neither this goal nor the very definition of "blight" and "slums" is self-evident. But both a functional, judgmental definition and a more operational, structural one employ the rubric "substandard." Under the judgmental definition, "blight" and "slum" refer to dwellings which are not "decent, safe, and sanitary." [2] They are likely to be dilapidated, overcrowded, filthy, vermin-infested fire traps. Under the structural definition, architectural characteristics such as absence of bathtub or toilet, or of adequate wiring, comprise the components of "substandard." Despite its greater judgmental latitude, the former definition is more appropriate for our purposes, since the latter often operates as a criterion of architectural obsolescence rather than of housing quality.

The benefits inhering in the goal of eliminating blight and slums are not self-evident, because it is not at once obvious that what is gained exceeds what is lost. Slum dwellings represent low-quality housing. The usual overcrowding of such dwellings implies that the typical dwelling unit per household is also of very low quantity. Furthermore, these units are typically inhabited by poor families. The nub of the ambiguity is simply that, given the technical characteristics of the commodity which supplies housing services, so long as there exist poor families the existence of a significant supply of low-quality, low-quantity housing units might represent an optimal use of resources in this market. If so, their elimination would not render even *positive gross* benefits, but would introduce suboptimal resource utilization—i.e., it would render *negative gross* benefits.[3]

On the demand side, the existence of poverty makes the demand for low-quality, low-quantity housing eminently reasonable. Housing, being such a considerable part of the total budget, is a good place to economize with a highly limited budget, especially for families newly arrived in cities, who had experienced rural or foreign housing conditions that were considerably worse. On the supply side, the durability of housing makes it most efficient to meet the demand for such housing, not through new construction, but by means of a "filtering" downward of the existing housing stock through aging, structural conversion to permit occupancy of smaller units, and depreciation of maintenance.[4] "Filtering" is not restricted to the lowest portion of the housing stock; the great majority of the stock goes through a life cycle downward through lower and lower quality uses. Most new construction occurs in the upper half of housing use, and most retirements in the lowest use categories; thus, most units pass through a wide range of use levels during their lifetime. Since housing mobility is greater at the higher-income levels than at the lower, filtering is largely initiated by middle- and higher-income groups releasing their present accommodations in favor of newly constructed dwellings. Conversion occurs via changes in vacancy rates and relative price changes. Thus, a stock of old, worn housing, cut up into small units in the process of downward conversion, is the market's efficient way of providing housing services to the poor. If the overall pattern is unsatisfactory, the problem is poverty, not inefficiency in the housing market.

The above argument applies to low-quality housing. A slum is low-quality housing, but it is something more as well. And it is in the respects in which slums are something more that we may find the source of benefits from

[2] "Blight" refers to a process, and can refer to one or more structures, whether residential or not. "Slum" refers to a cluster of structures, usually residential, in an advanced stage of "blight."

[3] "Gross" in the sense that it is exclusive of the resource costs of elimination through redevelopment.

[4] This treatment of "filtering" is heavily dependent upon William G. Grigsby, *Housing Markets and Public Policy* (Institute for Urban Studies, University of Pennsylvania, 1962).

slum elimination. I shall argue that there are at least three respects in which slums may represent suboptimal resource use:

1. There exist important neighborhood effect externalities in land use; these are likely to be especially significant in slum areas.
2. The profitability incentives to produce the particular *type* of low-quality housing that characterizes slums rest upon market biases which are either ethically disapproved or the inadvertent result of public policies.
3. The functioning of slums entails the creation of important social costs which are externalities to the actors involved.

Neighborhood Externalities. There are important externalities in the nature of housing services and hence in the value of the property which provides them. The housing consumed by a household consists not only of occupancy of a specific dwelling but also of the location of the dwelling and its neighborhood. The neighborhood consists of other residential dwellings, of commercial and industrial establishments, of public services such as schools, street lighting, and police protection, of recreational and cultural amenities, and, most of all, of people. In the simple model presented by Davis and Whinston, the quality of the housing services associated with a particular dwelling depends on the character of the dwelling, the amount of maintenance and repair devoted to it, and also on the character of dwellings in the neighborhood together with their state of maintenance-repair.[5] For each of the n pieces of property comprised by the neighborhood, the owner obtains the highest return if his property is undermaintained, while all or most others are well maintained. He obtains a smaller return if his, as well as all or most others, are well maintained, less if his and all or most others are poorly maintained, and least if his is well maintained while everyone else's is undermaintained. This is the payoff matrix of the "Prisoner's Dilemma" type of strategic game. Each owner has an incentive to let his property be undermaintained while others maintain their property well. But the very generality of this incentive means that it cannot be realized: all property will tend to be undermaintained. Yet this outcome is less satisfactory to all owners than the only other attainable outcome—namely, high maintenance for all. This latter could not be attained by atomistic behavior, since each owner singly would shy away from high maintenance, but it is an outcome which all could bring about simultaneously: i.e., each could agree to it contingent on everyone else's agreeing to it.

Thus, the important externality of neighborhood means that the outcome arrived at by atomistic choice will typically be suboptimal, in the sense that nonatomistic coordinated choice could make all owners better off than they would be when acting atomistically.

This type of externality is very general. It is by no means restricted to slum areas, and may be supposed to affect property in all areas. Moreover, neighborhood effects may not everywhere be such that low maintenance is suboptimal; in some situations, high maintenance may well be suboptimal. All of it depends on the specific payoff matrix appropriate to the particular market. Is the market any better able to adjust land uses to the complicated pattern of such externalities in upper-income areas than in lower-income areas? At first blush it might seem that suboptimal land use can occur anywhere, at any level, in any direction, and to any extent, depending only on accident. This conclusion may seem even more persuasive when one considers the many forms of land misuse: undermaintenance; or the vying character of housing services, such as single vs. multiple-occupancy dwellings, high-rise vs. walkup apartment buildings; or even the residential-commercial-industrial mix.

Yet there is a special link between this type of market suboptimality and slum areas. Neighborhood effects are generally recognized. Indeed, special social mechanisms have been devised to minimize their most adverse effects. Building codes and zoning are attempts to moderate some of the worst effects of land use externalities; they typically stipulate permissible lower limits in quality and quantity—never

5 Otto A. Davis and Andrew B. Whinston, "Economics of Urban Renewal," *Law and Contemporary Problems*, Vol. 26 (Winter 1961), pp. 105–117.

upper limits. The slum-blight linkage stems from the fact that zoning and building codes are likely to be less effective for low-quality areas than for high-quality areas. Low capital availability, high population density, and householders' ignorance and, often, lack of urban disciplines are among the reasons for this.

Profitability Bias in the Production of Slums. Slums do not simply happen. They represent a pattern of resource use which is made by man; they are produced. They are produced because they are profitable. It is the contention of the present section that this profitability stems partly from market circumstances which are not "normally approved" but rather are generally desired by the electorate to be publicly rectified. It also stems partly from certain existing public policies, which also are capable of rectification. The profitability of slums is not inevitable, nor does it rest on market forces that are ethically neutral.

Slums are produced both intensively and extensively. Intensive production means conversion of property to lower and lower use—and then, for lowest uses, to lower and lower quality levels of service. Extensive production means extending the spatial boundaries of slum concentrations. The two aspects often go hand in hand. The most important types of intensive production are converting dwellings to increasingly overcrowded occupancy, and allowing the state of the property to deteriorate progressively.

To say that slums are profitable to produce is not to say that all property owners obtain excessive returns. It means rather that high rewards are available to "innovators" and, initiative having already been taken, it pays others to follow suit, sometimes against their personal preferences. Profitable opportunities exist, and the dynamics of contagion through neighborhood effects magnifies the drift. Profitable opportunities exist because of characteristics of the demand for inferior housing and because of legal and financial policies.

On the demand side, slum dwellers have historically been not only poor but disadvantaged: large clusterings of recent immigrants and underprivileged minority groups, radically uninformed about the market and their legal rights, and too poor to invest in information. Moreover, the rest of the community has often superimposed on these disabilities the artificial disability of discrimination. This has become especially onerous in the present generation, when it is the Negro who is preponderantly the slum dweller. The problem of slums is not at present solely a problem of the Negro, but that it *is* the Negro who disproportionately inhabits the slums aggravates the problem. Discrimination against the Negro in employment and housing has been especially severe. In housing it takes the form of segregation; large areas of cities are effectively closed to Negro occupancy, despite the willingness to pay stipulated rents.

The impact of all this is a large, uninformed, highly inelastic demand for low-quality housing in concentrated areas. Expansion of quantity comes most profitably from conversion to overcrowding. Moreover, the higher cost of accelerated depreciation is not made up in rentals, but in the less noticeable way of neglecting to keep the property up to legally required standards. Thus, conversion to slum use often increases revenues without increasing costs and even sometimes decreases actual expenses. It is not at all atypical for property to be run down profitably to a state where the cost of bringing the structure up to the legally required minimum level exceeds the value of the property. The property in this case has *negative* social value.

The profitability of slum production based on these characteristics is akin to the adulteration of commodities based on consumer ignorance. The market response in such situations is not considered to be due to the interaction of "normally approved" market forces. The consumers are considered to be "unfairly" disadvantaged. Political consensus in the United States has typically called for protection to offset such disadvantage. Thus, one can argue that slum profitability is to this extent "socially inadvertent."

A number of "artificial" factors on the supply side enhance the profitability of slum production—"artificial," in the sense that they are inadvertent consequences of public policies rather than inherent characteristics of the market. The federal income tax law is one such factor: a landlord can advantageously report accelerated depreciation on his slum property, without attempting to offset the depreciation by maintenance outlays. Property completely depreciated for tax purposes will, despite the lack of maintenance, still retain most of its competitive market position relative to the rest of the neighborhood, because of neighborhood externalities and disabilities already mentioned on the demand side. The property can be profitably sold, since the buyer can take depreciation on the property anew while failing to maintain it, and resell it profitably in turn. Thus, the same property, many times dilapidated, is kept in lower and lower occupancy use while continuing to record depreciation for tax purposes. Slum property tends to be kept in use far longer, and to a much lower level of quality, than it would in the absence of these tax advantages.

The profitability of slum property attracts speculators to buy up and convert many non-slum structures to slum use. The properties are refashioned to make overcrowding possible, thus setting the stage for faster depreciation, and then the speculators typically sell them at higher prices, the aim being capital gains rather than slum incomes.[6]

The property tax is another factor that encourages slum use and discourages unslumming. Rarely reflecting the profitability of slum use, it *is* raised when investment is made for upward renovation and maintenance. Such asymmetric assessment response acts as a drag on capital expenditure to improve the quality of slum and near-slum property. The tax biases resource use into less capital-intensive uses of land. Other things being equal, there is a tendency to choose the lower of two capital intensities, and with it, lower maintenance and lower quality use.

Capital rationing has an even stronger effect. Credit is essentially unavailable for remodeling and repair in slum and nearslum areas.[7] This aborts attempts at unslumming or even at maintaining existing housing quality. Credit sources apparently turn down each application because they judge it separately on the marginal basis that, alone, it will fail to offset downward neighborhood pressure and will thus be itself overwhelmed by adverse neighborhood effects. This neglects the potentially significant impact that could be created

if the whole set of otherwise creditworthy applicants were approved.

Besides discouraging the maintenance and upgrading of property, the credit squeeze discourages homeownership in the area, encourages emigration, and thus tends to increase the supply of dwellings for cheap, quick sale—further encouraging speculative accumulations for slum creation. The dynamics of such creation is aided by asymmetry in the working of neighborhood externalities: low-income minorities are undesirables to majority groups, but not vice versa. The minorities can drive out the majority group just by their presence, but the opposite movement is much more difficult to produce: it requires providing attractions great enough to offset often considerable antipathies.

A final "superfluous" factor stimulating slum production is ethnic prejudice itself. First, it enhances the *internal* production of slums by aggravating the poverty, immobility, and weak market condition of slum dwellers, as noted above. Second, it enhances the *external* spread of slums because the resulting concentration pressure within the segregated area brings about differentially higher housing prices (for given quality) and lower quality than elsewhere, creates a strong pent-up demand for better quality and for lower-priced housing, and thus results in spillouts into majority areas, when the prospect of differential profits from minority-group members is enough to offset the prejudice of the seller or renter. Even a single incursion into a hitherto "poor" area is often enough to precipitate panic flight by majority-group members, followed by large-scale replacement by the minority group. Once such a breach has occurred, the pent-up demand pressure of the minority is often great enough to make conversion of the area to slum use profitable, whatever the area's initial socioeconomic character. Panic flight makes for property bargains attractive to speculators—bringing about an ownership pattern highly conducive to slum creation. Moreover, rapid extensive turnover of

6 David Laidler, "The Effects of Federal Income Taxation on Owner-Occupied Dwellings" (doctoral dissertation in process, University of Chicago, 1964).
7 See Jane Jacobs, *The Death and Life of Great American Cities* (Random House, 1961), Chaps. 15–16.

property itself favors slum creation, since it destroys stable neighborhood expectations.

Internal and external production of slums is favored by the same factors, since the strength of the incentives toward both depends on the extent of price differentials (for given quality) between "ghetto" and outside areas. On the other hand, given the strength of these enhancing factors, successful external spread acts as a safety valve, tending to decrease internal production. Thus, the greater the barrier to spread, the greater the internal production.

Our discussion has implicitly assumed a "tight" housing market. If the market is "loose," the above factors may be more than offset by supply ease, and thereby slums may remain unexacerbated, or unslumming may actually take place. In the latter case a spatial spread of minority groups, for example, would not be equivalent to a spread of slums. Even so, the presence of the factors listed here makes for a greater quantity and intensity of slums than would otherwise be true for the same overall supply and demand conditions. There is some indication that the market was tight in the 1940's through the late 1950's, and that this, together with substantial emigration, favored slum creation. Since the late 1950's a loosening has been in evidence, either stabilizing or even diminishing the extent of slums.

Insofar as exploitation is absent, quality level and money price are substitute forms of higher real prices. We argue that the former tends to be favored by gratuitous forces where "natural" forces dictate the level of real prices. Even if we "accept" the desirability of the real price level as part of an optimal resource allocation, this acceptance does *not* lead to social indifference about the form it takes. That it takes the form of slums may well have great social significance, since the mere physical existence of slums and the living patterns thereby favored have been strongly asserted to entail heavy social costs through important externalities. Thus, slums are neither natural nor inevitable, and they may not be desirable.

The Social Costs of Slums. It was indicated above that the existence of slums and hence their eradication could well have far-reaching effects on living patterns in the city. For many years slums have been alleged to generate important social evils: physical, psychological, and health hazards to inhabitants and passers-by; heavy resource costs to inhabitants of the rest of the city. These social costs presumably arise out of important externalities and are therefore "inadvertent." The interdictions in much of this literature are something as follows:

1. Slum dwellings are likely to be fire traps, significantly increasing the probability of general conflagration.
2. Given overcrowding, filth, and inadequate sanitary facilities, slum areas are likely to be a health menace, increasing the frequency and severity of illness both to inhabitants and outsiders (through contagion).
3. Slums breed crime.
4. Slums create personality and social adjustment difficulties.

It is beyond the scope of this paper to expatiate on these contentions. But the allegations are clearly serious and deserve careful evaluation. Substantiation would furnish strong grounds for holding that slums per se represent suboptimal resource use. The net elimination of slums would then qualify as rendering social benefits, independent of any other function it performed.

Summary. Old, low-quality housing is not in itself undesirable, especially if poverty exists. Its elimination carries no *a priori* benefits. Slums are, however, distinguishable from an optimal natural market response of this sort. They represent especially—unnecessarily—low-quality clusterings (if only because of overcrowding), and are largely brought about by important externalities and the side-effects of alterable social policies. Their mere existence may result in social costs which stem from externalities in the functioning of slums. Thus, elimination of slums could rectify a suboptimal market response. Redevelopment is one method of elimination. Our analysis indicates, however, that it is not the only one, since it shows that the slum-enhancing factors are amenable to social control. Thus, policies alternative to redevelopment can be derived from the same analysis that establishes the potential desirability of redevelopment.

OTHER GOALS OF THE URBAN RENEWAL PROGRAM

The elimination of blight and slums concerns only what is to be removed or destroyed. The other goals of the urban renewal program concern largely what is to be substituted. Do these goals carry additional sources of net benefits? The limited scope of this paper precludes any detailed examination, but a few conclusions can be sketched out.

On the whole, slum removal differs appreciably from the other goals. It can in principle involve almost exclusively the real incomes of the present slum landlords and their tenants —for example, by policies directed toward internalizing the externalities in the housing market. This is true of both redevelopment *and* nonredevelopment approaches to slum removal. Whatever income transfers (as opposed to aggregate effects) are involved concern primarily slum landlord/slum tenant relationships. But these other goals involve income transfers far more intrinsically, and the transfers often extend considerably beyond the parties to slum transactions. In general, slum clearance aims to correct market distortions; the other goals aim to subsidize particular land and/or consumption uses of particular groups.

The distinction is not hard and fast, however. There is reason to believe that slum clearance sometimes involves large income redistribution effects relative to its aggregate effects. Moreover, subsidization can in a dynamic setting have aggregate effects, and these several goals differ in their ratio of aggregate to transfer effects. Finally, I am chary of laying too great a methodological distinction between the level of income and its distribution. In any case, the present form of benefit-cost analysis enables the distinction to be made without underscoring.

Mitigation of Poverty. Intrinsically, redevelopment is neutral toward the mitigation of poverty. In practice, many projects may indeed have exacerbated poverty, by eliminating numerous units at one end of the housing stock while adding a smaller number much nearer the other end. In any case, the impact of a project on poverty depends on the particular features of the project, not on the fact of redevelopment. Features designed specifically to mitigate poverty are likely to involve a separable marginal cost. Thus proper evaluation of the program from this point of view must ask whether comparable resources applied outside the redevelopment format could have as much impact on poverty.

Decent, Safe, and Sanitary Housing for All. The housing portion at least, of this goal, can be met if the level of new construction becomes and stays high enough to accelerate filtering and hasten retirements from the housing stock. Since incentives for overuse and over extended structure lifetimes exist, new construction must be great enough to cause a substantial "oversupply" of housing in order to meet the goal. This necessitates shifting large amounts of resources to housing that would otherwise remain elsewhere—i.e., it involves subsidizing a particular consumption area—presumably at the expense of other areas. Such subsidization may at special times seem to carry an aggregative weight—as during a period of drastic housing shortage (relative to the availability of other goods). Such a situation does not seem to apply today. This goal is therefore treated as generating predominantly transfer effects, and an additional benefit category is not introduced for it.

Revival of Downtown Areas of Central City. This represents an attempt to enhance the economic attractiveness of the central city's downtown area relative to suburban areas, the former having been substantially damaged attendant on the process of suburbanization. To a large extent this goal envisages simply a subsidized transfer effect. A kind of aggregative effect, however, may also result. A major city represents a scale of population concentration large enough to make possible forms of specialized services—opera companies, museums, zoos, specialty shops—which would not be viable with lesser concentration. To the extent that the decentralizing impact of suburbanization decreases group concentrations below the relevant critical masses, subsidized enhancement of downtown can help reattain these endangered scale economies.

It must be noted that implementation of this goal competes with that of mitigation of poverty, since it aims to displace low-income residential and commercial uses by much higher income uses. In general, the list of goals does not form a consistent set—the specific fashioning of a project to enhance one goal frequently results in meeting the others less well.

Attraction of Middle-Income Families from Suburbs Back to the Central City. Like the preceding goal, much of this one's effect is simply that of income transfer. But there is an aggregate effect here too. The goal is advanced as a way of rectifying a progressive narrowing (homogenizing) of the population base in the central city toward lower income and social minority groups. The achievement of a more balanced population distribution can improve commercial diversification, the use of public services, and cultural and political vigor. Again like the preceding goal, implementation of this is likely to come at the expense of mitigation of poverty.

Attraction of Additional "Clean" Industry into the City. Since we operate on the assumption of full employment (or, at any rate, if this be dropped, on the assumption that the urban renewal program is too clumsy to be used countercyclically), attraction of clean industry can be treated as a pure transfer activity, subsidizing one land use on a specific site at the expense of other uses and other sites.

Implementation of this goal typically comes at the expense of most of the others we have mentioned.

Enhancement of the Budget Balance of the Central City Government. There are two distinct perspectives within which changes in the fiscal balance of the planning government are interpreted as generating net benefits. The first postulates that any marginal budgetary surplus enhances the ability of the local government to carry out valuable social coordinating functions and therefore renders net social benefits to the community. The second asserts that the health and functioning of the local government are not at issue at all, but rather a marginal budgetary surplus indicates that the redevelopment program instituted by the government created more market value than it used up, and created therefore net benefits. The dif-

ference between the two interpretations is fundamental. The second measures the values already created, the first measures the ability to create new values in the future.

The first stems from a model of local government finance somewhat as follows. The expenditure and revenue systems of the local government are strongly constrained externally. There exist important public expenditure needs; the tax base available to the government to finance these needs is limited. Therefore, when events affect the public fisc adversely this hampers the ability of the government to do what the electorate wants it to do. One might call this a model of imperfect responsive government: it adverts a crucial imperfection in the governmental process.

The application of this model to the present case involves the same trend of population movement that we have noted above. The growth of slums and suburbanization have tended to erode the city's property tax base, to give a lower rate of growth of sales tax revenue, and to bring in a population disproportionately constituting the poor, who require a larger volume of public services (for example, welfare and health services) than the groups whom they replaced. In addition, the central city has continued to render important services to suburbanites who work and shop in the central city and are currently outside the reach of *quid pro quo* taxation. Indeed, traffic, road, and direct transportation (e.g., city-operated transit systems) services and facilities have increased substantially in the past decade. Thus, the expenditure needs of the central city have risen and its traditional revenue sources have lagged behind. In this context it is argued that governmental programs which produce a marginal budgetary surplus (raising tax yields more than they incur outlays) are producing net benefits for the community, because they make possible additional desired public actions which were otherwise rationed by financial stringency.

This argument must be rejected. To support it would imply that the government ought to undertake programs, or reformulate existing uses, for the purpose of making "profits." This would seriously distort the role of government, since in a representative democracy that role is to do things which are explicitly undesirable to leave to profit-seeking actions of the private market. The governmental role would be significantly abdicated.

Moreover, the supposed dilemma begs the question. If existing modes of taxation prove inadequate under changing trends, why is there not resort to other forms? If present expenditure programs are crushing, relative to the willingness to pay, cannot some of these programs be reconsidered? Admittedly, some of the problems stem from the complex interrelationships of a metropolitan area with important externalities, yet without metropolitan government. But these call for a solution within the political process itself—to make that process more responsive to the balance of wants and resources. To corrupt the process further by changing the criterion for public action would seem to be folly. Thus, while I recognize the present financial difficulties of some city governments, I shall not count the impact of redevelopment of the city's treasury as either net benefit or loss.

The case for the second perspective is quite different. In this, the production of a marginal budgetary surplus has nothing to do with benefits to the government. It concerns the size of the costs incurred by the redevelopment project —public outlays—on the one hand, and the size of the value created by the project, as allegedly exemplified by changes in assessed valuation and thence by public revenues, on the other. The value is enjoyed by redevelopers of the prepared site, but the government is assumed to exact a payment in the form of higher taxes equivalent to this created value. Thus, what is involved here is not a kind of benefit different from those which we have already discussed, but only a special way by which benefits of the sort already considered can be counted.

Summary of Other Goals. Of the six goals other than slum elimination, all have important elements of subsidy, involving real income redistribution; but only two—revival of downtown areas and attraction of middle-income families—were judged to be capable of generating general benefits. Mitigation of poverty is very important. Its achievement is by no means intrinsic with redevelopment; it requires additional separable subsidy components. The

general benefits which allegedly may stem from downtown revival and attraction of middle-income families are broad and amorphous, so that measurement will be extremely difficult, if not even impossible in principle.

In addition to these characteristics, analysis of the six goals suggests to us here, just as it did for slum elimination, the kinds of suboptimality which redevelopment can help solve. It therefore also suggests that alternatives to redevelopment can also solve some of these same problems. Under mitigation of poverty, for example, a simple alternative is to make general grants to the poor with funds equal to the amount of the subsidy for the poor involved in any particular redevelopment project. And regarding provision for adequate housing to all, an alternative approach is more rigidly to enforce health and building codes. This would lead to spot rehabilitation and selective rent increases in the slum area. It would also tend to displace some of the very poor, as under the typical redevelopment project, and would improve housing quality in the relevant areas. But since the quality improvement would be far less radical than under typical redevelopment, relative housing prices would not change so adversely in the low end of the housing stock, and no price declines would occur in the upper end. The resource cost of such a package would be considerably less than under redevelopment.

THE STRUCTURE OF BENEFIT-COST COMPARISONS

It has been argued above that the proper benefit-cost procedure is to compare three alternatives: redevelopment (R), the status-quo (S), and a particular package of policy measures (M) designed to perform many of the same kinds of functions as R. Only if R performs favorably with respect to *both* S and M is it a desirable policy. It was noted that M is not unique; there may be many possible substitute packages. I do not attempt the selection of an appropriate M here, but the previous analysis makes it possible now to give examples of elements that might appear in M.

To combat slum formation we may consider reform of property tax assessment procedures;

provision of mortgage credit for dwellings in blighted and nearly blighted areas; more rigid enforcement of health and building codes; spot rehabilitation or demolition of individual dwellings not brought up to code regulations. To combat poverty and internal familial problems we may consider general-purpose monetary grants; informational services; programs for special education (like recent dropout educational programs in the city of Chicago and elsewhere) ; additional social work services. Other inclusions might be more adequate garbage disposal services and police protection, and open-occupancy programs to combat the segregation pressure that adds to the profitability of slum creation.

In computing benefits among S, R, and M, we must specify differences, not simply in their immediate impact, but over their expected future course. This is of real importance. We have indicated that slum creation is closely associated with a normal adaptation of durable capital stock in the housing market—that there is a "life cycle" through which items in the housing stock pass. Housing on present slum sites will be gradually retired on private initiative, the rate of retirement and nature of the replacement depending upon supply and demand conditions in the market. Moreover, unslumming (significant uncrowding and structure rehabilitation) sometimes voluntarily occurs, and at least one observer alleges this to be more than a rarity.[8] Thus, the status quo policy with respect to a particular site does not imply a permanent commitment to slum use.

In the same vein, redevelopment does not imply a permanent commitment to nonslum use on the site in question. Indeed, there are reports that certain types of redevelopment— with or without public housing—may accelerate the process of slum formation, not only by pushing slums elsewhere in response to dislocatees' demand, but by decreasing the nonslum lifetime of new structures.[9] These types of redevelopment encourage high crime rates and behavior that aggravates depreciation of property in neighborhoods where property is still new. Thus, some of the behavioral phenomena associated with slums may occur in environments dissociated from old, obsolescent structures.

One of the dimensions in the evaluation of benefits and costs is, therefore, the forces determining the useful lifetime of items in the housing stock. Other things being equal, running down the useful lifetime is a cost, and elongating it is a benefit. The relevant variable is the rate of depreciation of the stock. This is not congruent with either obsolescence or the rate of filtering, both of which more likely represent enhanced usefulness in the stock.

THE MEASUREMENT OF BENEFITS

We classify the housing stock into H_1 (low-quality units) and H_2 (nonlow-quality units).[10] H_1 consists of standard (H_{12}) and substandard (H_{11}) units. All of H_2 is assumed standard. A redevelopment project destroys h_{11} units of H_{11} —the redevelopment site—and substitutes h_{12} units of H_{12} and/or h_2 units of H_2. Commercial and industrial units may be involved, in addition to residential units, in either the demolition or the replacement.

The Impact of Redevelopment

Three types of impact are postulated: [11]

1. Improved resource efficiency through internalizing market externalities.
2. Differential real-income effects according to location, income level, owner-tenant status, and functional classification of property, as a result of changes in numbers and location of housing units and commercial and industrial property.
3. Changes in slum-generated social costs due to destruction of slum property.

8 Jacobs, op. cit. (see footnote 7, above) , Chap. 15.
9 See Harrison Salisbury, "The Shook-Up Generation," series of articles (March 24-30, 1958) in the New York Times; and Jacobs, op. cit., throughout.
10 The official definition of "housing unit" is "accommodation designed for the residence of a single household." More than one family may thus inhabit a single unit; moreover, the size of the unit is not fixed. Thus, the "unit" is not really a standard quantity of housing.
11 I omit highly diffuse impacts, such as architectural aesthetics or population balance, as not subject to measurement. They should not be excluded from consideration, but should be brought to the attention of the electorate. It is for them to call out a valuation for these impacts.

The first and third impacts are aggregate income effects, the second is a distributional effect. The first arises from the existence of important neighborhood externalities. Land use under the market is suboptimal because, where many landowners are involved, a lack of coordination leads them to act singly in a way that results in an inferior overall situation. Coordination would correct this. But coordination is costly, since it involves production of informational and organizational services, and undependable, since it must cope with the individual profitability from cheating. This problem of enforcement under voluntary agreement is especially difficult. Common ownership is the only complete answer.

This conclusion holds even more strongly when we broaden the type of externality involved to include not only maintenance decisions but also the more fundamental decisions about what type of structures to erect. Such decisions require, not simply coordinated decisions, but a single, integrated decision. For example, the choice may be between many small structures on individual plots or a single high-rise structure for the entire site. Only common—i.e., single—ownership of the entire site makes it possible to act on such a choice.

Thus, land assembly is required. Land assembly is costly and time-consuming, all the more so the more individual parcels that must be purchased. It is beset by private obstructionism and lesser (but also costly) forms of bargaining pressures. These costs can easily be great enough to dissuade private entrepreneurs from undertaking projects designed to internalize externalities.

Government redevelopment substantially cuts the cost of assembly by invoking the right of eminent domain. This bypasses the obstacle course of bargaining sequentially with individual parcel owners. Eminent domain enables land to be inexpensively assembled and employed in units large enough to internalize important neighborhood externalities. Thus, government site preparation—assembly, demolition, clearance—is in effect the creation of a new type of land input: land in neighborhood-sized lumps. It is as if a technical innovation were made, transforming the units of a certain input to new units with higher productivity. This transformation is the source of the external benefits. It represents net social gain.

Where externalities impose poor land use, redevelopment should increase the productivity of land in the redevelopment site, and therefore its value. But redevelopment also involves a replacement of h_{12} and/or h_2 for the loss of h_{11}. How does this affect the enhanced value in the site? Analysis of this takes us through the second, or redistributional impact, of redevelopment.

I argue, first, that as a good first approximation redevelopment does not affect either the total low-quality or total nonlow-quality demand for housing in the metropolitan area, since I assume that aggregate money income for each group of consumers is essentially unaffected, and that the only significant income redistribution occurs through income effects, which are fully reflected in a given demand function.

In the typical redevelopment project, most demolition occurs in H_{11}, a small amount of replacement occurs in H_{12}, and most replacement occurs in H_2, at a considerably higher quality level. The total number of all types of units constructed is less than the number destroyed.[12] Thus, typically, the supply falls in H_1 and rises in H_2, again with no change in demands. Both supply functions have an elasticity greater than zero because a high price encourages either new construction or conversion of existing units, the first being more important for H_2 housing, the second more important for H_1 housing. Under H_1, much of the downward conversion is not from H_2 to H_1, but within H_1 toward slum use. The elasticity is not infinitely great for H_2 because of

12 The Urban Renewal Administration (Housing and Home Finance) places the figures (as of 1964) at 0.8 unit of planned replacement (mostly in H_2) for every 1.0 unit demolished (mostly in H_1). More lopsided figures of .25 to 1.0 given in Martin Anderson, *The Federal Bulldozer* (MIT Press, 1964), reflect only actual replacement as of the date tabulated, and fail to allow for the substantial lag between demolition and final replacement. Actually, the long period of gestation means that both short-run and long-run analyses of redistribution impacts should be undertaken. The two would show quite different results. Planned public housing (h_{12}) is approximately 8 percent of planned replacements. In our simplified model we pretend that all demolitions occur in H_{11}. Actually, some occur in H_{12} as well—redevelopment tracts can have less than 100 percent blight.

the usual reasons, or for H_1 because of imperfect substitutability among different units and the costs of conversion. Under these assumptions, H_2 prices decline and H_1 prices rise. This induces some conversion, both from H_2 into H_1 and within H_1 itself, down toward slum use (through increased crowding). But no change in the demand for land should occur, since the conversion is accomplished by filtering of existing units. Thus, the change in relative unit prices should leave land prices unchanged.[13]

One type of effect on land prices is possible. If the above shifts affect the location of significant commercial, industrial, and public service properties in broad sections of the metropolitan area, they can affect the relative locational advantages of different areas, and thereby cause relative shifts in land prices. For simplicity, it is assumed that the sum of any such price changes over the whole area is zero.

Thus redevelopment increases the productivity of land in the redevelopment site (an aggregate effect); it differentially affects the size of, and therefore the price of, different portions of the housing stock (a redistribution effect), but without necessarily affecting land prices; and it may, where significant commercial and public service facilities are moved, affect relative locational advantages (a redistribution effect), thereby affecting land prices between the redevelopment site and elsewhere. Our purpose is to measure the first effect. But land values in the redevelopment site may show the effect on locational advantages as well. To isolate the first, we make use of our assumption that the sum of locational effects is zero, and that these effects are the only source of land price changes elsewhere. Then:

$$(1) \quad \Delta P_c^l = \Delta P_{sE}^l + \Delta P_{sL}^l ;[14]$$
$$(2) \quad \Delta P_{sL}^l + \Delta P_{\bar{s}L}^l = 0 ;$$
$$(3) \quad \Delta P_{\bar{s}}^l = \Delta P_{\bar{s}L}^l ; \text{ so}$$
$$(4) \quad \Delta P_s^l = \Delta P_{sE}^l - \Delta P_{\bar{s}}^l ; \text{ or}$$
$$(5) \quad \Delta P_{sE}^l = \Delta P_s^l + \Delta P_{\bar{s}}^l ;$$

where $\Delta P_s^l \equiv$ land price changes in the redevelopment site; $\Delta P_{sE}^l \equiv$ land price changes in the redevelopment site due to internalization of externalities; $\Delta P_{sL}^l \equiv$ land price changes in

the redevelopment site due to changes in locational advantages; $\Delta P_{\bar{s}}^l \equiv$ land price changes elsewhere than in redevelopment site (but within metropolitan area); $\Delta P_{\bar{s}L}^l \equiv$ land price changes elsewhere than the redevelopment site (but within the metropolitan area) due to changes in locational advantages. ΔP_s^l and $\Delta P_{\bar{s}}^l$ are observables, but ΔP_{sE}^l, ΔP_{sL}^l, and $\Delta P_{\bar{s}L}^l$ are not. Equation (5) derives the desired nonobservable as a function of observables only.

The third type of impact, relating to social costs of slums, depends on what happens to slums. From our analysis, there are three influences. First, slum property is physically eliminated. Second, some households dislocated from these destroyed units move into other already overcrowded slum units, increasing the degree of overcrowding (the rise in housing prices leads to their purchase of less housing than before). Third, there is conversion of property down to slum level for the first time. Thus, the net effect depends on the relative magnitudes of elimination, worsening, and spread of slums. On balance, a smaller physical area, and fewer total units, are likely to be at slum level. This effect will be smaller than the area and number of units demolished by redevelopment, and some exacerbation will have occurred in existing slums.

The influence of this on slum-generated costs depends on the particular composite of effects. Fire hazards depend on geographic extent and degree of overcrowding; health hazards depend more on overcrowding than on geographic area; personality problems depend more on the size of the real income effect and on household turnover. Thus, the overall impact depends on specifics. One complex that has general relevance, however, is neighborhood stability and diversity of opportunity. It has been argued that social rootlessness is more to blame for slum-generated behavior than is physical

13 An aggregate effect on land prices is conceivable, but likely to be unimportant. As a result of the net decrease in housing units, a substitute for filtering is new construction on low density land, especially in suburbs. This might raise land prices very slightly. I shall neglect this possibility in what follows.
14 Assuming no property taxes. These taxes will be treated later.

dilapidation or overcrowding.[15] Some types of redevelopment, by moving many people en masse, badly disrupt supportive social relationships. In addition, where projects emphasize extreme homogeneity they lay the groundwork for future destabilizing migration waves. Such redevelopment emphases can accelerate depreciation of property. They entail social costs.

Thus, the third type of benefit (and cost) from redevelopment is highly complicated. Some benefits are likely to be produced; but there are possibilities for substituting one kind of social disutility for another. The fact that one or both kinds may prove difficult to measure does not excuse planners and outside observers from giving them attention. We shall return to consider them more fully below.

Internalization of Externalities

Under this heading we seek to measure the increased productivity of land in the redevelopment site. A first approximation involves observing the difference between the highest price for which the local public authority (LPA) can sell the prepared site at competitive bidding and the price it paid for it, and then making the adjustment in equation (5) to remove any effect of locational advantage. Now, we must adjust for property taxation as well. The market price will reflect the diminution in value resulting from capitalized property tax. Since increased productivity will be reflected in higher taxes, the capitalization factor in the LPA's sale will exceed that factor in its purchase. To measure the full productivity change we must add back a tax adjustment factor to the price change. The following equations, all referring to land in the redevelopment site,[16] make this explicit:

Let V_E be the productivity value of site land attributed to nonlocational factors (factors which are subject to the externalities which the LPA project internalizes); and let P_E be the market value corresponding to these factors. Then P_E will be less than V_E by the capitalized value of anticipated taxes on this property (associated with nonlocational factors) : [17]

(6) $$P_E = V_E - t(P_E),$$

where $t(P_E)$, is the capitalized value of anticipated taxes, assuming that these taxes depend chiefly on market value.

Writing the change between before-and-after redevelopment values as ΔP_E, ΔV_E, we have:

(7) $$\Delta V_E = \Delta P_E + t(\Delta P_E).$$

Substituting equation (5) in equation (7) gives:

(8) $$\Delta V_E = (\Delta P_s + \Delta P_{\bar{s}}) + t(\Delta P_s + \Delta P_{\bar{s}}),$$

where

$$\Delta P_s \equiv \Delta P_s^l$$

and

$$\Delta P_{\bar{s}} \equiv \Delta P_{\bar{s}}^l.$$

Thus, to calculate the relevant change in value we must know the change in land prices for the site and for the rest of the metropolitan area, and the change in capitalized value of taxes for both. This is subject to a number of pitfalls. The price at which the LPA sells the prepared site may diverge substantially from the competitive market price. Absence of competitive bidding, disposition by convention to a single redeveloper, and specification of necessary redevelopment characteristics enormously complicate the problem of discovering the true market value of the site.

We implicitly assume that when the LPA buys property under eminent domain it shifts the same capitalized tax liability backward to the seller that a private purchaser would—thus, in equation (8) $V_{E0} = P_{E0} + t(P_{E0})$ and $V_{E1} = P_{E1} + t(P_{E1})$. The rationale is that the LPA expects to lose through backward shifting

15 For example, see Jacobs, *op. cit.,* Part I and Chap. 15.
16 Therefore, for simplicity we temporarily suppress superscript referring to "land" and subscript referring to site.
17 This is derived from the algebraic partitioning of total productivity and market values of land into a locational and nonlocational component. Thus, where

$$P = P_E + P_L \text{ and } V = V_E + V_L,$$
(6a) $$P = V - t(P), \text{ and hence}$$
(6b) $$P_E + P_L = [V_E - t(P_E)] + [V_L - t(P_L)].$$

when *it* disposes of the land: the expected value of the land is less by the capitalized value of newly expected tax. But actual practice may diverge from this.

It will be noted that our measure of increased value in the redevelopment site refers only to the value of land, not to the value of improvements on the land. This diverges from other treatments.[18] One main rationale for exclusion of changes in structure values is that we assume full employment: that is, that any investment in improvements on the site displaces other useful employment for the resources so used. Thus, we reject the explicit use of redevelopment as a countercyclical instrument of fiscal policy; it is too clumsy for that.

The full-employment assumption alone does not suffice to determine the benefits from site investment. Resources might be used here more advantageously than elsewhere, especially where lumpy ventures are involved. However, we largely eschew such differences, assuming competitive capital and construction markets —effectively treating site investment as representing only a marginal resource shift. Its productivity is thus assumed equal to that in other uses. This assumption, whenever incorrect, biases measured redevelopment benefits downward.

While changes in the value of site structures are excluded by our treatment, there are changes in the value of some structures that are not excluded. Redevelopment improves the neighborhood. Hence it improves the real value of housing services furnished by given bundles of land and improvements near enough to the redevelopment site to be affected. The value of the land sites and their structures thereby becomes enhanced. This is a real externality, not a pecuniary one, and should be counted as a benefit.

Unfortunately, actual measurement of this enhancement in value is enormously complicated, because the relative price repercussion resulting from redevelopment (due to dislocation and relative stock changes) and the relative location effects—both of which are distributional effects—are likely to impinge especially on just the units most affected by this externality; and the effects are likely to enhance the value of the land and structures as

well. Thus, the observed increased value of adjacent land and structures will be a composite of three forces, only one of which is an aggregate productivity effect. In principle, one can disentangle the separate influences by specifying the characteristics of redevelopment projects which differentially influence the strength of relative stock and dislocation, location, and neighborhood externality, forces. But in practice such specification will exceed the subtlety of available data.

A simple procedure that might be used is to determine whether the project is locationally neutral, or small enough to have only trivial relocation and relative housing stock effects. If *both* conditions are met, then the entire change in adjoining structure value can be treated as the result of externality enhancement. Otherwise, the value changes can be treated as entirely redistributional. *Erroneous* choice of the first option overstates benefits; *any* choice of the second understates benefits, mostly when it represents the worse side of the dichotomy.

Even so simple a procedure is faced with a serious problem—that of determining the boundary of significant neighborhood effect. If one decided in a specific case to include neighborhood enhancement, which structures should be included? Since many factors in addition to redevelopment are constantly at work changing relative prices of land sites and housing stock, the setting of boundaries by observing which prices rise is dangerous. Yet no simple but dependable method for setting boundaries suggests itself. Perhaps one would have to adopt the conservative procedure of including only a few blocks in each direction of the projects, and even here excluding directions in which structural or functional barriers to interplay with the project area exist.

In sum, we measure productivity changes by measuring changes in the redevelopment site land, adjusting for locational advantage changes and for tax capitalization. Changes in the value of improvements on the site are excluded, largely through the assumption of full employment, but spillover changes in the value of neighborhood land and structures are in-

18 See, for example, Davis and Whinston, *op. cit.* (see footnote 5, above) .

cluded to the extent that they represent externality enhancement.

A final point should be noted. We have discussed only the effects of redevelopment, not of the composite alternative to redevelopment and the status quo (policy M). Clearly, before redevelopment is practically decided on, some such concrete composite should be formulated and its consequences evaluated as with redevelopment.

Relative Changes in Housing Stock

Under our model of redevelopment, the replacement structures are basically different from those they supersede. One population moves out, essentially another moves in. The relative changes in the housing stock (subtractions from H_1, smaller additions to H_2) create the following groups of affected individuals:

1. Individuals with specific types of assets or goods and services previously being consumed but now removed as objects of choice.
2. Individuals with the same range of commodities open to choice but facing increased prices for some of them.
3. Individuals with specific types of assets or goods and services, hitherto not available, but now made available, and chosen.
4. Individuals with the same range of commodities open to choice, but facing lowered prices for some of them.

Group 1 applies largely to residential, commercial, and industrial inhabitants of property which is to be demolished as part of the project. Group 2 applies largely to inhabitants of structures which are close substitutes for those which are to be demolished. Group 3 applies to individuals who are potential customers for the new residential dwellings or commercial or public-service facilities produced as part of the project. Group 4 is similar to Group 3, except that its members need not actually move to the project site to be affected and, where they do make such a move, it is to structures and services which are similar to those already available—only the total *quantity* of such structures is affected by the project. Group 3,

on the other hand, is involved only where the project has made available novel types of residential, commercial, or public-service facilities and contains as members only individuals who have actually moved into them. Since location is sometimes an important aspect of such facilities, a combination of a type of such facilities already available elsewhere but in a distinctively different location might qualify as a novel facility.

An important asymmetry must be noted among the groups. Whereas in Groups 2, 3, and 4 any change in behavior is a voluntary response to changes in market signals—lower or higher prices for goods hitherto available, or availability of new goods—in Group 1 the change is coerced. Inhabitants of demolished structures are forced to move out. They alone are *precluded* from unchanged consumption in housing; others are simply induced to change by the desire to make a better adjustment, but need not if they do not wish it.

The welfare impact on these groups is as follows. If we assume first that all individuals had been in equilibrium with full information about alternatives prior to the project, then Groups 1 and 2 suffer welfare losses and Groups 3 and 4 experience welfare gains.

Group 1 suffers three types of loss:

1. Elimination of the chosen alternatives and others in the same neighborhood from the opportunity set of residential inhabitants—the necessity to choose less preferred alternatives.
2. Loss of accumulated capital in specific neighborhood adjustment by both residents and commercial enterprises.
3. Rise in the absolute price of the type of housing typically purchased by these inhabitants.

The size of the first factor depends on the heterogeneity of the housing stock. We must allow that differences believed by residents to be important do exist even in small sectors of the housing market. Thus significant discrepancies may be involved between first and lower choices.

The second factor concerns the adjustment of each household's whole pattern of nonhousing consumption and social interaction (for example, the making of friendships) to the opportunities presented by residing in a specific housing unit in a specific neighborhood. These investments in knowledge and decision-making are largely lost when a family moves out of a neighborhood. Not all such loss represents a welfare loss. Some such changes are voluntarily sought to obtain novelty or a widening of experience. But the involuntary mass eviction attendant on redevelopment is likely to represent an unwanted change for most dislocatees. An implication of this factor is that a family's preference for its chosen—and lived-in—housing over its previous second choice is greater after the family has dwelt there some time than at the time of its choice.

The first and second factors together constitute "moving costs" over and above the physical cost of transporting property and person, but are independent of one another. The first is a flow cost, the second a stock or capital cost. The first can be *directly* offset by the attractiveness of the new destination, the second much less so. We assume that physical moving costs are reimbursed as an integral part of redevelopment. This is a fair approximation to actual practice.[19] "Psychological" moving costs are not reimbursed.

Group 1 includes business establishments which are forced to terminate or relocate. Assuming that physical moving expenses are reimbursed, components of good will not bound up with specific location are transferable; locational advantages of the original site are, however, lost. For enterprises which terminate, the whole of good will is lost. These are of course distributional, not aggregate, effects.

The last factor, price rises, has a conventional effect. Those affected suffer a welfare loss measurable in terms of consumer surplus. One of the components of this effect, however, relates to the first factor. Families dislocated from their first choices in the precluded site do not in fact select what their second choices might have been if no price rises had occurred. Instead, higher housing costs induce them to choose less housing than previously—or less probably, lower-quality housing.[20]

The above consequences assume that the members of Group 1 were in full equilibrium before dislocation occurred. But there are real reasons, associated with significant lack of information on their part, for believing that their prior situation may have substantially diverged from equilibrium. If so, this will make a difference in the size of the first factor, but not of the other two. Eviction now need not necessarily lead to an inferior choice by each family. The explicit search, perhaps aided or entirely assumed by relocation authorities, could frequently turn up improvements over the original unit, in which case some families may actually benefit (perhaps some of those admitted to public housing). But the larger the number of families who are simultaneously dislocated and the tighter the housing market, the larger will be the proportion of dislocated who must settle for inferior choices. Moreover, the displaced will still lose accumulated neighborhood adjustment capital, and will still be faced with generally higher housing prices.

Measurement of these losses is difficult. The third factor could be measured by the conventional method of estimating consumer surplus via the demand function for housing, if the first factor were not important. If it *were* important, this would complicate the interpretation of movements along such a demand function. In view of our discussion about prior disequilibrium of residents, we may simplify without too much error by assuming that the first factor is negligible. Thus we treat housing transfers within a broad quality level as taking place between essentially homogeneous units. This assumption can be tested by sampling actual dislocatee experience.

Estimates of social capital adjustment costs will be of the money value of the minimum housing package improvement necessary to induce families to move from one neighborhood to another. The sample used should exclude families that like novelty.

Group 2 suffers only a price-rise effect. We measure this by the same means employed for Group 1. Any moves made by these families are voluntary—so no coerced adjustment cost is involved.

Group 3 experiences a quality-change effect

19 Martin Millspaugh, "Problems and Opportunities of Relocation," *Law and Contemporary Problems*, Vol. 26 (Winter 1961), pp. 8–11.
20 Less probably, because of the emphasis on higher quality in the relocation function of redevelopment projects.

(i.e., new housing opportunities), a price effect, and an adjustment effect. Since members of this group move voluntarily, they gain by the new first choice/second choice discontinuity. Since they are subject to neighborhood adjustment costs, the net gain is less by this amount, but the gain must exceed the cost. This is a weak constraint, since those who become members of Group 3 may do so because they like novelty. For them adjustment costs will be negligible or even negative. We shall treat such costs for Group 3 as a whole as zero. This suggests that we may measure the first gain by assuming that the differential price of the new housing is just high enough to equal the marginal purchasers' evaluation of the quality appreciation. Actual computation of consumer surpluses is of course very complicated and requires drastic simplifications.

Group 3 is subject to the effect of price declines—a gain for them—even though they do not remain in dwellings whose prices have fallen. Since they could have remained, their move indicates that the quality-price package represented by the new housing is preferred to the old housing at lower prices. Thus, the measure of "quality appreciation" should include this price effect, and will be in effect a composite measure of quality *and* price change.

Group 4 is nearly symmetrical with Group 2, Group 4 being gainers while Group 2 are losers. For this group quality differences resulting from redevelopment are not important; we can deal largely in price and quantity changes. The biggest effect here, then, is the increase in supply (H_2) with its resulting decrease in prices; members of this group benefit whether or not they move into the redevelopment site. Any adjustment costs resulting from moving are likely to be trivial, as with Group 3—since members will voluntarily move within the same neighborhood or to a "better one." The price effect can be measured by the method used for Group 2.

We have largely discussed effects on residents. Effects on businesses are much the same, requiring translation of effects into profits. If we include property owners in this class, we can classify them as follows: owners of property on the site; owners of improvement properties patronized by Groups 1 and 2; and owners of nonsite improvement property patronized by

Group 4. The first class of owners gains a producer's surplus in anything but a perfectly discriminating arrangement with the LPA. The second gains a quasi-rent as a result of increased demand; the third loses symmetrically as a result of decreased demand.[21] Methods of calculation are essentially the same as for consumers.

The discussion of Groups 2, 3, and 4 has assumed prior optimal adjustment. Unlike the treatment of Group 1, dropping this assumption here makes no difference. Since all moves by these groups are voluntary, they represent anticipated improvements. It makes no difference that the groups could have been better off than they were before the project. Insofar as their subsequent move is induced by the project, it is *this* improvement only that we seek to measure.

Effects on Social Costs of Slum Living

This is an extremely difficult area for appropriate measurement—in fact, pessimism has often gone so far as to suggest that measurement attempts be abandoned. But something can be known, and important distinctions about order of magnitude can be made.

The problem of measurement here is, briefly, that the causal process between slum living and these dimensions of social cost is complicated and interrelated with other causal factors; it has only a probabilistic influence; outcomes are difficult to read; changes in the arguments of the functional relationship typically have only minor short-run effects, the important ones being long-run; lastly, even where proper effects are isolable, they are likely to be observable only qualitatively. Exhaustive relevant dollar measurement is far from obviously feasible.

Our four categories of social cost are (1) fire hazards, (2) health menace, (3) crime, (4) personality and social adjustment difficulties. For each of these, our task is to measure, not the total costs generated by slums, but the

21 Owner-occupiers are composites of property owners and consumers. Their gains as the one are offset by their losses as the other. On balance, their owner role predominates since their opportunities are capitalized (frozen) there but not for their consumer role.

change in these total costs, throughout the metropolitan area, brought about by the redevelopment complex of demolition, dislocation, and replacement. The analytic building block of such measurement is to find, where possible, the money value of resources which the affected individuals would be willing to incur to avoid the costs imposed on them. Where this is not possible, we attempt to find the magnitude of the cost consequences in terms of the original dimensions—such as number of serious illness days, or of deaths.

Fire Hazards. Costs here involve two elements: the slum-connected differential loss and damage to property and human life; the differential fire-protection costs to prevent life and property losses from being greater. For property loss, fire insurance records are appropriate. Measurement of the value of human life is a highly controversial question, but a number of relevant procedures can be suggested. (This particular measurement problem is common to most areas in the public sector, and extended discussion is beyond our present scope.) Human disability is not well measured by medical expenses alone since, like fire-protection services, these limit rather than prevent damages. A component that would measure lost productivity and the personal valuation of suffering should be added.

Differential fire-protection costs can be approximated roughly by actual fire department expenditures, although this may entail a bias. It is claimed that actual service levels are inadequate in slums, relative to nonslum areas.[22] If we measured the change in fire-protection needs due to redevelopment by a before-after service comparison we would understate the difference, since the "before" (and presumably higher) figure would have been below actual needs. But this bias is offset to some extent by the fact that inadequate protection leads to higher damages. One might even crassly argue that the political determination of service levels marginally equates the extra cost of service with the "social value" of additional expected fire damage—so that the bias is exactly offset. Less crassly, the absence of the necessary data makes the assumption attractive for purposes of simplification.

A basic complication of our procedure is that we must separate out the fire hazard effect of the slum itself from that of its special population. Redevelopment demolishes structures, but redistributes the population elsewhere. Insofar as kind of use influences fire hazard and is influenced by type of population, a gross association between fire and slum will overstate the net relationship. Isolating the effect of slums proper should be amenable to multiple regression, in which fire hazard per $1,000 assessed valuation is made a function of family income level, population density, and percentage of substandard dwellings, the last reflecting slums.

Health Hazards. As noted above, medical services do not prevent illnesses perfectly, or even cure them perfectly, but they limit the ravages more or less. Thus, as with fire hazards, our measure contains two components: differential protective, therapeutic services; and differential morbidity and fatality.

Measuring these components is considerably more difficult than the corresponding ones for fire. The first should be measured by the value of medical services, but this value is not easy to obtain for the specific geographic population. Moreover, sliding scales of compensation for such services, extending down to free care, complicate valuation. On the other hand, it is not easy to point out a bias in differential adequacy of *public* health and medical services; if anything, a disproportionate amount of these goes to slum inhabitants.

Morbidity and fatality figures are even more difficult to obtain for the slum population, since such households are likely to seek medical care in a smaller percentage of illnesses than nonslum households do. Specific sampling studies might be required. The problem of evaluating the social cost of human illness and death is the same as with fire.

Also as with fire, we must isolate the effect of slums proper from that of the selective characteristics of the slum population, since the latter effect remains after redevelopment. The population influence is especially important here, and especially difficult to separate out. As with fire, multiple regression should be used,

22 For example, see Max R. Bloom, "Fiscal Productivity and the Pure Theory of Urban Renewal," *Land Economics*, Vol. 38 (May 1962), p. 140.

but observations would be expressed in per capita terms rather than, as with fire, in assessed valuation terms.

Crime. Public protective services here (unlike the preceding categories) do have substantial deterrent effect. The level of police protection authorized by the political process does bear a closer relation to the amount the public is willing to pay to *avoid* losses due to crime than do services under the preceding categories. The relation is far from perfect, since it is probably criminal apprehension as much as deterrence that is increased by enlarging the level of police services, and not even apprehension is dependably related to budget size. But if we posit that the police budget, say, is a fair first-approximation measure, then we are able to bypass some very difficult problems concerning the human cost of crime—assault, robbery, rape, murder, etc.—where such cost probably far exceeds the value of the property involved.

Our method here, with a very healthy dose of error (especially because of population selectivity), compares slum with nonslum per capita costs. The measuring procedure is much like that for our earlier categories, with per capita units preferable to area or value of property units.

Personality and Social Adjustment Difficulties. For this category we possess especially poor measures. The more personal, psychiatric types of difficulties are rarely deterred and—for this socioeconomic level of the population—rarely treated or cured. Only when they reach the level of severe psychosis is even a third level of action resorted to: custodial or mildly adjustive care. For what may well be a wide ocean of unhappiness, despair, misery, frustration, anger, and fright, we have no operational measuring rods. Broad qualitative judgments about both psychic states and the processes which might bring them into being are all that we possess. We cannot either stringently establish the truth of slum-generated costs here or measure them. Since I personally believe the qualitative argument that slums do generate costs in this category, I am prepared to suggest that our exclusion of any measure here imparts a downward bias—possibly an important one—to our specified total of external social costs due to slums.

But we are unable to specify the direction of the bias in estimating how these costs are affected by the redevelopment project as a whole, when account is taken of the pattern of relocation.

For the more obviously family and neighborhood group types of difficulty the problem is somewhat easier. These are difficulties which *are* attacked by explicit actions—in this case, family social work, settlement house activities, neighborhood clubhouse activities, and so on. Some deterrence is present and some amelioration. On the basis of slight information, one is inclined to believe that the combined deterrent-ameliorative efficacy of these services—even in prospect—is less than for the other categories. Moreover, these services are the only ones which seem to give us an operational entree to measurement in this overall category. If we use total social work budgets as we have other protective services, we shall avowedly be omitting the submerged portion of the iceberg.

To summarize the discussion of changes in slum-connected social costs, I believe these alleged costs probably exist, but even a rough measurement is extremely difficult. It may be even more difficult to find out how they are affected by redevelopment, when relocation is taken into account. Some components are easier to measure than others, but all results should be taken with real reservation.

Reservation about even the direction of change stems from the possibility that the effects of massive relocation in spreading slums could significantly offset the effects of redevelopment in eliminating them. If in particular projects, or even in general, findings should indicate that the former effect is slight, our procedures become more useful—since most remaining biases then run in the same direction of understanding benefits from redevelopment.

A final point should be made. Some observers (probably including myself) believe that this social cost category is the most important of all: urban renewal programs will stand or fall ultimately on how significant are these benefits. Yet we have been deeply pessimistic about being able to obtain relevant dollar figures to use as offsets to project costs. To base important policy decisions on only the dollar amounts that *can* be computed, just because these *are* the only dollar amounts, would be most dangerous; the underestimation of the most truly distinctive benefits of the program might be crucial. Wherever possible, therefore, money magnitudes should be supplemented by the vector of nonmonetary consequences, e.g., serious illness days, murders, incidence of psychosis. While the investigator may not be able to discover unique consensual tradeoffs in the community among these different kinds of consequences, society has the option of discovering them by a form of simulation—the governmental decision-making process.

AN ILLUSTRATIVE NUMERICAL EXAMPLE [23]

The numerical illustration briefly presented in conclusion is intended, not as a serious empirical application, but only as an exercise designed to highlight some of the statistical problems that may be encountered. The scope of this study was too small to enable us to collect important bodies of data; in what follows below, therefore, we indicate some of the places where a larger study could reasonably hope to improve data quality and quantity appreciably.

The example relates to the three projects in Chicago which had been terminated early enough to make data available: Michael Reese, Hyde Park "B," and Blue Island. Of the three, only Michael Reese is a large project; Hyde Park "B" is a small strip in the much larger overall Hyde Park–Kenwood Project. The first two began in 1956, the third in 1959; they all terminated in 1961 or 1962. For each project we measure all three types of consequence, but to facilitate estimation we omit from internalization benefits the spillover effects on the value of neighborhood land and structures (these are extremely difficult to obtain within the limited scope of our empirical study).

Internalization Benefits

For simplicity, we use the simple model of equation (5) above [24] (omitting superscripts):

(5) $$\Delta P_{sE} = \Delta P_s + \Delta P_{\bar{s}}$$

where ΔP_s is the land price change in the redevelopment site; ΔP_{sE} is the land price change

in the redevelopment site due to internalization; $\Delta P_{\bar{s}}$ is the land price change elsewhere in the metropolitan area (location advantage adjustment). Further, only Michael Reese is large enough and strategically enough located to warrant any consideration of a locational advantage shift. This is not likely to be important enough to be picked up by our statistical technique.[25] But the present scope precludes any attempt at calculating the correction. A larger empirical study should invest resources here to attempt the correction, since this is a marginal case. Our present procedure, then, will simply assume that $\Delta P_{\bar{s}} = 0$.

Our purpose is to calculate site land-value changes due to internalization, measured as the difference between 1955 and 1962 (Michael Reese and Hyde Park "B") , or between 1958 and 1962 (Blue Island) . These periods are long enough, however, so that general forces affecting land values in the city as a whole could have had noticeable effect. We must adjust site-value changes for these general influences, to isolate the effects of redevelopment. Our method is to "explain" part of land value movements in terms of per capita income and population, and to subtract this explained portion of site-value changes from the gross change in order to obtain the site-value change due to redevelopment. Thus, the explained portion

(9) $$_{Y,N}P = a + b_1 Y + b_2 N,$$

where $_{Y,N}P$ is "Y-N explained" land prices, Y is per capita income, and N is population.[26]

Direct estimation of equation (9) requires data on site values, population, and income which are not available. A major empirical study could construct series for site population and land prices, since elaborate and laborious operations are involved. But this is certainly beyond the scope of even moderate applications. We therefore substitute indirect estima-

[23] Data accumulation and calculations were performed by Robert Puth.
[24] Thereby omitting the tax capitalization adjustment of equation (8) above. This imparts a downward bias to our estimates. It can be rectified by estimating a tax capitalization factor.
[25] The method suggested in my "Economic Evaluation of Urban Renewal."
[26] Our estimation actually used Y as aggregate income, because of data problems.

tion, depending heavily on interpolation from Cook County data. Our model is:

$$(10) \qquad _R\Delta P_s = \Delta P_s - _{Y,N}\Delta P_s,$$

where $_R\Delta P$ is redevelopment induced land changes; and postsubscript s refers to the redevelopment site.

Our indirect estimation from Cook County data is obtained from the assumption that:

$$(11) \qquad \frac{_{Y,N}\Delta P_s}{_{Y,N}\Delta P_c} = \frac{\text{mean}(P_s)_{0,1}}{\text{mean}(P_c)_{0,1}},$$

where postsubscript c refers to Cook County data and subscripts 0,1 refer to preproject and postproject dates. We estimate (9) for Cook County and then calculate $_{Y,N}\Delta P_c$. We can obtain mean $(P_c)_{0,1}$. The one type of data we possess about the site is $\Delta P_s/\text{mean} (P_s)_{0,1}$. Algebraic manipulation of (10) and (11) shows that from these we can determine $_R\Delta P_s$.

Our data to estimate the coefficients in (9) are for 1947–1961: income and population figures from *Sales Management,* land values from the Cook County Tax Assessor's Office. The latter are assessed valuations inflated to a market value basis. Following official assessment prac-

tice, we assume assessments are 40 percent of true market values. Our land value series is clearly inadequate. Somewhat better results can be obtained from direct approximations to market valuations in *Olcott's Land Values Blue Book of Chicago,* but these are available only on a lot-by-lot basis, and aggregation is terribly cumbersome. A larger study than the present one should certainly attempt to get better land figures. The data appear in Table 1.

Equation (9) was estimated as:

$$(12) \quad _{Y,N}P_c = - \; 10{,}857{,}084 + 1.79Y_c$$
$$+ \; 3554.76N_c.$$

Our direct estimation of gross site-value changes is shown in Table 2, and is based on market values for a standard lot (100 by 125 feet). Given these, we compute land value changes attributable to redevelopment in Table 3.

Redistribution Effects

We deal here with real income redistribution through the (largely) price effects of relative changes in the housing stock. We have suggested that dislocatees lose most, and those re-

Table 1 Land Prices, Aggregate Income, and Population, Cook County, 1947–1961

Years	Land Prices (P_c)	Aggregate Income (Y_c)	Population (N_c)
1947	$18,399,558	$ 7,416,982	4,225.7
1948	19,666,323	8,176,791	4,305.8
1949	19,574,018	8,425,620	4,522.7
1950	19,984,798	8,137,803	4,490.7
1951	22,045,478	8,967,124	4,548.8
1952	22,052,150	9,173,481	4,601.8
1953	22,448,690	9,583,494 [a]	4,607.1
1954	22,839,805	9,993,506	4,667.5 [a]
1955	22,947,800	10,769,380	4,727.9
1956	25,716,518	11,476,197	4,866.1
1957	27,345,985	11,684,475	4,881.8
1958	28,316,530	11,757,304	4,944.8
1959	31,196,125	12,814,366	5,049.1
1960	31,543,940	13,428,844	5,119.8
1961	32,199,125	13,352,979	5,165.7

Source: Column 1 from Cook County Tax Assessor's Office; columns 2 and 3 from *Sales Management.*
[a] Value interpolated.

Table 2 Changes in Standard-Lot Land Values During Redevelopment Project, 1955, 1958, 1962 (land values per standard lot) [a]

Changes	Hyde Park "B"	Michael Reese	Blue Island
Preproject Land Value [b]	$12,500	$ 5,750	$5,000
Postproject Land Value [c]	20,000	10,500	7,250
Change, Absolute	7,500	4,750	2,250
Percent Change (mean land value as base)	46%	58%	37%

Source: Olcott's Land Values Blue Book of Chicago, volumes for 1955, 1958, 1962.
[a] 100 × 125 feet.
[b] For Hyde Park and Michael Reese this is 1955; for Blue Island, 1958.
[c] 1962 for all projects.

Table 3 Changes in Redevelopment-Site Land Values Due to Redevelopment ($_R\Delta P_S$), 1955, 1958, 1962

Changes	Hyde Park "B"	Michael Reese	Blue Island
1. Actual Percentage Change ΔP_s/mean (P_s) [a]	46%	58%	37%
2. Percentage Change Explained by Y and N $_{Y,N}\Delta P_s$/mean (P_s) [b]	23%	23%	13%
3. Percentage Change Due to Redevelopment $_R\Delta P_s$/mean (P_s)(line 1 − line 2)	23%	35%	24%
4. Absolute Change Due to Redevelopment, per Standard Lot ($_R\Delta P_s$)	$ 3,738	$ 2,844	$ 1,470
5. Initial Total Market Value of Acquired Land (L_0)	$49,506	$1,596,433	$45,559
6. Terminal Total Market Value of Acquired Land (L_1) [c] Adjusted for Y and N	$79,080	$3,315,618	$74,333
7. Total Change Due to Redevelopment (L) (line 6 − line 5)	$29,574	$1,719,235	$28,774

Source: Line 1 from Table 2 above. Line 2 from Table 1 and equation (9) above. Line 4 from Olcott's Land Values Blue Book of Chicago, 1955, 1958, 1962. Lines 5–7, Ibid., 1955, 1958, 1961, 1962; from Chicago Land Clearance Commission, Michael Reese-Prairie Shores Redevelopment Project: Final Project Report, 1962 (for column 2); and line 3.
[a] Actual site mean: for Hyde Park, $16,250; Michael Reese, $8,125; Blue Island, $6,125.
[b] Explained Cook County mean: Hyde Park, $28,434,954; Blue Island, $29,704,660.
[c] For columns 1 and 3, L_0 is the figure adjusted for Y,N; for column 2, L_1 is the adjusted figure.

placing them in the redevelopment site gain most. The former, but not the latter, are likely to be poor and members of racial minorities. Thus, the redistribution is politically potent.

But dislocatee worsening is not inevitable. Significant prior suboptimality, along with active relocation efforts by the LPA, could reverse this. Besides, real worsening will occur only if the number of simultaneous dislocatees is large relative to the size of the market. A small project will have little or no effect on housing prices elsewhere.

In addition to the question of the actuality of real influence is that of circumstances where

such influences can be detected. Redistribution effects are most noticeable if the market is tight. If the market is loose, dislocation effect may appear solely in terms of decreased vacancy rates, or, at most, in prices falling somewhat more slowly than they would have in the absence of redevelopment. Such effects either do not much affect well-being, or are too subtle to be detected by most statistical procedures.

In the projects studied here, all three factors are present: we suspect prior disequilibrium, the number of dislocatees is small relative to the market and, most important of all, the overall market was significantly loosening during the period. It is doubtful whether, in this context, the small, if any, tightening effect of redevelopment could be detected.

For actual measurement, two procedures are suggested by the constraints of our small scope, first, to obtain differences in actual rentals paid by relocatees from relocation authority records, second, to compare preproject site rentals with postproject rentals in areas heavily affected by dislocatees. Both prove inconclusive. Under the first, relocatees from Chicago projects somewhat more recent than those we are studying paid slightly higher rents after dislocation (median rents rose by $6) ,[27] but most moved from substandard to standard housing in the process; thus no estimate of even the direction of real rental changes can be given. This is an area, however, where a larger study might well improve the quality of data. The relocation experience of specific families might be followed.

The second procedure is no more promising, even for larger studies, since it rests on finding areas comparable except for relocation impact. The combination of substantial market loosening, and locational and population differences among areas superficially similar in terms of housing, will probably overwhelm systematic redevelopment impact by statistical "noise." We have been unable to produce figures that adjust for these complications.

The data are not persuasive, let alone decisive. But for all their paucity, they may be consistent with the tenor of our introductory remarks: dislocatees in these projects may not have been much hurt, if at all. We shall therefore proceed on the assumption that at least *negative* redistribution effects were not important. This assumption is being made, *not* on the basis of lack of data, but on the strength of the moderating circumstances mentioned above which we are pretty sure were operative in the present case. Lack of data is not a general warrant for assumption of zero effects, since the attendant circumstances might well favor strong impacts. The lack of direct measurement of them would not justify their exclusion, especially if their direction were known.

Effects in Slum-Generated Social Costs

We have probed some of the voluminous literature on the twin problems of slum-generated costs and of the effect of redevelopment and

public housing on these costs. We found suggestive treatments of parts of these problems, but no definitive studies, no sources from which quantification, even in dimensions other than money, can reliably be made. To attempt such a study ourselves is beyond our scope—and would probably be even beyond the scope of an expanded study on these lines. Still needed are additional studies out of the allied social sciences.

But we may sketch some gross tendencies abstracted from the literature. Slum concentration very likely increases fire hazards appreciably; physical configuration and use characteristics strongly suggest this. Since the sheer spatial area of concentration is important, redevelopment, on balance, probably decreases this hazard.

Overcrowding and filth demonstrably increase morbidity. Relocation into standard dwellings would decrease this hazard, but health hazards due to poverty and group practices will be untouched. The sketchy data of the last section indicating appreciable dislocatee movement from substandard to standard housing suggests that redevelopment does decrease social costs relating to health.

Crime is more related to poverty and specific population than to physical surroundings. But spatial configuration may have relevance, by increasing personality difficulties, or by affecting productivity (through illness, deterioration of aspirations, etc.) , or through homogeneity of deprived population. Redevelopment might therefore have some latitude. If redevelopment, including relocation, improves neighborhoods on balance, then it might well decrease crime. On the other hand, the dislocation process may itself generate an offsetting impact: uprooting people from their accustomed locale may have traumatic personality effects, encouraging crime. Such an effect may be only transitional, however, lasting only until new roots are fixed.

On balance, then, redevelopment may slightly decrease crime; but this effect will become apparent only after some time as offsetting transitional effects disappear and as the long-run impact of slums on behavior is gradually moderated (especially in new generations) .

Much the same can also be said about the

[27] Relocation Office, Urban Renewal Administration, Chicago, Illinois. Figures from our projects are not available.

Table 4 Summary Table of Benefit-Cost Analysis (*in thousands of dollars*)

Project Costs and Benefits	Blue Island	Hyde Park "B"	Michael Reese
I. Resource Costs of Project			
1. Gross Project Costs (GPC)	$396	$638	$6,235
2. Less Initial Value of Land (L_0)	46	49	1,596
3. Equals Total Resource Costs (TC)	350	589	4,639
II. Benefits Produced by Project			
1. Increased Productivity of Site Land ($L_1 - L_0$)	$ 29	$ 30	$1,719
2. Increased Productivity of Neighboring Land and Improvements (Spillover)	+	+	+
3. Decreased Social Costs Associated with Slums (ΔSC)	+	+	+
Total Costs Not Offset by Site Land Benefit (I.3 minus II.1)	$321	$559	$2,920

Source: Line I₁ from *Urban Renewal Characteristics 1962*, Urban Renewal Administration, 1962. Line I₂ (columns 1 and 2) *Olcott's Land Values Blue Book of Chicago*, 1956, 1962 issues; column 3 from Chicago Land Clearance Commission, *Michael Reese-Prairie Shores Project: Final Project Report*, 1962. (Assessed valuation figures converted to market value on assumption that former is 40 percent of latter.) Line II.1 from Table 3, line 7.

last category: poverty and population will account for most of the difficulty. But spatial situational factors will count too, since depressed, unhealthy, overcrowded surroundings can warp individual and family interactions. Moreover, under these circumstances, unhappiness and mental illness may be easier to evoke than crime—but may also be harder to measure. Redevelopment should have an ameliorative effect over time, depending, as with crime, on relocation's achieving some situational improvement. The eventual impact on human happiness may be very important. But numbers are not available.

In sum, if we conclude that relocation did not much spread or aggravate slums elsewhere, then we may tentatively infer that redevelopment probably decreased social costs in all five categories, most probably in fire and health, least in crime. But no quantification can be offered here, not even in the dimension natural to each kind of social cost.

These benefits may be very important. When we bring together our *quantified* benefits with a rough estimate of the order of magnitude of project costs in the next section, the latter far outweigh the former. Redevelopment is not justified in terms of land productivity alone. Jus-

tification must rest most strongly on the importance of this present category, the most distinctive type of benefit under renewal. We thus cannot use lack of data as an excuse for omitting this category: to do so would give redevelopment a seriously biased hearing. This warning holds especially when we compare redevelopment with the status quo. But it also holds, though in lesser degree, for comparison with the modified public-policy package as well, because the configuration of effects on slums differs under the two alternatives.

Summary of Benefit-Cost Analysis

We are now in a position to summarize these numerical estimates. They are presented in Table 4, which is structured to give the reader an idea of the magnitude between overall resource costs and benefits.[28] Spillover benefits and benefits associated with decreasing the social costs of slums are marked with pluses.

[28] The basic organizing relationships are:
(1) $$GPC = AC + R$$
(2) $$AC = L_0 + I_0$$
where $GPC \equiv$ Gross Project Cost
$AC \equiv$ Cost of Acquired Real Estate in Site (Acquisition Cost)

To simulate a decision-making context, site-land benefits are subtracted from total resource costs on the bottom line, so as to indicate how much spillover and social cost benefits would have to be worth to decision-makers in order that the total exceed total costs from the projects listed. Benefits associated with subsidization to achieve "public goals" (like population heterogeneity, university expansion, architectural beauty) would appropriately be added at this point to determine the grand balance.

$L_0 \equiv$ Market Value of Land Acquired in Site

$I_0 \equiv$ Market Value of Improvements Acquired in Site

$R \equiv$ Resource Expenditures in Project Other than AC

(3) $\quad TC = I_0 + R \quad$ where $TC \equiv$ Total Resource Costs of Project

(since I_0, but not L_0, is lost to society through Project)

so

(4) $\quad TC = (AC - L_0) + R = GPC - L_0$

(5) $\quad TB = (L_1 - L_0) + \text{(spillover)} + (\Delta SC)$

Efficiency in Public Urban Renewal Expenditures Through Benefit-Cost Analysis

JAMES C. T. MAO

STATEMENT OF THE PROBLEM

The purpose of this paper is to present a conceptual framework for the benefit-cost analysis of public urban renewal expenditures and to demonstrate the practicability of this framework through a case study. Since public renewal decisions are reached outside the market mechanism, some index of efficiency is needed for judging which projects are worthwhile and which are not. As the reader is aware, a number of studies have been made to appraise the *particular* impact of public urban renewal expenditures. Marris, Lichfield, Hartman, and others have studied the effects of renewal on the housing welfare of relocatees.[1] San Francisco, Indianapolis, and other cities have analyzed the effects of renewal on the condition of local finances.[2] But at the time this study was undertaken, no writer had produced in a single framework an evaluation broad enough to encompass all the different effects of renewal.[3] In fact, there did not exist an internally consistent theoretical scheme for making such an overall appraisal. The framework suggested in this paper, I hope, will help close this important gap in the literature on urban renewal.

The technique employed here is essentially that of benefit-cost analysis, or what is known in industry and business as capital budgeting.

The application of benefit-cost analysis to urban renewal decisions poses certain special questions of a theoretical nature: *one*, What are the benefits and costs of urban renewal from the viewpoint of society as a whole? *two*, What criteria should be used in ranking urban re-

Reprinted by permission of the *Journal of the American Institute of Planners*, XXXII, No. 2 (March 1966), 95–107.

1 See P. Marris, "The Social Implications of Urban Redevelopment," *Journal of the American Institute of Planners*, XXVIII (August, 1962), 180–186; Nathaniel Lichfield, "Relocation: The Impact on Housing Welfare," *Journal of the American Institute of Planners*, XXVII (August, 1961), 199–215; and Chester W. Hartman, "The Housing of Relocated Families," *Journal of the American Institute of Planners*, XXX (November, 1964), 266–286.

2 See, for example, "Relationship of Redevelopment in San Francisco to Increased Assessed Values and Tax Revenues," a mimeographed report prepared by the San Francisco Redevelopment Agency, dated January 2, 1964.

3 The only possible exception is Nathaniel Lichfield's pioneering attempt to appraise the costs and benefits of three redevelopment projects in California. See his *Cost-Benefit Analysis in Urban Redevelopment* (Berkeley: Real Estate Research Program, University of California, 1962). In Lichfield's study, the repercussions of urban renewal were traced in relation to the various affected groups such as consumers, producers, and so forth, whereas in this study the repercussions are traced directly in relation to the basic objectives of urban renewal.

newal projects? *three,* How should intangible benefits and costs be treated in the appraisal? *four,* How should the social cost of capital used in urban renewal be computed? These questions are taken up next. A detailed analysis of the East Stockton (California) Urban Renewal Project is then presented, and its purpose is to illustrate the applicability of benefit-cost analysis as a tool for evaluating the efficiency of public renewal expenditures. Finally, a summary of results and some of the conclusions suggested by my findings are outlined.

THEORETICAL ASPECTS

The efficiency of any form of expenditures, whether private or public, can be evaluated only in terms of the objectives which these expenditures are intended to achieve. Hence, the question: What is the nature and purpose of urban renewal?

Urban renewal as used here refers to that program under which local governments are given federal subsidies and the power of eminent domain to condemn sites, to demolish buildings, and to resell the cleared sites to those who would redevelop them according to predetermined plans. Thus the term, for our purposes, excludes some urban rehabilitation. The social and economic benefits of the urban renewal program are expected by the federal government to be manifold. The Housing and Home Finance Agency described the costs of slums and blight in these words:

> The human cost of slums and blight is enormous. Disease, crime, and juvenile delinquency are much more frequent in rundown areas than elsewhere. The economic cost is huge, too. As blight spreads, it creates greater and greater needs for municipal services, while at the same time blighted areas return less and less tax revenue to the city. Businesses suffer from slums and blight too. Inefficient sites, lack of room for expansion, traffic congestion, poor housing and community facilities for employees, and inadequate transportation—all of these create higher operating costs for business, force many of them to abandon their locations for modern and efficient sites.[4]

Benefits and Costs of Urban Renewal

There are, then, at least three distinct benefits which the federal government expects from its urban renewal program: *one,* superior pattern of resource allocation, *two,* social benefits of slum clearance, and *three,* improved fiscal position of local governments. The first benefit is generally accepted by all students of urban renewal. Renewal permits a city to refashion and rebuild its physical plant according to modern conceptions of urban efficiency. Without going into the causes of urban blight,[5] it may be observed that one of the characteristics of blight is the misallocation of land resources. Whether a particular urban renewal project actually improves resource allocation is a matter of empirical verification rather than of theoretical deduction. If there is an improvement, however, it will result from one or more of three transformations in land use: (1) Transformation in income class—land is transferred from low-income users to high-income users. (2) Transformation in density—land is transferred from low to high density uses. Not infrequently, however, renewal plans have prescribed reductions in project area density. In such instances, renewal may result in a reduction rather than an increase in the value of project area land. (3) Transformation in activity—land is transferred from residential to industrial or commercial uses, or vice versa. If this type of transformation is interpreted broadly, we may also include the widening and rerouting of streets and the dedication of project area land to schools and parks.

The effects of these transformations on property values are not confined to the project area. When a renewal plan significantly alters existing densities and urban patterns, the indirect effect on city-wide property values may well exceed the direct effect on renewal area property values. However, if only minor changes in densities and urban patterns are effected, then the

4 Housing and Home Finance Agency, *20 Questions on Urban Renewal* (Washington, D.C., 1963) , p. 1.
5 A blighted area is one where renewal would produce a net social gain, but where private action is lacking because of the presence of certain obstacles. Cf. Otto A. Davis and Andrew B. Whinston, "The Economics of Urban Renewal," *Law and Contemporary Problems,* XXVI (Winter, 1961), 111.

policy maker can reasonably focus his attention only on properties in the project area and its immediate neighborhood.

Consider next the social benefits of slum clearance. The federal government provides certain safeguards for the housing welfare of residents displaced by urban renewal activities. More specifically, a local redevelopment agency is required by law to provide former residents with decent, safe, and sanitary housing, conveniently located and at prices or rents within the means of these residents.[6] It should not be thought, however, that relocation will invariably result in an improvement in the housing welfare of relocatees. After analyzing relocation in a number of cities, Marris observed that people tended to be relocated in neighborhoods which were quite similar to those that were cleared and that relocation so far has made only marginal improvement in the housing welfare of relocatees.[7] The preceding statement, of course, does not imply that urban renewal can never bring about any improvement in the living conditions of relocatees. It is not inconceivable that if low-cost housing is available in the city, relocation could significantly improve the housing welfare of those relocated. The Marris observations, however, show that we cannot take for granted the expected gain in housing welfare.

We should also ask ourselves such questions as: If housing and environment are improved, will there be reduction in rates of crime, fires, disease, and juvenile delinquency? Will we need fewer policemen and firemen in the city to provide the same protection as before? To the extent that renewal does reduce the costs of providing these services, this reduction constitutes a tangible social benefit.

Finally, consider the effects of urban renewal on the fiscal position of the local government. The spreading of slums creates an especially heavy demand for certain types of municipal services, while at the same time slums cut significantly into the revenue productivity of the tax system. Hence, in addition to demoralizing their inhabitants, slums constitute an economic drain on the city's treasury. Hopefully, the spreading of slums may be arrested or even reversed when an area is redeveloped and the former residents relocated. Hence, improvement in local finances is still another benefit which urban renewal is designed to produce.

Let us turn now from the benefits to the costs of urban renewal. Conceptually, the social costs of renewal (costs to the community as a whole, or to any persons within it) include the disruptive influence of relocation on the pre-renewal residents, and the value of resources used up in the renewal process. There does not exist an objective basis for assigning a monetary value to the first group of costs. The second group of costs include costs of relocation, costs of survey, planning and administration, costs of public improvements, costs of demolition, value of improvements demolished, and any possible land value write-down.

In Table 1, the social costs of renewal are

6 As directed in Housing and Home Finance Agency, *Urban Renewal Manual*, Part 16, chap. 3, par. 3.110.
7 See P. Marris, *op. cit.*, p. 182.

Table 1   The Social Costs and Benefits of Urban Renewal

Benefits	*Costs*
1. Better allocation of resources	1. Survey and planning costs
a. Increase in property value	2. Administrative expenses
b. Value of public improvements installed	3. Demolition cost
c. Aesthetic and cultural value of planned communities	4. Value of improvements demolished
2. Social implications of slum clearance	5. Cost of public improvements
a. Reduction in crime, disease, fires, and juvenile delinquency	6. Relocation costs
b. Improvement in housing welfare	a. Economic
c. Savings in the costs of municipal services	b. Noneconomic
3. Improvement in local finances	7. Land value write-down

matched against the social benefits of renewal. The items in the table, especially those on the side of benefits, are suggestive rather than definitive. Thus, "improvements in housing welfare" appears on the side of benefits. If in a particular project, relocation actually resulted in a deterioration in the housing welfare of those relocated, then we would have a negative benefit, which is equivalent to a cost.

The Problem of Criterion

Suppose the benefits and costs of various renewal projects have been ascertained. What criteria shall the authority use for the purpose of ranking projects according to their relative attractiveness? There is also the question of how large the total renewal budget should be. At the purely theoretical level, these decisions can be resolved as follows. Resources employed in public investments have alternative uses in the production of marketable goods and services and will therefore have a price which measures their opportunity cost, the value of the resources in alternative use. Designate this opportunity cost as the social cost of capital. A renewal project then is worthwhile if the present value of its benefits, discounted at the social cost of capital, exceeds the corresponding present value of its costs. Since urban renewal projects have a time dimension, discounting is necessary to establish the value at a given point in time (present value) of expenditures to be made over a period of time.

More formally, consider a project which will produce social benefits (before the deduction of cost of capital) of B_1, B_2, ... B_n in time periods $1,2, \ldots n$ (that is, say, B_1 of benefit in the first year, B_2 in the second, . . .). If the social cost of capital, i, is a constant, then the present discounted value of future benefits is given by the expression:

$$(1) \qquad B = \sum_{t=1}^{n} \frac{B_t}{(1+i)^t},$$

the standard expression for interest or discounting. Assume the costs of the project to be K_1, K_2, ... K_n in time periods $1,2 \ldots n$. The present value of future costs is given by a similar expression:

$$(2) \qquad K = \sum_{t=1}^{n} \frac{K_t}{(1+i)^t}$$

Next, define the net social contribution, W, of a project as the difference between B and K:

$$(3) \quad W = B - K = \sum_{t=1}^{n} \frac{B_t}{(1+i)^t} - \sum_{t=1}^{n} \frac{K_t}{(1+i)^t}$$

As a decision rule, the government should undertake a project only if the value of its net social contribution, W, is greater than zero. Moreover, in order to maximize net social contributions the government should keep on expanding its total renewal budget until no additional project makes a further contribution to net social benefit. For the marginal project, $W = 0$.

In order to explore the conditions under which W is equal to zero, it is useful to define a new concept: the marginal efficiency, or internal rate of return of a project.[8] The marginal efficiency, r, of a project is that discount rate which will equate the present value of the entire series of present and future benefits to the present value of the entire series of present and future costs. Symbolically, r is defined by the following equation:

$$(4) \qquad K = \sum_{t=1}^{n} \frac{B_t}{(1+r)^t}$$

Now for any project which makes some positive contribution to net social benefit, $W \geq 0$, or alternatively:

$$(5) \qquad \sum_{t=1}^{n} \frac{B_t}{(1+i)^t} - \sum_{t=1}^{n} \frac{B_t}{(1+r)^t} \geq 0$$

8 In the literature of economics, r is traditionally referred to as the marginal efficiency of investment. We have followed this standard terminology, although, strictly speaking, r measures the average return for the project as a whole. It is a marginal concept in so far as it reveals the contribution of any one project to the renewal program, assuming decisions are always made in terms of adding or subtracting projects. Cf. O. Eckstein, "Investment Criteria for Economic Development and the Theory of Intertemporal Welfare Economics," *Quarterly Journal of Economics*, LXXI (February, 1957), 59–60, n. 8.

To satisfy this condition, r, the marginal efficiency of the project must be equal to or greater than i, the social cost of capital. The rule for maximizing social benefit, therefore, can be stated alternatively. The government should rank renewal projects according to their marginal efficiencies and should undertake all projects for which r, the marginal efficiency is equal to or greater than i, the social cost of capital.

The Social Cost of Capital

The marginal efficiency of a project is a rate of return, calculated *before* the deduction of the cost of capital invested. A public urban renewal project, therefore, is profitable or not depending on whether its marginal efficiency is greater than, equal to, or less than the social cost of capital. Since urban renewal expenditures are borne by both the federal and local governments, the social cost of public capital devoted to renewal is measured by taking a weighted average of the cost of federal and local funds.

What is the social cost of federal financing? The opportunity cost idea requires that this social cost be estimated by tracing the federal funds to their sources and by determining the returns which these funds would have earned if they had been left in private hands. This sounds like a major research assignment, and indeed it can be. Fortunately, work on this subject was carried out a few years ago by Professor Otto Eckstein in connection with his research on water resources development.[9] Since his study is readily available, we shall restrict our discussion to a brief restatement of his assumptions, conclusions, and qualifications.

In his study, Eckstein experimented with two alternative models of tax changes. The two models differed primarily in their incidence, one being most burdensome to low-income families and the other to high-income families. Model A called for a decrease in the personal exemption of the federal income tax and an increase in federal excise taxes, whereas Model B called for a proportionate increase in both the personal and the corporate income taxes. In both cases, Eckstein found the social cost of capital to be between five and six percent. That is, the money would have yielded a five to six percent return if left in private hands.

Eckstein was quick to point out that his conclusions were valid only if the time preference of the present generation is accepted for the intertemporal allocation of resources, that is, valid only if our present understanding of future benefits to be derived remains true for the future.[10] Society as a whole, however, may on ethical grounds decide to save a greater share of current income for future consumption than what the people are willing to vote for individually in the market place. In that case, the opportunity cost of capital diverges from its social cost, which now becomes a politically-determined rate. We might add that if society does use a low rate to evaluate its renewal projects, then efficiency considerations require that the same rate be applied to public investments in all other fields.

In urban renewal, when the cleared land has been sold for redevelopment, a deficit known as "net project cost" usually results. Under existing law, two-thirds of this cost is borne by the federal government and one-third by the local government. The social cost of local funds depends on the method used by the local government in financing its one-third share of the net project cost. Since local tax systems are regressive, whenever local tax money is used the social cost of capital is similar to that of federal funds in Eckstein's Model A, in which the tax burden fell chiefly on the lower income classes. Whenever borrowed funds are used, the interest rate on local debt is the best indicator of opportunity cost and hence the best measure of the social cost of capital.[11]

The Treatment of Intangible Benefits and Costs

The task of evaluating urban renewal projects would be considerably simpler if there were no

9 J. V. Krutilla and O. Eckstein, *Multiple Purpose River Development* (Baltimore: The Johns Hopkins Press, 1958), chap. 4.
10 Krutilla and Eckstein, *op. cit.*, pp. 125–127. For more recent discussions of this topic, see S. A. Marglin, "The Social Rate of Discount and the Optimal Rate of Investment," *Quarterly Journal of Economics*, LXXVII (February, 1963), 95–111, and his "The Opportunity Costs of Public Investment," *Quarterly Journal of Economics*, LXXVII (May, 1963), 274–289.
11 We do not use the interest on U.S. obligations as a measure of the cost of federal financing because the federal government's two-thirds share of net project cost is completely tax financed.

intangible benefits and costs. In reality, the nature of urban renewal is such that many of its benefits and costs do not have monetary values that can be determined objectively. What significance shall be assigned to these intangibles in the overall evaluation of renewal projects?

We propose the following method of treating intangibles. First, discount all project expenditures to the present at the social cost of capital. The sum of the present values is the total tangible cost of the renewal project. Next, assume the marginal efficiency of the project to be the same as the social cost of capital and discount all tangible benefits to the present at that rate. The sum of the present values is the total tangible benefit of the renewal project. Now, if total tangible cost exceeds total tangible benefit, the difference is the value which society must assign to the intangibles in order for the project to break even. If total tangible benefit exceeds total tangible cost, then the project's marginal efficiency is higher than the social cost of capital, even if society assigns a net value of zero to the intangibles. In both situations, the policy maker might experiment with assigning monetary values to intangibles on a subjective basis.

This method of treating intangibles also highlights a major difficulty in appraising urban renewal projects. Since there is no objective basis for evaluating intangibles, there can be no independent estimate of the marginal efficiency, r, of a particular project. But as Robert Coughlin has said, "It is only by comparing the comparable things and measuring the measurable things and then setting them aside that the planner will really be able to concentrate on those things which seem noncomparable and immeasurable." [12]

AN APPLICATION

The objective of the preceding section has been to devise a method for appraising the efficiency of public renewal expenditures. Let us now examine the practicability of this method by applying it to the East Stockton (California) Urban Renewal Project.[13] Since several approximations have been made, the reader may wish

to regard the figures as merely illustrative of the types of results to be obtained.

Background and Location of the Project

The East Stockton Urban Renewal Project covered a 189-acre residential slum in Stockton, California. Lots in the area were all undersized —25 by 50 feet. There were no curbs, gutters, sidewalks, or sanitary and storm sewers. About 90 percent of all the dwelling units in the area were unfit for human habitation. There was a lack of recreational facilities for adults and children. Compared with the city as a whole, the area experienced above-average rates of crime, disease, fires, and juvenile delinquency.

Physically, the 189-acre project was situated less than two miles directly east of Stockton's central business district. Except for a small protruding section at the southeast corner, the project area was rectangular in shape. See Figure 1.

Data in Table 2 bring out the extent to

Table 2 Land Uses in East Stockton Before and After Urban Renewal (in Acres)

	Before	After
Residential: single-family	120.8	64.0
Residential: multi-family	None	8.2
Parks and Schools	None	10.0
Industrial and Commercial	7.6	37.0
Streets, Alleys, and Proposed		
Cross-Town Freeway	60.4	69.6
Total	188.8	188.8

Source: Redevelopment Agency of the City of Stockton.

which renewal altered land uses in the project area. Broadly speaking, a residential slum was cleared and replaced by a planned residential community with some nonresidential reuses. See

12 Robert Coughlin, in his review of Roland N. McKean, "Efficiency in Government through Systems Analysis," *Journal of the American Institute of Planners,* XXVI (November, 1960), 340–341.
13 Unless otherwise stated, basic data pertaining to the project were all supplied by the Redevelopment Agency of the City of Stockton.

Figure 1   Diagram of Stockton.

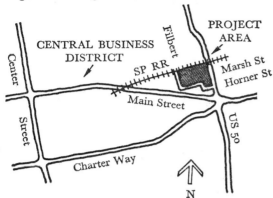

Figures 2 and 3 for the "before" and "after" land-use maps.

Effect of Urban Renewal on Property Value

One important benefit of urban renewal is the resulting improvement in resource allocation. Since renewal in East Stockton did not significantly alter city-wide densities and urban patterns, the tangible aspects of this benefit can be approximated by the combined increase in the value of project area land and the value of neighborhood properties.[14] Such an approximation requires the resolution of three problems: the delimitation of the neighborhood area; the selection of an appropriate time period for determining the full impact of renewal; and the removal, from observed changes in property value, of any effect which is extraneous to urban renewal.

Since the effects of urban renewal are ever-widening, any rule used to delimit the neighborhood must necessarily be arbitrary. Fortunately, the East Stockton project is bounded by a railroad track on the north, a major highway on the east and a main thoroughfare on the south which tended to block the spread of indirect effects. The renewal neighborhood is, therefore, defined to include an additional 17 blocks outside the project, but within these boundaries. (Figure 1.) The presence of artificial barriers on three sides of the project minimized the arbitrary nature of the boundaries chosen.

The next practical problem of estimation is the selection of an appropriate time period for

measuring the effect renewal has on property values. The many stages through which urban renewal passes from inception to completion is a time-consuming process. In the case of East Stockton, the official redevelopment plan was approved by the federal government in July, 1959. During five years after that date, properties were acquired and cleared, and some 82 percent of the cleared land was sold. Hence we feel that the period 1959–64 is long enough to capture at least a major portion of the impact of renewal.

Finally, there is the problem of isolating from the observed changes in property value all effects extraneous to urban renewal. Real estate value in Stockton generally has risen steadily in recent years, partly because of growth in real income and in population, and partly because of the falling purchasing power of the dollar. Our objective, of course, is to identify the part of the observed increase in property value which is strictly attributable to urban renewal.

The increase in the value of project area land is easiest to measure, since the data are kept in official files of the Redevelopment Agency. The Agency paid a total of $666,218 for the 189 acres of land in the project area. This amount was paid out over a period of time with the midpoint estimated at June 30, 1960. By the summer of 1964, approximately $1,121,000 worth of land had already been sold, and the expectation was that all of the remaining land would be sold before 1967 for an additional $255,000. Discounting these amounts to June 30, 1960, at an assumed social cost of capital of 6 percent, we get a total present value of $893,849. Hence the Redevelopment Agency realized a "profit" of $227,631 on the project area land.[15]

The value of properties in the project neighborhood (defined above) totaled about $6 mil-

14 In view of the proposed cross-town freeway, the reader may well question the statement that urban renewal in East Stockton did not significantly alter existing densities and urban patterns. Our position is that a cross-town freeway would have been built whether or not East Stockton was renewed. Hence, the changes which the freeway will bring about cannot be attributed to urban renewal in East Stockton.

15 Although real estate prices have risen generally in recent years, we are assuming that land value in the project area would have remained static in the absence of urban renewal.

Figure 2 East Stockton before redevelopment. Source: Redevelopment agency of the city of Stockton.

lion in 1964. To compute the increase in the value of these properties between 1959 and 1964, the most reliable and objective approach would be to use actual sales records as a basis. In checking through records at the local title insurance company, no property in this area was found which was sold in 1959 and resold in 1964. However, there were a number of sales consummated in the 1963–64 period. The problem, then, is to determine the amount which these houses, in their 1963–64 conditions, would have sold for in 1959.

The price which one of these houses (in its 1963–1964 condition) would have commanded in 1959 is a type of information which only an appraiser familiar with local real estate values could provide. Records kept at the local multiple listing center showed that two realtors and one builder were directly or indirectly involved in more than 50 percent of all real

estate transactions in the renewal neighborhood. In separate interviews, these three specialists were asked to identify, from the list of recent sales, those properties with which they were personally familiar. These interviews produced a consensus that property values in the 17-block area west of the project and in the triangular area south of the project have risen about 25 percent and 13 percent, respectively, during those five years. The triangular area is outside the city limits, and the unavailability of city water and sewer services was given as the reason for the relatively smaller increase in property value in this area.

Now that the increase in neighborhood property values has been estimated, what portion of that increase shall we count as a benefit of urban renewal? Consider the triangular area to the south of the project. During 1959–64, property value there increased by about 13 percent,

Figure 3   East Stockton after redevelopment. Source: Redevelopment agency of the City of Stockton.

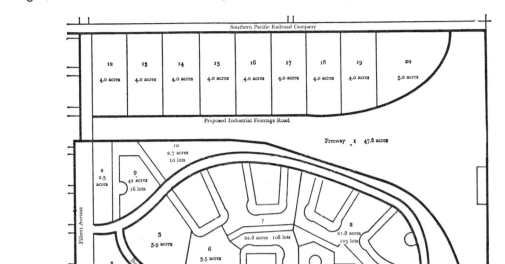

compared with about 8 percent for properties in Stockton generally. Since relatively few of the former residents of East Stockton were re-located in this area, the bulk of the 5 percent net increase in value is attributable to the beneficial effect of improved neighborhood conditions.

In the 17-block area west of Filbert Street, the net increase in property value was about 17 percent, reflecting the combined impact of a considerable influx of relocatees into this area and of improved neighborhood conditions. Our objective, however, is to determine that portion of the increase which resulted strictly from an improvement in neighborhood conditions. We know that since the 17-block area has the advantages of being within the city limits, urban renewal must have benefited this area at least as much as it benefited the triangular area. Hence, we estimate the revitaliz-

ing effect of slum removal on property values to be somewhere between 5 and 17 percent for the area immediately west of the renewal project. In the following calculations, an intermediate 10 percent is assumed to be representative of the change that occurred in this neighborhood.

Using 5 percent for the triangular area and 10 percent for the 17-block area, we find that the removal of slums in East Stockton increased property value in the neighborhood by about $415,500.[16] Adding this figure to the $227,631 Agency "profit," we obtain $643,000 as an esti-

16 In 1964, property values in the 17-block area and the triangular area totaled $4.2 million and $1.8 million, respectively. These figures represented increases of 25 percent and 13 percent over their corresponding values in 1959. The 1959 property values for these two areas must have been $3.36 million and $1.59 million, respectively. 10% × $3.36 million + 5% × $1.59 million = $415,500.

mate of the combined increase in the value of project area land and neighborhood properties.

Effect of Urban Renewal on Local Finances

Urban renewal affects local finances in two important ways: first, through its effect on property value and hence on property tax revenue; second, through its effect on the amount of expenditures needed to maintain a certain level and quality of municipal services.[17]

Urban renewal in East Stockton was estimated to increase the value of project area land and neighborhood properties by $643,000. This figure is a reasonably accurate estimate of the *net* effect of improved resource allocation on total property value. Using an effective tax rate of 2.8 percent, we estimate the associated increase in property tax at $18,000. Note that we attribute no tax revenues to improvements that have been or will be built in the project area. These improvements merely take the place of construction which would otherwise have occurred elsewhere, had East Stockton not been renewed.

Urban renewal also affects local finances through its effect on the amount of expenditures needed to maintain a certain level and quality of municipal services. While urban renewal does not automatically eliminate slums, it can substantially cut down the private and social costs of slum living. Take, for instance, the effect of renewal on reducing fire hazards. The per capita cost of fire protection depends in part on the density of the development and moral character of the population, and in part on the type, design, and construction of the properties. Because renewal demolishes fire traps and relocates former residents in low-income housing of standard quality, we may expect a reduction in the cost of fire protection as well as in realized fire losses.

The savings in the cost of fire protection can be estimated as follows. Assume the cost of fire protection to be closely correlated with the number of fire calls. In 1959, the year before relocation started, East Stockton had 21 building fire calls as compared with 340 calls for the city of Stockton. At that time, population in East Stockton totaled about 2,000 as compared with 83,000 for the entire city. A

resident of East Stockton, therefore, required about two and a half times as much fire protection as that received by an average resident. In 1959, the city spent a total of $1.2 million for fire protection. On the assumption that project residents will require only average protection after relocation, renewal reduced the cost of fire protection by about $42,000 annually.[18] Capitalizing the annual saving of $42,-000 at the estimated social cost of capital of 6 percent, we get $700,000 as the value of all present and future savings in fire protection costs.

Similar computations put the estimated annual savings in police protection at $70,000, with a capitalized value of $1,167,000 and the estimated annual savings in health protection at $25,500, with a capitalized value of $425,000.

Effect of Urban Renewal on Housing Welfare

Between August, 1959 and June, 1962, the Redevelopment Agency helped to relocate a total of 719 households. Of these households, 50 percent were Negro, 40 percent Mexican, and the remainder white. These 719 households were also among the poorest in the nation, with annual median incomes of about $3,000 for families and $1,300 for single persons. How did relocation affect the housing welfare of these pre-renewal residents of East Stockton?

Consider first the effect of relocation on housing expenditures. For families, median

17 Are we not counting the benefits of renewal twice if we include both the increased property value and the tax increment that flows from this increase? It would indeed be double counting if we did that, but we do not. The improvement in local finances is treated as an intangible benefit distinct from the related but separate event of an increase in tax revenue. A healthy fiscal position is essential to the vitality of a city. Hence any improvement in local finances constitutes a social benefit.

18 The saving is projected on the basis of the average, rather than the marginal relationship between the cost of fire protection and the amount of services provided. The average cost, of course, may or may not be an accurate measure of the cost of providing an additional unit of service. Therefore, unless fire protection is a constant-cost "industry," the use of average cost might have introduced an error into our estimated saving. Because Stockton has a fairly sizable population, it is likely that fire protection is being supplied under conditions of increasing cost. Any possible error, therefore, results in an underestimation of the true saving.

monthly rental remained constant at $45 before and after relocation. For single persons, the amount increased from $25 to $35. Among owner occupants, relocation resulted in significant increases in house value for both families and single persons. Before relocation, the median price of houses for all families was $3,600; after relocation, the median price was $8,000. For all single persons, the corresponding increase in median value of house was from $3,200 to $6,000.

On the whole, then, the former residents of East Stockton did pay more for their housing after relocation. The next logical question is whether these former residents experienced any improvement in housing amenities. Detailed statistics show: (1) a significant reduction in overcrowding for families; (2) no change in average occupancy for single persons (to whom the question of overcrowding does not apply); (3) a significant improvement in the quality of housing for both families and single persons; and (4) a dispersal of Negro and Mexican households from the concentration that existed in East Stockton.

The above analysis suggests that housing amenities improved for the former residents after they were relocated. This improvement, however, was purchased at the cost of higher housing expenses, especially for those residents who were home-owners. The question, therefore, arises: How many of these households believed that they actually benefited from relocation? To answer this question, the Redevelopment Agency in 1961 resurveyed a portion of the residents who were then relocated in Stockton. In all, Agency staff called on 437 households, but were able to get in touch with only 257 respondents. Of these 257 replies, 85 percent were affirmative.

Total Cost of Renewal and its Financing

The costs of the East Stockton Project, expended over a ten-year period, totaled $4.7 million. Within this total, the single largest item was the cost of improvements demolished, $2.3 million; the next largest items were the cost of site improvements, $0.7 million, and the cost of public and supporting facilities, $0.6 million. Included in Table 3 is a detailed tab-

ulation of these individual costs, with the dates on which these costs were incurred. Costs are dated because the timing of these costs is essential to the application of the benefit-cost analysis. Theoretically, costs are not incurred until real resources are actually used up. To simplify analysis, the assumption is made here that real costs are incurred when payments are made by the local redevelopment agency.

The key concept in understanding the financing of any urban renewal project is that of the "net project cost." Net project cost is legally defined as the difference between the cost of surveying, planning, acquiring and clearing the land, and the proceeds from resale of the cleared land. As mentioned earlier, this net project cost is shared, two-thirds by the federal government and one-third by the local government. The opportunity cost of federal funds has been estimated at around 5.5 percent. The local share in the case of East Stockton was all borrowed money, on which the interest rate was 4.4 percent. Assuming a marginal tax rate of 40 percent, the investor who purchased these tax-exempt securities received a yield comparable to a 7.3 percent corporate bond. This rate of 7.3 percent measured the opportunity cost of Stockton's one-third share of the net project cost. Overall, we get a weighted average of 6 percent (i in Equation 5) as the opportunity cost of resources used up in the East Stockton Project.

Overall Evaluation

The final phase of this case study is an overall evaluation of the efficiency of the East Stockton Project. To facilitate this evaluation, Table 3 summarizes the amounts and the timing of all the tangible social benefits and costs that were associated with the project.

Let us evaluate the efficiency of the project as if today were December 31, 1958, the approximate date when the Redevelopment Agency of Stockton incurred the bulk of its survey and planning costs. The social cost of capital is assumed to be 6 percent per annum. Discounting all costs at 6 percent back to December 31, 1958, we get a total present value of $3,800,105. Next, discount all benefits back to December 31, 1958 at an assumed marginal ef-

Table 3 Summary of Tangible Social Benefits and Costs of the East Stockton Urban Renewal Project

Benefit	Amount	Date of Reckoning		Cost	Amount	Date of Reckoning
I. Increase in the value of project area land	$ 227,631	June 30, 1960	I.	Survey and Planning	$ 113,190	Dec. 31, 1958
			II.	Project execution expenditures		
II. Increase in the value of neigh- borhood prop- erties	415,500	June 30, 1964	a.	Administra- tive, travel and office furniture	201,535	June 30, 1961
III. Value of public improvements: school and parks *	822,980	June 30, 1966	b. c.	Legal services Acquisition expenses, salaries of relocation staff, and other related	113,800	Dec. 31, 1960
IV. Reductions in costs of munici- pal services				items	387,466	Dec. 31, 1960
			d.	Site clearance	93,135	June 30, 1961
a. Savings in fire protec- tion cost	700,000	Jan. 1, 1964	e.	Disposal, lease, reten- tion costs	59,228	June 30, 1964
b. Savings in health pro- tection cost	425,000	Jan. 1, 1964	f.	Project in- spection	32,731	Dec. 31, 1962
c. Savings in police pro- tection cost	1,167,000	Jan. 1, 1964	g.	Value of im- provements demolished	2,342,418	June 30, 1961
			III.	Site Improve- ments	701,315	June 30, 1964
			IV.	Public and supporting facilities	551,980	Dec. 31, 1967
			V.	Relocation pay- ments	84,715	June 30, 1961

* We are assuming that these public investments have net social values equal to their costs. On the right side of the table, these costs are included under items III and IV.
Source: Benefits represent the author's estimates; costs are from the official budget of the Redevelopment Agency of Stockton; information on the timing of expenditures was supplied by the fiscal officer of the Agency.

ficiency of 6 percent. The total present value of all benefits is found to be $2,701,382. (See Table 4.) The present value of costs, therefore, exceeds the present value of benefits by $1,098,723. This is the value which society must place on the net intangible benefits if the project is to earn the assumed social cost of capital of

6 percent. Are the net intangible benefits associated with the project worth $1,098,723? This is a question which each reader must answer for himself. Similar computations show that if the social cost of capital is 6 percent, assigning yearly marginal efficiencies of 7, 8, 9, and 10 percent to the East Stockton Project

Table 4 Overall Evaluation of East Stockton Urban Renewal Project (in dollars)

Assumed Marginal Efficiency (percent per annum)	Present Value of Tangible Benefits	Present Value of Tangible Costs	Required Value of Intangible Benefits: Col. (3) minus Col. (2)
	Social Cost of Capital: 6%		
6%	2,701,382	3,800,105	1,098,723
7%	2,278,827	3,800,105	1,521,278
8%	1,883,603	3,800,105	1,916,502
9%	1,678,585	3,800,105	2,121,520
10%	1,455,403	3,800,105	2,344,702
	Social Cost of Capital: 4%		
4%	4,067,594	4,063,505	(4,089)
5%	3,111,054	4,063,505	952,451
6%	2,701,382	4,063,505	1,362,123
7%	2,278,827	4,063,505	1,784,678
8%	1,883,603	4,063,505	2,179,902
	Social Cost of Capital: 2%		
2%	7,774,233	4,355,826	(3,418,407)
3%	5,340,796	4,355,826	(984,970)
4%	4,067,594	4,355,826	288,232
5%	3,111,054	4,355,826	1,244,772

Source: Based on costs and benefits as estimated in Table 3.

puts the required value of intangibles at $1,-521,278, $1,916,502, $2,121,502 and $2,344,702 respectively.

The above computations were carried out using 6 percent as the annual social cost of capital. How would the results be affected if a different social cost of capital were used? Table 4 also summarizes the results of our experimentation with a social cost of capital of 4 percent and 2 percent. The data illustrates two general relationships which the reader may already have deduced from our earlier discussion of the criterion problem. First, a higher social cost of capital decreases the present value of renewal costs, which in turn increases the marginal efficiency of the project. But the increase in marginal efficiency is always smaller than the corresponding increase in the social cost of capital. Second, for the project to achieve a given marginal efficiency, the minimum value which society must place on the net intangible benefits varies inversely with the social cost of capital.

The above observations are interesting, but in what ways could the policy maker have made use of these findings, let us say five or six years ago, when the decision to undertake urban renewal in East Stockton was actually reached? As indicated above, this paper is neutral with respect to the valuation of intangibles and the selection of a social cost of capital. Once these are determined, our analysis shows how the marginal efficiency of an urban renewal project can be computed. To illustrate, suppose it were decided for the East Stockton Project that net intangible benefits were worth about $1,000,000 and that the social cost of capital equalled 4 percent. Our computation shows a marginal project efficiency of about 5 percent. Since the social cost of capital was only 4 percent, the conclusion would be that the project was a worthwhile undertaking.[19] This is how benefit-cost analysis can be used to improve the efficiency of public investment in general and renewal expenditures in particular.

19 This conclusion would not necessarily follow, however, if the East Stockton Project had been but one of several mutually exclusive alternatives. In such a case, the marginal efficiencies of these alternatives should all be determined, and the project with the highest return should be undertaken.

SUMMARY AND CONCLUSIONS

The purpose of this paper has been to bridge the gap between theory and practice in measuring the efficiency of public expenditures for urban renewal. Granted the need for public renewal expenditures, the question arises as to how the total amount and the composition of such expenditures are to be determined. We suggested that the technique of benefit-cost analysis be used to measure the efficiency of government expenditures when such expenditures absorb scarce resources.

The application of benefit-cost analysis requires the identification and the quantification of the benefits and costs associated with specific urban renewal projects. The benefits of urban renewal are threefold: improved resource allocation, improved local finances, and social benefits of slum clearance. The costs are the resources used up in the renewal programs and the disruptive influence of relocation on the prerenewal residents. The specific problems of

measurement were illustrated by a case analysis involving the East Stockton Project.

The case study revealed that four factors were especially important in determining the efficiency of the East Stockton Project: the savings in local government expenditures, the value of prerenewal structures demolished, the value of net intangible benefits, and the social cost of capital. Great care should be exercised in generalizing these results to other types of renewal projects. The East Stockton Project involved the total clearance of a residential slum, and hence the conclusions regarding project efficiency were strictly applicable only to this type of development. The efficiency of other types of projects may well be governed by other factors. The specific nature of our findings points up the direction of needed future research. Other types of urban renewal projects need to be evaluated. The ultimate purpose of such studies should be to provide data from which generalizations can be derived on the critical factors affecting broader classes of renewal projects.

Urban Renewal: A Strategy for Information and Analysis

LOWDON WINGO, JR.

One of the difficulties in probing the rationale of urban renewal policy is the lack of consensus about both what the program is and what it ought to be. It certainly began as a housing program: its antecedents were instituted in large degree to improve the welfare of the low income consumers of housing services. Other interests have injected new viewpoints and objectives which have diluted considerably the housing goals. City planners have shaped many of the federal and local viewpoints which measure the aims of the program in terms of the redesign and reconstruction of the city. Central business district interests have seen in the program the possibility of the massive effort necessary to arrest the drain of urban decentralization and to refocus the economic and social life of the region on its core—a revitalized, transformed central business district. What

is urban renewal? It depends on whom you ask.

In a narrow sense urban renewal addresses the processes which influence the condition of the city's physical plant. The plant ages, becomes obsolescent, and is consumed in the production of shelter and other services. It is also constantly being renewed through the market processes in the form of capital replacement investment. Nevertheless, whatever the overall picture, the *intra*metropolitan picture is very different. Extremes which are buried in the regional averages are quickly revealed, particularly in the different rates of capital replacement in the various parts of the city. Some areas get left behind with deteriorating physi-

Reprinted by permission of the *Journal of the American Institute of Planners*, XXXII, No. 3 (May 1966), 143–154.

cal plants even in periods of overall growth, while others experience not only capital replacement but enhancement of their physical plant.

Urban renewal decision-making, then, focuses on the older parts of the region, while treating them in the context of overall regional development. The phenomena with which it must deal are essentially aspects of the intrametropolitan processes at work shaping the spatial organization of the metropolitan region. Accordingly, an information system for urban renewal decision-making can build on the state of knowledge of intraregional processes and the special informational requirements of urban renewal decisions.

A broader construction of the urban renewal problem would embrace the critical ecological dimensions which accompany the differential rates of replacement of the plant in various parts of the city. It is clearly not coincidental that characteristics of the metropolitan social structure are closely related to the condition and rate of replacement of the region's housing stock—poor people, for example, consume only the dwelling services of a deteriorating, obsolete segment of the stock. The relationship between marginal firms and old, poorly maintained commercial structures is similarly clear. Because there tend to be concentrations of such deteriorated structures in the city, the "problem" of blight exists.

The emergence of blight in the physical plant of the city is the formal justification for the development of an urban renewal program and policy. But the deterioration of structures and the use or misuse of the land on which they are situated proceed from a concurrence of many factors. The elimination of blight is simple, if expensive. Altering the processes—pathological or benign—which bring it about is another matter. Nevertheless, a useful restatement of the *policy problem* of urban renewal would shift the emphasis away from efforts to arrest blight directly and toward the determination of how much and what kinds of community actions should be taken to achieve specified levels of conservation of the physical plant of the community. The evolution of urban renewal policy has produced institutional arrangements of an extraordinarily complex nature as well as a special set of policy tools

and approaches. The policy takes the form of a particular sequence of decisions involving numerous public and private agents exercising a multitude of interests and viewpoints.[1]

THE CHARACTER OF THE URBAN RENEWAL PROBLEM: ITS EVOLUTION

This very dissensus suggests the value of a review of the evolution of public policy dealing with the physical state of the city, for urban renewal is the product of this evolution. Public concern over the slum can be traced back into the nineteenth century when it was basically a social problem growing out of the poverty of immigrants who poured into old housing surrounding the central business area, where their labor market was concentrated. In the early part of the twentieth century the State of New York adopted a series of tenement codes under the police powers to compel a modicum of capital replacement by owners on behalf of the health and safety of tenants.

In the 1920's recognition of the effects of external diseconomies among certain classes of land use motivated the development and judicial validation of zoning. "Superior uses," such as housing, were protected from the blighting effects (social costs) which certain "inferior uses," such as industrial activities, imposed upon them. While zoning may have restrained some effects of deterioration in the upper strata

---

1 Recent research activities supported by the Urban Renewal Administration promise to raise significantly the level of analysis, projection, and policy formulation in urban renewal. The Community Renewal Program in Pittsburgh developed a model to make conditional predictions about the spatial distribution of land use and the state of the physical plant of the central city. See Community Renewal Program, Department of City Planning, Pittsburgh, Pa., Progress Report No. 5, *Simulation Model* (January, 1964), and Progress Report No. 6, *TOMM (Time Oriented Metropolitan Model)* (January, 1964). A parallel program of analysis in San Francisco proposed to approach the problem through the analysis and simulation of land, housing, plant, and investment markets. See Arthur D. Little, Inc., *San Francisco Community Renewal Program—Purpose, Scope and Methodology*, a Progress Report to the Department of City Planning of the City and County of San Francisco, (August, 1963). These efforts reflect the desire of the Urban Renewal Administration to bring about a more sophisticated analytical format than has yet developed out of local urban renewal programs.

of the housing stock, it seems to have been less successful in improving slum housing conditions. The New Deal housing reformers determined to tackle the problem head-on with direct public intervention in the housing market. Where private investment was not forthcoming, the public would build new housing for slum occupants directed toward two effects: to provide a high quality component to the low income stocks, and to drive down rents in the private stock by expanding the supply. This latter effect was later compromised by the coupling of public housing to slum clearance, so that frequently the stock was not expanded at all. When this policy became too expensive for public housing, the clearance objective was suppressed.

Housing codes proliferated after World War II. Like the New York tenement codes, they set standards under the police powers compelling certain minimal capital replacement in the housing stock as a whole. They sought to establish limits to permissible disinvestment, that is reduction of capital value, in the low income stock. At the same time national housing policy emphasized rapid expansion of the total stock. That strategy focused on the expansion of supply in the profitable upper and middle income housing markets, relying on the "filtering down" of the vacated older dwellings to expand the stock for the lower income markets. By *current* standards such a strategy might well be construed as the deliberate acceleration of blight. The rapid rate of urban growth and the release of pent-up wartime demand obscured the extent to which the filtering process actually worked for the lower income groups.

The National Housing Act of 1949 introduced urban redevelopment as an approach to reduce the effects of blight in residential areas. It recognized that public investment alone could not master the problem of low income housing and thus revised the role of public investment to one of eliminating the obstacles to private investment in blighted areas. This it did under the assumption that externalities (effects upon the site by nearby land uses), site assembly limitations, and demolition (site preparation) costs were the principal obstacles to private investment.

The Housing Act of 1954 evolved from the awareness that the redevelopment of slums could not take place on a sufficient scale to equal the rate at which new blight was taking place. It took a more sophisticated view of the complexity of differential real estate investment flows. It was concerned with the broad processes of blight in lieu of the focus on the slum, and so brought together an arsenal of policies: public absorption of inflated property values and investment in new social overhead in blighted areas; "spot clearance" of blighting land uses and structures; zoning, housing, and building codes with strong enforcement provisions; private credit; community organization; and others. The strategy, then—eliminate the worst housing, rehabilitate the declining, stabilize and conserve the good. The "planned outcome" emerged as an important policy dimension, and the social welfare housing goals were diluted.[2] In the 1961 Act the Community Renewal Program made its appearance as a general staff function to develop community-wide strategies to combat blight in the city as a whole.[3]

Two correlative developments deserve note. First, nonresidential renewal has rapidly increased in importance: earlier acts permitted up to 10 percent of a project to be used for nonresidential (i.e., consumer service) use; now 40 percent of a project site may be planned for industry or commercial activity. Again the policy has shifted away from housing objectives to an attack on the many dimensions of urban deterioration. Metropolitan planning activities have been stimulated and supported by the Urban Renewal Administration's 701 program as a complementary activity to urban renewal, recognizing the regionwide nature of the processes at work in urban growth and change.

In short, the evolution of public policy has shifted the policy focus from the slum area to the neighborhood, to the central city, and ultimately to the region; from limited concerns with the lowest housing strata to the total hous-

2 The program has been well described in David M. Walter, "A New Pattern for Urban Renewal," and in Ashley A. Foard and Hilbert Fefferman, "Federal Urban Renewal Legislation," in *Law and Contemporary Problems XXV*, (Durham, N.C.: Duke University, August, 1960), 635–84.
3 See S. Leigh Curry, Jr., "The Community Renewal Process," *The Federal Bar Journal*, XXI (Summer, 1961), 358–71.

ing stock and even to the state of the physical plant of the region; from a policeman-and-policed relationship between local governments and parts of the private housing sector to an intricate net of public-private relations into which are drawn neighborhood organizations, financial institutions, welfare agencies, local interest groups, and the complex array of housing, planning, land use, and transportation agencies from every level of government. The motivating force in this evolution of policy has been, of course, the changing perception of the problem. Accordingly, we have to begin with the observation that we address the problem at a particular state in its evolution: it will change further, perhaps in response to new information availabilities, but at the last, new institutions for providing information and analysis need to comprehend this fact. Further, we have to begin with a view of urban renewal as comprehending a multitude of interests each with its own expectations and criteria for urban renewal policy.[4]

THE CHARACTER OF THE URBAN RENEWAL PROBLEM: ITS CONTENT

What, then, is urban renewal concerned about? Legislative preambles set forth the purpose of eliminating *slums* and *blight* in cities, but these are descriptive rather than operational terms, and there is precious little authoritative commentary on their meanings. Thus it becomes necessary to clothe these with interpretation.

The slum is the more ambiguous of these terms. The legislative authors possibly construed slums as being exaggerated cases of concentrated blight in residential areas—the high priority target of renewal efforts. It is no longer possible, however, to so restrict the meaning, for the slum is in many cases a genuine social community in the culture of poverty with all of the institutions of support and adjustment and accommodation new urban migrants as well as low income groups need. Because it is more than merely a housing problem, the slum attracts the special attention and concern of a variety of public and private activities. In short, the slum is an organic part of the complex urban society which serves important so-

cial and economic functions for the region as a whole.[5] It is no mystery why these characteristics should focus on the poorest housing stock in the region; the crucial consideration here is that programs addressed to remedy the slum problem as a problem of physical blight will find themselves face to face with a bewildering set of social and economic dimensions.

In the literature "blight" seems to refer to the condition of physical plant which has been the subject of net disinvestment over a period of time. It is identified with properties on which outlays for repair, maintenance, renovation, and modernization have been less than those needed to maintain the property in its original condition, or at a stable level of economic productivity. When disinvestment takes place in such a degree and in such ways as apparently to result in a substantial misallocation of the community's resources or in systematic inefficiencies in the region's productive activities, it becomes a policy problem. While the current state of urban renewal policies emphasizes the arrest of blight over the mitigation of slums, we should ultimately find ourselves centrally concerned with identification of desired rates of capital replacement in terms of the productivity of site *and* plant together.

In general, the phenomena of blight fit comfortably within a framework of economic analysis because of the central role of resource allocation. The problem of the slum as a socio-economic-physical phenomenon presents issues much more complex for the development of public policy. The primary interest here focuses on the processes of blight and the proper role of public policies attendant thereon.

Net disinvestment in improved real estate can be viewed as the resultant of two sets of

4 Robert A. Dahl has provided a penetrating study of the local politics of urban renewal in *Who Governs?* (New Haven and London: Yale University Press, 1961). Richard U. Ratcliff has studied the interaction of private investment decisions with public renewal policies in *Private Investment in Urban Redevelopment*, Research Report 17 (Berkeley: The University of California, The Real Estate Research Program, 1961). Both amply illustrate the complexities of the urban renewal policy making.
5 For an informative analysis of the impact of urban renewal on the social organism of the slum, see Peter Marris, "A Report on Urban Renewal in the United States," in Leonard J. Duhl, (ed.), *The Urban Condition* (New York: Basic Books, 1963).

factors. One set embraces the developments which tend to reduce the productive capacity of the facility: aging, technological obsolescence, and sheer capital consumption. The way in which a structure ages is largely a matter of the character of its construction and the physical factors of the environment which are basically exogenous to our consideration. Obsolescence, by contrast, can be viewed as a by-product of a dynamic society in which innovation and fashion constantly generate the marketing of new and preferred items. Previously produced items find themselves in a position of market inferiority. The housing market demonstrates in classic fashion the way in which obsolescence takes place: new styles, postwar innovations in construction and the use of space, and new household technologies have given the prewar housing stock a position of market inferiority. Factory obsolescence takes place when new processes, new equipment, or more efficient spatial organization give new plants an advantage in production costs over earlier plants, a process which has frequently been pointed to as a primary factor in the headlong movement of many of Boston's centrally located industrial activities to the new peripheral industrial areas along famed Route 128. Finally, structures are "consumed" simply by use at a rate reflected by maintenance costs.

The other set of factors consists of the elements affecting the demand for urban improved urban real estate through their impact on the income earning expectations of the real estate in various uses. These are as complex and myriad as the kinds of use which are possible, but in general have to do with levels of social overhead, externalities among economic activities, and access to inputs and to markets. If *A* is the most profitable use of site *K*, anything which influences the profitability of *A* at *K* will influence the flow of investment in the improvements on *K*: *A's* competitive position in its market and its future prospects is the significant datum.

While the capital consumption factors are easily conceptualized, the capital replacement factors involve the total web of regional and interregional economic relationships. Physical blight is not a simple phenomenon; it is a symptom of various kinds of changes taking place in the urban economy. To say that capital

disinvestment takes place in segments of the urban plant is not to say that this is an economic pathology. We must go one step further and determine the degree to which imperfections in the markets are misallocating community resources, either in the sense that they can be reallocated to yield a higher net return, or in the sense that disadvantages are thereby imposed on the community which justify our efforts to divert some public and private investment flows. Renewal policies may impair productive efficiency, but even this may be warranted if the social gains are great enough. At the other extreme are the prospects that both efficiency and social returns can be realized by appropriate diversion of investment flows. What we are left with, then, is an examination of the determinants of the rate of capital-replacing investment in the city's physical plant. More specifically, we need to be concerned with the differential rates of replacement which produce blight in particular parts of the city.

THE VARIETIES OF BLIGHT

Recently the urban renewal problem has been the focus of a number of theoretical explorations by economists interested, first, in characterizing the economic dimensions of the problem, and, second, in specifying policy criteria in urban renewal programs (Davis and Whinston, Rothenberg, Bailey, Schaaf, Baumol, Lessinger, Bloom, and others). Their work has demonstrated that the reduction of the flow of capital-replacing investment can stem from either of two quite distinct effects (at the level of theory, if not on the ground). The first will be labeled the *externalities effects,* and the second, the *structural effects.* Since dominance of either in a specific situation could lead to quite different policy conclusions and require different analytical information, it is worth exploring both briefly.

Davis and Whinston have discussed the case in which the productivities of *A* and *B* are interdependent, where policy making is completely decentralized. They expand on the prospect that a "Prisoner's Dilemma" situation typifies much, if not all, urban blight, such that investment by both *A* and *B* in their adjoining properties will yield high joint returns, say of 7 percent when alternative investments are yielding 4 percent. If A invests in his property and B does not follow suit, B will obtain some benefits from A's investment without any investment of his own, while A's returns will be depressed because of the blighted condition of B. Each can be assured a minimum return of 4 percent by declining the property investment and will perhaps accrue a considerably greater return, should the other improve his property unilaterally. On the other hand, to invest would make possible a moderately high return but expose one to the considerably lower return if the other failed to follow suit. In short, both are trapped by the uncertainty of the other's behavior into the position where the optimum strategy for each independently produces lower returns than in the case in which each was required to follow a strategy which would maximize the yield to both. A coalition is possible only where each understands the pay-off possibilities to the other as well as his own, and where this condition does not exist the intervention of a third party empowered to require this behavior of both is necessary to maximize the returns to both.

Davis and Whinston see this interdependence trap as the central phenomenon in blight.[6] A will not invest in his property because if B does not follow suit he will lose, and B is better off not to follow suit, so that capital-replacing investment declines and blight follows or intensifies. Only the intervention of government constraining all to invest can realize the maximum returns to the total amount of investment. The government internalizes the problem to achieve the optimum allocation of resources by setting up the investment constraints in the form of minimum standards. This concept of the processes of blight and its remedy, although only recently articulated in this form, has been implicit in much of the evolution of urban renewal policies.

A contrasting case, however, is where although A's productivity depends on B, B's is independent of A. Thus B can behave without calculating the effects of his behavior on A, and A must adjust his behavior to his best estimate of what B is likely to do. A may suffer uncompensated losses which discourage investment in his building capital at that location. (He may also realize gains.) Where there are many A's,

B will be considered a blighting influence or nuisance subject to regulation or even to being "redeveloped out," by spot clearance. To the extent that such externalities condition the productivity of establishments situated in urban areas, the altered yield of capital renewing investment in physical plant in areas affected by them can be expected to influence quite directly the differential proliferation of blight.

The structural effects of blight derive from the urban economy itself where the etiological processes involved in urban blight develop. The simple fact is that much disinvestment in the urban physical plant can be construed as a response to changes in the technological, social, and economic organization of the metropolitan region. Since World War II, popular tastes, rising family incomes, and national housing policy have conspired to generate the low density, scattered single family housing tracts around the metropolitan hinterlands. Suburbia has now become a way of life to child-oriented middle income families whose demand is probably the most active factor in the housing market. The older stock filtering down to lower income groups was quite logically subject to disinvestment of capital, which is to say it was increasingly sensitive to blight as we have defined it. This effect was, of course, mitigated where growth of demand for suburban housing was more rapid than the growth of supply and decentralization was deferred. In static or declining areas one would expect to find the blight in the old stock much more rapid. At any rate, the changing structure of demand for housing is possibly the most powerful factor in blighting the older stock.

Changing technologies of transportation and communication have played powerful roles in recent years in the reorganization of the metropolitan economy. These have had the effect of vastly increasing the supply of space accessible to the entire web of urban activities. Land values tend to be based in part on differential transportation costs and such changes could obviously not produce effects in any neutral fashion. These developments have reshuffled the comparative advantages of location and

6 Otto Davis and Andrew Whinston, "The Economics of Urban Renewal," in *Law and Contemporary Problems*, XXVI (St. Paul: West Publishing Co., Winter, 1961), 105–118.

the resulting widespread changes in the land values have been generally accompanied by disinvestment at the disadvantaged locations of the older housing and nonhousing physical plant of the city. Continued investment in transportation systems in metropolitan regions is likely to vastly increase this effect.

The changing technology of production has contributed to this restructuring of the city. The new technologies tend to make intensive use of both space and capital and rely on higher skills than their predecessors. On all these counts decentralized industrial locations are by far the most economical, and the major share of new investment is taking place in the metropolitan hinterlands. This trend not only accelerates disinvestment in the older central city industrial areas but accelerates the processes of decentralization by reducing the employment ties between the central city and the suburbs.

Accompanying all of these structural changes has been the reorganization of consumer services with new orientation toward the rich, middle class markets for goods and services now spread over the scattered suburban margins of the region. The suburban shopping center is the principal institution of this change. As its popularity has grown so has the market for CBD outlets declined. At some point the decline must be reflected in disinvestment in the intensely built up retail core of the CBD. This perhaps more than anything else is the source of demands for commercial renewal of the urban core.

Blight, then, is not a simple pathology of improperly maintained structures. Its causal factors are myriad and complex, and whether it is good or bad depends on what public policy is trying to achieve: if the only alternative to cheap, dilapidated housing is expensive dilapidated housing—or no housing at all—it is likely that the former will be preferred by low-income, disadvantaged groups and by the political elements who seek to defend their interests. The short run symptoms of changes in the profitability of elements of the housing stock will be manifested as changes in the vacancy rates and rent levels in that part of the stock. The way in which these occur, and their persistence, may offer us important indicators of coming changes in real estate investment

flows which are almost assuredly the long range response to these new demand conditions. Where rents and occupancy rates are rising, capital replacement is likely to be high, and the investment in new additions to this part of the stock is likely to increase. Where they are declining, it can be expected that capital

THE URBAN RENEWAL POLICY PROBLEM: HOW TO HELP WHOM TO OPTIMIZE WHAT AND WHERE

replacement will decline until there is a net disinvestment leading ultimately to a blighted condition.

Though we may feel that the arrest of urban blight is not an operational goal for public policy, still no other simple, operational characterization of the problem can describe urban renewal as it is actually carried on. It is hardly possible to specify an objective function that will satisfy all interests, nor does it appear feasible to order goal statements in such a way as to avoid important conflicts. Why this should be so is no mystery. The state of the community's physical plant cannot be viewed analytically as a problem divorced from the complex social, economic, and political processes which take place in it. Therefore a policy with other than just cosmetic objectives must intervene in these processes and must engage the multitude of interests as well as public and private purposes involved in the urban economy.

Any reading of the urban renewal literature will bring out a variety of goal statements which purport to represent the public interest in urban renewal. The elimination of slums is perhaps the goal statement with the longest and most vigorous history in the housing movement; as suggested earlier, it embraces many more problems than the condition of the region's physical plant. The arrest of blight is more recent and more practical in terms of the policy tools available. Municipalities have strongly supported renewal programs because they promised to increase the fiscal resources of hard-pressed central cities by expanding the tax base with new structures and new activities in the urban core. Rejuvenation of the central business district—and the related conservation of property values there—has drawn the support of powerful property and retail interests who have seen in renewal programs effective tools to improve the levels of services, to provide new sites for the expansion of economic activities downtown, and to lure the wealth of the suburban markets back to the center. Civic groups have espoused urban renewal programs in the hope that the flight of high income and leadership groups to the suburbs could be arrested. And the middle class generally has seen urban renewal as a program to achieve aesthetic qualities in urban life which the private market, with its presumptions about the public taste, seems incapable of realizing. Then, improvement of the housing welfare of the urban resident has been strongly put forth at the federal level as an important aim of the program from the beginning. Although other purposes of the urban renewal program have increased their relative significance, the housing objectives are still of primary importance.

The point is that all of these—and others—are legitimate objectives of the program. The complex nature of the program depends on the participation of a considerable array of interests, groups, and agencies, each of which imprints its own purposes on it. In the private sector, urban renewal confronts property owners and their associations; consumer interests; civic groups; taxpayer organizations; investment bankers; redevelopment entrepreneurs; and design, aesthetic, and architectural interests. On the public side, not only do the three levels of government become involved, but they become involved at many points. At the local level alone urban renewal touches on the functions of municipal agencies responsible for planning, for public works, for social welfare services, for transportation, for education, and for public safety, as well as for housing and redevelopment. Similarly, many state and federal agencies find themselves involved in the urban renewal decision-making process. Since each of these groups and agencies needs to interpret urban renewal activities in the light of its own mission, its participation will require information inputs germane to that mission.

Accordingly, these multiple interests and their respective objectives raise questions about the value of a normative model in the evaluation of alternative urban renewal policies. To select one objective as primary and all the others as secondary in seeking optimum policies simply would not reflect the structure of decision-making in a fashion consistent with the real world. Instead, a more useful approach would attempt to expedite and rationalize the existing structure of decision-making by improving the information environment for all of the public and private interests involved; this fundamentally is the strategy which underlies this paper.

SOME SUGGESTIONS FOR
A STATISTICAL SYSTEM FOR
REGIONAL HOUSING POLICY DECISIONS

Making such a strategy explicit carries with it a number of implications for the development of an information system to improve the character of urban renewal decisions and policies.

1. It places emphasis on the use of positive models (simulations of the real world which seek to define causal relationships and predict the consequences of alternative policies) and their information requirements in contrast to the use of normative models (which seek to identify a *best* course of action, given some description of the decision maker's objectives) with their more particular information requirements. The outputs of such a program will be variables with a high degree of relevance for various kinds of decision-makers involved in the urban renewal decision processes.

2. Communication and interpretation of relevant information for the various decision-makers emerge as crucial functions if each is to integrate such information effectively into his plans and policies.

3. New institutions will be required to monitor changes in improved real estate and in the transactions which affect it, if the timeliness of the information is to be maintained. Immediacy of the information will be important to all parties, and an integrated system of information and analysis can provide this by permitting new information to be played through the system to suggest in advance changes in significant dimensions which appear to be in the offing or which are likely to follow from actions of the participants.

4. A critical dimension of such an information system is the institutional arrangements

through which the information becomes translated into action.

In the following suggestions for such a system these institutional imperatives should be considered implicit.

An integrated information system such as that proposed by Perloff and Leven [7] can be expanded and elaborated specifically to facilitate housing policy decisions, recognizing that these decisions are indeed related to other developmental issues equally central to the urban renewal policy problem. Ultimately, we are concerned with the whole web of policies for urban development, of which urban renewal is but one aspect, but decisions will continue to be made about individual kinds of problems, and the information needs will derive from the way in which the problems are perceived by the present set of institutions. Indeed, a set of accounts can serve not only the particular purpose of providing each agent with more reliable information for his decision needs, but of making him sensitive to the interdependencies between his behavior and that of others.

Finally, housing policy for a metropolitan region is not a monolithic, highly centralized set of decisions. It engages every governmental level. It involves zoning, housing, and building codes of municipalities. It will be strongly influenced by regionwide service and resource policies. It involves a substantial part of the urban land market, of local public expenditures to support the housing stock, and of the whole real estate market apparatus, including investment institutions. The function of an information system here ought to be the coordination through common information and analysis of the activities and programs influencing the supply and demand conditions surrounding the urban housing stock.

A system of statistical information for urban renewal policies should be designed to serve a number of purposes directly associated with the decision-making process. In the first place, it should provide identification by appropriate and consistent criteria of the sectors of the urban physical plant which require intervention in one form or another by public agencies. In other words, it should offer current information and analysis on the state of the housing stock and the changing composition of housing demand.[8] More than this, however, the system will need to reflect critical causal and associative relations among variables, if it is to serve well as a policy instrument. It should be able to facilitate diagnosis of the undesirable states of portions of the physical stock of the community as they develop. It should facilitate projection of the impact of changes in important exogenous variables on the stock of community physical capital. It should facilitate the "testing" of policy alternatives in terms of

7 Werner Hirsch in his article, "Design and Use of Regional Accounts," which appeared in the May 1962 issue of the *American Economic Review,* has suggested that intraregional accounts should be, in effect, really disaggregated regional accounts under the assumption that many regional issues are strongly influenced by the intraregional character or distribution of the factors involved.

William Niskanen, in an article, "The Use of Intrametropolitan Data," shifted the focus to the analysis and projection of intraregional problems having unique systemic characteristics arising from behavioral variables whose significance depends on their locational or spatial dimensions. (Werner Z. Hirsch, ed., *Elements of Regional Accounts,* The Johns Hopkins Press, 1964.) He has recommended the development of predictive models of intraregional growth and change for the basic information system. Britton Harris in "An Accounts Framework for Intrametropolitan Models" (Hirsch, ed., *ibid.*), advances Niskanen's theme by clarifying the relationship of intraregional accounts to intraregional models. Systematic intraregional accounts will facilitate the development of intraregional models, but the causal structure of such models will require a great deal of information not appropriate to the accounts framework. Beyond this, it seems clear that intraregional accounts will have significant roles in decision-making apart from the analytical use of intrametropolitan models. Finally, Harris notes that intraregional accounts can advance metropolitan analysis by providing the informational bases for comparative analysis of metropolitan phenomena.

Harvey Perloff and Charles Leven, in "Toward an Integrated System of Regional Accounts: Stocks, Flows and the Analysis of the Public Sector," (Hirsch, ed., *ibid.*), like Hirsch, see intrametropolitan accounts as disaggregated regional accounts, but in an integrated system of accounts and associated information which tie natural, capital, and human resource accounts (assets) into a set of income, product, and interindustry accounts (flows). This development not only makes it feasible to trace effects through the information system, but generates hypotheses about functional relationships for supporting econometric analysis.

8 The Perloff-Leven system of accounts includes a "non-human resource account" tabulating the area and value of land, the floor area, base area, and value of buildings, and the value of equipment. Disaggregated by area, this account would provide valuable information to supplement the dwelling unit information. See Perloff and Leven, *op. cit.* pp. 191–194.

their consequences for significant variables, and should thus aid in decision-making. Analyses of the feasibility of various alternatives may similarly be expedited by the availability of a flow of statistical information. Finally, an information system should provide mechanisms for monitoring crucial variables with the kind of immediacy needed for "in flight" policy corrections while programs are in operation. These requirements suggest the need for several layers of information of varying degrees of generality. An information system incorporating these qualities is described in the Appendix to this article.

First, an integrated regional information system would seem to be almost indispensable to provide a constant background of changing regional aggregates against which to view changes in the community's physical capital. The need for information for the region as a whole on the capital stock, human resources, and governmental transactions has been emphasized by Perloff and Leven for policy-making generally.[9] The regional housing market, labor markets, public services, and land resources are all features of urban growth and change whose interdependencies make regional performance a significant datum for urban renewal. Second, we need a constant flow of information about the interrelationships among parts of the urban region. This is the kind of information which would be the output variables of such intraregional models as proposed by Harris and Niskanen.[10] Here we are concerned with the changing functional roles played by parts of the region in the regional economy and the linkages among them: suburban-central city relationships, the regional organization of distributive activities, the relationships between homes and workplaces, and so forth.

Another sector of the information system needs to focus on political jurisdictions simply because they are the source of the institutions, authorities, and fiscal resources through which the public decisions concerning the region's physical plant are made. Indeed, urban renewal legislation is addressed to such jurisdictions to be agents of the program. Different policies among regional jurisdictions can exert a substantial influence on the investment flows which bring about changes in the character and distribution of activities throughout the region. Consequently, such information has as a major objective highlighting the way in which the individual locality is participating in regional growth and change.

Finally, we are concerned about the simple distribution of important aggregates among parts of the city, and how these tend to respond to changing regional and local aggregates. This level of information deals with the characteristics of small areas such as, perhaps, census tracts. The purpose of such information is to identify the "grain" of local conditions of blight, and so to make possible the diagnosis of blight which is primarily an effect of surrounding conditions from the more general case of structural blight, which is largely a demand phenomenon.

It goes without saying that of equal importance to the content of such an information system is the establishment of a framework for and a process of continuing analysis of the data, interpretation of changes, and communication of the implications of the developing information to the array of public and private decision-makers who are jointly responsible for the differential flows of investment into (and disinvestment out of) the region's physical plant. The use of common information can provide a powerful element of coordination and predictability to the behavior of various public and private decision-makers. Such information will be used in common only if it provides a clearly superior base on which to formulate policies and make investments.

To make such a system superior by itself would be a costly proposition. The physical plant of our cities represents a large proportion of the total wealth of the nation and the flows of investment induced by its growth and change are a significant fraction of our gross national product. We are, in effect, warranted to make some commitments of financial resources to the management of this vast national asset. Actually, to the extent that such a system would supplement other information institutions within the context of a regional informa-

9 With the addition of income information, this information could be derived directly from disaggregation of the Perloff-Leven "human resource account." See Perloff and Leven, *op. cit.*, pp. 194-7.
10 See footnote 4.

tion system, the costs of data gathering, analysis, projection, interpretation, and communication of information about the changing character of the urban plant would probably not exceed the order of magnitude of current public and private expenditures for information on and analysis of these matters. As urban renewal and housing policies continue to increase their roles in the growth and development of our cities, they will have to be seen as continuing processes which require as indispensable inputs continuing flows of organized statistical information and ongoing institutions for its analysis, interpretation, and communication. Only in this way will it be possible for the urban community to determine what kinds of urban development alternatives are possible and to select the most effective set of public and private instrumentalities to work for the desired alternative in the conservation and development of the urban physical plant.

APPENDIX
A STATISTICAL INFORMATION SYSTEM FOR REGIONAL HOUSING POLICY MAKING

The following information system is based on several assumptions. Since urban renewal and housing policies of government tend to intervene in specific ways around specific projects or developments, a reasonably detailed breakdown of information is desirable. The system should also be able to reflect the dominant spatial interdependencies on both the supply and demand sides of the metropolitan housing market. This means that the organization of the system will reflect an interrelated set of hypotheses joining the major variables, some of which are suggested below. It is also based on assumptions about specific kinds of data which clearly are not readily available everywhere, but to the extent that it can put into perspective the need for such information, it can help to make the case for its development.

The most obvious set of data needed to inform decisions about investment flows in the housing market is some description of the stock of housing units broken down by important functional characteristics and by its distribution among the various parts of the region. We can characterize this in the following fashion:

(1) $\quad _k x_i =$ the number of housing units of class k located in subarea i.

k represents the classification of housing stock into quality and function groups such that each should ideally behave as a homogeneous good on the market. The functional differentiae would distinguish size and character of construction (for example, detached, semi-detached, walk-up apartment, elevator apartment, and so forth). Qualitative differentiae would introduce age, condition of structure, and internal services. Every group k then would be distinguished from all other such groups either in terms of the character of the unit or its quality. The subscript i introduces the spatial structure of the housing market, as defined by the way in which the region is broken down into subareas for analysis. i might be a simple grid square in a coordinate system covering the whole region. On the other hand, the externalities effect in urban blight argues for a system of subareas which would help to distinguish problems characterized by externalities from those of more general character in the housing stock. Thus, where possible, it would be useful to have subareas defined with an eye to degrees of homogeneity with respect to k.

On the demand side, two dimensions of housing market need to be brought to the fore. On the assumption that the household is the most appropriate consuming unit, the information system needs to emphasize those household characteristics most closely associated with consumption patterns. Let

(2) $\quad _h z_j =$ the number of households of class h who are functionally associated with area j.

The classification system h is based on socioeconomic characteristics such as household size and composition, income, race, and similar variables. For all practical purposes, j represents the household's functionally associated subarea, that in which is located the activity exerting the primary locational attraction of the household. In most cases this would be the employment site of these households, since the home-work relationship effectively structures large parts of the housing market in space.

$_hz_j$ is, of course, closely associated with the occupational-industrial structure of the regional economy disaggregated by subareas. Under some circumstances j might represent something other than an employment area: for students it could be the area in which a college or university is located; for retired persons it could be the area in which medical facilities exist.

At this point, we have a subregional distribution of the housing stock by market classes. In addition, we have the demand side of the market structured by consumption aspects and distributed really in terms of dominant locational determinants. The supply and demand aspects can be brought together to define an occupancy variable thus:

$_{hk}W_{ij}$ = that part of $_{k^{\wedge}i}$ occupied by $_hz_j$, or the number of class h households based in area j occupying k class housing in area i.

In this expression, ij is the journey-to-work relationship, while hk is the more conventional mapping of households of various characteristics on the qualitatively structured housing stock. Vacancy rates can then be defined as follows:

(3)
$$_kg_i = \frac{_kx_i - _kW_i}{_kx_i},$$

where

$$_kW_i = \sum_h \sum_j {}_{hk}W_{ij}$$

and
$$i, j = (1, 2, 3, \quad q, \quad n), (i \neq j)$$
$$h = (1, 2, 3, \ldots .m)$$
$$k = (1, 2, 3, \ldots .l)$$

for any segment of the stock defined by location and class of housing.

Ultimately the datum of interest in regional housing policy (or urban renewal decisions) is the succession of changes in the variable $_{hk}W_{ij}$. They reflect the outcome of housing market processes at work in the regional economy, but more than this, they suggest the appropriate form of housing policy objectives. Thus, one might identify one set of values for $_{hk}W_{ij}$, say $_{hk}W_{ij}$, which is the preferred set, or the regional housing policy goals. Then, the policy objectives emerge quite directly. They are the actions designed to close the gap between the current values of $_{hk}w_{ij}$ and $_{hk}W_{ij}$. Clearly the values of $_{hk}W_{ij}$ are derived from a number of more general determinations. The ij relationship depends on the planned distribution of employment areas throughout the region. It depends on the projected character of the regional transportation system and on the institutional and behavioral variables which influence the locational and travel decisions of future users. The h values are for the most part exogenous and will derive from projections of the regional economy and population. The k values will be considerably influenced by the existing stock of housing, as well as by the region's view of what constitutes improvement in the level of housing welfare.

In addition to these stock-occupancy data, we need a related slate of information to explain changes in these data which would include at least the following:

$_aY_i$ = the performance index of public service a in area i; and,
$_aC_i$ = the cost of producing service a at level Y in i.

There is much evidence that variations in levels of such public services as education, public safety, recreation, and transportation (and of such private services consumed by households, such as retailing) have a substantial influence on the character of the local housing market.

(4)
$$_{hk}W_{ij} = f\,(_aY_i)$$
$$\text{and } _aY_i = f\,(_aC_i, _bY_i \ _kA_i, _ku_i)$$
$$\text{where } a, b = (1, 2, \ldots \ldots .p), (a \neq b)$$
$$i, j = (1, 2, \ldots q, \ldots n), (i \neq j),$$
and 1, 2, q = areas constituting local gov't-unit Q
$_kA_i$ = the average assessed value of k-class units in i.
$_ku_i$ = aggregate real property tax rate of k in i

The construction of such indices may involve some difficulty and may not be very elegant, but an instrumental understanding of the regional housing market would not be complete without introducing some such variables, even in the form of ordinals or rankings. Clearly many public sector actions to achieve housing goals will take place through planned changes in levels of public services. Such performance indices offer analytical opportunities for relating such actions to their impacts.

(5) $_k r_i$ = index of the mean price of housing services of class k in area i.

Although such information is not easy to come by, it will be indispensable in the general analysis of the regional housing market, in approximately the following form:

(6) $_k r_i = f\,(_k x_j,\, _h z_j,\, _k g_i)$
and $_{hk} w_{ij} = f\,(_k r_i)$
for all j, h, and k
where $j = (1, 2, 3, \ldots \ldots n)$

Then we need to know something about the flow of resources into construction:

(7) Let $_k V_i$ = the total value of improvements made to housing of class k in area i, and

(8) $_k V_i$ = the total cost of new units of class k constructed in area i during a specified period of time.

Both of these variables are measures of gross flows of investment into sectors of the housing stock, but they respond to different circumstances and produce outcomes of different dimensions. We can, for example, posit an implicit rate of depreciation of the stock of k-class units in i which over a period of time would be reflected in qualitative downward shifts among classes. The degree of such a shift should be, in part, a function of $_k v_i$. On the other hand, the flow of capital into segment ki might be sufficiently great as to produce upward qualitative shifts. The creation of new units (and hence $_k V_i$) tends to affect only the top qualitative strata of the stock, in contrast. Then, the lagged relation would be

(9) $(_k x_i)_t = f\,(_k V_i,\, _k V_i,\, _k x_i)_{t-1}$
(10)   And, let $_k(uA)_i$ = real property tax costs (average of k in i).

These variables need to be related to the service performance indices to fill out the picture of how public sector financial policies influence the character of local housing markets, so that

(11) $_k V_i,\, _k V_i = f[_k(uA_j,\, _N r_j,\, _k g_i)]$
where $j = (1, 2, .\, i, \ldots n)$
Finally, we need a set of variables representing land uses:

(12) $_K s_i$ = the area of land devoted to land use K in area i, where k represents land in private use, a land in public use, and o designates vacant land, all subsets of K, then

(13) $_k V_i = f\,(_o s_i)$

Other analytical variables will be germane to specific relationships, and this brief discussion does not purport to be exhaustive. Even as attenuated as it is in this presentation, metropolitan housing market analysis can represent a very large and complex problem. The key variable $_{hk} w_{ij}$ in a region divided into a hundred rather large zones and dealing with ten consumer classes and ten housing classes can have as many as one million values simply to describe the structure of the housing even without identifying the analytical relations and sequences. The important role of analysis is not only to provide some predictive power with respect to the variable $_{hk} w_{ij}$ but to do so with generalizations capable of simplifying the entire structure. Thus, for example, the ij relations in the housing market have received some powerful analysis in recent years by Lowry, Herbert and Stevens, Kain, Harris, and others, so that these relations have been collapsed into distance or access expressions. Beverly Duncan suggested further generalizations about hij relations in the association of occupational-industrial groups with varying lengths of the journey to work, which can be substantiated by recent transportation studies. In fact, the considerable quantity of analysis of metropolitan housing markets and transportation systems which has accumulated in the last few years in the United States already provides powerful clues to the important structural relations implicit in regional housing policy.

Criteria for Appraising Governmental Housing Programs

LEO GREBLER

My assignment has all the attractions of a trip into territory strewn with land mines. On one side is the *Wertfreie* economics which really denies that we have any business dealing with our subject, except to predict the likely results of alternative courses of action. On the other side is the professional tradition of the political economist concerned with ends and norms as well as means. Straight ahead of us loom the forbidding problems of measuring utilities and defining the public interest. Next to this land mine lies the booby trap of performance standards. Nearby is the explosive role of politics in economic decisions. And throughout our territory are scattered the tempting but precarious side trips into other disciplines bearing on housing welfare. It will be a miracle if we can find the narrow path between so many hazards.

First, we must ask why there should be any interference with the market—other than the time-honored local controls in the form of building and housing codes, etc. Here, an easy answer is given by the cynic who tells us that politicians have discovered and learned to exploit the vote-getting potentials of housing programs. The trouble with this position is that the vote potentials must express widespread disenchantment with the performance of the housing sector. This disenchantment still needs to be explained and may at least in part be explainable in economic terms.

An easy answer is also supplied by reference to historical accidents. In this view, government housing programs are the result of the collapse of the mortgage market during the Great Depression, the search for pump-priming devices, and the aftermath of World War II, plus the notorious difficulty in terminating governmental activities that become entrenched in our system. Historical conditions may indeed explain the initiation and specific form of governmental programs. Moreover, federal legislation to meet housing emergencies has demonstrated to many people's satisfaction that the government "can do something about it." But historical conditions cannot account fully for the persistence and intensification of public programs in so many countries where a great variety of circumstances has led to the same result: increased government intervention in housing.

Another easy answer comes from some of the specialists who have become so thoroughly imbued with their subject that they endow housing with top social priority without giving much consideration to competing individual or collective wants. The main trouble here is a myopic view of the world that does not help in solving the problem of resource allocation among alternative uses.

Finally, an easy answer is furnished by those who, as a matter of faith or intellectual conviction, accept the competitive system under consumer sovereignty as the most efficient and equitable organizing principle. But the question is to what extent the housing market and the related mortgage market conform to the underlying theoretical models.

I suggest that economic criteria for federal interference with the market be derived from economic performance standards for the housing sector.[1] This concentration on economic criteria does not mean we are insensitive to noneconomic aspects of housing. It simply delineates the area in which we can hope to apply whatever professional skills we possess. As for noneconomic aspects, we simply bow to that archradical, Benjamin Disraeli, who said: "The best security for civilization is the dwelling, and upon proper and becoming dwellings depends more than anything else the improvement of mankind. Such dwellings are the nursery of all domestic virtues, and without a becoming home the exercise of those virtues is impossible."[2]

From *American Economic Review*, I (May 1960), 321–332. Reprinted by permission of the American Economic Association and the author.

1 There are, of course, additional general criteria for assessing any governmental programs, as well as the pervasive problem of computing the cost of public credit and subsidies. This paper deals with criteria specific to the housing sector.
2 Quoted from Robert Moore Fisher, *Twenty Years of Public Housing* (Harper & Bros., 1959), p. 62.

PERFORMANCE STANDARDS

Borrowing from the concept of "workable competition," one may specify standards of workable performance of the housing sector. The most important standards underlying this paper are as follows:

1. A housing supply sufficient to allow each consumer unit demanding separate living quarters to occupy a dwelling unit of its choice in respect to size, location and environment, tenure, and quality, subject only to the economic restraint of price. Absence of other than price restraint.

2. A supply of dwelling units, as described, at prices each household can pay without undue, continuous strain on its budget. The point of strain may be defined as a ratio of occupancy cost or rent to income.

3. A supply of vacant dwelling units distributed geographically and by size, quality, and price, etc., in such manner that it allows people to move without excessive friction.

4. An efficient market organization, including adequate market information available to consumers as well as suppliers.

5. A reasonably operative market mechanism which, together with effective local controls, causes depreciation to lead ultimately to the end of the line: abandonment, physical removal, and replacement of the asset (though not necessarily on the same site).

6. New building sufficient for both replacement and growth.

7. Steady progress in meeting rising individual and community housing standards, including more widely shared gains in consumers' housing satisfactions.

8. A financial system which allocates external funds for housing on the basis of anticipated net yields and risk evaluations in comparison with alternative investments, and which leaves no credit gaps identifiable on this criterion.

9. Reasonable stability of the housing sector within the framework of stable growth of the economy as a whole.

10. Meeting the above performance standards at minimum and reasonably balanced private and social costs.[3]

To what extent have our performance standards been met? What are the obstacles to better performance? Have the federal programs removed or at least moderated some of these obstacles? Within my time limits, I cannot go over the entire list of standards. Let it merely be mentioned that we have gone a long way in augmenting the housing supply to the point where involuntary doubling-up of families is minimal and overcrowding limited to a relatively small segment of the population, though it is more frequent among Negroes and certain other minority groups than among whites. The increase in vacation and weekend cottages even foreshadows the emergence of a new standard of two housing units per family—two houses in every garage! Also, the quality of housing has unquestionably improved in the past ten years. With these preliminaries, I shall now concentrate on a few selected performance standards which involve resource allocation (mainly Nos. 7 and 10 above); the institutional framework within which the market operates (mainly Nos. 5, 6, and 8); housing assistance to certain groups of the population (mainly Nos. 2 and 7); and economic stability (No. 9).

RESOURCE ALLOCATION

Certain federal programs which operate over a broad range of the housing sector have come to be used as vehicles for raising the allocation of resources to housing over and above the share obtained from consumer decisions and the interplay of market forces. These are the mortgage insurance programs backstopped by the mortgage purchases of the Federal National Mortgage Association, which now holds more than 5 billion dollars of loans.

If this is their objective, have the programs

3 Obviously, a paper twice as long as this one could be devoted to justifying and specifying in detail these performance standards. It may merely be noted that our performance standards differ from the common housing need estimates and the objectives set forth in the "Declaration of National Housing Policy" in the Housing Act of 1949 in that they do not employ physical criteria such as "substandard" housing or "decent home." There are serious questions concerning the economic meaning of such terms and their application to quantitative housing goals. Moreover, standards of "adequate" housing change over time. Consequently, the notion of eliminating "substandard" housing once and for all, in ten or twenty or thirty years, is highly unrealistic.

succeeded? Unfortunately, our profession has done little to throw light on this question. So far as I know, there are only two comprehensive analyses of the over-all quantitative impact of the programs on residential construction, and they come to almost diametrically opposite conclusions. According to one, the effect during the postwar years has been merely to raise the price but not the real output of construction.[4] According to the other, the programs can be credited with a substantial increase in output.[5] Here is a challenging unfinished piece of business, as intriguing from a methodological viewpoint as it is important for policy formation.

If the allocation of resources to housing has been adversely affected by high acquisition cost of housing,[6] the federal programs have done next to nothing to attack the problem. The few steps in the direction of federally-sponsored technological research have been timid and halting.[7] Mortgage insurance at best has made a modest contribution by helping develop merchant builders operating on a larger scale. The federal government has tread lightly in using the substantial leverage of its programs for greater progress in removing costly restrictive practices, which are often ossified in building codes. Instead of direct attack, the programs offer a compensatory device. They have sought to soften the impact of high real costs by reducing down payments and outlays for debt service. But the postwar injection of easier credit may have actually intensified the increase of construction costs and house prices. An industry thriving on easy terms may have lacked the discipline and incentive to innovate, strive for technological advance, and develop better marketing techniques.

On the whole, then, there remains real doubt whether the mortgage insurance and FNMA programs have contributed substantially to resource reallocation in favor of housing. There are indications that past allocation trends adverse to this sector may have been reversed in the postwar period. The share of housing expenditures in total consumption, which fell for at least three decades before World War II, has increased.[8] The long-run decline in the share of residential construction in GNP (in real terms)[9] seems to have come to a halt. As yet we cannot say with confidence that these reversals of past trends reflect a basic shift in consumer taste, associated among other things with more

leisure, renewed cultural emphasis on family and home, and suburbanization. In any event, it appears that reallocation of resources in favor of housing depends mainly upon fundamental changes in our way of living and on prolonged prosperity, and that the federal credit programs may at best facilitate these changes.

IMPROVEMENT OF INSTITUTIONAL ARRANGEMENTS

Have the federal programs improved the performance of the housing sector by promoting

4 R. J. Saulnier, Harold G. Halcrow, and Neil H. Jacoby, *Federal Lending and Loan Insurance* (Princeton University Press for NBER, 1958), pp. 336–47.
5 George F. Break, "The Growth and Significance of Federal Loan Guaranties and Insurance" (manuscript for publication by the Nat. Planning Asso.), Chap. 5.
6 Between 1915 and 1957, residential construction costs as measured by the Boeckh index increased by 394 per cent. In the same period, the wholesale price index for all commodities (BLS) rose by about 160 per cent and the consumer price index (BLS) by 177 per cent. Between 1926 and 1957, the wholesale price index for commodities other than farm products and food increased by 76 per cent. In the same period, the index of residential construction costs rose by 172 per cent. The increase in construction costs would remain disproportionate even if it were possible to allow for the insufficient reflection of productivity increase in available cost indexes and for their resulting upward bias. For more extensive discussion of trends in construction costs, see Grebler-Blank-Winnick, *Capital Formation in Residential Real Estate* (Princeton University Press for NBER, 1956) pp. 278–79 and Appendix C. We need not, nor can we, examine here whether the disproportionate long-term rise in construction costs is due to the large labor-cost content in residential building, or lagging technological advance, or the supply cost curve of lumber, or higher standards imposed in part by building codes and similar regulations, or restrictive practices.
7 Special aids were extended to prefabricators under the veterans emergency housing program of 1946, which collapsed after a short life. Technological research was also stimulated by the research provisions of the Housing Act of 1948, but appropriations for this activity were terminated after a short while. Experience would indicate that crash programs and a monolithic approach, such as prefabrication, are doomed to failure.
8 Between 1909 and 1946 the share of housing expenditures in total consumption declined from 19 to 12 per cent exclusive of household utilities and from 24 to less than 14 per cent inclusive of utilities. Cf. J. Frederic Dewhurst and associates, *America's Needs and Resources* (Twentieth Century Fund, 1955), Appendix 4–5. Between 1946 and 1957, the current BLS reports which use a somewhat different method of calculation show an increase from 9.4 per cent exclusive of utilities to 12.4 per cent.
9 Cf. Grebler-Blank-Winnick, *op. cit.*, Chap. IX.

better institutional arrangements? I shall illustrate by reference to two of our performance standards.

As has been demonstrated by at least a hundred years of urbanization, the market mechanism combined with local codes has failed to meet our test of providing for replacement of depreciated assets. The durability of houses is not the only nor even a sufficient reason—witness the market-induced scrapping of other durables. There is the additional and perhaps more important fact that the removal of dwellings is determined mainly by forces external to the housing market; that is, the demand for other uses for the sites of dwellings. The sites demanded for other uses are not necessarily, nor are they often in fact, those with the most heavily depreciated residential structures. Consequently, the external forces determining the scrapping of houses have not produced sustained, vigorous replacement. Inadequate local codes or their lax, timid, and often downright corrupt enforcement have added to this difficulty. As a housing expert recently reminded us, we have been fairly successful in driving the unsafe jalopy off our highways, but concerted and continuous efforts to cast out unsafe dwellings have been rare.[10] Also, while the demand and supply forces perpetuating slums are complex, public action could at least mitigate one of these forces: the low marginal cost of operating slums. The low cost often reflects real-estate taxation based on faulty assessment practices which fail to take proper account of actual net income.

Largely because the housing sector has provided for growth rather than replacement, its performance in meeting rising individual and community standards has been less satisfactory than that of markets for other goods and services. To be sure, rising standards have been achieved by improvement of existing dwellings as well as by new construction. But dwelling standards are inseparable from environmental standards, which are again largely controlled by forces external to the housing market. We can marvel at venerable New England homes around the village green, so well maintained and improved with up-to-date equipment. Generally, however, the market cannot induce capital improvements when old property is in a sea of neglected houses or an area with inadequate

community facilities or when it fronts on a major traffic artery.

The urban renewal and public housing programs can be credited with some progress in the removal of depreciated housing. If scrapping is to be accelerated, however, more effective use must be made of market forces and regulatory and real-estate tax policies that can help accomplish the objective.[11] In the absence of these, we face the unpleasant prospect that urban surgery at immensely growing public expense will still be necessary thirty or fifty years from now.

To cope with this problem, a so-called "workable program" for slum prevention and elimination is now required of local governments before they can qualify for federal assistance for urban renewal and public housing. In my observation, there has been altogether too much pussyfooting in using this device. Here, as well as in other programs, a much more forceful *quid pro quo* policy seems necessary. Under such a policy, federal assistance would be denied or scaled down substantially if the local government failed to give tangible evidence of continuous, effective, and cumulative action.

Another case where opportunities for better institutional arrangements have been used half-heartedly is the mortgage market. Again, one can credit the Federal Home Loan Bank System with improving the secondary liquidity position of savings and loan associations and the mortgage insurance programs and FNMA

10 John Searles, *J. of Housing*, Sept., 1959, p. 295.
11 As for more imaginative and forceful local actions, one might consider surcharges to slum owners for fire protection and perhaps other public services clearly associated with certain defined conditions of their property (Martin J. Bailey, "Note on the Economics of Residential Zoning and Urban Renewal," *Land Econ.*, Aug., 1959). In addition to using eminent domain for land assembly in urban renewal projects, this power, under appropriate amendments to state laws, could perhaps also be employed to condemn the illegal, low-value improvements alone instead of both land and improvements. This method would not only be less expensive but would force owners more effectively to place new improvements on the site or sell the site to others for improvements. Further, since the scrapping of deteriorated housing is often impeded by the difficulty of assembling large numbers of parcels for new large-scale private development, the use of eminent domain without write-down of land values might be examined so as to solve the problem of "holdouts." These examples are given not to advocate specific measures but rather to illustrate the range of actions which might be explored.

with improving the marketability of residential mortgages. But the mere existence of these programs has also lulled us into apathy on the much-needed reform of state laws which inhibit the interregional flow of mortgage funds or make mortgage loans unnecessarily costly or risky. The marketability of conventional loans is still severely limited. Regional and local differences in effective mortgage interest rates seem to be still far greater than is justified by loan origination and servicing costs, given equal risks. The Voluntary Home Mortgage Credit Program is only a token measure to improve borrowers' access to lending facilities in remote areas and small towns where imperfect competition in the mortgage market is most pronounced.[12]

Instead of attacking directly these and other defects in institutional arrangements which establish the ground rules for the market, the federal programs again offer largely compensatory devices. Federal investment in mortgages through FNMA has made up in part for imperfections of the mortgage market. Federal grants and loans for urban renewal have been allowed to divert the energy of local governments from local action to efforts to obtain their share of federal assistance.

ASSISTANCE TO SELECTED POPULATION GROUPS

For a long time, housing subsidies to certain groups of the population have been justified on the argument that poor housing inflicts large costs on society. However, the simple correlations between substandard housing and social disorders costly to the community are rightly no longer accepted as proofs of causal relationships. But I suggest a case can still be made for the proposition that improved housing and residential environment would enhance the productive contribution of substantial parts of our population and therefore yield "external economies," quite apart from social and human values.[13] In addition, more energetic housing code enforcement would aggravate the pressing problem of rehousing those who live in slums for reasons of economic necessity (by no means all slum dwellers). And minority groups, especially Negroes, are faced in the market with non-price

restraints in the form of area and concomitant housing quality restrictions. Hence, our performance standard of more widely shared gains in housing has economic as well as social connotations. No statistics are needed to demonstrate that we have still a long way to go in meeting this standard, though it is clear that housing policy alone cannot solve the problems of poverty, personal or group maladjustments, or prejudice.

Here, we have a monolithic type of federal assistance: the embattled public housing program. The new rental housing project in public ownership and management, usually institutional, designed for long-term use and set apart from the rest of the community, has practically become the only solution offered.[14] This solution has been found wanting not only by many communities but even by a large number of actual and potential beneficiaries.

Our proverbial ingenuity in finding pragmatic solutions to problems by trial and error seems to have failed us. As has been said correctly, a nation can try out only one fiscal policy at a time but there can be many different kinds of public housing policies.[15] We have allowed little experimentation with alternative approaches, such as subsidies to families rather than projects, or the use of existing housing or short-term minimum housing, or expanded social services for problem families, or subsidies for the purchase of low-cost single-family houses

12 The Voluntary Home Mortgage Credit Program was authorized in the Housing Act of 1954 to help provide funds for FHA and VA loans in small communities and remote areas as well as for minority housing in any area. The main *modus operandi* is to funnel loan applications which were previously turned down to lenders co-operating in the program.
13 Curiously, one finds this proposition quite often in reports by economists and "conservative" businessmen on missions to underdeveloped countries. But it should also hold for advanced nations.
14 In addition, federal assistance has been offered in the form of mortgage insurance on specially advantageous credit terms for housing those who are dislocated by urban renewal and similar projects. This device, however, is ineffective for many groups requiring relocation. To the large extent that FNMA under its special assistance program buys the mortgages on relocation housing, the real instrument of assistance is federal credit rather than mortgage insurance.
15 Martin Meyerson and Edward C. Banfield, *Politics, Planning and the Public Interest: The Case of Public Housing in Chicago* (Glencoe: The Free Press, 1955), p. 283.

rather than rental projects which are expensive to build and operate, or public credit alone instead of cash subsidies. We have yet to redefine what groups of the population subsidized housing should serve in a high-level economy, as distinguished from the days when the slogan "one-third of the nation ill-fed, ill-clothed and ill-housed" carried greater conviction. By allowing individual localities to experiment with a wide range of methods, it may also be possible to substitute cost criteria for the present physical criteria in determining how far and how fast the nation is willing to go in housing subsidies for selected groups of the population.[16]

HOUSING PROGRAMS AND ECONOMIC STABILITY [17]

The question of criteria for the adjustment of federal housing programs to the objectives of economic stabilization policy has become the subject of lively debate. According to one view, the commitment of the federal government to assist the housing sector implies what is tantamount to an exemption of this sector from the vicissitudes of economic fluctuations. An opposite view holds that the achievement of better housing is clearly subordinate to the larger objective of stable economic growth.

Conflicting value judgments such as these cannot be wholly resolved in economic terms, but neither can they be resolved without economic criteria. One of these concerns time dimensions. Housing goals, as expressed in the preamble to the basic Housing Act of 1949, can only be attained over a long period of time. Consequently, temporary modifications of the government's support of housing need not seriously interfere with the accomplishment of housing goals. Economic stabilization policies, on the other hand, necessarily have a much shorter time horizon, and unremitting governmental support of housing at times of inflationary pressures can seriously interfere with the attainment of stabilization objectives. These differences in time dimensions themselves suggest that the gains in national welfare resulting from more effective stabilization policies will exceed the gains that can be obtained from uninterrupted efforts to maximize housing goals.

A second and related economic consideration is the effect of temporary restraints of housing credit on the long-term demand for homes. In the case of goods or services with shorter consumption periods or acquired on impulse, the potential demand that is frustrated by tighter credit terms may be killed rather than deferred. In the case of housing, however, short-run credit restraints are likely to result in deferral rather than permanent loss of demand. Few homes are bought on impulse. Consumers adjust the quality of their housing but slowly to changes in their income or asset holdings. The time when a family first purchases a home is conditioned largely by the family life cycle in which a span of one or two years is negligible. Consequently, most of the demand eliminated by credit restraint is likely to be reactivated when financial conditions become more favorable to borrowers, provided that employment and income remain high.

Third, varying the intensity of government aid to housing is not discriminatory when such action merely modifies temporarily the special benefits conferred on this sector of the economy. If the intensity of federal assistance is at times relaxed in the interest of economic stability, this can be considered a reasonable price for long-run benefits received by all those, including builders, who stand to gain from the preferred status of the housing sector.

Fourth, occasional restraint on the housing sector can be good housing policy as well as a necessary or desirable tool of economic stabilization policy. Maximum output of new residential construction is not the only criterion of good housing policy, at least in the short run. Other criteria are the maintenance of reasonable stability in the housing market itself and the prevention of excessive increases in construction costs and land prices. Incessant stimu-

16 On these points, cf. Robert Moore Fisher, *op. cit.*, which provides the first comprehensive analysis of economic aspects of the federal public housing program.
17 This section draws largely on the author's, *Housing Issues in Economic Stabilization Policy* (NBER, Occasional Paper 72) . See also his paper, "The Role of Residential Capital Formation in Postwar Business Cycles," Conference on Savings and Residential Financing (sponsored by the United States Savings and Loan League) , 1959 *Proceedings*. These papers discuss also the marked fluctuations of residential construction financed by government-insured loans and their relationship to the inflexible maximum interest rates on such loans.

lation of new building can seriously interfere with these objectives.

Fifth, a policy of incessant stimulation of housing may adversely affect the flow of funds into other "high-priority" sectors of the economy instead of those activities which the proponents of ever normal or ever rising residential building would consider less urgent than housing. Neither business investment nor consumer credit is highly sensitive to the usual moderate changes in the cost of borrowing. Consequently, increased financing for housing in tightening capital markets may draw funds away from the capital improvement programs of state and local governments, which are probably more sensitive to credit, as is housing.

To be sure, all of these considerations must be balanced against the impact of credit restraints and relaxations on residential construction itself. Long-term business planning, continuity of production at optimum scale, and efforts at cost reduction can be frustrated if builders must adjust their operations to discretionary alterations in the intensity of federal aid as well as changes in general credit availability and monetary policy. This point argues for cautious and sparing use of federal housing credit policies for economic stabilization purposes. But it does not vitiate the principle of integrating these policies with general stabilization objectives so long as federal credit aids have a major impact on the housing market.

NEED FOR REAPPRAISAL

In conclusion, I suggest that our federal housing programs are in urgent need of reappraisal which, if not agonizing, ought to be at least bold, imaginative, and searching. Instead of continuing and expanding activities which were developed to deal with the problems of yesteryear, we must re-examine their place in a high-level economy and in the light of the federal government's commitments under the Employment Act. Such re-examination may still conclude that financial assistance by the federal government is required to achieve socially desirable results as defined by the community-at-large. We may still find that the forces with which we are dealing are so stubborn that compensatory financial aid, the mainstay of the

present programs, is the only feasible alternative. The point is that we have insufficiently tested the potentials of that kind of government action which is designed to improve energetically the institutional framework in which the market operates, including local controls, and to attack directly some of the forces which have impinged on the performance of the housing sector, such as the high acquisition cost of housing.

Here are some of the questions such a reappraisal may examine. Should it be the purpose of federal programs to reallocate resources in favor of the housing sector generally, or should federal aid focus on housing assistance to groups deemed to be at a disadvantage? Would sustained federal aid to improve the technology and reduce the cost of construction be more effective in assisting the housing sector than the indirect measures we now employ? How can we make the most of federal assistance by effective *quid pro quo* arrangements with state and local governments? Is mortgage insurance still necessary to protect lenders against a debacle in the mortgage market when the federal government is committed to a policy of maintaining reasonably full employment, which of itself should protect us from financial disaster? Does the economic position of veterans as a group, as compared to non-veterans, justify the perpetuation of housing benefits for veterans of World War II, which have already been extended far beyond the original expiration date? And if the insurance programs are unnecessary as protective devices but serve other purposes, such as resource reallocation or improved marketability of mortgages or implementation of the Employment Act, are they the best means of accomplishing these purposes? Or should federal mortgage insurance be reserved for investments which the market clearly could not be expected to make without assistance, such as housing for certain groups of the aged, or urban renewal projects, or especially low-cost construction? Has the stress on encouraging home ownership in our programs pushed this type of tenure beyond real consumer preferences and, by promoting suburbia, hastened the very decay of central city areas which the urban renewal program seeks to cure?

Obviously, hard choices will be involved in

this kind of reappraisal. It is not enough to say that federal programs can do all of these things and more of each. By scattering our efforts in response to special pressures and without clearly focused objectives, we are in danger of meeting none of these objectives really well. Finally, in appraising benefits and costs it will be necessary to apply a much broader concept of the social cost of housing programs than the cost to the federal government, however

computed. We must include such items as the cost of institutional arrangements left unimproved as compensatory federal aid reduced the pressure for dealing with them directly; the cost to the public of failure to promote technological advance or of stultifying it; and even the alternative uses of insurance premiums collected in the case of apparently self-supporting programs such as FHA.

Economic Questions in Urban Redevelopment

LOUIS WINNICK

America's experience with federally-supported urban redevelopment has been quite limited. The great bulk of the present program is still in the execution and planning stage. Yet, short as experience has been, there have already appeared very many riddles and more than a few misconceptions. Those who have given time and thought to the rationale of city planning find themselves troubled by recurring questions on the means and goals of urban redevelopment. In this paper I will touch upon only three of these questions, although you have my complete assurance that the list of perplexities is much longer. These three deal with (1) the nature of subsidy, (2) induced capital formation, and (3) some problems connected with the pricing of redevelopment facilities.

THE NATURE OF SUBSIDY

There is a prevailing notion that, because urban redevelopment usually requires a public outlay, there is also necessarily a subsidy either to the developer or to the occupants of the new real estate. Thus there has been an outcry from the press and the public that it is morally wrong to subsidize hotels, office buildings, or luxury apartments on urban renewal sites—the now notorious $8,000-a-year penthouse in one New York City project comes to mind. In consequence, strong pressure is exerted to confine land write-down aids to housing, particularly

to so-called "low-income" or "middle-income" housing.

Few economists would agree with the view that every public outlay for a private venture represents a subsidy or, while we are on the point, with the widely-held corollary view that there is no subsidy unless there is a budgeted public outlay.

A subsidy is defined as a negative tax. A tax is not a tax unless there is an unrequited transfer of private resources to the public treasury. Obviously, a payment to government is not a tax if the payer receives at least an equivalent return of goods or rights; i.e., his balance sheet remains unaffected by the transaction, as when a private dealer purchases Treasury securities or when a household is assessed for a sewer which adds at least equal value to the resale price of his dwelling. And, to determine the incidence of a tax, we must look not to the payer of record but to the person who has suffered a shrinkage in income, consumption, or net worth.

By the same token, public outlays for urban redevelopment will not constitute a subsidy to private parties unless it can be shown that the latter have been made economically better off. Putting aside some subtleties, chiefly with respect to consumer surplus, it is legitimate to

From *American Economic Review*, LI, No. 2 (May 1961), 290–298, 302–304. Reprinted by permission of the American Economic Association and the author.

conclude that when a private user pays the going market price or rent for possession of real estate, he has received no subsidy regardless of how large may be the public expenditure associated with the transaction.

I can best illustrate this point by taking an example outside of the federal urban redevelopment program. Some of you know of the current plan of a number of communities in New Jersey to reclaim a large tract of swampy meadowland which is located close to New York City and which has considerable potential as a site for industry. Let me assume that draining and diking one hundred acres of this marshland will entail a cost of $3.00 per square foot or a total expenditure of roughly 13 million dollars. Let me further assume, not too unrealistically, that in a free and open auction to industrial developers the reclaimed land will command a price of $1.50 per square foot or 6.5 million dollars. That is, given active bidding by informed investors who have evaluated the net earnings potential of the reclaimed tract relative to competitive opportunities, $1.50 per foot is deemed to be the maximum price which just makes the purchase worthwhile. Clearly, neither the successful bidder nor his future tenants have been given a subsidy notwithstanding a net community outlay of 6.5 million dollars. The community outlay represents an expenditure made necessary by a physical defect in the site for which nature is to blame. If there is a subsidy, it is to the community-at-large which expects to derive widely-disseminated benefits from new industry. The community is, of course, free to decide whether these social gains are worth the social costs.

The economics of reclaiming slum land are not different from the economics of reclaiming swampland. In both cases, public assistance may be needed to bridge the gap between costs and re-use value and the expenditure of public resources is (or should be) justified by anticipated social benefits. Condemnation awards for even the most deteriorated real estate are usually generous and the costs of tenant relocation and building demolition are far from negligible. To be sure, if a site has very great promise, it is not at all impossible that private developers will offer a price equal to (or, for that matter, higher than) the full costs of acquisi-

tion and clearance. In this event, urban redevelopment can proceed without public outlay. In the case of most redevelopment projects, however, the income potential of the replacement real estate will not warrant full payment for the site. And the cost-value gap may be further widened if the urban renewal agency specifies something less than the highest economic use of the site (e.g., town houses instead of apartment houses or apartment houses instead of office buildings), or if it insists on higher standards (e.g., larger amounts of open space) than tenants are willing to pay for by higher rent. A public outlay then becomes obligatory to close the spread between costs and market value. But as long as the highest market value is received on resale, the public grant for land writedown will not be a subsidy to the developer or to his tenants, however much a subsidy it may be to the community-at-large. The presumptive purpose of public outlay is to overcome a cost disadvantage, not to give a price advantage.

INDUCED CAPITAL FORMATION

If these conclusions on the nature of subsidy are correct, we can next turn to a second question of some importance: To what extent will publicly-aided redevelopment prove a tool for accelerating economic growth; i.e., for increasing the nation's stock pile of productive capital facilities—housing, factories, office buildings, and so forth? Or will public action succeed in merely redistributing a given volume of investment; i.e., in changing the geographic location of capital facilities that would have been built in other places?

Many of those who most enthusiastically support a massive urban redevelopment program seem to believe that public outlays for slum clearance and rehabilitation will result in a large volume of additional private investment. Certainly, urban redevelopment stands high on the list of those who wish to step up our economic growth. At the same time, many of those who fear a bigger program because of its inflationary consequences must also, at least implicitly, subscribe to the notion of accelerated investment. Since government outlays for the acquisition of slum land represent a nonexhaustive payment (i.e., a transfer in ownership of existing assets rather than a claim against current production), the objections of the non-enthusiasts would appear to be based principally on the expectation that slum clearance will bring forth an excessive volume of private capital formation.

Both hopes and fears may be groundless. They derive from the fact that, to date, each dollar of public outlay for redevelopment has been accompanied by several dollars of private investment. To take a hypothetical but representative project, a municipality acquires and clears ten acres of slums, in or near the center of the city, at a cost of 8.7 million dollars. The cleared site is sold at open auction for 2.7 million dollars to an apartment developer who proceeds to build a 24 million dollar apartment project. A public expenditure of 6 millions (a 4 million federal outlay and a 2 million municipal outlay) is thus accompanied by four times as much private capital formation. Moreover, additional private investment may take place adjacent to the redevelopment site—retail stores or, now that the character of the area has changed, other new apartment houses, *ex post*, a total of five, six, or more dollars of private investment will be attributed to each dollar of public investment.

Plainly, we cannot accept, uncritically, this narrative as evidence that the multiplier effect of public urban redevelopment is anywhere near the size indicated. As Leo Grebler and others have already pointed out, there are a number of reasons for believing that urban redevelopment will stimulate only a moderate amount of incremental investment.

A net increase in aggregate investment could be attributed to urban redevelopment only if it were demonstrated that the new real estate improvements, or the act of producing them, would cause space users (households and firms) to enlarge their aggregate expenditures for building space; or better yet, only if it were demonstrated that consumers were induced to hold more structure capital per unit than would have been the case in the absence of a public redevelopment plan.

Such an increase in, say, residential capital formation could arise from several circumstances. (With minor substitutions, chiefly on the relation between site efficiency and profits,

my arguments would apply also to business demand for commercial and industrial space.)

Forced Spending. Since the presence of substandard and obsolete structures is usually a precondition for the selection of an urban redevelopment site, slum clearance results in a shrinkage of the aggregate inventory of cheap housing space. Although some of the dislocated households will dissolve, we can observe from actual surveys that most find substitute locations, generally at higher rents; i.e., willingly or unwillingly, they are forced to hold a larger amount of residential capital. We can conclude, therefore, that to the degree that urban redevelopment accelerates the demolition of old structures, the resulting increase in the national rent bill is a factor making for a higher rate of capital formation.

A Better Accommodation to Existing Demand. Because locations are differentiated, i.e., because each location has some unique characteristics, it is conceivable (and even probable) that a redevelopment project will not only attract customers away from other sites for new housing but will cause additional tenants to enter the new-housing market; i.e., to upgrade their present housing. For example, practically every neighborhood, even the poorest, contains residents who are underhoused with respect to income and preferences but who have been unable to find suitable quarters in their present neighborhood where, for sentimental or business reasons, they insist on remaining. Cases in point are local political leaders, storekeepers, doctors, and others with a strong desire to live close to their employment. Of course, such effective but unsatisfied demand is a rarity in the American economy, and it is proper to ask why unaided private developers have not sought to accommodate it. The answer is that the real-estate market is far from perfect. The supply curve for one of the critical inputs—land—is quite discontinuous. The acquisition of a site in a highly developed area involves many parties at interest and many legal complexities. The unaided private developer who tries to piece together an acre of land at a predetermined point in the city finds it an arduous and often unsuccessful task, inasmuch as it may entail negotiations with twenty owners and an equal number of lessees having various legal rights. Each of these parties at interest can seek to exact a monopolist's price or flatly reject any and all offers. To be sure, even under such adverse circumstances most builders can assemble a limited amount of plottage. But the market prospects of a small-scale development surrounded by an expanse of slum and blight are not often promising.

With urban redevelopment powers, such impediments to land assembly are readily overcome. Through eminent domain the municipality can acquire sites of almost any size and can therefore create a neighborhood environment with maximum market potential. It is reasonable to assume that, price aside, a large-scale project in a protected environment will not only win tenants away from competitive sites but may also generate new demand.

Price. Finally, urban redevelopment could lead to an appreciable increase in aggregate demand if, as a result of land writedown, the new real estate were offered at a bargain rent. However, as was seen, the economic rationale of the federal land writedown program has been to eliminate a cost disadvantage rather than to confer a price advantage. The resale price of a site is set by an open auction so that the amount of land writedown given will be no more than is necessary to achieve a competitive market rent. To be sure, there may be economics of scale in building and operating a large-scale project. But, presumably, the extra profit potential is already reflected in the winner's bid price. In short, as the urban redevelopment program is presently conceived, we cannot, in principle, place much weight on bargain pricing as a means for stimulating additional demand. The subject of pricing is so important, however, that it will be discussed more fully later on.

Summarizing, as long as the objective of urban redevelopment aids is to eliminate cost disadvantages rather than to subsidize occupants, new investment demand will be generated chiefly through forced spending and through product differentiation. It is not possible, of course, to make a priori estimates of the market response to these two forces. But, in my opinion at least, this response will not be very great. Public pressures to limit tenant dislocation and forced spending are, to put it mildly, overwhelming. And, as in other markets, product differentiation without price advantage tends to result mainly in interproduct shifts in demand rather than new demand. This is particularly true in the market for real estate where the existing product is seldom scrapped but lingers indefinitely on the market, offering powerful price competition to the new product.

Most likely the principal accomplishment of urban redevelopment will be to alter the locale of investment rather than to induce new investment. Let me emphasize, however, that the redistribution of urban investment is a gain hardly to be scorned. In fact, given a pervasive tendency toward population decline in both large and small cities, the paramount urban need may well be a more satisfactory rearrangement of residence and industry rather than a substantial increase in the aggregate real-estate inventory.

PRICING PROBLEMS

Land Writedown versus Rent Writedown. Turning next to some practical problems in pricing, let me refer once more to the hypothetical apartment project described earlier in this paper—the one which required a land writedown of 6 million dollars. Such a writedown was needed, it was said, to cover the difference between cost and market value. Given the specifications of the plan, had the private developer paid full costs for the site, he would have had to obtain a rental of approximately $56.00 a month per room. In the judgment of all concerned, such a rent was deemed to be $6.00 above the going market rent of $50.00 a room. A land writedown grant was made to wipe out this $6.00 handicap.

But according to this analysis the term "land writedown" is surely a misnomer for the term "rent writedown." The real object of public aid is to bring rent down to a competitive market level. Obviously, a rent reduction could be achieved by writing down not the cost of land alone but any of the capital or operating costs upon which rent is based. And, as a matter of financial arithmetic, land writedown is hardly the most effective way to reduce rents to market level. In fact, an aid program restricted solely to land writedown will be an unnecessarily limited program. This conclusion follows from the fact that land costs, even when high, do not ordinarily have a major impact on rents. Thus, in the case of our hypothetical apartment project, a 70 per cent writedown of land costs from 8.7 to 2.7 million dollars succeeded in reducing rents by little more than 10 per cent. Had the site been conveyed free of charge (i.e., had there been a 100 per cent land writedown), the lowest rent attainable through land writedown would have been approximately $48.00 per room, a total reduction of 15 per cent.

Suppose, now, that in a given redevelopment area the lowest rent which can be attained after a 100 per cent writedown is substantially higher than what tenants will pay. Then, either the redevelopment plan must be revised or some more powerful form of aid will have to be given. What can we suggest? An obvious proposal is that the present federal land writedown formula be abandoned in favor of outright cash grants in whatever amount is necessary to bring rent down to market level. However, other tools can be thought of. One of these is the more imaginative use of liberal FHA Section 220 mortgages to reduce debt service charges (and therefore the rent) of redevelopment housing. A much bolder step in the same direction is New York State's Mitchell-Lama Law. Under this law the builder of a (limited profit) private housing project can obtain from the state or municipality a fifty-year, 3½ per cent mortgage equal to 90 per cent of costs. He can further obtain from the municipality a 40 per cent abatement in real estate taxes. Applying both of these aids to our hypothetical apartment house would have further lowered rent from $50.00 to $32.00 per month per room—a rent writedown three times as great as that which resulted from land writedown.

Our urban redevelopment programs could be immeasurably improved by adopting rent writedown tools in substitution for, or in supplementation of, land writedown grants. Were municipalities to evolve a Mitchell-Lama type formula, three important advantages would accrue.

First, because the rent-reducing power of municipal tax and credit aids is so great a municipality is enabled to redevelop (assuming that it were wise to do so) high-cost–low-value neighborhoods; i.e., highly unfavorable slum areas where even a 100 per cent land writedown is insufficient to bring rent down to market level. A municipality could thus widen its program by choosing neighborhoods which are now out of the economic reach of a land writedown formula. In many cities such neighborhoods may be precisely the ones where it is most urgent to encourage private investment or to bring in a different class of population; e.g., families with school age children to areas with under-utilized schools and white middle-class families to neighborhoods which are tending toward racial and social imbalances.

Second, because cash land writedown grants could in many instances be dispensed with, a municipality would be able to carry out a very considerable amount of redevelopment outside of the federal program. This is a gain not to be lightly dismissed, since the municipality is set free from the delays and uncertainties of Congressional action and federal control.

Third, armed with a combination of tax, credit, and land writedown aids, a municipality could, if it so desired, inaugurate a pricing policy which went beyond the mere elimination of cost disadvantage; i.e., it could engage in outright subsidy. By setting rents below the going market level, a municipality could then tap additional layers of housing demand and thereby help overcome a housing shortage, should one exist. The extra volume of housing investment thus obtained would, of course, depend upon the community's demand elasticity for housing with respect to price. While new demand could be generated by bargain prices on any quality-class of housing, luxury as well as nonluxury, there is reason to believe that consumer response per given amount of rent reduction would be greatest if subsidy were limited to so-called "middle-income" housing. Admittedly, a program of housing subsidy would be laden with very many dangers and inequities. A full discussion of merits and pitfalls would however carry us too far afield.

Some would attribute to tax and credit aids still a fourth advantage; namely, that, unlike cash writedowns, no government costs are involved. That is, since the municipal loan would be repaid and since the tax yields on the new real estate, even after partial tax abatement, would usually equal or exceed the taxes paid on the former slum site, it is believed that the public escapes a burden. I do not have space to debate this point. Suffice it to say, that a fifty-year, $3\frac{1}{2}$ per cent loan is an extremely scarce economic good—a privilege for which the private market would gladly pay a price. For example, if the municipality would permit me to replace my twenty-five year, $5\frac{1}{2}$ per cent home mortgage with a $3\frac{1}{2}$ per cent loan for an equivalent term, I would be willing to pay a premium (in cash or additional real estate taxes) of up to $240 per $1,000 of loan. The revenue foregone through the use of municipal credit and tax aids—quite apart from the cost to the federal treasury of additional tax-exempt municipal bonds—constitutes a public cost, whether or not it appears in the budget. Whether such aids constitute a subsidy or not depends on how they are used.

Rationing Public Aids. My final thought is that, unless a deliberate policy of subsidy is embarked upon, the amount and type of aid should be strictly rationed in accordance with the cost-value equation of each redevelopment project. If public resources are not to be misused, no more or less aid should be given than is required by the market to fulfill the plan. For example, slum site A in the central core may be an area of great potential market appeal. An analysis may indicate that 1,000 new apartment units could be rented at $60.00 a room and that such a rental would be sufficient to meet all the costs of redevelopment. Here the only aid which should be given is land assembly. Slum site B may be an area of moderate market appeal, with a rent potential of say $40.00 a room. Such a rent might be attained solely through the use of a long-term, low-interest mortgage. By contrast, slum site C is an area in which not only are site costs high but which is also so low in status that it would be difficult to attract tenants unless rents are set appreciably below the minimum market rent for new housing in the city as a whole. That is, to attract the required number of occupants a rent of $20.00 per room may have to be offered, perhaps $15.00 less than the next best opportunity in the new-housing market. In such cases, it may be necessary to mobilize the full panoply of public aids.

The urban renewal administrator should also recognize that a project is underpriced if, at the predetermined rent, demand exceeds the available supply; i.e., if more tenants of the wanted type apply than there are available units. An oversubscribed apartment project indicates that more aid has been given than is necessary for the success of the plan and that the tenants (or developers) are receiving what may be an unintended subsidy. Conversely, weak demand for a project would be evidence that a still lower rent and a larger dosage of aid is needed if the objectives of the plan are to be reached. Incorrect pricing not only means an overuse of public resources or a wastage of private investment, but it may also thwart the community's redistribution plan. Thus, putting $25.00 per room housing in a popular $60.00 per room neighborhood could significantly weaken the chances of attracting families to neighborhoods of much lower status. When orchestra seats are made available at balcony prices, balcony seats tend to go begging.

Let me close by repeating that the few points touched upon in this paper barely scratch the surface of deeper quandaries to which our urban redevelopment program has given birth. How does one balance economic and noneconomic factors in selecting a site and in choosing the optimal type of replacement real estate? What yardsticks should be applied in determining whether the benefits of a given redevelopment scheme justify its costs? And what principles can be established (welfare economists, please note) for the compensation of dislocated occupants?

Unless urban redevelopment policy obtains a prominent place on the economist's agenda, it will be shaped in accordance with the wishes of special-interest groups. We will then be giving credence to Henry Wallich's remark that just as experience is another word for mistakes we have already made, policy is another word for mistakes we are about to make.

DISCUSSION

IRVING MORRISSETT

I would consider "the nature of subsidy" in a rather different light than that explained by Mr. Winnick. He defines a subsidy as a negative tax. I would agree that a "tax is an unrequited transfer of private resources to the public treasury," but not that a subsidy is an unrequited transfer of public resources to a private treasury. A subsidy is more usefully defined as payment made by government for the purpose of persuading or making it possible for the recipient to do something he otherwise would not do. The subsidy is usually conditional upon the performance of the specified act: the farmer must grow or not grow certain crops, the shipowner must continue to run ships, and the urban redeveloper must offer facilities below cost or undertake some other act that would not be dictated by market forces. Taxes are sometimes levied for the purpose of persuading people to do something they otherwise would not do—the high liquor tax, for example, is intended partly to discourage riotous living. But taxes usually are collected for other purposes, such as redistributing income (we refer to the opposite of this as a "transfer payment," not a subsidy) or paying for government activities.

In my definitions, a subsidy is efficient if it gets the job done—that is, if it is successful in modifying the action of the recipient as desired—without paying more than is necessary to modify his actions. It is "excessive" if more than the minimum necessary to modify his actions is paid. Mr. Winnick's definition of a subsidy corresponds to my definition of an excessive subsidy; in his lexicon, there is no subsidy if the payments made are just sufficient to get the job done. But this is peculiar terminology. It is common gossip, well founded I believe, that the urban redevelopment program involves subsidies. The subsidies are given to a local government or redevelopment authority in consideration of the carrying out of a certain approved plan. The subsidies do not go to private parties, because they are directed toward the objective of modifying the behavior of the local authority. The effects of the approved plan do, however, carry beyond the original federal-local relationship. The redevelopment plan specifies land uses that are to be permitted or encouraged; and although the original subsidy may not make a $10,000 penthouse available at a bargain rate of $8,000, it cannot be divorced from responsibility for making an $8,000 penthouse available at a location where it otherwise would not be. The original subsidy usually is a necessary condition for setting in motion a comprehensive plan, the results of which must be judged as a whole.

I am uncertain about the meaning of Mr. Winnick's assertion that the purpose of a subsidy is to eliminate a cost disadvantage. I can understand that a redevelopment plan typically reduces the cost of using particular land for more or less specified purposes. But the reference to elimination of cost disadvantages sounds very much like the concept of "cost equalization" which has so often derailed intelligent consideration of tariff and public utility problems. The questions of "what costs" and "whose costs" could lead analysts into great and unnecessary confusion. The simpler and relevant question is: How much of the cost must be met by subsidy in order to get responsible recipients to carry out the agreed-upon plan?

The point of the third section of Mr. Winnick's paper is well taken: there is no compelling reason for confining the form of urban renewal grants to defrayal of land acquisition costs. There are two essential contributions that government makes to urban renewal. First and most important is eminent domain coupled with a comprehensive plan. The second is subsidy. As Mr. Winnick points out, both the scope and flexibility of urban renewal plans could be increased by making wider use of tax and interest rebates as well as land writedowns.

The middle section of the paper deals with one aspect of what is the heart of the urban renewal problem—the heart being the value of the benefits derived. Subsidies have two general purposes. One is to substitute public value judgments or "tastes" for private judgments, as in the subsidization of symphony orchestras. The other purpose is to encourage the production of goods and services which benefit third parties. If a subsidy is involved, such indiscriminate, nonmarketable benefits usually constitute only a part of the benefits of production, as with the certain private benefits and assumed public benefits of our ship-building subsidy program. If all of the benefits of production are indiscriminate, as with national defense and city parks, the activity is usually socialized and there is no subsidy in the sense in which I have used the word.

From among the many possible indiscriminate benefits of urban renewal, Mr. Winnick has selected induced capital formation and shed light on some of the most important analytical problems related to it. If new capital is only diverted from one location to another by a renewal program, there is a gain only if benefits are calculated for an area that excludes the location from which the investment project was enticed. There are several routes by which net additions to capital formation may come, as Mr. Winnick points out. The sheer destruction of low-grade and obsolete capital goods—industrial, commercial, or residential—may induce replacement which otherwise would have occurred much more slowly. The same result can be obtained with a well-placed bomb, and in both cases the human as well as the monetary costs of destruction must be weighed against the benefits of the increased capital.

A second kind of capital formation attributable to urban renewal, as suggested by Mr. Winnick, is encouraged by the availability of new construction sites of types not previously available to meet the needs or desires of prospective investors. Still another type of real capital gain,

if not of capital formation, which Mr. Winnick might have added is the increase of efficiency in the use of existing capital. A city exists for the purpose, among others, of facilitating the production of a wide variety of goods and services. It can perform its facilitating functions poorly or well. Presumably these functions will be performed better as the result of a redevelopment program which would mean greater efficiency in the use of both private and social capital.

The difficulties of assessing the magnitude and impact of induced capital formation are illustrative of the problems encountered in assessing the whole range of possible benefits of urban redevelopment. The monetary costs of redevelopment are fairly ascertainable, and the nonmonetary costs are identifiable if not easily measured. But on the benefit side, both the monetary and the nonmonetary effects are for the most part quite difficult to identify and measure. The benefits of urban redevelopment constitute a large and important underdeveloped area of urban research.

1 2 3 4 5 6 7 8 9 10 11 12 13 14 15   75 74 73 72 71 70 69